ADVANCED
QuickC®

ADVANCED
QuickC®

Werner Feibel

Osborne **McGraw-Hill**
Berkeley, California

Osborne **McGraw-Hill**
2600 Tenth Street
Berkeley, California 94710
U.S.A.

For information on translations and book distributors outside of the U.S.A.,
write to Osborne **McGraw-Hill** at the above address.

A complete list of trademarks appears on page 697.

ISBN 0-07-881352-2

For my parents, who have always encouraged and supported me in my efforts, and for Luanne

CONTENTS

ACKNOWLEDGMENTS

Many people deserve thanks for making this book possible. The following people were particularly helpful and encouraging throughout the project:

I wish first to thank the people at Osborne/McGraw-Hill, who are always helpful, friendly, and very good at their jobs—it is a pleasure to work with them. Jeff Pepper and Liz Fisher deserve special thanks for keeping me on track and on schedule throughout the project. Fran Haselsteiner and the production staff worked hard and did an excellent job turning the material I sent them into a finished product on a very tight schedule. For all their efforts, I thank them. Thanks also to Judy Wohlfrom for her design work on the book.

Gratitude is also due to Nelson Johnson for his technical review of the chapters. His very helpful criticisms and suggestions kept unfortunate errors out of the book and added numerous good points. His extensive knowledge of C and sound programming sense greatly improved the code and the text. The copy editor, Bob Wanetick, did an excellent job of catching errors and oversights. His ability to note very subtle inconsistencies, sometimes separated by several pages or even several chapters, was truly impressive, and I thank him for applying his skills to *Advanced QuickC*.

Finally, I owe my friends another round of thanks for again putting up with me and my deadlines. In particular, I want to thank Luanne, Alexa, Dan, Dylan—still little, but growing all the time—and Scott. Work is always much easier and more fun when you have good friends to relax with.

—W.F.

INTRODUCTION

In many ways the easiest part of learning a programming language such as C is learning the syntax. Once you've learned the syntax, you want to start building interesting and useful programs, but you often find that such projects require more complex data structures and techniques than C provides directly.

This book contains information and code to help you overcome this obstacle to building more useful programs. The goal is to provide you with a broad collection of functions and programs to get you started on your programming projects. The book also includes background information and discussions of how the data structures, algorithms, and functions work so you'll be able to extend and add to the resources provided here.

The early chapters discuss useful data structures: stacks, queues, linked lists, and trees. You'll also find functions for creating and manipulating such data structures.

Chapter 1 introduces you to stacks and queues; Chapter 2 discusses recursion and provides examples of recursive functions. Recursion, a very powerful programming technique, is important in handling some data structures. Chapter 3 includes an extensive discussion of trees. In addition to discussing simple trees and providing the code for building and searching them, the chapter includes information and functions for working with balanced trees, which offer a much more efficient way of using tree structures.

Chapters 4 through 7 develop general-purpose applications, most of which use the data structures and recursive techniques described in the earlier chapters. Many of the capabilities provided in these chapters—such as parsing, sorting, and data compression—can be used in a wide range of programs.

In Chapter 4 you'll find algorithms for sorting a collection of values and or for searching a body of data for a particular value. The functions implementing these algorithms can be used in your programs. You'll also find a program for exploring the different functions, to help you decide which sorting routines might be most useful for your purposes.

Chapter 5 provides algorithms and functions for parsing mathematical expressions. In effect, the chapter develops a calculator. The calculator can handle common mathematical operations as well as exponentiation, and can also handle variables.

Chapter 6 shows you how to compress your text files so they take up less space on your disk. The chapter also contains algorithms for encrypting text files. If you like doing cryptogram puzzles, you'll find the encryption program in this chapter particularly entertaining and useful. The program lets you encode files you've created and also lets you work on deciphering text that has already been encrypted.

Chapter 7 shows you how to work more closely with DOS and with low-level services on your computer. The chapter includes numerous functions for gaining access to such services as the clock on your computer, the screen, the keyboard, and so forth. You'll also learn how to create, delete, modify, and hide files.

Chapters 8 through 10 show how to use C for more specialized purposes. Chapter 8 discusses random number generation and provides you with several generators. These generators are used in Chapter 9 to run simulations of various processes, such as waiting in line at a bank, tossing coins, and manufacturing light bulbs. Chapter 10 provides the tools you need to evaluate the simulations or to analyze other types of information. You'll find statistical techniques for summarizing data, for testing hypotheses about your information, and for creating mathematical models of your data.

Chapter 11 discusses graphs and shows how they can be used

to find the shortest route between two places, to solve maze puzzles, and to represent other types of puzzles.

The chapters include a great deal of source code—about 650KB worth of functions and programs. I've tried to document the code extensively, to make it easier to follow and to modify. You should study the code, play with the programs, and explore the effects of making changes in the code.

The main purpose of a book such as this is to teach you something about more advanced programming topics. To make this easier, I've tried to make the code reflect the concepts under discussion, rather than trying to make the code faster but more difficult to follow. Once you understand how an algorithm and the function implementing it work, you can always go in and make the function more efficient. It's much more difficult to go the other way—to learn an algorithm from fast, but generally more cryptic, code.

WHAT YOU SHOULD KNOW

This book assumes that you have programmed in C before, and that you are familiar with the fundamental syntax and concepts of C. In case your C is a bit rusty, there's a very brief refresher summary in Appendix A. If you're new to C, you'll probably be better off with a book such as *Using QuickC* (by Werner Feibel, Osborne/McGraw Hill, 1988) before you tackle the topics in this book.

You should also be familiar with QuickC or Microsoft C 5.0. There is a fairly detailed summary of QuickC commands in Appendix C if you need a refresher on that programming environment. The code uses constructs contained in the Draft Proposed ANSI Standard C. This means the programs should be easily transportable to other C implementations, provided these conform to the ANSI Standard.

Although some of the chapters discuss fairly specialized topics, the book attempts to include any background or contextual information you might need. It does not assume any prior knowledge in these topic areas.

—Werner Feibel

PROGRAM SOURCE FILES

This book contains dozens of programs to illustrate and exercise the data structures and algorithms developed in the book. Many of the programs are designed for experimentation and exploration, and some can be quite entertaining to use, such as the cryptogram program in Chapter 6.

The complete source code for all the programs is included, so you can simply copy the programs from the book. However, if you want to save yourself the task of entering the programs, the source code for all the functions and programs in this book is available on two 360KB diskettes. The diskettes contain over 600KB of source files. To order the diskette, just use the form.

DISKETTE ORDER FORM

Please send me __ set(s) of the source code diskettes for *Advanced QuickC*.

Name _____

Company (if applicable) _____

Street address _____

City _____ State _____ ZIP _____

Amount enclosed $_____

U.S.A. orders: $22 per set ($20 plus $2 shipping and handling. In Mass., please add $1 sales tax per set.)
Foreign orders: $25 per set ($20 plus $5 shipping and handling.)

Please send this form, along with your check or money order, to

Werner Feibel
P.O. Box 2499
Cambridge, MA 02238

Osborne/McGraw-Hill assumes NO responsibility for this offer. This is solely an offer of Werner Feibel and not of Osborne/McGraw-Hill.

1

STACKS AND QUEUES

In this book you'll find many programs that do useful and interesting things. A surprising proportion of these programs relies on a fairly small number of strategies and data structures. In this chapter you'll look at two widely used and very versatile data structures.

A common task in programs is manipulating lists, or sequences, of elements —whether numbers, words, or a combination of these. Two of the simplest things to do with lists are adding elements to a list and removing elements from a list. In this chapter, you'll look at lists in which such changes are always made at either end —that is, the front or the back —of the list.

You can use two fundamental strategies for manipulating such lists, or sequences, differentiated by the order in which elements are added and removed. One strategy is always to remove the most recent element added; that is, the last element added to the list will be the first element removed. Such a sequence is often called *LIFO*, for "last in, first out." Examples of LIFO sequences include

- Archeological strata, or layers, representing settlements at a particular time. Settlements build on top of one another, so the most recent settlement will be the top one. These layers are excavated in a last-in-first-out sequence, since the most recent settlement is the first one excavated.

- Function calls in a running program. When a particular function (let's say **main( )**) is executing in a program, a call to another function (let's say to **first( )**) will temporarily suspend execution of **main( )** while **first( )** is executing. If **first( )** calls another function (**second( )**) during execution, **first( )** will be suspended temporarily while **second( )** executes. Once **second( )** finishes, control will transfer back to **first( )**, the most recently suspended program. For example, suppose each of the functions in the listing below calls the next one. The functions would be suspended in sequence, from **main( )** through **fifth( )**. Functions would be reactivated in the reverse order, however; that is, **fifth( )** would be reactivated after **sixth( )** completed, then **fourth( )** would be reactivated after **fifth( )** finished, and so forth.

```
main()
first()
second()
third()
fourth()
fifth()
sixth()
```

- Stacked trays and plates in a cafeteria. You always get the top one, and you always add a tray or plate to the top.

The other strategy is always to remove the "oldest" element from the list, that is, to remove the element added the longest time ago, which is the first element in the list. This strategy is often called *FIFO*, for "first in, first out." Examples of FIFO sequences include

- Lines in banks or cafeterias
- Waiting lists that are administered in strict sequence
- Program schedulers, which turn over control to jobs in the order in which the control requests are received

STACKS

A *stack* is a LIFO sequence. To represent a stack, you need two things: a place to store its elements and a means of getting to the most recently added element in the stack.

Representing a Stack

You could represent a stack of double values with the following data structure:

```
#define MAX_VALS   50   /* maximum number of elements in stack */

struct dbl_stack {
     /* vals is a MAX_VALS element array of double */
        double   vals [ MAX_VALS];
        int      top;
};
```

This structure groups the two elements of a stack. The top member will always indicate the next available cell in the stack's array, that is, in the **vals[]** member.

Similarly, you could represent a stack of strings with the following data structure:

```
#define MAX_VALS   50   /* maximum number of elements in stack */
#define SHORT_STR  15   /* maximum length for a stack entry */

struct stack {
     /* vals is a MAX_VALS element array of strings */
        char   vals [ MAX_VALS] [ SHORT_STR];
        int    top;    /* indicates the next stack cell to be filled */
};
```

As with the stack of double values, this structure groups the two elements of a stack: the **vals[]** array of (**string**) elements and **top**, which indicates the next available cell in the **vals[]** member. In this case, the next available element is itself an array, so **top** effectively specifies the first cell of this character array. For example, if **top** were 10, the next character added to the array would be stored in cell **vals[10][0]**.

Stack Operations

Later in this chapter, you'll build functions that work with stacks of strings; this representation provides a flexibility that will come in handy when you build a calculator. For this reason, you'll work with the second stack example, **stack**, rather than with a **dbl_stack**, in this chapter. You could just as easily write functions such as the following for stacks containing other types of values. Think about how you would do this as you work with these examples. In later chapters, you'll use other definitions of stack elements and modify the stack functions accordingly.

The only destructive operations you will need to carry out on stacks are adding and removing elements. You will find it useful to check whether a stack is empty or full and to examine such other things as the stack's size and the contents of the top stack slot. It is also useful to have a general procedure for initializing a stack.

Initializing and Examining a Stack

The following macros and functions let you initialize a stack, test whether there are any elements in the stack or whether the stack is full, and so forth. You should type these into your computer, adding to and modifying them as needed. See Appendix C of this book or Chapter 2 of *Using QuickC* (by Werner Feibel, Osborne/McGraw-Hill, 1988) for a brief summary of commands for using the QuickC editor.

```
/* Macros and functions for manipulating stacks.
   File assumes defs.h has been read.
*/

/* For all three macros, A should be a pointer to stack */
#define STACK_EMPTY(A)    (!((A)->top))           /* is stack empty? */
#define STACK_FULL(A)     ((A)->top == MAX_VALS)  /* is stack full? */
#define STACK_SIZE(A)     ((A)->top)              /* nr elements in stack */
```

```
struct stack {
    /* vals is a MAX_VALS element array of strings */
        char vals [ MAX_VALS] [ SHORT_STR];
        int  top;    /* indicates the next stack cell to be filled */
};


/* *************
    stack function DECLARATIONS
************* */
void        disp_stack ( struct stack *);
void        init_stack ( struct stack *);
void        show_stack_top ( struct stack *);
int         stack_height ( struct stack *);
int         stack_is_empty ( struct stack *);
int         stack_is_full ( struct stack *);


/* *************
    stack function DEFINITIONS
************* */
/*
   void init_stack ( struct stack *stack_ptr)
   ********************************************************
   Initialize each cell in the stack to NULL_STR;
   set top of stack (next element to add) to 0.
   CALLS :  strcpy ();
   GLOBALS : MAX_VALS
   PARAMETERS :
            struct stack *stack_ptr : pointer to stack being initialized.
   RETURN : <none>
   USAGE : init_stack ( &st);
   ********************************************************
*/
void init_stack ( struct stack *stack_ptr)
{
        int  index;

        for ( index = 0; index < MAX_VALS; index++)
                strcpy (stack_ptr -> vals [ index], null_str);
        stack_ptr -> top = 0;
}


/*
   int stack_is_empty ( struct stack *stack_ptr)
   ********************************************************
   Test whether stack_ptr is empty.
   If the_stack.top == 0, then stack is empty,
   so negating value returns the correct answer.
   CALLS :
   GLOBALS :
   PARAMETERS :
            struct stack *stack_ptr : pointer to stack being checked.
   RETURN : TRUE if stack is empty; FALSE otherwise.
   USAGE : result = stack_is_empty ( &st);
   ********************************************************
*/
int stack_is_empty ( struct stack *stack_ptr)
{
        return ( !(stack_ptr -> top));  /* if zero, return true */
}
```

```
/*
   int stack_is_full ( struct stack *stack_ptr)
   ***********************************************************
   Test whether stack_ptr is full.
   If stack_ptr -> top == MAX_VALS, then stack is full.
   CALLS :
   GLOBALS : MAX_VALS
   PARAMETERS :
           struct stack *stack_ptr : pointer to stack being checked.
   RETURN : TRUE if stack is full; FALSE otherwise.
   USAGE : result = stack_is_full ( &st);
   ***********************************************************
*/
int stack_is_full ( struct stack *stack_ptr)
{
        return ( stack_ptr -> top == MAX_VALS); /* if equal, return true */
}




/*
   void  show_stack_top ( struct stack *stack_ptr)
   ***********************************************************
   Display the top stack element, but DO NOT pop the element.
   CALLS : printf (); STACK_EMPTY ()
   GLOBALS :
   PARAMETERS :
           struct stack *stack_ptr : pointer to stack being checked.
   RETURN : <none>
   USAGE : show_stack_top ( &st);
   ***********************************************************
*/
void  show_stack_top ( struct stack *stack_ptr)
{
        if ( !STACK_EMPTY ( stack_ptr))
                printf ( "Top stack element: %s\n",
                        stack_ptr -> vals [ stack_ptr -> top - 1]);
}


/*
   int  stack_height ( struct stack *stack_ptr)
   ***********************************************************
   Return the number of elements currently in the stack
   CALLS :
   GLOBALS :
   PARAMETERS :
           struct stack *stack_ptr : pointer to stack being checked
   RETURN : number of elements currently in stack.
   USAGE : size = stack_height ( &st);
   ***********************************************************
*/
int  stack_height ( struct stack *stack_ptr)
{
        return ( stack_ptr -> top);
}


/*
   void disp_stack ( struct stack *st)
   ***********************************************************
```

```
        Display the contents of the stack.
        CALLS : printf ();
        GLOBALS :
        PARAMETERS :
                struct stack *stack_ptr : pointer to stack being displayed.
        RETURN : <none>
        USAGE : disp_stack ( &st);
        ***************************************************
*/
void disp_stack ( struct stack *st)
{
        int index;

        for ( index = st -> top - 1; index >= 0; index--)
                printf ( "stack.top == %d : value == %s\n",
                        index, st -> vals [ index]);
}
```

The file **defs.h** contains the constant definitions used by these and other functions. The following listing shows the contents of **defs.h** as required by the stack functions.

```
/* Contents of file defs.h, as required for stack and other functions. */

#define INVALID_VAL   -99999.999
#define MAX_VALS      50    /* maximum stack size */

#define MAX_STR       100
#define SHORT_STR     15     /* length for a short string, used in stacks */

#define BLANK_CHAR    ' '
#define NULL_CHAR     '\0'

#define FALSE         0
#define TRUE          1

char    *null_str = "";
char    *blank_str = " ";
```

init__stack( )

The **init__stack( )** function initializes each cell in the array member to **NULL__STR** and sets **(*stack__ptr).top** to 0. The value of the top member of a stack represents the index of the next cell in the stack array to be filled. Thus, if this value is 0, there are no elements in the stack.

Recall that the *structure pointer operator* ($-$>) is a shorthand way of accessing a member in a structure when you're working with a pointer to the structure. The following two statements are equivalent and show what the —> does:

```
/* the following two assignment statements are equivalent */

stack_ptr -> vals [ 12] = val;

/* dereference the stack pointer, to get at the stack itself
   --- (*stack_ptr) ---
   then access the structure's vals member --- (*stack_ptr).vals [ 12]
   The parentheses are necessary because of the relative precedence of
   . and *
*/
(*stack_ptr).vals [ 12] = val;
```

stack_is_empty() and STACK_EMPTY()

The **stack_is_empty()** function checks the value of the top member of the stack passed as an argument. If this member has the value 0, then the stack is empty. To return the appropriate truth value, the zero result is negated to produce a nonzero, or true, result. Note that the parameter here is actually a pointer to a stack rather than a stack; this is to save storage, since the system would need to make a local copy of the stack when **stack_empty()** was called. Making such copies often requires you to increase the stack space used for your program; copying also takes time.

The **STACK_EMPTY()** macro accomplishes the same thing more quickly. This macro substitutes the negation of the top member of the stack to which the macro's argument is pointing. The stack functions in this chapter use **STACK_EMPTY()** rather than **stack_is_empty()**.

stack_is_full() and STACK_FULL()

The **stack_is_full()** function checks whether the top member equals the predefined stack size limit, **MAX_VALS**. If this is the case, the stack is full (since the next cell to be filled has an index beyond the maximum index allowed for the stack array). Again, a pointer to a stack is used, to save storage and time.

The **STACK_FULL()** macro accomplishes the same thing more quickly. This macro substitutes an expression testing the equality of the top member and **MAX_VAL**. The macro takes a pointer to a stack as its argument. The stack functions in this chapter use **STACK_FULL()** rather than **stack_is_full()**.

**show_stack_top( ), disp_stack( ),
stack_height( ), and STACK_SIZE( )**

The **show_stack_top( )** function displays the value currently at
the top of the stack. Function **disp_stack( )** displays the entire
stack, one element per line. Function **stack_height( )** returns the
number of elements in the stack. Finally, the macro **STACK_
SIZE( )** provides a quicker means of returning the stack size than
does the **stack_height( )** function, because the macro simply substitutes the value of the stack's top member in an expression during
preprocessing rather than requiring a function call at run time.

Adding to and Removing
from the Stack

Because of the way stacks are defined, the only place you can modify
a stack is at the top. To add an element, you add it to the top of the
stack —that is, in the first available cell. To remove an element, you
remove the topmost value in the array and adjust the top of the stack
indicator accordingly. These two actions —adding to and removing
from a stack —are known as *pushing* and *popping* the stack, respectively. The following functions let you push and pop the specified
stack:

```
/* Functions for pushing and popping a stack.
   Add to file stack.c.
*/


/* Add to function declaration section of stack.c */
char        *pop_stack ( struct stack *);
int         push_stack ( char *, struct stack *);

/* function definitions */

/*
    int push_stack ( char *val, struct stack *stack_ptr)
    *********************************************************
    Add an element to a stack, first checking whether the stack is full.
    If the stack is full, the function does nothing.
    CALLS : STACK_FULL (); strcpy ()
    GLOBALS : TRUE, FALSE
    PARAMETERS :
            char *val : string being added to stack;
            struct stack *stack_ptr : pointer to stack being augmented.
    RETURN : int specifying whether something was added to stack
    USAGE : did_add = push_stack ( str, &st);
    *********************************************************
```

```
*/
int push_stack ( char *val, struct stack *stack_ptr)
{
    /* if stack is not full, add the element,
       AND increment the top of stack marker.
    */
    if ( !STACK_FULL ( stack_ptr))
    {
            strcpy ( stack_ptr -> vals [ (stack_ptr -> top)++], val);
            return ( TRUE);
    }
    else    /* if stack is full, indicate that push was unsuccessful */
            return ( FALSE);
}


/*
    char *pop_stack ( struct stack *stack_ptr)
    *****************************************************
    Remove an element from a stack, if possible;
    return the element to the calling function;
    adjust the top of the stack to reflect the pop.
    CALLS : STACK_EMPTY ()
    GLOBALS :
    PARAMETERS :
            struct stack *stack_ptr : pointer to stack being popped.
    RETURN : string popped from stack.
    USAGE : strcpy ( str, pop_stack ( &st));
    *****************************************************
*/
char *pop_stack ( struct stack *stack_ptr)
{
        if ( !STACK_EMPTY ( stack_ptr))
                return ( stack_ptr -> vals [ --stack_ptr -> top]);
        else
                return ( null_str);
}
```

push_stack( )

The **push_stack( )** function takes two arguments: a string value and a pointer to a stack. The second parameter must be a pointer so that the new element remains in the stack once **push_stack( )** has finished its work. Recall that in C, parameters are passed by value; that is, only a copy of the value stored in an argument is passed ordinarily. This means there is no way of changing the actual variable directly unless you pass in the address of the variable you want to change.

The **push_stack( )** function first checks whether the stack is full; if so, it does not change the stack. The function does return a value of FALSE(0) in that case, to indicate that the push was unsuccessful.

The use of the structure pointer operator twice in **push_stack( )** makes the central expression very compact. The expression indicating the array subscript effectively says, "Get the top member of the stack to which **stack_ptr** is pointing, using the current value of **top** to do this, and *then* increment the **top** member by 1." The parentheses around **stack_ptr —>top** are there for clarity; they are not necessary, since the structure pointer operator has a higher precedence than the increment operator. Thus, the assignment statement says, "Assign **val** to the cell at the top of the stack to which **stack_ptr** is pointing; then adjust the top-of-stack indicator after making the assignment."

pop_stack( )

A similar kind of syntax is used to access a particular stack cell in function **pop_stack** and to adjust the top-of-stack indicator. This time, however, the prefix version of the decrement operator (--) is used when specifying the index of the cell to pop. The **top** member always indicates the *next* cell to be *filled*, which means that the last value pushed onto the stack is in the cell whose index is 1 less than the current top-of-stack value. Once this element has been popped, the new value of top is retained as the new top-of-stack indicator, since the cell just emptied by the pop is now the next one to be filled.

Exercising the Stack

The following program lets you test the stack functions. The only new element required for the program is the **main( )** function; so if you've got the other functions on disk, you need to type just **main( )**. The files **defs.h** and **stack.c** contain the data structures, preprocessor constants, and function definitions from the earlier listings.

```
/* Program to exercise stack functions.
   Program reads stack routines and definitions from file stack.c
*/

#include <stdio.h>
#include <stdlib.h>
#include <string.h>
/* read files containing preprocessor directives and function definitions */
#include "defs.h"
#include "stack.c"

main ()
{
        struct stack st;
        int          index;
        char         *outcome, message [ SHORT_STR];
```

```
/* show how much storage the stack requires. */
    printf ( "%d\n", sizeof (st));
    init_stack ( &st);          /* initialize the stack */

/* get values for the stack */
    do
    {
            printf ( "? ");
            gets ( message);
            push_stack ( message, &st);
    }
    while ( strcmp( message, null_str));

/* display the values by looping through the stack */
    for ( index = st.top; index >= 0; index--)
    {
            outcome = pop_stack ( &st);
            if ( outcome != null_str)
                    printf ( "%d: %s\n", st.top, outcome);
            else
                    printf ( "nothing left in stack\n");
    }

/* get more values for the stack */
    do
    {
            printf ( "? ");
            gets ( message);
            push_stack ( message, &st);
    }
    while ( strcmp ( message, null_str));

/* display the values by calling disp_stack () */
    disp_stack ( &st);
}
```

You can compile this program to memory in the QuickC environment, or you can create an executable file with QuickC, Microsoft C 5.0, or any other C compiler that adheres to the Draft Proposed ANSI Standard. Suppose you have the program in a file called **xstack.c**. To compile this file to executable form in QuickC,

1. Type **qc xstack** at the main DOS command line.
2. Once in QuickC, press ALT-R, followed by C, to get the compiler options menu.
3. In the dialog box for this menu, press X to have QuickC compile to an **exe** file.

Play with the program to get a better feel for how stacks work and to test the limits of the functions. For example, try entering a string that is longer than **SHORT—STR** characters. What happens if you push a string onto the stack after pushing such a long string?

The **MAX—VALS** of 50 defined in **stack.c** is arbitrary. If you decide to make it larger, however, you may need to increase the stack size in the QuickC run-time options. To do this, press ALT-R-O (that is, press the ALT and R keys simultaneously, then type the letter O). In the resulting dialog box, press ALT-S to get into the **Stack Size** text box. Set this to a larger value (such as 4096 or 8192), and press RETURN. Then compile and run your program as you normally would.

USING STACKS: A SIMPLE POSTFIX CALCULATOR

In this section, you'll build a program to serve as a simple four-function calculator. This program will use stacks to store values during the computations. The calculator will use a *postfix*, or *reverse Polish*, notation.

Infix Notation

You're probably used to writing mathematical expressions such as the following:

```
7.5 + 39.3 - 16.2
```

Let's look briefly at the structure of this expression. Elements such as + and − are known as *operators*. They specify what is to be done with the values surrounding them. These values, such as 7.5 and 16.2, are called *operands*. They represent the values used by the operators to produce results or new operands for other operators. Thus, the preceding expression has the structure

```
    7.5        +        39.3        -        16.2
<operand> <operator> <operand> <operator> <operand>
```

The + and the − operators each take two operands and return a single value. For example, the addition operator, +, combines the operands 7.5 and 39.3 and produces a single result, 46.8, the sum of the two operands. Similarly, the subtraction operator, −, takes the resulting 46.8 and subtracts its second operand, 16.2, from this value, returning a single value, 30.6, as the result.

Operators that take two operands and return a single result are called *binary operators*. In the preceding notation, each binary operator is placed between its operands. This notation is called *infix* notation and is the one taught in school.

In mathematical expressions, addition and subtraction are usually performed from left to right in the order encountered — unless the expression also involves multiplication or division. Recall from algebra that multiplication and division have precedence over addition and subtraction. Thus, the following expression would come out to 17.5, not 22.5, because multiplication has precedence over addition:

```
2.5 + 5 * 3
```

To make the expression come out to 22.5, you need to use parentheses to control the order in which the operations are carried out.

```
(2.5 + 5) * 3
```

This example points out one of the disadvantages of infix notation: the need for parentheses to specify how the computations are to be done.

Postfix Notation

In the 1950s Jan Łukasiewicz, a Polish logician, developed parenthesis-free notational systems for writing mathematical expressions. In these systems, an operator either precedes its operands (prefix, or Polish, notation) or follows the operands (postfix, or reverse Polish, notation). The advantage of these systems is that you never need parentheses to specify the order of evaluation.

You'll use postfix notation in the calculator you'll build in this chapter. First, however, let's look briefly at how postfix notation works. The following are two expressions in infix and postfix versions:

```
3 + 7   /* infix notation: <left operand> <operator> <right operand> */
3 7 +   /* postfix notation: <left operand> <right operand> <operator> */

2.5 + 5 * 3   /* infix notation */
2.5 5 3 * +   /* postfix notation */
```

The first pair of expressions illustrates the major difference between infix and postfix versions: In the former, the operator is preceded by a left operand and followed by a right operand; in the latter, the operator is preceded by *both* operands.

Let's look carefully at the second pair of expressions, because these show how to determine the order of the terms in the expression. From the infix version, you can determine that the answer will be 17.5 because the expression reduces to 2.5 + 15; that is, the right operand for the addition operator is the 15 that results from the multiplication. In infix form, this amounts to the following sequence of steps:

```
5   *   3     /* == 15 */
2.5 +   15    /* == 17.5 */
```

You can break the postfix version up as follows to produce the same result:

```
5   3   *     /* == 15 */
2.5 15  +     /* == 17.5 */
```

You generally evaluate expressions from left to right. You can use that method to see how computations are done with postfix expressions. To evaluate a postfix expression,

1. If the expression contains only an operand, you are done; otherwise, proceed to step 2.

2. Find the leftmost operator. In the preceding case, this was *.

3. Find the two operands immediately preceding this operator — in this case, 3 and 5.

4. Carry out the required operation, using the operand immediately to the left of the operator as the right operand and the operand farther away as the left operand. In this case, the computation is: 5 * 3.

5. Substitute the result for the three terms used in the computation. In your case, 15 replaces the terms 5, 3, and *.

6. Repeat steps 1 through 5 until you are left with a single value. In your case, another pass through the algorithm adds 2.5 and 15 to produce a final result.

To see why parentheses are unnecessary with postfix notation, let's look at another version of our expression. The following are infix and postfix versions of an expression in which addition is to be performed before multiplication:

```
(2.5  +  5)  *  3          /* infix notation */
2.5   5  +  3  *           /* postfix notation */
```

Using the algorithm, you would go through the following steps to solve this expression:

1. Find + as the leftmost operator.

2. Compute 2.5 + 5.

3. Substitute the result for the terms 2.5, 5, and +, leaving 7.5 3 *.

4. Find * as the leftmost operator the second time through the algorithm's loop.

5. Compute 7.5 * 3.

6. Substitute the result for 7.5, 3, and *, leaving 22.5.

7. Stop, since there is just a single operand and no more operators.

In a postfix expression, operators always appear in the order in which they will be applied. These operators are always preceded by their operands, even though the operands may be quite complex, involving other expressions.

Creating a Postfix Expression

Let's look at one more example. Later, you'll create a function for converting to postfix automatically. For now, to create a postfix expression, just try to determine what each operator's operands are. To write the postfix expression, simply put these operands immediately before the operator. Sometimes you may need to work to get the operand, as in the expressions where it was necessary to compute 5 * 3 to get the right operand for the addition operator.

Let's build the postfix form of the following expression:

```
7.5 + 35 * (7 - 3.5) + 6 / 3
```

The left operand for the first addition operator is obviously 7.5. The right operand is not so clear; it will turn out to be some value resulting from the multiplication. So to determine the right operand for the first addition operator, you need to evaluate the portion of the expression involving the multiplication operator. To do this, put the addition problem on hold temporarily while you resolve the multiplication.

The left operand for the product is also clear: It is 35. The right operand will be the result of the subtraction in the parentheses. Therefore, to complete the operands for the multiplication operator, you first need to carry out the subtraction. The left operand for the subtraction is 7; the right operand is 3.5. Therefore, the postfix form of the subtraction term is

```
7    3.5    -       /* postfix form of term involving subtraction operator */
 ~~   ~~~

    L    R          /* L == left operand; R == right operand */
```

This becomes the right operand for the multiplication operator. Thus the multiplication term becomes

```
35      7   3.5    -    *
~~      ~~~~~~~~
L           R
```

This whole expression is, in turn, the right operand for the first addition operator. So, we have

```
7.5        35    7  3.5  -    *        +
~~      ~~~~~~~~~~~~~~~~~~~
L                    R
```

This entire, long expression is the left operand for the second addition operator. (When you evaluate the larger expression, the preceding expression will be reduced to a single number.) To find the right operand for that operator, you first need to deal with the division operator, since division has higher precedence than addition. The postfix form for the division term is simply

```
6   3    /
~~  ~~
L   R
```

Putting these elements together, we get the following as the postfix version of the original expression:

```
7.5   35  7  3.5  -  *  +        6  3  /        +
~~~~~~~~~~~~~~~~~~~        ~~~~~~
L                         R
```

Evaluating a Postfix Expression

Now let's evaluate this expression. To do this, you work your way from left to right. As long as you encounter operands, you move on, putting each operand aside for eventual use. The easiest way to do this is to push the operands onto a stack as you encounter them. After the first four operands in the expression have been processed, such a stack would look as follows:

```
3.5            /* top stack element */
7
35
7.5
```

When you encounter an operator, you pop the topmost operand from the stack; this becomes the right operand. To get the left operand, pop the stack again. Thus after encountering the $-$ operator, you have $7 - 3.5$ as an expression to be solved, and the stack looks as follows:

```
35    /* top stack element */
7.5
```

The result of the subtraction is 3.5. Push this result back onto the stack, since it will be the right operand for the multiplication operator, which is the next element encountered in the expression.

To process the multiplication operator, pop the first and second elements from the top of the stack for the right and left operands, respectively. Thus you have $35 * 3.5$ to solve, and the stack contains only the element 7.5.

The product of 35 and 3.5 is 122.5. Push this value back onto the stack.

The addition operator is the next element encountered. To apply this operator, pop the 122.5 and the 7.5 from the stack, and carry out the addition. Then push the result onto the stack. The stack again contains a single element: this time, 130.

The next two elements in the expression are operands, so these are pushed onto the stack, resulting in the following:

```
3
6
130
```

To apply the division operator, pop 3 and 6, and solve $6 / 3$. Then push the result, 2, onto the stack again.

To apply the final operator, +, pop 130 and 2, and add them. The answer of 132 is the result of evaluating the expression with which you began.

Implementing a Postfix Calculator

In the next few pages, you'll build a simple four-function calculator for evaluating postfix expressions. For this version, you'll need to enter the expression in postfix form. Later, you'll write routines for converting an infix expression to postfix.

To compile the following program to memory in QuickC, you'll need to use a Quick library, since one of the functions called is not built into QuickC. See Appendix B for a discussion of how to build such a library. To compile to an executable file, follow the steps outlined earlier.

The central function is **solve_postfix( )**, which evaluates a postfix expression. To do its work, this function keeps operands in a stack as it evaluates the expression. The actual computations are done by **do_add( )**, **do_mult( )**, **do_sub( )**, and **do_div( )**.

Notice that the program uses stacks of strings, converting to numbers when necessary for computing. A stack of strings is more flexible than the **dbl_stack** defined earlier and will be useful when converting from infix to postfix. This approach is somewhat slower, however, since the extra conversions take time. Later in the book you'll use recursion to build the elements of a more efficient calculator.

Having worked with this version, you shouldn't find it too difficult to rewrite this program to work with a **dbl_stack**. The computational functions will become much easier. Don't forget that you'll need to change the stack manipulation functions as well.

Let's look at the main program and its routines first, before looking at the auxiliary routines used when doing the work.

```
#include <stdio.h>
#include <stdlib.h>
#include <string.h>
#include "defs.h"
#include "stack.c"
#include "utils.c"

#define ADD_OP        "+"
#define MULT_OP       "*"
#define SUB_OP        "-"
#define DIV_OP        "/"
#define BADVAL_STR    "-99999.999"

#define SHOW_WORK     1      /* show intermediate results */

struct stack st;

/* "Local" function declarations for 4-function calculator */
void        do_add ( struct stack *), do_mult ( struct stack *);
void        do_sub ( struct stack *), do_div ( struct stack *);
double      solve_postfix ( char *, struct stack *);

main ()
{
        double      result;
        char        express [ MAX_STR];
        char        entry [ MAX_STR];

        init_stack ( &st);          /* initialize the stack */
        printf ( "? ");
        gets ( express);

        printf ( "expression == %s\n", express);
        result = solve_postfix ( express, &st);

        printf ( "Answer == %15.6lf\n", result);
}


/*
    void do_mult ( struct stack *stack_ptr)
    ********************************************************
    Multiply top two values on the stack, and push the product onto stack.
    CALLS : atof (); empty_str (); f_to_str (); pop_stack (); push_stack ();
    GLOBALS : BADVAL_STR, SHORT_STR
    PARAMETERS :
          struct stack *stack_ptr : pointer to stack for storing product
    RETURN : <none>
    USAGE : do_mult ( &my_stack);
    ********************************************************
*/
void do_mult ( struct stack *stack_ptr)
{
        double left, right, result;
        char   *str;
        int    count = 0;

        str = pop_stack ( stack_ptr);
        count += ( empty_str ( str) ? -1 : 1);
        right = atof ( str);
        str = pop_stack ( stack_ptr);
        count += ( empty_str ( str) ? -1 : 1);
```

```
        left = atof ( str);
        if ( count != 2)
                push_stack ( BADVAL_STR, stack_ptr);
        else
        {
                result = left * right;
                push_stack ( f_to_str ( result, SHORT_STR), stack_ptr);
        }
}


/*
   void do_div ( struct stack *stack_ptr)
   ************************************************************
   Divide top two values on the stack, and push the quotient onto stack.
   CALLS : atof (); empty_str (); f_to_str (); pop_stack (); push_stack ();
   GLOBALS : BADVAL_STR, SHORT_STR
   PARAMETERS :
           struct stack *stack_ptr : pointer to stack for storing quotient
   RETURN : <none>
   USAGE : do_div ( &my_stack);
   ************************************************************
*/
void do_div ( struct stack *stack_ptr)
{
        double left, right, result;
        char   *str;
        int    count = 0;

        str = pop_stack ( stack_ptr);
        count += ( empty_str ( str) ? -1 : 1);
        right = atof ( str);
        str = pop_stack ( stack_ptr);
        count += ( empty_str ( str) ? -1 : 1);
        left = atof ( str);
        if ( count != 2)
                push_stack ( BADVAL_STR, stack_ptr);
        else
        {
                result = left / right;
                push_stack ( f_to_str ( result, SHORT_STR), stack_ptr);
        }
}


/*
   void do_add ( struct stack *stack_ptr)
   ************************************************************
   Add the top two values on the stack, and push the sum onto stack.
   CALLS : atof (); empty_str (); f_to_str (); pop_stack (); push_stack ();
   GLOBALS : BADVAL_STR, SHORT_STR
   PARAMETERS :
           struct stack *stack_ptr : pointer to stack for storing sum
   RETURN : <none>
   USAGE : do_add ( &my_stack);
   ************************************************************
*/
void do_add ( struct stack *stack_ptr)
{
        double left, right, result;
        char   *str;
        int    count = 0;

        str = pop_stack ( stack_ptr);
        count += ( empty_str ( str) ? -1 : 1);
        right = atof ( str);
```

```
        str = pop_stack ( stack_ptr);
        count += ( empty_str ( str) ? -1 : 1);
        left = atof ( str);
        if ( count != 2)
                push_stack ( BADVAL_STR, stack_ptr);
        else
        {
                result = left + right;
                push_stack ( f_to_str ( result, SHORT_STR), stack_ptr);
        }
}


/*
    void do_sub ( struct stack *stack_ptr)
    ************************************************************
    Subtract top two values on the stack, and push the difference onto stack.
    CALLS : atof (); empty_str (); f_to_str (); pop_stack (); push_stack ();
    GLOBALS : BADVAL_STR, SHORT_STR
    PARAMETERS :
            struct stack *stack_ptr : pointer to stack for storing difference
    RETURN : <none>
    USAGE : do_sub ( &my_stack);
    ************************************************************
*/
void do_sub ( struct stack *stack_ptr)
{
        double left, right, result;
        char    *str;
        int     count = 0;

        str = pop_stack ( stack_ptr);
        count += ( empty_str ( str) ? -1 : 1);
        right = atof ( str);
        str = pop_stack ( stack_ptr);
        count += ( empty_str ( str) ? -1 : 1);
        left = atof ( str);
        if ( count != 2)
                push_stack ( BADVAL_STR, stack_ptr);
        else
        {
                result = left - right;
                push_stack ( f_to_str ( result, SHORT_STR), stack_ptr);
        }
}


/*
    double solve_postfix ( char *express, struct stack *st)
    ************************************************************
    Solve a postfix expression and return the result.
    CALLS : atof (); do_add (); do_div (); do_mult (); do_sub ();
            empty_str (); pop_stack (); push_stack ();
            remove_wd (); show_stack_top (); strcmp (); strcpy ();
    GLOBALS : ADD_OP, DIV_OP, MULT_OP, SHORT_STR, SHOW_WORK, SUB_OP
    PARAMETERS :
            char *express : postfix expression to solve
            struct stack *st : stack used for computations
    RETURN : result of evaluating postfix expression.
    USAGE : result = solve_postfix ( my_postfix, &my_stack);
    ************************************************************
*/
double solve_postfix ( char *express, struct stack *st)
{
        char    curr_term [ SHORT_STR];
        char    *outcome;
```

```
while ( !empty_str ( express))
{
        strcpy ( curr_term, remove_wd ( express));
        if ( strcmp ( curr_term, ADD_OP) == 0)
                do_add ( st);
        else if ( strcmp ( curr_term, MULT_OP) == 0)
                do_mult ( st);
        else if ( strcmp ( curr_term, SUB_OP) == 0)
                do_sub ( st);
        else if ( strcmp ( curr_term, DIV_OP) == 0)
                do_div ( st);
        else
                push_stack ( curr_term, st);
        if ( SHOW_WORK)
                show_stack_top ( st);
}
outcome = pop_stack ( st);
return ( atof ( outcome));
}
```

Function **main( )** gets the postfix expression, and then it calls
solve_postfix( ) to do the work. Finally, **main( )** reports the result
of evaluating the expression.

solve_postfix( )

The **solve_postfix( )** function processes the postfix expression, one
token at a time. If the token is an operator, the function calls the
function appropriate for computing with the operator; should the
token be an operand, the function pushes the token onto a stack
containing other operands waiting to be used. Depending on the
value of the manifest constant, **SHOW_WORK**, **solve_postfix( )**
may show the intermediate results, in the form of the top stack
element as each token is processed.

do_mult( ), etc.

The four operator functions, **do_mult( )** through **do_sub( )**, all
work the same way: They pop two operands from the stack, convert
each of these from string to numerical form, carry out the appropriate computation, and push the result back onto the operand stack.
Because the stack contains strings, this result is first converted to a
string using a function called **f_to_str( )**, which you'll look at in
a bit.

Each of the operator functions requires two operands to do its
work. If there are too few operands on the stack, the functions push a
default error value, **BADVAL_STR** onto the stack. To determine

whether this should happen, the functions use the **int** variable **count**. This value is initialized to 0 during definition. The value is incremented by 1 each time a valid operand is popped from the stack. If the functions do not have two operands to work with, the functions return **BADVAL—STR**. The test for determining how to change **count** uses the conditional operator (**? :**) to specify the appropriate change, depending on whether or not the string just read is empty. The latter outcome indicates that there is nothing on the stack to pop.

The **solve—postfix( )** and the **do—xxx( )** functions use several other functions to help do their work, most notably the stack functions in **stack.c** as well as functions **remove—wd( )** and **f—to—str( )** in file **utils.c**. The following listing shows the contents of **utils.c**:

```
/* Partial contents of file utils.c */

/* **************
   string function DECLARATIONS
************** */
int        char_pos ( char *str, int ch);
void       delete ( char *str, int start, int how_many);
int        empty_str ( char *);
char       *remove_wd ( char *);

/* *********************
   miscellaneous function DECLARATIONS
********************* */
char       *f_to_str ( double, int)

/* **************
   string function DEFINITIONS
************** */

#define LPAREN    "("
#define RPAREN    ")"


/*
   int char_pos ( char *str, int ch)
   ***********************************************************
   Return the array subscript corresponding to the first occurrence of the
   specified character in the string.
   If the character does not occur in the string, the function returns -1.
   CALLS :
   GLOBALS : NULL_CHAR;
   PARAMETERS :
           char *str : string to search for occurrence of character.
           int ch : character to seek in str.
   RETURN : int representing array subscript of 1st occurrence of ch in str.
   USAGE : where = char_pos ( str, ch);
   ***********************************************************
*/
int char_pos ( char *str, int ch)
{
        int index;
```

```
    /* The function only searches, continuing until either
       the character is found OR end of string is reached.
    */
        for ( index = 0; ( str [index] != ch) && ( str [ index] != NULL_CHAR);
            index++)
                ;

    /* if end of string (i.e., character NOT found), return -1,
       else return subscript (index value) at which character was found.
    */
        if (str [ index] == NULL_CHAR)
                return ( -1);
        else
                return ( index);
}



/*
    void delete ( char *str, int start, int how_many)
    ***********************************************************
    Delete a specified number of characters from a string,
    beginning at a specified position in the string.
    NOTE: The starting position refers to the actual position of the
          character in the string, NOT in the array.
          Thus, the first starting position in the string is 1 NOT 0.

    CALLS : strlen()
    GLOBAL : NULL_CHAR
    PARAMETERS :
            char *str : string from which characters are to be deleted;
            int start : position (NOT array subscript index) of first character
                        to delete;
            int how_many : number of characters to delete.
    USAGE : delete ( str, 2, 27);
    ***********************************************************
*/
void delete ( char *str, int start, int how_many)
{
        int index1, index2;

    /* if starting position is an invalid value, start with 1 */
        if ( start < 1)
                start = 1;
    /* if # of chars to delete would go past end of string,
       just delete to end of string.
    */
        if ( start + how_many - 1 > strlen ( str))
                how_many = strlen ( str) + 1 - start;

    /* leave all characters before start position alone;
       begin changing characters at character (start - 1),
       (because arrays begin at index 0)
       begin moving new characters from position (start + how_many - 1);
       substitute the characters indexed by index2 for those indexed by
       index1.
       continue until the end of the string has been reached.
    */
        for ( index1 = start - 1, index2 = start + how_many - 1;
              str [ index2] != NULL_CHAR; index1++, index2++)
        {
                str [ index1] = str [ index2];
        }
        str [ index1] = NULL_CHAR;    /* terminate the string properly */
}
```

```
/*
    int  empty_str ( char *str)
    *********************************************************
    Return TRUE if str is empty

    CALLS : strlen()
    GLOBAL : NULL_CHAR
    PARAMETERS :
            char *str : string to test;
    RETURN : TRUE if string is empty; FALSE otherwise
    USAGE : result = empty_str ( str);
    *********************************************************
*/
int  empty_str ( char *str)
{
        return ( !strlen ( str));   /* strlen == 0 if empty, so negate */
}




/*
    char *remove_wd ( char *str)
    *********************************************************
    Remove the first word from a string; a word is any sequence of characters
    followed by a blank. Strip this word from the string being processed.
    If no blanks are found in the specified string, the entire string is
    returned as the word.
    CALLS : char_pos(), delete(), strcpy()
    GLOBALS : BLANK_CHAR, MAX_STR, NULL_CHAR
    PARAMETERS :
            char *str : string from which to remove a word.
    RETURN : string containing first word found in str.
    USAGE : new_word_str = remove_wd ( str);
    *********************************************************
*/
char *remove_wd ( char *str)
{
        int index, where;
        int char_pos ( char *, int);
        char temp [ MAX_STR];

    /* remove any leading blanks from string */
        while ( !char_pos ( str, BLANK_CHAR))
                delete ( str, 1, 1);

    /* find position of first blank in string.
       If a blank is found, copy everything up to (but not including)
       If no blank is found, return entire string as the new word,
       then empty the original string.
    */
        where = char_pos ( str, BLANK_CHAR);
        if ( where >= 0)
        {
            /* copy word into temp */
                for ( index = 0; index < where; index++)
                        temp [ index] = str [ index];
                temp [ index] = NULL_CHAR;      /* terminate temp properly */
                delete ( str, 1, where + 1);   /* remove word from str */
        }
        else
        {
                strcpy ( temp, str);       /* copy str to temp */
                str [ 0] = NULL_CHAR;      /* set str to empty string */
        }
        return (temp);
}
```

```
/* **********************
   miscellaneous function DEFINITIONS
********************** */

/*
    char *f_to_str ( double val, int max_len)
    ***********************************************************
    Convert a double value to a string with length <= max_len
    The function checks whether zeros need to be added after the
    decimal point, and adds them, adjusting the number of remaining
    digits written;
    The function actually writes 3 digits fewer than the maximum length
    allowed --- to leave room for a sign, decimal point and \0.

    CALLS : ecvt (), strcpy()
    GLOBALS : MAX_STR, NULL_CHAR
    PARAMETERS :
            double val : value to be converted to string.
            int  max_len : longest string that can be built.
    RETURN : string containing number converted to string form.
    USAGE : str_value = f_to_str ( val, max_size);
    ***********************************************************
*/
char *f_to_str ( double val, int max_len)
{
        char  temp_str [ MAX_STR], str [ MAX_STR];
        char  *str_ptr;
        int   sign_val, pt_pos, index, small_len;

        str_ptr = str;         /* use str_ptr to build the string */
    /* Turn the number into a string, using ecvt() library function.
        max_len : maximum string length allowed.
        The 3 places subtracted are for: sign, decimal point, \0
    */
        strcpy ( temp_str, ecvt ( val, max_len - 3, &pt_pos, &sign_val));

    /* if the number is negative, sign_val == 1 */
        if ( sign_val)
                *str_ptr++ = '-';

    /* if zeros are needed right after decimal point ---
        that is, if the number is less than .1
    */
        if ( pt_pos < 0)
        {
                /* if the number is so small that more fractional
                    zeros are required than are allowed in the string,
                    just fill the allowable number of places with zeros.
                */
                if ( -pt_pos > (max_len - 3))
                        pt_pos = -max_len + 3;
                /* small_len keeps function from writing too long a
                    string in the event of a very tiny value;
                */
                small_len = max_len - 3 + pt_pos;
                *str_ptr++ = '.';
                for ( index = pt_pos; index < 0; index++)
                        *str_ptr++ = '0';
                pt_pos = 0;
        }
        else   /* if number is large enough to cause no special problems. */
        {
                /* transfer the digits left of the decimal point */
                for ( index = 0; index < pt_pos; index++)
                        *str_ptr++ = temp_str [ index];
```

```
            *str_ptr++ = '.';
    }

/* transfer the digits right of the decimal point */

        for ( index = pt_pos; temp_str [ index] != NULL_CHAR; index++)
            *str_ptr++ = temp_str [ index];

        *str_ptr = NULL_CHAR;     /* terminate resulting string properly */
        return ( str);
}
```

remove—wd( )

Function **remove—wd( )** copies the first word of a string (that is, the first sequence of characters followed by a blank or the end-of-string marker) to another string and removes the word from the original string. The function first removes any leading blanks, then determines the position of the next blank, and copies all characters up to (but not including) the blank to a new string. The function deletes the same characters from the original string and returns the string containing this word.

To do its work, **remove—wd( )** calls **char—pos( )**, which returns the position at which a specified character first appears in a string, and **delete( )**, which deletes a specified section of a string.

f—to—str( )

Function **f—to—str( )** converts a floating point value to string form. The function makes the resulting string as long as you request. To do its work, **f—to—str( )** calls a run-time library function, **ecvt( )**. This library function converts a **double** to a string but does not put a decimal point or sign into the string. **ecvt( )** does, however, tell you where the decimal point should go and whether the value is positive or negative.

f—to—str( ) essentially copies the string created by **ecvt( )**, inserting characters where needed. The conversion function first deals with the sign and inserts a − if the value is negative. The function then checks whether the decimal point is so far to the left that leading zeros need to be added to the number. For example, a value less than 0.10 (such as 0.09) would require at least one leading zero. After inserting the decimal point at the desired position, the function keeps copying until it comes to the end of the string returned by **ecvt( )** or until the string being built has reached the maximum length allowed.

The function actually builds a string three characters shorter than the maximum length allowed by the user. This is necessary to accommodate a sign character, the decimal point, and the null character that ends the string.

Converting from Infix
to Postfix

The preceding calculator is useful for computations only once you've created a postfix expression. You're more used to working with infix expressions, so let's turn the task of creating a postfix expression over to the program. In this section you'll look at the routines for converting from infix to postfix form.

The following listing shows the routines used to accomplish this. Add function **expand—str( )** to your **utils.c** file. Assume the other functions in the listing are in a separate file, **pfutils.c**, because these functions assume that a stack data structure has been defined. The functions in **utils.c** are more generally applicable and do not require a stack structure. You'll use those functions in other programs.

```
/* Function for putting blanks around specified characters
   --- e.g. parentheses.  Add to file utils.c.
*/

/* Add the following to the function declarations in utils.c */
char    *expand_str ( char *, char, char)

/*
    char *expand_str ( char *str, char ch1, char ch2)
    ***********************************************************
    Surround any occurrences of either specified character
    blanks in the string parameter.
    CALLS :
    GLOBALS : BLANK_CHAR, MAX_STR, NULL_CHAR
    PARAMETERS :
            char *str : string to be expanded
            ch1, ch2 : characters to be surrounded by spaces
    RETURN : expanded string, with characters surrounded by spaces.
    USAGE : strcy ( str, expand_str ( str, ch_one, ch_two));
    ***********************************************************
```

```
*/
char *expand_str ( char *str, char ch1, char ch2)
{
        char temp [ MAX_STR];
        int   index = 0, str_ind = 0;

        strcpy ( temp, str);

    /* As long as there are characters in temp, transfer them to
       str --- surrounding occurrences of ch with blanks.
    */
        while ( (temp [ index] != NULL_CHAR) && ( str_ind < MAX_STR))
        {
                if ( (temp [ index] != ch1) && ( temp [ index] != ch2))
                        str [ str_ind++] = temp [ index++];
                else    /* if current character is one to be padded */
                {
                        /* make sure string will not get too long */
                        if ( str_ind < MAX_STR - 3)
                        {
                                str [ str_ind++] = BLANK_CHAR;
                                str [ str_ind++] = temp [ index];
                                str [ str_ind++] = BLANK_CHAR;
                        } /* if enough room left in str */
                        index++;
                }    /* if current character is to be padded */
        }            /* while there are characters to process in temp */

    /* terminate newly built string properly */
        if ( str_ind < MAX_STR)
                str [ str_ind] = NULL_CHAR;
        else
                str [ --str_ind] = NULL_CHAR;

        return ( str);
}



/* ***************** Contents of file pfutils.c ****************** */

/* **********************
   postfix utility function DECLARATIONS
********************** */
char          *to_postfix ( char *);
int           precedes ( char *, char *);


/* **********************
   postfix utility function DEFINITIONS
********************** */

/*
   char *to_postfix ( char *str)
   ********************************************************
   Convert an infix expression to postfix form;
   currently understands * / + - operators.
   CALLS : get_out (); handle_op (); handle_rparen (); init_stack ();
           pop_stack (); push_stack (); strcat (); strcmp (); strcpy ();
   GLOBALS : blank_str, MAX_STR, LPAREN, NULL, null_str, RPAREN, SHORT_STR
   PARAMETERS :
           char *str : infix string to convert to postfix.
   RETURN : string representing postfix version of expression
   USAGE : strcpy ( postfix_str, to_postfix ( infix_str));
   ********************************************************
```

```
*/
char *to_postfix ( char *str)
{
        char   op_str [ MAX_STR];      /* string to hold operators */
    /* infix and postfix (output) string, respectively */
        char   in_str [ MAX_STR], out_str [ MAX_STR];
    /* current token, and string popped from stack, respectively */
        char   curr_wd [ SHORT_STR], next_cand [ SHORT_STR];
    /* used to determine whether a string is contained in another */
        char   *test_str;
    /* used to identify invalid infix expressions */
        int    val_count = 0;
        extern struct stack st;

    /* declarations for functions called only by to_postfix (). */
        char   *handle_op ( char *, struct stack *, char *, int *);
        char   *handle_rparen ( struct stack *, char *, int *);
        void   get_out ( char *);

    /* initialize stacks and strings */
        init_stack ( &st);
        strcpy ( op_str, "* / + -");   /* string containing operators */
        strcpy ( in_str, str);
        strcpy ( out_str, null_str);   /* string for postfix expression */

    /* process the infix string */
        while ( strcmp (in_str, null_str))
        {
                strcpy ( curr_wd, remove_wd (in_str));

            /* if curr_wd is a left parenthesis */
                if ( !strcmp ( curr_wd, LPAREN))
                {
                        push_stack ( curr_wd, &st);
                        continue;

                }

            /* if curr_wd is a right parenthesis */
                if ( !strcmp ( curr_wd, RPAREN))
                {
                        strcpy ( out_str,
                                handle_rparen ( &st, out_str, &val_count));
                        continue;     /* get next token */
                }   /* if RIGHT PARENTHESIS */


            /* if token is an operator or an operand */
                if ( (test_str = strstr ( op_str, curr_wd)) != NULL)
                {
                        strcpy ( out_str,
                                handle_op ( curr_wd, &st,
                                        out_str, &val_count));
                        continue;
                }     /* if an operator was found */
                else  /* if the token is an operand, add to out_str */
                {
                        strcat ( out_str, curr_wd);
                        strcat ( out_str, blank_str);
                        val_count++;
                }     /* if tcken is an operand */
        }   /* while in_str is not empty */
```

```
/* Copy remaining operators from stack to postfix expression */
    strcpy (next_cand, pop_stack ( &st));
    while ( strcmp ( next_cand, null_str))
    {
            strcat ( out_str, next_cand);
            strcat ( out_str, blank_str);
            val_count--;
            if ( val_count < 0)
                    get_out( out_str);
            strcpy (next_cand, pop_stack ( &st));
    }   /* while there is something on the stack */

    if ( val_count != 1)
            get_out( out_str);
    return ( out_str);
}


/*
    int precedes ( char *op1, char *op2)
    ************************************************************
    Test relative precedence of two operators passed in;
    return TRUE if first operator has precedence >= second operator.
    Routine currently knows about * / + -, and gives left parentheses
    an arbitrarily low precedence.
    CALLS : empty_str (); strcpy (); strstr ()
    GLOBALS : FALSE, TRUE, MAX_STR, NULL
    PARAMETERS :
            char *op1 : first operator for comparison
            char *op2 : second operator for comparison
    RETURN : whether op1 has precedence >= precedence of op2
    USAGE : if ( precedes ( str1, str2)
    ************************************************************
*/

int precedes ( char *op1, char *op2)
{
        char    *test_str;
        char    level_0 [ MAX_STR], level_1 [ MAX_STR], level_10 [ MAX_STR];
        int     prec1, prec2;

    /* if one or both operators is null, return a value right away */
        if ( empty_str ( op1))
                return ( FALSE);
        if ( empty_str ( op2))
                return ( TRUE);

    /* initialize strings for operators at each precedence level */
        strcpy ( level_0, "* /");
        strcpy ( level_1, "+ -");

    /* Check whether op1 is found in any of the precedence strings */
        if ( (test_str = strstr ( level_0, op1)) != NULL)
                prec1 = 0;
        else  if ( (test_str = strstr ( level_1, op1)) != NULL)
                prec1 = 1;
        else /* if op1 is anything else, most notably, a left parenthesis */
                prec1 = 10;

    /* Check whether op2 is found in any of the precedence strings */
        if ( (test_str = strstr ( level_0, op2)) != NULL)
                prec2 = 0;
```

```
        else if ( (test_str = strstr ( level_1, op2)) != NULL)
                prec2 = 1;
        else    /* if op2 is anything else, most notably a left parenthesis */
                prec2 = 10;

    /* if op1 has higher precedence than op2, return TRUE */
        /* if (prec1 <= prec2)
                return ( TRUE);
        else
                return ( FALSE); */
        return ( (prec1 <= prec2) ? TRUE :  FALSE);
}


/*
    char *handle_op ( char *curr_wd, struct stack *st,
                      char *out_str, int *val_count)
    **********************************************************
    Process operators while converting from infix to postfix.
    Basic algorithm compares current operator token with stack top.
    If current has higher or equal precedence, old stack top is repushed, and
    current is pushed onto stack --- becoming new top.
    If current has lower precedence, then top operator is appended to postfix
    structure, and next top is popped --- to repeat the process.
    This continues until stack is empty or current is pushed onto the stack.
    CALLS : pop_stack (); precedes (); push_stack ();
            stack_empty (); strcmp (); strcpy ();
    GLOBALS : blank_str, null_str, SHORT_STR
    PARAMETERS :
            char *curr_wd : current operator token;
            struct stack *st : pointer to stack holding operators temporarily
            char *out_str : (postfix) string being built.
            int *val_count : value used to check whether expression is valid.
    RETURN : postfix string being built is returned to calling routine.
    USAGE : strcpy ( pf_str, handle_op ( popped_top, &st, pf_str, &count));

    **********************************************************
*/
char *handle_op ( char *curr_wd, struct stack *st,
                  char *out_str, int *val_count)
{
        char next_cand [ SHORT_STR];

    /* if stack is empty, push operator onto temp */
        if ( stack_empty ( st))
                push_stack ( curr_wd, st);
        else    /* if there are operators on stack already */
        {
            /* get top operator from stack */
                strcpy (next_cand, pop_stack ( st));
            /* while current popped operator has higher
               precedence than current token, add
               popped operator to postfix expression.
            */
                while ( precedes ( next_cand, curr_wd))
                {
                        strcat ( out_str, next_cand);
                        strcat ( out_str, blank_str);
                        (*val_count)--;
                        if ( *val_count < 0)
                                get_out ( out_str);
                    /* get top operator from stack */
                        strcpy (next_cand, pop_stack ( st));
                }
```

```
                /* if a popped operator has lower
                   precedence than current token,
                   push popped operator back onto stack.
                */
                if ( strcmp ( next_cand, null_str))
                        push_stack ( next_cand, st);
                /* push current token onto stack */
                push_stack ( curr_wd, st);
        }  /* if there are operators on the stack */

        return ( out_str);
}



/*
    char *handle_rparen ( struct stack *st, char *out_str, int *val_count)
    *********************************************************
    Process operators preceding a right parenthesis while converting
    from infix to postfix. Algorithm pops stack elements and appends
    them to the end of the postfix expression being built, until the
    element popped is a left parenthesis, at which point both parentheses
    are discarded, and the function returns the modified postfix expression.
    CALLS : get_out (); pop_stack (); stack_empty (); strcmp (); strcpy ();
    GLOBALS : blank_str, LPAREN, null_str, RPAREN, SHORT_STR
    PARAMETERS :
            struct stack *st : pointer to stack holding operators temporarily
            char *out_str : (postfix) string being built.
            int *val_count : value used to check whether expression is valid.
    RETURN : postfix string being built is returned to calling routine.
    USAGE : strcpy ( pf_str, handle_op ( &st, pf_str, &count));
    *********************************************************
*/
char *handle_rparen ( struct stack *st, char *out_str, int *val_count)

{
        char next_cand [ SHORT_STR];

        strcpy ( next_cand, pop_stack ( st));

    /* pop until the left parenthesis is found */
        while ( strcmp ( next_cand, LPAREN))
        {
            /* if something was popped,
               add it to the postfix string
            */
            if ( strcmp (next_cand, null_str))
            {
                    strcat ( out_str, next_cand);
                /* add a blank to separate tokens */
                    strcat ( out_str, blank_str);
                /* binary operator reduces # elems */
                    (*val_count)--;
                    if ( *val_count < 0)
                            get_out ( out_str);
            }
            else   /* if nothing left on stack */
                    get_out ( out_str);
            strcpy ( next_cand, pop_stack ( st));
        }

        return ( out_str);
}
```

```
/*
   void get_out (char *str)
   **********************************************************
   Print a "Bad expression" message and exit program.
   Called only by to_postfix ().
   CALLS : exit (); printf ()
   GLOBALS :
   PARAMETERS :
           char *str : string specifying desired message.
   RETURN : <none>
   USAGE : get_out ( "a");
   **********************************************************
*/
void get_out (char *str)
{
        printf ( "Invalid expression. Exiting. Str == %s\n", str);
        exit ( 1);
}
```

The central routine will take a string containing an infix expression and return a postfix version of the string. The original string has the following restrictions:

- Tokens must consist of numbers, one of the four operators, and left or right parentheses.

- All operators must have at least one blank to either side of them.

    Let's look at the functions.

to—postfix( )

The actual conversion is done by the function **to—postfix( )**. This function calls several other ones while doing its work and uses two important data structures: a stack on which to store operators and left parentheses, and a string in which the function builds the postfix expression. The basic strategy in **to—postfix( )** is to take tokens from the infix string one at a time and process them according to the following algorithm:

0. If the infix string is not empty, get a token from the string and proceed to step 1. Otherwise, pop each element from the operator stack and add it to the end of the postfix string, and exit when the stack is empty.

1. If the token is a left parenthesis, push it onto the operator stack. Repeat step 0.

2. If the token is a right parenthesis, pop elements off the operator stack and add these to the end of the postfix string until the left parenthesis is found. When the left parenthesis is found, stop popping the stack. Do *not* add the left parenthesis to the postfix string. Repeat step 0.

3. If the token is an operator, check whether the operator stack is empty. If so, push the current token onto the operator stack. Repeat step 0.

4. If the token is an operator but the operator stack is not empty, pop the operator stack and compare the relative precedence of the popped operator and the current token. (For purposes of this comparison, assume that left parentheses have a lower precedence than actual operators.)

5. If the popped operator has higher precedence than the current token, add the popped operator to the end of the postfix string, and pop the operator stack again. Repeat the comparison in this step as long as the stack has elements to pop and the popped operator has higher precedence than the current token. If the popped operator has lower precedence, proceed to step 6. If the stack is empty, go to step 3.

6. If the popped operator has lower precedence than the current token, push the popped operator back onto the operator stack, and *then* push the current token onto the operator stack. Repeat step 0.

7. If the token is an operand, add it to the end of the postfix string. Repeat step 0.

Let's work through an example using this algorithm. Take the expression used earlier: $7.5 + 35 * (7 - 3.5) + 6 / 3$. To illustrate the algorithm, you'll need to keep track of four values: current token (**token**), popped operator (**popped**), top stack value (**top‒val**), and the postfix string (**pf**) as shown in Figure 1-1. The figure also specifies the step that brought about the particular values on the

token	popped	top_val	pf								count	step
7.5	---	null	null								0	0
---	---	null	7.5								1	7
+	---	null	7.5								1	0
---	---	+	7.5								1	3
35	---	+	7.5								1	0
---	---	+	7.5	35							2	7
*	---	+	7.5	35							2	0
*	+	null	7.5	35							2	4
*	---	+	7.5	35							2	6
---	---	*	7.5	35							2	6
(	---	*	7.5	35							2	0
---	---	(	7.5	35							2	1
7	---	(	7.5	35							2	0
---	---	(	7.5	35	7						3	7
-	---	(	7.5	35	7						3	0
-	(	*	7.5	35	7						3	4
-	---	(	7.5	35	7						3	6
---	---	-	7.5	35	7						3	6
3.5	---	-	7.5	35	7						3	0
---	---	-	7.5	35	7	3.5					4	7
)	---	-	7.5	35	7	3.5					4	0
)	-	(	7.5	35	7	3.5					4	2
)	(	*	7.5	35	7	3.5	-				3	2
+	---	*	7.5	35	7	3.5	-				3	0
+	*	+	7.5	35	7	3.5	-				3	4
+	+	null	7.5	35	7	3.5	-	*			2	5
+	---	null	7.5	35	7	3.5	-	*	+		1	3
---	---	+	7.5	35	7	3.5	-	*	+		1	3
6	---	+	7.5	35	7	3.5	-	*	+		1	0
---	---	+	7.5	35	7	3.5	-	*	+	6	2	7
/	---	+	7.5	35	7	3.5	-	*	+	6	2	0
/	+	null	7.5	35	7	3.5	-	*	+	6	2	4
/	---	+	7.5	35	7	3.5	-	*	+	6	2	6
---	---	/	7.5	35	7	3.5	-	*	+	6	2	6
3	---	/	7.5	35	7	3.5	-	*	+	6	2	0
---	---	/	7.5	35	7	3.5	-	*	+	6	3	3	7
---	/	+	7.5	35	7	3.5	-	*	+	6	3	3	0
---	---	+	7.5	35	7	3.5	-	*	+	6	3 /	2	0
---	+	null	7.5	35	7	3.5	-	*	+	6	3 / +	2	0
---	---	null	7.5	35	7	3.5	-	*	+	6	3 / +	2	0

Figure 1-1. Step-by-step creation of postfix expression

line. Don't worry about the **count** column; we'll discuss that in a bit. When a value is undefined or irrelevant, the entry contains - - -.

Try solving the postfix expression by hand to help consolidate your mastery of postfix expressions.

handle—op( ) and handle—rparen( )

To do its work, **to—postfix( )** calls two functions: **handle—op( )** (to process operators) and **handle rparen( )** (to move operators until a left parenthesis is found on the stack).

The **handle—op( )** function is responsible for steps 4 through 6 in the algorithm, and the **handle—rparen( )** takes care of step 7. The **to—postfix( )** function does steps 0 through 3 itself.

precedes( )

To determine relative precedence, **handle—op( )** calls the function **precedes( )**, which returns TRUE if the first operator passed in has precedence higher than or equal to the precedence of the second operator. For **handle—op( )**, the first operator is the popped operator, and the second operator is the current token. (By assigning greater precedence to the popped operator when the two operators have equal precedence, you ensure that the expression is evaluated from left to right.)

The strategy in **precedes( )** is to test the operator against strings that contain all the operators at a particular precedence level. Thus **level—0** contains the multiplication and division operators, which have the same precedence. The addition and subtraction operators are listed in **level—1**. By determining the level string in which an operator is found, the function can determine the relative precedence. To add other operators at a particular level, just change the contents of the level string. To add other precedence levels, define and initialize strings for those levels, and add the appropriate conditional (**else if**) clauses to the **if** construct.

Notice the column labeled "count" in the illustration. This column records the value of **count**, a local variable in function **to—postfix( )**. This variable provides a quick and easy way to determine whether the postfix expression is syntactically correct.

Essentially, the **count** variable records the number of operands in the function. Each time an operand is added to the postfix expression (**out—str**), the value of **count** is increased by 1, because the number of operands in the expression has increased by 1. Each time a binary operator is added to the expression, the value of **count** is *decreased* by 1. (Recall that a binary operator takes two operands and returns a single value, or operand. Thus, the presence of a binary operator in the expression effectively reduces the number of operands by one.)

The value of **count** is updated as changes are made to the postfix expression. When you have finished building the postfix expression, the value of **count** must be 1, because you will end up with a single result when you finish evaluating a proper postfix expression. If the value of **count** ever becomes 0 or less once you've started building the expression, the expression is incorrect. For example, if **count** is less than 0, the expression has too many operators; if **count** equals 0, the expression has been processed without a result. As soon as the function finds that **count** has a nonpositive value, it ends the program, since the expression is invalid.

expand—str( )

Many people are used to typing parentheses right next to values, with no intervening spaces. For this reason, the calculator does not require these blanks. The function that converts from infix to postfix expects these blanks, however. The **expand—str( )** function puts these blanks around any parentheses it finds in your expression. This function simply moves characters from one string to another. Any time it encounters one of the two specified characters — in our case, left and right parentheses — the function adds a blank before and after the character.

You could also call this function to put blanks around operators, but be careful when dealing with the subtraction operator. Putting blanks around the subtraction operator will also put a blank between a minus sign and a number. To avoid this, you might want to require a minus sign to be separated by blanks but process the other operators with **expand—str( )**.

To incorporate these functions into the calculator program, you just need to add the function declarations and definitions to the appropriate source files (such as **utils.c** or **pfutils.c**). You also need to add three lines to your **main( )** function to include the **pfutils.c** file, to expand the infix string, and to convert it to postfix form. The following listing contains the revised **main( )**:

```c
/* Revised main() function for four-function calculator.
   Program now takes infix expressions as input
*/

#include <stdio.h>
#include <stdlib.h>
#include <string.h>
#include "defs.h"
#include "stack.c"
#include "utils.c"
#include "pfutils.c"         /* NEW line --- to read postfix utils file */

#define ADD_OP        "+"
#define MULT_OP       "*"
#define SUB_OP        "-"
#define DIV_OP        "/"
#define BADVAL_STR    "-99999.999"

#define SHOW_WORK     1     /* show intermediate results */

struct stack st;

/* "Local" function declarations for 4-function calculator */
void        do_add ( struct stack *), do_mult ( struct stack *);
void        do_sub ( struct stack *), do_div ( struct stack *);
double      solve_postfix ( char *, struct stack *);

main ()
{
        double      result;
        char        express [ MAX_STR];
        char        entry [ MAX_STR];

        init_stack ( &st);            /* initialize the stack */
        printf ( "? ");
        gets ( express);

    /* The following two lines are new --- to convert to postfix */
        strcpy ( express, expand_str ( express, '(', ')'));
        strcpy ( express, to_postfix ( express));

        printf ( "expression == %s\n", express);
        result = solve_postfix ( express, &st);

        printf ( "Answer == %15.6lf\n", result);
}
```

Suggestions and Projects

The calculator you've built is somewhat flexible and useful. You can extend and modify it in several ways, however, and you may want to do so.

A couple of straightforward extensions involve the use of command line arguments. You might want to make it possible to specify on the command line whether to show intermediate results — that is, to set the value of a variable such as **SHOW_WORK** at run time. A second possibility would be to let the user enter the infix expression on the command line. To do this, your main program (or some other function) would need to construct the infix expression from the command line arguments.

You might want to make the calculator able to use other operators, such as exponentiation, logarithms, and so forth. If you do this, keep in mind that you may be introducing new precedence levels and nonbinary operators. For example, a logarithm operator is a *unary operator*: It takes one value and returns another value, the logarithm of its operand.

Another possibility is to make the calculator able to handle variable names. For example, if you allowed just single-character variable names and distinguished between uppercase and lowercase, you could have 52 variables in an expression. To add this capability, you would need to add a mechanism for determining or getting values for the variables and a way of dealing with the variables while processing the expressions.

Once you've got the calculator this far, you might make it possible to specify a function name (and possibly a file name), have the calculator get the formula for the function from the specified file, and then solve the formula for the specific values you have.

QUEUES

At the beginning of the chapter, you read about strategies for handling lists of elements: the LIFO strategy used in stacks, which you've just seen, and the FIFO strategy used in queues, which you'll look at now.

A *queue* is a list structure in which the first element added to the list is also the first element removed from the list. Additions are always made at the end of the list, and deletions are always made from the beginning of the list. It's like a line at the bank: You get on at the end of the line, and you leave from the front of the line when your turn comes.

The following structure provides one representation of a queue:

```
#define MAX_VALS    50    /* maximum number of elements in queue */
#define SHORT_STR   15    /* maximum size of elements in a queue of strings */

struct queue {
    /* the actual queue elements are stored in an array of strings */
        char    vals [ MAX_VALS] [ SHORT_STR];
        int     front, /* first occupied cell; first to be emptied */
                back;  /* next cell to be filled */
};
```

This structure is very similar to the template for a stack that we've been using. The major difference is the extra **int** member in the queue structure, which indicates the beginning of the list. This information is needed because elements are removed from the front of the list.

It is not feasible to move all remaining elements forward each time an element is removed from the front of the queue. Therefore, when an element is removed, the value of the **front** member of the queue is simply increased by 1.

What happens when you fill the last cell in the **vals[]** array? In a simple queue, this means you cannot add any more elements. However, suppose you had filled the queue and then removed 49 elements—that is, removed the strings in cells 0 through 48— leaving only the string in **vals[49]**. With a simple queue, you would not be able to add another element unless you moved the queue's element or elements forward.

One way around this problem is to use *circular queues*. The actual data structure for a circular queue is the same as for a regular, or linear, queue: a structure containing an array and two **int** members. A circular queue is used differently, however. When you have filled the last cell in the array—that is, the cell with index **MAX_VALS** **−1**—the next cell to be filled is **vals[0]**, assuming that cell is currently empty.

   The cells of the queue array are treated as if they were arranged in a ring, or circle. The **front** and **back** members are used to determine whether you can add (or remove) a queue element at a particular time. Figure 1-2 provides one way of thinking about circular queues.

   The members **front** and **back** indicate the next array element to be removed and the next element to be filled, respectively. These members' values chase each other around the circle. For example, if **front** and **back** had values 2 and 7, respectively, the queue would have five elements, in cells **vals[2]** through **vals[6]**. The next element to be removed is **vals[2]**; the next cell to be filled is **vals[7]**. Assuming one element is added and three are removed, the new values for **front** and **back** would be 5 and 8, respectively.

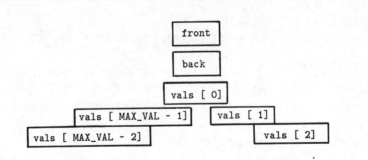

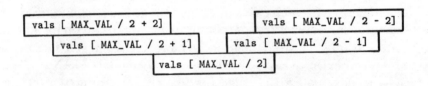

Figure 1-2.   Conceptual representation of circular queue structure

In a similar manner, if **front** were 49 and **back** were 4, the queue would have five elements: **vals[49]**, **vals[0]**, **vals[1]**, **vals[2]**, and **vals[3]**. If you remove an element from this queue, the new value of **front** will be 0, since **MAX_VALS** is 50 in your program. The largest array index is 49, so the value of **front** will wrap around to the start of the array.

Using the preceding approach for circular queues makes distinguishing a full queue from an empty one impossible. For example, suppose **front** = 5 and **back** = 4. In this case, the queue has only one empty slot. Adding an element changes the value of **back** to 5. The values of **front** and **back** are equal, and the queue is full. Now suppose **front** = 5 and **back** = 6. In this case, the queue contains one element. Removing the element would empty the queue but also would make **front** equal **back**.

To deal with this problem, you'll need to use one of the queue cells as a boundary, or "buffer," cell between **front** and **back**. This cell will be the cell immediately before the current value of **front**. The cell cannot be used to store an element, so a 50-cell circular queue can hold only 49 elements.

Queue-Handling Functions

You'll want functions for checking, displaying, and modifying queues, just as you have for manipulating stacks. The following listing contains the queue-handling functions. For the subsequent discussion, assume these functions are in a file called **queue.c**.

```
/* Contents of file queue.c --- queue definition and queue-handling functions.
   Definitions and functions assume file defs.h has been read.
*/

struct queue {
     /* the actual queue elements are stored in an array of strings */
        char    vals [ MAX_VALS] [ SHORT_STR];
        int     front, /* first occupied cell; first to be emptied */
                back; /* next cell to be filled */
};


/* **************
   queue function DECLARATIONS
*************** */
void    q_init ( struct queue *q_ptr);
int     q_full ( struct queue *q_ptr) ;
int     q_empty ( struct queue *q_ptr);
int     q_add ( char *str, struct queue *q_ptr);
```

```
char    *q_remove ( struct queue *q_ptr);
void    q_show_front ( struct queue *q_ptr);
void    q_show_back ( struct queue *q_ptr);
void    q_disp ( struct queue *q_ptr);


/* **************
   queue function DEFINITIONS
************** */

/*
   void q_init ( struct queue *q_ptr)
   ********************************************************
   Initialize each string cell to null_str;
   set front and back to 0.

   CALLS : strcpy ();
   GLOBALS : MAX_VALS
   PARAMETERS :
           struct queue *q_ptr : address of queue to initialize
   RETURN : <none>
   USAGE : q_init ( &my_queue);
   ********************************************************
*/
void q_init ( struct queue *q_ptr)
{
        int index;

        for ( index = 0; index < MAX_VALS; index++)
                strcpy ( q_ptr -> vals [ index], null_str);
        q_ptr -> front = 0;
        q_ptr -> back = 0;
}



/*
   int q_empty ( struct queue *q_ptr)

   ********************************************************
   Is the queue empty?
   Returns TRUE if front and back have the same value, FALSE otherwise.

   CALLS :
   GLOBALS : FALSE, TRUE
   PARAMETERS :
           struct queue *q_ptr : address of queue to check
   RETURN : TRUE if empty, FALSE otherwise
   USAGE : result = q_empty ( &my_queue);
   ********************************************************
*/
int q_empty ( struct queue *q_ptr)
{
        return ( (q_ptr -> front == q_ptr -> back) ? TRUE : FALSE);
}



/*
   int q_full ( struct queue *q_ptr)
   ********************************************************
   Test whether queue is full.
   Return TRUE if either of the following is the case:
   back == front - 1 (i.e., the "buffer" cell is the next one filled)
   or
   back == maximum index value (MAX_VAL - 1) AND front == 0 (i.e., the
```

```
    buffer --- in this case last --- cell is the next one filled)

    CALLS :
    GLOBALS : FALSE, MAX_VALS, TRUE
    PARAMETERS :
            struct queue *q_ptr : address of queue to check
    RETURN : TRUE if full, FALSE otherwise
    USAGE : result = q_full ( &my_queue);
    ***********************************************************
*/
int q_full ( struct queue *q_ptr)
{
    /* full if next cell to be filled is the boundary cell just
       before front. The second part of the || operator handles
       the case where front and back are on either side of the
       wraparound point --- that is, if back = 49 and
       front = 0.
    */
        if ( (q_ptr -> back == q_ptr -> front - 1) ||
            ( ( q_ptr -> back == MAX_VALS - 1) && ( q_ptr -> front == 0)))
                return ( TRUE);
        else
                return ( FALSE);
}



/*
    void q_show_front ( struct queue *q_ptr)
    ***********************************************************
    Display the first element in the queue

    CALLS : printf (); q_empty ();
    GLOBALS :
    PARAMETERS :
            struct queue *q_ptr : address of queue to be displayed.
    RETURN : <none>

    USAGE : q_show_front ( &my_queue);
    ***********************************************************
*/
void q_show_front ( struct queue *q_ptr)
{
        if ( !q_empty ( q_ptr))
                printf ( "First element (%d) : %s\n",
                        q_ptr -> front, q_ptr -> vals [ q_ptr -> front]);
}



/*
    void q_show_back ( struct queue *q_ptr)
    ***********************************************************
    Display the last element in the queue

    CALLS : printf (); q_empty ();
    GLOBALS : MAX_VALS
    PARAMETERS :
            struct queue *q_ptr : address of queue to be displayed.
    RETURN : <none>
    USAGE : q_show_back ( &my_queue);
    ***********************************************************
*/
void q_show_back ( struct queue *q_ptr)
{
```

```
       if ( !q_empty ( q_ptr))
               if ( q_ptr -> back == 0)
                       printf ( "Last element (%d) : %s\n",
                                MAX_VALS - 1,
                                q_ptr -> vals [ MAX_VALS - 1]);
               else
                       printf ( "Last element (%d) : %s\n",
                                q_ptr -> back - 1,
                                q_ptr -> vals [ q_ptr -> back - 1]);
}


/*
   void q_disp ( struct queue *q_ptr)
   *********************************************************
   Display the entire queue

   CALLS : printf ();
   GLOBALS : MAX_VALS
   PARAMETERS :
           struct queue *q_ptr : address of queue to be displayed.
   RETURN : <none>
   USAGE : q_disp ( &my_queue);
   *********************************************************
*/
void q_disp ( struct queue *q_ptr)
{
        int  bak, frnt;

    /* bak and frnt are used to store changeable copies of
       back and front.
    */
        bak = q_ptr -> back;
        frnt = q_ptr -> front;

    /* if the queue does not wrap around,
       write the values from frnt through bak - 1.

    */
        if ( frnt < bak)
        {
                for ( ; frnt < bak; frnt++)
                        printf ( "%d : %s\n", frnt,
                                 q_ptr -> vals [ frnt]);
        }
    /* else if the queue elements wrap around from cell MAX_VALS - 1
       past cell 0, display all the elements through the highest index
       in the queue, then display the cells from 0 through bak - 1.
    */
        else if ( frnt > bak)
        {
                for (  ; frnt < MAX_VALS; frnt++)
                        printf ( "%d : %s\n", frnt,
                                 q_ptr -> vals [ frnt]);
                for ( frnt = 0; frnt < bak; frnt++)
                        printf ( "%d : %s\n", frnt,
                                 q_ptr -> vals [ frnt]);
        }
    /* else if neither of the above cases holds, the queue is empty. */
        else
                printf ( "Queue is empty.\n");
}


/*
   int q_add ( char *str, struct queue *q_ptr)
   *********************************************************
   Add an element to the queue, if possible.
```

```
        CALLS : q_full (); strcpy ();
        GLOBALS : FALSE, MAX_VALS, TRUE
        PARAMETERS :
               char *str : string to add to queue;
               struct queue *q_ptr : address of queue to be modified.
        RETURN : TRUE if element was added, FALSE otherwise
        USAGE : result = q_add ( "str to add", &my_queue);
        ************************************************************
*/
int q_add ( char *str, struct queue *q_ptr)
{
        if ( !q_full ( q_ptr))          /* if queue is not full */
        {
               /* assign value, then increment back indicator. */
               strcpy (q_ptr -> vals [ ( q_ptr -> back)++], str);

               /* Compute remainder when dividing by MAX_VALS,
                  to make sure the next value is within the valid
                  range. For example, a value of 50 would be
                  wrapped around to 0, which is the remainder when
                  50 is divided by 50.
               */
               q_ptr -> back %= MAX_VALS;
               return ( TRUE);
        }
        else
               return ( FALSE);
}


/*
   char *q_remove ( struct queue *q_ptr)

   ************************************************************
   Remove an element from the queue, if possible.

   CALLS : q_empty (); strcpy ();
   GLOBALS : MAX_VALS, SHORT_STR
   PARAMETERS :
           struct queue *q_ptr : address of queue to be modified.
   RETURN : string removed from queue or null_str
   USAGE : strcpy ( mystr, q_remove ( &my_queue));
   ************************************************************
*/
char *q_remove ( struct queue *q_ptr)
{
        char temp [ SHORT_STR];

        if ( !q_empty ( q_ptr))         /* if queue is not empty */
        {
               /* remove the element in cell front;
                  then increase the value of front to be ready
                  to remove the next element.
               */
               strcpy ( temp, q_ptr -> vals [ (q_ptr -> front)++]);
               q_ptr -> front %= MAX_VALS;
               return ( temp);
        }
        else
               return ( null_str);
}
```

q_init()

This function initializes each string element in the queue's array

q—init( )

This function initializes each string element in the queue's array (every **vals[ ]** element) to an empty string. The function also initializes the structure's **front** and **back** members to 0.

q—empty( )

This function returns TRUE if the queue has no elements. This is the case if the **front** and **back** members are equal. Notice that the function is passed a pointer to the queue rather than being passed the entire queue. This saves the time and memory required to copy the queue for the function.

q—full( )

This function returns TRUE if the queue is full—that is, if it has **MAX—VALS** − 1 elements. This is the case if the only cell to be filled is the one immediately preceding the cell with subscript **front**. The function tests this by determining whether **back** == **front** − 1 or whether **back** == **MAX—VALS** −1 while **front** == **0**.

q—show—front( ) and q—show—back( )

These functions display the first and last elements in the queue, respectively. If the queue is empty, the functions display a message to that effect. Notice again that the parameter for each function is a pointer to a queue rather than a queue.

q—disp( )

This function displays each element in the queue along with its array subscript. The function must handle two cases. In the first case, the queue's occupied cells do not wrap around from the high subscript values past 0. The value of **front** is smaller than the value of **back** in this case. The second case is for queues whose first element is in a cell with a higher subscript than the subscript of the last element; that is, the queue wraps around. To handle the second case, the function first displays all the elements with the high subscripts and then displays the elements with the low subscripts.

q—add( )

This function adds an element at the end of the queue, if possible. The function returns TRUE if the string was added and FALSE if the queue is already full. When changing the value of **back**, the function applies the modulus operator to make certain the resulting subscript is within the valid range (0 through **MAX__VALS** − 1).

q__remove( )

This function removes and returns an element from a queue. If the queue is empty, the function returns an empty string. This function also uses the modulus operator to make sure values for **front** are valid.

Exercising the Queue-Handling Functions

The following listing contains a program you can use to exercise the queue-handling functions:

```
/* Program to exercise queue-handling functions */

#include <stdio.h>
#include <stdlib.h>
#include <string.h>
#include "defs.h"
#include "queue.c"


struct queue  q;

main ()
{
        char str [ MAX_STR];
        char info [ MAX_STR];
        int  result;

        q_init ( &q);
        for ( result = 0; result < MAX_VALS - 1; result++)
                q_add ( "a", &q);

        do
        {
                printf ( "Add  Remove  Front  Back  Display  Quit? ");
                gets ( str);
                switch ( str [ 0])
                {
                        case 'a' :
                                printf ( "Add what string? ");
                                gets ( info);
                                result = q_add ( info, &q);
                                if ( result)
                                        printf ( "Done\n");
                                else
                                        printf ( "Queue is full\n");
```

```
                         break;
             case 'r' :
                         strcpy ( info, q_remove ( &q));
                         if ( strcmp ( info, null_str))
                                   printf ( "%s\n", info);
                         else
                                   printf ( "Empty queue.\n");
                         break;
             case 'f' :
                         q_show_front ( &q);
                         break;
             case 'b' :
                         q_show_back ( &q);
                         break;
             case 'd' :
                         q_disp ( &q);
                         break;
             case 'q' :
                         continue;
             default :
                         printf ( "invalid entry\n");
                         break;

             }
     }
     while ( strcmp ( str, null_str));
     q_disp ( &q);
}
```

A Task Scheduler

Queues are commonly used in programs where tasks must be done
in sequence and the list of tasks may change during program execution. In this section you'll use queues to represent tasks being processed by a simple scheduler, which allocates limited processing
time to tasks in sequence.

The scheduler will manage a list of tasks that must be worked on
in sequence. The tasks require variable amounts of time to be completed. The scheduler, however, is allowed to give each task only a
limited amount of time before moving on to the next task. For
example, suppose the scheduler had the following list of tasks and
was allowed to allocate only 5 seconds to a task before moving on:

```
Task    Time required (secs)
A       3
B       24
C       7.3
D       4
```

The scheduler would take the first task, A, from the queue and work on it. Since this task takes only 3 seconds, the scheduler could complete the task before moving on. The scheduler then would remove the next task, B, from the queue, and work on it. After 5 seconds, the scheduler must stop working on this task and move on to the next.

The scheduler would save the remainder of the task — requiring 19 more seconds — by adding the interrupted task to the end of the queue, that is, after task D. Following this, the scheduler would remove task C from the queue and work on it for 5 seconds. After adding the remainder of task C to the queue, the scheduler's task queue would look as follows:

Task	Time required
D	4
B	19
C	2.3

On the next time through the task queue, the controller would finish tasks D and C, leaving just task B to process. This will take three more cycles.

The following listing contains the main program and a function to carry out such a scheduler's work. The **utils.c** file is the same one used earlier for the calculator program.

```c
/* Task scheduler program */

#include <stdio.h>
#include <stdlib.h>
#include <string.h>
#include "defs.h"
#include "queue.c"
#include "utils.c"

/* maximum time allowed on task each pass, before moving to next task. */
#define MAX_PER_TASK   5.0

struct queue q;

main ()
{
        char    temp [ MAX_STR], info [ MAX_STR];
        double  total_time = 0.0;
        void    process_task ( struct queue *, double *);

        printf ( "Please enter information in the following form:\n\n");
        printf ( "<Single-letter task name>  <time><Return>\n\n");
        printf ( "Name and time must be separated by at least one blank.\n");
        printf ( "Just press Return when all tasks have been entered.\n\n");

    /* get the task information */
        printf ( "? ");
        gets ( info);
```

```
        while ( strcmp ( info, null_str))
        {
                strcpy ( temp, remove_wd ( info));
                strcat ( temp, info);
                q_add ( temp, &q);
                printf ( "? ");
                gets ( info);
        }

    /* process the tasks */
        while ( !q_empty ( &q))
                process_task ( &q, &total_time);

        printf ( "Total processing time == %.2lf seconds.\n", total_time);
}



/*
    void process_task ( struct queue *q_ptr, double *time)
    **********************************************************
    Process a task until it is done or until the maximum time per task
    has been used. If the task is done, discard it, otherwise add the
    partially done task to the end of the queue, for later processing.

    CALLS : atof (); f_to_str (); printf (); q_add (); strcat (); strcpy ();
    GLOBALS : MAX_PER_TIME, MAX_STR, NULL_CHAR, SHORT_STR
    PARAMETERS :
            struct queue *q_ptr : address of queue containing task info.
            double *time : address of variable containing total elapsed time.
    RETURN : <none>
    USAGE : process_task ( &my_queue, &my_time);
    **********************************************************
*/
void process_task ( struct queue *q_ptr, double *time)
{
        char    str [ MAX_STR],  /* to hold the element from queue */
                *temp,  /* used to discard task name during computations */
                name;
        double  value;
        int     result;  /* used to determine whether q_add worked */

    /* get the front queue element --- the current task */
        strcpy ( str, q_remove ( q_ptr));
        temp = str;
        name = str [ 0];  /* get the task's name */
        value = atof ( ++temp);  /* convert rest of string to number */

    /* if the entire task can be done in one cycle,
       adjust total work time, discard task when done, and report
    */
        if ( value <= MAX_PER_TASK)
        {
                *time += value;
                printf ( "Task %c (%.2lf secs) completed.\n",
                        str [ 0], value);
        }
    /* else if task needs another cycle,
       process task for a cycle, adjust total time, adjust task time,
       add task to back of queue, and report
    */
        else
        {
                *time += MAX_PER_TASK;
                value -= MAX_PER_TASK;
                /* leave only task name in str ---
                   to make adding number (in string form) cleaner
                */
                str [ 1] = NULL_CHAR;
                /* add "number" to element string */
```

```
strcat ( str, f_to_str ( value, SHORT_STR - 1));
result = q_add ( str, q_ptr);
printf ( "Task %c processed, time remaining == %.2lf secs.\n",
         str [ 0], value);
   }
}
```

Let's see how this program works.

main( )

The **main( )** function first explains the required input format to the user. Then the program gets the task information from the user. The user must provide two items of information: a one-character name for the task and the amount of time the task will require. The user enters this on one line, possibly with a space between the name and the time.

If there is a space, then the **remove_wd( )** function first removes the "string" corresponding to the task name and copies it into the string (**str**) that will be added to the queue. The program then adds the time (which had been read as part of a string and is, therefore, in string form) to the end of **str**. Function **remove_wd( )** had removed all leading blanks from the string it was processing; this serves to store both items of information in **str** without a blank separating them.

If there is no blank between name and time in the original string, the entire input string is added to **str** from the call to **remove_wd( )**. In that case, an empty string is added in the call to **strcat( )**.

Once all the tasks and their time requirements have been entered, the program begins to act as the controller. The core of the program is the next-to-last statement in **main( )**. This **while** loop keeps processing as long as there are tasks to work on.

process_task( )

The actual task processing and time adjustment is performed by **process_task( )**. This function gets a task from the queue and tries to complete it within the allowable time (**MAX_PER_TASK**). If that is possible, the task is discarded and the function reports that the task is done. If the task requires too much time to finish within one cycle, the function works on the task as long as possible, adjusts the time still required on the task, and adds the task to the end of the queue.

The string element added to the queue actually contains two pieces of information: a single letter representing the task's name and the amount of time required for the task. To store both of these items within a character array, the function must convert the numerical value **back** to a string; it does this by calling function **f_to_str( )**, which is in **utils.c** and was discussed earlier.

The string element is built by retaining the first character (that is, the character with subscript 0) as the task name, converting the remaining time to a string, appending this "stringized" number to the string, and adding the resulting string to the queue.

Suggestions and Projects

You've seen a simple example using a queue. You can use the same general strategy to create a "To do" list scheduler, in which you add tasks to a list, work on them in sequence, and move a task to the end of the list if you were unable to finish it. Try modifying the necessary functions — mainly **process_task( )** — to handle such an application.

Earlier in the chapter, you used a string to hold the postfix expression in your four-function calculator. You could also use a queue, in which case you would have to change several of the functions, such as **to_postfix( )** and **solve_postfix( )**.

You might want to try a more complex example, one involving multiple queues. For example, write a program to handle an airport check-in and seating-assignment process. Assume you have three baggage-check lines. Each of these lines is feeding its customers into the same seating-assignment line; thus you have three queues being emptied into a fourth queue.

SUMMARY

In this chapter, you've learned something about stacks and queues, two data structures that will be very useful in later programs and in much of what you do.

In Chapter 2 you'll look at recursion, a very powerful programming technique that is ideal in situations where you don't know in advance how often something will need to be done or how large something will be. You'll also look at another useful data structure: linked lists.

2

RECURSION AND LINKED LISTS

In Chapter 1 you learned about stacks and saw an example of using stacks to create a four-function calculator. In this chapter, you'll use stacks to examine how recursion, a very powerful programming technique, works. After that, you'll use recursion to manipulate yet another useful data structure, linked lists.

FUNCTION CALLS

In Chapter 1 you saw that the flow of control in a sequence of nested function calls could be represented by a stack. In an example, you had the following sequence of function calls:

```
main() calls first()        /* 1 */
first() calls second()      /* 2 */
second() calls third()      /* 3 */
third() calls fourth()      /* 4 */
fourth() calls fifth()      /* 5 */
fifth() calls sixth()       /* 6 */
```

When **main()** calls **first()**, execution of **main()** is suspended temporarily, and the current state (variable values, current instruction, and so forth) of **main( )** is saved. Function **first( )** then starts executing. When **first( )** calls **second( )**, the state for **first( )** is saved and **second( )** starts executing.

Suspended functions are saved in a stack structure and are reactivated from the most recently suspended to the function suspended the longest. Thus, after step four in the example, the suspended function stack would look as follows:

```
third()
second()
first()
main()
```

Function **fourth( )** would be executing. Later, while function **sixth( )** is executing, the suspended function stack looks as follows:

```
fifth()
fourth()
third()
second()
first()
main()
```

To reactivate a function, it is popped from the suspended function stack, and the function continues executing from the state it had when suspended. Thus, the last function to finish is **main( )**, since it will be the last function popped from the stack.

RECURSION

In principle, any function can call any other function. Ordinarily, functions will call other functions. For example, **second( )** calls **third( )** above as a step in carrying out the task **second( )** is to accomplish.

A *recursive function* is one that calls *itself* to do part of the function's work. This means that one version of the function is put on hold while a different version is activated.

Just like other functions, a recursive function generally has a task or a computation to perform. If the task is simple enough to be solved right away — that is, if there is only one thing to do — the function solves it and returns control to the calling function. On the other hand, if there is more work to be done, the function calls a copy of itself to work on a slightly easier version of the problem. This continues until one of the calls occurs with a version of the problem simple enough to do its work right away. The version of the function executing at that point will do its work and then return control to the more complex version of the same function, which will be at the top of the suspended function stack. Let's look at some examples of recursive functions.

Counting Recursively

The function **count( )** in the following listing counts to the value passed as an argument when the function is called. In addition, the function provides information about the current environment. The function does its work by calling simpler versions of itself until the function only has to count to 1. At that point, the currently executing version of **count( )** simply writes the value and then returns control to its calling function.

```
/* Program to count recursively, and also to write information about
   current level of recursion.
   Program illustrates recursive function call.
*/

#include <stdio.h>

int level;

/* Count from 1 to the specified number. Work is done by calling
   the function recursively, then counting upwards from 1, as control
   is returned to the calling functions to do their work.
   While doing its work, this version of the function also
   displays information regarding the level of recursive calls.
*/
void count ( int val)
{
    /* Write some information about the level of recursion. */
        printf ( "Starting count, level %3d; val == %3d\n",
                ++level, val);

    /* the actual recursion occurs if the condition is true.
       Otherwise, control simply passes to the next statement.
    */
        if ( val > 1)
                count ( val - 1);

    /* Main task line for function count().
       After a return from another call to count(), control returns
       to this point.
```

```
        */
            printf ( "\t\t\t\t\t**** Displaying val: %3d\n", val);

        /* Write some more information about the level of recursion. */
            printf ( "Leaving count, level %3d; val == %3d\n",
                    level--, val);
    }
    main ()
    {
            void count ( int);
            int  how_high;         /* value to which count should go. */

            printf ( "Count to what value? ");
            scanf ( "%d", &how_high);
            level = 0;
            count ( how_high);
    }
```

The following listing shows the output for this program when **how—high** has the value 5. The actual counting is done in the "Displaying val" lines.

```
Count to what value? 5
Starting count, level   1; val ==    5
Starting count, level   2; val ==    4
Starting count, level   3; val ==    3
Starting count, level   4; val ==    2
Starting count, level   5; val ==    1
                                          **** Displaying val:   1
Leaving count, level    5; val ==    1
                                          **** Displaying val:   2
Leaving count, level    4; val ==    2
                                          **** Displaying val:   3
Leaving count, level    3; val ==    3
                                          **** Displaying val:   4
Leaving count, level    2; val ==    4
                                          **** Displaying val:   5
Leaving count, level    1; val ==    5
```

Count()

This function actually does the counting. Let's see how the function calls in this program work. Program execution begins with **main( )**, which executes several statements and then calls **count( )**, with an argument of 5 (the value of **how—high**). When **count( )** is called, **main( )** is suspended temporarily and is pushed onto the suspended function stack.

Function **count( )** starts executing, with its parameter, **val,** having the value 5. (We'll refer to this version of the function as **count(5)**, where 5 represents the actual parameter value for that function call.) The function prints its "Starting count" message and then calls another version of itself, with an argument of 4 (**val** −1). With this call, **count(5)** is pushed onto the suspended function stack while **count(4)** executes.

This version of the function also writes the "Starting count" message and then calls another version of **count( )**, with an argument of 3. After **count(4)** has been pushed onto the suspended function stack, this stack looks as follows:

```
count ( 4)      /* top of stack */
count ( 5)
main ()
```

With the stack in this condition, **count(3)** is executing. After writing its message, **count(3)** calls **count( )** with an argument of 2. Function **count(3)** is added to the suspended function stack at this point.

Function **count(2)** writes its message and then passes an argument of 1 to another version of **count( )**. While **count(1)** is executing, the suspended function stack looks as follows:

```
count ( 2)      /* top of stack */
count ( 3)
count ( 4)
count ( 5)
main ()
```

There are now four versions of **count( )** on hold; each version decided the task was still too difficult to perform and called **count( )** with a slightly easier version of the problem—in this case, the task of counting to a smaller number.

When the actual parameter is 1, **count( )** is able to carry out the task that has been set—counting to 1. Thus, **count(1)** does not make another recursive call; rather, **count(1)** does its job—displaying the value stored in a local variable, the parameter **val**. (In its current form, the function also displays some additional information to make it easier to follow the execution sequence.)

Once **count(1)** has finished, control transfers back to the calling function, which is the top function on the suspended function stack. Thus, **count(2)** is reactivated and is finally able to do its task —writing the current value of **val**. Notice that both **count(1)** and **count(2)** had different values for **val**. This is because each version of the function has allocated its own storage for this parameter. The parameter is passed by value, which means any changes to the parameter are confined to the function and are not passed back out to the calling function. Thus, none of the versions of **count( )** knows about or has access to the values of the other versions' parameters.

After **count(2)** finishes, the values 1 and 2 are displayed, along with other messages. When **count(2)** finishes, **count(3)** is popped from the suspended function stack, and it writes *its* current value for **val**, 3. Control is then passed to **count(4)**, which had called **count(3)**. After **count(4)** is popped, the suspended function stack looks as follows:

```
count ( 5)      /* top of stack */
main ()
```

Eventually, control will return to **main( )**. By then, the successive function completions will have displayed the values 1 through 5, in order. As far as function suspension and suspended function stack manipulation go, recursive functions behave in the same way as other functions.

Because the same function is being called each time, however, it is possible to make a sequence of recursive calls that would never terminate or, rather, would terminate when all the system's available memory was exhausted during execution. Let's look at some rules and examples about defining recursive functions.

To aid in the discussion, let's look at an unembellished version of the **count( )** function from our earlier example; this will make it easier to identify individual components of a recursive function's definition. Notice that the entire function is just two statements: an **if** construct and a call to **printf( )**.

```
/* Unembellished version of recursive count () function */

/* Count from 1 to the specified number. Work is done by calling
   the function recursively, then counting upwards from 1, as control
   is returned to the calling functions to do their work.
*/
void count ( int val)
{
     /* the actual recursion occurs if the condition is true.
        Otherwise, control simply passes to the next statement.
     */
     if ( val > 1)
             count ( val - 1);

     /* Main task line for function count().
        After a return from another call to count(), control returns
        to this point.
     */
     printf ( "\t\t\t\t**** Displaying val: %3d\n", val);
}
```

Without the statements that write information about the recursion
level, this function turns out to be very simple. A recursive function must include the following types of statements:

1. A test to determine whether the function can avoid calling
   itself again, that is, to determine whether the function can
   simply do its work and terminate. In the preceding function,
   this is the **if** statement testing whether (**val > 1**).

2. A statement that calls the function itself. This call *must* be
   made with parameter values that will eventually make the test
   condition take on a value that will bypass the recursive call. In
   the preceding function, this is accomplished by calling the
   function with arguments that approach the termination value
   of 1.

3. The statements needed to carry out the task of the function. In
   the preceding function, this would be the call to **printf( )**.

A recursive function *must* test whether a recursive call is
necessary before making such a call. If you write your function so
that the function calls itself first and then tests whether it's all
right to stop, the function will never terminate. Thus, the follow-

ing version of the recursive function will never terminate. You will eventually get a run-time error when there's no more room for the system to store environments for all the versions of the function being created through the recursive calls.

```
/* Incorrect recursive function */

/* NOTE:   DO NOT USE THIS VERSION OF THE RECURSIVE FUNCTION.
   This version will terminate in a run-time error.
*/

void count ( int val)
{
    /* The recursion occurs first in this version.
       The function will keep calling itself, so that no version
       of the function will ever get to test whether it can stop.
       The program will eventually terminate with a run-time error.
    */
    count ( val - 1);
    if ( val > 1)
            printf ( "\t\t\t\t**** Displaying val: %3d\n", val);
}
```

Similarly, the following version of the function is incorrect because the value of **val** used in each call is larger than the current value and is thus moving *away* from the termination value of 1. This version will also end in a run-time error.

```
/* Incorrect recursive function */

/* NOTE:   DO NOT USE THIS VERSION OF THE RECURSIVE FUNCTION.
   This version will terminate in a run-time error.
*/

void count ( int val)
{
        if ( val > 1)
                count ( val + 1);  /* val grows, so won't terminate */

    /* Main task line for function count().
       After a return from another call to count(), control returns
       to this point.
    */
        printf ( "\t\t\t\t**** Displaying val: %3d\n", val);
}
```

Thus, although recursive calls look just like any other function calls, you need to take particular care to use them only in certain places and only with particular types of parameter values.

Table 2-1.   Fibonacci Numbers

Number	Value	Source
fib(1)	1	definition
fib(2)	1	definition
fib(3)	2	fib(1)+fib(2)
fib(4)	3	fib(2)+fib(3)
fib(5)	5	fib(3)+fib(4)
fib(6)	8	fib(4)+fib(5)
fib(7)	13	fib(5)+fib(6)
fib(8)	21	fib(6)+fib(7)

Remember: A recursive function must always test whether it can stop *before* calling another version of itself. If a recursive call is made, the parameters in some call should eventually have values that will make further recursive calls unnecessary.

Fibonacci Numbers

Let's look at another example of recursion. In this case, the recursive function will actually contain more than one recursive call. The recursive function computes a Fibonacci number. *Fibonacci numbers* are elements in a mathematical series that show up in all sorts of contexts. The definition of a Fibonacci number is simple, and it is recursive.

The first two Fibonacci numbers, **fib(1)** and **fib(2)**, are defined as 1. Subsequent Fibonacci numbers are formed by adding the two preceding Fibonacci numbers. Thus, **fib(3)** is the sum of **fib(2)** and **fib(1)** and so forth: **fib(3) == fib(2) + fib(1) == 1 + 1 == 2; fib(4) == fib(3) + fib(2) == 2 + 1 == 3.** Table 2-1 lists the first few Fibonacci numbers.

The following program computes the desired Fibonacci number:

```
/* Program to compute a specified Fibonacci number.
   Program also illustrates recursion.
*/

#include <stdio.h>
#include <math.h>

/* Function to compute the specified Fibonacci number.
   If x is 1 or 2, the function returns 1; otherwise the
   function returns the sum of the two preceding Fibonacci numbers.
*/
long fib ( int x)
{
        if ( x > 2)  /* if x > 2, compute the number */
                return ( fib ( x - 1) + fib ( x - 2));
        else    /* by definition, fib( 2) and fib( 1) == 1 */
                return ( 1);
}


main ()
{
        long fib (int), fibans;
        int seed;

        printf ( "Number? ");
        scanf ( "%d", &seed);
        fibans = fib ( seed);
        printf ( " fib (%2d) == %ld\n", seed, fibans);
}
```

fib( )

This function computes the specified Fibonacci number. Notice
the structure of the recursive function, **fib( )**. Before making a
recursive call, the function tests whether it can stop. If so, a specific value (1) is returned, and the function returns control to the
calling function; if not, the function calls itself *twice*. This is per-
fectly valid but just a bit more unusual than simple recursion
where a function calls itself only once.

   fib(4) is the sum of **fib(3)** and **fib(2)**. But **fib(3)** itself is the
sum of **fib(2)** and **fib(1)**. Thus, if you don't keep track of the two
preceding Fibonacci numbers, you need to do lots of work each
time one of the higher Fibonacci numbers is computed.

Table 2-2. Calls Required to Compute Fibonacci Numbers

Value	Fibonacci Nr. (fib(value))	Number of Calls Required
5	5	9
10	55	109
15	610	1219
20	6765	13529
25	75025	150049
30	832040	1664079

A recursive function for computing Fibonacci numbers can be very inefficient after the first few values. Table 2-2 shows the number of calls to **fib( )** required to compute various Fibonacci numbers.

Try to modify the **fib( )** function to provide the information in Table 2-2. To do this, you need to have some way of keeping track of each entry into the **fib( )** function.

Anything you can do recursively you can also do nonrecursively. In many cases, such as that of Fibonacci numbers, the non-recursive, or *iterative,* version is much more efficient. Write a nonrecursive version of **fib( )**.

Tower of Hanoi

Let's look at one more example: the Tower of Hanoi puzzle. The pieces of this puzzle consist of three poles and some number of disks that can be put on the poles to build towers. The disks are all of different sizes.

At the start, all the disks are on one tower, the source, and are in order of size — smallest disk at the top, largest on the bottom — as in Figure 2-1, which shows a 4-disk problem. The puzzle requires you to move all the disks from the source tower to a target tower in as few moves as possible.

Figure 2-1.   4-disk Tower of Hanoi problem

There are two restrictions on your moves:

- You may move only one disk at a time.
- You may never put a larger disk on top of a smaller one.

The simplest version of the problem is obviously the 1-disk problem. To solve this version, you simply need to move the disk from the source tower to the target and you are done.

The 2-disk version illustrates the restrictions. Figure 2-2 shows the towers for a 2-disk problem. To solve this, you can move the top disk on source (the smaller disk) to either temp or target. The simplest solution is

1. Move the smaller disk from source to temp.

2. Move the larger disk from source to target.

3. Move the smaller disk from temp to target.

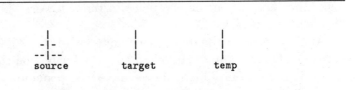

Figure 2-2.   2-disk Tower of Hanoi problem

If you had started your solution by moving the smaller disk to target, you would be unable to put the larger disk on the target tower because of the second restriction. You would therefore have to put it on temp, move the smaller disk to source again, and then move the larger to target. Only then would you be able to put the smaller disk on target. This solution would require five moves instead of three.

Although it is not evident, the solution for the 2-disk problem actually uses a strategy that reduces the problem to a 1-disk version. The general strategy is to move all disks except the bottom one from source onto temp and then move the remaining disk from source to target. Once this 1-disk problem has been solved, the solution solves the remaining problem by moving the disk from temp onto target. This last move is again just a solution to a 1-disk problem, but with a different source tower.

The 3-disk problem shows this strategy in a more complex case. Figure 2-3 shows the starting configuration for the 3-disk version.

To solve the 3-disk problem, break it into the following subproblems:

1. Solve the 2-disk problem from source to temp.

2. Move the remaining disk from source to target.

3. Solve the 2-disk problem from temp to target.

The second subproblem is the 1-disk problem you saw earlier. To solve the first subproblem, treat it as a simple 2-disk problem.

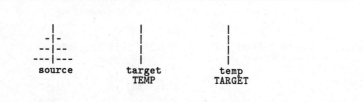

Figure 2-3.   3-disk Tower of Hanoi problem

Thus, the goal is to get the second disk onto TARGET. (The names in uppercase letters refer to the towers as seen from the context of the first 2-disk subproblem.) To accomplish this, move the top disk onto TEMP, and then move the middle disk onto TARGET. To complete the solution to this subproblem, move the smallest disk from TEMP to TARGET.

It turns out that you need seven moves to solve the 3-disk problem: three moves to solve the 2-disk subproblem from source to temp, one move to solve the 1-disk subproblem from source to target, and three moves to solve the 2-disk subproblem from temp to target.

The following listing contains a program that will solve the 4-disk version of the problem. The program uses function **hanoi( )** to do the work. This function will work with towers of any height.

```
/* File Hanoi.C */
/* Program to solve the Tower of Hanoi problem.
   Program also illustrates use of recursion.
*/

#include "defs.h"
#undef MAX_VALS
#define MAX_VALS 15
#define NOINDENT    0
#define INDENT      1

#include "stack.c"
/* define source, temp, target, respectively */
struct stack  A, B, C;
int    level = 0;

/* function declarations */
void   hanoi ( int, struct stack *, struct stack *, struct stack *);
void   show_towers ( int);


/* function to solve tower of hanoi problem */
void hanoi ( int height, struct stack *src,
            struct stack *target, struct stack *temp)
{
    /* used to count number of calls to hanoi() */
      level++;

    /* if 1 disk on source, move it to target */
      if ( height == 1)
      {
              push_stack ( pop_stack ( src), target);
              show_towers ( NOINDENT);       /* display towers */
```

```
        }
        else /* if there's still work to be done */
        {
            /* solve (n-1)-disk subproblem from source to temp */
                hanoi ( height - 1, src, temp, target);
                push_stack ( pop_stack ( src), target);
                show_towers ( INDENT);          /* display towers */

            /* solve (n-1)-disk subproblem from temp to target */
                hanoi ( height - 1, temp, target, src);
        } /* else if there's still work to be done */
}   /* function hanoi () */


/* display contents of tower of hanoi stacks */
void show_towers (int moved)
{
        char *spaces = "                              ";

        if ( moved)     /* if label is to be indented */
                printf ( "%s", spaces);
        printf ( "A:\n");
        disp_stack ( &A);
        if ( moved)
                printf ( "%s", spaces);
        printf ( "B:\n");
        disp_stack ( &B);
        if ( moved)
                printf ( "%s", spaces);
        printf ( "C:\n");
        disp_stack ( &C);
        printf ("\n");
}


main ()
{
        init_stack ( &A);
        init_stack ( &B);
        init_stack ( &C);

    /* create initial configuration */
        push_stack ( "4", &A);
        push_stack ( "3", &A);
        push_stack ( "2", &A);
        push_stack ( "1", &A);

    /* display initial configuration */
        show_towers ( NOINDENT);

    /* solve tower of hanoi problem */
        hanoi ( 4, &A, &B, &C);

        printf ( "%d calls to hanoi()\n\n", level);

    /* display final configuration */
        show_towers ( NOINDENT);
}
```

This program uses stacks to represent the towers. We've changed the maximum stack size for this program by changing **MAX_VALS**, using the **#undef** and **#define** preprocessor directives. To manipulate the stacks, the program uses the functions contained in **stack.c**, which you created in the previous chapter.

hanoi( )

This recursive function actually solves the problem. The function first checks whether **src**, the source or starting tower, contains only one element. If so, the function solves the problem by moving the disk from **src** to **target** and returns control to the calling function.

If the function is unable to do its work, **hanoi( )** calls itself with a smaller problem, (n−1)-disks. Notice that the subproblem is to move the smaller tower from **src** to **temp**. This call solves the first subproblem in our strategy. Once it's done, the **src** tower has been cleared of everything except the bottom disk. This disk is moved to **target**, solving subproblem 2. The function then makes another recursive call to solve a smaller problem —this time, moving the smaller tower from **temp** to **src** to solve the remaining subproblem.

show_towers( )

This function displays the contents of the three towers, which are named **A**, **B**, and **C** in the program. Notice that the function refers to the towers by their global names rather than by source, temp, and target. The towers play different roles at different points in the solution; the global names do not change, however. The calls to **show_towers( )** are included to enable you to follow the solution process.

Run the program, and then compare the program's execution with the following outline of the strategy we've been discussing:

I.   Solve the 3-disk problem from A to C
   A. Solve the 2-disk problem from A to B
      1. Solve the 1-disk problem from A to C
      2. Solve the 1-disk problem from A to B
      3. Solve the 1-disk problem from C to B

     B. Solve the 1-disk problem from A to C

     C. Solve the 2-disk problem from B to C

         1. Solve the 1-disk problem from B to A

         2. Solve the 1-disk problem from B to C

         3. Solve the 1-disk problem from A to C

II. Solve the 1-disk problem from A to B

III. Solve the 3-disk problem from C to B

     A. Solve the 2-disk problem from C to A

         1. Solve the 1-disk problem from C to B

         2. Solve the 1-disk problem from C to A

         3. Solve the 1-disk problem from B to A

     B. Solve the 1-disk problem from C to B

     C. Solve the 2-disk problem from A to C

         1. Solve the 1-disk problem from A to C

         2. Solve the 1-disk problem from A to B

         3. Solve the 1-disk problem from C to B

The preceding program displays the contents of the towers after each step. To write this information to a file instead of to the screen, use the DOS redirection operator. For example, if you save the program under the names **hanoi.c** and **hanoi.exe**, you can save the tower information in a file, **hanoi.dat**, by typing the following on the DOS command line:

```
hanoi > hanoi.dat
```

Modify the program to handle an arbitrary number of disks. Keep in mind, however, that the number of calls will increase as you add more disks. Adding a disk will more than double the number of steps required to solve the problem. Specifically, if you want to solve the problem for n disks, the solution will require $2^n - 1$ steps.

Although your algorithm can handle any number of disks in principle, the program will really be able to handle only a relatively small number of disks, because each recursive call eats up additional stack memory.

Incidentally, legend has it that there is a tower with 64 disks on it and that monks are solving this version of the problem by transferring one disk per second. When they have finished transferring the disks to the target tower, the universe will come to an end. You may as well keep working on your own programs, however, since this won't happen for almost 600 billion years.

Some Final Words on Recursion

The preceding examples were designed to give you a feel for how recursion works and to make you more comfortable thinking about recursive solutions.

Despite the fact that they can be inefficient, recursive functions will be very useful throughout this book as well as in many other programming contexts. Such functions will be particularly valuable in situations where you don't know in advance how many elements the program will be handling.

We'll see that making use of the suspended function stack to control the progress of a sequence of recursive function calls can provide a means of making sure the program always ends up back at the correct location.

LINKED LISTS

Recursion plays a role in manipulating another important data structure: a linked list. In this section you'll find out about linked lists and how to build them.

A *linked list* is a sequence of data elements in which each element in the sequence points to its successor. These pointers provide the links that hold the list together. The only way to access an element in the middle of the list is start at the beginning of the list and follow the pointers through the list, element by element, until you reach the target element. Linked lists are *sequential access* data structures, since you must traverse a list in sequence.

This is very different from an array, where the structure itself provides a means of finding and accessing individual elements. In an array, you can access any element at random by simply computing an offset from the array's starting address. Because you can access any element at any time, arrays are often called *random access* data structures.

The advantage of a linked list is that you need not know in advance the number of elements you'll need. With an array, you would need to allocate all the storage when the program or function started up. With a linked list, you can allocate storage for an element dynamically, when you need it.

Self-Referential Structures: Building Blocks for Linked Lists

Before we look at the functions for building linked lists, let's look at the representation of linked lists. The basic element of a linked list is a node. This node must contain at least two items of information: the node's data and a pointer to the next node.

The following structure serves to represent such a node, which we'll call an **lnode** to associate it with a linked list.

```
/* Node for a linked list.
    Two members: data, and a pointer to another node lnode.
    Note: MAX_STR must be defined somewhere.
*/

struct lnode {
        char   data [ MAX_STR];
        struct  lnode *next;       /* pointer to another lnode */
};
```

This structure has two members. The **data** member contains the actual information to be stored in the node—in this case, a string. The **next** member is a pointer to another **lnode**. Such nodes can be used to make arbitrarily long chains of such structures, linked together by the **next** members of each **lnode**.

The first **lnode** in a linked list is often referenced by a pointer to **lnode**—that is, an ordinary pointer, not a structure member. This pointer will reference an **lnode**, whose **next** member may, in turn, point to another **lnode**. The list may contain as many **lnode** elements as your implementation can handle. The **next** member

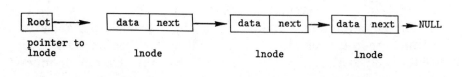

Figure 2-4. Linked list data structure

of the last **lnode** in the list should be a **NULL** pointer. Figure 2-4 shows a three-element list with **root** as the starting pointer.

The following listing shows functions for manipulating linked lists and for allocating the storage required for an **lnode**. Use the name **lists.c** for the file containing these functions.

```
/* File Lists.C
   Functions to manipulate and display linked lists
   Note : File assumes defs.h has been read.
*/

#include <malloc.h>

/* Node for a linked list.
   Two members: data, and a pointer to another lnode.
*/
struct lnode {
        char   data [ MAX_STR];
        struct  lnode *next;      /* pointer to another lnode */
};

char *bad_str = "INVALID VALUE";

/* **********
   linked list function DECLARATIONS
********** */
struct lnode *back_of_list ( struct lnode *, struct lnode *);
struct lnode *front_of_list ( struct lnode *, struct lnode *);
struct lnode *get_node ( struct lnode *);
struct lnode *middle_of_list ( struct lnode *, struct lnode *);
void         show_list ( struct lnode *);


/* **********
   linked list function DEFINITIONS
********** */

/* allocate space for and initialize a structure;
   return pointer to it
```

```
*/
struct lnode *get_node ( struct lnode *item)
{
        void *malloc ( size_t);

    /* allocate enough space to store an lnode */
        item = (struct lnode *) malloc ( sizeof ( struct lnode));

    /* if allocated, initialize the structure */
        if (item != NULL)
        {
                item->next = NULL;
                strcpy ( item->data, null_str);
        }
        else
                printf ( "Nothing allocated\n");
        return ( item);              /* return the pointer */
}


/* add the structure pointed at by new to
   the front of the list pointed at by list.
*/
struct lnode * front_of_list ( struct lnode *new, struct lnode *list)
{
        new->next = list;
        list = new;
        return (list);
}


/* add new lnode to end of list to which list points. */
struct lnode *back_of_list ( struct lnode *new, struct lnode *list)
{
        if ( list == NULL)
        {
                list = new;
                return ( list);
        }
        else
        {
            /* return results of most recent search. */
                list->next = back_of_list ( new, list->next);
                return ( list);
        }
}


/* add lnode to list at position corresponding to data member's
   relative position
*/
struct lnode *middle_of_list ( struct lnode *new, struct lnode *list)
{
        if ( list == NULL)
        {
                list = new;
                return ( list);
        }
        else if ( strcmp ( list->data, new->data) > 0)
        {
```

```
            new->next = list;
            list = new;
            return ( list);
     }
     else
     {
         /* return results of most recent search. */
         list->next = middle_of_list ( new, list->next);
         return ( list);
     }
}
```

```
/* display contents of the list */
void show_list ( struct lnode *list)
{
     if ( list != NULL)
     {
            printf ( "%s\n", list->data);
            if ( list->next != NULL)
                  show_list ( list->next);
     }
}
```

The following listing contains a **main( )** function for exercising
the functions in **lists.c**.

```
/* Program to build and display linked lists */

#include <stdio.h>
#include <stdlib.h>
#include <string.h>
#include "defs.h"
#include "lists.c"


main ()
{
     struct lnode *temp, *root = NULL;
     char    info [ MAX_STR], *tempstr;
     int     selection, done = FALSE;

     printf ( "Add to 1) front; 2) middle; or 3) back of list? ");
     gets (info);
     selection = atoi ( info);

     temp = get_node ( temp);
     while ( (temp != NULL) && ( !done))
     {
            printf ( "Data? ");
            gets ( info);
            strcpy ( temp->data, info);
            if ( strcmp ( temp->data, null_str))
            {
                  switch ( selection)
                  {
```

```
                              case 1:
                                      root = front_of_list ( temp,
                                                               root);
                                      break;
                              case 2:
                                      root = middle_of_list ( temp,
                                                               root);
                                      break;
                              default:
                                      root = back_of_list ( temp,
                                                            root);
                                      break;
                      }    /* END switch */
              }   /* END if data is nonzero */
              else
                      done = TRUE;

              temp = get_node (temp);
      }

      if ( root != NULL)
              show_list ( root);
      printf ( "Show which node? ");
      gets ( info );
      selection = atoi ( info);
      while ( selection != -1)
      {
              show_node ( root, selection);
              printf ( "Show which node? ");
              gets ( info );
              selection = atoi ( info);
      }

      printf ( "Delete what value? ");
      gets ( info);
      while ( strcmp (info, "-1"))
      {
              root = del_val_node ( root, temp, info);
              if ( root != NULL)
                      show_list ( root);
              else
                      printf ( "list is now empty\n");
              printf ( "Delete what value? ");
              gets ( info);
      }

      printf ( "Delete which node? ");
      gets ( info );
      selection = atoi ( info);
      while ( selection != -1)
      {
              root = del_node ( root, temp, selection, tempstr);
              if ( root != NULL)
                      show_list ( root);
              else
                      printf ( "list is now empty\n");
              printf ( "Delete which node? ");
              gets ( info );
              selection = atoi ( info);
      }
}
```

This program produced the following three sessions when asked to add to the front, middle, and back of the list, respectively.

```
Add to 1) front; 2) middle; or 3) back of list? 1
Data? 2
Data? 7
Data? 3
Data? 8
Data? 0
   8.00
   3.00
   7.00
   2.00


Add to 1) front; 2) middle; or 3) back of list? 2
Data? 2
Data? 7
Data? 3
Data? 8
Data? 0
   2.00
   3.00
   7.00
   8.00


Add to 1) front; 2) middle; or 3) back of list? 3
Data? 2
Data? 7
Data? 3
Data? 8
Data? 0
   2.00
   7.00
   3.00
   8.00
```

The program lets you build lists using three different insertion methods. Let's look at the list functions.

get—node( )

This function allocates storage for an **lnode** structure and returns a pointer to this storage. The allocated space can be used to create a new element to add to a linked list. To do its work, the function calls the predefined function **malloc( )**, which actually gets and allocates the appropriate storage. If storage cannot be allocated, the function returns a **NULL** pointer.

front—of—list()

The basic strategy in **front—of—list()** is to make the **next** member of the **new** structure point to the beginning of the list— that is, to the same place as **list**. Once this is accomplished, the contents of **list** are modified to point to the same **lnode** as **new**. Thus, the list is built as follows: 2; then 7, 2; then 3, 7, 2; then 8, 3, 7, 2. Figure 2-5 shows the sequence of steps involved when adding to the front of the list. The names in parentheses correspond to **root** and **temp**, respectively, in the **front—of—list()** function.

back—of—list()

This function adds a new **lnode** at the end of the current list. The function first checks whether the current list is empty, in which case the new **lnode** becomes the only element in the list. If this is not the case, the function calls itself with the next element in the list as the "root" of the list. Each of these recursive calls is made with a shorter list; so the calls must eventually reach the end of the list. At that point, the new **lnode** is added to the list. This innermost call returns the one-element list to its calling function, which returns a two-element list to its calling function, and so forth.

middle—of—list()

This function adds a new **lnode** in its "size place"—that is, in a location based on the data member. The basic strategy in **middle—of—list()** is as follows:

    If the end of the list has been reached—that is, if the **next** member of the current **lnode** (**list** —> **next**) is a NULL pointer— make **list**—>**next** point to the same **lnode** as **new**, and return this value (and control) to the calling function. Otherwise, the function will need to do some more processing. If the function is not at the end of the list, then **list**—>**data** exists (since **list** is pointing to an **lnode**). If the **data** member of **list** is greater than the **data** member of **new**, the new structure should be inserted

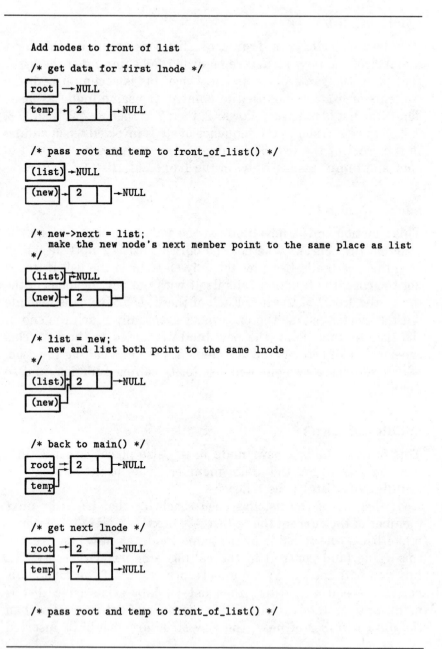

Figure 2-5.   Sequence of actions for adding to the front of a list

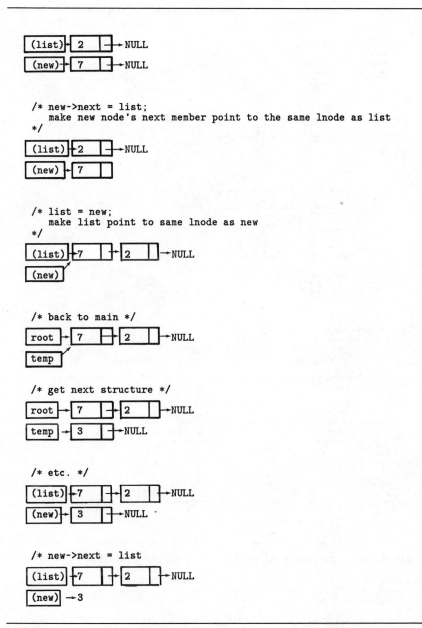

Figure 2-5.   Sequence of actions for adding to the front of a list
(*continued*)

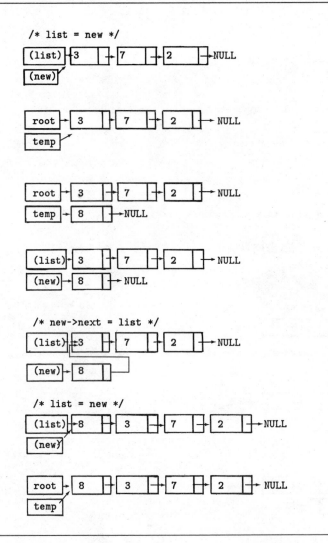

Figure 2-5.   Sequence of actions for adding to the front of a list
(*continued*)

just before the **lnode** to which **list** is pointing. Once this is
accomplished, the value of **list** is changed to point to the **lnode**
referenced by **new**. The new address stored in **list** is returned to
the calling function.

If **list** is pointing to something but the **data** member of this **lnode** is *less than* **new —>data**, then the function must keep searching for the proper place to insert the **lnode** to which **new** points. The function accomplishes this by calling itself with a shortened version of the list, namely, one starting with the **lnode** referenced by **list —>next**. The idea is that if **list —>data** is still too small, the **data** member of the next **lnode** in the ordered list may be larger.

When the recursive call returns with the modified list referenced by **list —>next**, the new structure has been inserted at the appropriate point. The current version of the function can then return its value, **list**, to the calling function. Once that's done, the various versions of the function will return the appropriate values to *their* calling functions. Figure 2-6 shows a list before (a) and after (b) a particular value has been added at the appropriate position.

Try working through the steps in building an ordered list using the same input as in the example for **front_of_list( )**.

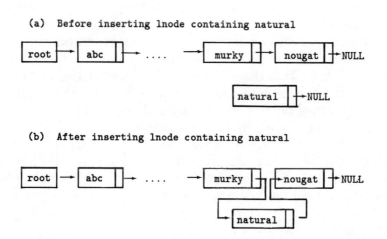

Figure 2-6.   Inserting a node into a linked list

show__list( )

This function displays the contents of the list, starting with the first element. This recursive function is somewhat different from those you've seen so far. The function tests whether the list is empty to determine what to do. If the list is empty, the function does nothing; it simply returns control to the calling function; otherwise, the function writes the value of the current element's **data** member. Then the function calls itself with a shorter list, the one referenced by the value in **list—> next**.

This function can easily be rewritten in a nonrecursive manner, and it is more efficient that way. In its present form, the function is a clean example of recursion. Try writing a nonrecursive version on your own. The recursive form of the function can be modified easily if you want to display the list from last element to first. To do this, simply move the **printf( )** statement *after* the inner **if** statement.

The list exerciser program

There are two items of note in the list exerciser program. First, each **lnode** is allocated as it's needed. The **get__node( )** function is responsible for getting this storage (if possible), initializing the structure, and returning a pointer to the storage allocated. By calling **get__node( )** only when you need another **lnode**, you can minimize the amount of storage required to run your program.

A second point concerns the returns from the list-building functions. Notice that the same variable is used twice in expressions involving a list-building function—once as the variable to which a returned pointer is assigned and once as an argument to the function. Let's see why this was necessary.

The following program helps show why a returned value is needed in this particular situation. The program contains a modified version of the **front__of__list( )** function, which writes information about the locations at which various things are happening.

```
/* Program to add to the front of a linked list, and to display
   information about the locations where things are occurring.
   Program helps illustrate importance of return values for certain
   functions.
*/

#include <stdio.h>
#include <stdlib.h>
#include <malloc.h>
#include "defs.h"
#include "slink.c"

struct lnode *new_front_of_list ( struct lnode *, struct lnode *);

/* add the structure pointed at by new to
   the front of the list pointed at by list.
*/
struct lnode *new_front_of_list(struct lnode *new, struct lnode *list)
{
        printf ( "FRONT: &list == %u; list == %u; ", &list, list);
        printf ( "&new == %u; new == %u\n", &new, new);
        new->next = list;
        list = new;
        printf ( "front: &list == %u; list == %u; ", &list, list);
        printf ( "&new == %u; new == %u\n", &new, new);
        return (list);
}


main ()
{
    /* Function declarations */

        struct lnode *temp, *root = NULL;
        char    info [ MAX_STR];
        int     selection;
        int     done = FALSE;

        temp = get_node ( temp);
        while ( (temp != NULL) && ( !done))
        {
                printf ( "\n\nData? ");
                gets ( info);
                strcpy ( temp -> data, info);
                if ( strcmp ( temp->data, null_str))
                {
                        printf ( "MAIN: &root == %u; root == %u; ",
                                &root, root);
                        printf ( "&temp == %u; temp == %u\n",
                                &temp, temp);
                        root = new_front_of_list ( temp, root);
                        printf ( "main: &root == %u; root == %u; ",
                                &root, root);
                        printf ( "&temp == %u; temp == %u\n",
                                &temp, temp);

                }
```

```
                else
                        done = TRUE;

                temp = get_node (temp);
        }

        if ( root != NULL)
                show_list ( root);
}
```

When run with the same data as in the previous example, this program produced the following:

```
Data? 2
MAIN: &root == 4406; root == 0; &temp == 4408; temp == 4610
FRONT: &list == 4296; list == 0; &new == 4294; new == 4610
front: &list == 4296; list == 4610; &new == 4294; new == 4610
main: &root == 4406; root == 4610; &temp == 4408; temp == 4610


Data? 7
MAIN: &root == 4406; root == 4610; &temp == 4408; temp == 4714
FRONT: &list == 4296; list == 4610; &new == 4294; new == 4714
front: &list == 4296; list == 4714; &new == 4294; new == 4714
main: &root == 4406; root == 4714; &temp == 4408; temp == 4714


Data? 3
MAIN: &root == 4406; root == 4714; &temp == 4408; temp == 4818
FRONT: &list == 4296; list == 4714; &new == 4294; new == 4818
front: &list == 4296; list == 4818; &new == 4294; new == 4818
main: &root == 4406; root == 4818; &temp == 4408; temp == 4818


Data? 8
MAIN: &root == 4406; root == 4818; &temp == 4408; temp == 4922
FRONT: &list == 4296; list == 4818; &new == 4294; new == 4922
front: &list == 4296; list == 4922; &new == 4294; new == 4922
main: &root == 4406; root == 4922; &temp == 4408; temp == 4922


Data?
8
3
7
2
```

Let's see how this program does its work. The goal of each call to **front_of_list( )** is to add a new **lnode** to the front of the list. This means that **root** will point to a new **lnode** after each call to **front_of_list( )**. More specifically, this means that the contents of storage location 4406 (the location at which **root**'s value is stored) should be different after each call to **front_of_list( )**.

Let's look at the output within **front_of_list( )** to see whether this can happen. First, notice the address and contents of **list**, the parameter corresponding to **root** in the function. This variable has the same contents as **root**, but this address is stored at a different location. This is because all that has been passed to the function is a *copy* of the address stored in **root**, that is, stored at location 4406. The address of **root** itself, 4406, has not been passed.

Because the value passed is an address, you can make changes in the variable located at that address. For example, after making **list** point to the same place as **new**, you could make changes in ***list**, the variable to which **list** is pointing. Because ***list** is an alias for ***root**, these changes would remain after you left the function.

However, you could *not* change the contents of **root** itself, even though you could change the address stored in **list**. This is because **root** and **list** are not aliases. By returning the desired address from the function and assigning this address directly to **root** in the calling function, you manage to make **root** point to a new **lnode** after the function call. (You could also accomplish this by passing a pointer to a pointer to structure—**struct lnode****—but that would take us too far from our topic.)

Deleting Nodes from a Linked List

Once you've built a linked list, you may want to remove an element from it. The following listing contains routines for doing this in two different ways: by specifying the ordinal position of the node to be removed (first, fifth, or last, for example) and by specifying the **data** value of the node to be removed. There is also a function for showing the **data** value of a specified **lnode**. Assume the function declarations and definitions in the listing have been added to file **lists.c**.

```
/* Additions for Lists.C
   Functions to delete and display linked list nodes
   Add these functions to Lists.C.
*/
```

```
/* **********
   new linked list function DECLARATIONS
********** */
struct lnode *del_node (struct lnode *, struct lnode *, int, char *);
struct lnode *del_val_node ( struct lnode *, struct lnode *, char *);
char         *return_val_node ( struct lnode *, char *);
void          show_node ( struct lnode *, int);
void          show_val_node ( struct lnode *, char *);


/* **********
   new linked list function DEFINITIONS
********** */


/* Delete the node at position which_node in list;
   assign the data value of this node to *result,
   and return a pointer to root of the revised list.
*/
struct lnode *del_node ( struct lnode *base, struct lnode *prev,
                         int which_node, char *result)
{
        struct lnode *curr;   /* current node under consideration */
        int    index = 1;

        curr = base;   /* set curr to point to first node */
        prev = NULL;   /* first node has no predecessor */

    /* if list is empty or user wants to delete a non-existent node */
        if ( (base == NULL) || ( which_node < 0))
        {
                result = bad_str;
                return ( base);
        }

    /* if user wants to delete first element. */
        if ( which_node == 1)
        {
                result = base -> data;
                base = base -> next;
                return ( base);
        }

        if ( which_node)  /* if deleting a node other than last one */
            /* traverse list until the specified node is reached
               or until then end of the list is reached.
            */
            for ( index = 1;
                  (index < which_node) && (curr != NULL); index++)
                {
                        prev = curr;
                        curr = curr -> next;
                }

    /* if deleting last element, and list has only 1 element */
        else if ( curr -> next == NULL)
        {
                result = curr -> data;
                base = NULL;   /* list is now empty */
                return ( base);
        }
```

```
        else             /* find last element in list */
                while ( ( curr != NULL) && ( curr -> next != NULL))
                {
                        prev = curr;
                        curr = curr -> next;
                        index++;
                }

        if ( prev != NULL)  /* if node other than first was deleted */
        {
                if ( curr != NULL) /* if there is a current element */
                {
                        /* return value stored at current node */
                        result = curr -> data;
                        /* make current point to the node after the one
                           to be deleted.
                        */
                        curr = curr -> next;
                        /* make the deleted node's predecessor point to
                           the node after the one deleted.
                        */
                        prev -> next = curr;
                }
                else  /* if end of list was reached before deleting */
                        result = bad_str;
        }         /* if prev != NULL */
        else
                result = bad_str;
        return ( base);
}


/* Delete the node with the value specified in val from the list,
   and return a pointer to root of the revised list.
*/
struct lnode *del_val_node ( struct lnode *base, struct lnode *prev,
                             char *val)
{
        struct lnode *curr;
        int    index = 1;

        curr = base;    /* make curr point to first element of list */
        prev = NULL;    /* first element has no predecessor */

    /* if there is nothing to delete */
        if ( base == NULL)
        {
                printf ( "ERROR : Empty list; no node deleted.\n");
                return ( base);
        }

    /* if the first node matches the value to be deleted. */
        if ( strcmp ( strstr ( base -> data, val), null_str))
        {
                base = base -> next;
                return ( base);
        }

    /* find the node whose data member has the specified value */
        for ( ; ( curr != NULL) &&
                ( !strcmp ( strstr ( curr -> data, val), null_str)); )
```

```
        {
                prev = curr;
                curr = curr -> next;
        }

    /* if the value was not found in the list */
        if ( curr == NULL)
        {
                printf ( "Value not found; nothing deleted.\n");
                return ( base);
        }

        if (curr != NULL) /* if there's a current element, delete */
        {
                curr = curr -> next;
                prev -> next = curr;
        }

        return ( base);
}


/* Show the value stored at a specified node.
   Node is specified by passing its position in list to function,
   with first element having position 1, etc.
   To see the last node in the list, pass 0 to the functiuon.
*/
void show_node ( struct lnode *base, int which_node)
{
        struct lnode *temp;
        int    index = 1;

        temp = base;

    /* if which_node is invalid, set it to show last element */
        if (which_node < 0)
                which_node = 0;

        if ( which_node)    /* if want to see a node other than last */
            /* traverse list until specified node is reached
               or until the end of the list has been reached.
            */
                for ( index = 1;
                        (index < which_node) && (temp != NULL); index++)
                            temp = temp -> next;
        else /* if user wants to see last element */
            /* traverse list to the end */
                while ( ( temp != NULL) && ( temp -> next != NULL))
                {
                        temp = temp -> next;
                        index++;
                }
        if ( temp != NULL)
                printf ( "node %d == %s\n", index, temp -> data);
        else
                printf ( "No such node\n");
}
```

```
/* Show the node with the value specified in val from the list. */
void show_val_node ( struct lnode *base, char *val)
{
        struct lnode *curr;

        curr = base;    /* make curr point to first element of list */

    /* if there is nothing to show */
        if ( base == NULL)
                printf ( "ERROR : Empty list.\n");

    /* if the first node matches the value to be shown. */
        if ( strcmp ( strstr ( base -> data, val), null_str))
                printf ( "%s\n", base -> data);

    /* find the node whose data member has the specified value */
        for ( ; ( curr != NULL) &&
                ( !strcmp ( strstr ( curr -> data, val), null_str)); )
                curr = curr -> next;

    /* if the value was not found in the list */
        if ( curr == NULL)
                printf ( "Value not found.\n");
        else
                printf ( "%s\n", curr -> data);
}


/* Return node containing the string specified in val from list. */
char *return_val_node ( struct lnode *base, char *val)
{
        struct lnode *curr;

        curr = base;    /* make curr point to first element of list */

    /* if there is nothing to show */
        if ( base == NULL)
                printf ( "ERROR : Empty list.\n");

    /* if the first node matches the value to be shown. */
        if ( strcmp ( strstr ( base -> data, val), null_str))
                return ( base -> data);

    /* find the node whose data member has the specified value */
        for ( ; ( curr != NULL) &&
                ( !strcmp ( strstr (curr -> data, val), null_str)); )
                curr = curr -> next;

    /* if the value was not found in the list */
        if ( curr == NULL)
        {
                printf ( "Value not found.\n");
                return ( null_str);
        }
        else
                return ( curr -> data);
}
```

show_node( )

This function displays the **data** member of the specified **lnode**. To specify an element for display, pass the ordinal position of the node you want to see as the second argument, beginning with 1 for the first node. If you pass a 0 as the second argument, the function will display the value of the *last* **data** member in the list.

The basic strategy in **show_node( )** is to use **temp** to point to the nodes in the list and to traverse the list until **temp** points to the node you want to see or until the function reaches the end of the list. Notice that the **for** loop to move to the desired node seems to stop one short of the node you want, since one of the termination conditions is **index > which_node**. Because **temp** starts out pointing to the first element, **index** actually represents the number of nodes you need to move to get to the desired one. For example, to get to the second node, you need to move just one node.

If you want to see the last element in the list, the function traverses the list until **temp** points to an element whose **next** member is **NULL**, because this node will be the last one in the list; the function will display the **data** member from this node. Thus, the two tests for this **while** construct will stop the traversal if either the end of the list or the last element has been reached.

show_val_node( )

This function displays the entire **data** member of the first node that contains a string that you specify. (See the vocabulary-testing program later in this section for an example using this function.)

return_val_node( )

This function returns the string contained in the **data** member of the first node that contains a string that you specify. (See the vocabulary-testing program later in this section for an example using this function.)

del—node( )

This function deletes a specified **lnode** from a linked list. The function takes four arguments: a pointer to the start of the list, a pointer to the **lnode** preceding the one being deleted, an **int** specifying the ordinal position of the **lnode** to delete, and a pointer to a **double** for passing the value of the deleted element back from the function. The function returns a pointer to the beginning of the revised list.

To specify a node to delete, give the node's ordinal position in the list, beginning with 1 for the first element as the value of **which—node**. To delete the last element, pass 0 as the actual value for the third parameter. The value of the node being deleted is passed back in *****result**, the variable to which the fourth parameter is pointing.

The function first checks for some special cases: an empty list or an invalid **lnode** to be deleted. In these cases, the function assigns **INVALID—VAL** to *****result**, and returns a **NULL** pointer. Another special case is if the first node in the list is to be deleted. In this case, the value of this node's **data** member is assigned to *****result**, and **base** is set to point to the second **lnode** in the list.

For other cases, the function uses **curr**, a pointer to an **lnode**, to specify the current element during the search process. This pointer is used to traverse the list. The **prev** pointer is used to reference the **lnode** preceding the one currently under consideration. Essentially, **prev** follows **curr** through the list until the function reaches the node to be deleted.

The search for the desired **lnode** is similar to the one used in **show—node( )**—using **index** to keep count of the number of nodes traversed. The actions taken each time through the loop differ in **del—node( )**, however, since both **curr** and **prev** must be updated each time. The case of a single-element list in which you want to delete the last (and only) element is also handled separately, since there is no need to assign a value to **prev**.

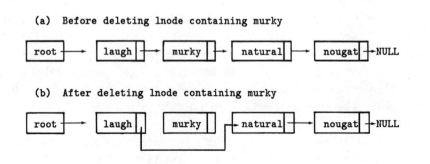

(a) **Before deleting lnode containing murky**

(b) **After deleting lnode containing murky**

Figure 2-7. Deleting a node from a linked list

Once the desired node has been found, the function assigns the appropriate information to ***result** and makes the preceding node point to the node following the one being deleted. Figure 2-7 shows a linked list before (a) and after (b) a particular node has been deleted.

del—val—node( )

This function also deletes a node. However, you identify the node by passing a string specifying the value of the node you want to delete. The function takes three arguments: a pointer to the start of the list to be modified, a pointer to the **lnode** preceding the one to be deleted, and a **char** representing the value of the node to be deleted.

The function again deals first with some special cases: an empty list and the case in which the first node's **data** member matches the value to be deleted. If neither case occurs, the function searches until it finds a match between **val** and a **data** member or until the search reaches the end of the list without finding the specified value. In the first case, the **lnode** is simply deleted; in the second case, nothing is deleted, and the function returns a message to that effect. To check whether it has found the node to delete, the function **del—val—node( )** compares **val** with the value of **data** for the **lnode**.

Example: A Vocabulary-
Testing Program

Not surprisingly, linked lists are very useful in programs that display or build lists of information. We'll look at an example of such a program in this section.

The program, **vocab.c**, reads a list of words from a specified file and puts them into a list in a sorted sequence. The program will then let you do various things with this list, including displaying the entire list, adding an item to the list, deleting an item from the list, and displaying a particular item.

In this example, the file contains a French vocabulary list. Each entry begins with a French word, followed by its English approximation. Let's assume the following list is stored in the file **french.dat:**

```
parler  speak
courir  run
comprendre  understand
vendre  sell
femme,la    woman
lire   read
entrer     enter, come in
maison,la    house
acheter    buy
```

The following program uses linked lists to get these vocabulary items into the program:

```
/* Vocabulary testing program */

#include <stdio.h>
#include <stdlib.h>
#include <string.h>

#include "defs.h"
#include "utils.c"
#include "lists.c"

/* Function declarations */
struct lnode *do_add ( struct lnode *, struct lnode *, FILE *);
struct lnode *do_delete ( struct lnode *, struct lnode *, char *);
void   do_show ( struct lnode *, char *);
void   do_test ( struct lnode *, char *);
struct lnode *get_list ( FILE *, struct lnode *, struct lnode *);
```

```
main ( int argc, char *argv [])
{
        struct lnode *temp, *root = NULL;
        char    choice [ MAX_STR];
        int     selection;
        char    *tempstr;
        FILE    *fp;


    /* if no file name was specified */
    if ( argc <= 1)
    {
            printf ( "Usage:  vocab <file name>\n");
            exit ( 1);
    }
    else  /* if a file was specified, try to open and read it */
    {
            fp = fopen ( argv [ 1], "a+");
            if ( fp != NULL)
            {
                /* read the entries from the file, put in list */
                root = get_list ( fp, root, temp);
                rewind ( fp);

                /* the main loop for a session */
                do
                {
                        printf ("S)how <word>; A)dd ");
                        printf ("entry; D)elete entry;\n");
                        printf ("E)ntire list; N)umber <#>;");
                        printf (" Q)uit;\nYour selection? ");
                        gets ( choice);

                        switch ( toupper (choice [ 0]))
                        {
                                case 'S':  /* show a node */
                                        do_show(root, choice);
                                        break;
                                case 'A':  /* add a node */
                                        temp = get_node(temp);
                                        root = do_add ( root,
                                                        temp, fp);
                                        break;
                                case 'D':  /* delete a node */
                                        root = do_delete(root,
                                                temp, choice);
                                        break;
                                case 'E':  /* entire list */
                                        show_list ( root);
                                        break;
```

```
                                case 'N':  /* show node */
                                        selection =
                                            atoi ( ++tempstr);
                                        show_node (root,
                                                    selection);
                                        break;
                                case 'Q':  /* quit */
                                        break;
                                case 'T':  /* test user */
                                        do_test ( root,
                                                    choice);
                                        break;
                                default :
                                        break;
                        }
                }
                while ( toupper (choice [ 0]) != 'Q');

                fclose ( fp);
            }  /* else, if file was opened */
        }  /* else, if file was specified */
}


/* show the first node containing the specified string */
void do_show ( struct lnode *base, char *choice)
{
        char *tempstr = &choice [ 1];

    /* delete leading blanks from the string */
        while (choice [ 1] == BLANK_CHAR)
                delete ( choice, 2, 1);
        show_val_node ( base, tempstr);
}


/* add an entry to the list and to the file. */
struct lnode *do_add(struct lnode *base, struct lnode *temp, FILE *fp)
{
        char info [ MAX_STR];
        int   selection;

        printf ( "entry? ");
        gets ( info);
        selection = fputs ( info, fp);
    /* report success or failure */
        if ( !selection)
                printf ( "Successful\n");
        else
                printf ( "Unsuccessful.\n");
        fputs ( "\n", fp);
```

```
    /* add node to list */
        strcpy ( temp -> data, info);
        base = middle_of_list ( temp, base);
        return ( base);
}


/* delete a node from the list */
struct lnode *do_delete ( struct lnode *base, struct lnode *temp,
                          char *choice)
{
        char *tempstr = &choice [ 1];

        while (choice [ 1] == BLANK_CHAR)
                delete ( choice, 2, 1);
        base = del_val_node ( base, temp, tempstr);
        return ( base);
}


/* test user by presenting the foreign word,
   and asking for English equivalent
*/
void do_test ( struct lnode *base, char *choice)
{
        char response [ MAX_STR], clue [ MAX_STR], entry [ MAX_STR];
        char *tempstr = &choice [ 1];

    /* remove leading blanks */
        while (choice [ 1] == BLANK_CHAR)
                delete ( choice, 2, 1);

    /* get just the entry string */
        strcpy ( entry, return_val_node ( base, tempstr));
    /* get the foreign word */
        strcpy ( clue, remove_wd ( entry));

    /* test user */
        printf ( "%s? ", clue);
        gets ( response);
    /* if user's answer is in the English part of entry */
        if ( strstr ( entry, response) != NULL)
                printf ( "Correct.\n");
        else
        {
                printf ( "Sorry, %s == %s\n", clue, entry);
        }
}
```

```
/* read the entries from a file and add them to an ordered list. */
struct lnode *get_list ( FILE *fp, struct lnode *base,
                         struct lnode *temp)
{
        char outcome [ MAX_STR], info [ MAX_STR];


        strcpy ( info, fgets ( outcome, MAX_STR, fp));
        while ( strcmp ( info, null_str))
        {
                temp = get_node ( temp);
                strcpy ( temp -> data, info);
                printf ( "%s", temp -> data);
                base = middle_of_list ( temp, base);
                strcpy ( info, fgets ( outcome, MAX_STR, fp));
        }
        return ( base);
}
```

The program lets you do several things with the vocabulary list. In its current form, the program is designed for teaching the vocabulary. You can ask the program to show you the information about any French or English word by typing S followed by the word whose entry you want to see. The program uses **strstr( )** to find the entry, so you need not specify the entire line to see an entry.

You can also let the program get the entry at any particular position in the list by pressing N followed by a number. In this way you can learn the vocabulary without knowing what's in the list.

You can add entries to the list by selecting the **Add** option. The program will write this new entry to the file. If you choose to delete an entry from the list, the program will do so in memory but will not remove the entry from the file. You can, of course, remove the entry with your editor.

You can also have the program test you on particular entries. In its current form, you must tell the program the word on which you want to be tested. The program will then display the French word and ask you to type its English counterpart.

get—list( )

This function reads lines from the file referenced by **fp** and adds each line to an ordered list. The function returns this list.

do—add( )

This function adds an entry to the list and also writes this entry to the vocabulary file from which the list was read. The function returns the modified list.

do—delete( )

This function deletes the specified node from the list *in memory*. The vocabulary file is not affected. To determine the node to delete, the function takes everything in the user's command line after the **D**. To ensure that leading blanks are not used in the search, the function deletes them from the string before searching for the string in the list.

do—show( )

This function displays the complete value for the first string that contains the string passed to as **choice** parameter. This function, like **do—delete( )**, deletes any leading blanks; so they will not influence the outcome of the search.

do—test( )

This function displays the foreign-language portion of the entry specified by the user (via parameter **choice**). The function then reads and evaluates the user's answer. If the answer is contained in the English portion of the entry, the answer is considered correct.

Extensions to the Vocabulary Tester

One extension you can make to the program is to give it the ability to select an entry at random and display this entry. This would be similar to the **Number** option, except that the program would select the entry to be displayed.

Similarly, you can give the program the ability to select random entries and test you on them. Once this is in place, you may want to add the ability to keep track of the percentage of correct responses. You might also give the program the ability to test you by presenting either the French or the English word, depending on how you wish to be tested.

Uses for Linked Lists

Linked lists are a very versatile data structure. They can be defined to hold just about any type of information you want, simply by changing the basic **lnode** structure. You don't need to specify the number of elements the list will contain; rather, you can add to and delete from the list as your program requires. The uses to which you can put linked lists are limited only by your imagination and ingenuity.

You can use linked lists to implement stacks. To push an element onto the stack, you would use a function such as **front—of— list( )**; to pop an element from the list, you would call **del—node( )** with **which—node** equal to 1.

Because you could allocate storage for nodes dynamically, you would not need to specify a maximum stack size in advance. The stack would be defined as full if you could no longer allocate storage for another **lnode**; the stack would be empty if the pointer to the start of the list were a **NULL** pointer. There would be no need for a **top** member, since the next element would always be added or removed at the front of the list.

Similarly, you could implement linear queues using linked lists. To add to a queue, you would use a function such as **front— of—list( )**; to remove an element, you would delete the last element (that is, you would pass 0 as the value for **which—node**).

The **middle—of—list( )** function lets you sort information by inserting each value at its appropriate position as you build the list. Such a sorting technique is known as an insertion sort; you'll find out more about this and several other sorting algorithms in Chapter 4.

SUMMARY

In this chapter, you learned about recursion as a programming technique and saw some examples of recursive functions for accomplishing various tasks. You also learned about linked lists and saw how recursion can be used to build and display them.

In the next chapter, you'll learn about another important data structure, trees, and you'll see how recursion is used to build and traverse trees.

3

TREES

In the last chapter, you learned about linked lists. You saw that the **middle—of—list( )** function enabled you to sort data by building a linked list with the data in "size places." The routine for accomplishing this task was recursive but fairly straightforward. Recall that one limitation of linked lists is that you can get to inner nodes only by going through the nodes that precede your target in the list. If the list is long, this can be time-consuming.

One step toward decreasing the work required to traverse a list is to subdivide the list into two "sublists." One of these would contain the "large" values; the other would contain the "small" values. Both of these sublists would be sorted. When you had a new element to add, you could decide whether the element belonged in the small or the large sublist. Adding an element to a sublist that is about half the size of the original list can save considerable time.

In this chapter, you'll see how a tree structure lets you accomplish such a reduction. A tree also lets you reduce your sublists into even smaller sublists. This recursive-problem subdivision saves you even more time.

EXAMPLE: SORTING THE MAIL

Suppose you have to alphabetize letters addressed to the following people:

```
Madison
Washington
Jefferson
Adams
Harrison
Pierce
Lincoln
Truman
Roosevelt
Hoover
McKinley
```

Let's try to sort these letters using a sublist strategy. Suppose it's possible to sort these letters in a very large open space so that you can lay them out in front of you in whatever configuration you wish. Your strategy will be to take the name on the first letter encountered as the boundary between "small" and "large" names. Any names earlier than the boundary value in alphabetical order ("small" names) will be put in the small pile, or sublist; other names will go into the large sublist. After making Madison the boundary value, you have the following:

```
              Madison
              (boundary)
```

The next letter (to Washington) goes into the large-name pile, which you'll put on the right, as in the following illustration. Similarly, Jefferson goes into the small-name pile on the left, also shown in the illustration.

```
                     Madison
                     (boundary)

(small sublist)                      (large sublist)
   Jefferson                           Washington
```

The next letter, Adams, clearly goes into the left pile, based on Madison as the boundary. At this point, you need to decide how to handle the sorting within the small and large sublists. One possibility is to use the same strategy that got you this far. Think of Jefferson as also being a boundary — between those "smaller" than Jefferson and those "larger" than that name. In that case, Adams goes to the "small-small" sublist.

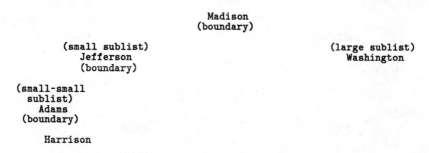

This strategy can be carried even further by making Adams a boundary between "small-small-small" values and "small-small-large" values, that is, those values smaller than Adams and those larger than Adams but smaller than Jefferson. At this point, Harrison is added to the sublist.

```
                        Madison
                        (boundary)

        (small sublist)                    (large sublist)
           Jefferson                          Washington
           (boundary)

    (small-small
       sublist)
        Adams
      (boundary)

         Harrison
```

When Pierce is added, Washington becomes a boundary. Pierce is added to the smaller sublist bounded by Washington, since Pierce comes between Madison and Washington alphabetically. Notice that Pierce is in the larger sublist relative to the boundary set by Madison.

Lincoln precedes Madison but follows Jefferson alphabetically. Therefore, Lincoln is in the small-large sublist — small for Madison, large for Jefferson. The following illustration shows your sorting after Pierce and Lincoln are added:

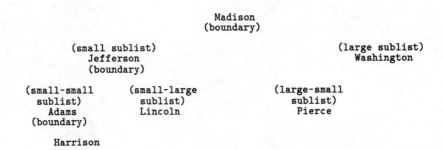

Notice that Truman becomes a boundary right after being added because the next name in the list, Roosevelt, is larger than Pierce but smaller than Truman. Therefore, Roosevelt must be added to one of Truman's sublists—in this case, the small sublist. The next illustration shows the configuration of the sorted letters after Hoover and McKinley are added:

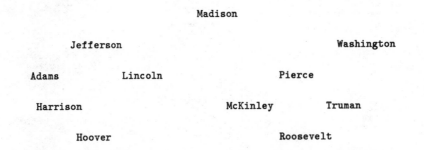

If these letters were all spread out as in our illustrations, it certainly would be easy to pick up the letters in sorted order. You could simply find the smallest name (down in the lower left pile) and pick it up, pick up the smallest of the remaining letters, and so forth.

The basic strategy you'll use to read such lists in order has the same general structure as the solution to the Tower of Hanoi problem in Chapter 2. The top level of subproblems, as shown in the next illustration, is as follows:

1. Read the smaller sublist for Madison.
2. Read Madison.
3. Read the larger sublist for Madison.

```
SMALLER SUBLIST FOR MADISON
                                        READ MADISON
                                                      LARGER SUBLIST FOR MADISON

                                        Madison

              Jefferson                                        Washington

      Adams              Lincoln                      Pierce

          Harrison                              McKinley          Truman

              Hoover                                  Roosevelt
```

As in the Tower of Hanoi problem, the first subproblem actually consists of the following second-level subproblems, indicated in the illustration below:

1. Read the smaller sublist for Jefferson.
2. Read Jefferson.
3. Read the larger sublist for Jefferson.

```
  SMALLER SUBLIST FOR MADISON
                                    Madison
  SMALLER FOR JEFFERSON
        READ JEFFERSON
              LARGER FOR JEFFERSON

              Jefferson                                    Washington

      Adams              Lincoln                      Pierce

          Harrison                              McKinley          Truman

              Hoover                                  Roosevelt
```

To get this far, subproblem 1 would have called the smaller sub-problem 1.1 (small list for Jefferson) recursively. To solve 1.1, you would go to yet another level of subproblem:

1. Read the smaller sublist for Adams.
2. Read Adams.
3. Read the larger sublist for Adams.

At this level, things will finally start to happen. Notice there is no smaller sublist for Adams; therefore, that job is done. The next step is to read Adams. Subproblem 1.1.3 requires additional work:

1. Read the smaller sublist for Harrison.
2. Read Harrison.
3. Read the larger sublist for Harrison.

Again, there is no smaller subproblem. The next step is to read Harrison. Our sorted list so far contains Adams and Harrison, in that order.

The next outstanding subproblem is 1.1.3.3—read the larger sublist for Harrison. This problem requires the following actions:

1. Read the smaller sublist for Hoover.
2. Read Hoover.
3. Read the larger sublist for Hoover.

Since there is no smaller sublist for Hoover, the next step is to pick up Hoover and add this letter to the end of our (two-element) ordered list. There is also no larger sublist for Hoover, so you are done with Herbert.

By finishing with Hoover, you've also managed to finish the larger sublist for Harrison. This, in turn, solves the larger sublist for Adams. So far, you've resolved the sublists for Adams, Harrison, and Hoover, and all three are currently in the list and in order.

This solves the smaller sublist for Jefferson; you can now add Jefferson to the list. The next step is to solve the larger sublist for Jefferson. This happens when you find that there are neither smaller nor larger sublists for Lincoln and you add Lincoln to the sorted letter sequence.

Once you're finished with Jefferson, you've completed the smaller sublist for Madison. You then add Madison to the list, since this is the next task. Finally, you need to solve the larger sublist for Madison. This will require additional recursive calls. Try working your way through the right side of your sorted letter configuration. Later in the chapter you'll find a function for accomplishing the same thing.

TREES

In the previous section you saw how to sort information in a manner that is more efficient than the sequential traversal required with linked lists. The traversal strategy you used in the letter example is still sequential; however, the strategy simply took advantage of the current configuration to minimize the number of steps required to put an element in its proper place. Essentially, the strategy was a divide-and-conquer approach, where each new element was placed by moving it to its proper position in simpler sublists until finally you added the new element to an empty list.

Trees are a common data structure for such an approach in terms of sublists (or subtrees, as you'll see). Like linked lists, trees are made of nodes that contain both information and pointers to other nodes. In a linked list, each **lnode** pointed to exactly one other **lnode**; for a tree, on the other hand, nodes may point to more than one other node of the same type. As with linked lists, the first node in the tree is generally accessed by means of a simple pointer to the appropriate type of node. We'll refer to the first node as the *root* of the tree.

The number of pointer members a tree's nodes have determines the type of tree. For example, the following structure defines a node for building a *binary tree*, in which each node has pointers to two other nodes of the same type.

```
/* Definition for a tree node */

struct tnode {
        char            data [ MAX_STR];
    /* pointers to the left, or smaller, sublist and the
       right, or larger, sublist, respectively.
    */
        struct tnode *left, *right;
};
```

The **left** and **right** members point to the nodes that serve as boundaries in the left and right sublists, respectively. Thus, **left** and **right** point to the roots of the left and right subtrees, respectively. The examples in this chapter will involve binary trees.

Similarly, if you were building a *ternary tree*, your **tnode** structure would have three pointers to **tnode** members — perhaps, **left**, **right**, and **middle**. A *quadtree* has up to four branches at each node, so the basic element for a quadtree would need four pointer members. Quadtrees are very important in artificial intelligence work concerned with machine vision.

Let's look at a few examples of trees. The following illustration shows a very simple tree:

```
                        Madison
```

This tree consists of only one element, whose "value" is Madison, which is the string stored in the node's **data** member. Both the **left** and **right** members are null.

The following is also a tree:

```
                        (root)
                        Madison

    (right sublist)                         (right sublist)
       Jefferson                               Washington
```

This tree consists of three elements: the boundary, or root, value (Madison), and the nodes to which the **left** and **right** members point — Jefferson and Washington, respectively. Both of these nodes have null pointers as the values for their **left** and **right** members. Jefferson and Washington are known as successors, or *children*, of

Madison. In turn, Madison is the *parent* node for Jefferson and Washington. These sublists are also trees, since single nodes are trees, as you saw in the previous example.

Nodes in a binary tree can have zero, one, or two children. A node with no children at the bottom of one of the subtrees is called a *leaf*, or a terminal node. All other nodes in a tree are called *interior* nodes.

Building a Binary Tree

In the letter-sorting example, you actually built a binary tree. In this section, you'll develop the functions needed to do this in a program. As you build the tree, each new element will be inserted in its "size place."

To sort the letters, you took the name on the first letter and added it to an empty letter collection. You automatically made this name a boundary value for subdividing subsequent names into those smaller and larger than the first name's value. This first boundary value was the root of the tree.

You compared subsequent elements with the root, using alphabetical order as the comparison criterion. If the name preceded the root name, you moved it to the left (small) sublist; if the name followed the root name alphabetically, you moved it to the right (large) sublist. If there was already an element at the head of the sublist, you compared the new name with this "second-level" boundary value, moving it to the left or the right as the comparison dictated. This step was repeated as long as there were boundary values at the top of each sublist. Eventually, you came to a point where there was no element to compare, that is, to an empty list. You attached the new element at that point. If you think of each of the lower-level boundary values as being roots of local trees (contained inside the original tree and smaller than the original tree) beginning with that node, you will recognize this last action as the local counterpart of adding the first element to the original list.

The following listing contains functions for allocating storage for a **tnode** and adding a **tnode** to a binary tree.

```
/* **********
   tree function DECLARATIONS
********** */
struct tnode *get_tnode ( struct tnode *);
struct tnode *add_to_tree ( struct tnode *, struct tnode *);


/*
   struct tnode *get_tnode ( struct tnode *item)
   *********************************************************
   Allocate space for and initialize a tnode structure for
   for simple tree; return pointer to the storage allocated.

   CALLS : malloc (); printf (); sizeof ();
   GLOBALS :   NULL
   PARAMETERS :
           item : pointer to storage allocated for allocated tnode.
   RETURN : a pointer to the allocated tnode
   USAGE : temp = get_tnode ( temp);
   *********************************************************
*/
struct tnode *get_tnode ( struct tnode *item)
{
        void *malloc ( size_t);

    /* allocate enough space to store a tnode */
        item = (struct tnode *) malloc ( sizeof ( struct tnode));

    /* if allocated, initialize the structure */
        if (item != NULL)
        {
            /* initially, node does not point to any nodes */
                item -> left = NULL;
                item -> right = NULL;
                strcpy ( item->data, null_str);
        }
        else
                printf ( "Nothing allocated\n");
        return ( item);              /* return the pointer */
}


/*
   struct tnode *add_to_tree ( struct tnode *new,
                     struct tnode *root)
   *********************************************************
   Add new tnode at appropriate spot in simple tree.

   CALLS : add_to_tree (); strcmp ();
   GLOBALS : NULL
   PARAMETERS :
           new : new tnode to be added to tree;
           root : tree to which tnode is to be added;
   RETURN : pointer to modified tree.
   USAGE : root = add_to_tree ( temp, root, &successful);
   *********************************************************
*/
```

```
struct tnode *add_to_tree ( struct tnode *new, struct tnode *root)
{
        if ( root == NULL)  /* if (local) tree is empty, just add */
        {
                root = new;
                return ( root);
        }
        else  /* go left or right, depending on comparison */
        {
                /* if new value <= current node value,
                   add to left subtree
                */
                if ( strcmp ( new -> data, root -> data) <= 0)
                        root -> left = add_to_tree ( new, root->left);
                else    /* add to right subtree */
                        root->right = add_to_tree ( new, root->right);
                return ( root);
        }   /* move down a subtree */
}
```

get—tnode()

This function allocates storage for a **tnode** structure and returns a pointer to the location of this storage. If the function is unable to allocate the required storage, the function returns a null pointer. To do its work, **get—tnode()** calls **malloc()**, the Run-Time library function declared in the header file **malloc.h** distributed with your QuickC system. If successful, the function also initializes the **data** and the two pointer members.

add—to—tree()

This function adds a **tnode** to the specified tree at the position the element should have, given the current tree and the contents of the new node's **data** member.

The function works as follows: If the tree passed as a parameter is empty, the new element is added and becomes the root of the tree; otherwise, the program decides whether to continue its search down the left or the right subtree. If the **data** member of the new node precedes or is identical to the **data** value in the root node, the function will continue down the left subtree; otherwise, the search continues down the right subtree.

If the function needs to continue searching, it calls itself, with the element referenced by the **left** or **right** member of the root node (depending on whether the function is to go left or right) as the new root parameter; that is, the recursive call is made with the root of either the left or the right subtree as its argument. Eventually, the recursive calls will come to a point where the most recent local tree is empty, at which point the new node is added.

For example, to add Madison, Washington, and Jefferson to the tree, **add—to—tree( )** would be used as follows:

1. Call **add—to—tree( )** with **root** (initialized to **NULL**) as the argument.

   ▪ Add Madison to the empty tree; that is, set **root** to point to the node containing Madison as its **data** value.

2. Call **add—to—tree( )** with the root as the argument again and with Washington as the node to be added. After comparing Madison with Washington, call **add—to—tree( )** with **Madison —> right** as the local root node and Washington as the node to be added.

   ▪ Add Washington to the empty tree (at **Madison —> right**).

3. Call **add—to—tree( )** with the root as the argument again but with Jefferson as the node to be added this time. After comparing Madison with Jefferson, call **add—to—tree( )** with **Madison —> left** as the local root node and Jefferson as the node to be added.

   ▪ Add Jefferson to the empty tree (referenced by **Madison —> left**).

Traversing Binary Trees

Once you've built a tree, you can display its contents in several ways. The process of moving through a tree is often known as *tree traversal*. In this section you'll learn about some of the possible tree traversal sequences and develop routines to carry them out.

Perhaps the most common order for displaying a tree is in its sorted sequence. Recall that you built your trees by putting smaller values in the left subtrees. Thus, to display a tree in order, you'll need to show the leftmost nodes first and work your way over to the right.

This turns out to be very simple if you use recursion.

Because all the items in the left subtree precede the root element which, in turn, precedes the elements in the right subtree, the general strategy for an in-order traversal is as follows: First display the left subtree, then the root, and then the right subtree. Another common order of display is the left subtree, then the right subtree, and then the root. This *postorder sequence* is very common in processing mathematical expressions. Essentially, postorder traversal amounts to displaying or processing a postfix expression. For example, consider a tree whose nodes can contain either operands or operators, such as the following. (You can do this with the tree structure you've been using.)

```
          +

    7           5
```

The postfix form of the expression in the tree would be

```
7    5    +
```

Notice that this sequence corresponds to left subtree, right subtree, root. If you substitute operand for subtree and operator for root, you'll see this even more clearly. This traversal sequence is often known as a *postfix sequence*.

Earlier, we mentioned that you can also create prefix expressions, in which the operator precedes its two operands. If you had such an expression in a tree, the situation would call for a *preorder*, or *prefix*, *traversal*.

The prefix form of the preceding example is

```
+    7    5
```

This corresponds to displaying the root value, then the left subtree, and then the right subtree—or operator, left operand, right operand.

Incidentally, notice that our in-order traversal essentially amounts to an infix traversal, where 7, +, and 5 correspond to left operand, operator, and right operand, respectively.

```
7    +    5
```

Notice that in all three cases — in-order, preorder, and postorder — the sequence involved either a root or a subtree. In each case, the root element corresponded to operators, and the subtrees corresponded to operands. If these subtrees were complex operands — that is, operands requiring further evaluation — then the root of the subtree would again be an operand. All simple operands are leaf nodes.

The following functions display a tree in sorted order, prefix order, and postfix order, respectively. Notice that the functions differ only in the placement of the **printf( )** statement. Since **printf( )** is where the display functions actually do their work, and since this statement always displays the **data** value of the current (root) element, the location of this statement will determine what kind of traversal is involved.

```
/* routines to display a tree in sorted, prefix and postfix order */

/* ***********
   tree function DECLARATIONS
*********** */
void show_tree ( struct tnode *);
void show_preorder ( struct tnode *);
void show_postorder ( struct tnode *);


/*
   void show_tree ( struct tnode *tree)
   ********************************************************
   Display contents of the tree, using an in-order traversal.

   CALLS : printf (); show_tree ();
   GLOBALS : NULL
   PARAMETERS :
           tree : pointer to tree to be displayed.
   RETURN : none
   USAGE : show_tree ( root);
   ********************************************************
*/
void show_tree ( struct tnode *tree)
{
        if ( tree != NULL)
        {
            /* show left subtree first */
                if ( tree -> left != NULL)
                        show_tree ( tree -> left);
            /* display root */
                printf ( "%s\n", tree->data);
            /* then show right subtree */
                if ( tree -> right != NULL)
                        show_tree ( tree -> right);
```

```
        }    /* if tree not empty */
}


/*
    void show_preorder ( struct tnode *tree)
    ************************************************************
    Display contents of a tree, using prefix order traversal.

    CALLS : printf (); show_preorder ();
    GLOBALS : NULL
    PARAMETERS :
            tree : pointer to tree to display.
    RETURN : none
    USAGE : show_preorder ( root);
    ************************************************************
*/
void show_preorder ( struct tnode *tree)
{
        if ( tree != NULL)
        {
            /* display root value first */
                printf ( "%s\n", tree->data);
            /* then display left subtree */
                if ( tree -> left != NULL)
                        show_preorder ( tree -> left);
            /* finally, right subtree */
                if ( tree -> right != NULL)
                        show_preorder ( tree -> right);
        }    /* if tree is not empty */
}

/*
    void show_postorder ( struct tnode *tree)
    ************************************************************
    Display contents of a tree, using postfix order traversal.

    CALLS : printf (); show_postorder ();
    GLOBALS : NULL
    PARAMETERS :
            tree : pointer to tree to display.
    RETURN : none
    USAGE : show_postorder ( root);
    ************************************************************
*/
void show_postorder ( struct tnode *tree)
{
        if ( tree != NULL)
        {
            /* show left subtree first */
                if ( tree -> left != NULL)
                        show_postorder ( tree -> left);
            /* then right subtree */
                if ( tree -> right != NULL)
                        show_postorder ( tree -> right);
            /* finally, show root value */
                printf ( "%s\n", tree->data);
        }
}
```

show—tree( )

This function traverses the tree and displays the contents of each node. The presentation is in order — in our case, based on an alphabetical sorting. When the "alphabet" is defined in terms of a character set, such as ASCII, the ordering is called *lexicographic*. For the sake of the examples, alphabetic and lexicographic orderings are very similar. For example, in a lexicographic ordering, *Apple* would precede *apple*, since *A* precedes *a* in the ASCII character set. An alphabetical ordering would not give precedence to either, since case does not matter in an alphabetical ordering.

If the pointer members of the current node are not null pointers (that is, the function hasn't reached the end of a subtree), then the **show—tree( )** function calls itself to move further down the left subtree. This continues until the function reaches one of the bottom, or leaf, elements in the tree. This element has a null pointer for the value of its **left** member. Since this version of the function fails the **if** test, it does nothing except return control to its calling function.

After returning from the recursive call down the left subtree, the function displays the **data** value stored at the current node. The function then calls itself to travel down the right subtree, writing those values where appropriate. The recursion ensures that all nodes are eventually visited and makes it unnecessary to keep track of where you are in the tree. The sequence of the function calls — **show—tree( )** for left subtree, **printf( )** for current **data** value, **show—tree( )** for right subtree — ensures that the tree will be displayed in sorted order.

show—postorder( )

This function displays the contents of a tree in postfix order, that is, left subtree, right subtree, root. The postfix label refers to mathematical expressions often being represented in a tree; in such cases, the root nodes are operators, and the leaf nodes are operands. To evaluate a postfix expression, you would get the left operand (left subtree), then the right operand (right subtree), and finally the operator (root).

Notice that this function has the same structure as **show—tree( )** and **show—preorder( )** — traversing first the left subtree and then the right. The difference is simply in the placement of the **printf( )**

statement that actually displays the value of the current node. Since the operator is the last item retrieved in a postfix expression, the root node should be the last one displayed. There is another difference, of course: Each function calls itself rather than **show_tree( )**.

show_preorder( )

This function displays the contents of a tree in prefix order, that is, in a notation where an operator precedes its left and right operands. To display a tree in prefix order, the function needs to write the operator (root) information first, then the information for the left operand (left subtree), and finally that for the right operand (right subtree).

Again, the only thing needed to change the sequence of the original display function is a change in the location of the **printf( )** call.

Breadth-First Tree Traversal

Another common way to traverse a tree is by levels in the tree. In this traversal, the root is displayed first. Next, the roots of the left and right subtrees are displayed, in that order. Then the roots of the second level of subtrees are displayed from left to right. The following illustration shows a tree:

A *breadth-first traversal* of this tree would visit the nodes in the following order:

6   4   8   2   5   7   9   1   3

In a breadth-first traversal, all the nodes at one level are visited before any nodes at the next level. This is in contrast to a *depth-first traversal*, such as an in-order traversal, in which the routine first moves to the lowest level in a subtree.

A breadth-first traversal strategy is more difficult to implement than a depth-first traversal. To see how it's done, let's look at a small example: the top three levels of the tree in the preceding illustration. For each node, you'll want to keep track of what gets displayed and what nodes are accessible at that point.

At the top level, you display the contents of the root node. You are also able to access the nodes referenced by **root —> left** and **root —> right**.

At the second level, you move from left to right, as required earlier. Thus, at this level, the values of **root —> left —> data** and **root —> right —> data** are displayed. (To make it simpler, let's refer to **root —> left** and **root —> right** as **lroot** and **rroot**, respectively.) At the top level, **lroot —> data** and **rroot —> data** can be displayed.

At the second level of the tree, the following four nodes are accessible:

```
lroot -> left
lroot -> right
rroot -> left
rroot -> right
```

At each of the two levels you've traversed so far, the nodes whose values are displayed contain information about the nodes to be displayed at the next level. If you read the nodes accessible from a specific level—reading from left to right—you will have the sequence in which the nodes are displayed. To read from left to right actually involves a small-scale motion (from **left** to **right** members at a level) *and* a large-scale one (from the left to the right node at the next-higher level).

In Chapter 1, you learned that queues can be used to store elements that must be processed in the order in which they "arrive." You'll use a queue to help keep the nodes to be displayed in sequence. The following function displays the contents of a tree in a breadth-first sequence:

```
/* function for traversing list in breadth-first order. */

void breadth_first ( struct tnode *);

/*
    void breadth_first ( struct tnode *tree)
    *************************************************************
    Traverse and display binary tree breadth-first, that is, by
    level, and from left to right within subtree pairs at each level.
    Requires qlnode data structure and the routines called below.

    CALLS : back_of_qlist (); del_qnode (); get_qnode (); printf ();
    GLOBALS : NULL
    PARAMETERS :
            tree : pointer to tree to display.
    RETURN : none
    USAGE : breadth_first ( root);
    *************************************************************
*/
void breadth_first ( struct tnode *tree)
{
        struct qlnode *qroot = NULL, *qtemp;
        struct tnode  *temp, *qreturn;

    /* get a node with which to add to the queued list */
        qtemp = get_qnode ( qtemp);
    /* make the qlnode's data member point to the tree's root */
        qtemp -> tn = tree;
    /* add qlnode to queued list */
        qroot = back_of_qlist ( qtemp, qroot);

    /* continue while the queued list is not empty */
        while ( qroot != NULL)
        {
            /* get pointer to front node --- for display */
            qroot = del_qnode ( qroot, qtemp, 1, &qreturn);
            temp = qreturn;
            /* display the tnode's value */
            printf ( "%s\n", temp -> data);
            /* if tnode has a left child, add it to queued list */
            if ( temp -> left != NULL)
            {
                    qtemp = get_qnode ( qtemp);
                    qtemp -> tn = temp -> left;
                    qroot = back_of_qlist ( qtemp, qroot);
            } /* if tnode has left child */

            /* if tnode has a right child, add it to queued list */
            if ( temp -> right != NULL)
            {
                    qtemp = get_qnode ( qtemp);
                    qtemp -> tn = temp -> right;
                    qroot = back_of_qlist ( qtemp, qroot);
            }   /* if tnode has right child */
        } /* while queued list is not empty */
}
```

breadth—first( )

This function traverses the specified tree level by level. Within levels, the function traverses the tree from left to right. The function uses a linked list that is manipulated like a queue. This list contains pointers to nodes in the tree. The sequence in which elements are added to this queued list corresponds to the sequence in which the tree nodes are displayed.

The function builds a list of pointers to nodes from the tree, ordered by level, as it turns out. The first element added to the list is the tree's root node, which will be displayed first.

After adding this node, the function continues processing until the queued list is empty. The **while** loop carries out the following tasks:

1. Getting the **tnode** referenced by the front list element to display and removing this pointer (to **tnode**) from the list

2. Displaying the **data** value for the target node

3. Adding the root of the left subtree to the queued list for display

4. Adding the root of the right subtree to the queued list for display

Steps 3 and 4 ensure that all the nodes are added to the list and that they are added in the correct sequence. The queue properties of the list ensure that the elements are removed from the list in the correct order for display.

To do its work, **breadth—first( )** uses a **qlnode** data structure. This is similar to an **lnode**; however, the **data** member is a pointer to **tnode** instead of a string. The following listing contains the declaration for this data structure and routines needed for adding to and removing from a linked list of **qlnode** elements. Assume you've put these functions in a file named **ql.c**; later on, you'll put the definition of a **qlnode** in a separate file, named **types.h**.

```
/* QL.C : Functions to create a simple queue using linked lists.
   Data structures and routines used by breadth_first () ---
   to store pointers to tnodes in a queued list.
   The qlnode declaration should be put in file types.h;
   the functions for manipulating qlnodes should be put in file lq.c.
*/
```

```
#include <malloc.h>

/* Node for a q-list.
   Two members: tn, and a pointer to another node like this one.
   Put in file types.h
*/
struct qlnode {
        struct  tnode  *tn;         /* pointer to a node in a tree */
        struct  qlnode *next;       /* pointer to another qlnode */
};


/* **********
   linked list function DECLARATIONS
********** */
struct qlnode *back_of_qlist ( struct qlnode *, struct qlnode *);
struct qlnode *del_qnode ( struct qlnode *, struct qlnode *, int,
                           struct tnode **);
struct qlnode *front_of_qlist ( struct qlnode *, struct qlnode *);
struct qlnode *get_qnode ( struct qlnode *);


/* **********
   linked list function DEFINITIONS
********** */

/*
   struct qlnode *get_qnode ( struct qlnode *item)
   ************************************************************
   Allocate space for and initialize a queued list structure;
   return pointer to the structure.

   CALLS : malloc (); printf ();
   GLOBALS : NULL
   PARAMETERS :
   item : pointer to storage allocated for the qlnode .
   RETURN :  pointer to the allocated storage.
   USAGE :  qtemp = get_qnode ( qtemp);
   ************************************************************
*/
struct qlnode *get_qnode ( struct qlnode *item)
{
    /* allocate enough space to store an qlnode */
       item = (struct qlnode *) malloc ( sizeof ( struct qlnode));

    /* if allocated, initialize the structure */
       if (item != NULL)
       {
               item->next = NULL;
               item->tn = NULL;
       }

       else
               printf ( "Nothing allocated\n");
       return ( item);             /* return the pointer */
}


/*
   struct qlnode *front_of_qlist ( struct qlnode *new,
                         struct qlnode *list)
   ************************************************************
   Add new queued list node to the front of an existing list.
```

```
    CALLS :
    GLOBALS :
    PARAMETERS :
    new : pointer to the node being added;
          list : pointer to the list being modified.
    RETURN : pointer to the modified list.
    USAGE : qroot = front_of_qlist ( qtemp, qroot);
    **********************************************************
*/
struct qlnode * front_of_qlist ( struct qlnode *new,
                                 struct qlnode *list)
{
        new->next = list;
        list = new;
        return (list);
}


/*
    struct qlnode *back_of_qlist ( struct qlnode *new,
                        struct qlnode *list)
    **********************************************************
    Add new queued list node to the back of an existing list.

    CALLS : back_of_qlist ();
    GLOBALS : NULL
    PARAMETERS :
    new : pointer to the node being added;
          list : pointer to the list being modified.
    RETURN : pointer to the modified list.
    USAGE : qroot = back_of_qlist ( qtemp, qroot);
    **********************************************************
*/
struct qlnode *back_of_qlist ( struct qlnode *new,
                               struct qlnode *list)
{
        if ( list == NULL)
        {
                list = new;
                return ( list);
        }
        else
        {
            /* return results of most recent search. */
                list->next = back_of_qlist ( new, list->next);
                return ( list);
        }
}


/*
    struct qlnode *del_qnode (struct qlnode *base, struct qlnode *prev,
                        int which_node, struct tnode **result)
    **********************************************************
    Delete the node at position which_node in list;
    assign the tn value of this node to *result,
    and return a pointer to root of the revised list.
```

```
        CALLS :
        GLOBALS : NULL
        PARAMETERS :
                base : pointer to start of queued list being modified;
                prev : pointer to node preceding one being deleted;
                which_node : ordinal position of node being deleted;
                result : pointer to pointer to node being deleted.
        RETURN : pointer to modified queued list.
        USAGE : qroot = del_qnode ( qroot, qprev, 10, &temp);
        ********************************************************
*/
struct qlnode *del_qnode ( struct qlnode *base, struct qlnode *prev,
                           int which_node, struct tnode **result)
{
        struct qlnode *curr;    /* current node under consideration */
        int    index = 1;

        curr = base;    /* set curr to point to first node */
        prev = NULL;    /* first node has no predecessor */

     /* if list is empty or user wants to delete non-existent node */
        if ( (base == NULL) || ( which_node < 0))
        {
                *result = NULL;
                return ( base);
        }

     /* if user wants to delete first element. */
        if ( which_node == 1)
        {
                *result = base -> tn;
                base = base -> next;
                return ( base);
        }

        if ( which_node)      /* if deleting node other than last one */
                /* traverse list until the specified node is reached
                   or until the end of the list is reached.
                */
                for ( index = 1;
                        (index < which_node) && (curr != NULL); index++)
                        {
                                prev = curr;
                                curr = curr -> next;
                        }
     /* if deleting last element, and list has only 1 element */
        else if ( curr -> next == NULL)
                {
                        *result = curr -> tn;
                        base = NULL;    /* list is now empty */
                        return ( base);
        }
        else            /* find last element in list */
                while ( ( curr != NULL) && ( curr -> next != NULL))
                        {
                                prev = curr;
```

```
                        curr = curr -> next;
                        index++;
                }
        if ( prev != NULL)  /* if node other than first was deleted */
        {
                if ( curr != NULL) /* if there is a current element */
                {
                /* return value stored at current node */
                        *result = curr -> tn;
                /* make current point to the node after the one
                        to be deleted.
                */
                        curr = curr -> next;
                /* make the deleted node's predecessor point to
                        node after the one deleted.
                */
                        prev -> next = curr;
                }
                else  /* if end of list was reached before deleting */
                        *result = NULL;
        }       /* if prev != NULL */
        else
                *result = NULL;
        return ( base);
}
```

Searching a Tree

A common action involving trees is a search for values in a tree.
Recall that one of the advantages of a tree over a linked list is that
you can determine whether an element is in a tree in fewer steps
than you need to search for an element in a linked list. The following
function lets you search for a specified value in a tree.

```
/* routine to find a specified tnode in a tree */

struct tnode *find_tnode ( struct tnode *, struct tnode **, char *);

/*
   struct tnode *find_tnode ( struct tnode *tree,
                                struct tnode **prev, char *val)
   **********************************************************
   Function to find a specified value in a tree;
   function returns a pointer to the desired node, and also
   passes back a pointer to the node preceding the desired one.

   CALLS : strcmp ();
   GLOBALS : NULL
```

```
    PARAMETERS :
            tree : pointer to root of tree being searched;
            prev : pointer to pointer to tnode, to return node
            preceding the desired one;
            val : string specifying value being sought.
    RETURN : pointer to desired node.
    USAGE : temp = find_tnode ( root, &prev, "target");
    ***********************************************************
*/
struct tnode *find_tnode ( struct tnode *tree, struct tnode **prev,
                              char *val)
{
        if ( tree != NULL)
        {
            /* search until val is found or end of tree is reached */
                while ( (tree != NULL) && (strcmp (tree->data, val)))
                {
                    /* before moving on, set predecessor */
                    *prev = tree;
                    /* move left or right, depending on comparison */
                    if ( strcmp ( tree -> data, val) < 0)
                            tree = tree -> right;
                    else
                            tree = tree -> left;
            } /* while not found and not at end of tree */
        }         /* if tree is not empty */
        return ( tree);
}
```

find_tnode( )

This function searches for a specified value in a tree. The function
returns a pointer to the node containing the value or a null pointer if
the value is not found in the tree. The function uses a tree's ordering
properties to minimize the number of nodes that need to be checked
before an answer is possible.

The function also passes back a pointer to the node preceding the
one you're looking for. This makes it possible to make changes at the
node and ensure that these will be made properly in the tree. For
example, later you'll see some functions that will let you perform
arbitrary rotations on a node in a tree.

The parameter to which this predecessor information is passed is
a pointer to pointer to **tnode** (**tnode). Therefore, you must pass the

address of a **tnode** pointer variable to the function. For example, the following listing shows how you might call this function:

```
struct tnode *temp1, *temp2, *root;

temp1 = find_tnode ( root, &temp2, "hello");
```

Deleting from a Tree

It is more difficult to delete a node from a tree than it is to insert or find a node. A deletion routine must check for several possibilities and be able to modify the tree by changing the subtree structure.

The simplest case is that in which the value to be deleted is a leaf node, that is, a node that has no children. You just need to delete the pointer to such a node from its parent.

The more complex case arises when the node being deleted is an interior node, that is, one that has at least one child. In such a case, the general strategy is to move the node to be deleted downward in the tree until it becomes a leaf node. Such "rebranching" is done by exchanging two nodes and modifying their subtrees accordingly; you accomplish this by using either of two functions, **l—rotate( )** or **r—rotate( )**.

For example, suppose you had the tree shown in part (a) of the following illustration and you wanted to exchange the relative levels of Madison and Pierce:

```
                    Madison
          Lincoln           Pierce
                      McKinley    Roosevelt
                                      Truman
                                  Washington
                (a)
```

```
                    Pierce
        Madison              Roosevelt
    Lincoln    McKinley          Truman
                                    Washington
            (b)
```

```
            Pierce
    Lincoln          Roosevelt
        Madison              Truman
            McKinley         Washington
            (c)
```

```
                Pierce
        Lincoln        Roosevelt
              McKinley      Truman
        Madison              Washington
                (d)
```

To decide how to do this, let's determine how the modified tree would look. After the exchange, Madison would be the root of a subtree of Pierce. Since Madison precedes Pierce lexicographically, it would become the left subtree.

Pierce already has a left subtree; you'll need to do something about this. McKinley precedes Pierce but follows Madison. Therefore, McKinley must become part of Madison's right subtree. At the start, Pierce is the root of Madison's right subtree; however, Pierce is now the parent node for Madison and so is no longer a right subtree. In fact, Madison has no right subtree, since Pierce kept *its* right subtree and is moving its left subtree to Madison. Because Madison has no right subtree, McKinley becomes the root of this right subtree.

After the exchange, the tree looks as shown in part (b) of the illustration. Such an exchange is known as a *left rotation*. In a left rotation, a parent node is exchanged with its *right* child. After the exchange, the original parent node is the *left* child of the new parent node. Thus, Pierce was originally the right child of the node with value Madison. After the exchange, Madison is the left child of Pierce. The net effect of a left rotation is to move the original parent node down one level and to the left and to move the right child up one level.

Now, suppose you wanted to exchange Madison and Lincoln. You could use a *right rotation* to accomplish this. This rotation exchanges a parent node and its *left* child. After the exchange, the original parent will be the *right* child. Thus, after the rotation, Madison will be the right child of Lincoln. Since Lincoln was a leaf node, it had no right subtree to shift; therefore, Madison will not have a left child. McKinley is unaffected as the right child of Madison. The resulting tree is shown in part (c) of the illustration.

Finally, you could do another left rotation to exchange Madison and McKinley. McKinley would become Lincoln's right child, and Madison would become a leaf as the left child of McKinley, as in part (d). At that point, you could easily delete Madison from the tree, since it would be a leaf node.

The following listing contains functions for doing left and right rotations:

```
/* routines for rotating the root node to the left or to the right */

struct tnode *l_rotate ( struct tnode *);
struct tnode *r_rotate ( struct tnode *);

/*
    struct tnode *l_rotate ( struct tnode *tree)
    *********************************************************
    Rotate a node down and to the left, at the same time
    moving the node's right child up and to the left.
    Function is for nodes in simple trees.

    CALLS :
    GLOBALS : NULL
    PARAMETERS : tree : pointer to node around which to rotate
    RETURN : pointer to new root of modified tree portion.
    USAGE : root = l_rotate ( root);
    *********************************************************
```

```
*/
struct tnode *l_rotate ( struct tnode *tree)
{
        struct tnode *temp = tree;

        if ( tree != NULL)
        {
                tree = tree -> right;
                temp -> right = tree -> left;
                tree -> left = temp;
        }
        return ( tree);
}

/*
   struct tnode *r_rotate ( struct tnode *tree)
   *********************************************************
   Rotate a node down and to the right, at the same time
   moving the node's left child up and to the right.
   Function is for nodes in simple trees.

   CALLS :
   GLOBALS : NULL
   PARAMETERS : tree : pointer to node around which to rotate
   RETURN : pointer to new root of modified tree portion.
   USAGE : root = r_rotate ( root);
   *********************************************************
*/
struct tnode *r_rotate ( struct tnode *tree)
{
        struct tnode *temp = tree;

        if ( tree != NULL)
        {
                tree = tree -> left;
                temp -> left = tree -> right;
                tree -> right = temp;
        }
        return ( tree);
}
```

l__rotate( ) and r__rotate( )

Function l__rotate moves the top of the right subtree to make it the new root and moves the ex-root to the top of the new root's left subtree. Thus, function l__rotate moves the root node down and to the left.

Function r__rotate( ) moves the top of the left subtree to make it the new root and moves the ex-root to the top of the new root's right subtree. Thus, function r__rotate moves the root node down and to the right.

Both of these functions are called by other functions as needed. You should *not* use these functions to rotate an arbitrary element. If you did, the subtree you were rotating would be lost from the original tree. Later, you'll develop some rotation functions to use when you want to rotate arbitrary nodes in a tree.

Remember: Do not use **l_rotate( )** and **r_rotate( )** to rotate arbitrary tree elements.

The node-deletion function uses the following general strategy, involving rotations, to delete a node from a tree:

1. If the node is a leaf, delete it.
2. If the node is not a leaf, use left and right rotations to move the node down the tree until the node becomes a leaf node. Then delete the node.

Function **del_tnode( )** in the following listing implements step 2 by trying to rotate down and to the right until it can no longer do so. The function then tries to rotate down and to the left until that is no longer possible. At that point, the function is at a leaf node and can simply delete it.

The following listing deletes the first node encountered that has the specified value.

```
/* routines to delete a node from a simple tree.
   Note, del_tnode () function will not work with
   AVL trees introduced elsewhere.
*/

int tree_leaf ( struct tnode *);
struct tnode *del_tnode ( char , struct tnode *);

/*
    int tree_leaf ( struct tnode *item)
    ********************************************************
    Return TRUE if specified function is leaf node -- has no children.

    CALLS :
    GLOBALS : FALSE, NULL, TRUE
    PARAMETERS :
            item : pointer to tnode being examined.
    RETURN : TRUE or FALSE
    USAGE : result = tree_leaf ( root);
    ********************************************************
```

```
*/
int tree_leaf ( struct tnode *item)
{
        if ( ( item -> left == NULL) && ( item -> right == NULL))
                return ( TRUE);
        else
                return ( FALSE);
}



/*
   struct tnode *del_tnode ( char *str, struct tnode *tree)
   ***********************************************************
   Delete node with specified value from tree, return modified tree.
   NOTE : This function works ONLY with simple trees.

   CALLS : del_tnode (); l_rotate (); printf (); r_rotate ();
           strcmp (); tree_leaf ();
   GLOBALS : NULL
   PARAMETERS :
           str : value of tnode to be deleted;
           tree : pointer to root of tree from which to delete node.
   RETURN : pointer to modified tree.
   USAGE : root = del_tnode ( "leaving", root);
   ***********************************************************
*/
struct tnode *del_tnode ( char *str, struct tnode *tree)
{
    /* if there are no more nodes to check, and still no match,
       indicate failure.
    */
    if ( tree == NULL)
    {
            printf ( "Value not found, returning NULL\n");
            return ( NULL);
    }
    /* if the value has been found */
    if ( strcmp ( str, tree -> data) == 0)
    {
            /* if value is in a leaf, just delete it, return NULL */
            if ( tree_leaf ( tree))
                    return ( NULL);
            else  /* if node has children */
            {
                    /* shuffle node to bottom, toward right first.
                       Note that you need a left child to move right
                       --- because the left child replaces the root.
                    */
                    if ( tree -> left != NULL)
                    {
                            tree = r_rotate ( tree);
                        /* after rotating, try to delete from
                           new, lower position.
                        */
                            tree = del_tnode ( str, tree);
                    }
                    else /* if can't go right anymore, go left. */
                    {
                            tree = l_rotate ( tree);
                        /* after rotating, try to delete from
                           new, lower position.
```

```
                                   */
                        tree = del_tnode ( str, tree);
                } /* else left rotate */
        } /* if node has children */
}   /* if value has been found */
else /* if value does not match */
{
        /* if value precedes current value, search left */
        if ( strcmp ( str, tree -> data) < 0)
                tree->left = del_tnode ( str, tree->left);
        else  /* if value follows current value, go right */
                tree->right = del_tnode ( str, tree->right);
}
return ( tree);
}
```

tree_leaf( )

This function returns **TRUE** if the specified **tnode** is a leaf (that is, if both the **left** and **right** members of the node are null pointers) and **FALSE** otherwise.

del_tnode( )

This function deletes the first node having the specified value and returns the modified tree. The function first tests a special case to see whether it can stop with minimal work.

If the local root passed in is a null pointer, it means the specified value was not in the tree. In this case, the function returns a null pointer to the calling function, which is usually another version of **del_tnode( )**. The result is that the original tree remains unchanged after all the recursive function calls have been completed.

If a node containing the specified value is found, the function checks whether the node is a leaf and, if so, deletes it. The function is done and can return control to the calling function.

If the node is not a leaf, the function rotates the node down and to the right as far as possible. After that, the function rotates down and to the left as far as possible. The function keeps searching after each rotation by calling itself with the node at its new, lower position as root. When done, the function will be at a leaf, which it can delete.

In its current form, the function is blind in that it doesn't try to move down the shorter subtree: It has no way of determining whether the left or the right subtree from any node is shorter. (In subsequent sections, you'll modify and extend your tree-manipulation tools to provide such information and make various tree functions more efficient. It will be your task to write a modified function for deleting tree nodes more efficiently.)

If the specified value does not match the value of the current node, the function continues searching down the left or the right subtree, as appropriate. This continuation takes the form of a recursive call to **del__tnode( )** with a child node as the new local root.

Exercising Binary Tree Routines

The following program lets you build a binary tree and then traverse it in the order you specify. The listing also includes a file for displaying the contents of a tree sideways on the screen.

```
/* program to exercise binary tree routines.
   Listing also contains function to display tree sideways on screen.
*/

/* Program to test tree handling functions */

#include <stdio.h>
#include <stdlib.h>
#include <string.h>
#include "defs.h"
#include "trees.h"
#include "types.h"
#include "ql.c"
#include "trees.c"

#define MAX_MENU 10


/* menu for the selections possible with this program */
char *menu [ MAX_MENU] = {"0) Quit", "1) Add Node", "2) Delete Node",
                "3) Inorder", "4) Preorder", "5) Postorder",
                "6) Breadth-First", "7) Display",
                "8) Find Node"};

/* Function DECLARATION */
void disp_tree ( struct tnode *, int);


/*
    void show_menu ( char *menu [], int menu_size)
    **********************************************************
    Display the specified menu, which is an array of strings.
    menu_size indicates the number of strings in the menu.
    Function also prompts user for a choice.
```

```
      CALLS : printf ()
      GLOBALS : MAX_MENU
      PARAMETERS :
            char *menu [] : array of strings, containing menu.
            int menu_size : number of items in menu.
      USAGE : show_menu ( menu, 10);
      *********************************************************
*/
void show_menu ( char *menu [], int menu_size)
{
      int count;

      printf ( "\n\n");

   /* if programmer claims menu has more than maximum allowed items,
      bring the value into line.
   */
      if ( menu_size > MAX_MENU)
            menu_size = MAX_MENU;

   /* display the individual strings in the array */
      for ( count = 0; count < menu_size; count++)
            printf ( "%s\n", menu [ count]);
      printf ( "\n\n");

   /* prompt user */
      printf ( "Your choice? (%d to %d) ", 0, menu_size - 1);
}


main ()
{
      struct tnode   *temp, *temp2, *root = NULL;
      struct qlnode  *qtemp, *qroot = NULL;
      char           info [ MAX_STR];
      int            selection;
      void           wait ( void);

      /* repeat this loop until user wants to quit */
      do
      {
            show_menu ( menu, 9);
            gets ( info);
            selection = atoi ( info);

         /* switch on user's menu selection */
            switch ( selection)
            {
                  default:
                        break;
                  case 0:
                        break;
                  case 1:                  /* add node */
                        temp = get_tnode ( temp);
                        if ( temp != NULL)
                        {
                              printf ( "Value? ");
                              gets ( temp -> data);
                        }
                        else
                              printf ( "no node allocated\n");
                        root = add_to_tree ( temp, root);
                        break;
```

```
                         case 2:            /* delete node */
                                 printf ( "Delete what value?");
                                 gets ( info);
                                 root = del_tnode ( info, root);
                                 break;
                         case 3:            /* inorder traversal */
                                 show_tree ( root);
                                 wait ();
                                 break;
                         case 4:            /* preorder traversal */
                                 show_preorder ( root);
                                 wait ();
                                 break;
                         case 5:            /* postorder traversal */
                                 show_postorder ( root);
                                 wait ();
                                 break;
                         case 6:            /* breadth-first */
                                 breadth_first ( root);
                                 wait ();
                                 break;
                         case 7:            /* display tree */
                                 disp_tree ( root, 0);
                                 wait ();
                                 break;
                         case 8:            /* find node */
                                 printf ( "Find what value?");
                                 gets ( info);
                                 temp = find_tnode ( root, &temp2,
                                                 info);
                                 if ( temp != NULL)
                                         printf ( "%s\n", temp->data);
                                 else
                                         printf ( "%s not found\n",
                                                 info);
                                 wait ();
                                 break;
                 }
         }
         while ( selection != 0);
}


/*
   void wait ()
   ********************************************************
   Pause to let user see displayed material.

   CALLS : gets (); printf ();
   GLOBALS :
   PARAMETERS : none
   RETURN : none
   USAGE : wait ();
   ********************************************************
*/
void wait ()
{
         char *resp = " ";

         printf ( "<Return> to continue ");
         gets ( resp);
}
```

```
/*
    void disp_tree ( struct tnode *tree, int slevel)
    ********************************************************
    Display contents of the tree on the screen; display is sideways.

    CALLS : disp_tree (); printf ();
    GLOBALS : NULL
    PARAMETERS :
          tree : pointer to tree to display;
          slevel : current level of nesting in the tree.
    RETURN : none
    USAGE : disp_tree ( root, 0);
    ********************************************************
*/
void disp_tree ( struct tnode *tree, int slevel)
{
        int  index;
        char *filler = "      ";  /* for filling space to show level */

        if ( tree != NULL)
        {
                /* display left subtree first */
                if ( tree -> left != NULL)
                        disp_tree ( tree -> left, slevel + 1);
                /* write filler for each level traversed */
                for ( index = 0; index < slevel; index++)
                        printf ( "%s", filler);
                /* display node value */
                printf ( "%s\n", tree->data);
                /* display right subtree */
                if ( tree -> right != NULL)
                        disp_tree ( tree -> right, slevel + 1);
        }
}
```

show_menu( )

This function displays the contents of a string array. This array contains a menu of the options available in the current program. The function needs to know the array you want to display and the number of elements in the array.

main( )

The **main( )** function in this exerciser program is simply a loop that displays a menu, gets a selection from the user, and carries out the actions appropriate for the selection. In this case, the actions consist of calls to specific tree-handling functions.

wait( )

This function simply prompts the user to press RETURN.

disp__tree( )

This function displays the specified tree in a sideways tree structure. The function uses an in-order traversal, displaying the nodes in sorted order from smallest to largest.

The function uses a parameter, **level**, to keep track of the number of levels from root at which the current node is located. The function keeps calling itself with a node farther down in the tree until it reaches a leaf node. At that point, the function simply returns control to the calling function.

The calling version of the function will write the **data** value of the current node, indented by an amount proportional to the number of levels from the root. This process continues until the entire left subtree has been displayed. After displaying the root value, the function calls itself recursively to do the same thing for the right subtree. This time, the calling function does nothing upon regaining control, since the current node's **data** value has already been displayed. (Later, you'll develop a routine to draw the tree vertically.)

Balanced Trees

Earlier, you read that trees can be searched and built more quickly than linked lists. The magnitude of the gain depends on how "even," or "balanced," the tree being searched is. One common measure of balance is based on the difference in height of all pairs of left and right subtrees at each level.

The height of a subtree is the maximum number of nodes you need to traverse to get to a leaf in the subtree, starting at the root of the subtree. We'll use both "height" and "depth" to refer to the same attribute of trees; thus, a tree with height 5 can also be described as 5 levels deep.

Using such a measure, the tree in the following illustration is reasonably balanced. Each subtree in a pair is of roughly equal height, and most parents have either two or zero children. Both the left and the right subtrees of Madison have height 2 (left: Jefferson, Adams and Jefferson, Harrison; right: Washington, Truman). Similarly, both subtrees of Jefferson are the same height (one level). The only imbalance occurs in the subtrees for Washington: The left subtree has height 0; the right subtree has height 1.

```
                          Madison

            Jefferson                              Washington

      Adams        Harrison                              Truman
```

On the other hand, suppose you had the following list of names:

```
Adams
Coolidge
Fillmore
Hayes
Jackson
Polk
Wilson
```

If you built a tree out of the elements in the order in which they appeared in the list, your tree would look like the following:

```
      (0) Adams (6)
          (0) Coolidge (5)
              (0) Fillmore (4)
                  (0) Hayes (3)
                      (0) Jackson (2)
                          (0) Polk (1)
                              (0) Wilson (0)
```

The heights of the trees are in parentheses next to the root for each subtree. Notice that the trees of a leaf both have height 0, since such a node has no children.

This tree is not balanced. The height of the left subtree for Adams is 0, while the right subtree is 6 levels deep. Similarly, going down the right side, the left subtree at each level has height zero, while each right subtree reaches to the bottom of the tree. Similarly, the tree in the next illustration is also quite unbalanced.

```
                        Lincoln
          LB Johnson                      Polk
        A Johnson            McKinley            Washington
      Hayes             Madison     Monroe    Truman     Wilson
    Arthur
Adams       Fillmore
        Coolidge
```

In this case, the left and right subtrees have the same number of nodes, but they are distributed quite differently. The right side of the tree is nicely balanced; the left side is very skewed.

Earlier, you used rotations to shuffle nodes to the bottom of a tree so that you could delete them. You can also use rotations to balance a tree. For example, you could use l**_rotate( )** three times to make Hayes the root in the one-sided tree shown earlier. The first call would use Adams as the parameter, the second would use Coolidge, and the third would use Fillmore. After these three calls, the tree would look like this:

```
                Hayes
          Fillmore    Jackson
      Coolidge              Polk
    Adams                       Wilson
```

This tree is balanced for the two outermost subtrees but imbalanced in the lower subtrees: Only the root node has two children; all other interior nodes have one child.

To see what needs to be done to balance such a tree, think of the left and right subtrees as trees in their own right. To deal with the right subtree, you will want to do a left rotation to make Polk the local root. Recall that left rotations move a node down and to the left.

This new node in the left subtree increases the height of that subtree by one. At the same time, a left rotation decreases the height of the right subtree by one, since a node from that subtree is moved up to replace the old root. For the left subtree in the preceding illustration, you will need to do a right rotation to make Coolidge the local root and Fillmore a right subtree of Coolidge.

When these rotations have all been carried out, the resulting tree will look as follows:

```
                        Hayes

             Coolidge                Polk

         Adams     Fillmore     Jackson   Wilson
```

Such rotations become useful only if you can automate the balancing process; that is, you'll want to have the tree-building functions keep track of the degree of balance after each insertion. When the tree becomes unbalanced, the program should take the appropriate steps to balance it.

AVL Trees

In the previous section, you used subtree height to provide an informal measure of balance. In *AVL trees*, the relative heights of left and right subtrees are used to determine when the tree is unbalanced. An AVL tree is a binary tree in which left and right subtrees at a given level always differ by, at most, one level. Such trees are named after two Russian mathematicians, G. M. Adel'son-Vel'skii and E. M. Landis, who first showed how to build and maintain such balanced trees.

To build and manipulate AVL trees, you'll need to modify the definition of a **tnode** structure. In addition to the **data** member and the **left** and **right** pointer members, you'll add members in which to store the height of the node's left and right subtrees. The following structure declaration shows the extended **tnode** for AVL trees:

```
/* data structure declaration for balanced trees.
   Put this declaration in file avl.h
*/



/* Node for a tree. Five members:
   data, two height values and two pointers to other tnodes
*/
struct tnode {
        char    data [ MAX_STR];
        int     l_ht, r_ht;             /* heights of subtrees */
        struct  tnode *left, *right; /* pointers to other tnodes */
};
```

Several, but not all, of our tree-handling functions will need to be
changed to accommodate this new version of the **tnode**. Some of
these changes are very minor, such as adding initialization for the
new members in function **get_tnode( )**. Other changes are much
more involved, as you'll see in this section.

The following listing shows the functions that need to be changed
to handle the extended tree nodes:

```
/* AVL.C : functions for handling AVL trees.
   Change these functions from definitions for simple trees.
*/

#include <malloc.h>

#define MAX2(x,y)    ( ((x) > (y)) ? (x) : (y) )

/* **********
   tree function DECLARATIONS
********** */
/* Changed or New functions for AVL trees */
struct tnode *add_to_tree ( struct tnode *, struct tnode *, int *);
struct tnode *get_tnode ( struct tnode *);
struct tnode *l_rotate ( struct tnode *);
struct tnode *r_rotate ( struct tnode *);

/* **********
   tree function DEFINITIONS
********** */
/*
   struct tnode *get_tnode ( struct tnode *item)
   *******************************************************
   Allocate space for and initialize a tnode structure for
   AVL tree; return pointer to the storage allocated.

   CALLS : malloc (); printf (); sizeof ();
   GLOBALS :   NULL
   PARAMETERS :
           item : a pointer to the storage allocated for the
                  requested tnode.
```

```
        RETURN : a pointer to the allocated tnode
        USAGE : temp = get_tnode ( temp);
        *********************************************************
*/
struct tnode *get_tnode ( struct tnode *item)
{
    /* allocate enough space to store an tnode */
        item = (struct tnode *) malloc ( sizeof ( struct tnode));

    /* if allocated, initialize the structure */
        if (item != NULL)
        {
            /* initially, node does not point to any nodes */
                item -> left = NULL;
                item -> right = NULL;
                item -> l_ht = 0;
                item -> r_ht = 0;
                strcpy ( item->data, null_str);
        }
        else
                printf ( "Nothing allocated\n");
        return ( item);              /* return the pointer */
}


/*
        struct tnode *add_to_tree ( struct tnode *new,
                        struct tnode *root, int *done)
        *********************************************************
        Add tnode at appropriate spot in AVL tree.

        CALLS : add_to_tree (); l_rotate (); r_rotate (); strcmp ();
        GLOBALS : NULL
        PARAMETERS :
                new : new tnode to be added to tree;
                root : tree to which tnode is to be added;
                done : variable for indicating whether node was added.
        RETURN : pointer to modified tree.
        USAGE : root = add_to_tree ( temp, root, &successful);
        *********************************************************
*/
struct tnode *add_to_tree ( struct tnode *new, struct tnode *root,
                        int *done)
{
        int    feedback;

        *done = 0;                   /* nothing done so far */
    /* if tree (or subtree) is empty, add the new node */
        if ( root == NULL)
        {
                root = new;
                root -> l_ht = 0;
                root -> r_ht = 0;
                *done = 1;        /* node being added */
                return ( root);
        }
        else
        {
            /* if new data <= current data, will need to go left. */
                if ( strcmp ( new -> data, root -> data) <= 0)
                {
                        root -> left = add_to_tree ( new, root->left,
                                                &feedback);
```

```
        /* height of left subtree increases,
           since routine went left.
        */
            root -> l_ht += feedback;
    }
    else     /* go right, since new data > current data */
    {
            root-> right = add_to_tree ( new, root->right,
                                            &feedback);
        /* height of right subtree increases,
           since routine went right.
        */
            root -> r_ht += feedback;
    }    /* else if going right */

/* if something was added (feedback), and the
   heights of the two subtrees are unequal,
   may need to balance tree.
*/
    if ( feedback && (root -> l_ht != root -> r_ht))
    {
        /* if left subtree is more than one level deeper
           than right subtree, move local root down the
           right subtree.
        */
            if ( (root->r_ht - root->l_ht) < -1)
            {
                /* if left subtree below the one about to
                   be balanced is also deeper, rotate
                   right, to pull top of left subtree up.
                */
                    if ( ( (root->left)->r_ht
                            - (root->left)->l_ht)    < 0)
                        root = r_rotate ( root);
                /* if right subtree below one about to be
                   balanced is deeper, rotate left in
                   lower subtree, to balance that part,
                   then move local root down and right.
                */
                    else
                    {
                            root->left =
                                l_rotate ( root->left);
                            root = r_rotate ( root);
                    }
            }
        /* else if right subtree is more than one level
           deeper than left subtree
        */
            else if ( (root->r_ht - root->l_ht) > 1)
            {
                    if ( ( ( root->right)->r_ht
                            - ( root->right)->l_ht)  > 0)
                        root = l_rotate ( root);
                    else
                    {
                            root->right =
                                r_rotate ( root->right);
                            root = l_rotate ( root);
                    }
            }
            else /* if no imbalance after adding node */
                *done = 1;   /* job is done */
```

```
                    }    /* if something was added */
                return ( root);
        }    /* if root != NULL */
}


/*
    struct tnode *l_rotate ( struct tnode *tree)
    ***********************************************************
    Rotate a node down and to the left, at the same time
    moving the node's right child up and to the left.
    Function is for nodes in AVL trees.

    CALLS : MAX2
    GLOBALS : NULL
    PARAMETERS : tree : pointer to node around which to rotate
    RETURN : pointer to new root of modified tree portion.
    USAGE : root = l_rotate ( root);
    ***********************************************************
*/
struct tnode *l_rotate ( struct tnode *tree)
{
    /* pointer to root being moved downward */
        struct tnode *old_root = tree;

    if ( tree != NULL)
    {
        /* make the top of the right subtree the new root */
            tree = tree -> right;
        /* transfer new root's left subtree to old root's right */
            old_root -> right = tree -> left;
        /* make old root the top of the new one's left subtree */
            tree -> left = old_root;
        /* if a left subtree had been transferred above */
            if ( old_root -> right != NULL)
                /* height of the new right subtree ==
                    height of the left subtree transferred
                    + 1 for the top of the old left subtree
                */
                old_root->r_ht = 1 +
                                    MAX2 (old_root->right->r_ht,
                                          old_root->right->l_ht);
            else /* if no subtree was transferred */
                    old_root -> r_ht = 0;
        /* height of new root's subtree ==
            height of subtree headed by old root
            + 1 for the old root node.
        */
            tree -> l_ht = 1 + MAX2 ( tree->left->l_ht,
                                      tree->left->r_ht);
    }    /* if tree != NULL */
    return ( tree);
}

/*
    struct tnode *r_rotate ( struct tnode *tree)
    ***********************************************************
    Rotate a node down and to the right, at the same time
    moving the node's left child up and to the right.
    Function is for nodes in AVL trees.
```

```
        CALLS : MAX2
        GLOBALS : NULL
        PARAMETERS : tree : pointer to node around which to rotate
        RETURN : pointer to new root of modified tree portion.
        USAGE : root = r_rotate ( root);
        ********************************************************
*/
struct tnode *r_rotate ( struct tnode *tree)
{
        struct tnode *old_root = tree;

        if ( tree != NULL)
        {
                tree = tree -> left;
                old_root -> left = tree -> right;
                tree -> right = old_root;
                if ( old_root -> left != NULL)
                        old_root->l_ht = 1 +
                                        MAX2 (old_root->left->l_ht,
                                              old_root->left->r_ht);
                else
                        old_root -> l_ht = 0;
                tree -> r_ht = 1 + MAX2 ( tree->right->l_ht,
                                          tree->right->r_ht);
        }   /* if tree != NULL */
        return ( tree);
}
```

get—tnode( )

As it did earlier, this function allocates space for a **tnode**, if possible, initializes the members of this node, and returns a pointer to the storage allocated.

add—to—tree( )

As it also did earlier, this function adds an element to a sorted tree. This time the process is much more complex, however, since the function must balance the tree, if necessary, after adding an element.

The function uses the **l—ht** and **r—ht** members of the tree nodes to determine when to rebalance the tree. If the tree is empty, the function simply adds the new element. If there are other elements in the tree, the function moves through the tree until it reaches the location at which the new element should be inserted and adds the element. This part of the process is the same as for the simple tree nodes you used earlier.

After adding the element, the function checks whether it needs to rebalance, that is, if the **r__ht** and **l__ht** values for a particular node differ by more than one. If the left subtree is deeper, the general action will be to move the local root element down and to the right, thus adding to the right subtree's depth. If the right subtree is deeper, the move will be down and to the left.

Let's look at two examples that show how the balancing is done. The first example builds a tree from the following elements, read in the order listed:

```
Massachusetts
Georgia
Rhode Island
Delaware
Kentucky
California
```

After the first five elements have been added, the tree looks like the following illustration. Figures in parentheses are the values of **l__ht** and **r__ht** for the node. In the illustration, the tree is still balanced.

```
                    (2) Massachusetts (1)
          (1) Georgia (1)              (0) Rhode Island (0)
   (0) Delaware (0)        (0) Kentucky (0)
```

When California is added, the tree looks like this:

```
                    (3) Massachusetts (1)
          (2) Georgia (1)              (0) Rhode Island (0)
   (1) Delaware (0)        (0) Kentucky (0)
(0) California (0)
```

Adding this element makes the tree unbalanced: The root node has a left subtree two levels deeper than the right subtree. The eventual solution will be a right rotation to move Massachusetts down to the right and to move Georgia, the top of the left subtree, up to become the new root.

Before deciding on the appropriate action, the function checks the subtrees of Georgia. If Georgia's left subtree is longer, then a simple right rotation will suffice, since such a rotation decreases the height of the left subtree. Thus, the **add_to tree( )** function simply does a right rotation involving Georgia and Massachusetts. Determine what the resulting tree will look like.

The next example illustrates the other possible outcome if the left subtree is deeper. This time, build the same tree, except, for the last element, add Louisiana instead of California. Thus, after the first five elements have been added, the tree again looks like the one shown earlier (before the addition of California). After Louisiana is added, the tree looks like the next illustration. Notice that the height of the left subtree for Massachusetts is still 3, since you must go through Georgia and Kentucky to reach Louisiana, the node farthest from the root.

```
                    (3) Massachusetts (1)

            (1) Georgia (1)              (0) Rhode Island (0)

(0) Delaware (0)        (0) Kentucky (1)

                            (0) Louisiana (0)
```

This time, when the function checks Georgia's subtrees, the right subtree will be deeper. Recall that a right rotation decreases the height of the left subtree. In this case, such an action would increase the discrepancy between Georgia's left and right subtrees. To avoid this, the function first does a left rotation involving Georgia as the local root and Kentucky as the element that will become the new local root. This action increases the height of the left subtree by 1 and decreases the height of the right subtree by 1. After this rotation, the tree looks like this:

```
                    (3) Massachusetts (1)

            (2) Kentucky (1)              (0) Rhode Island (0)

    (1) Georgia (0)        (0) Louisiana (0)

(0) Delaware (0)
```

Now you can do a right rotation to move Kentucky up to become the new root and to move Massachusetts down to become the head of Kentucky's left subtree.

The reasoning is similar if you happen to be moving down the right subtree in these comparisons.

Function **add_to_tree( )** uses the parameter **done** and the local variable **feedback** to keep track of when some action has been taken in the function call. Thus, if one of the recursive function calls added a node, this call would return a 1 in the variable referenced by **done**. This 1 would be picked up by the local variable **feedback** in the calling function and would be added to the height of the left or the right subtree, as appropriate.

l_rotate and r_rotate

These functions are used by **add_to_tree( )** to perform the same task they did for the simpler **tnode** structure. Now, the functions also must update the height members for the nodes the function moves.

After a left rotation, two members are affected: the **right** member of the old root and the **left** member of the new root. In the function, **old_root** refers to the old root, and **tree** always refers to the current root—initially the old root and then the new root.

Let's look at an example to see how the height adjustments work, using the following illustration of a subtree:

```
                    DO

                        RE

                    MI

                FA
```

If you do a left rotation using DO as the root,

- The node containing RE will become the new root.

- The subtree with MI as its root will become the right subtree for DO.

- The node containing DO will become the top of the left subtree for RE.

Because of the second point, **old—root—>r—ht** must be adjusted. The new **r—ht** for this node is based on the height of the subtree beginning with MI. This subtree's height is equal to the height of MI's left or right subtrees, whichever is larger. In this case, the left subtree has height 1, and the right subtree has height 0. This value is added to 1—for the level added by MI. Thus, the **r—ht** for DO becomes 2.

Similarly, RE's **l—ht** must be adjusted. This value is based on the height of DO's subtrees (0 and 2). Again, you need to add 1 for the level added by the node containing DO; therefore, the height of RE's left subtree is $1 + 2$, or 3.

Work through the adjustments required for right rotations on your own to test your grasp of what's involved in rotating nodes in a tree.

Routines You May Want to Change

In addition to the routines that you need to change when working with AVL trees, you may want to modify some other routines to provide information about subtree heights at each node.

All the display routines—**show—tree( )**, **show—preorder( )**, **show—postorder( )**, **breadth—first( )**, and **disp—tree( )**—are candidates for such changes. You would need only to add instructions to display additional information.

Function **del—tnode( )** will not work for AVL trees, since the current version of the function does not know anything about heights. Try to write a version of this function that will work with AVL trees. *Do not use the current version with AVL trees.*

Remember: Do not use the current version of function **del—tnode( )** for deleting from AVL trees.

Displaying a Tree Vertically

In this section, you'll find routines used to display a binary tree vertically, with the root at the top of the tree and subtrees spaced below and to either side of the root. This task is much more involved than the sideways tree display provided by **disp—tree( )**.

Essentially, a vertical tree can be drawn using a breadth-first traversal. Thus, your basic strategy will be similar to the one used to display a tree in a breadth-first sequence: You'll store the nodes to be displayed in a queued list and use the nodes in the list to add the next nodes to the list. This time, however, you'll put in "dummy" nodes to represent empty spots in the tree. These will provide the information needed to determine where to write values.

The function takes advantage of the number of possible nodes at a given level being both a power of two and one more than all the possible nodes up to that level. You can have only one node at the root. At the first level below the root, you can have at most two nodes (left and right subtrees). At level 2, the most nodes you can have is four, which equals 2^2 and is one more than the three nodes up to that point. At level 3, you can have eight possible nodes, and so forth. The function uses this information to determine when the tree is moving to another level.

The following functions allow you to display the specified tree vertically. Function **put_entry()** does the actual writing for **draw_tree()**.

```
/* routines for drawing a binary tree vertically */

void draw_tree ( struct tnode *);
void put_entry ( char *, int);

/*
    void draw_tree ( struct tnode *tree)
    ************************************************************
    Draw a specified tree vertically.
    Assumes qlnode data structure and associated functions.

    CALLS : back_of_qlist(); del_qnode(); get_qnode(); get_tnode();
            printf(); put_entry(); strcmp(); strcpy();
    GLOBALS : NULL
    PARAMETERS : tree : pointer to tree to be displayed.
    RETURN : none
    USAGE : draw_tree ( root);
    ************************************************************
*/
void draw_tree ( struct tnode *tree)
{
#define MAX_WIDTH  80

        int    nr_done = 1, level = 1, space = MAX_WIDTH,
               index, max_level, nr_dummy = 0, adding = TRUE;
        struct qlnode *qroot = NULL, *qtemp;
        struct tnode  *temp, *qreturn, *dummy, *last;

        dummy = get_tnode ( dummy);
        last = get_tnode ( last);
        strcpy ( last -> data, blank_str);
        qtemp = get_qnode ( qtemp);
        qtemp -> tn = tree;
```

```
        qroot = back_of_qlist ( qtemp, qroot);
        max_level = 1 + MAX2 ( tree -> l_ht, tree -> r_ht);

        while ( ( strcmp ( qroot->tn->data, blank_str))
                && ( level <= max_level + 1))
        {
            /* get an element to display */
            qroot = del_qnode ( qroot, qtemp, 1, &qreturn);
            temp = qreturn;

            /* if another level of nodes added to queued list */
            if ( nr_done >= ( 1 << level))
            {
                    space /= 2;   /* 2 * nodes --> 1/2 the space */
                    level++;      /* adjust level number */
                    nr_dummy = 0; /* curr level not all dummies */
                    printf ( "\n");
                    if ( space <= 2)
                            printf ( " no room to write.\n");
            }

            /* if the node is just a filler, just write blanks */
            if ( temp == dummy)
            {
                    for ( index = 0; index < space; index++)
                            printf ("%c", BLANK_CHAR);
            }
            else    /* if a real node, add in allotted space. */
                    put_entry ( temp -> data, space);
            nr_done++;   /* another node displayed */

            /* if still adding nodes to the queued list */
            if ( adding)
            {
                /* if there's a left subnode to add, add it */
                if ( temp -> left != NULL)
                {
                        qtemp = get_qnode ( qtemp);
                        qtemp -> tn = temp -> left;
                        qroot = back_of_qlist ( qtemp, qroot);
                }
                else  /* if no left subnode, add dummy node */
                {
                        qtemp = get_qnode ( qtemp);
                        qtemp -> tn = dummy;
                        qroot = back_of_qlist ( qtemp, qroot);
                        nr_dummy++;
                }     /* if no left subnode */

                /* if there's a right subnode to add, add it */
                if ( temp -> right != NULL)
                {
                        qtemp = get_qnode ( qtemp);
                        qtemp -> tn = temp -> right;
                        qroot = back_of_qlist ( qtemp, qroot);
                }
                else  /* if no right subnode, add dummy */
                {
                        qtemp = get_qnode ( qtemp);
                        qtemp -> tn = dummy;
                        qroot = back_of_qlist ( qtemp, qroot);
                        nr_dummy++;
                }     /* if no right subnode */
            }   /* if adding */
        } /* while qroot != NULL */
        if ( level > max_level + 1)
```

```
{
        /* add last node to ensure routine stops */
        qtemp = get_qnode ( qtemp);
        qtemp -> tn = last;
        qroot = front_of_qlist ( qtemp, qroot);
}
while ( strcmp ( qroot->tn->data, blank_str))
{
    /* get an element to display */
        qroot = del_qnode ( qroot, qtemp, 1, &qreturn);
        temp = qreturn;

        /* if the node is just a filler, just write blanks */
        if ( temp == dummy)
        {
                for ( index = 0; index < space; index++)
                        printf ("%c", BLANK_CHAR);
        }
        else   /* if a real node, add in allotted space. */
                        put_entry ( temp -> data, space);
        } /* if still adding nodes to the queued list */
        printf ( "\n");
}


/*
   void put_entry ( char *str, int size)
   **********************************************************
   Actually display contents of tree being drawn vertically.

   CALLS : printf (); strlen ();
   GLOBALS : BLANK_CHAR;
   PARAMETERS : str : value to be displayed;
                size : # columns available for displaying.
   RETURN : none
   USAGE : put_entry ( "hello", 40);
   **********************************************************
*/
void put_entry ( char *str, int size)
{
        int  length, index, spaces, half;

        length = strlen ( str);
        if ( length < size - 1)
        {
                spaces = size - length;
                half = spaces / 2;
                for ( index = 0; index < half; index++)
                        printf ( "%c", BLANK_CHAR);
                printf ( "%s", str);
                if ( spaces % 2)   /* if an odd number of spaces */
                        printf ( "%c", BLANK_CHAR);
                for ( index = 0; index < half; index++)
                        printf ( "%c", BLANK_CHAR);
        }
        else
                for ( index = 0; index < size - 1; index++)
                        printf ( "%c", str [ index]);
                printf ( "%c", BLANK_CHAR);
}
```

draw—tree( )

This function displays a binary tree vertically. To do its work, the function keeps track of the possible nodes (children) at each level of the tree that are filled and determines the appropriate spacing for displaying the information at different levels.

The function uses the queued list you saw earlier. This time, however, the function adds dummy nodes to the list so that the display will contain blanks for empty nodes.

To determine when to stop, the function checks whether all the levels in the tree have been put in the list and displayed. This happens when the function is about to move to a level that would be deeper than the largest height of any subtree.

The **draw—tree** function decides what to display and then calls **put—entry( )** to write the actual information.

put—entry( )

This function actually displays an entry. The function is passed the information and the current level, which it uses to determine how much space to allocate for the information.

For example, the function assumes a maximum width of 80 columns. The function also assumes you haven't done any other writing since the last call. Function **put—entry( )** simply starts writing from the current cursor position. The root element can have all 80 columns for its display. Function **put—entry( )** centers the root node's information within these 80 columns.

The next level can contain two nodes, so each is allotted 80 / 2, or 40, columns. Again, the function centers values that are shorter than the allotted width. The next level can have four nodes, so each node is allowed 20 columns to display its information. Notice that after four levels (16 possible nodes), each node gets only 5 columns to display its information. The function actually truncates the information after four columns to leave space between values. This means you can't display trees more than five levels deep, since there would not be any space to write the node's value.

Rotating Arbitrary Nodes

The following functions let you carry out left and right rotations. Unlike functions **l—rotate( )** and **r—rotate( )**, these functions can be used to find and move elements you specify. The earlier functions really assume you are working from the root; therefore, there is no need to keep track of the predecessor node. On the other hand, you should *not* use the following functions if you want to rotate around the top-level root of your tree.

```
/* functions for rotating around an arbitrary value */

struct tnode *l_roll ( struct tnode *, char *);
struct tnode *r_roll ( struct tnode *, char *);


/*
    struct tnode *l_roll ( struct tnode *tree, char *str)
    ************************************************************
    Routine for rotating left around an arbitrary node in a tree
    --- except for the root node of the tree.
    NOTE : function is designed for AVL trees, and will not work with
    simple tree nodes.

    CALLS : find_tnode (); MAX2 ();
    GLOBALS : NULL
    PARAMETERS :
            tree : pointer to root of tree having nodes rotated;
            str : value of node around which to rotate;
    RETURN : pointer to modified tree
    USAGE : root = l_roll ( root, "target");
    ************************************************************
*/
struct tnode *l_roll ( struct tnode *tree, char *str)
{
    /* pointer to root being moved downward */
        struct tnode *old_root, *temp, *prev;

        temp = find_tnode ( tree, &prev, str);
        old_root = temp;
        if ( (temp != NULL) && ( temp -> right != NULL))
            {
            /* make the top of the right subtree the new root */
                temp = temp -> right;
            /* move new root's left subtree to old root's right */
                old_root -> right = temp -> left;
            /* make old root the top of new one's left subtree */
                temp -> left = old_root;
            /* if a left subtree had been transferred above */
                if ( old_root -> right != NULL)
                    /* height of the new right subtree ==
                        height of the left subtree transferred
                        + 1 for the top of the old left subtree
                    */
                        old_root->r_ht = 1 +
```

```
                                         MAX2 (old_root->right->r_ht,
                                               old_root->right->l_ht);
                else /* if no subtree was transferred */
                        old_root -> r_ht = 0;
            /* height of new root's subtree ==
               height of subtree headed by old root
               + 1 for the old root node.
            */
                temp -> l_ht = 1 + MAX2 ( temp->left->l_ht,
                                          temp->left->r_ht);
        }   /* if temp != NULL */
        if ( strcmp ( temp -> data, prev -> data) < 0)
                prev -> left = temp;
        else
                prev -> right = temp;
        return ( tree);
}


/*
    struct tnode *r_roll ( struct tnode *tree, char *str)
    ************************************************************
    Routine for rotating right around an arbitrary node in a tree
    --- except for the root node of the tree.
    NOTE : function is designed for AVL trees, and will not work with
    simple tree nodes.

    CALLS : find_tnode (); MAX2 ();
    GLOBALS : NULL
    PARAMETERS :
            tree : pointer to root of tree having nodes rotated;
            str : value of node around which to rotate;
    RETURN : pointer to modified tree
    USAGE : root = r_roll ( root, "target");
    ************************************************************
*/
struct tnode *r_roll ( struct tnode *tree, char *str)
{
        struct tnode *old_root, *temp, *prev;

        temp = find_tnode ( tree, &prev, str);
        old_root = temp;
        if ( ( temp != NULL) && ( temp -> left != NULL))
        {
                temp = temp -> left;
                old_root -> left = temp -> right;
                temp -> right = old_root;
                if ( old_root -> left != NULL)
                        old_root->l_ht = 1 +
                                        MAX2 ( old_root->left->l_ht,
                                               old_root->left->r_ht);
                else
                        old_root -> l_ht = 0;
                temp -> r_ht = 1 + MAX2 ( temp->right->l_ht,
                                          temp->right->r_ht);
        }   /* if temp != NULL */
        if ( strcmp ( temp -> data, prev -> data) < 0)
                prev -> left = temp;
        else
                prev -> right = temp;
        return ( tree);
}
```

l—roll() and r—roll()

These functions rotate to the left and to the right, respectively. They are used for rotating an arbitrary node (for example, to see what a tree would look like after a rotation).

To carry out such a rotation, you need to specify the root of the tree and the value of the node you wish to rotate. To ensure that the rotations are actually done in the tree, the function uses **prev**, a pointer to a **tnode**, to keep track of the node preceding the one you will rotate. This ensures that a node from the tree will always point to the subtree you are rotating.

Remember: Don't use the rotation functions **l—roll( )** and **r—roll( )** to rotate around the root node of a tree.

Exercising the Tree Routines

The following program lets you exercise the tree-handling functions developed in this chapter. You'll see numerous applications of trees throughout this book.

```
/* Program to test AVL tree handling functions */

#include <stdio.h>
#include <stdlib.h>
#include <string.h>
#include "defs.h"
#include "avl.h"
#include "types.h"
#include "ql.c"
#include "avl.c"

#define MAX_MENU 15


/* menu for the selections possible with this program */
char *menu [ MAX_MENU] = {"0) Quit", "1) Add Node", "2) Delete Node",
                          "3) Inorder", "4) Preorder", "5) Postorder",
                          "6) Breadth-First", "7) Display",
                          "8) Draw Tree", "9) Find Node",
                          "10) Left Rotate", "11) Right Rotate"};
```

```
/*
   void show_menu ( char *menu [], int menu_size)
   ***********************************************************
   Display the specified menu, which is an array of strings.
   menu_size indicates the number of strings in the menu.
   Function also prompts user for a choice.

   CALLS : printf ()
   GLOBALS : MAX_MENU
   PARAMETERS :
           char *menu [] : array of strings, containing menu.
           int menu_size : number of items in menu.
   USAGE : show_menu ( menu, 10);
   ***********************************************************
*/
void show_menu ( char *menu [], int menu_size)
{
        int count;

        printf ( "\n\n");

        /* if programmer claims menu has more than maximum allowed
           items, bring the value into line.
        */
        if ( menu_size > MAX_MENU)
                menu_size = MAX_MENU;

        /* display the individual strings in the array */
        for ( count = 0; count < menu_size; count++)
                printf ( "%s\n", menu [ count]);

        printf ( "\n\n");

        /* prompt user */
        printf ( "Your choice? (%d to %d) ", 0, menu_size - 1);
}


main ()
{
        struct tnode   *temp, *temp2, *root = NULL;
        struct qlnode *qtemp, *qroot = NULL;
        char          info [ MAX_STR];
        int           selection, outcome;
        void          wait ( void);

        /* repeat this loop until user wants to quit */
        do
        {
```

```
show_menu ( menu, 12);
gets ( info);
selection = atoi ( info);

/* switch on user's menu selection */
switch ( selection)
{
        default:
                break;
        case 0:
                break;
        case 1:                   /* add node */
                temp = get_tnode ( temp);
                if ( temp != NULL)
                {
                        printf ( "Value? ");
                        gets ( temp -> data);
                }
                else
                        printf("no node allocated\n");
                root = add_to_tree ( temp, root,
                                        &outcome);
                break;
        case 2:                   /* delete node */
                printf("Sorry, no deletion routine ");
                printf( "for AVL trees;\nyou'll ");
                printf ( "have to write your own.\n");
                break;
        case 3:                   /* inorder traversal */
                show_tree ( root);
                wait ();
                break;
        case 4:                   /* preorder traversal */
                show_preorder ( root);
                wait ();
                break;
        case 5:                   /* postorder traversal */
                show_postorder ( root);
                wait ();
                break;
        case 6:                   /* breadth-first */
                breadth_first ( root);
                wait ();
                break;
        case 7:                   /* display tree */
                disp_tree ( root, 0);
                wait ();
                break;
```

```
            case 8:             /* draw tree */
                draw_tree ( root);
                wait ();
                break;
            case 9:             /* find node */
                printf ( "Find what value?");
                gets ( info);
                temp = find_tnode ( root, &temp2,
                                    info);
                if ( temp != NULL)
                        printf ( "%s\n", temp->data);
                else
                        printf ( "%s not found\n",
                                info);
                wait ();
                break;
            case 10:            /* rotate left */
                printf ( "Rotate on what node?");
                gets ( info);
                temp = l_roll ( root, info);
                if ( temp != NULL)
                        printf ( "%s\n", temp->data);
                else
                        printf ( "%s not found\n",
                                info);
                draw_tree ( temp);
                wait ();
                break;
            case 11:              /* rotate right */
                printf ( "Rotate on what node?");
                gets ( info);
                temp = r_roll ( root, info);
                if ( temp != NULL)
                        printf ( "%s\n", temp->data);
                else
                        printf ( "%s not found\n",
                                    info);
                draw_tree ( temp);
                wait ();
                break;
        }
    }
    while ( selection != 0);
}


/*
    void wait ()
```

```
          **********************************************************
          Pause to let user see displayed material.

          CALLS : gets (); printf ();
          GLOBALS :
          PARAMETERS : none
          RETURN : none
          USAGE : wait ();
          **********************************************************
*/
void wait ()
{
        char *resp = " ";

        printf ( "<Return> to continue ");
        gets ( resp);
}
```

Suggestions and Activities

Because they are such a versatile data structure, there are many
things you can do with trees.

Ternary Trees

In this chapter, you've looked at only binary trees, but there are
other tree configurations. Develop the data structures and functions
for working with ternary trees—trees with pointer nodes to left,
right, and middle subtrees. Some of the functions will require only
minor changes, while others will need to be modified considerably.

For example, you'll need to change the **add—to—tree( )** function,
including the criteria for deciding the direction in which to rotate.
You'll also need to change the rotation routines, since you may be
rotating to or from a middle subtree.

Drawing Trees

The current version of **draw—tree( )** is not really suited for trees
deeper than three levels (up to 15 total elements) and is impossible to
use after five levels, as the five columns allowed at the fourth level
are rarely enough space to display a node's value.

You may want to modify the **draw_tree( )** and the **put_entry( )** functions to allow a node's value to spill over into the next node if no value is to be written for that node.

SUMMARY

In this chapter, you learned about trees, one of the most widely used data structures. You developed routines for building, searching, and transforming binary trees, whether simple trees or AVL trees.

In the next chapter, you'll look at two common tasks in programs: sorting information and searching for particular information in a larger collection. You'll see that you've already developed some sorting routines among your functions for linked lists and trees.

4

SORTING AND SEARCHING

Two very common activities in programs are sorting information on some basis and searching for a particular item of information in a larger body of data. In this chapter, you'll look at some algorithms for sorting data and for searching through a file or another body of data.

As you'll see, different algorithms are likely to be useful for different data or in different contexts. The effectiveness of an algorithm also depends strongly on the data structures being used.

ALGORITHM EFFECTIVENESS

One way of measuring the effectiveness of an algorithm is to estimate the number of assignments or exchanges required to complete the algorithm. This information is usually expressed in terms of the number of elements in the collection. Comparisons between elements generally are not included when estimating performance, since comparisons take much less time than assignments and exchanges.

In Chapter 2, we saw that the number of steps required to solve the Tower of Hanoi problem was $2^n - 1$, where n is the number of disks. For example, if you have 5 disks, it will take $2^5 - 1$, or 31, steps to solve the problem. In such a case, you speak of the *running time*, or *performance*, of the algorithm. The Tower of Hanoi algorithm has running time proportional to 2^n.

Similarly, an algorithm to add all n elements in an array has running time proportional to n, since you need to read each element in the array and add it to the sum.

To say that an algorithm's performance is proportional to n^2 is the same as saying that the algorithm will require n^2 times some constant (such as 1/2 or 2 or even 100) assignments or exchanges. It's common to omit the constants when discussing an algorithm's performance. Performance figures almost always refer to the *average* behavior of an algorithm. Actual running times depend on various things, most notably the extent to which the data are ordered at the outset.

SORTING

Numerous algorithms have been developed for *sorting* values in a program, that is, for putting the values into a sequence based on some aspect of the values.

Among sorting algorithms, there is a general trade-off between algorithm simplicity and efficiency. For example, you can sort a collection of data by searching through the data repeatedly, removing the smallest value on each pass and adding this value to the sorted collection. This algorithm is very simple to implement but is quite slow if you have a large collection of data.

There are several things to keep in mind when deciding on a sorting algorithm for a particular task. (In subsequent sections, you'll look at some of these issues as you develop your sorting algorithms.)

First, the number of elements can make a difference. For small collections —on the order of a hundred or so items —the difference in performance among algorithms may not be noticeable; however, number of elements becomes a factor for large data collections. For example, an algorithm proportional to n will be about 1000 times faster than an algorithm proportional to ^{22} for a 1000-item collection.

Second, the data structure you use makes a difference. As you'll see, sorting algorithms suitable for data stored in arrays are different from those suitable for information in linked lists or trees.

Third, you will need different algorithms to sort data on disk—when the collection is too large to sort in memory, for example—than to perform the entire sort in memory. You'll see that the algorithms for these two situations are quite different.

Fourth, the choice of algorithm may also be dictated by the degree of ordering that the data have at the start of the sorting process. For example, some "good" algorithms become very inefficient if the data are almost in order or are in reverse order.

Finally, information about the range and types of values being sorted can also help guide the selection of an algorithm. For example, suppose you have a very large number of cases taking on a small range of values. You may be better off simply tallying the frequencies with which the values appear than actually sorting the data.

Selection Sort

One of the simplest sorting algorithms is a *selection sort*. The strategy is to find the smallest element in an array and exchange it with the value in the first cell, then find the smallest element in the remainder of the array and exchange it with the value in the second cell, and continue until you have reached the end of the array.

The following program implements such a selection sort. The functions **disp—array()**, **swap—int()**, and **wait()** are general utility functions. We'll put them in a file named **sortutil.c**; you may want to do the same or possibly add them to your **utils.c** file. You should put **select—sort()** into a file named **sorts.c**. Later, we'll assume the sorting routines are all in a file that has this name.

```
/* Program to illustrate selection sort algorithm */

#include <stdio.h>
#include <stdlib.h>
#include <string.h>

#define MAX_VALS 100        /* maximum number of elements in array */

int vals [ MAX_VALS];       /* array containing values to be sorted */

/* *************
   Miscellaneous Function DECLARATIONS
************* */
void    disp_array ( int [], int, int);
void    swap_int ( int *, int *);
void    wait ( void);
void    select_sort ( int [ ], int);

/* *************
   Miscellaneous Function DEFINITIONS
************* */
/* Swap two int values passed as parameters */
void swap_int ( int *first, int *second)
{
        int temp;        /* to store one of the values during swap */

        temp = *first;
        *first = *second;
        *second = temp;
}


/* display contents of an array, nr_per_line elements on each line. */
void disp_array ( int info [], int size, int nr_per_line)
{
        int    index;

        for ( index = 0; index < size; index++)
        {
                printf ("%7d", info [ index]);
             /* if nr_per_line elements have been written, send \n */
                if ( (index % nr_per_line) == (nr_per_line - 1))
                        printf  ("\n");
        }   /* for index = 0 ..  */
}
```

```c
/* pause to let user see displayed material */
void wait ()
{
        char *resp = " ";

        printf ( "<Return> to continue ");
        gets ( resp);
}



/* sort an array of int, by finding the smallest element
   in each pass through the array
*/
void  select_sort ( int info [ ], int size)
{
        int  outer, inner;

    /* for each element of the array */
        for ( outer = 0; outer < size - 1; outer++)
        {
            /* for all elements that have not yet been sorted */
                for ( inner = outer + 1; inner < size; inner++)
                        if ( vals [ inner] < vals [ outer])
                                swap_int ( &vals [ outer],
                                           &vals [ inner]);
        }   /* for each array element */
}



main ()
{
        int     index;

    /* generate an array of pseudorandom integers */
        for ( index = 0; index < MAX_VALS; index++)
                vals [ index] = rand ();

        disp_array ( vals, MAX_VALS, 10);
        wait ();

        select_sort ( vals, MAX_VALS);
        printf ( "After selection sort:\n");
        disp_array ( vals, MAX_VALS, 10);
        wait ();
}
```

This program produced the following session:

```
   41  18467   6334  26500  19169  15724  11478  29358  26962  24464
 5705  28145  23281  16827   9961    491   2995  11942   4827   5436
32391  14604   3902    153    292  12382  17421  18716  19718  19895
 5447  21726  14771  11538   1869  19912  25667  26299  17035   9894
28703  23811  31322  30333  17673   4664  15141   7711  28253   6868
25547  27644  32662  32757  20037  12859   8723   9741  27529    778
12316   3035  22190   1842    288  30106   9040   8942  19264  22648
27446  23805  15890   6729  24370  15350  15006  31101  24393   3548
19629  12623  24084  19954  18756  11840   4966   7376  13931  26308
16944  32439  24626  11323   5537  21538  16118   2082  22929  16541
<Return> to continue
After selection sort:
   41    153    288    292    491    778   1842   1869   2082   2995
 3035   3548   3902   4664   4827   4966   5436   5447   5537   5705
 6334   6729   6868   7376   7711   8723   8942   9040   9741   9894
 9961  11323  11478  11538  11840  11942  12316  12382  12623  12859
13931  14604  14771  15006  15141  15350  15724  15890  16118  16541
16827  16944  17035  17421  17673  18467  18716  18756  19169  19264
19629  19718  19895  19912  19954  20037  21538  21726  22190  22648
22929  23281  23805  23811  24084  24370  24393  24464  24626  25547
25667  26299  26308  26500  26962  27446  27529  27644  28145  28253
28703  29358  30106  30333  31101  31322  32391  32439  32662  32757
<Return> to continue
```

disp_array()

This function displays an array of **int** values, writing a specified number of values on a single line. The function writes the values in the desired format, keeping track of the number of values written on the current line. When the maximum number of values have been written on the line, the function writes a newline character. The function takes three arguments: the array to display, the size of the array, and the number of values to write on each line.

swap_int()

This function exchanges the values of the two parameters passed in by using pointers to **int**. This routine is useful for exchanging values, as in the selection sort algorithm. You'll probably want to develop such swapping functions for any common data types, or you might want to work on developing a generic swapping routine.

wait( )

This function merely prompts the user to press RETURN before continuing.

select—sort( )

This function actually sorts the specified array, using two loops. The outer loop is executed for each cell in the array. The first time through this loop, the smallest element is put into place, in cell 0 of the array. The second time through, the next-smallest value is put in cell 1. If the array is of size n, this loop is executed n times.

The inner loop compares each cell in the remaining array with the cell currently being filled. If the value in the cell indexed by **inner** is smaller than the value in the cell having subscript **outer**, the values in the two cells are exchanged.

Each time through the inner loop, the function needs to check fewer cells, since all the early cells will have been filled. For example, after 20 cells (0 through 19) have been filled, the inner loop needs to check only 79 cells (21 through 99). At this point, **outer** will be 20, since cell 20 is the one currently being filled. After 80 cells have been filled, the inner loop needs to check only 19 more cells, and so on.

On the average, the inner loop will be executed roughly $n/2$ times for each time through the outer loop. Thus, the function will check about $n * n/2$, or $n^2/2$, cells. This means that the selection sort function's running time is proportional to n^2.

To see this, define a global variable, **calls**, in your program, initialize the variable to 0, and increment it each time through the inner loop. The relevant portion of the revised function is shown in the following listing. Notice that you'll need to add curly braces, since the inner loop becomes a compound statement.

```
/* new inner loop to write calls information for selection sort */

for ( inner = outer + 1; inner < size; inner++)
{
        calls++;                /* new line */
        if ( vals [ inner] < vals [ outer])
                swap_int ( &vals [ outer], &vals [ inner]);
}
```

If you recompile and run the program, you'll find that the function checks 4950 cells for an array of 100 elements — 50 fewer than our approximation of $n^2/2$. You actually check an average of $(n - 1)/2$ elements, because the cell currently being filled is not checked again. Thus, the first time you need to check only 99 cells rather than 100.

Bubble Sort

The *bubble sort* is another algorithm that is easy to implement but not very efficient. The basic strategy is to let the largest values "bubble" to the top of the array by interchanging the values in adjacent cells if the element in the lower cell has a larger value than the element in the next cell.

For example, the following listing shows the exchanges made while sorting five elements. To identify them, let's assume the leftmost element is in spot A, the next element is in spot B, and so on, to the rightmost element, in spot E.

```
Comparison  list after comparison
            23      7       39      128     12
A-B         7       23      39      128     12
B-C         7       23      39      128     12      (no exchange)
C-D         7       23      39      128     12      (no exchange)
D-E         7       23      39      12      128     (top value is sorted)
A-B         7       23      39      12      128     (no exchange)
B-C         7       23      39      12      128     (no exchange)
C-D         7       23      12      39      128     (D value is sorted)
A-B         7       23      12      39      128     (no exchange)
B-C         7       12      23      39      128     (C value is sorted)
A-B         7       12      23      39      128     (A and B are sorted)

            A       B       C       D       E
```

Notice that after bubbling a value to its position, you don't look at the value again. This saves time, since you won't ever make any exchanges once an element has been moved to its proper position.

The following listing shows a function for doing a bubble sort on an array of integers. You should add this function to your **sorts.c** file.

```
/* void bbl_sort ( char *vals [], int size)
   Sort an array of integers by letting "largest" remaining integer
   work its way to the top of the array on each pass.
*/

void bbl_sort ( int vals [], int size)
{
        int  low, hi, top;    /* for looping through array */

        top = size;    /* highest element that needs to be compared */
        while ( top > 0)
        {
                for ( low = 0, hi = 1; hi < top; low++, hi++)
                {
                        /* if vals [ low] > vals [ hi], exchange them */
                        if ( vals [ low] > vals [ hi] )
                                swap_int ( &vals [ low], &vals [ hi]);
                }   /* END for hi < top */
                top--;        /* another integer has been placed. */
        }  /* END while top > 0 */
}  /* END bbl_sort () */
```

bbl_sort( )

On each pass, this function bubbles a value up to the current
value of **top** in the array. As the remaining largest value reaches
its position, the top of the array to search becomes lower. The
outer (**while**) loop will be executed n times, if n is the number of
values. The inner loop will again be executed an average of $n/2$
times for each pass through the outer loop. Thus, the running
time of the bubble sort is also proportional to n^2.

Shaker Sort—A Double Bubble Sort

In the bubble sort, we let large values move upward in the array.
This was arbitrary: We could just as well have let small values
move downward in the array. The *shaker sort* is a variant of the
bubble sort that does both of these things simultaneously.

The following listing shows a function to do a shaker sort on an
array of integers. The major differences between this function
and **bbl_sort( )** are in the continuation condition for the **while**
loop and in the addition of a second inner loop that moves downward in the array.

```
/* void shaker_sort ( char *vals [], int size)
   Sort an array of integers by letting  "largest" remaining integer
   work its way to the top of the array on each pass.
*/

void shaker_sort ( int vals [], int size)
{
        int  low, hi, top, bottom;   /* for looping through array */

        top = size;  /* highest element that needs to be compared */
        bottom = 0;

        while ( top > bottom)
        {
                for ( low = bottom, hi = bottom + 1;
                      hi < top; low++, hi++)
                {
                        /* if vals [ low] > vals [ hi], exchange */
                           if ( vals [ low] > vals [ hi] )
                                   swap_int ( &vals [low], &vals [hi]);
                }   /* END for hi < top */
                top--;       /* another integer has been placed. */

                for ( hi = top, low = top - 1;
                      hi > bottom; hi--, low--)
                {
                        /* if vals [ hi] < vals [ low], exchange */
                           if ( vals [ hi] < vals [ low] )
                                   swap_int ( &vals [hi], &vals [low]);
                }   /* END for hi < top */
                bottom++;   /* another integer has been placed. */
        }  /* END while top > bottom */
}   /* END shaker_sort () */
```

shaker_sort( )

On one pass through the array, the function lets the current largest value move to its position near the top. On the next pass, the algorithm lets the current smallest value move downward to its position. Like the bubble sort, the shaker sort moves the "ceiling" downward as the top cells are sorted. It also moves the "floor" upward as the lower part of the array is sorted. Thus, the array remaining to sort shrinks toward the center cells from both sides. The last cells to be sorted will be near the center of the array.

Although this algorithm needs fewer exchanges than the bubble sort, the difference is in the constant, not in the factor that depends on n. Therefore, the shaker sort also is proportional to n^2.

Exercising Sorting Routines

The following program lets you exercise the selection, bubble, and shaker sorts. The listing also includes a version of the shaker sort function that illustrates a simplified version of the sorting process on screen.

```c
/* Program to exercise sorting algorithms, to sort array of int. */

#include <stdio.h>
#include <stdlib.h>
#include <string.h>
#include "sortutil.c"
#include "sorts.c"

#define MAX_VALS    15
#define MAX_STR     80
#define MAX_MENU    20


/* define and initialize string array */
int    vals [ MAX_VALS];

/* menu for the selections possible with this program */
char *menu [ MAX_MENU] = { "0) Quit",
                           "1) Bubble", "2) Fancy Bubble",
                           "3) Shaker", "4) Fancy Shaker",
                           "5) Selection", "6) Fancy Selection"};

int  level = 0;


/* display the specified menu, which is an array of strings.
   menu_size indicates the number of strings in the menu.
   Function also prompts user for a choice.
   CALLS : printf ()
   GLOBALS : MAX_MENU
   PARAMETERS :
           char *menu [] : array of strings, containing menu.
           int menu_size : number of items in menu.
*/

void show_menu ( char *menu [], int menu_size)
{
        int count;

        printf ( "\n\n");

    /* if programmer claims menu has more than maximum allowed items,
           bring the value into line.
        */
        if ( menu_size > MAX_MENU)
                menu_size = MAX_MENU;
```

```
        /* display the individual strings in the array */
        for ( count = 0; count < menu_size; count++)
                printf ( "%s\n", menu [ count]);

        printf ( "\n\n");

        /* prompt user */
        printf ( "Your choice? (%d to %d) ", 0, menu_size - 1);
}


main ()
{
        int  index, outcome;
        char info [ MAX_STR];
        int  selection, to_find;

        /* repeat this loop until user wants to quit */
        do
        {
                show_menu ( menu, 7);
                gets ( info);
                selection = atoi ( info);

                fill_array ( vals, MAX_VALS);
                disp_array ( vals, MAX_VALS, 10);


                /* switch on user's menu selection */
                switch ( selection)
                {
                        default:
                                break;
                        case 0:
                                break;
                        case 1:                 /* bubble */
                                bbl_sort ( vals, MAX_VALS);
                                disp_array ( vals, MAX_VALS, 10);
                                break;
                        case 2:                 /* fancy bubble */
                                printf ( "Not implemented.\n");
                        /* fancy_bbl_sort ( vals, MAX_VALS);
                                disp_c_array ( vals, MAX_VALS, 70); */
                                break;
                        case 3:                 /* shaker */
                                shaker_sort ( vals, MAX_VALS);
                                disp_array ( vals, MAX_VALS, 10);
                                break;
                        case 4:                 /* fancy shaker */
                                fancy_shaker_sort ( vals, MAX_VALS);
                                disp_c_array ( vals, MAX_VALS, 70);
                                break;
                        case 5:                 /* selection */
                                select_sort ( vals, MAX_VALS);
                                disp_array ( vals, MAX_VALS, 10);
                                break;
```

```
                case 6:                        /* fancy selection */
                        printf ( "Not implemented.\n");
                      /* fancy_select_sort ( vals, MAX_VALS);
                         disp_c_array ( vals, MAX_VALS, 70); */
                         break;
                }
        }
        while ( selection != 0);
}


void fancy_shaker_sort ( int vals [], int size)
{
        int  low, hi, top, bottom;    /* for looping through array */
        int  index;
        for (index = 0; index < size; index++)
                vals [ index] = vals [ index] % 26 + 97;

        top = size;  /* highest element that needs to be compared */
        bottom = 0;

        while ( top > bottom)
        {
                for ( low = bottom, hi = bottom + 1;
                     hi < top; low++, hi++)
                {
                    /* if vals [ low] > vals [ hi], exchange them */
                        if ( vals [ low] > vals [ hi] )
                                swap_int ( &vals [ low], &vals [ hi]);
                }   /* END for hi < top */
                vals [top] = toupper (vals [top]);   /* mark as done */
             /* display current state of ordering */
                disp_c_array ( vals, MAX_VALS, 70);
                top--;        /* another integer has been placed. */
                if ( top == 0)
                        vals [ top] = toupper ( vals [ top]);

                for ( hi = top, low = top - 1;
                     hi > bottom; hi--, low--)
                {
                    /* if vals [ hi] < vals [ low], exchange them */
                        if ( vals [ hi] < vals [ low] )
                                swap_int ( &vals [ hi], &vals [ low]);
                }   /* END for hi < top */
                vals [bottom] = toupper (vals [bottom]); /* done */
             /* display current state of ordering */
                disp_c_array ( vals, MAX_VALS, 70);
                bottom++;     /* another integer has been placed. */
                if ( bottom == top)
                        vals [ bottom] = toupper ( vals [ bottom]);
        }  /* END while top > bottom */
}  /* END fancy_shaker_sort () */
```

fancy_shaker_sort( )

This function converts the values in the array to values within the range of the lowercase ASCII characters and sorts them using a shaker sort. To illustrate the sequence of steps, the function displays the entire array of characters each time it brings an element to its proper position, with the newly sorted element converted to uppercase before being displayed. Thus, at any time, all uppercase characters in the list have been sorted.

Try writing a **fancy_bbl_sort( )** to illustrate the same thing for that algorithm. Keep in mind that you cannot convert a character to uppercase until the sorting algorithm no longer uses it.

The following listing shows a session using the **fancy_shaker_sort( )** function.

```
Your choice? (0 to 12) 4
    41   18467    6334   26500    19169   15724   11478   29358   26962   24464
  5705   28145   23281   16827     9961

hpghqmeaulnlfdy

Ahpghqmedulnlfy

AhghpmedqlnlfuY

ADhghpmefqlnluY

ADghhmefplnlqUY

ADEghhmflplnqUY

ADEghhflmlnpQUY

ADEFghhllmnpQUY

ADEFghhllmnPQUY

ADEFGhhllmnPQUY

ADEFGhhllmNPQUY

ADEFGHhllmNPQUY

ADEFGHhllMNPQUY

ADEFGHHllMNPQUY

ADEFGHHlLMNPQUY

ADEFGHHLLMNPQUY

ADEFGHHLLMNPQUY
```

Write **fancy_select_sort( )** and **fancy_bbl_sort( )** functions to show the sorts on screen.

To do its work, the exerciser program calls various utility functions. You saw some of these earlier. The new functions are shown in the following listing. The program assumes these are in file **sortutil.c**.

```
/* display the contents of an array, in character format. */
void disp_c_array ( int info [], int size, int nr_per_line)
{
        int    index;

        printf ( "\n");
        for ( index = 0; index < size; index++)
        {
            /* if character is printable */
                if ( isprint ( info [ index]))
                        printf ("%c", info [ index]);
                else
                        printf ( "?");
            /* if nr_per_line elements have been written, send \n */
                if ( (index % nr_per_line) == (nr_per_line - 1))
                        printf  ("\n");
        }   /* for index = 0 ..  */
        printf ( "\n");
}


/* fill an array with specified number of pseudorandom values */
void fill_array ( int vals [], int size)
{
        int index;

        for ( index = 0; index < size; index++)
                vals [ index] = rand ();
}
```

disp_c_array( )

This function displays the contents of an integer array, but as characters (**%c**) rather than decimal values. This makes it possible to use the character's case as information in the list. As with **disp_array( )**, the function writes a specified number of values on a line and then moves to the next line.

The function assumes the array has already been converted to values within the printable character range, although the function **disp_c_ array( )** does test to make sure this is the case. To test this, it uses the **isprint( )** macro predefined in the file **ctype.h** included with QuickC and other compilers that adhere to the Draft Proposed ANSI Standard. This macro returns TRUE (a nonzero value) if the character is printable and FALSE (0 in C) if the character is not printable—for example, if it's a control character.

fill_array( )

This function fills the specified array with the required number of pseudorandom integers. The function calls the Run-Time library function **rand( )** to accomplish this.

Insertion Sort

The strategy behind an *insertion sort* is similar to the process of sorting a hand of cards: You can take a card, move it to its location in sequence, and move the remaining cards left or right as needed.

For example, suppose you had the poker hand in the following illustration and you wanted to order the cards. One ordering would be by suit (clubs, diamonds, hearts, spades) and then by value (2 through ace) within each suit. The arrows indicate the actions taken, and the number below each arrow indicates the step's position in the sequence of actions required to put each card in place. After the steps have been carried out, the cards will be in the sequence shown in the next line down.

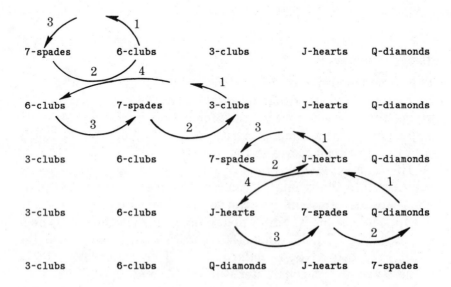

Notice that the first step is always to move the value to be sorted to temporary storage—to free a cell and to allow later reinsertion into a new cell.

After the first two elements in the array are sorted, the remaining elements are inserted in relation to these. Any cells that need to be displaced are moved in the appropriate direction to make room for the value being relocated.

The following listing contains a function for performing an insertion sort. You may want to add this function to file **sorts.c** and add a menu option in the exerciser program.

```
/* insertion sort routine */
void  insert_sort ( int vals [], int size)
{
        int  low, hi, temp;

        for ( hi = 1; hi < size; hi++)
        {
                temp = vals [ hi];  /* value currently being moved */
        /* compare from previous cell downward */
                low = hi - 1;
        /* while still cells to compare,
           and while new value still goes lower
        */
                while ( (low >= 0) && ( temp < vals [ low]))
                {
                        /* move the earlier cells upward */
                        vals [ low + 1] = vals [ low];
                        /* move to next lower cells */
                        low--;
                }      /* while still not ready to insert */
                vals [ low + 1] = temp;   /* store current value */
        }    /* for hi < size */
}
```

insert_sort( )

This function sorts the elements of an array by inserting each element in its proper place in the sorted portion of the array. To make room, the algorithm pushes any larger values to the right in the array. This algorithm is also proportional to n^2 in its average behavior. The insertion sort needs to do little work, however, if the array is already ordered for the most part.

If you try your hand at writing a **fancy_insert_sort( )**, keep in mind that the cell values are not fixed in this algorithm. This means that you can't simply convert a character to uppercase after putting it in a cell, because the character may be needed for comparisons. The best you can do is make the character uppercase while displaying the array but leave the actual value in the array lowercase.

Variants on Insertion Sorts

Various steps are possible to make the insertion sort algorithm a bit faster. For example, the algorithm finds the cell in which to put the current value by backtracking from the current value's cell until it reaches a cell whose value is smaller than the current value. This search for the target cell can be made faster by taking advantage of the fact that all cells before the current one are already ordered.

This strategy, sometimes known as a *binary insertion sort*, works as follows. Suppose you want to put the value in cell 26 in its proper location. Suppose further that this value will eventually be put in cell 4. Instead of comparing the values in cells 25, 24, and so on down to cell 4, the binary insertion strategy first checks cell 13, the cell halfway between the start of the array and the current cell. If the current value is smaller, the algorithm must go down even further. In the next step, you would check cell 6— the cell halfway between the lowest cell and the last one checked, 13, which was still too large. This strategy of bisecting the remaining cells enables you to find the target cell much more quickly. Once there, however, the algorithm must still move all 22 cells up to insert the value in cell 4. Thus, binary insertion can save time during the comparison process but not during the shifting.

Shell Sort

An insertion sort works well when the array is mostly sorted at the outset. The number of exchanges is minimized in such an array; this saves time, since the exchanges and shifts take more time than comparisons. Small values high up in the array are especially costly, since they make it necessary to move lots of elements up, which takes time. In 1959, Donald Shell modified the insertion sort in an ingenious way that improved the sorting performance considerably. The resulting algorithm has become known as the *Shell sort*.

In an ordinary insertion sort, movement is one cell at a time. For example, when values in an array are moved up, the value in cell X is moved to cell $X + 1$. It takes more than 20 moves to transfer the value in cell 26 to cell 5 with an insertion sort.

Shell suggested sorting in several passes. Early passes would sort only elements separated by some number of other elements. For example, the first pass through an array might sort elements 13 positions apart. After this pass, elements 0, 13, 26, 39, and so on, would be sorted. Elements 1, 14, 27, 40, and so on, would also be sorted. This pass moves small values far down in the array, with few exchanges. In effect, after this pass, the array would consist of 13 sorted data sets, all interleaved. Chances are good that values of similar size will be close to each other, which means fewer exchanges will be needed.

A second pass might sort for values separated by four cells — 0, 4, 8, 12, and so on. After this pass, the array would be reasonably ordered. To finish off what has now become a much easier job, the third pass through the data would be the ordinary insertion sort, in which moves are to adjacent cells.

It turns out that a Shell sort is proportional to $n^{1.25}$, rather than to the n^2 we've been seeing with the other algorithms. To illustrate what this difference in order of magnitude is, Table 4-1 shows the

Table 8-3.   Running Times for n^2 and $n^{1.25}$ Algorithms

n	n^2	$n^{1.25}$	$n^2/n^{1.25}$
10	100	18	5.5
100	10,000	316	31.6
500	250,000	2364	105.8
1000	1,000,000	5623	177.8
5000	25,000,000	42044	594.6

relative running times for n^2 and $n^{1.25}$ algorithms at various sample sizes. For 500 elements, an $n^{1.25}$ algorithm is about 100 times faster than an n^2 algorithm; for 5000 elements, an algorithm such as the Shell sort is almost 600 times faster than an n^2 algorithm.

The advantages of Shell sort over an ordinary insertion sort become increasingly pronounced as the array size increases. This is one reason the Shell sort is one of the most commonly used sorting algorithms. The algorithm is efficient and the function logic is straightforward.

Part of the trick in making the Shell sort effective is to select a good range of gaps between elements in successive passes. Surprisingly, no one has completely analyzed the Shell sort. However, much empirical research has been done on the behavior of the Shell sort using various gap sequences. It turns out that values based on the following calculation produce a good collection of gap sizes. On the other hand, powers of 2 tend to produce inefficient gaps.

1. The last, and smallest, gap will always be 1, to get the final, sorted array.

2. The second-smallest gap should be (3 * current—gap + 1), that is, 4.

3. Subsequent gaps are generated using the formula in step 2. Thus, the next-smallest gap is (3 * 4 + 1), or 13.

4. The process stops with the *second*-largest gap that is smaller than the array size.

This calculation generates the following gap sizes:

1	4	13	40	121	364

If you're working with an array of 300 elements, the largest gap your Shell sort routine should use is 40, which satisfies the criteria in step 4. You could also make a pass with a gap size of 121, if you wished; empirical studies show, however, that the extra pass doesn't save you enough exchanges to make it worthwhile.

The following listing implements a Shell sort. Notice how the function computes the highest gap to use. Effectively, the Shell sort function is simply an insertion sort within a loop. The outer loop's continuation condition is to make a pass through the array for each gap size generated in the sequence.

In each pass, the array is sorted for different-sized gaps. Thus, the first "insertion" sort would involve cells separated by 40, as above, the second pass would be with a gap of 13, and so on down to 1.

```c
/* shell sort function */
void  shell_sort ( int vals [], int size)
{
        int  low, hi, temp, gap = 1;

    /* generate gap sizes */
        do
                gap = 3 * gap + 1;
        while ( gap < size);
        gap /= 3;    /* to avoid using gaps that are too big */
        gap /= 3;    /* to avoid using gaps that are too big */

    /* for decreasing gap sizes do the following loop */
        for ( ; gap >= 1; gap /= 3)
            {
                for ( hi = gap; hi < size; hi++)
                    {
                    /* value currently being moved */
                        temp = vals [ hi];
                    /* compare from previous cell downward */
                        low = hi - gap;
                    /* while still cells to compare,
                        and while new value still goes lower
                    */
                        while ( (low >= 0) && ( temp < vals [ low]))
                            {
                            /* move the earlier cells upward */
                                vals [ low + gap] = vals [ low];
                            /* move to next lower cells */
                                low -= gap;
                        }     /* while still not ready to insert */
                    /* store current value */
                        vals [ low + gap] = temp;
                }     /* for hi < size */
        }    /* for gap > 1 */
}
```

shell__sort( )

This function performs a Shell sort on the integer array passed as a parameter. The function first determines the largest **gap** to use, based on the array size; then it does additional passes, sorting cells at smaller gaps in the sequence. These passes are simply insertion sorts looking at elements separated by **gap** elements.

Think about what you might show in a **fancy__shell__sort( )** function; that is, determine how you could show the progress of the algorithm on the screen. Then write a **fancy__shell__sort( )** routine.

Quicksort

The *quicksort* algorithm was developed by C.A. Hoare in 1962 and is one of the most commonly used sorting algorithms. Quicksort uses a divide-and-conquer algorithm to accomplish its sorting task.

The algorithm breaks down the entire array into a number of smaller arrays, which are sorted by a recursive call to another version of the algorithm. The basic technique is to move two "walls," or partitions, toward each other. An ascending wall moves from the left side of the array (lowest subscript) upward; a descending wall moves from the right side of the array (highest subscript) downward. The ascending wall is designed to catch large values that need to be moved up in the array; the descending wall catches small values that need to be moved down.

In a pass in the quicksort algorithm, large and small are defined in relation to some reference value that is selected at the start of the algorithm. Whenever the ascending wall finds a value larger than the reference value, the wall stops moving. Similarly, when the descending wall finds a value smaller than the reference value, that wall stops. If the two walls have not yet passed each other, the values in the cells at the two walls are exchanged; thus, a large value is moved up and a small value is moved down. After making such an exchange, the walls continue their movement until they find new values to exchange or until they pass each other.

When they pass each other, the two walls stop. At this point, all values to the left of the descending wall are less than the reference value, and all values to the right of the ascending wall are larger than the reference value. Within these smaller partitions, however, the values are still jumbled.

The next step is to perform quicksorts on these smaller arrays. The original call to quicksort had an ascending wall beginning with subscript 0 and a descending wall beginning with subscript MAX— VALS − 1. One recursive call to quicksort will work with an array that goes from 0 to the cell whose subscript is the value of **descending** just before the recursive call; a second call will use the array beginning at **ascending** and continuing to the highest subscript in the current array.

The following listing shows various intermediate states when using quicksort to order a 15-element array. Uppercase elements are the current values of the ascending and descending walls on entry to quicksort or when two values are exchanged. The reference value for each call is shown at the top of the steps for that call. The indentation reflects the call's level of recursion.

```
reference value == e:  /* quick_sort ( vals, p, d) */
P h q g h u m e a y l n l f D    /* P, D walls */
D h q g h u m e a y l n l f P    /* exchange d, p */
d A q g h u m e H y l n l f p    /* exchange a, h */
d a E g h u m Q h y l n l f p    /* exchange e, q */
/* walls will pass each other */

    /* sort smaller left partition */
    reference value == a:  /* quick_sort ( vals, d, e) */
    D a E g h u m q h y l n l f p
    A D e g h u m q h y l n l f p
    /* walls will pass each other */

        /* no left partition, so sort smaller right one */
        reference value == d:  /* quick_sort ( vals, d, e) */
        a D E g h u m q h y l n l f p
        a D e g h u m q h y l n l f p

    /* sort smaller right partition */
    reference value == h:  /* quick_sort ( vals, g, p) */
    a d e G h u m q h y l n l f P    /* G, P walls */
    a d e g F u m q h y l n l H p    /* exchange f, h */
    a d e g f H m q U y l n l h p
```

```
/* etc. */
reference value == f:  /* quick_sort ( vals, g, h) */
a d e G f H m q u y l n l h p
a d e f F G h m q u y l n l h p
```

```
    reference value == g:  /* quick_sort ( vals, g, h) */
    a d e f G H m q u y l n l h p
    a d e f G h m q u y l n l h p
```

```
reference value == l:  /* quick_sort ( vals, m, p) */
a d e f g h M q u y l n l h P
a d e f g h H q u y l n l M p
a d e f g h h L u y l n Q m p
a d e f g h h l L y U n q m p
```

```
    reference value == l:  /* quick_sort ( vals, h, l) */
    a d e f g h H l L y u n q m p
    a d e f g h h L L y u n q m p
```

```
       reference value == h:  /* quick_sort ( vals, h, l) */
       a d e f g h H L l y u n q m p
       a d e f g h H l l y u n q m p
```

```
    reference value == n:  /* quick_sort ( vals, y, p) */
    a d e f g h h l l Y u n q m P
    a d e f g h h l l M u n q Y p
    a d e f g h h l l m N U q y p
```

```
       reference value == m:  /* quick_sort ( vals, m, n) */
       a d e f g h h l l M N u q y p
       a d e f g h h l l M n u q y p
```

```
          reference value == q:  /* quick_sort ( vals, u, p) */
          a d e f g h h l l m n U q y P
          a d e f g h h l l m n P q y U
          a d e f g h h l l m n p Q y u
```

```
             reference value == y:  /* quick_sort ( vals, y, u) */
             a d e f g h h l l m n p q Y U
             a d e f g h h l l m n p q U Y
```

```
adefghhllmnpquy
```

Notice that by the first recursive call to the quicksort algorithm —
with D being the value of the leftmost cell and E the value of the
rightmost cell for the smaller array — all values to the right of the
E come later in an ordering than the reference value (e). Similarly, all values to the right of the G (in the call with G and P as
walls) are greater than the reference value.

The first recursive call to the lower partition ends after one
more level of recursion (with adjacent elements D and E as the
walls). When the lower end is done, the elements **a**, **d**, and **e** are in
order.

The function then applies the same divide-and-conquer strategy to the higher end of the array, that is, the partition from G to P. The next recursive call in this partition eventually orders the **f**, **g**, and **h** elements. (The other **h** will eventually work its way down.) This process of sorting smaller and smaller partitions continues until all the elements are sorted.

The following function implements a quicksort algorithm to order an array of integers:

```
/* quicksort function */

void  quick_sort ( int vals [], int left, int right)
{
    /* ascending is left wall, descending is right wall */
    int     ascending = left, descending = right, ref_val;

    /* select the comparison value */
    ref_val = vals [ ( left + right) / 2];
    do
    {
        /* while element smaller than reference value,
           move left wall upwards
        */
        while ( vals [ ascending] < ref_val)
                ascending++;
        /* while element larger than reference value,
           move right wall downwards
        */
        while ( vals [ descending] > ref_val)
                descending--;
        /* if the walls haven't passed each other,
           exchange the values
        */
        if ( ascending <= descending)
                swap_int ( &vals [ ascending++],
                                &vals [ descending--]);
    }   /* END do loop */
    while ( ascending <= descending);

    /* if descending wall has not yet reached left partition,
       call quick_sort again with this smaller array
    */
    if ( left < descending)
            quick_sort ( vals, left, descending);
    /* if ascending wall has not yet reached right partition,
       call quick_sort again with this smaller array
    */
    if ( right > ascending)
            quick_sort ( vals, ascending, right);
}  /* END quick_sort () */
```

quick_sort( )

This function sorts an array using a quicksort algorithm. The function can be broken into three major portions: initialization, exchanges, and recursion.

During initialization, the function sets the **ascending** and **descending** indexes to the left and right walls, respectively. The function also selects a reference value. In the algorithm here, the middle element in the array is selected. The reference value selected can strongly affect quicksort's performance; for example, if the reference value turns out to be the smallest or the largest value in the array, the algorithm will make one pass without accomplishing anything.

Large and small values are exchanged for the entire partition. This phase groups elements based on their size relative to **ref_val**.

The recursive phase involves calling **quick_sort( )** to work on the same task for a smaller partition. This process continues in the recursive calls until the entire array is sorted. As you'll see, the recursion phase is one place where the quicksort implementation can be fine tuned.

Quicksort is proportional to $n * log(n)$, where log is the logarithm function. To see what this means, look at Table 4-2, which shows the number of steps needed to sort arrays of different sizes. As you can see, the performance of an $n * log(n)$ algorithm is even better than that of an $n^{1.25}$ algorithm. Keep in mind, however, that such performance figures are for average performance—depending on the initial data, among other things.

Table 4-2.   Times for $n * log(n)$ Algorithms

n	$n * log(n)$
10	10 * 1 == 10
100	100 * 2 == 200
500	500 * 2.7 == 1350
1000	1000 * 3 == 3000
5000	5000 * 3.7 == 18495

Drawbacks of Quicksort

One factor that keeps quicksort from being universally used is that its behavior changes drastically depending on the array being sorted. For example, quicksort works extremely hard when the data are almost in order from the start. In some situations, quicksort will actually run proportionately to n^2.

Choice of a reference value also makes a difference. Partitions that are roughly equal in size can be sorted more quickly than partitions that are very uneven in size. Small partitions are almost too simple for quicksort: It's inefficient to call quicksort to exchange two values, as happened in the example shown earlier. Large partitions are likely to require more recursive calls to finish than smaller partitions.

Quicksort's recursive properties can also cause problems, especially in computers with limited memory or in programs with limited stack space for storing suspended functions: It's possible to overflow the stack by making too many levels of recursive calls.

Remedies for Quicksort

The first and third phases of a quicksort function lend themselves most readily to changes. Both portions can be modified to make the function behave more efficiently over a broader range of situations.

You can get quite fancy when selecting a reference value. One method that is easy and reasonably effective is to select three array elements as candidate reference values. The middle value of these three will become the actual reference value. By selecting the median of several values, you greatly decrease the likelihood that your reference value will be extremely large or extremely small.

The recursion phase is also a good candidate for improvements in the algorithm. A common modification is to be more selective about when to make a recursive call with a smaller partition. If the partition is too small, recursion becomes quite inefficient. To deal with this, the function could be modified to perform a simpler sort (such as an insertion sort) on partitions smaller than some cutoff size. For example, partitions containing about 20 or fewer elements can be sorted just as efficiently with an insertion sort. The quicksort routine will never know that the sorting was not done recursively.

To make this change, you simply need to expand the **if** statements in the recursion phase. You would need to test for the size of the array still remaining to be sorted: If it's smaller than some cutoff size, the function should call **insert_sort( )** or another sorting algorithm; if larger, the function should call itself, as it currently does.

The Microsoft C Run-Time library includes a quicksort function, **qsort( )**, that you can use to sort arrays of any type, provided you can specify the size of each cell in the array. You may want to study the **qsort( )** function if you have the source code for the Microsoft Run-Time library.

Sorting Arrays of Structures

Let's sort a different type of information, to raise some important issues about sorting data. You'll sort an array of structures, using one of the structure's members as the key for sorting.

The programs in this section use the following structure definition:

```
/* structure definition for sorting routines */

#define MAX_EDUC   15
#define MAX_ELEM   5

struct ed {
        char    major [ MAX_EDUC];
        double gpa;
} struct_array1 [ MAX_ELEM];
```

The following program sorts an array of structures using the **gpa** member of the structure. The program does *not* sort correctly, however.

```
/* Program to "sort" an array of structures ---
      based on value of gpa members.
      Program exchanges only gpa members, not the entire structures ---
      because an array of structures has been used.
      NOTE: This program sorts incorrectly.
*/
```

```
#include <stdio.h>
#include <stdlib.h>

#define MAX_EDUC  15
#define MAX_ELEM  5
#define MAX_STR   80

struct ed {
        char    major [ MAX_EDUC];
        double gpa;
} struct_array1 [ MAX_ELEM];


/* get values for members of an ed structure */
void get_struct ( struct ed *stuff)
{
        char info [ MAX_STR];

        printf ( "Major? ");
        gets ( stuff->major);

        printf ( "GPA? ");
        gets ( info);
        stuff->gpa = atof ( info);
}

main()
{
        void get_struct ( struct ed *);
        void bbl_sort ( struct ed [], int);
        void show_struct ( struct ed);
        int  index;

        /* initialize structure array */
        for ( index = 0; index < MAX_ELEM; index++)
                get_struct ( &struct_array1 [ index]);

        /* display values of structures in array */
        for ( index = 0; index < MAX_ELEM; index++)
        {
                printf ( "%d: ", index);
                show_struct ( struct_array1 [ index]);
        }

        /* sort structures */
        bbl_sort ( struct_array1, MAX_ELEM);

        /* display values of structures in sorted array */
        printf ( "\n\nAfter sorting array of structures\n");
        for ( index = 0; index < MAX_ELEM; index++)
        {
                printf ( "%d: ", index);
                show_struct ( struct_array1 [ index]);
        }
}


/* void bbl_sort ( struct ed stru [], int size)
   Sort array of structures by letting "largest" remaining structure
   work its way to the top of the array on each pass.
*/

void bbl_sort ( struct ed stru [], int size)
{
        double temp;           /* for exchanging pointers */
        int  low, hi, top;     /* for looping through array */
```

```
        top = size;  /* highest element that needs to be compared */
        while ( top > 0)
        {
                for ( low = 0, hi = 1; hi < top; low++, hi++)
                {
                        /* if stru [ low].gpa > stru [ hi].gpa, swap */
                        if ( stru [ low].gpa >  stru [ hi].gpa)
                        {
                                /* NOTE: only gpa members are being
                                   swapped.
                                */
                                temp = stru [ low].gpa;
                                stru [ low].gpa = stru [ hi].gpa;
                                stru [ hi].gpa = temp;
                        }
                }    /* END for hi < top */
                top--;          /* another string has been placed. */
        } /* END while top > 0 */
}  /* END bbl_sort () */


/* display contents of an ed structure */
void show_struct ( struct ed stru)
{
        printf ( "%s major, gpa == %6.2lf\n", stru.major, stru.gpa);
}
```

For a sample session, this program produced the following:

```
Major? astron
GPA? 3.5
Major? bio
GPA? 2.7
Major? chem
GPA? 3.7
Major? math
GPA? 3.65
Major? psych
GPA? 3.4
0: astron major, gpa ==    3.50
1: bio major, gpa ==    2.70
2: chem major, gpa ==    3.70
3: math major, gpa ==    3.65
4: psych major, gpa ==    3.40


After sorting array of structures
0: astron major, gpa ==    2.70
1: bio major, gpa ==    3.40
2: chem major, gpa ==    3.50
3: math major, gpa ==    3.65
4: psych major, gpa ==    3.70
```

This program is supposed to sort structures based on the values of the **gpa** member in each of the structures. Unfortunately, the result is not what you would want. The sorting function has simply exchanged the **gpa** members in the structures it compared but left the other members with their original structures.

To sort properly, it is easier to use an array of pointers to structures. The sorting routine would then exchange pointers. This version will actually change the order in which the structures are referenced. The following program accomplishes this by using an array of pointers to a structure:

```
/* Program to sort an array of structures ---
   based on the value of the gpa members.
   Program uses structure pointers, so the structures themselves
   are reordered.
*/

#include <stdio.h>
#include <stdlib.h>

#define MAX_EDUC   15
#define MAX_ELEM   5
#define MAX_STR    80

struct ed {
        char    major [ MAX_EDUC];
        double gpa;
} struct_array [ MAX_ELEM],    /* array of structures */
  *ptr_array [ MAX_ELEM];      /* array of pointers to structures */

void get_struct ( struct ed *stuff)
{
        char info [ MAX_STR];

        printf ( "Major? ");
        gets ( stuff->major);
        printf ( "GPA? ");
        gets ( info);
        stuff->gpa = atof ( info);
}

main()
{
        void get_struct ( struct ed *);
        void bbl_sort_ptr ( struct ed *[], int);
        void show_struct ( struct ed);
        int  index;

    /* initialize structure array */
        for ( index = 0; index < MAX_ELEM; index++)
                get_struct ( &struct_array [ index]);
```

```
        /* make pointers reference the structure array elements */
        for ( index = 0; index < MAX_ELEM; index++)
                ptr_array [ index] = &struct_array [ index];

        /* display the structures referenced by the pointers */
        for ( index = 0; index < MAX_ELEM; index++)
        {
                printf ( "%d: ", index);
                show_struct ( *ptr_array [ index]);
        }

        /* sort the structures referenced by the pointers */
        bbl_sort_ptr ( ptr_array, MAX_ELEM);

        /* display the sorted structures. */
        printf ( "\n\nAfter sorting array of pointer to structs\n");
        for ( index = 0; index < MAX_ELEM; index++)
        {
                printf ( "%d: ", index);
                show_struct ( *ptr_array [ index]);
        }

}




/* void bbl_sort_ptr ( struct ed *stru [], int size)
   Sort an array of structure pointers by letting "largest" remaining
   structure work its way to the top of the array on each pass.
*/

void bbl_sort_ptr ( struct ed *stru [], int size)
{
        struct ed *temp;      /* for exchanging pointers */
        int  low, hi, top;    /* for looping through array */

        top = size; /* highest element that needs to be compared */
        while ( top > 0)
        {
                for ( low = 0, hi = 1; hi < top; low++, hi++)
                {
                        /* if *stru [ low].gpa > *stru [ hi].gpa, swap */
                        if ( stru [ low]->gpa >  stru [ hi]->gpa)
                        {
                                temp = stru [ low];
                                stru [ low] = stru [ hi];
                                stru [ hi] = temp;
                        }
                }   /* END for hi < top */
                top--;        /* another string has been placed. */
        } /* END while top > 0 */
} /* END bbl_sort_ptr () */




/* display contents of an ed structure */
void show_struct ( struct ed stru)
{
        printf ( "%s major, gpa == %6.2lf\n", stru.major, stru.gpa);
}
```

This program produces the following, given the same responses as in the previous example:

```
Major? astron
GPA? 3.5
Major? bio
GPA? 2.7
Major? chem
GPA? 3.7
Major? math
GPA? 3.65
Major? psych
GPA? 3.4
0: astron major, gpa ==   3.50
1: bio major, gpa ==   2.70
2: chem major, gpa ==   3.70
3: math major, gpa ==   3.65
4: psych major, gpa ==   3.40


After sorting array of pointer to structures
0: bio major, gpa ==   2.70
1: psych major, gpa ==   3.40
2: astron major, gpa ==   3.50
3: math major, gpa ==   3.65
4: chem major, gpa ==   3.70
```

This program sorts the structures properly. This time, the entire structure is moved—by making a different pointer reference the structure.

Notice that the arrow operator is only used for the comparison in the test condition, in function **bbl_sort_ptr( )**. After the comparison has been made, addresses, not structure members, are transferred. On the other hand, when showing the array, you need to use the indirection operator to get the actual structure, because the array element is a pointer. *Inside* the **show_struct( )** function, the arrow operator is not needed, because the entire structure, rather than a pointer to the structure, has been passed.

In this program, the information was first read into a static array of structures. Then the locations of these structures were assigned to the structure pointers in **ptr_array[ ]** to allocate storage for the structures.

Sorts on Lists and Trees

In the preceding two chapters, you built ordered lists and ordered trees. The functions used were actually sorting functions. The algorithms were essentially insertion sorts, since the list or tree was built by adding the new element.

The list-sorting algorithm is in function **middle__of__list( )**, and the tree-sorting algorithm is in function **add__to__tree( )**. Both of these algorithms work with sequential data structures, as opposed to random access structures, such as arrays.

The sorting algorithms you've seen so far in this chapter have worked with arrays and have therefore been random access algorithms. One consequence of this is that you can exchange arbitrary elements in the array with each other. In a sequential algorithm, on the other hand, you can get to an element only by going through its predecessors.

Sequential data structures require different sorting strategies. In the next section, you'll look at some algorithms for sorting a very common sequential access data structure: a text file.

SEQUENTIAL ACCESS STRUCTURES: FILES

You'll often want to store your information in external files. If each item in the file is the same length, you can find a random element by simply moving to the appropriate offset in a file. In most files, however, entries use different amounts of space. In this case, you need to access the file sequentially — reading each entry in the file until you reach the one you want. Reading the contents of such files is straightforward — unless the files are compressed or encrypted in some way.

You may need to sort the contents of a file for some reason. In that case, sequential access to find arbitrary elements becomes unacceptably time-consuming. Confronted with such a problem, you should consider the data, the state of the file to be sorted, and the goal of the sorting.

For example, if all you want to do is add a new entry in the proper place in an already sorted list, your strategy will be different than if you needed to sort an unordered list of items in a file.

Similarly, if you have just a few entries, all of which you can keep in memory while sorting, you can sort by building a tree or a linked list. On the other hand, if you have too many entries to keep in memory, you will need to store some of your work on disk.

Simple Sequential Sorts

Let's look at the simple case requiring you to sort material in a file. If you know that the file is small enough to fit into memory, you can build a tree containing the file entries and then write this tree in sorted order to a new file.

A second simple case arises if all you want to do is add a new entry at the appropriate spot in an already ordered file. To do this, open a second file, and write the entries from the original file into the new file, using the following rules:

1. While the entry just read from the original file "precedes" the new entry, write the entry just read to the new file. If this is true, go to step 2; when it is no longer true, go to step 3.

2. Get another entry from the original file, and repeat step 1.

3. If the new entry precedes the entry just read from the original file, write the new entry to the new file, and then write the older entry to the new file. Then proceed to step 4.

4. While there are still entries in the old file, get an entry from the old file, and write it to the new file.

The following program lets you apply either of the above methods to a file you specify. The program expects three command line entries from you: sorting method to use, old file name, and new file name.

```
/* Program to exercise simple external sorting routines */

#include <stdio.h>
#include <stdlib.h>
#include <string.h>
#include "defs.h"
```

```
#include "avl.h"
#include "types.h"
#include "lq.c"
#include "avl.c"

#define ADD_SWITCH      'a'      /* to add new entry to file */
#define SORT_SWITCH     's'      /* to sort a simple file in memory */

char *empty_line = "\n";         /* files must end with a blank line */

/* Function DECLARATIONS */
void add_to_file ( char *, char *, char *);
void sort_small_file ( char *, char *);
void write_tree ( struct tnode *, FILE *);


/* main function --- calls add_to_file () or sort_small_file (),
   depending on command line information.
   Command line arguments must be (in order):
   -a to add a new entry to existing file OR
   -s to sort a simple file in memory, thenb write to a new file.
   <old file name>, <new file name>
*/
main ( int argc, char *argv [])
{
        struct tnode *root = NULL, *temp;
        char         new [ MAX_STR];

        if ( argc < 4)
        {
                printf ( "Usage: fsort ");
                printf ( "<-a -s> <old file> <new file>\n");
                exit ( 1);
        }
        else    /* if user has supplied all necessary arguments */
        {
                if ( tolower ( argv [ 1] [ 1]) == ADD_SWITCH)
                {
                        printf ( "New entry? ");
                        gets ( new);
                        add_to_file ( new, argv [ 2], argv [ 3]);
                }
                else if ( tolower ( argv [ 1] [ 1]) == SORT_SWITCH)
                        sort_small_file ( argv [ 2], argv [ 3]);

                else    /* if not a valid switch */
                {
                        printf ( "-a == Add new element; ");
                        printf ( "-s == Sort old file\n");
                        printf ( "Exiting program.\n");
                        exit ( 1);
                }
        }  /* if valid command line */
}


/* add a new entry to an existing, ordered file ---
   by writing entries to a new file, inserting new entry at
   the appropriate place.
```

```
*/
void add_to_file ( char *new, char *old_name, char *new_name)
{
        FILE    *fp, *new_fp, *fopen ();
        char    curr [ MAX_STR], buff [  MAX_STR];

        fp = fopen ( old_name, "r");
        if ( fp != NULL)
        {
                new_fp = fopen ( new_name, "w");
                if ( new_fp != NULL)
                {
                        fgets ( curr, MAX_STR, fp);
                        /* while still getting info from file, AND
                        value just read still precedes new info.
                        */
                        while ( strcmp( curr, empty_line) &&
                                (strcmp( curr, new) <= 0))
                        {
                                fputs ( curr, new_fp);
                                fgets ( curr, MAX_STR, fp);
                        }
                        /* add new entry, including a \n */
                        fputs ( new, new_fp);
                        fputs ( empty_line, new_fp);
                        /* write last value read from old file ---
                        to new file.
                        */
                        if ( strcmp ( curr, empty_line))
                                fputs ( curr, new_fp);
                        fgets ( curr, MAX_STR, fp);
                        /* write rest of old file to new location */
                        while ( strcmp( curr, empty_line))
                        {
                                fputs ( curr, new_fp);
                                fgets ( curr, MAX_STR, fp);
                        }
                }    /* if new file was opened */
        } /* if old file was opened */
}




/* write contents of tree to specified file */
void write_tree ( struct tnode *tree, FILE *fptr)
{
        if ( tree != NULL)
        {
                if ( tree -> left != NULL)
                        write_tree ( tree -> left, fptr);
                fputs ( tree -> data, fptr);
                if ( tree -> right != NULL)
                        write_tree ( tree -> right, fptr);
        }    /* if tree != NULL */
}
```

```
/* sort a small disk file in memory, then write sorted
   information (in form of a tree) to nre file, in order.
*/
void  sort_small_file ( char *old_name, char *new_name)
{
        FILE            *fp, *new_fp, *fopen ();
        struct tnode    *root = NULL, *temp;
        char            curr [ MAX_STR], buff [  MAX_STR];
        int             result;

        fp = fopen ( old_name,      .*.
        if ( fp != NULL)
        {
                new_fp = fopen ( new_name, "w");
                if ( new_fp != NULL)
                {
                        /* allocate memory for new tree node */
                        temp = get_tnode ( temp);
                        fgets ( curr, MAX_STR, fp);
                        /* while still stuff to add from file,
                        and still possible to add to tree.
                        */
                        while ( strcmp( curr, empty_line) &&
                                (temp != NULL))
                        {
                                strcpy ( temp -> data, curr);
                                /* add newly read data to tree */
                                root = add_to_tree ( temp, root,
                                              &result);
                                temp = get_tnode ( temp);
                                fgets ( curr, MAX_STR, fp);
                        } /* while still something to do. */
                        write_tree ( root, new_fp);
                } /* if new file was opened */
        }   /* if old file was opened */
}
```

add—to—file()

This function adds a new entry to an existing file by writing the old file and the new entry to a new file. The function assumes the existing file is already sorted, and the new entry is written at the appropriate point in the new file.

write—tree()

This function writes the information stored in a sorted tree to the specified file, with the information written in order. This function has the same structure as **show—tree()**, except for the actual output statement—**fputs()** in **write—tree()**, rather than **printf()** as in **show—tree()**.

sort—simple—file( )

This function reads a file from disk, builds a sorted tree containing the file entries, and then writes this sorted tree in order to a new file. The function uses **write—tree( )** to do its work.

A More Complicated File Sort

A somewhat more complicated problem arises if you need to add an entire file to a second one. In this case, assume both files are already sorted and that they need to be merged with each other.

The basic strategy will be to compare values taken from each file, writing the smaller value of the pair to a third file. Once a value is written, a new value is selected from the appropriate file to replace the written value in the next comparison. For example, suppose you had files containing the material in the following listing:

```
file 1: 4      10      16      23      93
file 2: 3      7       39
```

Let's use **v1** and **v2** to refer to the current values from files 1 and 2, respectively. The merging process would use the following steps:

1. Read a value from each file.
2. While values are read from both files, compare the two values. If **v1** "precedes" **v2**, write **v1** to the new file; otherwise, write **v2** to the new file. If the end of one file has been reached, go to step 4; otherwise, go to step 3.
3. Read a new value from the file whose value was just written to the new file. That is, if **v1** was just written, read a new **v1** from file 1; otherwise, read a new **v2** from file 2. Repeat step 2.
4. While there are still values in the file not yet completed, read a value from the file and write the value to the new file. For example, if file 1 is not yet ended (but file 2 is), transfer the remainder of file 1 to the new file.

The following listing shows a function for merging two sorted
files:

```c
/* merge sort function */
void merge_sort ( char *f1, char *f2, char *f3)
{
        FILE *fp1, *fp2, *fp3;
        char *str1, *str2, *str3;

        fp1 = fopen ( f1, "r");
        fp2 = fopen ( f2, "r");
        fp3 = fopen ( f3, "w");
        if ( ( fp1 != NULL) && ( fp2 != NULL) && ( fp3 != NULL))
        {
                fgets ( str1, MAX_STR, fp1);
                fgets ( str2, MAX_STR, fp2);
                /* while still getting info from both files */
                while ( strcmp( str1, empty_line) &&
                        strcmp( str2, empty_line) )
                {
                        if ( strcmp ( str1, str2) <= 0)
                        {
                                fputs ( str1, fp3);
                                fgets ( str1, MAX_STR, fp1);
                        }
                        else  /* if str2 should be written */
                        {
                                fputs ( str2, fp3);
                                fgets ( str2, MAX_STR, fp2);
                        }
                }

                if ( strcmp ( str1, empty_line) == 0)
                {
                        while ( strcmp ( str2, empty_line))
                        {
                                fputs ( str2, fp3);
                                fgets ( str2, MAX_STR, fp2);
                        }
                }

                if ( strcmp ( str2, empty_line) == 0)
                {
                        while ( strcmp ( str1, empty_line))
                        {
                                fputs ( str1, fp3);
                                fgets ( str1, MAX_STR, fp1);
                        }
                }
                fputs ( empty_line, fp3);
                fclose ( fp3);
        }    /* if all files were opened */
        else
                printf ( "Too few files opened.\n");
}
```

merge—sort( )

This function merges the contents of two already sorted text files and writes the results to a third file. The function takes three file names as arguments.

The function first tries to open all three files. If successful, the function processes entries until one of the files is empty. Each time through this loop, the function writes a value to the file referenced by **fp3**. The function then reads another value from either **fp1** or **fp2**, depending on whether **str1** or **str2** was written. When one of the files is empty, the function writes the remaining entries from the surviving file to the new file.

Projects and Suggestions

You can extend and combine the preceding external sorting routines to handle even more complex sorting problems. For example, it is fairly straightforward to create a **merge—sort( )** function that merges three files into a fourth one. Try it.

A more challenging task is to sort a sequential access file that is too long to be sorted in memory. There are numerous algorithms in the literature for accomplishing this; however, many of them insist on knowing the size of the file in advance or can handle only files of certain sizes.

You can build a function to accomplish this task by combining simpler techniques. For example, you could use the function **sort—small—file( )** to sort as much of the file as possible in memory. Once this was done, you would write the resulting tree to a disk file. After freeing the memory allocated for the tree, you would build another tree with additional material from the file being sorted and write this tree to a different disk file. You could then use **merge—sort( )** to combine these two sorted files into a third file. If your original file was completely read into the two trees, the third file is your sorted file and you're done. If you still have material in the original file, you'll need to read another tree, merge this material with your third file, and so forth.

SEARCHING

All this sorting should, surely, have a purpose. Often, the goal is to be able to find an item of information quickly at some later time. You shouldn't be surprised to learn that numerous algorithms have been developed to make *searching* more efficient. In this section, you'll look at some simple search algorithms.

Sequential Search: Arrays, Lists, and Trees

The easiest way to search for an entry in an array (or a file) is to work your way through the array until you find the value or reach the end of the array. This search strategy does not assume that the array is already sorted. On the average, you will search through about half of an array before you find the value you're seeking. Thus, a *sequential search* algorithm for arrays is proportional to n.

The following listing shows a sequential search function for searching an array. (You've already seen a sequential search routine for linked lists, in Chapter 2.)

```
/* sequential search algorithm */
int seq_search ( int target, int vals [], int size)
{
        int index;

        for ( index = 0; ( index < size)
                        && ( vals [ index] != target); index++)
                ;
        if ( vals [ index] == target)
                return ( target);
        else
                return ( INVALID_INT);
}
```

seq_search( )

This function searches for a specified value by examining element after element until it finds the value or the entire array has been examined.

Binary Search

If you know an array is sorted, you can take advantage of this fact and the random access property of arrays to speed up a search considerably. The most common algorithm that makes use of an array's ordering is a *binary search* algorithm.

A binary search algorithm searches for a value by trying to isolate smaller and smaller partitions in which the value can be found. Each partition is half the size of the preceding one. For each partition being examined, the function selects an element whose cell is in the middle of the partition being tested. Because the array is sorted, you can determine whether to continue looking in the lower or the higher set of values.

For example, suppose you want to find a value in a 100-cell array.

1. Select the middle cell of the array as the boundary.

2. If the boundary value is smaller than the value being sought, look further, using the right part of the array.

3. If the boundary value is larger than the value being sought, look further, using the left part of the array.

4. If you are down to single-cell partitions and still have no luck, the function is done, and the value is not in the array.

The following listing implements a binary search algorithm. (In Chapter 3, you saw a routine for searching a binary tree in which the search directions were determined by the relative standing of the two values being compared.)

```
/* binary search algorithm */
int bin_search ( int target, int vals [], int size)
{
        int index, low = 0, hi = size - 1;

        while ( low <= hi)
        {
                index = ( low + hi) / 2;
                if ( target > vals [ index])
                        low = index + 1;
                else if ( target < vals [ index])
                        hi = index - 1;
                else
                        break;
```

```
       }
       printf ( "After loop, index = %d; val == %d; target = %d\n",
               index, vals [ index], target);
       if ( target == vals [ index])
               return ( target);
       else
               return ( INVALID_INT);
}
```

bin__search()

This function does a binary search for a specified value in the array passed as a parameter. If the value is found in the array, the function returns the value; otherwise it returns a predefined value indicating failure.

Each time through the loop, the function compares the target value against the value in the center cell of the current array — the cell with subscript **index**. If the value in this cell precedes the target value, the function searches farther in the right part of the array defined by the cell following **index** and the rightmost cell of the remaining array. On the other hand, if the target value precedes the element in cell **index**, the search continues in the array to the left, bounded by the leftmost cell and the cell with subscript **index** − 1. If neither of these cases holds, then **target** must equal **vals [index]**, in which case the value has been found in the array. The function can then return the value.

At each step through the loop, **bin__search()** halves the number of cells left to search. Effectively, this means you need to search roughly one cell for each power of two needed to create an array as large as the one you're searching. For example, if you were searching an array of 32 (2^5) elements, you would need to examine about 5 cells to find the value if it's in the array. The first cell checked would cut the number of remaining cells to 16; the second would cut it to 8; the third to 4; and so on. For this reason, the **bin__search()** algorithm is proportional to the logarithm to base 2 of n, $log_2 (n)$.

The binary search has clear speed advantages over an ordinary sequential search, provided the array is sorted to begin with. The algorithm is easy to code and is considerably faster than sequential search.

Projects and Suggestions

Various tricks have been developed to fine tune the binary search algorithm, making it even faster. A common variant, *interpolation search*, tries to use more precise information about the most likely location of the element. For example, if you were looking up the word *search* in a dictionary, you would open the book near the end of the dictionary, since the letter *s* comes after the middle of the alphabet.

Similarly, an interpolation search compares the target value against a cell whose position in the current partition corresponds roughly to the expected location of the value. Write an interpolation search function.

Although you can get far with these simple search algorithms, very large data structures, such as dictionaries, usually call for much faster search techniques. You may want to find out something about *hashing*, a very fast access technique. Computer science books on algorithms or data structures often discuss hashing.

SUMMARY

In this chapter, you learned about some common techniques for sorting information and for searching for information in existing data structures, the two tasks that are among the best studied in computer science. Hundreds of algorithms and variants exist to accomplish these tasks.

In the next chapter, you'll look at another very common task in programs: parsing expressions. You'll build a more sophisticated calculator using the parsing algorithms.

5

PARSING
EXPRESSIONS

In Chapter 1, you saw how to implement a four-function calculator using stacks. The calculator worked by creating a postfix version of the expression you entered and solving the postfix problem. In this chapter, you'll develop a calculator that has even more power and that doesn't need to convert to postfix to solve your expression.

PARSING

To evaluate an expression, a calculator first needs to know the status or role of each element, or *token*, in the expression. In a four-function calculator, each element must be either an operator or an operand. The calculator must somehow be able to distinguish between the two types of elements.

The process of breaking an expression down into constituent elements and associating a role, or purpose, with each element is known as *parsing*. For example, in Chapter 1, the function **to—postfix( )** served as a parser by identifying individual elements of an expression and deciding whether each token was an operator or an operand. To categorize an element, a parser uses a definition of the possible types of elements and information about where each can occur.

A Simple Sentence Parser

Let's look at a very simple parser that breaks down strings of words into sentence components. We'll assume this parser understands only nouns, verbs, articles, and adjectives. The parser also accepts only the following limited vocabulary of words:

Nouns—book, car, cheese, goat, house, lawn, mold, window

Verbs—has, hit, jumped, lost, missed, needs, painted, was

Adjectives—green, heavy, polite, rambunctious, soft, third

Articles—a, the

This parser uses the following rules to determine the components of a sentence:

1. A sentence consists of a subject and a predicate.
2. A subject consists of a noun possibly preceded by an adjective possibly preceded by an article; that is, a subject consists of an optional article, an optional adjective, and a required noun, in that order. Thus, "a heavy cheese," "green goat," and "the lawn" can all be subjects, whereas "window third" and "the heavy" cannot.
3. A predicate consists of a verb possibly followed by what is usually called an object. As it turns out, an object has the same components and characteristics as a subject. Therefore, we'll use the term *subject* for both these cases. Thus, a predicate has a verb and may have an article, an adjective, or a noun. The noun is required if either an article or an adjective is included after the verb. In short, a predicate is a verb possibly followed by a subject. Thus, "jumped" and "needs the mold" are both

predicates, whereas "has soft" is not. The invalid predicate needs to add a noun or drop the adjective. If *any* part of a subject is included after the verb, the noun must be included.

4. A noun consists of any of the words given as nouns in the preceding list.

5. An adjective consists of any of the words given as adjectives in the list.

6. An article consists of any of the words listed as articles.

7. A verb consists of any of the words listed as verbs.

In these rules, a sentence is defined in terms of subjects and predicates. Subjects and predicates are defined in terms of parts of speech (articles, nouns, and so on). These are, in turn, defined in terms of specific examples, or *literals*. The rules used by a parser are known as the *grammar* for the parser.

A grammar is often expressed formally as a set of *rewrite rules*, or *productions*. These are often written as a sequence of definitions, with the element being defined placed on the left and the definition of the element placed to the right.

The following listing shows the rewrite rules for our parser:

```
<sentence> := <subject> <predicate>

<subject> := {<article>} {<adjective>} <noun>

<predicate> :=  <verb> {<subject>}

<article> := "a" || "the"

<adjective> := "green" || "heavy" || "soft" || "third"

<noun> := "book" || "lawn" || "mold" || "window"

<verb> := "has" || "jumped" || "needs" || "was"
```

This notation system is known as a *Backus-Naur form*, or *BNF, notation*, after the developers of the system. We'll use := to mean "is defined as." The element to the left of the := is the component being defined; the sequence to the right represents the production for that element. Thus, a sentence is produced by a subject and a predicate. Components are included in the order in which they appear in the production: A sentence begins with a subject, which is followed by a predicate.

Elements in angle brackets (<>) are eventually defined in terms of other components in a separate production. This means that the parser needs to do more processing before it has finished with the component. Elements that appear on the left side of a production are known as *nonterminals*, because they require further processing.

A subject is defined in terms of three other components: article, adjective, and noun, in that order. The article is specified within curly braces ({}) to indicate that the element is optional: You may, but need not, include an article. The adjective is also optional. The noun, however, is required. Thus, the simplest subject would consist only of a noun.

An article is defined as being either of two strings: "a" or "the". The two vertical bars (||) indicate that either the element to the left *or* the element to the right is included. An adjective and a noun are also defined in terms of specific strings.

Notice that the candidates for article, adjective, and noun are not in angle brackets. These elements are literal strings. When the parser reaches one of these elements, it has finished processing that component. For this reason, such literal elements are known as *terminals*. Terminal elements never appear on the left side of a production.

After the production for noun has been included in the grammar above, the parser knows everything it needs to know about a sentence subject. The predicate component is defined in the next production as a verb followed by an optional subject. Again, a verb is defined in terms of terminal elements.

Let's see how this parser would do its work on a sentence. We'll parse "The heavy car needs windows."

The parser takes this sentence and tries to find a subject and a predicate, as in the first production. To find a subject, the parser checks first for an article and then for an adjective. If it finds neither of these, it proceeds, looking next for a noun. Once a noun is found, the subject has been identified, and the parser can look for the predicate. To find the predicate, the parser first looks for a verb and then looks for a subject.

The following program illustrates such a parser. Function **sentence( )** generates random sentences using the words available in the grammar. Function **parse( )** calls two other functions to parse the sentence into a subject and a verb.

The program uses four global arrays and four global integers to represent the terminals for each part of speech and the size of the arrays for each part of speech. For example, in the following program, the array **article[]** contains only two elements: "a" and "the".

```
/* Program to generate and parse sentences based on
   the following grammar:

   <sentence> := <subject> <predicate>

   <subject> := {<article>} {<adjective>} <noun>
   <article> := "a" || "the"
   <adjective> := "green" || "heavy" || "polite" ||
                  "rambunctious" || "soft" || "third"
   <noun> := "book" || "car" || "cheese" || "goat" ||
             "house" || "lawn" || "mold" || "window"

   <predicate> := <verb> {<subject>}
   <verb> := "has" || "hit" || "jumped" || "lost" ||
             "missed" || "needs" || "was"
*/


#include <stdio.h>
#include <stdlib.h>
#include <string.h>
#include "wrk\defs.h"
#include "wrk\utils.c"

#define MAX_TERMS  10    /* maximum # of terminals per category */

/* valid words  for parser. */
char article [ MAX_TERMS] [ SHORT_STR] = {
      "the", "a"};
char adjective [ MAX_TERMS] [ SHORT_STR] = {
      "green", "heavy", "third",
      "soft", "polite", "rambunctious"};
char noun [ MAX_TERMS] [ SHORT_STR] = {
      "car", "cheese", "goat", "house",
      "window", "mold", "lawn", "block"};
char verb [ MAX_TERMS] [ SHORT_STR] = {
      "has", "jumped", "needs", "was",
      "painted", "hit", "lost", "missed"};

/* sizes for each of the terminal arrays */
int  nr_art = 2, nr_adj = 6, nr_noun = 8, nr_verb = 8;
```

```
/* Function DECLARATIONS */
char *get_subject ( void);
char *get_word ( char [] [ SHORT_STR], int);
char *match ( char [] [ SHORT_STR], int, char **);
char *maybe_get_word ( char [] [ SHORT_STR], int, int);
char *parse ( char *);
char *predicate ( char *);
char *sentence ( void);
int  starts_with ( char *, char *);
char *subject ( char *);


/* Function DEFINITIONS */
main ()
{
        char phrase [ MAX_STR];
        int  index, seed, how_often;

        printf ( "seed ( 0 .. 32767)? ");
        gets ( phrase);
        seed = atoi ( phrase);
        srand ( seed);
        printf ( "Create how many sentences? ");
        gets ( phrase);
        how_often = atoi ( phrase);

        for ( index = 0; index < how_often; index++)
        {
                strcpy ( phrase, sentence ());     /* get sentence */
                printf ( "%s\n", phrase);          /* display it */
                strcpy ( phrase, parse ( phrase)); /* parse it */
                printf ( "After parsing: %s\n\n", phrase);
        }
}


/*
   char *get_word ( char term [] [ SHORT_STR], int size)
   ************************************************************
   Select a word at random from the specified array; return word.

   CALLS : rand (); strcat (); strcpy ();
   GLOBALS : SHORT_STR
   PARAMETERS :
          term : array containing terminals;
          size : # elements in array
   RETURN : pseudorandom word
   USAGE : strcpy ( my_word, get_word ( verb, nr_verb));
   ************************************************************
*/
char *get_word ( char term [] [ SHORT_STR], int size)
{
        int  which;
        char temp [ SHORT_STR];

        which = rand () % size; /* get index of word */
        strcpy ( temp, term [ which]);
        strcat ( temp, " ");    /* add space before next word */
        return ( temp);
}
```

```
/*
   char *maybe_get_word (char term [][ SHORT_STR], int size, int odds)
   ************************************************************
   Possibly select and return a word at random from specified array;
   Likelihood of deciding to select a word == odds / size.
   If yes, select it and return the word.

   CALLS : rand (); strcat (); strcpy ();
   GLOBALS : null_str, SHORT_STR
   PARAMETERS :
           term : array containing terminals;
           size : # elements in array
           odds : # values for which a word will be returned.

   RETURN : pseudorandom word
   USAGE : strcpy ( my_word, maybe_get_word ( verb,
                                              nr_verb, nr_verb - 1);
   ************************************************************
*/
char *maybe_get_word ( char term [] [ SHORT_STR], int size, int odds)
{
        int   which, yes;
        char temp [ SHORT_STR];

        yes = ( rand () % size) < odds;

        if ( yes)   /* if OK to get a word */
        {
                which = rand () % size;    /* get index of word */
                strcpy ( temp, term [ which]);
                strcat ( temp, " ");   /* space before next word */
                return ( temp);
        }
        else /* if no word is to be generated */
                return ( null_str);
}




/*
   char *sentence ()
   ************************************************************
   Generate a sentence, consisting of a subject and a predicate.

   CALLS : get_subject (); get_word (); rand (); strcat (); strcpy ();
   GLOBALS : MAX_STR
   PARAMETERS :  get_subject (); rand (); strcat (); strcpy ();
   RETURN : grammatical sentence based on grammar at top of file.
   USAGE : strcpy ( my_sent, sentence ());
   ************************************************************
*/
char *sentence ()
{
        char   sent [ MAX_STR], temp [ MAX_STR];
        int    option;

    /* get subject */
        strcpy ( temp, get_subject ());
        strcpy ( sent, temp);
```

```
    /* get verb */
        strcpy ( temp, get_word ( verb, nr_verb));
        strcat ( sent, temp);

        option = rand () % 2;   /* decide whether to get subject */

        if ( option)
        {
                strcpy ( temp, get_subject ());
                strcat ( sent, temp);
        }
        return ( sent);
}


/*
   char *get_subject ()
   *********************************************************
   Generate a subject;
   possibly get article, possibly get adjective, get noun.

   CALLS : get_word (); maybe_get_word (); strcat (); strcpy ();
   GLOBALS : MAX_STR, nr_adj, nr_art, nr_noun, null_str, SHORT_STR
   PARAMETERS : none
   RETURN : string containing a subject.
   USAGE : strcpy ( my_subj, get_subject ());
   *********************************************************
*/
char *get_subject ()
{
        char  subj [ MAX_STR], temp [ SHORT_STR];

        strcpy ( subj, null_str);

    /* possibly get article */
        strcpy ( temp, maybe_get_word ( article,
                                        nr_art, nr_art - 1));
        strcpy ( subj, temp);

    /* possibly get adjective */
        strcpy ( temp, maybe_get_word ( adjective,
                                        nr_adj, nr_adj - 2));
        strcat ( subj, temp);

    /* get noun */
        strcpy ( temp, get_word ( noun, nr_noun));
        strcat ( subj, temp);

        return ( subj);
}


/*
   char *parse ( char *str)
   *********************************************************
   Parse sentence into subject and predicate.
```

```
        CALLS : predicate (); strcat (); strcpy (); subject ();
        GLOBALS : MAX_STR
        PARAMETERS :
                str : string to parse.
        RETURN : parsed string, with main components separated by //.
        USAGE : strcpy ( new_str, parse ( my_expression));
        ********************************************************
*/
char *parse ( char *str)
{
        char subj [ MAX_STR];

        strcpy ( subj, subject ( str));      /* get subject */
        strcat ( subj, " // ");              /* add separator */
        strcat ( subj, predicate ( str));    /* get predicate */

        return ( subj);
}




/*
    char *subject ( char *str)
    ********************************************************
    Parse sentence portion to identify components of a subject;
    return these components if found.

    CALLS : strcat (); strcmp (); strcpy ();
    GLOBALS : MAX_STR, null_str, SHORT_STR
    PARAMETERS :
            str : string in which to find subject.
    RETURN : subject portion from str.
    USAGE : strcpy ( my__subj, subject ( expression));
    ********************************************************
*/
char *subject ( char *str)
{
        char subj [ MAX_STR], temp [ SHORT_STR];

        strcpy ( subj, null_str);  /* initialize subject string */

    /* get article, if present */
        strcpy ( temp, match ( article, nr_art, &str));
        if ( strcmp ( temp, null_str))  /* if found, add to subject */
        {
                strcat ( subj, temp);
                strcat ( subj, " * ");  /* add separator */
        }

    /* get adjective, if present */
        strcpy ( temp, match ( adjective, nr_adj, &str));
        if ( strcmp ( temp, null_str))
        {
                strcat ( subj, temp);
                strcat ( subj, " * ");  /* add separator */
        }
```

```
    /* get noun */
        strcpy ( temp, match ( noun, nr_noun, &str));
        if ( strcmp ( temp, null_str))
                strcat ( subj, temp);
        else /* if not getting anything */
                return ( null_str);

        return ( subj);
}


/*
   char *predicate ( char *str)
   ************************************************************
   Parse sentence portion to identify components of a predicate;
   return these components if found.

   CALLS : natch (); strcat (); strcmp (); strcpy ();
   GLOBALS : MAX_STR, null_str
   PARAMETERS :
           str : string in which to search for predicate.
   RETURN : predicate portion of str.
   USAGE : strcpy (my_pred, predicate ( expression);
   ************************************************************
*/
char *predicate ( char *str)
{
        char pred [ MAX_STR], temp [ MAX_STR];

        strcpy ( pred, null_str);  /* initialize predicate string */

    /* get verb */
        strcpy ( temp, match ( verb, nr_verb, &str));
        if ( strcmp ( temp, null_str))
                strcat ( pred, temp);
        else
                return ( null_str);

    /* get a subject component, if possible */
        if ( strcmp ( str, null_str))
        {
                strcpy ( temp, subject ( str));
            /* if subject found, add it */
                if ( strcmp ( temp, null_str))
                {
                        strcat ( pred, " * ");
                        strcat ( pred, temp);
                }
        }
        return ( pred);
}


/*
   int  starts_with ( char *str1, char *str2)
   *********************************************************
   Return TRUE if string under consideration begins with
   specified element --- e.g., remainder of sentence begins
   with the sentence component currently being sought.
```

```
        CALLS : strcmp (); strcpy (); strstr ();
        GLOBALS : FALSE, MAX_STR, TRUE
        PARAMETERS :
                str1 : reference string;
                str2 : test string
        RETURN : TRUE if str1 starts with material in str1.
        USAGE : strcpy ( my_str, starts_with ( reference, test_str);
        *******************************************************
*/
int  starts_with ( char *str1, char *str2)
{
        char info [ MAX_STR];

        while ( *str1 == ' ')      /* remove leading blanks */
                str1++;
        strcpy ( info, strstr ( str1, str2));    /* look for match */

    /* if str1 starts with str2, info and str1 should match */
        if ( strcmp ( info, str1) == 0)
                return ( TRUE);
        else
                return ( FALSE);
}



/*
   char *match ( char info [] [ SHORT_STR], int size, char **str)
   *************************************************************
   Return the word that matches the current front of the
   remaining sentence.

   CALLS : remove_wd, starts_with (); strcpy ();
   GLOBALS : null_str, SHORT_STR
   PARAMETERS :
           info : array of terminals to check;
           size : array size;
           str : pointer to string -- so everything changes.
   RETURN : string containing value that was matched, or null_str.
   USAGE : srcpy ( lone_wd, match ( verb,
   *************************************************************
*/
char *match ( char info [] [ SHORT_STR], int size, char **str)
{
        int  index;
        char temp [ SHORT_STR];

    /* look through array for match with first word of sentence */
        for ( index = 0; ( index < size) &&
                        ( !starts_with ( *str, info [ index]));
                        index++)
                ;
        if ( index == size)      /* if no match found */
                return ( null_str);
        else                     /* if something matched */
        {
            /* remove word from sentence */
                strcpy ( temp, remove_wd ( *str));
                return ( info [ index]);
        }
}
```

The program generates and parses "sentences" such as the following:

```
a polite goat has a soft house

the polite cheese lost

the house missed a car

the polite window painted a soft cheese

the heavy mold has a third cheese

a heavy block needs the third car

a rambunctious lawn painted a lawn

heavy goat painted soft cheese
```

Clearly, productions do not guarantee meaningful sentences; they merely specify how to generate *grammatical* sentences. A parser does not work with the meaning of a sentence—just with the locations and roles of words in the sentence. Parsing is merely a mechanical syntactic translation process and not a sophisticated type of language processing; that is, a parser is concerned with only the function of a word in relation to a grammar, not with the meaning of the word.

sentence( )

This function generates a sentence satisfying the definition in the production for a sentence. The function calls **get—subject( )**, which generates a phrase conforming to the production for a subject. Next, **sentence( )** calls **get—word( )** to generate a verb.

Finally, **sentence( )** determines whether to get a second subject to follow the verb. This decision depends on whether the pseudorandom integer returned by **rand( )** is even or odd: If it's odd, **sentence( )** calls **get—subject( )** again. Thus, about half the sentences should have second subjects.

get—subject( )

This generates at least a noun and possibly also an article and an adjective, in the proper positions, to return as a subject phrase. To get the words, **get—subject( )** calls **maybe—get—word( )** (for the optional article and adjective) and **get_word( )** (for the noun, which is always included).

get_word( )

This function selects an element at random from the specified array. For example, when the program needs a verb, the **verb[]** array is passed as the first parameter to **get_word( )**. This function then calls **rand( )** to determine which element from the array to return.

maybe_get_word( )

This function may select an element at random from the array specified; in this way, it works just like **get_word( )**. The difference between the functions is that **maybe_get_word( )** may return a value from the array or return an empty string.

The likelihood that any value will be selected at all is determined by the second and third parameters passed to function **maybe_get_word( )**. The likelihood is computed by first getting a pseudorandom value between 0 and **size − 1** and seeing whether the value is smaller than **odds**. For example, if the array's size were 8 elements (0 through 7) and **odds** were 5, then the likelihood would be 5 / 8 that any array value at all would be selected.

parse( )

This function controls the parsing process, although the real work actually is done by other functions. The **parse( )** function first calls **subject( )** to return the subject of the sentence. After assimilating the string returned by **subject( )**, function **parse( )** calls **predicate( )** to return the second major component of the sentence. The **parse( )** function then returns the analyzed string to the function that called **parse( )**—in this case, **main( )**.

Notice that in doing its work **parse( )** essentially moves down in the productions by calling functions to identify the intermediate level of elements—subject and predicate. Each of those functions, in turn, processes the sentence to an even lower level—that of individual parts of speech—by checking whether the current elements fit in lower-level rewrite rules.

subject( )

This function identifies the subject of a sentence portion and further distinguishes the subject's optional article and adjective as well as its required noun. The function returns the subject in a string in which the constituent parts of a subject are separated by special delimiter characters. To accomplish this, **subject( )** calls an even lower level function, **match( )**, which tries to match the next word in the current string with a terminal of the appropriate type.

predicate( )

This function returns the predicate portion of a sentence, broken into its constituent elements—required verb and optional subject. The **predicate( )** function calls **match( )** to return a verb. If there is still something in the string to be analyzed—that is, if there is a second subject—the function calls **subject( )** to return it.

   Notice that there is a direct correspondence between the conditional call to **subject( )** in **predicate( )** and an optional subject's inclusion in the production for a predicate. In general, you'll see that the productions for a grammar can be very helpful in guiding the code to parse the grammar.

match( )

This function returns a string corresponding to a specific word from the sentence if the word is found in the array for the appropriate part of speech. At each call, **match( )** will be looking for a match on a particular part of speech. The function works by looping through the array, comparing each array element with the string whose analysis is currently under way. If the function finds a match, it returns the appropriate array element; otherwise, the function returns a null string.

   To do its work, **match( )** calls **starts—with( )** to answer the simple, "yes/no" question about whether the current array element is also the first word in the string and is, therefore, the terminal sought.

starts—with( )

This function returns TRUE if the comparison string (first parameter) starts with the specified string (second argument).

A Simple Math Parser

Let's look at another simple parser, one that understands only expressions involving the four arithmetic operators and numbers. This parser does not understand parentheses; therefore, for this example, assume that all operators have the same precedence.

This parser works with three types ef elements: expression, operator, and operand. To decide what to do with the elements in an expression, the parser uses the following set of rules:

1. An expression is formed by a single operand or by an operand followed by an operator and another operand. This second operand can, in turn, be followed by an operator and another operand. This operator-operand sequence can be repeated at the end of the expression.

2. An operator is any of the following: $+ - * /$.

3. An operand is a number.

In these rules, an expression is defined in terms of operators and operands. Operators are defined in terms of special symbols, and operands are defined as numbers; thus, the terminals in the grammar for such expressions will be operators and numbers.

The following listing shows the productions for this grammar:

```
<expression> := <operand> || <operand> <operator> <expression>

<operand> := number

<operator> := "+" || "-" || "*" || "/"
```

The productions for this grammar are recursive, since an expression is defined in terms of itself. Using "expression" to specify the third element in an expression makes it easy to allow multiple operator-operand pairs in an expression. The last element in the original expression will always be a single-operand expression.

Such recursive definitions are quite common, and they will prove handy later. You've already seen examples of such recursive definitions; for example, you know that a tree can be defined as a root node or as a root node with pointers to one or more other trees or subtrees.

Essentially, the recursive definition of *expression* says that an expression consists of a single operand or of an operand followed by an operator and either a single operand or an operand followed by another operator and operand, and so on. For example, the following are all valid expressions in our grammar:

```
      4              /* single operand definition */
/* expression */
     7.5      /        4
/* operand operator expression */
      3       *      7.5 / 4
/* operand operator expression */
      6       +    3 * 7.5 / 4
/* operand operator expression */
    23.5      *        2
/* operator operand expression */
```

Let's see how a parser for this grammar would evaluate an expression such as

```
6       +    3 * 7.5 / 4
```

Recall that in the grammar used here, the operators all have equal precedence, so this parser will generally give different answers than the "algebra parser" you learned in school. Recall also, from the sentence example, that the parser keeps processing until it reaches a terminal. When it reaches a terminal, the parser returns the value of the terminal to the calling context. Eventually, the calling context will have enough elements to carry out its task. Let's work through the example to see this process in action.

The parser looks for a single operand or an operand followed by more material. The parser immediately finds the 6. At this point, the parser searches for more information and finds an operator. The parser has now identified two elements, the operand 6 and the operator +. These will be used once the parser returns a second operand. To get this second operand, the parser searches for an expression.

An expression is a nonterminal. Therefore, the parser needs to do additional processing. Just as it did at the beginning of the original expression, the parser finds an operand, but it keeps searching in order to evaluate this inner expression. After finding the 3, the parser returns the operator *. At this point, there are two operand-operator pairs on hold, each waiting for a second operand. The two pending computations are shown in the following listing:

```
6    +

        3    *
```

If a parser has identified an operand and an operator in an expression, then it needs to look for another expression. Thus, the parser finds the operand 7.5 and the operator / as part of this third expression. There are now three levels of pending computations:

```
6    +

        3    *

                7.5    /
```

The parser again needs to find and evaluate an expression. This time, it returns the operand 4, which turns out to be the entire expression. The parser has finally reached the end of its parsing for the original expression. The 4 is returned to the calling context, which is the pending computation 7.5 /. This computation now has all the required elements and can return 1.875 as its result.

This result is returned to the calling context, the pending computation 3 *. After this computation is completed, the result, 5.625, is returned to the next pending computation. After the addition has been done, the sum, 11.625, is returned as the result of the original expression.

Notice that this parser evaluates from right to left, since it descends to the lowest grammar level required to evaluate an element, that is, to return a terminal. It turns out that a right-to-left evaluation is easier for the very common type of parser you'll build in this chapter.

By coincidence, the result in the preceding example is equal to the one you would get using the rules of algebra. This will not always happen in other cases. For example, change the original expression to the following, and use the parser to evaluate the expression. Compare the result with the one you get using algebra.

```
6        +    3 * 7.5 / 4  -  2
```

In the next section, you'll build a parser capable of handling operator precedence as well as parentheses in expressions. Keep in mind that the parser essentially puts an analysis on hold while it does additional analyses at lower levels in the grammar. Once the lower levels of analysis have been completed, the results are returned to calling contexts, which had suspended further actions until those results were returned. Thus, the top grammar levels are the last to be resolved when an expression is parsed.

This process is very similar to what happens during function calls. Because the process of parsing an element (such as an expression) can require processing nested examples of the same type of element (the inner expressions), the parsing is recursive.

A Recursive Descent Parser

In this section, you'll build a parser that uses the descending strategy illustrated earlier and that works with a grammar involving recursive definitions of elements. This parser is an example of a very common parsing strategy that has been used in compilers and other programs requiring translation. This recursivme strategy of descending through lower levels of a grammar is very common and is known as *recursive descent parsing*.

The recursive descent parser will use a grammar very similar to the rules of algebra, with which you're familiar. The parser will be able to handle the four arithmetic operators (+, −, *, /), a unary negation operator (−), as well as an exponentiation operator (^), which lets you raise an element to a specified power. The parser will also be able to handle parentheses used to override the predefined operator precedence. Additionally, the parser will be able to handle variables used in expressions.

To provide you with some guidelines for a programming task, the grammar will also include the beginnings of an ability to handle named functions. Your challenge will be to modify the program developed later in the chapter to handle such function calls.

Operator Precedence Rules

The parser will use the following precedence for the valid operators:

1. Unary negation (−) will have the highest precedence.
2. The exponentiation operator (^) will have the second-highest precedence.
3. The multiplicative operators (*, /) will have the next-highest precedence.
4. The additive operators (+, −) will have the lowest precedence.
5. Parentheses can be used to override the default precedence.

These rules, along with the fact that operators at the same level of precedence can be applied in any order, make the grammar behave like the rules of algebra, despite the parser's customarily evaluating from right to left where precedence rules do not dictate the order.

Variables and Functions

The grammar includes a definition for a variable and a partial definition for a function. A variable is specified by a single alphabetic character; for example, **a**, **A**, and **q** are all variable names. Variable names are case insensitive; thus, **a** and **A** refer to the same variable in the grammar.

Functions are specified by the function name followed by a list of arguments within parentheses. A function name contains only alphabetic characters and must be at least two letters long. If the function contains no arguments, then the name is followed by an empty pair of parentheses. Otherwise, the expression must include information about the arguments. One possibility is to provide values or expressions for each argument to the function, separated by commas. You should think about how best to specify arguments prior to trying to add function-parsing ability to your program.

Grammar for Parser

The parser you'll build uses the following partial grammar. As earlier, the parser will analyze mathematical expressions involving any of five binary operators, one unary operator (negation, or minus), parentheses, variables, and (once you add the capability) function calls. In the grammar, you'll need to add productions for specifying arguments to functions.

Expressions will again consist of operands and operators. This time, however, you'll distinguish among different types of operands, depending on the operators involved. The top level of the grammar will consist of operands connected by additive operators (+, −), because these operators have the lowest precedence. We'll refer to operands connected by additive operators as *terms*. Thus, the top-level definition for an expression is

```
<expression> := <term> ||
                <term> "+" <expression> ||
                <term> "-" <expression>
```

Notice again that the definition of *expression* is recursive. Thus, at the top level — the last level to be resolved — expressions consist of terms, additive operators, and inner expressions.

Terms, in turn consist of operands that are connected by multiplicative operators (*, /). Before computing an additive expression involving terms — that is, involving additive operators — you need to evaluate components involving multiplicative operators. We'll refer to such operands as *factors*. Thus, the definition for a term is

```
<term> := <factor> ||
          <factor> "*" <term> ||
          <factor> "/" <term>
```

This definition also is recursive. Before evaluating any expression components involving multiplicative operators, you need to evaluate any elements using the exponentiation operator. Thus, factors can be defined in terms of operands involving exponentiation. The production is as follows:

```
<factor> := <subfactor> || <subfactor> "^" <factor>
```

That is, a factor involves operands involving the exponentiation operator. We'll call such operands *subfactors*. At this level, we'll find terminal elements. A subfactor may consist of constant values — in this case, numbers. The grammar can also handle variables; so a subfactor can also consist of a variable. Similarly, a function may consist of a function call, although this component won't be implemented in the parser you'll build here.

Parentheses and the unary (minus) operator are also processed at the level of subfactors. In addition to containing a constant, a variable, and a function call, a subfactor also may consist of an expression inside parentheses or may be preceded by a minus sign. The productions for a subfactor and for the remaining nonterminals in this definition are as follows:

```
<subfactor> := <constant> ||
               <variable> ||
               <function call> ||
               "(" <expression> ")" ||
               "-" <subfactor>
```

```
<constant> := number

<variable> := "a" || "A" || "b" || "B" ... "Y" || "z" || "Z"

<function call> := <function name>
                    "(" {<subfactor>} {, <subfactor} ")"

<function name> := letter letter {letter}
```

Ultimately, a subfactor should always evaluate to a number after enough processing. For example, a variable should be evaluated by a determination of the value associated with that variable and the returning of this value. Similarly, the result of a function call should evaluate to a specific value.

The general strategy for a parser using such a grammar would be

1. Find term.
2. While the expression is not finished, find additive operator (+, −), and go to step 3.
3. If additive operator was found, find expression, and go back to step 2.

The first task requires further processing and can be broken down into the following tasks:

1. Find factor.
2. While the term is not finished, find multiplicative operator (*, /), and go to step 3.
3. If multiplicative operator was found, find term, and go back to step 2.

Again, the first of these subtasks requires processing at a lower level. Thus, to find a factor, the parser needs to perform the following actions:

1. Find subfactor.
2. While the factor is not yet finished, find an exponentiation operator (^), and go to step 3.
3. If exponentiation operator was found, find factor, and go back to step 2.

Finally, the first subtask here, find subfactor, consists of the following steps:

1. Look for minus sign. If found, multiply value resulting from rest of subfactor by −1.
2. Check for left parenthesis. If found, find expression. Discard right parenthesis following expression.
3. Else if not a left parenthesis, look for a function call. If found, handle the function evaluation.
4. Else if not a function call, look for a variable name. If found, get value for the variable, and return this value.
5. Else if not a variable, return the value found, since it should be a number.

A Sample Evaluation

Let's use the preceding breakdown to work through an example. We'll parse the following expression:

```
-(7.5 + 5) * 3 / y
```

The general trend is to go downward in the productions for processing; that is, expression handler calls term handler, calls factor handler, calls subfactor handler, and so forth. The trend is to go upward when returning values; for example, constant → subfactor → factor → term → expression.

The first step in parsing the expression is to find a term. To do this, you first need to look for a factor; to do *this*, however, you first need to find a subfactor.

To find a subfactor, check for a minus sign. In this case, you find one; this means the resulting subfactor will be multiplied by −1 before being returned. After flagging this fact, the parser continues its search for a subfactor in the remainder of the expression, which has now lost its leading minus sign.

To find another subfactor, check for a minus sign again. You don't find one, since it has been removed. The parser does find a left parenthesis, however. The parser discards the parenthesis and searches for an expression in the remainder of the original expression, which is

```
7.5 + 5) * 3 / y
```

To handle an expression, first find a term. To do this, find a factor, and to do *this*, find a subfactor. This time, the subfactor-handling component finds a number, 7.5, immediately. After looking unsuccessfully for an exponentiation operator, the subfactor handler returns this value to the calling context—the factor-handling portion. Notice that the 7.5 is not multiplied by −1: Because of the parentheses, the negation applies to the entire inner expression currently being evaluated, not just to the 7.5.

After the 7.5 is returned as the value of the subfactor, the remaining expression looks as follows:

```
+ 5) * 3 / y
```

The factor-handling component looks for an exponentiation operator after having a value returned for the subfactor. No such operator is found, so the component has nothing more to do. Thus, the factor component consisted of a single subfactor. This value, 7.5, is returned to the calling context, the term-handling component.

This component looks for a multiplicative operator in the next token from the original expression. Since no such operator is found, the term handler passes the value on to its calling context, the expression handler.

This component looks for an additive operator, which it finds. This operator is saved along with the value that has already been returned (7.5), while the component evaluates the expression that should follow such an operator.

To parse the 5, the expression handler calls the term-handling component, which calls the factor-handling component, which, in turn, calls the subfactor component. Again, the resulting value is a constant, 5. This is returned to the factor-handling component, which returns it to the term-handling component, which returns it to the expression handler. At this point, the inner expression has been parsed. A calculator can now compute the sum, 12.5, resulting from evaluating the inner expression.

The expression handler returns this value to the calling context. Recall that in this case, the subfactor-handling routine made the call (to evaluate the expression within parentheses). This expression has been evaluated, the result being 12.5. The right parenthesis is discarded, and the subfactor-handling component can return the value of the subfactor. Before it does so, however, the value is multiplied by −1, since the entire subfactor has been evaluated.

At this time, the remaining expression is

```
* 3 / y
```

The −12.5 is returned to the factor handler, which passes it on to the term handler, since the next token is not an exponentiation operator. Thus, the −12.5 is passed to the term-handling component. This component stores the value and looks for a multiplicative operator. This time, the component finds the *. This operator is stored for eventual use, while the parser evaluates the term that should follow such an operator.

To do this, the parser tries to find a factor by first trying to find and return a subfactor. In this case, the result is 3, the value of the constant found by the subfactor component. The term component takes this result and multiplies it by the previously stored value, −12.5. The result, −37.5, is stored while the term-finding component looks for another multiplicative operator. The / is found and is stored while the component looks for a term.

To accomplish this, the parser tries to find a factor, first trying to find and return a subfactor. In this case, the subfactor component finds a **y**, which is identified as a variable. The parser gets the value associated with this variable—probably from information supplied with the expression—and returns the value. Suppose this value is 8. The subfactor component returns 8 to the factor-handling component, which returns the value to the term handler.

The term handler divides the −37.5 previously stored by the returned value, 8, for a result of −4.6875. The term handler then looks for another multiplicative operator. When none is found, the component returns the value −4.6875 to the expression handler. This component looks for another additive operator. Since none is found, the expression handler returns its value to the calling context as the value of the original expression.

The following listing shows the sequence of steps taken in parsing the expression. At each step, the listing shows the current token being processed, the remaining expression, the currently active handler (marked with an asterisk), and the current intermediate result.

token	curr express	express	term	factor	sub	result
-	(7.5+5)*3/y	*				
-	(7.5+5)*3/y		*			
-	(7.5+5)*3/y			*		
-	(7.5+5)*3/y				*	
(	7.5+5)*3/y				*	
7.5	+5)*3/y	*				
7.5	+5)*3/y		*			
7.5	+5)*3/y			*		
7.5	+5)*3/y				*	7.5
7.5	+5)*3/y			*		7.5
7.5	+5)*3/y		*			7.5
7.5	+5)*3/y	*				7.5
+	5)*3/y	*				
5	)*3/y	*				
5	)*3/y		*			
5	)*3/y			*		
5	)*3/y				*	5
5	)*3/y			*		5
5	)*3/y		*			5
5	)*3/y	*				5
5	)*3/y	*				12.5
)	*3/y				*	12.5
*	3/y				*	-12.5
*	3/y			*		-12.5
*	3/y		*			-12.5
3	/y		*			-12.5
3	/y			*		-12.5
3	/y				*	3
3	/y			*		3
3	/y		*			3
/	y		*			3
y			*			3
y				*		3
y					*	8
y				*		8
y			*			.375
			*			-4.6875
		*				-4.6875

Notice that the parser passes a token from the topmost production (expression) down until the token reaches a production that can handle it; thus, the minus sign is not processed until function **subfactor( )**.

After this operator has been processed, the parser finds the left parenthesis, at which point control jumps back out to **express( )**. This is the one place in the current grammar where such a long move occurs. To process the next token (7.5), the parser passes the token down again. This time, transfer of control is more orderly, as the result is passed back up to **express( )**.

Function **express( )** processes and stores the addition operator and then passes the next token down until it can be processed in **subfactor( )**. This token evaluates to 5, and the result is passed back up to **express( )**, which then adds its two elements to produce 12.5.

At that point, control passes to the calling function, which in this case was **subfactor( )** (because of the left parenthesis). Function **subfactor( )** discards the right parenthesis. Since the entire subfactor has now been processed, the function can return it—but only after multiplying the value by −1 (because of the unary negation operator that had been processed at the start of the expression).

This result, −12.5, is passed up until one of the productions can deal with the next token (*). Since function **term( )** handles multiplicative operators, that function continues the processing: It saves the operator and passes the next token down to be processed. Function **subfactor( )** eventually evaluates this token as 3 and passes the value back up.

When the value reaches function **term( )**, this function saves the value and keeps looking for multiplicative operators. In this case, the function finds the division operator (/), which it saves, and then passes the next token (**y**) down to be processed.

This token is eventually identified in **subfactor( )** as a variable with a value of 8. This result is once again returned up until it reaches **term( )**. Since there are no more multiplicative operators (or tokens of any kind, for that matter), **term( )** evaluates its most recent elements, 3/8. This quotient becomes the multiplier for the other computation **term( )** had on hold. The product of −12.5 ∗ .375, −4.6875, is passed to the calling function, which was **express( )**. At this point, **express( )**, finding nothing more to process, returns control to the calling function, which now has the value of the entire expression.

Notice that the term elements were evaluated from right to left; that is, 3 / y was evaluated before −12.5 ∗ 3. Recall that this is one of the features of the recursive descent parsing strategy you've been using.

Implementing a Parser

The following functions represent the heart of a parser that works with the grammar presented earlier and used in the preceding examples. The functions **express( )**, **term( )**, **factor( )**, and **subfactor( )** are responsible for processing nonterminals. The lower-level functions **constant( )**, **variable( )**, and **funct( )** are designed to return specific values to the **subfactor( )** function. Put these functions in a file called **parse.c**.

```
/* Parse.C: Expression parser functions.
   Functions work with the following grammar: */

<expression> := <term> |
                <term> + <expression> |
                <term> - <expression>

<term> := <factor> |
          <factor> * <term> |
          <factor> / <term>

<factor> := <subfactor> |
            <subfactor> ^ <factor>

<subfactor> := <constant> |
               <variable> |
               <function> |
               ( <expression> ) |
               - <subfactor>


<constant> := int | double

<variable> := letter

<function> := <identifier> ( {<subfactor>} {, <subfactor>} )
```

```
<identifier> := letter letter {letter}
*/

#define MAX_STR       100

#define NO_OP         0
#define ADD_OP        1
#define SUBT_OP       2
#define MULT_OP       4
#define DIV_OP        8
#define EXP_OP        16
#define L_PAREN       32
#define R_PAREN       64
#define FN_NAME       128
#define VAR_NAME      256
#define CONST_VAL     512

/* values for variable array */
extern double  var_vals [ 26];
extern int     tok_val;
extern int     size;



/* Function DECLARATIONS */
double express ( void);
double term ( void);
double factor ( void);
double subfactor ( void);
double funct ( void);
double variable ( void);
double constant ( void);


/*
   double express ()
   ***********************************************************
   Parse using expression production: term || term op expression

   CALLS : express (); get_token (); next_token (); term ();
   GLOBALS : ADD_OP, SUBT_OP, tok_val
   PARAMETERS : none
   RETURN : value of expression
   USAGE : result = express ();
   ***********************************************************
*/
double express ()
{
        double result;

        result = term ();              /* get first operand */
        tok_val = next_token (&size);  /* find out about next token */

        while ( ( tok_val == ADD_OP) || ( tok_val == SUBT_OP))
        {
                switch ( tok_val)   /* handle + and - differently */
                {
                        case ADD_OP :
                                get_token ( size);
                                tok_val = next_token (&size);
                                result += express ();
                                break;
```

```
                        case SUBT_OP :
                                get_token ( size);
                                tok_val = next_token ( &size);
                                result -= express ();
                                break;
                        default :
                                break;
                }   /* switch on tok_val */

                tok_val = next_token ( &size);
        }
        return ( result);
}


/*
    double term ()
    **********************************************************
    Parse term using production: factor || factor op term

    CALLS : factor (); get_token (); next_token (); term ();
    GLOBALS : DIV_OP, MULT_OP, tok_val
    PARAMETERS : none
    RETURN : value of term component
    USAGE : result = term ();
    **********************************************************
*/
double term ()
{
        double result;

        result = factor ();             /* get first operand */

        tok_val = next_token ( &size); /* find out about next token */

        while ( ( tok_val == MULT_OP) || ( tok_val == DIV_OP))
        {
                switch ( tok_val)   /* handle * and / differently */
                {
                        case MULT_OP :
                                get_token ( size);
                                tok_val = next_token ( &size);
                                result *= term ();
                                break;
                        case DIV_OP :
                                get_token ( size);
                                tok_val = next_token ( &size);
                                result = safe_division ( result,
                                                        term ());
                                break;
                        default :
                                break;
                }   /* switch on tok_val */

                tok_val = next_token ( &size);
        }
        return ( result);
}
```

```
/*
   double factor ()
   *********************************************************
   Parse factor using production: subfactor || subfactor op factor

   CALLS : factor (); get_token (); next_token ();
           pow (); subfactor ();
   GLOBALS : EXP_OP, tok_val
   PARAMETERS : none
   RETURN : value of factor component
   USAGE : result = factor ();
   *********************************************************
*/
double factor ()
{
        double result;

        result = subfactor ();
        tok_val = next_token ( &size);

        while ( tok_val == EXP_OP)
        {
                switch ( tok_val)
                {
                        case EXP_OP :
                                get_token ( size);
                                tok_val = next_token ( &size);
                                result = pow ( result, factor ());
                                break;
                        default :
                                break;
                }   /* switch on tok_val */

                tok_val = next_token ( & size);
        }
        return ( result);

}


/*
   double subfactor ()
   *********************************************************
   Parse subfactor using production:
   constant || variable || function || (expression) || "-" subfactor

   CALLS : constant (); express (); funct (); get_token ();
           next_token (); printf (); subfactor (); variable ();
   GLOBALS : CONST_VAL, FN_NAME, L_PAREN, R_PAREN, SUBT_OP,
             tok_val, VAR_NAME
   PARAMETERS : none
   RETURN : value of subfactor
   USAGE : result = subfactor ();
   *********************************************************
*/
double subfactor ()
{
        double result;
        int    coeff = 1;
```

```
        tok_val = next_token ( &size);

        if (tok_val  == SUBT_OP)
        {
                coeff = -1;
                get_token ( size);
                tok_val = next_token ( &size);
        }

    /* Treat each of the following differently:
       (, function call, variable name, number.
    */
        switch ( tok_val)
        {
                case L_PAREN :
                        get_token ( size);
                        /* printf ( "After removing (: %s : %s\n",
                                   curr_tok, exp_str); */
                        result = express ();
                        tok_val = next_token ( &size);
                        if ( tok_val != R_PAREN)
                                printf ( "Missing )\n");
                        else
                                get_token ( size);
                        break;
                case FN_NAME :
                        get_token ( size);
                        result = funct ();
                        break;
                case VAR_NAME :
                        get_token ( size);
                        result = variable ();
                        break;
                case CONST_VAL :
                        get_token ( size);
                        result = constant ();
                        break;
                default :
                        break;
        }  /* switch tok_val */

        return ( coeff * result);
}



/* This one is for you to implement
   double funct ()
   ********************************************************
   CALLS :
   GLOBALS :
   PARAMETERS :
   RETURN :
   USAGE :
   ********************************************************
*/
double funct ()
{
        /* your implementation goes here */
}
```

```
/*
   double constant ()
   ***********************************************************
   Determine value of and returns a constant element.

   CALLS : atof ();
   GLOBALS : curr_tok
   PARAMETERS : none
   RETURN : value of constant element.
   USAGE : my_const = constant ();
   ***********************************************************
*/
double constant ()
{
        double val;

        return ( atof ( curr_tok));
}


/*
   double variable ()
   ***********************************************************
   CALLS : var_info ();
   GLOBALS : curr_tok
   PARAMETERS : none
   RETURN : return the value associated with specified variable name
   USAGE : my_var = variable ();
   ***********************************************************
*/
double variable ()
{
        double value;

        value = var_info ( curr_tok);
        return ( value);
}
```

express( )

This function implements the definition of an expression; that is,
it finds terms, additive operators, and expressions. The function
first gets a term, assigning the term's value to **result**. Then,
express( ) processes elements in the expression as long as it finds
an additive operator as the next token.

The function processes and notes the operator. The value of the
element following the operator is added to or subtracted from
result, depending on the operator. The second operand is returned
from a call to **express( )** on the right side of a compound assignment statement, as in

```
result += express ();
```

The resulting sum (or difference) is returned when **express( )** returns control to the calling function.

The functions **next—token( )** and **get—tok( )** are used to move through the original expression. They are described later, and the listings for them are included.

term( )

This function uses the same strategy as **express( )**, except that **term( )** looks for multiplicative operators and calls **factor( )** and **term( )** for its operands. Thus, the function evaluates the first operand and stores the value in **result** temporarily.

While the remaining expression begins with a multiplicative operator, **term( )** removes the operator, noting its type. The function then multiplies or divides the value of **result** by the operand returned from the call to **term( )**. Function **term( )** returns the resulting product or quotient when it returns control to the calling function (usually **express( )** or another version of **term( )**).

factor( )

This function finds subfactors and handles the exponentiation operator. The strategy is the same as for **express( )** and **term( )**. Unlike those functions, however, **factor( )** needs to handle only one operator.

subfactor( )

This function returns actual values to the higher-level functions. Function **subfactor( )** first checks whether the current token is a unary negation operator (a minus sign). If so, the value of **coeff** is changed to −1, which will be used as a multiplier for the value to be returned before exiting function **subfactor( )** and returning to the calling function.

Notice that this function does not check for the binary subtraction operator. The grammar, sequence of calls, and descent rules ensure that only the **express( )** function handles subtraction operators.

Once **subfactor( )** has determined whether a minus sign is involved, it checks whether the next token is a left parenthesis, a function name, a variable name, or a constant (a numerical value).

If the next token is a left parenthesis, the function discards it and calls **express( )** to look for an expression. When control returns to the **subfactor( )** function after this expression is evaluated, that function removes and discards the right parenthesis from the remainder of the original expression.

If the next token is a function name, **subfactor( )** calls the routine you write to evaluate functions.

If the next token is a variable name, **subfactor( )** calls function **variable( )** to get the value associated with the specified variable.

If the next token is a constant, the function calls **constant( )** to evaluate the number. The value is stored in **result**, which will eventually be returned by **subfactor( )** to the calling function (usually **factor( )**).

variable( )

This function simply gets a value associated with the current variable and returns that value. The variable's value comes either from an array of values or from a separate string containing the values of each variable used in the expression. You may want to implement this process differently.

To do its work, **variable( )** calls function **var—info( )**. This latter function actually checks whether there is an array element or whether it's necessary to get a value from the "variable string," **var—str**.

You can combine functions **variable( )** and **var—info( )**, if you wish. The main reason for keeping them separate is to give you the option of changing the way variables are processed and values are determined without changing the communication between functions such as **subfactor( )** and **variable( )**.

funct( )

This is a routine you should write for yourself. It should be able to determine the values for each parameter passed between the parentheses or should call other routines that can. This will probably mean you'll want to call **expression( )** for the arguments to a function call.

You'll then need to identify the function requested, for example, sine, square root, tangent. Finally, to actually evaluate the function call, you'll need to carry out the computations required for the function. Some functions will require a simple call to Run-Time library routines; for others, you may have to do your own calculations.

constant( )

This function determines the numerical value of the current token and returns that value to the calling function.

The following listing contains a program to exercise the parser and also shows the code for the functions called by the parsing routines but not shown in the previous listing. The listing contains some general utility routines, which you'll probably want to put in your **utils.c** file.

```
/* Program to exercise parser.
   Grammar is in Parse.c
*/

#include <stdio.h>
#include <stdlib.h>
#include <string.h>
#include <ctype.h>
#include <math.h>
#include "defs.h"
#include "utils.c"

/* global definitions */
char    *exp_str, *var_str, curr_tok [ MAX_STR];
int     tok_val = 0, size;

/* values for variable array */
double  var_vals [ 26];

/* Function DECLARATIONS */
int     array_offset ( int);
void    get_token ( int);
int     next_token ( int *);
double  var_info ( char *);
int     non_zero ( double);
double  safe_division ( double, double);

#include "parse.c"

main ( int argc, char *argv [])
{
        int     index;
        double  outcome;
        char    vars [ MAX_STR], expr [ MAX_STR];
```

```
        do    /* loop while user enters an expression */
        {
                /* initialize variable array */
        for   (index = 0; index < 26; index++)
                        var_vals [ index] = 0.0;

                printf ( "? ");
                gets ( expr);           /* get expression */
                exp_str = expr;
                if ( argc > 1)          /* if user will use variables */
                {
                        printf ( "? ");
        gets ( vars);    /* get variable values */
                        var_str = vars;
                }

                printf ( "%s\n", exp_str);  /* show expression */
                printf ( "%s\n", var_str);  /* show variable values */

                outcome = express ();           /* parse and solve */
                printf ( "%.3lf\n", outcome);  /* display solution */
        }
        while ( strcmp (expr, null_str));
}


/*
   int  next_token ( int *places)
   **********************************************************
   CALLS : isalpha (); isdigit ();
   GLOBALS : ADD_OP, CONST_VAL, DIV_OP, EXP_OP, exp_str,
           FN_NAME, L_PAREN, MULT_OP, R_PAREN, SUBT_OP, VAR_NAME
   PARAMETERS :
           *places : a pointer to int representing the number
                     of places the token requires.
   RETURN : code for the token found
   USAGE : my_tok_info = next_token ( &tok_size);
   **********************************************************
*/
int  next_token ( int *places)
{
        int   type, index = 0, spaces = 0;

        while ( *exp_str == ' ')        /* remove leading blanks */
                exp_str++;

        curr_tok [ index] = *exp_str;  /* get first character */
        switch ( curr_tok [ index])
        {
                case '( ' :
                        type = L_PAREN;
                        spaces = 1;
                        break;
                case ')' :
                        type = R_PAREN;
                        spaces = 1;
                        break;
                case '+' :
                        type = ADD_OP;
                        spaces = 1;
                        break;
```

```
                    case '-' :
                            type = SUBT_OP;
                            spaces = 1;
                            break;
                    case '*' :
                            type = MULT_OP;
                            spaces = 1;
                            break;
                    case '/' :
                            type = DIV_OP;
                            spaces = 1;
                            break;
                    case '^' :
                            type = EXP_OP;
                            spaces = 1;
                            break;
                    default :
                            if ( isalpha ( curr_tok [ index]))
                            {
                                    if ( !isalpha ( *(exp_str + 1)))
                                    {
                                            type = VAR_NAME;
                                            spaces = 1;
                                    }
                                    else   /* if function name */
                                    {
                                            type = FN_NAME;
                                            spaces = 1;
                                            while (isalpha
                                                    (*(exp_str + spaces)))
                                                    spaces++;
                                    }
                            }
                            else if ( isdigit ( curr_tok [ index]) ||
                                    ( curr_tok [ index] == '..'))
                            {
                                    type = CONST_VAL;
                                    spaces = 1;
                                    while (isdigit(*(exp_str + spaces)) ||
                                            (*(exp_str + spaces) == '.'))
                                            spaces++;
                            }
                    }
            } /* switch */
            *places = spaces;
            return ( type);
    }


    /*
       int array_offset ( int ch)
       ****************************************************
       CALLS : tolower ();
       GLOBALS :
       PARAMETERS :
               ch : character whose value is sought.
       RETURN : array subscript for letter in which to seek value.
       USAGE : index = array_offset ( my_char);
       ****************************************************
    */
    int array_offset ( int ch)
    {
            return ( tolower (ch) - 'a');
    }
```

```
/*
   double var_info ( char *str)
   ************************************************************
   CALLS : array_offset (); atof (); non_zero (); remove_wd ();
            str_cpy ();
   GLOBALS : MAX_STR, var_vals [];
   PARAMETERS :
            str : the token for which a value is to be found.
   RETURN : value of the element identified by the token.
   USAGE : my_result = var_info ( my_str);
   ************************************************************
*/
double var_info ( char *str)
{
        int     index;
        char    temp [ MAX_STR];
        double result;

        index = array_offset ( str [ 0]);

        if ( non_zero ( var_vals [ index]))
                return ( var_vals [ index]);
        else
        {
                strcpy ( temp , remove_wd ( var_str));
                result = atof ( temp);
                var_vals [ index] = result;
                return ( result);
        }
}


/*
   void get_token ( int size)
   ************************************************************
   CALLS :
   GLOBALS :
   PARAMETERS :
            size : # of cells to get from the original expression.
   RETURN : none
   USAGE : get_token (23);
   ************************************************************
*/
void get_token ( int size)
{
        int index;

        for (index = 0; (index < size) && (*exp_str != '\0'); index++)
                curr_tok [ index] = *exp_str++;
        curr_tok [ index] = '\0';
}


/*
   double safe_division ( double numer, double denom)
   ************************************************************
   Divide num by denom, checking for division by zero before doing so.
   Return quotient or default value (INVALID_VAL) on division by zero.
   CALLS : non_zero ();
   GLOBALS : INVALID_VAL
   PARAMETERS :
            double numer : numerator of division expression;
            double denom : denominator of division expression.
   USAGE : quotient = safe_division ( numer, denom);
   ************************************************************
```

```
*/
double safe_division ( double numer, double denom)
{
        int non_zero ( double);

        if ( non_zero ( denom))
                return ( numer / denom);
        else
                return ( INVALID_VAL);
}



/*
   int non_zero ( double val)
   ************************************************************
   Return TRUE if value differs from 0 by more than a specified
   amount.

   CALLS :
   GLOBALS : FALSE, TOLERANCE, TRUE
   PARAMETERS :
        val : number to comapre with 0.
   RETURN : TRUE if value differs from 0 by more than TOLERANCE,
            false otherwise.
   USAGE :  my_int = non_zero ( my_dbl);
   ************************************************************
*/
int non_zero ( double val)
{
        if ( (( val - 0.0) > TOLERANCE) || ((val - 0.0) < -TOLERANCE))
                return ( TRUE);
        else
                return ( FALSE);
}
```

non—zero( )

This function returns TRUE if the argument differs by more than a predefined amount from 0.0 and FALSE if the argument differs by less than this amount. Such a function is essential when testing **double** values for equality. Two **double** values are equal only if their bit pattern representations are identical; this is extremely unlikely if the two values are the result of computations, in which frequent rounding occurs.

safe—division( )

This function divides the first argument (**numer**) by the second argument (**denom**) and returns the quotient. Before doing so, however, the function checks whether the denominator, **denom**, is 0; if it is, the function returns a predefined error value.

next_token( )

This function finds the next token in an expression string and returns the code for that token. The code specifies what the token's role is in the expression. The codes, which are generally assigned to the **int** variable, **tok_val**, are defined as preprocessor manifest constants. The function first removes any leading blanks, which means you can put blanks in your expressions to make them easier to read.

In the process of determining the token's code, **next_token( )** counts the number of characters in the token. This value is returned to the calling routine through a pointer parameter. The information is needed by function **get_token( )**, which actually removes the token from the original expression.

get_token( )

This function actually removes the desired number of characters from the remainder of the original expression. The number of characters to remove is passed in as the only argument. The function copies the characters removed to the variable **curr_tok**.

var_info( )

This function does the dirty work for function **variable( )**. Function **var_info( )** first checks whether the specified variable already has a value, in which case the value stored in the array **var_vals[]** is used. If the variable does not yet have a value, the function removes the first token from **var_str** and determines its numerical value. This value is returned to the calling routine and is used in subsequent computations.

array_offset( )

This very specialized function is used to compute the subscript value corresponding to the specified variable in the global array **var_vals[]**. Function **array_offset( )** determines the offset of the specified variable name from **a** to determine which array value to use.

main( )

The **main( )** function in the exerciser program loops to let you enter expressions and values for variables until you are done. You can evaluate expressions with or without variables. If you want to include variables in your expressions, call the program with a command line argument. The function uses **argc** to determine whether you will be entering a function string. If **argc** is greater than 1, the program assumes you want to include variables. Thus, any character after the program name will tell the program to expect a string containing values for the variables in the expression.

Using QuickC to Compile and
Run the Parser in Memory

One of QuickC's most attractive features is the capability for compiling a program to memory and running the program without making a permanent code file. This feature decreases the compilation time considerably. To take advantage of this, you'll need to have a Quick library that contains the Run-Time library functions (such as **pow( )**) not built into the QuickC environment. See Appendix B for a brief summary of how to build and use a Quick library and how to incorporate such libraries into your program when compiling to memory.

You can even set a Run-Time option to pass a command line argument to the program. To do this, press ALT-R O to call up the Run menu and to select the Run-Time Option. (That is, hold the ALT and R keys and press O.) Your cursor will be in the Command Line text box in the dialog box for Run-Time options. Just type the command line argument you want to use, and press RETURN. Once back in the editor, you can just press the F5 function key to continue compilation.

A Sample Session

The following program will provide a record of calls to the major parsing functions (**express( )**, **term( )**, **factor( )**, and **subfactor( )**)

```
? -(7.5 + x)*y/z
? 3 5 7
  starting express:
    starting term:
      starting factor:
        starting subfactor:
          starting express:
            starting term:
              starting factor:
                starting subfactor:
                result == 7.500
                leaving subfactor:
                result == 7.500
                result == 7.500
                leaving factor:
              result == 7.500
              result == 7.500
              leaving term:
            result == 7.500
              starting express:
                starting term:
                  starting factor:
                    starting subfactor:
                    result == 3.000
                    leaving subfactor:
                  result == 3.000
                  result == 3.000
                  leaving factor:
                result == 3.000
                result == 3.000
                leaving term:
              result == 3.000
              result == 3.000
              leaving express:
            result == 10.500
            leaving express:
          result == -10.500
          leaving subfactor:
        result == -10.500
        result == -10.500
        leaving factor:
      result == -10.500
        starting term:
          starting factor:
            starting subfactor:
```

Figure 5-1.   Sample output from "talking" parser

```
                    result == 5.000
                     leaving subfactor:
                   result == 5.000
                   result == 5.000
                   leaving factor:
                 result == 5.000
                   starting term:
                     starting factor:
                       starting subfactor:
                       result == 7.000
                       leaving subfactor:
                     result == 7.000
                     result == 7.000
                     leaving factor:
                   result == 7.000
                   result == 7.000
                   leaving term:
                 result == 0.714
                 leaving term:
               result == -7.500
               leaving term:
             result == -7.500
             result == -7.500
             leaving express:
           -7.500
```

Figure 5-1.   Sample output from "talking" parser (*continued*)

and of intermediate values while parsing an expression. To accomplish this, three utility functions have been added, along with calls to these functions in each of the parsing functions.

To provide additional information concerning level of nesting, the program includes an external variable, **level**, whose value represents the number of major parsing functions currently active or temporarily suspended. The value of **level** is increased by 1 each time a parsing function is activated and is decreased by 1 each time such a function ends. The display functions indent by an amount proportional to the current value of **level**. Figure 5-1 shows a sample run of the program.

```
/* Program to exercise parser, and display progress of parser. */

#include <stdio.h>
#include <stdlib.h>
#include <string.h>
#include <ctype.h>
#include <math.h>
#include "defs.h"
#include "utils.c"

#define MAX_STR        100

#define NO_OP           0
#define ADD_OP          1
#define SUBT_OP         2
#define MULT_OP         4
#define DIV_OP          8
#define EXP_OP         16
#define L_PAREN        32
#define R_PAREN        64
#define FN_NAME       128
#define VAR_NAME      256
#define CONST_VAL     512

/* global definitions */
char    *exp_str, *var_str, curr_tok [ MAX_STR];
int     tok_val = 0, size, level = 0;

/* initial values for variable array */
double  var_vals [ 26];

/* Function DECLARATIONS */
double express ( void);      /* changed from earlier parser program */
double term ( void);        /* changed from earlier parser program */
double factor ( void);      /* changed from earlier parser program */
double subfactor ( void);   /* changed from earlier parser program */
double funct ( void);
double variable ( void);
double constant ( void);
int     array_offset ( int);
void    get_token ( int);
int     next_token ( int *);
double var_info ( char *);
int     non_zero ( double);
double safe_division ( double, double);
void    enter ( char *);
void    leave ( char *);
void    qt ( double);

main ( int argc, char *argv [])
{
        int     index;
        double  outcome;
        char    vars [ MAX_STR], expr [ MAX_STR];

        do
        {
                for  (index = 0; index < 26; index++)
                        var_vals [ index] = 0.0;

                printf ( "? ");
```

```
                   gets ( expr);
                   exp_str = expr;
                   if ( argc > 1)
                   {
                           printf ( "? ");
                           gets ( vars);
                           var_str = vars;
                   }

                   printf ( "%s\n", exp_str);
                   printf ( "%s\n", var_str);

                   outcome = express ();
                   printf ( "%.3lf\n", outcome);
           }
        while ( strcmp (expr, null_str));
}


/*
   int  next_token ( int *places)
   ********************************************************
   CALLS : isalpha (); isdigit ();
   GLOBALS : ADD_OP, CONST_VAL, DIV_OP, EXP_OP, exp_str,
           FN_NAME, L_PAREN, MULT_OP, R_PAREN, SUBT_OP, VAR_NAME
   PARAMETERS :
           *places : a pointer to int representing the number
                     of places the token requires.
   RETURN : code for the token found
   USAGE : my_tok_info = next_token ( &tok_size);
   ********************************************************
*/
int  next_token ( int *places)
{
        int   type, index = 0, spaces = 0;

        while ( *exp_str == ' ')
                exp_str++;

        curr_tok [ index] = *exp_str;
        switch ( curr_tok [ index])
        {
                case '(' :
                        type = L_PAREN;
                        spaces = 1;
                        break;
                case ')' :
                        type = R_PAREN;
                        spaces = 1;
                        break;
                case '+' :
                        type = ADD_OP;
                        spaces = 1;
                        break;
                case '-' :
                        type = SUBT_OP;
                        spaces = 1;
                        break;
                case '*' :
                        type = MULT_OP;
                        spaces = 1;
                        break;
```

```
                case '/' :
                        type = DIV_OP;
                        spaces = 1;
                        break;
                case '^' :
                        type = EXP_OP;
                        spaces = 1;
                        break;
                default :
                        if ( isalpha ( curr_tok [ index]))
                        {
                                if ( !isalpha ( *(exp_str + 1)))
                                {
                                        type = VAR_NAME;
                                        spaces = 1;
                                }
                                else   /* if function name */
                                {
                                        type = FN_NAME;
                                        spaces = 1;
                                        while (isalpha
                                                (*(exp_str + spaces)))
                                                spaces++;
                                }
                        }
                        else if ( isdigit ( curr_tok [ index]) ||
                                ( curr_tok [ index] == '.'))
                        {
                                type = CONST_VAL;
                                spaces = 1;
                                while (isdigit(*(exp_str + spaces)) ||
                                        ( *(exp_str + spaces) == '.'))
                                        spaces++;
                        }
        }  /* switch */
        *places = spaces;
        return ( type);
}



/*
    int array_offset ( int ch)
    *********************************************************
    CALLS : tolower ();
    GLOBALS :
    PARAMETERS :
            ch : character whose value is sought.
    RETURN : array subscript for letter in which to seek value.
    USAGE : index = array_offset ( my_char);
    *********************************************************
*/
int array_offset ( int ch)
{
        return ( tolower (ch) - 'a');
}


/*
    double var_info ( char *str)
```

```
        ***********************************************************
        CALLS : array_offset (); atof (); non_zero (); remove_wd ();
                str_cpy ();
        GLOBALS : MAX_STR, var_vals [];
        PARAMETERS :
                str : the token for which a value is to be found.
        RETURN : value of the element identified by the token.
        USAGE : my_result = var_info ( my_str);
        ***********************************************************
*/
double var_info ( char *str)
{
        int     index;
        char    temp [ MAX_STR];
        double result;

        index = array_offset ( str [ 0]);

        if ( non_zero ( var_vals [ index]))
                return ( var_vals [ index]);
        else
        {
                strcpy ( temp , remove_wd ( var_str));
                result = atof ( temp);
                var_vals [ index] = result;
                return ( result);
        }
}


/*
    void get_token ( int size)
    ***********************************************************
    CALLS :
    GLOBALS :
    PARAMETERS :
            size : # of cells to get from the original expression.
    RETURN : none
    USAGE : get_token (23);
    ***********************************************************
*/
void get_token ( int size)
{
        int index;

        for (index = 0; (index < size) && (*exp_str != '\0'); index++)
                curr_tok [ index] = *exp_str++;
        curr_tok [ index] = '\0';
}


/*
    double safe_division ( double numer, double denom)
    ***********************************************************
    Divide num by denom, checking for division by zero before doing so.
    Return quotient or default value (INVALID_VAL) on division by zero.
    CALLS : non_zero ();
    GLOBALS : INVALID_VAL
    PARAMETERS :
            double numer : numerator of division expression;
            double denom : denominator of division expression.
    USAGE : quotient = safe_division ( numer, denom);
    ***********************************************************
```

```
*/
double safe_division ( double numer, double denom)
{
        int non_zero ( double);

        if ( non_zero ( denom))
                return ( numer / denom);
        else
                return ( INVALID_VAL);
}



/*
   int non_zero ( double val)
   ************************************************************
   Return TRUE if value differs from 0 by more than a specified
   amount.

   CALLS :
   GLOBALS : FALSE, TOLERANCE, TRUE
   PARAMETERS :
       val : number to comapre with 0.
   RETURN : TRUE if value differs from 0 by more than TOLERANCE,
            false otherwise.
   USAGE :  my_int = non_zero ( my_dbl);
   ************************************************************
*/
int non_zero ( double val)
{
        if ( (( val - 0.0) > TOLERANCE) || ((val - 0.0) < -TOLERANCE))
                return ( TRUE);
        else
                return ( FALSE);
}



/*
   double funct ()
   ************************************************************
   CALLS :
   GLOBALS :
   PARAMETERS :
   RETURN :
   USAGE :
   ************************************************************
*/
double funct ()
{
        /* Your code here */
}



/*
   double constant ()
   ************************************************************
   Determine value of and returns a constant element.

   CALLS : atof ();
   GLOBALS : curr_tok
   PARAMETERS : none
   RETURN : value of constant element.
   USAGE : my_const = constant ();
   ************************************************************
```

```
*/
double constant ()
{
        double val;

        return ( atof ( curr_tok));
}


/*
   double variable ()
   ********************************************************
   CALLS : var_info ();
   GLOBALS : curr_tok
   PARAMETERS : none
   RETURN : return the value associated with specified variable name
   USAGE : my_var = variable ();
   ********************************************************
*/
double variable ()
{
        double value;

        value = var_info ( curr_tok);
        return ( value);
}


/* ************ Functions changed from earlier program ************ */

/*
   double express ()
   ********************************************************
   Parse using expression production: term || term op expression

   CALLS : express (); get_token (); next_token (); term ();
   GLOBALS : ADD_OP, SUBT_OP, tok_val
   PARAMETERS : none
   RETURN : value of expression
   USAGE : result = express ();
   ********************************************************
*/
double express ()
{
        double result;

        level++;
        enter( "express");
        result = term ();
        qt ( result);
        tok_val = next_token (&size);

        while ( ( tok_val == ADD_OP) || ( tok_val == SUBT_OP))
        {
                switch ( tok_val)
                {
                        case ADD_OP :
                                get_token ( size);
                                tok_val = next_token (&size);
                                result += express ();
                                break;
                        case SUBT_OP :
                                get_token ( size);
                                tok_val = next_token ( &size);
```

```
                                      result -= express ();
                                      break;
                          default :
                                      break;
                   }   /* switch on tok_val */

                   tok_val = next_token ( &size);
          }
          qt ( result);
          leave ( "express");
          level--;
          return ( result);
}



/*
   double term ()
   ***********************************************************
   Parse term using production: factor || factor op term

   CALLS : factor (); get_token (); next_token (); term ();
   GLOBALS : DIV_OP, MULT_OP, tok_val
   PARAMETERS : none
   RETURN : value of term component
   USAGE : result = term ();
   ***********************************************************
*/
double term ()
{
        double result;

        level++;
        enter( "term");
        result = factor ();
        qt ( result);
        tok_val = next_token ( &size);

        while ( ( tok_val == MULT_OP) || ( tok_val == DIV_OP))
        {
                switch ( tok_val)
                {
                        case MULT_OP :
                                get_token ( size);
                                tok_val = next_token ( &size);
                                result *= term ();
                                break;
                        case DIV_OP :
                                get_token ( size);
                                tok_val = next_token ( &size);
                                result = safe_division ( result,
                                                          term ());
                                break;
                        default :
                                break;
                }   /* switch on tok_val */

                tok_val = next_token ( &size);
        }
        qt ( result);
        leave ( "term");
        level--;
        return ( result);
}
```

```
/*
   double factor ()
   ************************************************************
   Parse factor using production: subfactor || subfactor op factor

   CALLS : factor (); get_token (); next_token ();
           pow (); subfactor ();
   GLOBALS : EXP_OP, tok_val
   PARAMETERS : none
   RETURN : value of factor component
   USAGE : result = factor ();
   ************************************************************
*/
double factor ()
{
        double result;
        /* int    tok_val; */

        level++;
        enter( "factor");
        result = subfactor ();
        qt ( result);
        tok_val = next_token ( &size);

        while ( tok_val == EXP_OP)
        {
                switch ( tok_val)
                {
                        case EXP_OP :
                                get_token ( size);
                                tok_val = next_token ( &size);
                                result = pow ( result, factor ());
                                break;
                        default :
                                break;
                }   /* switch on tok_val */

                tok_val = next_token ( & size);
        }
        qt ( result);
        leave ( "factor");
        level--;
        return ( result);
}


/*
   double subfactor ()
   ************************************************************
   Parse subfactor using production:
   constant || variable || function || (expression) || "-" subfactor

   CALLS : constant (); express (); funct (); get_token ();
           next_token (); printf (); subfactor (); variable ();
   GLOBALS : CONST_VAL, FN_NAME, L_PAREN, R_PAREN, SUBT_OP,
             tok_val, VAR_NAME
   PARAMETERS : none
   RETURN : value of subfactor
   USAGE : result = subfactor ();
   ************************************************************
*/
```

```
double subfactor ()
{
        double result;
        /* int    tok_val; */
        int    coeff = 1;

        level++;
        enter( "subfactor");
        tok_val = next_token ( &size);


        if (tok_val  == SUBT_OP)
        {
                coeff = -1;
                get_token ( size);
                tok_val = next_token ( &size);
                /* result = subfactor (); */
        }

        switch ( tok_val)
        {
                case L_PAREN :
                        get_token ( size);
                        /* printf ( "After removing (: %s : %s\n",
                                    curr_tok, exp_str); */
                        result = express ();
                        tok_val = next_token ( &size);
                        if ( tok_val != R_PAREN)
                                printf ( "Missing )\n");
                        else
                                get_token ( size);
                        break;
                case FN_NAME :
                        get_token ( size);
                        result = funct ();
                        break;
                case VAR_NAME :
                        get_token ( size);
                        result = variable ();
                        break;
                case CONST_VAL :
                        get_token ( size);
                        result = constant ();
                        break;
                default :
                        break;
        } /* switch tok_val */

        qt ( coeff * result);
        leave ( "subfactor");
        level--;
        return ( coeff * result);
}


/* ***** Functions for displaying program execution ***** */

/*
   void enter ( char *str)
```

```
     **********************************************************
     Display function name upon entry, indent depending on level.

     CALLS : printf ();
     GLOBALS :
     PARAMETERS :
             str : name of routine in which this is being called.
     RETURN :  none
     USAGE : enter ( "my_routine");
     **********************************************************
*/
void enter ( char *str)
{
        int index;

        for ( index = 0; index < level; index++)
                printf ( "  ");
        printf ( "starting %s:\n", str);
}


/*
    void leave ( char *str)
    **********************************************************
    Display function name upon exit, indent depending on level.

    CALLS : printf ();
    GLOBALS :
    PARAMETERS :
            str : name of routine in which this is being called.
    RETURN :  none
    USAGE : leave ( "my_routine");
    **********************************************************
*/
void leave ( char *str)
{
        int index;

        for ( index = 0; index < level; index++)
                printf ( "  ");
        printf ( "leaving %s:\n", str);
}


/*
    void qt ( double val)
    **********************************************************
    Print value of parameter, indent depending on level.

    CALLS : printf ();
    GLOBALS :
    PARAMETERS :
            val : value to display.
    RETURN : none
    USAGE : qt, val_to_show);
    **********************************************************
*/
void qt ( double val)
{
        int  index;

        for ( index = 0; index < level; index++)
                printf ( "  ");
        printf ( "result == %.3lf\n", val);
}
```

enter( ) and leave( )

These functions display a message and the function name on entering and leaving a parsing function, respectively. The functions indent the message by an amount proportional to the current value of the external variable, **level**.

qt( )

This function displays the current value of the parameter passed in. The function also indents an amount proportional to the value of **level**.

Extending the Parser

Let's add more operators to the parser to illustrate one way of extending the grammar. You'll add the binary logical operators AND (&&) and OR (||). Assume these operators have lower precedence than any of the operators the current version of the parser can handle, just as they do in C. Furthermore, assume that the logical AND operator has higher precedence than the logical OR operator.

This means you'll want the parser to resolve expressions involving AND operators after dealing with expressions containing arithmetic operators. Similarly, you'll want to resolve OR operators after dealing with operands connected by AND operators. We'll use *conjuncts* as the name for operands connected by AND operators and *disjuncts* to refer to operands connected by OR operators.

By the reasoning used earlier, this means you'll want to define disjuncts at the top of the grammar and conjuncts just below them. Thus, you'll need to add the following two productions to the grammar:

```
<disjunct> := <conjunct> ||
              <conjunct>  "||" <disjunct>

<conjunct> := <expression> ||
              <expression>  "&&" <conjunct>
```

To process the new operators, you'll need to add preprocessor definitions for AND—OP and OR—OP. You'll also need functions for processing conjuncts and disjuncts corresponding to the new productions. The **next—token( )** function needs to know about the new operators as well. Instead of calling **express( )** after a left parenthesis in **subfactor( )**, the function now needs to call **disjunct( )**. Note that this changes the production for a subfactor to the following, in which a disjunct is substituted for an expression:

```
<subfactor> := <constant> ||
               <variable> ||
               <function call> ||
               "(" <disjunct> ")" ||
               "-" <subfactor>
```

Finally, the main program must start its parsing by calling **disjunct( )**, which will call **conjunct( )**, which, in turn, will call **express( )**.

The following listing shows the functions and definitions that were added or changed when the binary logical operators were added to the grammar. The listing also contains two preprocessor definitions that you will need to add to your parser.

```
/* Functions for parsing binary logical operators.
   The following functions must be added or changed from the
   original parser. The new functions, conjunct () and
   disjunct (), must also be declared.
*/

#define AND_OP    1024
#define OR_OP     2048

/* New Function DECLARATIONS */
double  conjunct (void);
double  disjunct (void);

main ( int argc, char *argv [])
{
        int     index;
        double  outcome;
        char    vars [ MAX_STR], expr [ MAX_STR];

        do
        {
                for (index = 0; index < 26; index++)
                    var_vals [ index] = 0.0;

                printf ( "? ");
                gets ( expr);
```

```
                    exp_str = expr;
                    if ( argc > 1)
                    {
                            printf ( "? ");
                            gets ( vars);
                            var_str = vars;
                    }

                    printf ( "expression: %s\n", exp_str);
                    printf ( "variables: %s\n", var_str);

                    outcome = disjunct ();
                    printf ( "%.3lf\n", outcome);
            }
            while ( strcmp (expr, null_str));
    }


/*
    double subfactor ()
    ************************************************************
    Parse subfactor using production:
    constant || variable || function || (expression) || "-" subfactor

    CALLS : constant (); disjunct (); funct (); get_token ();
            next_token (); printf (); subfactor (); variable ();
    GLOBALS : CONST_VAL, FN_NAME, L_PAREN, R_PAREN, SUBT_OP,
              tok_val, VAR_NAME
    PARAMETERS : none
    RETURN : value of subfactor
    USAGE : result = subfactor ();
    ************************************************************
*/
double subfactor ()
{
        double result;
        /* int      tok_val; */
        int     coeff = 1;

        tok_val = next_token ( &size);


        if (tok_val   == SUBT_OP)
        {
                coeff = -1;
                get_token ( size);
                tok_val = next_token ( &size);
                /* result = subfactor (); */
        }

        switch ( tok_val)
        {
                case L_PAREN :
                        get_token ( size);
                        /* printf ( "After removing (: %s : %s\n",
                                curr_tok, exp_str); */
                        result = disjunct ();
                        tok_val = next_token ( &size);
                        if ( tok_val != R_PAREN)
                                printf ( "Missing )\n");
                        else
                                get_token ( size);
                        break;
```

```
                    case FN_NAME :
                            get_token ( size);
                            result = funct ();
                            break;
                    case VAR_NAME :
                            printf ( "VAR_NAME\n");
                            get_token ( size);
                            result = variable ();
                            printf ( "result = %.3lf\n", result);
                            break;
                    case CONST_VAL :
                            get_token ( size);
                            result = constant ();
                            break;
                    default :
                            break;
            } /* switch tok_val */

            return ( coeff * result);
}


/*
    int  next_token ( int *places)
    ********************************************************
    CALLS : isalpha (); isdigit ();
    GLOBALS : ADD_OP, AND_OP, CONST_VAL, DIV_OP, EXP_OP, exp_str,
              FN_NAME, L_PAREN, MULT_OP, OR_OP, R_PAREN,
              SUBT_OP, VAR_NAME
    PARAMETERS :
            *places : a pointer to int representing the number
                      of places the token requires.
    RETURN : code for the token found
    USAGE : my_tok_info = next_token ( &tok_size);
    ********************************************************
*/
int  next_token ( int *places)
{
        int  type, index = 0, spaces = 0;

        while ( *exp_str == ' ')
                exp_str++;

        curr_tok [ index] = *exp_str;
        switch ( curr_tok [ index])
        {
                case '(' :
                        type = L_PAREN;
                        spaces = 1;
                        break;
                case ')' :
                        type = R_PAREN;
                        spaces = 1;
                        break;
                case '+' :
                        type = ADD_OP;
                        spaces = 1;
                        break;
```

```
            case '-' :
                    type = SUBT_OP;
                    spaces = 1;
                    break;
            case '*' :
                    type = MULT_OP;
                    spaces = 1;
                    break;
            case '/' :
                    type = DIV_OP;
                    spaces = 1;
                    break;
            case '^' :
                    type = EXP_OP;
                    spaces = 1;
                    break;
            case '&' :
                    if ( *(exp_str + 1) == '&')
                    {
                            type = AND_OP;
                            spaces = 2;
                    }
            case '|' :
                    if ( *(exp_str + 1) == '|')
                    {
                            type = OR_OP;
                            spaces = 2;
                    }
            default :
                    if ( isalpha ( curr_tok [ index]))
                    {
                            if ( !isalpha ( *(exp_str + 1)))
                            {
                                    type = VAR_NAME;
                                    spaces = 1;
                            }
                            else   /* if function name */
                            {
                                    type = FN_NAME;
                                    spaces = 1;
                                    while (isalpha
                                            (*(exp_str + spaces)))
                                            spaces++;
                            }
                    }
                    else if ( isdigit ( curr_tok [ index]) ||
                        ( curr_tok [ index] == '.'))
                    {
                            type = CONST_VAL;
                            spaces = 1;
                            while (isdigit(*(exp_str + spaces)) ||
                                    ( *(exp_str + spaces) == '.'))
                                    spaces++;
                    }
      } /* switch */
      *places = spaces;
      return ( type);
}
```

```
/*
   double conjunct ()
   **********************************************************
   Parse conjunct using production: disjunct || disjunct op conjunct

   CALLS : conjunct (); disjunct (); get_token (); next_token ();
   GLOBALS : AND_OP, tok_val
   PARAMETERS : none
   RETURN : value of factor component
   USAGE : result = factor ();
   **********************************************************
*/
double conjunct ()
{
        double result;
        long int   temp_val;
        /* int     tok_val; */

        result = express ();
        temp_val = (long) result;
        tok_val = next_token ( &size);

        while ( tok_val == AND_OP)
        {
                switch ( tok_val)
                {
                        case AND_OP :
                                get_token ( size);
                                tok_val = next_token ( &size);
                                result = conjunct ();
                                if ( temp_val && non_zero ( result))
                                        temp_val = TRUE;
                                else
                                        temp_val = FALSE;
                                result = (double) temp_val;
                                break;
                        default :
                                break;
                }   /* switch on tok_val */

                tok_val = next_token ( &size);
        }
        return ( result);
}

/*
   double disjunct ()
   **********************************************************
   Parse disjunct using production: disjunct || disjunct op disjunct

   CALLS : disjunct (); express (); get_token (); next_token ();
   GLOBALS : OR_OP, tok_val
   PARAMETERS : none
   RETURN : value of factor component
   USAGE : result = factor ();
   **********************************************************
*/
double disjunct ()
{
        double result;
        long int   temp_val;
        /* int     tok_val; */
```

```
    result = conjunct ();
    temp_val = (long) result;
    tok_val = next_token ( &size);

    while ( tok_val == OR_OP)
    {
            switch ( tok_val)
            {
                    case OR_OP :
                            get_token ( size);
                            tok_val = next_token ( &size);
                            result = disjunct ();
                            if ( temp_val || non_zero ( result))
                                    temp_val = TRUE;
                            else
                                    temp_val = FALSE;
                            result = (double) temp_val;
                            break;
                    default :
                            break;
            }   /* switch on tok_val */

            tok_val = next_token ( &size);
    }
    return ( result);
}
```

Tasks and Suggestions

You can modify and extend the parser in various ways. In this section, you'll find suggestions for such extensions.

New Operators

One direction would be to add other operators, such as the modulus operator (%), logical and bitwise operators, and perhaps even an assignment operator. To do this, you would need to decide on the precedence for the new operators. Then you would need to add new components to the grammar, along with the productions needed to define these new components. The amount and type of modifications you'll need to make in the current version of the parser will depend on the operators and their precedence.

For example, you added binary logical operators (&&, ||) above and decided to give them lower precedence than the operators in the current grammar. You needed to modify the grammar by adding two productions. You also needed to add some functions and modify others.

For other operators, the required changes might be less drastic. For example, you might add a unary logical negation operator, giving it the same precedence as the unary arithmetic operator, or minus sign; that is, you would be adding a new operator but no new precedence levels. In that case, you would need to change function **subfactor( )** and function **next_token( )** to recognize and deal with this new operator.

Similarly, you might include the modulus operator among the multiplicative operators. In that case, functions **term( )** and **next_token( )** would need to be modified. Any time you add a new operator, you will need to add a preprocessor definition to represent the code for the new operator.

Showing and Saving Intermediate Values

It is fairly straightforward to show the value of an element or computation just as the value is being returned. If all you want to do is display a value, the task is simple; if you also want to display the partial expression whose value is being returned, the task becomes a bit more challenging, since you need to keep track, not only of the remaining part of the original expression, but also of the expression portion whose value is being displayed.

You can go even further and provide a means for storing these intermediate values, perhaps for later use. Again, the simple way is just to write each result to a file. A more complex approach would be to let the user provide a name for the value being saved so that other programs might be able to read the value of the result when necessary.

Looping on an Expression

For certain tasks, it's very useful to be able to repeat a computation over and over, with slight variations. You often see such loops in C programs. Here, however, we're talking about mathematical or logical expressions.

For example, suppose you wanted to generate a truth table for a logical statement involving some variables. This table would record whether the equation were TRUE or FALSE for each combination of variable truth values.

Similarly, suppose you wanted your calculator to generate a table showing the first 10 Fibonacci numbers. You could simply loop in an equation for generating Fibonacci numbers.

Named Formulas

Sometimes the computation for a particular function may be too complex to put into your original expression. In such a case, you can either put more of the information and work into your function-handling routine or provide a name for the required computation. Associated with this name would be the expression needed to carry out the desired task. When the calculator encountered a reference to such a function, it should get the expression and substitute it for the function call in the original expression at run time.

For example, suppose you needed to use the following formula for computing a distance between two points in an expression:

```
/* 3-dimensional distance formula. */

dist ( a, b, c, d, e, f) := sqrt ( (a-b)^2 + (c-d)^2 + (e-f)^2 )

/*
a:= ending x-coordinate
b:= starting x-coordinate

c:= ending y-coordinate
d:= starting y-coordinate

e:= ending z-coordinate
f:= starting z-coordinate
*/
```

This entire formula might be too long to include in your original expression. You could extend the parser to use the formula name, let's say **dist**, to find the expansion of this name and substitute the expanded version during the parsing process.

You can even make the calculator able to write or search files for such named formulas.

Error Handling

The current versions of the parser do no error checking on your expression. This means you will need to be certain the expression is valid if you expect to get a meaningful answer from the parser.

You should add error-checking capabilities to your parser.

You will need to decide what types of errors to look for and how to deal with them. At one extreme, the parser can simply stop as soon as it finds an error. At the other extreme, the parser may collect a catalog of errors, which it displays for you at the end of the parsing. At that point, you may want to have the parser let you enter the expression again.

SUMMARY

In this chapter, you learned about one common approach to parsing expressions: breaking an expression down into constituent parts based on a grammar that defines each of the parts. You saw how to build a very simple parser for sentences, and you built several versions of a parser for mathematical expressions.

Parsing is a much-studied activity, and there are numerous other approaches to parser design. Consult books on compiler construction to find out more about strategies for parsing. If you're interested in this topic, you should look into a program named **yacc** ("yet another compiler compiler"), which is used to generate parsers. The program is available in several versions. A public domain version is available on bulletin boards or from the C Users Group, P.O. Box 97, McPherson, Kansas 67460.

In the next chapter you'll look at various methods for transforming, compressing, and encrypting data.

6

DATA COMPRESSION
AND ENCRYPTION

Over the years, much work has been done on developing techniques for transforming data for different purposes. For example, data compression methods have been developed to make it possible to transmit long files more quickly and less expensively; data encryption algorithms have been developed to make the contents of a file readable only to those who know the algorithm underlying the encryption. Data encryption is a very active research area that has also prompted a great deal of work in the branch of mathematics called numerical analysis.

In this chapter, you'll look at a few simple data compression techniques. You'll find programs that will let you squeeze a file's contents into less space. You'll also look at some simple encryption strategies to let you transform your text files into encoded messages.

COMPRESSION
STRATEGIES

There are many approaches you can take to compressing text so that a message or a file takes less space. Some strategies rely on specialized knowledge (generally about a particular content area), and compress material by abbreviating specialized or common terms. For example, in medical papers you may find *EEG* instead of *electroencephalogram*, and in chemistry you may find *ADP* for *adenosine diphosphate*. Such a strategy is unlikely to shorten a document substantially, however. Moreover, it generally requires someone familiar with the content to "decompress" the material.

Other strategies shorten text by dropping certain letters or types of letters. For example, stenographers will often leave vowels or other letters out when taking notes. The following listing shows a paragraph followed by the same paragraph compressed using this approach. The compressed version of the paragraph is about two-thirds of the original length.

```
Can you read this sentence without difficulty? The next version
may take you much longer to read, since some of the characters have
been removed.
```

```
Cn u rd ths sntnc wtht dfclty? Th nxt vrsn may tk u mch lngr to rd,
snc som of th chrctrs hv bn rmvd.
```

Such a "stenography" approach can compress a message by a considerable amount. The compression technique essentially takes advantage of the fact that English text is generally redundant; that is, there is more information than you need to decipher a message. However, the compression strategy may vary, depending on context. For example, *hrs* might represent "horse" in one context, "hours" in another, and "Horus" in a third. Thus, it may be impossible to specify an exact algorithm that will handle all the cases.

You'll often need to modify or at least read the contents of a compressed file. Generally, you will want to work with the non-compressed version, that is, with the original, full message. It will be difficult—probably impossible—for a program to reconstruct the original material from a stenographer's version of the message, since the program would have to know about words and would even need some way of deciding which of two possible words was correct in a particular message.

Removing Spaces from a Text File

Other approaches compress a file more systematically, using strategies much easier to implement and much easier to reverse. For example, you might remove each space from a message, marking the removal by some means. One clever way of doing this was described by Joseph Sant in a *Computer Language* article ("A Simple Data Compression Technique," March 1987).

The strategy takes advantage of the fact that a simple ASCII text file contains only characters with codes up to 127, whereas you can store values up to 255 in the eight bits generally allocated for a character. If a character in your original file is followed by a space, 128 is added to the character's code, and the space is discarded. Characters not followed by a space are left unchanged. This simple technique can reduce the size of a file by a substantial amount.

When you use this strategy with a text file, the input file should contain only simple ASCII characters, between 0 and 127. The output file will contain a certain number of characters with codes above 127. Essentially, these "high," or extended, characters will consist of an ordinary character with a special marker—the leftmost bit being turned on—indicating that a space used to follow the character.

The following program lets you use this strategy to compress a text file. Function **despace( )** processes the file.

```
/* Program to compress a text file by removing spaces,
   and setting high-order bit of preceding character.
   File must be decompressed, or expanded using function enspace().
*/

#include <stdio.h>
#include <string.h>

#define SPACE_CHR        ' '    /* char to remove during compression */

void  despace ( FILE *, FILE *, long int *, long int *);

/* replace spaces in an ASCII text file with a marker on
   the character preceding the space
```

```
*/
void  despace ( FILE *src_ptr, FILE *target_ptr,
                long int *rd, long int *wrt)
{
        int    curr_ch, next_ch, ch;

        *rd = 0;
        *wrt = 0;
    /* remove leading blanks */
        while ( ((curr_ch = fgetc ( src_ptr)) == SPACE_CHR) &&
                   !feof ( src_ptr))
        {
                curr_ch = fgetc ( src_ptr);
                (*rd)++;
        }

    /* work as long as there are characters in source file */
        for ( ; !feof ( src_ptr); )
        {
                next_ch = getc ( src_ptr);
                (*rd)++;
                if ( next_ch == EOF) /* if source file done */
                {
                    /* write last character */
                        ch = putc ( curr_ch, target_ptr);
                        (*wrt)++;
                        continue;
                }
                if ( next_ch == SPACE_CHR)
                {
                    /* mark previous char, discard space */
                        curr_ch |= 128;
                    /* write modified character */
                        ch = fputc ( curr_ch, target_ptr);
                        (*wrt)++;
                    /* get another character */
                        curr_ch = fgetc ( src_ptr);
                        (*rd)++;
                }   /* if next character is a space */
                else   /* if not a space, write char */
                {
                        ch = fputc ( curr_ch, target_ptr);
                        (*wrt)++;
                    /* non-space becomes next char */
                        curr_ch = next_ch;
                }   /* if not a space */
        }    /* while source file is not empty */
}


main ( int argc, char *argv [])
{
        FILE       *src_ptr, *target_ptr;
        long int   nr_read, nr_written;

        if (argc <= 2)   /* if too few parameters */
        {
                printf ( "Usage: despace <source> <target>\n");
                exit ( 1);
```

```
      }
      else    /* if user provided two file names */
      {
          /* open source file */
             src_ptr = fopen ( argv [ 1], "r");
             if ( src_ptr == NULL)
             {
                    printf ( "Source file not found\n");
                    exit ( 1);
             }

          /* open output file */
             target_ptr = fopen ( argv [ 2], "w");
             if ( target_ptr == NULL)
             {
                    printf ( "Target file not be opened\n");
                    exit ( 1);
             }

          /* remove spaces from source file, write to target. */
             despace ( src_ptr, target_ptr, &nr_read, &nr_written);

             fclose ( target_ptr);
             fclose ( src_ptr);
      }
      printf ( "%ld chars read; %ld chars written\n",
             nr_read, nr_written);
}
```

despace( )

This function actually transfers the contents of one text file to a second file. In the process, spaces and the characters preceding them are replaced by extended characters.

The function first removes any leading blanks. After that, the function keeps processing until the file referenced by **src_ptr** is finished. The **feof( )** routine is a Run-Time library macro that returns a nonzero value if the end of the file passed as an argument has been reached.

Once the function has a nonspace character in **curr_ch**, the next character is read from the source file. If **next_ch** is a space, the bitwise OR operator (|) is used to mark **curr_ch**. This operator is used to turn the high order bit to 1 in **curr_ch**. The function then writes the new value of **curr_ch** to the target file.

If **next_ch** is not a space, then the function writes **curr_ch** unchanged to the target file. The **next_ch** then becomes the **curr_ch**, and the function gets a new value for **next_ch**.

The function also keeps track of the number of characters read from the source file and the number written to the target file. These numbers will tell you how much space you save by removing the space character. Notice that the counter parameters are **long int** rather than just **int**: The maximum integer value (32,767) on a PC is not very large and is easily exceeded even by moderately short files.

You'll notice that the function reports reading a different number of characters than DOS claims the file has. This discrepancy has to do with the way DOS stores the end-of-line information. The percentages in this chapter are based on the number of characters the function claims to count.

The current version of **despace( )** does not know how to handle multiple spaces in succession; thus, it removes at most one space at a time, except at the very start of the file. You may want to modify the function to discard repeated spaces.

Function **despace( )** assumes the source file is a genuine ASCII file. The function does not check whether the source file already contains extended characters. Modify the function to add such a check.

Function **despace( )** reduced the size of the text file for Chapter 5 by about 17%. Depending on the file, you may reduce the size of your file by as much as 20%. Generally, however, the reduction is more likely to be in the 15% to 18% range.

The output file from function **despace( )** is not a simple ASCII file: It will contain graphics characters from the extended character set on your computer. If you look at the file with your QuickC editor, you will see all sorts of unusual characters.

Restoring Spaces to a Compressed File

You will need to put spaces back into a decompressed file before you can edit it with an ordinary text editor, such as the QuickC editor. The following program contains a function, **enspace( )**, that replaces the extended characters in the file with ASCII characters and spaces.

```
/* Program to restore spaces to a compressed file.
   File must have been created using function despace ().
*/

#include <stdio.h>
#include <string.h>

#define SPACE_CHR      ' '        /* char restore during expansion */

void enspace ( FILE *, FILE *, long int *, long int *);


/* Restore spaces to a compressed file, by reconverting an
   extended ASCII character to a regular ASCII character
   followed by a space.
*/
void enspace ( FILE *src_ptr, FILE *target_ptr,
               long int *rd, long int *wrt)
{
        int        curr_ch, next_ch, ch;

        *rd = 0;
        *wrt = 0;
    /* while not at the end of the compressed file */
        for ( ; !feof ( src_ptr); )
        {
                curr_ch = fgetc ( src_ptr);  /* read char */
                (*rd)++;
                if ( curr_ch == EOF)    /* don't process if EOF */
                        continue;
                if ( curr_ch > 128)     /* if high-order bit is on */
                {
                        /* curr_ch & 127 sets high-order bit to 0,
                           which leaves original character.
                        */
                        ch = fputc ( curr_ch & 127, target_ptr);
                        (*wrt)++;
                        /* add space indicated by high-order bit */
                        ch = fputc ( SPACE_CHR, target_ptr);
                        (*wrt)++;
                }      /* if high-order bit is on */
                else  /* if just a regualr ASCII character */
                {
                        ch = fputc ( curr_ch, target_ptr);
                        (*wrt)++;
                }
        }    /* while source file is not empty */
}


main ( int argc, char *argv [])
{
        FILE       *src_ptr, *target_ptr;
        long int   nr_read, nr_written;
```

```
        if (argc <= 2)    /* if not enough command line argument */
        {
                printf ( "Usage: despace <source> <target>\n");
                exit ( 0);
        }
        else /* if user provided all necessary information */
        {
            /*  open source file */
                src_ptr = fopen ( argv [ 1], "r");
                if ( src_ptr == NULL)
                {
                        printf ( "Source file not found\n");
                        exit ( 0);
                }

            /*  open target file */
                target_ptr = fopen ( argv [ 2], "w");
                if ( target_ptr == NULL)
                {
                        printf ( "Target file could not be opened\n");
                        exit ( 0);
                }

          /* add spaces to source file, write to target */
                enspace ( src_ptr, target_ptr, &nr_read, &nr_written);

                fclose ( src_ptr);
                fclose ( target_ptr);
        }
        printf ( "%ld chars read; %ld chars written\n",
                nr_read, nr_written);
}
```

enspace( )

This function restores the spaces that had been removed by function **despace( )**. The expansion process also converts each extended character back to its original value. In short, function **enspace( )** restores the compressed file to its original form.

COMPRESSION BASED
ON LETTER PAIRS

One reason the **despace( )** function compresses a file as much as it does is that spaces occur very frequently in files—in fact, the space is generally the most common character in a text file.

You can develop more complex algorithms based on the occurrence of pairs of characters, or *digraphs*. For example, you could compress a file considerably if you could find a way to represent common digraphs in a single character. For example, suppose the digraph *he* occurred often in a text file. You could recode this pair of characters in a single byte, thereby saving one byte each time this digraph occurred—provided you could find a single-character code that was not being used for another purpose.

One possibility is to use the codes for nonprinting characters. For example, the ASCII characters 0 through 31 and 127 decimal are nonprinting characters. Only certain of these values—line feed (10), tab (9), and carriage return (13)—are likely to occur in a file. Two others, the null character (0) and the control-Z character (26), may occur in some files. That still leaves more than two dozen characters for recoding common digraphs in a single character.

In this section, we'll develop some routines for compressing a file using such a strategy.

Determining Digraph Frequencies

The first task is to identify the most common digraphs in text files. The exact frequencies will vary from file to file. However, certain digraphs are likely to be among the most common in just about any file. One such digraph is *he* and another is *th*. These digraphs occur often simply because the word *the* occurs so often. (In fact, in a million-word corpus of text, *the* occurs about 70,000 times; that is, about 7% of the words in a text file are likely to be *the*.)

From your knowledge of English, you can probably think of other digraphs that are likely to occur. The following listing contains other common ones:

```
in  or  ti  er  al  on
```

The following program lets you determine the frequencies of all possible digraphs for as many text files as you wish. After determining these frequencies, the program computes the relative proportion of occurrences associated with each digraph. Finally, the program finds all digraphs that contribute more than a specified minimal percentage.

```c
/* Program to compute digraph frequencies, store frequency
   information in an array, and rank order those digraphs that
   account for more than a minumum percentage of the digraphs.
*/

#include <stdio.h>
#include <stdlib.h>
#include <string.h>
#include <ctype.h>
#include "dilist.c"    /* linked list routines for digraph info */

#define MAX_STR    80
#define ALPHA      27   /* 0 is for non-alphabetic characters */
#define CUTOFF     .01  /* minimum digraph percentage for inclusion */

long int freq [ ALPHA][ ALPHA];   /* contains digraph frequencies */

/* Function DECLARATIONS */

int      array_index ( int);
long int count_diphthongs ( FILE *, long int [][ ALPHA]);
void     init_freq ( long int [][ ALPHA]);
void     other_files ( long int [][ALPHA], long int *);
void     rank_diphthongs ( FILE *, long int [ ][ ALPHA], long int);
void     write_diphthongs ( FILE *, long int [ ][ ALPHA], long int);


main ( int argc, char *argv[])
{
        FILE         *src_ptr, *target_ptr;
        struct lnode *root = NULL, *temp;  /* for ordering digraphs */
        long int     nr_digs = 0,      /* number of digraphs */
                     diphthongs = 0;  /* # of digraphs with letters */
        int          inner, outer,
                     over_1 = 0;   /* # digraphs above cutoff %age */
        double       val, val_sum = 0.0;

        if (argc <= 2)   /* if too few parameters */
        {
                printf ( "Usage: despace <source> <target>\n");
                exit ( 1);
        }
        else   /* if user provided two file names */
        {
            /* open source file */
                src_ptr = fopen ( argv [ 1], "r");
                if ( src_ptr == NULL)
                {
                        printf ( "Source file not found\n");
                        exit ( 1);
                }
```

```
                  /* open output file */
                     target_ptr = fopen ( argv [ 2], "w");
                     if ( target_ptr == NULL)
                     {
                             printf ( "Target file not be opened\n");
                             exit ( 1);
                     }

                     init_freq ( freq);  /* initialize frequency array */
                  /* count digraphs */
                     digraphs ( src_ptr, freq, &nr_digs);
                     fclose ( src_ptr);  /* close source file just done */

                  /* let user process other files if desired */
                     other_files ( freq, &nr_digs);

                     printf ( "%ld pairs\n", nr_digs);
                     fprintf ( target_ptr, "%ld pairs\n", nr_digs);

                  /* determine how many of the digraphs are diphthongs */
                     diphthongs = count_diphthongs ( target_ptr, freq);

                     write_diphthongs ( target_ptr, freq, diphthongs);

                     fprintf ( target_ptr, "\n\n Those over %.3lf:\n\n",
                               CUTOFF);

                  /* Build linked list of diphthongs making cutoff */
                     rank_diphthongs ( target_ptr, freq, diphthongs);

                     fclose ( target_ptr);       /* close log file */
            }      /* if user provided two file names. */
}


/* initialize frequency array to 0 */
void init_freq ( long int vals [ ][ ALPHA])
{
        int  outer, inner;

        for ( outer = 0; outer < ALPHA; outer++)
                for ( inner = 0; inner < ALPHA; inner++)
                        vals [ outer][ inner] = 0;
}


/*
   int array_index ( int ch)
   ********************************************************
   Return the subscript corresponding to character read ---
   0 if not alphabetic charactyer;
   otherwise, ordinal position in alphabet.

   CALLS : isalpha (); tolower ();
   GLOBALS :
   PARAMETERS :
           ch : character whose index is sought.
   RETURN : if ch is alphabetic character, ordinal position of
           chin alphabet; 0 otherwise.
   USAGE : index = array_index ( my_char);
   ********************************************************
```

```
*/
int array_index ( int ch)
{
        if ( isalpha ( ch))
                return ( tolower (ch) - 'a' + 1);
        else
                return ( 0);
}


/* process a source file, counting each digraph and recording
   these frequencies in the specified array.
*/
void digraphs ( FILE *src_ptr, long int vals [ ][ ALPHA],
                long int *count)
{
        int  first, second;  /* first and second character of pair */

        first = getc ( src_ptr);     /* get first character */

        for ( ; !feof ( src_ptr); )   /* continue until end of file */
        {
                second = getc ( src_ptr);  /* get 2nd character */
                if ( second == EOF)        /* stop if end of file */
                        continue;
              /* increment value in cell corresponding to digraph */
                vals [ array_index (first)][ array_index (second)]++;
                (*count)++;            /* another digraph processed */
              /* next digraph consists of second and a new letter */
                first = second;
        }     /* while source file is not done */
}


void other_files ( long int vals [][ALPHA], long int *nr_digs)
{
        char    next_file [MAX_STR], /* name of next file to open */
                *null_str = "";
        FILE    *src_ptr;

        do    /* open other files user reqeuests */
        {
                printf ( "File? ");
                gets ( next_file);
              /* if user specified a file, process it. */
                if ( strcmp ( next_file, null_str))
                {
                        src_ptr = fopen ( next_file, "r");
                        if ( src_ptr != NULL)
                                digraphs ( src_ptr, vals,
                                           nr_digs);
                        fclose ( src_ptr);
                }     /* if user specified a file to do */
        }
        while ( strcmp ( next_file, null_str));
}
```

```c
long int count_diphthongs (FILE *target_ptr, long int vals [][ ALPHA])
{
        int              outer, inner;
        long int nr_diphth = 0;

    /* loop through all array cells, except those with 0 subscript */
        for ( outer = 1; outer < ALPHA; outer++)
        {
                for ( inner = 1; inner < ALPHA; inner++)
                        nr_diphth += vals [ outer][ inner];
        }

        fprintf ( target_ptr, "\n\n%ld diphthongs\n", nr_diphth);
        return ( nr_diphth);
}


void  rank_diphthongs ( FILE *target_ptr, long int vals [ ][ ALPHA],
                        long int diphthongs)
{
        struct lnode *root = NULL, *temp;  /* for ordering digraphs */
        int              inner, outer,
                         over_1 = 0;    /* # digraphs above cutoff %age */
        double           val, val_sum = 0.0;

    /* Build list of diphthongs making cutoff */
        for ( outer = 1; outer < ALPHA; outer++)
        {
                for ( inner = 1; inner < ALPHA; inner++)
                {
                        val = vals [ outer][ inner] /
                             ( double) diphthongs;
                        if ( val >= CUTOFF)
                        {
                                over_1++;
                                val_sum += val;
                                temp = get_node ( temp);
                                temp -> data = val;
                                temp -> first = outer;
                                temp -> second = inner;
                                root = middle_of_list ( temp,
                                                       root);
                        }   /* if diphthong made cutoff */
                }   /* for second character of diphthong */
        }   /* for first character of diphthong */

        show_list ( target_ptr, root);
        printf ( "%d over .01; cumulative %%age== %.4lf\n",
                over_1, val_sum);
        fprintf ( target_ptr,
                "%d over .01; cumulative %%age== %.4lf\n",
                over_1, val_sum);
}


void write_diphthongs ( FILE *target_ptr, long int vals [][ ALPHA],
                        long int diphthongs)
```

```
{
        int outer, inner;

    /* write info about all occurring diphthongs */
        for ( outer = 1; outer < ALPHA; outer++)
        {
                for ( inner = 1; inner < ALPHA; inner++)
                        if ( freq [ outer][ inner] > 0)
                                fprintf ( target_ptr,
                                        "%c%c: %51d  (%.41f)\n",
                                        outer + 'a' - 1,
                                        inner + 'a' - 1,
                                        freq [ outer][ inner],
                                        freq [ outer][ inner] /
                                        ( double) diphthongs);
        }
}


/* ************************************************************** */
/* ************************************************************** */
/* Contents of Dilist.C, file containing linked list routines for
    doing frequency counts.
*/

#include <malloc.h>

/* Node for a linked list.
    Two members: data, and a pointer to another node like this one.
*/
struct lnode {
        double  data;
        int     first, second;
        struct  lnode *next;     /* pointer to another lnode */
};

char *bad_str = "INVALID VALUE";

/* ***********
    linked list function DECLARATIONS
*********** */
struct lnode *get_node ( struct lnode *);
struct lnode *middle_of_list ( struct lnode *, struct lnode *);
void         show_list ( FILE *, struct lnode *);


/* ***********
    linked list function DEFINITIONS
*********** */

/*
    ******************************************************
    Allocate space for and initialize a structure;
    return pointer to it.

    CALLS : malloc (); printf ();
    GLOBALS : NULL
    PARAMETERS :
            item : pointer to storage allocated.
    RETURN : pointer to storage allocated.
    USAGE : temp = get_node ( temp);
    ******************************************************
*/
```

```
struct lnode *get_node ( struct lnode *item)
{
        void *malloc ( size_t);

    /* allocate enough space to store an lnode */
        item = (struct lnode *) malloc ( sizeof ( struct lnode));

    /* if allocated, initialize the structure */
        if (item != NULL)
        {
                item->next = NULL;
                item -> data = 0.0;
                item -> first = 0;
                item -> second = 0;
        }
        else
                printf ( "Nothing allocated\n");
        return ( item);            /* return the pointer */
}




/*
    **********************************************************
    Add lnode to list at position corresponding to data member's
    relative position

    CALLS : middle_of_list ();
    GLOBALS : NULL;
    PARAMETERS :
            new : pointer to node to be added;
            list : pointer to list being expanded.
    RETURN : pointer to modified list.
    USAGE : root = middle_of_list ( temp, root);
    **********************************************************
*/
struct lnode *middle_of_list ( struct lnode *new, struct lnode *list)
{
        if ( list == NULL)
        {
                list = new;
                return ( list);
        }
        else if ( list->data <=  new->data)
        {
                new->next = list;
                list = new;
                return ( list);
        }
        else
        {
            /* return results of most recent search. */
                list->next = middle_of_list ( new, list->next);
                return ( list);
        }
}




/*
    **********************************************************
    Display contents of linked list.
```

```
        CALLS : show_list ();
        GLOBALS : NULL
        PARAMETERS :
                target_ptr : pointer to log file;
                listr : pointer to start of list being displayed.
        RETURN : none
        USAGE : show_list ( log_file, root);
        **************************************************************
*/
void show_list ( FILE *target_ptr, struct lnode *list)
{
        if ( list != NULL)
        {
                if ( list->next != NULL)
                        show_list ( target_ptr, list->next);
                printf ( "%c%c: %.4lf\n",
                        list->first + 'a' - 1,
                        list->second + 'a' - 1,
                        list->data);
                fprintf ( target_ptr, "%c%c: %.4lf\n",
                        list->first + 'a' - 1,
                        list->second + 'a' - 1,
                        list->data);
        }
}
```

In the program and in the following discussion, you'll see *diphthongs* used to refer to those digraphs that consist only of alphabetic characters. For example *az*, *qy*, and *tt* are diphthongs, but 'a?', '!+', and 'b=' are not. Thus, all diphthongs are digraphs, but the reverse is not the case.

array_index()

This function returns the index subscript of the character parameter. The subscript is computed by using the offset from *a* to **ch**. The **1** is added because the alphabetic characters start with subscript **1** in the frequency array. The cells with index 0 (in either first or second dimension) store information about digraphs consisting of at least one nonalphabetic character, that is, of digraphs that are not diphthongs.

init_freq()

This function simply initializes the cells of the frequency array **vals[]** to 0.

count_diphthongs()

This function sums the values in the cells whose subscripts are both based on alphabetic characters and returns this value.

write_diphthongs()

This function writes the frequencies and relative frequencies of each diphthong that appears at least once. The information is written to the specified file, rather than to the screen.

rank_diphthongs()

This function builds and writes (to screen and file) a linked list containing those diphthongs with relative frequencies above the value of CUTOFF. The function writes the contents of the linked list to the specified file and to the screen.

other_files()

This function gives the user a chance to process multiple files in the same sitting. The function calls **digraph()** to process the file and adds the file's digraph frequencies to the current frequency array.

If you specify a file that could not be found or opened, the function simply leaves the current pass through the loop and gets set to test the continuation condition again. If the file is empty, the continuation condition fails, and the loop stops; otherwise, the program simply lets you continue entering file names, ignoring the one that caused problems.

The following functions are for manipulating linked lists; the functions assume that you have declared an **lnode** structure. These functions are also used by programs later in the chapter. You should put the functions and the declarations in a file named **dilist.c**. The later programs read this file for the data structure and the functions.

get—node( )

This function returns a pointer to the storage allocated for a four-member structure. This function is very similar to the allocation function with the same name in your **lists.c** file, except that this structure has a **data** member of type **double**. Furthermore, the **lnode** here contains members for specifying the array indexes.

middle—of—list( )

This function is essentially the same as the function in **lists.c** from Chapter 2, except that the contents of the **lnode** structure are different. The function adds a node at its appropriate position in a linked list.

show—list( )

This function displays the contents of the specified linked list, as does the function with the same name in **lists.c**. The version in this program also writes this list to the specified file.

The current function also differs from the earlier **show—list( )** in that it displays the nodes from last—that is, largest relative frequency—to first. In this way, your list will be easier to follow. This is accomplished by moving the display statements after the recursive calls so that the function moves as far as possible in the list before writing.

main( )

The **main( )** function opens the first source file and calls **digraph( )** to do its work. The function makes sure that the user has entered enough information and that the files can be opened or created. Once the first file has been processed, **main( )** calls **other＿files( )** to let the user have more files processed.

The **main( )** function then writes various information to a file. To accomplish this, the program calls **write＿diphthongs( )**and other functions. Finally, the program calls **rank＿diphthongs( )**, which creates the list of those diphthongs that appeared more often than the relative frequency represented by CUTOFF.

The following relative frequencies are derived from using the program with the text of all the chapters in *Using QuickC* (by Werner Feibel, Osborne/McGraw-Hill, 1988).

```
Digraphs with relative frequencies over 0.010:

     freq.   rel. freq.

th: 17651   (0.0408)
he: 14424   (0.0333)
in: 12835   (0.0297)
er:  8629   (0.0199)
re:  8282   (0.0191)
on:  7741   (0.0179)
ti:  7078   (0.0164)
es:  6424   (0.0148)
at:  6064   (0.0140)
an:  5995   (0.0139)
ar:  5920   (0.0137)
ou:  5720   (0.0132)
te:  5642   (0.0130)
nt:  5538   (0.0128)
or:  5536   (0.0128)
to:  5443   (0.0126)
is:  5384   (0.0124)
st:  5324   (0.0123)
en:  5308   (0.0123)
le:  5125   (0.0118)
ra:  5050   (0.0117)
ng:  5036   (0.0116)
al:  4812   (0.0111)
io:  4656   (0.0108)
```

This listing contains all the diphthongs whose relative frequencies account for at least 1% of the characters. (You'll use these diphthongs in another file compression program.) The listing shows the diphthongs ranked from highest to lowest. These two dozen digraphs (about 4% of all the possible diphthongs) account for almost 40% of the diphthongs in *Using Quick C*.

A Compression Scheme Based on Digraph Frequencies

In this section, you'll develop a compression program that uses single-character codes to represent common digraphs. The strategy associates a code with each of the digraphs in the preceding list. The codes are those for the nonprinting characters that aren't commonly used.

The following program lets you compress or expand a file using a compression strategy based on digraph occurrences. The program contains two functions that transform the source files: **remove_dig( )**, which removes the digraphs and substitutes nonprinting character codes, and **add_dig( )**, which replaces nonprinting character codes with the appropriate digraph.

The two functions may look formidable because of their length. However, they are both very simple conceptually: Each is controlled by a **switch** statement. Function **remove dig( )** is actually called by another function, **dig_encode( )**. This makes it easier to keep an overview of the compression strategy in this long function by putting the source file handling elsewhere.

```
/* Program to compress a text file by recoding common digraphs
   as single-character codes.
*/

#include <stdio.h>
#include <string.h>

#define FALSE     0
#define TRUE      1
#define SPACE_CHR  ' '

/* single character codes associated with specified digraph */
#define TH_VAL    1
#define TI_VAL    2
#define TE_VAL    3
#define TO_VAL    4
#define HE_VAL    5
#define IN_VAL    6
#define IS_VAL    7
#define IO_VAL    8
#define ER_VAL    11
#define ES_VAL    12
#define EN_VAL    14
#define RE_VAL    15
#define RA_VAL    16
```

```
#define ON_VAL    17
#define OU_VAL    18
#define OR_VAL    19
#define AT_VAL    20
#define AN_VAL    21
#define AR_VAL    22
#define AL_VAL    23
#define NT_VAL    24
#define NG_VAL    25
#define ST_VAL    27
#define LE_VAL    28


/* Function DECLARATIONS */
void dig_encode ( FILE *, FILE *, long int *, long int *);
void remove_dig(FILE *, FILE *, int *, int *, long int *, long int *);
void add_dig ( FILE *, FILE *, long int *, long int *);


main ( int argc, char *argv [])
{
        FILE        *src_ptr, *target_ptr;
        long int    nr_read, nr_written;
        int         encode = TRUE;
        char        choice [ 10];

        if (argc <= 2)    /* if too few parameters */
        {
                printf ( "Usage: despace <source> <target>\n");
                exit ( 1);
        }
        else    /* if user provided two file names */
        {

                /* open source file */
                src_ptr = fopen ( argv [ 1], "r");
                if ( src_ptr == NULL)
                {
                        printf ( "Source file not found\n");
                        exit ( 1);
                }

                /* open output file */
                target_ptr = fopen ( argv [ 2], "w");
                if ( target_ptr == NULL)
                {
                        printf ( "Target file not be opened\n");
                        exit ( 1);
                }

                /* find out if user wants to encode or decode file */
                printf ( "encode? (n for NO) ");
                gets ( choice);
                if ( ( choice [ 0] == 'n') || ( choice [ 0] == 'N'))
                        encode = FALSE;
```

```
               if ( encode)    /* compress file */
                       dig_encode ( src_ptr, target_ptr,
                                   &nr_read, &nr_written);
               else            /* decompress file */
                       add_dig ( src_ptr, target_ptr,
                                &nr_read, &nr_written);

               fclose ( target_ptr);
               fclose ( src_ptr);
       }

       printf ( "%ld chars read; %ld chars written\n",
               nr_read, nr_written);
}



/* replace certain digraphs in an ASCII text file with
   a single-character code, taken from non-printing characters.
*/
void  dig_encode ( FILE *src_ptr, FILE *target_ptr,
               long int *rd, long int *wrt)
{
       int    curr_ch, next_ch, ch;

       *rd = 0;        /* # chars read from source */
       *wrt = 0;       /* # chars written to target */

    /* remove leading blanks */
       while ( ((curr_ch = fgetc ( src_ptr)) == SPACE_CHR) &&
               !feof ( src_ptr))
       {
               curr_ch = fgetc ( src_ptr);
               (*rd)++;
       }

    /* work as long as there are characters in source file */
       for ( ;  !feof ( src_ptr); )
       {
               next_ch = getc ( src_ptr);
               (*rd)++;
               if ( next_ch == EOF) /* if source file done */
               {
                   /* write last character */
                       ch = putc ( curr_ch, target_ptr);
                       (*wrt)++;
                       continue;
               }
               else    /* if not EOF, call remove_dig() */
               {
                       remove_dig ( src_ptr, target_ptr, &curr_ch,
                                   &next_ch, rd, wrt);
               }    /* if not a space */
       }    /* while source file is not empty */
}
```

```
/* Function to actually substitute a single-character code
   for specified digraphs. Function uses nested switch statements
   to match first and second characters against digraphs.
   Function always ends with the first character in the next
   pair having a value; calling routine must supply second character.
   Function currently uses the following digraphs:
   th ti te to at an ar al in is io er es en
   on ou or re ra nt ng he li
*/
void remove_dig ( FILE *src_ptr, FILE *target_ptr,
                  int *first, int *second,
                  long int *rd, long int *wrt)
{
        int  ch, got_dig = FALSE; /* TRUE if chars form a digraph */

        switch ( *first)
        {
                case 't' :    /* first char of digraph is t */
                        switch ( *second)    /* match second char */
                        {
                                case 'h' :
                                        ch = putc ( TH_VAL,
                                                        target_ptr);
                                        got_dig = TRUE;
                                        break;
                                case 'i' :
                                        ch = putc ( TI_VAL,
                                                        target_ptr);
                                        got_dig = TRUE;
                                        break;
                                case 'e' :
                                        ch = putc ( TE_VAL,
                                                        target_ptr);
                                        got_dig = TRUE;
                                        break;
                                case 'o' :
                                        ch = putc ( TO_VAL,
                                                        target_ptr);
                                        got_dig = TRUE;
                                        break;
                                default :
                                        break;
                        }
                        break;
                case 'a' :
                        switch ( *second)
                        {
                                case 't' :
                                        ch = putc ( AT_VAL,
                                                        target_ptr);
                                        got_dig = TRUE;
                                        break;
                                case 'n' :
                                        ch = putc ( AN_VAL,
                                                        target_ptr);
                                        got_dig = TRUE;
                                        break;
```

```
                        case 'r' :
                                ch = putc ( AR_VAL,
                                          target_ptr);
                                got_dig = TRUE;
                                break;
                        case 'l' :
                                ch = putc ( AL_VAL,
                                          target_ptr);
                                got_dig = TRUE;
                                break;
                        default :
                                break;
                }
                break;
        case 'i' :
                switch ( *second)
                {
                        case 'n' :
                                ch = putc ( IN_VAL,
                                          target_ptr);
                                got_dig = TRUE;
                                break;
                        case 's' :
                                ch = putc ( IS_VAL,
                                          target_ptr);
                                got_dig = TRUE;
                                break;
                        case 'o' :
                                ch = putc ( IO_VAL,
                                          target_ptr);
                                got_dig = TRUE;
                                break;
                        default :
                                break;
                }
                break;
        case 'e' :
                switch ( *second)
                {
                        case 'n' :
                                ch = putc ( EN_VAL,
                                          target_ptr);
                                got_dig = TRUE;
                                break;
                        case 's' :
                                ch = putc ( ES_VAL,
                                          target_ptr);
                                got_dig = TRUE;
                                break;
                        case 'r' :
                                ch = putc ( ER_VAL,
                                          target_ptr);
                                got_dig = TRUE;
                                break;
                        default :
                                break;
                }
                break;
```

```
case 'o' :
     switch ( *second)
     {
             case 'n' :
                     ch = putc ( ON_VAL,
                                 target_ptr);
                     got_dig = TRUE;
                     break;
             case 'u' :
                     ch = putc ( OU_VAL,
                                 target_ptr);
                     got_dig = TRUE;
                     break;
             case 'r' :
                     ch = putc ( OR_VAL,
                                 target_ptr);
                     got_dig = TRUE;
                     break;
             default :
                     break;
     }
     break;
case 'r' :
     switch ( *second)
     {
             case 'e' :
                     ch = putc ( RE_VAL,
                                 target_ptr);
                     got_dig = TRUE;
                     break;
             case 'a' :
                     ch = putc ( RA_VAL,
                                 target_ptr);
                     got_dig = TRUE;
                     break;
             default :
                     break;
     }
     break;
case 'n' :
     switch ( *second)
     {
             case 't' :
                     ch = putc ( NT_VAL,
                                 target_ptr);
                     got_dig = TRUE;
                     break;
             case 'g' :
                     ch = putc ( NG_VAL,
                                 target_ptr);
                     got_dig = TRUE;
                     break;
             default :
                     break;
     }
     break;
case 'h' :
```

```
                          switch ( *second)
                          {
                                  case 'e' :
                                          ch = putc ( HE_VAL,
                                                          target_ptr);
                                          got_dig = TRUE;
                                          break;
                                  default :
                                          break;
                          }
                          break;
                  case 's' :
                          switch ( *second)
                          {
                                  case 't' :
                                          ch = putc ( ST_VAL,
                                                          target_ptr);
                                          got_dig = TRUE;
                                          break;
                                  default :
                                          break;
                          }
                          break;
                  case 'l' :
                          switch ( *second)
                          {
                                  case 'e' :
                                          ch = putc ( LE_VAL,
                                                          target_ptr);
                                          got_dig = TRUE;
                                          break;
                                  default :
                                          break;
                          }
                          break;
                  default :
                          break;
          } /* switch on *first */

          if ( got_dig) /* if digraph was written, get new first char */
          {
                  *first = getc ( src_ptr);
                  (*rd)++;
          } /* if digraph was written */
          else    /* write first char, move second char forward */
          {
                  ch = putc ( *first, target_ptr);
                  *first = *second;
          } /* if just an ordinary character was written */
          (*wrt)++;   /* one char is always written, 0 or 1 are read */
}


/* Function to replace compressed character code read from
   source file with digraph character in target file.
*/
void add_dig ( FILE *src_ptr, FILE *target_ptr, long int *rd,
               long int *wrt)
```

```
{
        int    curr_ch, ch;

        *rd = 0;  /* # chars --- printing or not --- read */
        *wrt = 0; /* # printing chars written */

    /* remove leading blanks */
        while ( ((curr_ch = fgetc ( src_ptr)) == SPACE_CHR) &&
                !feof ( src_ptr))
        {
                curr_ch = getc ( src_ptr);
                (*rd)++;
        }

    /* work as long as there are characters in source file */
        for ( ; !feof ( src_ptr); )
        {
                switch ( curr_ch)  /* char just read from source */
                {
                        case TH_VAL :   /* code for 'th' */
                                ch = putc ( 't', target_ptr);
                                ch = putc ( 'h', target_ptr);
                                *wrt += 2;
                                break;
                        case TI_VAL :   /* code for 'ti' */
                                ch = putc ( 't', target_ptr);
                                ch = putc ( 'i', target_ptr);
                                *wrt += 2;
                                break;
                        case TE_VAL :
                                ch = putc ( 't', target_ptr);
                                ch = putc ( 'e', target_ptr);
                                *wrt += 2;
                                break;
                        case TO_VAL :
                                ch = putc ( 't', target_ptr);
                                ch = putc ( 'o', target_ptr);
                                *wrt += 2;
                                break;
                        case HE_VAL :
                                ch = putc ( 'h', target_ptr);
                                ch = putc ( 'e', target_ptr);
                                *wrt += 2;
                                break;
                        case IN_VAL :
                                ch = putc ( 'i', target_ptr);
                                ch = putc ( 'n', target_ptr);
                                *wrt += 2;
                                break;
                        case IS_VAL :
                                ch = putc ( 'i', target_ptr);
                                ch = putc ( 's', target_ptr);
                                *wrt += 2;
                                break;
                        case IO_VAL :
                                ch = putc ( 'i', target_ptr);
                                ch = putc ( 'o', target_ptr);
                                *wrt += 2;
                                break;
```

```
                    case ER_VAL :
                            ch = putc ( 'e', target_ptr);
                            ch = putc ( 'r', target_ptr);
                            *wrt += 2;
                            break;
                    case ES_VAL :
                            ch = putc ( 'e', target_ptr);
                            ch = putc ( 's', target_ptr);
                            *wrt += 2;
                            break;
                    case EN_VAL :
                            ch = putc ( 'e', target_ptr);
                            ch = putc ( 'n', target_ptr);
                            *wrt += 2;
                            break;
                    case RE_VAL :
                            ch = putc ( 'r', target_ptr);
                            ch = putc ( 'e', target_ptr);
                            *wrt += 2;
                            break;
                    case RA_VAL :
                            ch = putc ( 'r', target_ptr);
                            ch = putc ( 'a', target_ptr);
                            *wrt += 2;
                            break;
                    case ON_VAL :
                            ch = putc ( 'o', target_ptr);
                            ch = putc ( 'n', target_ptr);
                            *wrt += 2;
                            break;
                    case OU_VAL :
                            ch = putc ( 'o', target_ptr);
                            ch = putc ( 'u', target_ptr);
                            *wrt += 2;
                            break;
                    case OR_VAL :
                            ch = putc ( 'o', target_ptr);
                            ch = putc ( 'r', target_ptr);
                            *wrt += 2;
                            break;
                    case AT_VAL :
                            ch = putc ( 'a', target_ptr);
                            ch = putc ( 't', target_ptr);
                            *wrt += 2;
                            break;
                    case AN_VAL :
                            ch = putc ( 'a', target_ptr);
                            ch = putc ( 'n', target_ptr);
                            *wrt += 2;
                            break;
                    case AR_VAL :
                            ch = putc ( 'a', target_ptr);
                            ch = putc ( 'r', target_ptr);
                            *wrt += 2;
                            break;
```

```
                    case AL_VAL :
                            ch = putc ( 'a', target_ptr);
                            ch = putc ( 'l', target_ptr);
                            *wrt += 2;
                            break;
                    case NT_VAL :
                            ch = putc ( 'n', target_ptr);
                            ch = putc ( 't', target_ptr);
                            *wrt += 2;
                            break;
                    case NG_VAL :
                            ch = putc ( 'n', target_ptr);
                            ch = putc ( 'g', target_ptr);
                            *wrt += 2;
                            break;
                    case ST_VAL :
                            ch = putc ( 's', target_ptr);
                            ch = putc ( 't', target_ptr);
                            *wrt += 2;
                            break;
                    case LE_VAL :
                            ch = putc ( 'l', target_ptr);
                            ch = putc ( 'e', target_ptr);
                            *wrt += 2;
                            break;
                    default :  /* printing char was read */
                            ch = putc ( curr_ch, target_ptr);
                            (*wrt)++;
                            break;
                }  /* switch on curr_ch */
                (*rd)++;
                curr_ch = getc ( src_ptr);   /* get next char */
        }    /* while source file is not empty */
}
```

dig—encode()

This function reads from a source file and replaces any occurrences of specified digraphs with single-character codes. The actual replacement is done by function **remove—dig()**.

remove—dig()

This function actually replaces specified digraphs with single-character codes when writing to a target file. The function uses nested **switch** statements to check whether it has a digraph. For valid digraph starting characters, there are only a few possible second characters.

Currently, the function can handle 24 different digraphs. You can easily modify this by changing the **switch** statement and by making any necessary changes in the codes defined for the pre-processor (TH—VAL, for example).

add—dig()

This function replaces the compressed code for a digraph with the actual digraph when writing to a target file. The function uses a **switch** statement containing the codes for all the acceptable digraphs to check whether the current character needs to be replaced.

As with the **despace( )** function, the compression routines produce a file that contains more than printing characters. Figure 6-1 shows an example of such a file as seen by the QuickC editor.

This program compressed the text files for Chapters 1 through 5 of this book by about 20%. This is a substantial space savings, but is not much larger than the savings provided by the simpler **despace( )** function. The main gain with this strategy is a somewhat more consistent savings of about 20%.

Notice that the program compresses the original file by only about 20% despite the fact that the 24 digraphs account for almost 40% of the digraphs in a collection of files. This is because common digraphs tend to follow each other. For example, *th* is likely to be followed by *he*, since *the* is such a common word. However, when function **remove—dig( )** processes the *th*, the following *he* is lost, since the *h* is used for the first digraph. Counting and compressing behave differently.

Other Strategies

The space- and digraph-based strategies both use byte-sized encoding schemes. In the former strategy, the space character "piggybacks" on the character preceding it; in the digraph strategy, two characters are replaced by one, nonprinting character.

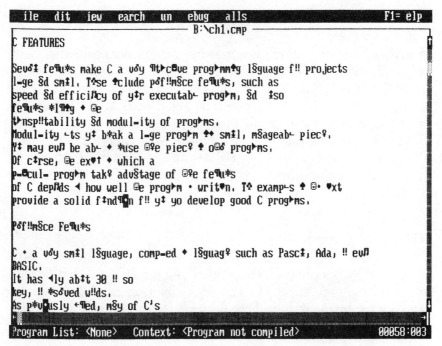

Figure 6-1.   Example of compressed file as seen by the QuickC editor

Another common compression technique actually uses a different number of bits to represent different characters. The general strategy behind *Huffman coding* (as this technique is called) is to find an encoding scheme that will let you represent frequently occurring characters in fewer bits than are required to represent characters that appear only rarely. This encoding scheme will let you minimize the number of bits required to encode a file.

In Huffman coding, character codes are stored in a tree. The least common characters are deeper in the tree than are those that occur frequently. A character's code depends on the path you need to take in the tree to get to the character. We won't look at Huffman coding here. If you're interested, look for more information in books about data structures or algorithms.

ENCRYPTING DATA

People have been hiding messages by various means for thousands of years. Over the centuries, many techniques have been developed for encrypting information. Currently, data encryption and decryption are very active research areas because of the concern about data security in government and industry.

In this section, we'll look at some simple encryption schemes. You'll develop functions to create and decipher cryptograms. You'll also develop some functions for gathering statistics about a message.

Offset Ciphers

One of the most common encryption techniques was used by Caesar to encode messages. A *Caesar cipher* is created by replacing each letter by the letter whose position in the alphabet is offset by the desired amount from the original letter.

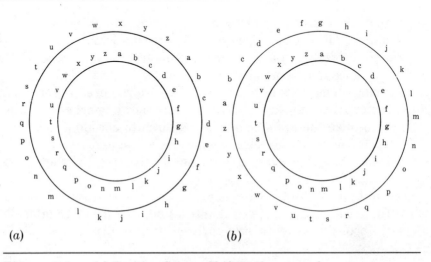

(a) (b)

Figure 6-2. (a) Positive Caesar Shift ($+3$): a → x, b → y, ...
                (b) Negative Caesar Shift (-6): a → g, b → h, ...

For example, if the offset were 2, the letter a would be replaced by c, b would be replaced by d, and so on up to x, which would be replaced by z. In such a cipher, the alphabet is treated as if the letters were represented in a ring: After z, the next letter is a. In a ring, a is offset from y by 2 and therefore replaces y in the cipher. Figure 6-2 shows the character replacements for two shifts, one positive and the other negative. The letter in the outer ring is substituted for its counterpart in the inner ring.

The following functions let you encode a message using the specified offset. The functions require an offset amount and an array in which to store the substitution information.

```
/* Functions to fill replacement array, given an offset value,
   and to encrypt a file using the offset cipher.
*/

/*
   ************************************************************
   Make substitutions based on offsetting letters by specified amount.

   CALLS : check_range ();
   GLOBALS : ALPHA
   PARAMETERS :
          code : array containing replacement chars, to be filled.
          offset : amount to offset for substitution.
   RETURN : none
   USAGE : set_offset ( my_array, -6);
   ************************************************************
*/
void set_offset ( int code [], int offset)
{
        int temp, index;

        for ( index = 0; index < ALPHA; index++)
        {
                temp = index + offset;
                if ( temp >= ALPHA)
                        code [ index] = temp - ALPHA + 'a';
                else if ( temp < 0)
                        code [ index] = temp + ALPHA + 'a';
                else    /* if normal */
                        code [ index] =  temp + 'a';
                code [ index] &= 127;
                check_range ( code [ index]);
        }   /* for each character */
}

/*
   ************************************************************
   Use specified array to encode message in source file.

   CALLS : feof (); fprintf (); fseek (); getc ();
          isalpha (); isupper (); printf (); putc ();
          rewind (); tolower ();
   GLOBALS : EOF, SEEK_END
```

```
       PARAMETERS :
               src_ptr : file containing message to be encoded;
               target_ptr : file to which to write encoded message;
               code : array containing letters to be substituted
                       while encoding.
       RETURN : none
       USAGE : translate_message ( src, log, encode_array);
       ********************************************************
*/
void translate_message ( FILE *src_ptr, FILE *target_ptr, int code [])
{
       int curr_ch, ch, out_index, seek_result;

       if ( src_ptr != NULL)
               rewind ( src_ptr);
       else
               printf ( "Couldn't rewind source file\n");

       seek_result = fseek ( target_ptr, OL, SEEK_END);
       if ( seek_result)
               printf ( "End of target file not found.\n");

       fprintf ( target_ptr, "\n");

       for ( ; !feof ( src_ptr); )
       {
               curr_ch = getc ( src_ptr);
               if ( curr_ch == EOF)
                       continue;
               if ( isalpha ( curr_ch))
               {
                       out_index = tolower ( curr_ch) - 'a';
                       if ( isupper ( curr_ch))
                               ch = putc ( toupper (
                                               code [ out_index]),
                                               target_ptr);
                       else
                               ch = putc ( code [ out_index],
                                               target_ptr);
               }
               else
                       ch = putc ( curr_ch, target_ptr);
       }

       fprintf ( target_ptr, "\n");
}



/*
   ********************************************************
   Check whether specified character is lower case alphabetic;
   complain if not.

   CALLS : printf (); wait ();
   GLOBALS :
   PARAMETERS :
           ch : character to check.
   RETURN : none
   USAGE : check_range ( 'P');
   ********************************************************
```

```
*/
void check_range ( int ch)
{
        if ( ( ch < 97) || ( ch > 122))
        {
                printf ( "%c: %d", '\07', ch);
                wait ();
        }
}




/*
    ********************************************************
    Pause to let user see displayed material.

    CALLS : gets (); printf ();
    GLOBALS :
    PARAMETERS :
    RETURN :
    USAGE : wait ();
    ********************************************************
*/
void wait ()
{
        char resp [ MAX_STR];

        printf ( "<Return> to continue ");
        gets ( resp);
}
```

set_offset( )

This function fills the array of substitution characters with the replacements for each character. A character's replacement is the character whose ordinal position is offset by a specified amount. Function **check_range()** makes sure characters are within the valid character range—in this case, between a and z.

check_range( )

This function checks whether the specified character is a lowercase alphabetic character. If so, the function does nothing; if the character is outside the valid range, the function reports this and waits for the user to press RETURN.

translate_message( )

This function reads a message from the specified source file, character by character. For each alphabetic character, the function substitutes the appropriate character from **code[ ]** before writing the character to the target file.

If a character is in uppercase, the function converts the replacement character to uppercase before writing it. Nonalphabetic characters are simply passed through unchanged.

Notice the use of the Run-Time library function **fseek( )**. This is used to place the file pointer at the end of the target file so that the **translate_message( )** won't accidentally destroy the contents of the file by writing over them.

The following listing shows a message encrypted in a Caesar cipher using functions from the preceding listing:

```
/* Cryptogram generated using a Caesar cipher. */

/* Jbppxdb ql bkzlab rpfkd pbq_qoxkpmlpb; lccpbq fp jfkrp qeobb */

Qefp jbppxdb fp bkzlafkd rpfkd x Zxbpxo zfmebo. Fk qefp
mxoqfzrixo zxpb, qeb lccpbq sxirb fp pbq xq jfkrp qeobb.
Qefp jbxkp qexq bxze zexoxzqbo fp obmixzba yv qeb zexoxzqbo
qexq zljbp qeobb mlpfqflkp bxoifbo fk qeb ximexybq.
```

Substitution Ciphers

Another class of encryption strategies works by replacing each character by another one selected by some pseudorandom process. The simplest example of such a cipher generates a substitution character at random. If this character is not yet being used as a replacement for another letter, the character becomes the substitute for the letter currently under consideration.

For example, the following listing shows an alphabet and the replacement characters after using a random substitution strategy:

```
/* Replacement characters for a cipher generated using
   random substitution.
   Format is <original character>: <replacement character>
*/

a: e       b: j       c: r       d: l       e: c       f: t
g: d       h: w       i: q       j: s       k: o       l: u
m: z       n: h       o: p       p: g       q: v       r: i
s: m       t: y       u: a       v: f       w: x       x: b
y: k       z: n
```

The function in the following listing lets you generate the substitutions based on a pseudorandom strategy. Once you've filled the substitution array, you can pass the array to **encode_ message( )**, just as you would when using an offset strategy.

```
/* Function to generate random substitutions for alphabetic chars. */
/*
    ***********************************************************
    Make random substitutions for each letter.

    CALLS : check_range (); rand ();
    GLOBALS : ALPHA, FALSE, TRUE
    PARAMETERS :
            code : aray containing replacement chars, to be filled.
            seed : for random number generation.
    RETURN : none
    USAGE : set_random_subst ( my_array, 34);
    ***********************************************************
*/
void set_random_subst ( int code [], int seed)
{
        int temp, index;
        int done [ ALPHA];   /* cell == TRUE if letter has been used */

        srand ( seed);

        for ( index = 0; index < ALPHA; index++)
                done [ index] = FALSE;

        for ( index = 0; index < ALPHA; index++)
        {
                temp = rand () % ALPHA;
            /* while letter has already been used, pick another */
                while ( done [ temp] || ( temp == index))
                        temp = rand () % ALPHA;
                code [ index] = (temp + 'a');
                code [ index] &= 127;
                check_range ( code [ index]);
                done [ temp] = TRUE;
        }
}
```

set_random_subst( )

This function uses the seed parameter to start a pseudorandom number-generation process. Each number is converted to an alphabetic character value. If the value just selected has not yet been used, the value replaces the letter represented by the array index. If the character selected has already been used, the function selects another replacement candidate. The function continues until a replacement has been found for each character.

Translating Encrypted Messages

If you need to decode a message that has been encrypted, you have several options. If the cipher was generated using an offset, you can try offsets one after the other until you hit upon the correct one. At most, you'll have to try 26 approaches to the problem. You need patience, but not necessarily logic, to solve a Caesar cipher.

Solving a cipher encrypted using a random substitution method can be much more difficult. It often helps to know how often each character appears in the message and to compare this text against relative frequencies of characters in English.

For example, e is the most common character in English text. Thus, you might try guessing that the most common letter in the encrypted message represents e. Similarly, t is the second most common letter in English text. The following listing shows the letters in descending order of their frequencies in a sample of English text. (The exact order will differ, based on the sample.)

```
e t a o n i s r h l d c u p f m w y b g v k q x j z
```

The following functions will let you compute the relative frequency with which each letter occurs in your message and let you rank-order and display those frequencies.

```
/* Program to count frequency of each character in a file. */

#include <stdio.h>
#include <string.h>
#include <ctype.h>
#include "dilist.c"

#define ALPHA     27
#define MAX_STR  100

int   ch_index ( int);
void  count_ch ( FILE *, long int [], long int *);
void  other_files ( long int [], long int *);
void  rank_freqs ( FILE *, long int [ ], long int);
void  show_ch_list ( FILE *, struct lnode *);
```

```
/*
 ***********************************************************
 Return array index of specified character:
 0 if not a letter; ordinal position in alphabet if a letter.

 CALLS : isalpha (); tolower ();
 GLOBALS :
 PARAMETERS :
        ch : character whose array index value is sought.
 RETURN : index value of specified character.
 USAGE : desired_index = ch_index ( my_char);
 ***********************************************************
*/
int ch_index ( int ch)
{
        if ( isalpha ( ch))
                return ( tolower ( ch) - 'a' + 1);
        else
                return ( 0);
}




/*
 ***********************************************************
 Count the number of occurrences of each character in a file.
 Non-letters are all grouped together.

 CALLS : feof (); getc (); rewind ();
 GLOBALS :
 PARAMETERS :
        src_ptr : file containing message to be analyzed;
        vals : array for storing frequency information;
        rd : address of variable containing # chars read.
 RETURN : none
 USAGE : count_ch ( src, freq_array, &nr_read);
 ***********************************************************
*/
void  count_ch ( FILE *src_ptr, long int vals [ ], long int *rd)
{
        int   curr_ch, ch;
        rewind ( src_ptr);

    /* work as long as there are characters in source file */
        for ( ; !feof ( src_ptr); )
        {
                curr_ch = getc ( src_ptr);
                (*rd)++;
                vals [ ch_index ( curr_ch)]++;
        }    /* while source file is not empty */
}
```

```
/*
    ************************************************************
    Rank order info about letter frequency and store in linked list.

    CALLS : get_node (); middle_of_list (); printf ();
    GLOBALS : ALPHA, NULL
    PARAMETERS :
            list : pointer to first element of ordered list;
            vals : frequency information;
            nr_ch : total chars read.
    RETURN : pointer to ordered list.
    USAGE : root = rank_freqs ( root, freq_array, nr_read);
    ************************************************************
*/
struct lnode *rank_freqs ( struct lnode *list,
                        long int freq [ ], long int nr_ch)
{
        struct lnode *temp = NULL;  /* for ordering digraphs */
        int         index;
        double      val;

        if ( list == NULL)
                printf ( "Starting rank with EMPTY list\n");

        /* Build ordered list of frequencies */
        for ( index = 1; index <= ALPHA; index++)
        {
                if ( nr_ch != 0)
                        val = freq [ index] / ( double) nr_ch;
                else
                        val = 0.0;
                if ( val > 1.0)
                        printf ( "%.4lf is > 1.0\n", val);
                temp = get_node ( temp);
                if ( temp != NULL)
                {
                        temp -> data = val;
                        temp -> first = index;
                        temp -> second = ' ';
                        list = middle_of_list ( temp, list);
                }
                else
                {
                        printf ( "Can't allocate node storage.\n");
                        break;
                }
        }   /* for each array cell */

        /* show_ch_list ( target_ptr, root); */
        if ( list == NULL)
                printf ( "Returning EMPTY list\n");

        return ( list);
}
```

```
/*
   ************************************************************
   Display contents of letter frequency list to screen.

   CALLS : printf ();
   GLOBALS : NULL
   PARAMETERS :
           list : pointer to list to be displayed.
   RETURN : none
   USAGE : show_ch_list ( root);
   ************************************************************
*/
void show_ch_list ( struct lnode *list)
{
        int index = 0;
        struct lnode *temp = NULL;

        temp = list;
        while ( temp != NULL)
        {
                printf ( "%c: %.4lf      ",
                        temp->first + 'a' - 1, temp->data);
                if ( ( index % 5) == 4)
                        printf ( "\n");
                index++;
                temp = temp -> next;
        }
}



/*
   ************************************************************
   Let user specify other files in which to count character
   frequencies, and call the counting routines.

   CALLS : count_ch (); fclose (); fopen (); gets ();
           printf (); strcmp ();
   GLOBALS : NULL, null_str
   PARAMETERS :
           vals : array containing character frequencies;
           nr_chr : pointer to variable containing total chars read.
   RETURN : none
   USAGE : other_files ( freq, &nr_read);
   ************************************************************
*/
void other_files ( long int vals [], long int *nr_chr)
{
        char      next_file [MAX_STR], /* name of next file to open */
                  *null_str = "";
        FILE      *src_ptr;

        do   /* open other files user requests */
        {
```

```
                    printf ( "File? ");
                    gets ( next_file);
                    /* if user specified a file, process it. */
                    if ( strcmp ( next_file, null_str))
                    {
                            src_ptr = fopen ( next_file, "r");
                            if ( src_ptr != NULL)
                                    count_ch ( src_ptr, vals,
                                                    nr_chr);
                            fclose ( src_ptr);
                    }    /* if user specified a file to do */
            }
            while ( strcmp ( next_file, null_str));
    }


main ( int argc, char *argv [])
{
            FILE        *src_ptr, *target_ptr;
            long int    nr_read = 0, val_sum = 0;
            long int    freq [ ALPHA];
            int         index;
            double      pct_sum = 0, pct;

            if (argc <= 2)    /* if too few parameters */
            {
                    printf ( "Usage: count <source> <target>\n");
                    exit ( 1);
            }
            else    /* if user provided two file names */
            {
                    /* open source file */
                    src_ptr = fopen ( argv [ 1], "r");
                    if ( src_ptr == NULL)
                    {
                            printf ( "Source file not found\n");
                            exit ( 1);
                    }

                    /* open output file */
                    target_ptr = fopen ( argv [ 2], "w");
                    if ( target_ptr == NULL)
                    {
                            printf ( "Target file not be opened\n");
                            exit ( 1);
                    }

                    for ( index = 0; index < ALPHA; index++)
                            freq [ index] = 0.0;

                    count_ch ( src_ptr, freq, &nr_read);
                    fclose ( src_ptr);

                    other_files ( freq, &nr_read);
```

```
              pct = (double) freq [ 0] / (double) nr_read;
              fprintf ( target_ptr, "*: %9ld    (%.4lf)\n",
                      freq [ 0], pct);
              val_sum += freq [ 0];
              pct_sum += pct;
              for ( index = 1; index < ALPHA; index++)
              {
                      pct = (double) freq [ index] /
                            (double) nr_read;
                      val_sum += freq [ index];
                      pct_sum += pct;
                      fprintf ( target_ptr,
                            "%c: %9ld    (%.4lf)\n",
                            index + 'a' - 1,
                            freq [ index],
                            pct);
              }
              fprintf ( target_ptr, "\n\n\n%9ld    (%1.4lf)\n\n",
                      val_sum, pct_sum);
              rank_freqs ( target_ptr, freq, nr_read);
              fclose ( target_ptr);
              fclose ( src_ptr);
      }
      printf ( "%ld chars read\n",
              nr_read);
}
```

count—ch( )

This function processes the source file and records the frequency
with which each alphabetic character occurs. Nonalphabetic
characters are all counted as equivalent.

To determine the cell in the frequency array that needs to be
incremented, the function calls **ch—index( )**. This function
returns the index of the cell containing information about the current character. Nonalphabetic characters are counted in cell 0.

ch—index( )

This function computes the specified character's ordinal position
in the alphabet. This value is used as the index for the character
in frequency and coding arrays. Nonalphabetic characters are
assigned 0 as their index.

rank_freqs( )

This function builds a linked list containing the index and relative frequency of each alphabetic character. The linked list is ordered, with the most frequent letter's node being at the end of the list.

To do its work, **rank_freqs( )** calls the linked list handling functions **get_node( )** and **middle_of_list( )**.

show_ch_list( )

This function displays the linked list, in order, on the screen.

Example

The following listing contains a message encrypted using a random substitution strategy. Function **set_random_subst( )** was used to encrypt the message.

```
/* Message encrypted using random substitution. */

Qhheyc: Heyaieu, qhwcichy --- em qhheyc qlcem, ywey qm yp mek,
qlcem ywey xc eic jpih xqyw, wefqhd wel ywcz gicfqpamuk qzgeiycl yp
am. Ywc lpryiqhc pt qhheyc qlcem qm phc pt ywc zpmy elzqiejuc teqywm
pt gwqupmpgwk, jcqhd qymcut eh qhheyc qlce ehl ywcictpic qherrcmmqjuc
yp lqmgippt, ywpadw Uproc tppuqmwuk maggpmcl wqzmcut yp wefc dqfch qy
e "juero ckc." Ezphd qhheyc qlcem zek jc zchyqphcl ywc jcuqct qh
phc'm ejquqyk yp rphlary e hcxmgegci, qh ywc diceyhcmm pt phc'm
rpahyik, qh ywc magciqpiqyk pt phc'm rqfquqneyqph, qh ywc qzgpiyehrc
pt phc'm gcimpheu etteqim ehl qh ywc qhycicmyqhd heyaic pt phc'm
lqmcemcm.

            ---- Ezjipmc Jqcirc, Ywc Lcfqu'm Lqryqpheik
```

This message contains the letter distribution shown in the following listing. The relative frequencies do not add up to 1.0 because the nonalphabetic characters (which generally account for about 20% to 25% of the characters in a file) are not included.

```
/* Relative letter frequencies in encrypted message. */

Relative Letter Frequencies:
e: 0.1006    i: 0.0799    n: 0.0695    t: 0.0680    a: 0.0666
o: 0.0621    s: 0.0562    r: 0.0355    h: 0.0355    d: 0.0266
l: 0.0237    f: 0.0237    p: 0.0178    c: 0.0178    y: 0.0148
m: 0.0148    b: 0.0148    u: 0.0133    g: 0.0104    v: 0.0089
w: 0.0044    k: 0.0030    z: 0.0015    x: 0.0000    q: 0.0000
j: 0.0000
```

A Cryptography Program

So far, you've seen some functions for generating two types of ciphers: offset and substitution. You've also seen some routines for computing frequency statistics for a message. These statistics can help you in your efforts to decipher a message.

In this section, you'll look at a program that lets you encode, decode, analyze, and guess at messages. Essentially, the program is an exerciser, not only for the routines already discussed, but also for some additional functions for displaying, analyzing, or storing various information.

The program works with two files: a source file containing a message to be encrypted or deciphered and a target file to which the translated message is written (and to which you may also have the program write replacement information and frequency statistics).

The program includes the following display capabilities:

- Show the original message
- Show the translated message
- Show frequency information
- Show replacement information

You can ask the program to make the following translations:

- Encrypt using an offset cipher
- Encrypt using a substitution cipher
- Decipher using an offset translation
- Decipher using an array of replacement characters specified by user

The program can also create, display, and store the following:

- An ordered list of letter frequencies
- A listing of replacement characters, based on an offset translation or on the user's guesses

- A translated version of the message, using a replacement array based on offsets or guesses

The following listing contains the program:

```c
/* Program for encoding and decoding cryptograms. */

#include <stdio.h>
#include <stdlib.h>
#include <string.h>
#include <ctype.h>
#include "dilist.c"


#define MAX_STR      100
#define MIN_STR      15
#define ALPHA        26
#define FALSE        0
#define TRUE         1
#define MINUS_SIGN   '-'
#define MAX_MENU     20    /* maximum menu choices */
#define ACTUAL_MENU  15    /* actual # menu choices in this program */

/* Function DECLARATIONS */
int          ch_index ( int);
void         check_range ( int);
void         count_ch ( FILE *, long int [], long int *);
int          get_int ( char *);
void         guess_ch ( int []);
int          open_both_files ( char *, char *);
struct lnode *rank_freqs ( struct lnode *, long int [], long int);
void         save_ch_list ( FILE *, struct lnode *);
void         save_code ( FILE *, int []);
void         set_offset ( int [], int);
void         set_random_subst ( int [], int);
void         show_code ( int []);
void         show_ch_list ( struct lnode *);
void         show_decoded_message ( FILE *);
void         show_menu ( char *[], int);
void         show_message ( FILE *);
void         translate_message ( FILE *, FILE *, int []);
void         wait (void);


char *null_str = "";

/* menu for the selections possible with this program */
char *menu [ MAX_MENU] = { "0) Quit",
                           "1) Show Message",
                           "2) Show Translated Message",
                           "3) Set Offset",
                           "4) Set Random Substitution",
                           "5) Sort Freqs",
```

```
                              "6) Show Freqs",
                              "7) Save Frequency Info",
                              "8) Guess Chars",
                              "9) Decode with Guesses",
                              "10) Translate Message",
                              "11) Show Replacement Array",
                              "12) Save Replacement Array",
                              "13) Show Guess Array",
                              "14) Save Guess Array"};

/* frequency with which each char appears in message */
long int    freq [ ALPHA + 1];       /* initalized to 0 */

/* user's replacement guesses */
int    guess [ ALPHA] = { '*', '*', '*', '*', '*', '*', '*', '*', '*',
                          '*', '*', '*', '*', '*', '*', '*', '*', '*',
                          '*', '*', '*', '*', '*', '*', '*', '*'};

/* replacement letters */
int    code [ ALPHA] = { 'a', 'b', 'c', 'd', 'e', 'f', 'g', 'h', 'i',
                         'j', 'k', 'l', 'm', 'n', 'o', 'p', 'q', 'r',
                         's', 't', 'u', 'v', 'w', 'x', 'y', 'z'};

FILE    *src_ptr, *target_ptr;


main ( int argc, char *argv [])
{
        long int    nr_ch = 0;
        int         offset,            /* cipher offset or seed */
                    selection;         /* menu selection */
        char        info [ MAX_STR];
        struct lnode *root = NULL, *temp = NULL;

        if (argc <= 2)    /* if too few parameters */
        {
                printf ( "Usage: count <source> <target>\n");
                exit ( 1);
        }
        else    /* if user provided two file names */
        {
            /* open source and target files.
               If not successful, exit with error.
            */
               if ( !open_both_files ( argv [ 1], argv [ 2]))
                       exit ( 1);

               /* get frequency data on source file. */
               count_ch ( src_ptr, freq, &nr_ch);
               rewind ( src_ptr);  /* move to front of file again */

               do         /* let user select from menu until done */
               {
                       wait ();
                       show_menu ( menu, ACTUAL_MENU);
                       gets ( info);
```

```
selection = atoi ( info);
switch (selection)
{
        case 0:
                break;
        case 1:  /* show original message */
                show_message ( src_ptr);
                break;
        case 2:  /* show decoded message */
                show_decoded_message (
                    target_ptr);
                break;
        case 3:  /* get, set cipher offset */
                offset = get_int ("Offset? ");
                set_offset ( code, offset);
                break;
        case 4:  /* set random cipher */
                offset = get_int ( "Seed? ");
                set_random_subst ( code,
                                        offset);
                break;
        case 5: /* rank order char freqs */
                root = rank_freqs ( root,
                            freq, nr_ch);
                break;
        case 6: /* show char frequency info */
                show_ch_list ( root);
                break;
        case 7: /* save char freq info */
                save_ch_list ( target_ptr,
                                    root);
                break;
        case 8: /* guesses for all chars */
                guess_ch ( guess);
                break;
        case 9: /* decode using guesses */
                translate_message ( src_ptr,
                    target_ptr, guess);
                break;
        case 10: /* encode with offset */
                translate_message ( src_ptr,
                    target_ptr, code);
                break;
        case 11: /* show replacements */
                show_code ( code);
                break;
        case 12: /* save replacement info */
                save_code ( target_ptr,
                                    code);
                break;
        case 13: /* show replacements */
                show_code ( guess);
                break;
```

```
                            case 14: /* save replacement info */
                                save_code ( target_ptr,
                                                guess);
                                    break;
                            default:
                                    break;
                    }  /* end switch (selection) */

            }
            while ( selection);    /* while user wants to work */

            fclose ( src_ptr);
            fclose ( target_ptr);
        }
}




/*
    void show_menu ( char *menu [], int menu_size)
    ************************************************************
    Display the specified menu, which is an array of strings.
    menu_size indicates the number of strings in the menu.
    Function also prompts user for a choice.

    CALLS : printf ()
    GLOBALS : MAX_MENU
    PARAMETERS :
            char *menu [] : array of strings, containing menu.
            int menu_size : number of items in menu.
    USAGE : show_menu ( menu, 10);
    ************************************************************
*/
void show_menu ( char *menu [], int menu_size)
{
        int count;
        char  *prompt = "Your choice (%d to %d)? ";

        printf ( "\n\n");

    /* if programmer claims menu has more than max allowed items,
        bring the value into line.
    */
        if ( menu_size > MAX_MENU)
                menu_size = MAX_MENU;

    /* display the individual strings in the array */
        for ( count = 0; count < menu_size; count++)
                printf ( "%s\n", menu [ count]);

        printf ( "\n\n");

    /* prompt user */
        printf ( prompt, 0, menu_size - 1);
}
```

```c
/*
    ************************************************************
    Let user enter the letter to be substituted for specified letter.

    CALLS : gets (); isalpha (); islower (); printf ();
            strcmp (); tolower ();
    GLOBALS : FALSE, MAX_STR, MINUS_SIGN, null_str, TRUE
    PARAMETERS :
            wrk : array of letter substitutions.
    RETURN : none
    USAGE : guess_ch ( guess_array);
    ************************************************************
*/
void guess_ch ( int wrk [])
{
        char   info [ MAX_STR];
        int    index, temp_ch, done [ ALPHA];

        for ( index = 0; index < ALPHA; index++)
        {
                done [ index] = FALSE;
        }
        for ( index = 0; index < ALPHA; index++)
        {
                if ( isalpha ( wrk [ index]) &&
                     islower ( wrk [ index]))
                        done [ wrk [ index] - 'a'] = TRUE;
        }
        do
        {
                printf ( "<Char><Guess> (-<char> to cancel guess) ");
                gets (info);
                if ( strcmp ( info, null_str) == 0)
                        break;
                info [ 0] = tolower ( info [ 0]);
                info [ 1] = tolower ( info [ 1]);
                if ( info [ 0] == MINUS_SIGN)
                {
                        temp_ch = wrk [ info [ 1] - 'a'];
                        if ( isalpha ( temp_ch) && islower ( temp_ch))
                                done [ temp_ch - 'a'] = FALSE;
                        wrk [ info [ 1] - 'a'] = '*';
                }
                else
                {
                        if ( done [ info [ 1] - 'a'])
                                printf ( "Letter already used.\n");
                        else
                        {
                                wrk [ info [ 0] - 'a'] = info [ 1];
                                done [ info [ 1] - 'a'] = TRUE;
                        }
                }
        }
        while ( strcmp ( info, null_str));
}
```

```
/*
    ************************************************************
    Make random substitutions for each letter.

    CALLS : check_range (); rand ();
    GLOBALS : ALPHA, FALSE, TRUE
    PARAMETERS :
            code : aray containing replacement chars, to be filled.
            seed : for random number generation.
    RETURN : none
    USAGE : set_random_subst ( my_array, 34);
    ************************************************************
*/
void set_random_subst ( int code [], int seed)
{
        int temp, index;
        int done [ ALPHA]; /* cell == TRUE if letter has been used */

        srand ( seed);

        for ( index = 0; index < ALPHA; index++)
                done [ index] = FALSE;

        for ( index = 0; index < ALPHA; index++)
        {
                temp = rand () % ALPHA;
            /* while letter has already been used, pick another */
                while ( done [ temp] || ( temp == index))
                        temp = rand () % ALPHA;
                code [ index] = (temp + 'a');
                code [ index] &= 127;
                check_range ( code [ index]);
                done [ temp] = TRUE;
        }
}




/*
    ************************************************************
    Make substitutions based on offsetting letters by specified amount.

    CALLS : check_range ();
    GLOBALS : ALPHA
    PARAMETERS :
            code : array containing replacement chars, to be filled.
            offset : amount to offset for substitution.
    RETURN : none
    USAGE : set_offset ( my_array, -6);
    ************************************************************
*/
void set_offset ( int code [], int offset)
{
        int temp, index;

        for ( index = 0; index < ALPHA; index++)
        {
```

```
                        temp = index + offset;
                        if ( temp >= ALPHA)
                                code [ index] = temp - ALPHA + 'a';
                        else if ( temp < 0)
                                code [ index] = temp + ALPHA + 'a';
                        else    /* if normal */
                                code [ index] =  temp + 'a';
                        code [ index] &= 127;
                        check_range ( code [ index]);
                }   /* for each character */
}


/*
    ************************************************************
    Use specified array to encode message in source file.

    CALLS : feof (); fprintf (); fseek (); getc ();
            isalpha (); isupper (); printf (); putc ();
            rewind (); tolower ();
    GLOBALS : EOF, SEEK_END
    PARAMETERS :
            src_ptr : file containing message to be encoded;
            target_ptr : file to which to write encoded message;
            code : array containing letters to be substituted
                    while encoding.
    RETURN : none
    USAGE : translate_message ( src, log, encode_array);
    ************************************************************
*/
void translate_message ( FILE *src_ptr, FILE *target_ptr, int code [])
{
        int curr_ch, ch, out_index, seek_result;

        if ( src_ptr != NULL)
                rewind ( src_ptr);
        else
                printf ( "Couldn't rewind source file\n");

        seek_result = fseek ( target_ptr, OL, SEEK_END);
        if ( seek_result)
                printf ( "End of target file not found.\n");

        fprintf ( target_ptr, "\n");

        for ( ; !feof ( src_ptr); )
        {
                curr_ch = getc ( src_ptr);
                if ( curr_ch == EOF)
                        continue;
                if ( isalpha ( curr_ch))
                {
                        out_index = tolower ( curr_ch) - 'a';
                        if ( isupper ( curr_ch))
                                ch = putc ( toupper (
                                        code [ out_index]),
                                        target_ptr);
```

```
                        else
                                ch = putc ( code [ out_index],
                                                target_ptr);
                }
                else
                        ch = putc ( curr_ch, target_ptr);
        }

        fprintf ( target_ptr, "\n");
}


/*
   ************************************************************
   Rank order info about letter frequency and store in linked list.

   CALLS : get_node (); middle_of_list (); printf ();
   GLOBALS : ALPHA, NULL
   PARAMETERS :
           list : pointer to first element of ordered list;
           vals : frequency information;
           nr_ch : total chars read.
   RETURN : pointer to ordered list.
   USAGE : root = rank_freqs ( root, freq_array, nr_read);
   ************************************************************
*/
struct lnode *rank_freqs ( struct lnode *list,
                        long int freq [ ], long int nr_ch)
{
        struct lnode *temp = NULL;  /* for ordering digraphs */
        int        index;
        double     val;

        if ( list == NULL)
                printf ( "Starting rank with EMPTY list\n");

    /* Build ordered list of frequencies */
        for ( index = 1; index <= ALPHA; index++)
        {
                if ( nr_ch != 0)
                        val = freq [ index] / ( double) nr_ch;
                else
                        val = 0.0;
                if ( val > 1.0)
                        printf ( "%.4lf is > 1.0\n", val);
                temp = get_node ( temp);
                if ( temp != NULL)
                {
                        temp -> data = val;
                        temp -> first = index;
                        temp -> second = ' ';
                        list = middle_of_list ( temp, list);
                }
                else
                {

                        printf ( "Can't allocate node storage.\n");
                        break;
```

```
                            }
                }    /* for each array cell */

                if ( list == NULL)
                            printf ( "Returning EMPTY list\n");
                return ( list);
}


/*
    ************************************************************
    Display contents of letter frequency list to screen.

    CALLS : printf ();
    GLOBALS : NULL
    PARAMETERS :
            list : pointer to list to be displayed.
    RETURN : none
    USAGE : show_ch_list ( root);
    ************************************************************
*/
void show_ch_list ( struct lnode *list)
{
        int index = 0;
        struct lnode *temp = NULL;

        temp = list;
        while ( temp != NULL)
        {
                printf ( "%c: %.4lf        ",
                        temp->first + 'a' - 1, temp->data);
                if ( ( index % 5) == 4)
                        printf ( "\n");
                index++;
                temp = temp -> next;
        }
}


/*
    ************************************************************
    Save contents of frequency list to specfied file.

    CALLS : fprintf (); fseek (); printf ();
    GLOBALS : NULL, SEEK_END
    PARAMETERS :
            target_ptr : pointer to file in which to save list;
            list : pointer to list to be written to file.
    RETURN : none
    USAGE : save_ch_list ( log, root);
    ************************************************************
*/
void save_ch_list ( FILE *target_ptr, struct lnode *list)
{
        struct  lnode *temp = NULL;
        int     counter = 0, seek_result;
```

```
        seek_result = fseek ( target_ptr, OL, SEEK_END);
        if ( seek_result)
                printf ( "End of target file not found.\n");

        fprintf ( target_ptr, "\nRelative Letter Frequencies:\n");

        temp = list;
        while ( temp != NULL)
        {
                fprintf ( target_ptr, "%c: %.4lf         ",
                        temp->first + 'a' - 1, temp->data);
                if ( ( counter % 5) == 4)
                        fprintf ( target_ptr, "\n");
                counter++;
                temp = temp -> next;
        }

        fprintf ( target_ptr, "\n");
}




/*
   ************************************************************
   Display unprocessed message on screen.

   CALLS : feof (); getc (); printf (); rewind ();
   GLOBALS : EOF
   PARAMETERS :
           src_ptr : pointer to file containing message.
   RETURN : none
   USAGE : show_message ( my_file);
   ************************************************************
*/
void show_message ( FILE *src_ptr)
{
        int ch;

        if ( src_ptr != NULL)
                rewind ( src_ptr);
        else
                printf ( "Can't read source file\n");

        for ( ; !feof ( src_ptr); )
        {
                ch = getc ( src_ptr);
                if ( ch == EOF)
                        continue;
                printf ( "%c", ch);
        }
}




/*
   ************************************************************
```

```
        Display message after it has been processed and written to file.

        CALLS : feof (); getc (); printf (); rewind ();
        GLOBALS : EOF, NULL
        PARAMETERS :
                f_ptr : file containing message to be displayed;
        RETURN : none
        USAGE : show_decoded_message ( log);
        ************************************************************
*/
void show_decoded_message ( FILE *f_ptr)
{
        int ch;

        if ( f_ptr != NULL)
                rewind ( f_ptr);
        else
                printf ( "Can't read source file\n");

        for ( ; !feof ( f_ptr); )
        {
                ch = getc ( f_ptr);
                if ( ch == EOF)
                        continue;
                printf ( "%c", ch);
        }
}


/*
    ************************************************************
    Return array index of specified character:
    0 if not a letter; ordinal position in alphabet if a letter.

    CALLS : isalpha (); tolower ();
    GLOBALS :
    PARAMETERS :
            ch : character whose array index value is sought.
    RETURN : index value of specified character.
    USAGE : desired_index = ch_index ( my_char);
    ************************************************************
*/
int ch_index ( int ch)
{
        if ( isalpha ( ch))
                return ( tolower ( ch) - 'a' + 1);
        else
                return ( 0);
}


/*
    ************************************************************
    Count the number of occurrences of each character in a file.
    Non-letters are all grouped together.

    CALLS : feof (); getc (); rewind ();
    GLOBALS :
```

```
    PARAMETERS :
            src_ptr : file containing message to be analyzed;
            vals : array for storing frequency information;
            rd : address of variable containing # chars read.
    RETURN : none
    USAGE : count_ch ( src, freq_array, &nr_read);
    ***********************************************************
*/
void  count_ch ( FILE *src_ptr, long int vals [ ], long int *rd)
{
        int    curr_ch, ch;

        rewind ( src_ptr);

    /* work as long as there are characters in source file */
        for ( ;  !feof ( src_ptr); )
        {
                curr_ch = getc ( src_ptr);
                (*rd)++;
                vals [ ch_index ( curr_ch)]++;
        }    /* while source file is not empty */
}


/*
    ***********************************************************
    Display replacement code on screen.

    CALLS : printf (); wait ();
    GLOBALS : ALPHA
    PARAMETERS :
            code : array containing replacement chars.
    RETURN : none
    USAGE : show_code ( code_array);
    ***********************************************************
*/
void  show_code ( int code [])
{
        int index;

        for ( index = 0; index < ALPHA; index++)
        {
                printf ( "%c: %c      ",
                        index + 'a', code [ index]);
                if ( ( index % 6) == 6)
                        printf ( "\n");
        }
}


/*
    ***********************************************************
    Save contents of frequency list to specfied file.

    CALLS : fprintf (); fseek (); printf ();
    GLOBALS : NULL, SEEK_END
```

```
        PARAMETERS :
                target_ptr : pointer to file in which to save list;
                code : array containing replacement chars.
        RETURN : none
        USAGE : save_ch_list ( log, root);
        **********************************************************
*/
void save_code ( FILE *target_ptr, int code [])
{
        int     index, seek_result;

        seek_result = fseek ( target_ptr, OL, SEEK_END);
        if ( seek_result)
                printf ( "End of target file not found.\n");

        fprintf ( target_ptr, "\nReplacement chars:\n");

        for ( index = 0; index < ALPHA; index++)
        {
                fprintf ( target_ptr, "%c: %c        ",
                        index + 'a', code [ index]);
                if ( ( index % 6) == 5)   /* 6 letters per line */
                        fprintf ( target_ptr, "\n");
        }   /* for each character */
        fprintf ( target_ptr, "\n\n");
}


/*
    **********************************************************
    Pause to let user see displayed material.

    CALLS : gets (); printf ();
    GLOBALS :
    PARAMETERS :
    RETURN :
    USAGE : wait ();
    **********************************************************
*/
void wait ()
{
        char resp [ MAX_STR];

        printf ( "<Return> to continue ");
        gets ( resp);
}


/*
    **********************************************************
    Prompt user for integer, and read user;s response.

    CALLS : atoi (); gets (); printf ();
    GLOBALS : MAX_STR
```

```
        PARAMETERS :
                message : string to display as prompt.
        RETURN : integer read.
        USAGE : selection = get_int ( "Your choice? ");
        ***********************************************************
*/
int  get_int ( char *message)
{
        char info [ MAX_STR];

        printf ( "%s ", message);
        gets ( info);
        return ( atoi ( info));
}




/*
    ***********************************************************
    Check whether specified character is lower case alphabetic;
    complain if not.

    CALLS : printf (); wait ();
    GLOBALS :
    PARAMETERS :
            ch : character to check.
    RETURN : none
    USAGE : check_range ( 'P');
    ***********************************************************
*/
void check_range ( int ch)
{
        if ( ( ch < 97) || ( ch > 122))
        {
                printf ( "%c: %d", '\07', ch);
                wait ();
        }
}




/*
    ***********************************************************
    CALLS : fopen (); printf ();
    GLOBALS : FALSE, NULL, TRUE
    PARAMETERS :
            src_name : name of source file;
            target_name : name of log file.
    RETURN : TRUE if both file opened; FALSE otherwise.
    USAGE : result = open_both_files ( "source", "log");
    ***********************************************************
*/
int open_both_files ( char *src_name, char *target_name)
{
```

```
/* open source file */
   src_ptr = fopen ( src_name, "r");
   if ( src_ptr == NULL)
   {
           printf ( "Source file not found\n");
           return ( FALSE);
   }
/* open output file */
   target_ptr = fopen ( target_name, "w+");
   if ( target_ptr == NULL)
   {
           printf ( "Target file not be opened\n");
           return ( FALSE);
   }
   return ( TRUE);
}
```

You've already used several of these functions, including **ch_index()**, **count_ch()**, **check_range()**, **rank_freqs()**, in earlier programs. Only the new functions will be mentioned here.

show_menu()

This function displays the menu of possible actions and prompts the user for a selection. You've seen this function in other situations. This function is very handy for programs where the user can keep cycling through the possible activities.

open_both_files()

This function tries to open the source and target, or log, files under the specified names. If successful, the program can proceed; otherwise, the program ends with an **exit()** call.

show_message() and show_decoded_message()

These two functions display the messages in the source and target files, respectively. Thus, **show_message()** displays the original message and **show_decoded_message()** displays the message from the target, or log, file.

show_ch_list() and show_code()

These functions display information on the screen. Function **show_ch_list()** displays the rank-ordered list of relative character frequencies. Function **show_code()** displays the contents of either the replacement array (**code[ ]**) or the array containing the user's guesses (**guess[ ]**).

save—ch—list( ) and save—code( )

These functions write information to the target file. Function **save—ch—list( )** writes the rank-ordered list of relative character frequencies. Function **save—code( )** writes the contents of either the replacement array (**code[ ]**) or the array containing the user's guesses (**guess[ ]**). Notice again how **fseek( )** is used.

guess—ch( )

This function lets the user guess at the likely replacement characters. For example, when trying to decipher a message, you may use the **rank—freqs( )** and **show—ch—list( )** functions to determine and display the most frequent letters. Using these data and the list of character frequencies in English text that you saw earlier in the chapter, you might start substituting characters in an effort to decipher the message.

Problems

The following listing contains some puzzles you may want to try solving. In some cases, the same message appears twice—encoded once with an offset cipher and once with a substitution cipher. All the cryptograms were created using the exerciser program. Use the program and try to decipher them.


```
/* Cryptogram puzzles */


Lzwjw sjw nwjq xwo egewflk af s esf'k wpaklwfuw ozwf zw wphwjawfuwk
kg emuz dmvaujgmk vakljwkk, gj ewwlk oalz kg dalldw uzsjalstdw
ugeeakwjslagf, sk ozwf zw ak af hmjkmal gx zak gof zsl. S nskl vwsd
gx uggdfwkk, sfv s hwumdasj vwyjww gx bmvyewfl, sjw jwimakalw af
usluzafy s zsl. S esf emkl fgl tw hjwuahalslw, gj zw jmfk gnwj al; zw
emkl fgl jmkz aflg lzw ghhgkalw wpljwew, gj zw dgkwk al sdlgywlzwj.
Lzw twkl osq ak, lg cwwh ywfldq mh oalz lzw gtbwul gx hmjkmal, lg tw
osjq sfv usmlagmk, lg osluz qgmj ghhgjlmfalq owdd, ywl yjsvmsddq
twxgjw al, lzwf escw s jshav vanw, kwarw al tq lzw ujgof, sfv klauc
al xajedq gf qgmj zwsv: keasdmfy hdwsksfldq sdd lzw laew, sk ax qgm
lzgmyzl al sk yggv a bgcw sk sfqtgvq wdkw.

          --- Uzsjdwk Vaucwfk, Lzw Haucoauc Hshwjk
```

Vqfyf pyf efym kfh ninfxvz bx p npx'z fjbzvfxwf hqfx qf fjcfybfxwfz
zi ndwq gdubwyidz ubzvyfzz, iy nffvz hbvq zi gbvvgf wqpybvprgf
winnbzfypvbix, pz hqfx qf bz bx cdyzdbv ik qbz ihx qpv. P epzv ufpg
ik wiigxfzz, pxu p cfwdgbpy ufsyff ik ldusnfxv, pyf yfodbzbvf bx
wpvwqbxs p qpv. P npx ndzv xiv rf cyfwbcbvpvf, iy qf ydxz iefy bv; qf
ndzv xiv ydzq bxvi vqf iccizbvf fjvyfnf, iy qf gizfz bv pgvisfvqfy.
Vqf rfzv hpm bz, vi tffc sfxvgm dc hbvq vqf irlfwv ik cdyzdbv, vi rf
hpym pxu wpdvbidz, vi hpvwq midy icciyvdxbvm hfgg, sfv sypudpggm
rfkiyf bv, vqfx nptf p ypcbu ubef, zfbaf bv rm vqf wyihx, pxu zvbwt
bv kbyngm ix midy qfpu: znbgbxs cgfpzpxvgm pgg vqf vbnf, pz bk mid
vqidsqv bv pz siiu p litf pz pxmrium fgzf.

            --- Wqpygfz Ubwtfxz, Vqf Cbwthbwt Cpcfyz

"Kag mdq axp, Rmftqd Iuxxumy," ftq kagzs ymz emup
"Mzp kagd tmud tme nqoayq hqdk itufq;
Mzp kqf kag uzoqeemzfxk efmzp az kagd tqmp ---
Pa kag ftuzw, mf kagd msq, uf ue dustf?"

"Uz yk kagft," Rmftqd Iuxxumy dqbxuqp fa tue eaz,
"U rqmdqp uf yustf uzvgdq ftq ndmuz;
Ngf, zai ftmf U'y bqdrqofxk egdq U tmhq zazq,
Itk, U pa uf msmuz mzp msmuz."

            --- Xqiue Omddaxx, Kag mdq Axp, Rmftqd Iuxxumy

Auiglkzmpl: Zvl jmynp nuwmzlu my myzluynzmiynp emxadzlx. Jiurlups
zvlxl emxadzlx flul xlzzple ws avsxmknp kiyznkz ij zvl emxadznyzx,
fmzv xdkv xmrapl nucdrlyzx nx zvl udemrlyznus picmk ij zvl zmrlx
kidpe xdaaps --- zvl xfiue, zvl xalnu, nye xi jiuzv. Fmzv zvl cuifzv
ij audelykl my rmpmznus njjnmux zvl auiglkzmpl knrl riul nye riul
myzi jnhiu, nye mx yif vlpe my vmcv lxzllr ws zvl rixz kidunclidx.
Mzx knamznp eljlkz mx zvnz mz ulodmulx aluxiynp nzzlyenykl nz zvl
aimyz ij auiadpxmiy.

Xnf: N zumzl aiadpnu xnsmyc, iu auihluw. ... Xi knpple wlkndxl mz
rnblx mzx fns myzi n fiiely vlne. Jippifmyc nul lqnraplx ij ipe xnfx
jmzzle fmzv ylf zllzv.

N alyys xnhle mx n alyys zi xodnyelu.
N rny mx byify ws zvl kiranys zvnz vl iucnymtlx.
Wlzzlu pnzl zvny wljiul nyswies vnx myhmzle sid.
Vnpj n pinj mx wlzzlu zvny n fvipl iyl mj zvlul mx rdkv lpxl.
Fvnz mx fiuzv eimyc mx fiuzv zvl zuidwpl ij nxbmyc xirlwies zi ei mz.
Plnxz xnme mx xiiylxz emxnhifle.
Xzumbl fvmpl sidu lrapislu vnx n wmc kiyzunkz.
Fvlul zvlul'x n fmpp zvlul'x n fiy'z.

             ---- Nrwuixl Wmlukl, Zvl Elhmp'x Emkzmiynus

```
Cvkkdgt xjhhji nzinz, ocjpbc ncz dn wt ivopmz ocz bziogzno xmzvopmz
gdqdib, rczi ncz azzgn ocz fidaz vo czm ocmjvo, dn vko oj yzqzgjk
pizskzxozy kjrzmn ja mzndnovixz, viy oj nziy yjxomdivdmzn agtdib,
zqzi rczi oczt cvqz wjpiy czm yjri viy ocdif oczt cvqz czm vo oczdm
hzmxt.

            --- Nvhpzg Wpogzm, Zmzrcji
```

```
Fc. Cthzocj Kptuiddic pixjtxn zlfipocj aclf yzi ptdjicxikk ..., oayic
o ktxelek oxj hlcskhcip aokztlx, ptyz foxq hzihsk oxj kyefwdik; oayic
kylrrtxn kejjixdq oxj kyoctxn owley ztf, yzix ok kejjixdq cexxtxn
alcpocj alc o aip rohik, oxj ok kejjixdq zodytxn onotx oxj kzostxn
ztk zioj; jltxn iuicqyztxn ptyz o bics oxj xlyztxn ptyz
rcifijtyoytlx.  ...  Fc. Cthzocj Kptuiddic pixjtxn ztk poq zlfipocj
oayic yztk aokztlx, pzthz tk hlxktjicij wq iutd-ftxjij fix yl wi
kqfwldthod la txylmthoytlx, oxj tk xly zidj wq kehz ricklxk yl jixlyi
yzoy kyoyi la jiir ptkjlf oxj ciadihytlx tx pzthz yzi ohylc sxlpk
ztfkida yl wi.

            --- Hzocdik Jthsixk, Yzi Ldj Hectlktyq Kzlr
```

TASKS AND SUGGESTIONS

If you're interested in cryptograms, you'll find lots of books on the topic and lots of puzzles in newspapers and magazines. In addition to the encryption strategies you've seen in this chapter, there are dozens of others. You might try implementing some of these and adding them to your program.

Partial Offset Ciphers

The Caesar cipher examined earlier used the entire alphabet to compute the offset values. You need not do this, however. For example, you might divide the alphabet into two or more groups. In a two-group split, group A might consist of the first 13 characters (*a* through *m*), and group B might consist of the rest.

You can then compute offsets independently for these groups. For example, you might use an offset of 4 to encrypt group A and an offset of −6 for group B. In this case, the replacement characters would be as shown in the following listing:

```
                  Group A                      Group B
Original   : a b c d e f g h i j k l m   n o p r q s t u v w x y z
Replacement: e f g h i j k l m a b c d   u v w x y z n o p q r s t
```

In this case, the offsets would be independent of each other, but the offset for each group would be computed using that group. You could also compute the offset for A using the letters in group B. The following listing shows what the replacements would be in that case for the same offsets. To find the replacement character for *a* in group A, go to group B and find the character that is offset by the appropriate amount from the first character in the group (because *a* is the first character in its group).

```
                  Group A                      Group B
Original   : a b c d e f g h i j k l m   n o p r q s t u v w x y z
Replacement: q r s t u v w x y z n o p   h i j k l m a b c d e f g
```

You might even use an offset cipher for one group and a replacement cipher for the other. Again, you could use each group for its own replacements, or you could use the other group for replacements.

Add functions to let you break your alphabet into at least two groups and to let you apply different encryption strategies to each group.

Keyword Ciphers

A large class of encryption techniques uses some predetermined *keyword* as the basis for a coding strategy. In such strategies, the letters of a keyword are the first ones used as replacements. The remaining letters in the alphabet are then used in order as replacements for the remaining characters in the original alphabet. See Dorothy L. Sayers's mystery novel *Have His Carcase* for an example of an elaborate keyword cipher.

The following listing shows the replacements for each of three different keywords: *decryption, wonderful,* and *programmability*. Notice what happens when the keyword contains repeated letters, as in the third example: The repetitions are simply discarded. Thus, *programmability* is written in somewhat abbreviated form, since about a third of its letters are repeated.

```
Original    : a b c d e f g h i j k l m n o p q r s t u v w x y z
Replacement: d e c r y p t i o n a b f g h j k l m q s u v w x z


Original    : a b c d e f g h i j k l m n o p q r s t u v w x y z
Replacement: w o n d e r f u l a b c g h i j k m p q s t v x y z


Original    : a b c d e f g h i j k l m n o p q r s t u v w x y z
Replacement: p r o g a m b i l t y c d e f h j k n q s u v w x z
```

Implement a keyword encryption function. Your function should let the user enter a keyword and should then generate the appropriate replacement array.

Ciphers Using Extended Character Sets

All the strategies you've looked at in this chapter have used only the alphabetic characters for encryption. You can create offset and substitution strategies in which the space character and the common punctuation characters (comma, period, hyphen, and so forth) are also used as replacements.

Such ciphers are considerably more difficult to solve. People generally make good use of the spatial layout of a message. The location of spaces gives you considerable cues concerning the message; for example, it helps you identify individual words. Short words such as *I*, or *a*, and *the*) can help you make good progress in deciphering a message. When another character is substituted for a space, the encrypted message becomes much more difficult to decipher because these visual cues are hidden.

Write encryption routines that will let you encode offsets or substitutions using an extended character set. Remember that you'll also need to modify the indexing routines.

Other Tools for Deciphering

If an encrypted message contains a single-letter word, the letter is almost certain to represent an *a* or *i*. Similarly, a three-letter word that appears multiple times in a message is likely to be *the*. If you can identify *the*, you've got over 10% of your problem solved.

Similarly, you can make use of digraph frequencies to help you identify the replacement patterns. You can use the digraph frequencies you computed earlier in this chapter or frequency lists from other sources, such as *Frequency Analysis of English Usage* by Francis and Kucera (Boston: Houghton Mifflin Co., 1982).

Write functions to look for one-letter words, and common two- and three-letter words and to compute relative frequencies of the most common digraphs.

Tiered Menus

Once your exerciser program is able to do all these things, your menu will be quite long. You may find it useful to develop routines for processing multiple menu layers. For example, the top level may let the user decide whether to show, translate, store, or compute. Once the user selects a top-level task, the program may ask for a lower-level selection. Thus, the program may ask you to specify what you want it to store.

Automated Guessing

Your encryption exerciser would be very convenient if the program could automatically substitute the most frequent letters in the message with their counterparts in a word frequency list. For example, once you have a frequency list, you may want the program to substitute the five most common letters in English text for the five most common letters in the cipher and then display the result.

Have Fun

You may find it enjoyable to use the program developed in this section to solve the cryptograms found in newspapers, books, and puzzle magazines, such as *Games* and others you can find in supermarkets and bookstores.

SUMMARY

In this chapter you learned about some functional and interesting ways to modify files. The first part of the chapter discussed two algorithms that compress text files by recoding certain characters or pairs in a more compact manner. You also developed some functions for doing certain analyses of text files, such as counting and ranking digraphs by frequency of occurrence.

The second part of the chapter developed functions that encrypt text files by means of two approaches. There was also a simple, general-purpose program for encrypting or deciphering messages.

The next chapter covers a very different topic. You'll learn how to gain access to certain DOS functions and will develop functions for using some of these services.

7

INTERACTING WITH DOS

Ordinarily, your C programs will perform tasks that are independent of the particular operating environment in which the program is running. For example, the C code for adding a series of numbers will be the same regardless of whether your program is to run under a DOS compiler such as QuickC or Microsoft C 5.0 or whether the program will run under a UNIX or XENIX operating system.

The actual program execution will, of course, depend on the low-level instructions generated by the compiler to accomplish the tasks in the operating environment. Your coding will not need to worry about these differences; after all, that's one of the advantages of high-level languages.

Sometimes, however, you may need to make use of services or functions provided by a particular operating system or machine. For example, your program may need to check the current time or date, or it may need to check how much space is available on a diskette. In such situations, you need some way of communicating directly with the operating system, or at least with one of its agents.

Under DOS, such communications are effected by means of interrupts. In this chapter, you'll learn something about software interrupts, and you'll find routines for making use of some of the more common functions and services provided by DOS and in the ROM-BIOS for your PC. Before jumping into a discussion of how to access DOS and put it to work for you, let's interrupt briefly to provide some background and context.

REGISTERS

Machines based on the Intel 8086 family of processors (including the 8088, the 80286, and others) do much of their work in machine registers of various sorts. These registers are 16 bits wide and are used to store various pieces of information when a program is running. When a program is executing, much of the action either takes place in these registers or is controlled by values currently stored in certain registers.

Of the 14 registers, 4 are general-purpose registers. These are known as AX, BX, CX, and DX, and they are used by the interrupt functions we'll be looking at. The AX register is generally known as the *accumulator register*, since input and output operations go through it and arithmetic operations are also performed in it. The BX register, or *base register*, is often used to store the base address of tables or address offsets. The CX register is often used as a counter for loops and is called the *count register*. Finally, the DX register, or *data register*, is used to store data used in computations.

Several other registers will also be used for some of the interrupts. The FLAGS register is used to signal errors or other special occurrences. Although this is a 16-bit register, individual bits in this register are used to indicate particular states or outcomes, such as overflow, zero result, and so forth. In the functions you'll look at, the FLAGS register is checked only to determine whether it is zero (no error) or nonzero (error). If there was an error, other registers will contain details or a code for the error.

Two other registers, the *index registers*, will be needed for certain functions. These registers are generally used to store addresses during other activities but may also be used to store intermediate results during computations. The two index registers are DI (destination index) and SI (source index). The DI register is used, for example, in a DOS service for renaming a file; the location of the new name string is stored in the DI register.

You can access an entire register at once, or you can access the high-order and low-order bytes of the register separately. When accessing the entire register, you would refer to, for example, AX. When accessing individual bytes, you would refer to the AH (high-order) and AL (low-order) bytes of AX, for example.

Your QuickC and C 5.0 implementations include a header file named **dos.h**. This file, which is not part of the Draft Proposed ANSI Standard, provides information and data structures for taking advantage of some of the services DOS can provide. The file contains a declaration for a REGS **union** type, which you can use to access the machine registers in your computer.

One version of the **union** is a structure whose members represent the most commonly used registers: the four general-purpose registers (AX, BX, CX, and DX), the FLAGS register, and the two index registers (DI and SI). Thus, each member of this structure is a 16-bit register. The other version of the **union** lets you access the individual bytes of a register. This version is a structure with members for the high- and low-order bytes of the four general-purpose registers—that is, AH, AL, BH, BL, CH, CL, DH, and DL.

The REGS **union** is used when you want to call DOS or the BIOS (Basic Input Output System) to perform a particular task, as you'll see in this chapter. Look at the declaration of the REGS **union** in the **dos.h** header file included with your QuickC or Microsoft C 5.0 package.

In addition to this **union** declaration, **dos.h** also contains the declarations for the Run-Time library functions you need to access the registers. In this chapter, you'll see how to use these functions to interact with DOS or the BIOS at a low level.

INTERRUPTS

An *interrupt* is essentially a signal from the program or elsewhere to the CPU. When an interrupt is made, the current activity stops temporarily while the desired task is carried out. Each interrupt has a numerical code associated with it; this code identifies the interrupt for the hardware, which then finds the code required to carry out the task specified by the interrupt.

There are two general ways of interrupting DOS via software. The first way uses a function call to pass an interrupt number directly to the operating system or the BIOS. The number passed corresponds to the interrupt requested. For example, software interrupt 0x25 is a request to do an absolute disk read, that is, to read a particular sector of the disk, regardless of whether this sector is part of a file or not. Microsoft provides a Run-Time library function, **int86()**, to call and execute interrupts directly.

The other way to interrupt DOS is to call a special software interrupt, 0x21, which provides access to additional DOS services. This interrupt is sometimes known as the *function dispatcher*, since its job is to get access to the appropriate DOS service. To use interrupt 0x21, you need to pass another value, which corresponds to the DOS service you want. For example, DOS service 0x36 tells you the amount of free disk space, and service 0x30 returns the DOS version number. The requested service number must be placed in a particular register before you call interrupt 0x21. This call is generally accomplished using either of two Run-Time library functions, **bdos()** or **intdos()**, that are provided to call the function dispatcher.

Most discussions of DOS interrupts and of the service functions accessible through these interrupts represent the codes for these interrupts in hexadecimal form. Thus, it's very common to see references to interrupt 0x21 (or 21H, for 21 *hex*) rather than to 33 (the decimal value corresponding to 0x21). We'll use hexadecimal representations here.

We'll be able to look at only a few of the many services available via the function dispatcher or directly through interrupts. For more information on DOS interrupts and DOS services, you might want to consult more-specialized books, such as Kris

Jamsa's *DOS: The Complete Reference* (Osborne/McGraw-Hill, 1987), Ray Duncan's *Advanced MS-DOS* (Bellevue, Wash.: Microsoft Press, 1986), or *Programmer's Reference Manual for IBM Personal Computers*, by Steven Armbrust & Ted Forgeron (Homewood, Ill.: Dow Jones-Irwin, 1986).

Cautions When Using DOS Interrupts

Be very careful when using DOS interrupts, especially if you're using interrupts or services that will actually change something on the disk. Before you use services that will reset the current date or that will write to particular parts of a disk, make very certain that you understand exactly how the interrupt or service works and that you know exactly what values you want to change and the new values to which you want to change them. You can get yourself into lots of trouble if you are sloppy here. Again, the references mentioned earlier can provide more details about the interrupts and services.

Caution: Interrupts can give you access to very privileged and critical areas of your disk, such as the directory area or internal settings. If you are not careful, you can easily change something inadvertently, damaging crucial files. Before you experiment with interrupts that will actually write or change information, back up your system. Also, be certain that you are sending the correct values *and* that the values are stored in the appropriate registers. You should get into the habit of doing as much error checking as possible when working with interrupts.

INTERRUPTING THROUGH THE FUNCTION DISPATCHER

There are two ways of getting access to the DOS or BIOS services: by going through the function dispatcher and by interrupting directly. The safer method is the one using the function dispatcher. By calling interrupts this way, you can be confident that your routines will work in the same way on different machines running DOS, as the function dispatcher "protects" your routines from hardware differences that may affect the way your machine actually does its work.

One drawback in using the function dispatcher is its speed. Sending indirect calls through interrupt 0x21 is slower than sending the interrupt directly to DOS or the BIOS. There are also certain services that are unavailable through the dispatcher. To get access to those services (such as the video functions) you need to interrupt directly.

In this section you'll learn how to request DOS services through the function dispatcher. The Run-Time library for QuickC and Microsoft C 5.0 includes the **bdos( )** and **intdos( )** functions for interrupting through the function dispatcher. The **bdos( )** function is for requesting simple services, and **intdos( )** is for services that require more information to be passed back and forth between your program and DOS.

int bdos (int fn__nr, int dx__val, int al__val)

The **bdos( )** Run-Time library function calls the function dispatcher (interrupt 0x21) to perform the service specified by the first argument, **fn__nr**. The **dx__val** parameter specifies the value to be placed in the DX register. If the desired function does not require a value in the DX register, you pass 0 for this parameter. Similarly, the third parameter specifies the 8-bit value to be placed in AL, the low-order byte of the AX register.

Thus, **bdos( )** is useful for DOS services that use only the DX and AX registers. (The service function number—that is, the first parameter to **bdos( )**—is actually stored in AH, the high-order byte of AX.) The function returns the **int** value stored in the 16-bit AX register after the interrupt. In this section, we'll look at some of the services that are accessible using **bdos( )**.

The nice thing about **bdos( )** is that you need not worry about any special data structures—you simply pass **int** values to the function. However, this simplicity is also a drawback of **bdos( )**:

The function is useful *only* for DOS services that involve just two of the general-purpose registers. Some service functions also involve the BX and CX registers or even some of the more specialized registers (such as for setting error or other flags). Do not use **bdos( )** for such interrupts.

0x1: Reading a Character from the Keyboard

DOS service function 0x1 gets a character from the input buffer (usually, the keyboard buffer) and echoes that character on the screen. This service function simply sits and waits until you type something into the keyboard buffer. To call this service, you need to request it by number; thus, the first argument to **bdos( )** would be 0x1, or simply 1 in this case.

Service 0x1 doesn't need any information to do its work; so you can use 0 for the second and third parameters. The service automatically echoes the character directly to the screen. You'll probably want to process the returned value so that your program can determine what character you've read. The following statement shows an example of a call to function **bdos( )**, requesting DOS service 0x1.

```
ret_val = bdos ( 0x1, 0, 0);
```

This statement accomplishes the following tasks:

1. It calls DOS function dispatcher (0x21) for the service function specified in the first parameter (in this case, 0x1).

2. It invokes the service function specified as the first argument. This service carries out its task based on the information, if any, stored in registers DX and AL. In the present example, the task is to read and display a character.

3. It returns the contents of the entire AX register after the service function has completed its work and has returned control to **bdos( )**.

The following program lets you type input for as long as you like. The program ends when you press CTRL-D.

```
/* Program to illustrate use of selected DOS software interrupts,
   and to illustrate use of run-time library function bdos().
*/

#include <stdio.h>
#include <dos.h>

void test_0x1 ( void);  /* routine to illustrate use of service 0x1 */


/* Illustrate use of bdos () for service function 0x1 ---
   read and echo a character from stdin.
*/
void test_0x1 ( )
{
        int resp;      /* return from call to bdos () */

        printf ( "Type your message, press Ctrl-D when done.\n");

    /* Repeat forever, or until a break.
       NOTE: You can also specify this as a preprocessor macro:
       #define FOREVER for ( ; ; )
    */
        for ( ; ; )
        {
            /* call function dispatcher */
            resp = bdos ( 0x1, 0, 0);
            resp &= 0xff; /* mask high order byte from resp */

            if ( resp == 0xd) /* if user typed return */
                    printf ( "%c", '\12'); /* send linefeed */
            else if ( resp == 0x4) /* if Ctrl-D */
                    break;              /* get out of loop */
        }   /* end forever */
}



main ()
{
        test_0x1 ();
}
```

There are several important points to notice about this example.

First, notice that the returned value, **resp**, is processed before use in tests. The input character is echoed to the screen immediately by the service function you have called. The value returned to **resp** is actually returned by function **bdos()** after the interrupt is completed. Recall that **bdos()** returns the contents of the entire AX register, whereas the character echoed on the screen is stored in the low-order byte, AL. The high-order byte, AH, can contain garbage or whatever was stored there the last time the register was used; therefore, you need to mask out the contents of the high-order byte before testing the character just typed.

Using the bitwise AND operator (&) is a quick way of accomplishing this. Thus, **resp & 0xff** zeros out the high-order byte and leaves the character value in **resp**. The example masks off the high-order byte in a separate statement for clarity. You can just as easily combine the **bdos( )** call and the masking in one step, as shown in the following line:

```
return = bdos ( 0x1, 0, 0) & 0xff;
```

A second point concerns the seemingly elaborate work involved when the user presses RETURN. The return character (0xd) simply sends a carriage return, which moves the cursor to the leftmost column. To actually move the cursor down to the next line, you need to send an additional line-feed character (0xa).

Such chores or niceties are usually done for you when you use higher-level functions, such as those in a Run-Time library. However, when you're working at the low level of DOS interrupts, you generally need to do many things yourself. This is one example.

Finally, notice that the control-D character "echoed" as a diamond on the screen. With DOS service function 0x1, the echo is automatic. You can filter out such special characters and handle them internally, rather than echoing them. You'll soon see another service function that will get input without echoing.

0x2: Writing a Character
to the Screen

DOS service function 0x2 writes a specified character to the standard output, which is generally the screen. The character you want to write is passed in as the value of **dx—val** when you call **bdos( )**. Again, you can pass 0 as the third parameter, since this service function does not use the contents of AL. For this service function, the first parameter to **bdos( )** will have to be 0x2, the code for the service function.

Thus, to accomplish the same thing as the call to **printf( )** in the preceding listing, you can substitute the following call to **bdos( )** for service function 0x2. Character '\12' is the line-feed character, represented as an octal code.

```
bdos ( 0x2, '\12', 0);
```

This instruction invokes **bdos( )** to have the function dispatcher start service function 0x2, which then writes the ASCII line-feed character to the screen.

0x3, 0x4, 0x5: Communicating with Ports and Printers

Service functions 0x3 and 0x4 let you communicate with the serial port on your computer. This port is generally COM1. Service 0x3 lets you read a character from the port. As such, the function is similar to service 0x1, but with a different input source. Function 0x4 lets you send a character to this port.

Service 0x3 has some drawbacks, particularly if the port is operating at a high transmission rate. Check the DOS documentation or one of the sources mentioned earlier for more details about this function and alternative ways of getting information from COM1.

Service function 0x5 lets you send a character to the printer, which is usually LPT1 or PRN. For example, you could use this DOS function to set up your printer before printing a document.

The following listing has functions you can use to call the services for communicating with the serial port and for sending information to a printer. You can incorporate the functions into programs, or you can simply use the actual function calls to **bdos( )** directly in your own code. The latter method can speed up the use of these services by saving the time required for an extra function call. The service requests are coded as separate functions for clarity in these listings.

```
/* Functions for communicating with serial and printer port,
   using bdos () function as the mediator, and using DOS services.

   If you need to increase speed, dispense with the functions,
   and simply put the calls to bdos() directly into your code.
   One way to do this, while keeping your code readable is to
   define the DOS service calls as macros. For example:

   #define SERIAL_RD  bdos ( 0x3, 0, 0) & 0xff
*/

/* Read a byte from the serial port, and return this value. */
int serial_rd ()
{
        int resp;

        resp = bdos ( 0x3, 0, 0) & 0xff;
        return ( resp);
}


/* Send a byte to the serial port. */
void serial_wrt ( int ch)
{
        ch &= 0xff;             /* just to make sure ch is a byte */
        bdos ( 0x4, ch, 0);    /* send ch to serial port */
}


/* Send a byte to the printer, usually LPT1 or PRN. */
void to_lpt ( int ch)
{
        ch &= 0xff;             /* just to make sure ch is a byte */
        bdos ( 0x5, ch, 0);    /* send ch to printer */
}
```

0x7, 0x8: Reading Without Echoing

Service functions 0x7 and 0x8 let you read a character from the standard input but without echoing this character to the screen. Thus, you can process the character internally and put it on the screen only if you wish. For example, the following listing uses function 0x8 instead of 0x1 to suppress echoing of the diamond when the user presses CTRL-D:

```
/* Program to illustrate use of selected DOS software interrupts,
   and to illustrate use of run-time library function bdos().
*/

#include <stdio.h>
#include <dos.h>

void test_0x8 ( void);  /* routine to illustrate use of service 0x8 */
```

```
/* Illustrate use of bdos () for service function 0x1 ---
   read and echo a character from stdin.
*/
void test_0x8 ( )
{
        int  resp;       /* return from call to bdos () */

        printf ( "Type your message, press Ctrl-D when done.\n");

        for ( ; ; )   /* repeat forever, or until a break */
        {
            /* call function dispatcher */
                resp = bdos ( 0x8, 0, 0);
                resp &= 0xff; /* mask high order byte from resp */

                if ( resp == 0xd)  /* if user typed return */
                {
                        bdos ( 0x2, 0xd, 0);       /* "echo" CR */
                        bdos ( 0x2, '\12', 0);   /* send linefeed */
                }
                else if ( resp == 0x4)  /* if Ctrl-D */
                        break;
                else /* if user types a "normal" character. */
                        bdos ( 0x2, resp, 0);   /* echo character */
        } /* end forever */
}


main ()
{
        test_0x8 ();
}
```

Function **test—0x8( )** lets you read the user's input, character by character, as in function **test—0x1( )**. In this case, however, the service function does not echo the character read. The function categorizes the character as a carriage return (0xd), control-D (0x4), or another character.

If the character is a carriage return, you need to send a line-feed character to move the cursor to the next line. However, in this function you also need to send the carriage return character, which must be echoed just like any other character.

If the character is control-D, the function breaks out of the loop, as before. This time the function does not echo the symbol that represents control-D. Other characters are simply echoed with a call to service function 0x2.

The difference between service functions 0x7 and 0x8 concerns their response to control-C and control-break characters. Service function 0x8 allows itself to be interrupted, as do most of the other service functions. Service function 0x7 ignores the break request and sends the control-C character through just like any other character.

0x9: Writing Strings

The services you've seen so far have all handled single characters. You can also use DOS to display an entire string, with service function 0x9. The string must end with a $ character, because the function displays until it finds this character. The following listing uses service function 0x9 to display the prompt string. Notice that the carriage return and the line feed are written separately after the string.

```
/* Program to illustrate use of selected DOS software interrupts,
   and to illustrate use of run-time library function bdos().
*/

#include <stdio.h>
#include <dos.h>

void test_0x8 ( void);  /* routine to illustrate use of service 0x8 */

/* Illustrate use of bdos () for service function 0x1 ---
   read and echo a character from stdin.
*/
void test_0x8 ( )
{
        int  resp;      /* return from call to bdos () */
        char *message =
               "Type your message, press Ctrl-D when done.$";

     /* write string through bdos (), wiht 0x9 as service code,
        with address of message as a parameter.
     */
        bdos ( 0x9, (unsigned) message, 0);
        bdos ( 0x2, 0xd, 0);    /* send CR */
        bdos ( 0x2, '\12', 0); /* send linefeed */

        for ( ; ; )   /* repeat forever, or until a break */
        {
             /* call function dispatcher */
                resp = bdos ( 0x8, 0, 0);
                resp &= 0xff; /* mask high order byte from resp */

                if ( resp == 0xd)  /* if user typed return */
                {
                        bdos ( 0x2, 0xd, 0);     /* "echo" CR */
                        bdos ( 0x2, '\12', 0);  /* send linefeed */
                }
                else if ( resp == 0x4)  /* if Ctrl-D */
                        break;
                else /* if user types a "normal" character. */
                        bdos ( 0x2, resp, 0);   /* echo character */
        } /* end forever */
}


main ()
{
        test_0x8 ();
}
```

0xb: Checking Input Status

The input service functions you've seen so far tend to sit and wait if there is nothing in the keyboard buffer. Under certain circumstances, this wastes time that could be better used doing other processing. One way of avoiding this is to check whether there is anything in the keyboard buffer. If the buffer contains a character, the program can then call an input-handling service to read the character.

DOS service function 0xb lets you check the buffer. Function **bdos( )** returns 0 if the keyboard buffer is empty and 0xff if there is something in the buffer. The following program uses service function 0xb to check whether the user has pressed a key. If so, the program echoes the character and waits for another character. While the buffer is empty, the program simply writes the uppercase alphabet over and over. To end the program, you would press CTRL-C.

```
/* Program to illustrate use of bdos () function and,
   more specifically, use of service 0xb --- check input status.
*/

#include <stdio.h>
#include <dos.h>

#define MAX_COUNT   26;  /* used to limit amount written on line */

void  text_0xb ( void);

/* Write to screen, until user presses a key.
Then stop until user presses another key.
Continue writing to screen, until ...
*/
void test_0xb ()
{
        int  count = 0, out, resp, ch;

        printf ( "Press any key to stop display; Ctrl-C to end.\n");
        resp = bdos ( 0x8, 0, 0); /* get a key, without echo. */

        for ( ; ; )
        {
                resp = bdos ( 0xb, 0, 0) & 0xff; /* keypress? */
                if ( resp == 0xff)   /* if yes ... */
                {
                        /* see what's in the keyboard buffer. */
                        ch = bdos ( 0x8, 0, 0) & 0xff;
                        /* write char twice, surrounded by *  */
                        bdos ( 0x2, '*', 0);
                        bdos ( 0x2, ch, 0);
                        bdos ( 0x2, ch, 0);
                        bdos ( 0x2, '*', 0);
                        /* get another character to start up again */
                        ch = bdos ( 0x8, 0, 0) & 0xff;
```

```
        }  /* end if keyboard buffer had a character */

        out = count % MAX_COUNT;  /* to generate letter rows */
        out += 'A';
        bdos ( 0x2, out, 0);
        bdos ( 0x2, ' ', 0);
        if ( ( count++ % 25) == 24)    /* if line is "full" */
        {
                bdos ( 0x2, 0xd, 0);  /* write CR, ... */
                bdos ( 0x2, 0xa, 0);  /* ... and linefeed */
        }  /* if time to go to next line */
    }  /* end forever */
}

main ()
{
    test_0xb ();
}
```

Your key presses will alternately start and stop the display. Your very first key press will start the display after the introductory message. At that point, function **test__0xb()** is waiting for you to do something. Recall that service functions (such as 0x8) wait until there is something in the keyboard buffer to read. As soon as you press a key, that character is read.

The function then enters the infinite **for** loop. The program displays characters and spaces, 50 to a line, as long as you have not pressed a key. Each time through the loop, service 0xb checks whether there is something in the keyboard buffer; if so, control is passed to service 0x8 to read the character. The character you typed is echoed twice, along with some other characters.

Since the call to 0x8 cleared the keyboard buffer of the character you typed, the next call stops the program until you press another key. The second call to service function 0x8 inside the **if** statement is not conditional on there being anything in the buffer. Thus, the program waits for you to press a key. Once you start the display again, service function 0xb keeps the program out of the **if** clause until you press another key.

0x19, 0x30: Other Simple
Service Functions

Service function 0x19 lets you determine the default disk drive. The function returns 0 in the low-order byte of AX through **bdos()** if the default drive is A, 1 if the drive is B, 2 if it's C, and so forth.

Service function 0x30 lets you determine the version of DOS currently running on your machine. This service returns information in both halves of the AX register. The low-order byte, AL, returns the major DOS version number (such as 1, 2, or 3); AH contains the minor version number (10, 11, and so on). *You* must get the constituent (byte-size) parts of this number after the return from **bdos( )**.

The easiest way to accomplish this is to get the low-order byte by masking the number with 0xff. This will leave only the low-order byte value. To get the value of the high-order byte, first mask the number with 0xff00—to zero out the low-order byte—and then right-shift the result by 8 bits.

The following listing shows how to use these two functions:

```
/* Program to illustrate use of bdos () function and
DOS services to determine default drive and DOS version.
*/

#include <stdio.h>
#include <dos.h>

main ()
{
        int resp, drive, major, minor;

    /* determine default drive */
        drive = bdos ( 0x19, 0, 0) & 0xff;
        printf ( "default drive = %c\n", drive + 'a');

    /* determine DOS version */
        resp = bdos ( 0x30, 0, 0);
        major = resp & 0xff;     /* major version in low-order byte */
    /* minor version in high order byte */
        minor = (resp & 0xff00) >> 8;
        printf ( "version %d.%d\n", major, minor);
}
```

The preceding service functions are all simple—they pass information via only two of the four general-purpose registers—and are all accessible using the Run-Time library function **bdos( )**. In the next section, you'll look at a Run-Time library function that enables you to call more-complex service functions. As with **bdos( )**, all service function requests will still go through the function dispatcher, interrupt 0x21.

int intdos (union REGS *inreg, union REGS *outreg)

Like **bdos( )**, the **intdos( )** function is used to effect a software interrupt and to execute a service function. Function **intdos( )** must be used instead of **bdos( )** when more than the DX register and the AL byte are involved in the call.

Function **intdos( )** also initiates a DOS software interrupt (0x21) for the function dispatcher, to request a specified operating system service. Unlike **bdos( )**, however, the **intdos( )** function passes information via unions that correspond to the general-purpose register and certain other registers. One version of the union works with entire registers; the other version works with individual bytes within registers. This REGS union is declared in the header file, **dos.h**.

The examples here assume that **inreg** and **outreg** are external variables, both defined as **union** REGS. Required values will be passed to the DOS service through **inreg**; results will be passed back to the calling function through **outreg**.

Before you call **intdos( )**, you need to put a value corresponding to the desired service into **inreg.h.ah**. You may also have to provide other information, depending on the service requested. In all cases, this information would be stored in the appropriate union member *before* calling **intdos( )**. The **intdos( )** function returns the value of register AX *after* the requested DOS service has done its work. The second pointer parameter, **&outreg**, also lets the function pass the contents of the entire REGS union back after the call.

Let's look at some examples to see how this works. We'll use separate functions to illustrate the service requests so as to make it easier to see the service at work.

0x36: Determining Available Disk Space

The following program tells you how much storage space is available on the default disk drive of your computer. The function

get—free—space( ) calls **intdos( )** for software interrupt 0x21 and requests DOS service 0x36, which ascertains and returns information about available disk space.

```
/* Program to determine available disk space.
   Program also illustrates use of DOS interrupts.
*/

#include <stdio.h>
#include <dos.h>

/* used to pass info to and from DOS services */
union REGS inreg, outreg;

long get_free_space ( void);

main ()
{
        long result;

        result = get_free_space ();
        printf ( "%ld total bytes free\n", result);
}


/* Determine available disk space on machine */
long get_free_space ()
{
        long  sectors, clusters, bytes, clusters_per_drive;
        long  total_free, disk_capacity;

     /* prepare inreg with the required information.
        The AH byte contains the DOS service requested;
        the DL byte contains drive about which you want information
     */
        inreg.h.ah = 0x36;      /* to ask for DOS service 0x36 */
        inreg.h.dl = 0x0;       /* to ask for current drive */

     /* Call the DOS interrupt 0x21, using intdos */
        intdos ( &inreg, &outreg);    /* to use interrupt 0x21 */

     /* results are stored in the registers.
        Total available space can be computed from:
        Sectors per cluster * Bytes per sector * Available Clusters
     */
        sectors = outreg.x.ax; /* sectors / cluster returned in AX */
        clusters = outreg.x.bx; /* return available clusters in BX */
        bytes = outreg.x.cx;    /* bytes per sector returned in CX */

     /* The following number is not needed to compute FREE space.
        It is useful for computing disk capacity, however.
     */
        clusters_per_drive = outreg.x.dx; /* clusters  in DX */

     /* Display information */
        printf ( "sectors == %d\n", sectors);
        printf ( "clusters == %d\n", clusters);
        printf ( "bytes == %d\n", bytes);
        printf ( "clusters_per_drive == %d\n", clusters_per_drive);
        total_free = bytes * sectors * clusters;
        disk_capacity = bytes * sectors * clusters_per_drive;
        printf ( "Total disk capacity == %ld\n", disk_capacity);
        printf ( "Total bytes free == %ld\n", total_free);
        return ( total_free);
}
```

This program produced the following output:

```
sectors == 4
clusters == 1636
bytes == 512
clusters_per_drive == 16318
Total disk capacity == 33419264
Total bytes free == 3350528
3350528 total bytes free
```

Once the DOS service function has been executed, the information needed to compute available disk space is returned in members of the union **outreg**. The number of sectors per cluster is returned in **ax**; the number of free clusters is returned in **bx**; the number of bytes per sector is returned in **cx**; and the total clusters on the disk are returned in **DX**. (See your DOS documentation or a book such as Kris Jamsa's *DOS: The Complete Reference* (Osborne/McGraw-Hill, 1987) for more information about how disks are organized into sectors and clusters.)

Notice that bytes were manipulated before calling **intdos( )**, whereas entire register values are returned. This is not uncommon when dealing with DOS interrupts and services. Generally, the number of the DOS service requested will be stored in **inreg.h.ah**, the high-order byte of AX. Additional information needed by a particular service may be stored in other bytes or registers.

0x2a, 0x2c: Getting Date and Time

The following program adds three new functions to the preceding program. Two of these use DOS services to do their work; the third, **how__long( )**, is used to compute the time elapsed between some starting point and a finishing point in your program.

```
/* Program to get current date
   and to time how long it takes to do this 1000 times.
   Program also illustrates use of DOS interrupts.
*/

#include <stdio.h>
#include <dos.h>

#define MAX_STR    80
#define FALSE       0
#define TRUE        1
```

```
union REGS inreg, outreg;
char  *null_str = "";

void   get_date ( int *, int *, int *);
double get_time ( void);
double how_long ( double, double);



/* function to get current date, and to pass information back
   in three pieces : month, date, year.
   Notice that month and date are stored in bytes, whereas year
   is stored in a 16 bit register value.
*/
void get_date ( int *month, int *day, int *year)
{
    /* Ask for DOS service 0x2a */
       inreg.h.ah = 0x2a;

    /* Call DOS interrupt 0x21 */
       intdos ( &inreg, &outreg);

       *month = outreg.h.dh;  /* current month returned in DH */
       *day = outreg.h.dl;    /* current day returned in DL */
       *year = outreg.x.cx;   /* current year returned in CX */
}



/* Function to get the number of seconds elapsed since
   midnight on the system clock.
*/
double get_time ()
{
       unsigned int hrs, mins, secs, hundredths;

    /* Request DOS service 0x2c */
       inreg.h.ah = 0x2c;

    /* Call interrupt 0x21 with the appropriate unions */
       intdos ( &inreg, &outreg);

       hrs = outreg.h.ch;    /* hours elapsed returned in CH */
       mins = outreg.h.cl;   /* minutes elapsed returned in CL */
       secs = outreg.h.dh;   /* seconds elapsed returned in DH */
       hundredths = outreg.h.dl; /* 1/100's secs returned in DL */

    /* Total elapsed time (in seconds) =
       3600 (secs / hr)  * hrs +
       60 ( secs / min) * mins +
       1 ( secs / sec) * secs +
       .01 ( secs per 1/100th sec) * hundredths.
```

```
        */
            return ( (double) hrs * 3600.0 + (double) mins * 60.0 +
                    (double) secs + (double) hundredths / 100.0);
}



/* Function to compute the number of seconds elapsed between
   start and finish
*/
double how_long ( double start, double finish)
{
#define FULL_DAY 86400.0  /* seconds in a 24 hr day */

    /* start == first elapsed time measurement;
       finish == second elapsed time measurement.
       If start > finish then the time must have passed midnight
       between start and finish of process.
       In that case, a formula adjustment is necessary.
    */
        if ( start > finish)
                return ( FULL_DAY - start + finish);
        else
                return ( finish - start);
}


main ()
{
        double start, finish;
        int    index, month, day, year;
        start = get_time ();     /* start timing */
        for ( index = 0; index < 1000; index++)
        {
                get_date ( &month, &day, &year);
        }
        finish = get_time ();    /* stop timing */
        printf ( "%d / %d / %d\n", month, day, year);
        printf ( "%10.2lf seconds elapsed\n",
                how_long ( start, finish));
}
```

The function **get—date( )** is used to determine the current date
on your machine. The DOS service function to provide this information is number 0x2a. The service returns the information in
three pieces, corresponding to month, day, and year. Notice that
month and day are returned in bytes, whereas the year is
returned in an entire 16-bit value. It turns out that this service
also returns the day of the week in numerical form. This informa-

tion is returned in AL, with Sunday being 0, Monday being 1, and so on. Modify the function to also provide this information to your program.

The **get_time( )** function uses DOS service function 0x2c to get information about the amount of time elapsed on the system clock since midnight. This time is reported in units ranging from hours down to hundredths of a second. Again, each of these values is returned in a different byte: hours in **outreg.h.ch**, minutes in **outreg.h.cl**, seconds in **outreg.h.dh**, and hundredths of a second in **outreg.h.dl**.

To time something in your program, just call **get_time( )** before starting the portion of the program that you want to time. This call assigns the amount of time elapsed between midnight and the time the program portion begins. When the timed portion is finished, call **get_time( )** again. The difference between the values returned by the second and first calls to **get_time( )** represents the amount of time the program portion took — provided you were not running this program around midnight.

If your first time reading is before midnight and your second reading is after midnight, the results will be incorrect if you simply subtract one value from the other, since elapsed time will start from 0 again at midnight. The **how_long( )** function returns the amount of time elapsed between two calls to function **get_time( )** and corrects the computations for the cases where you cross the midnight boundary. Check the code to see how this is done.

The program uses the three functions in the preceding listing to determine how long it takes to call DOS for the current date 1000 times.

0x2b, 0x2d: Setting the Time and Date

You can also change the values stored in the system time and date. Service function 0x2b will let you specify the month, day, and year to be used by the system. The call for this service is illustrated in function **set_date( )**, shown in the following listing:

```
/* function to set current date; information is passed
   in three pieces : month, date, year.
   Notice that month and date are stored in bytes, whereas year
   is stored in a 16 bit register value.
*/
int set_date ( int month, int day, int year)
{
        /* Ask for DOS service 0x2b */
        inreg.h.ah = 0x2b;

        inreg.h.dh = month;   /* send required values to service */
        inreg.h.dl = day;
        inreg.x.cx = year;

        /* Call DOS interrupt 0x21, the function dispatcher */
        intdos ( &inreg, &outreg);

        return ( !outreg.h.al);  /* BECOMES true is successful */
}


/* routine to let user exercise set_date () function. */
void test_set_date ()
{
        int     outcome, index, month, day, year;
        char    info [ MAX_STR];

        /* get required information */
        printf ( "month? ");
        gets ( info);
        month = atoi ( info);
        printf ( "day? ");
        gets ( info);
        day = atoi ( info);
        printf ( "year? ");
        gets ( info);
        year = atoi ( info);
        if ( year < 100)            /* adjust centuries on year. */
                year += 1900;
        outcome = set_date ( month, day, year);
        if ( outcome)
                printf ( "Date set successful\n");
        else
                printf ( "Date set UNsuccessful\n");
}
```

The date, which is stored in a byte (half register), must be a number between 1 and 31, inclusive. The month must be between 1 and 12, inclusive, and it is also stored in a byte. The year must be a value between 1980 and 2099, inclusive; the year is stored in an entire register. Any other values are considered invalid and will cause the service function to fail in its task.

The **oureg.h.al** member contains information about whether the date was changed successfully. If the value is 0, the date was changed; if the value is 0xff, the call failed.

To change the time information stored in the system clock, you need to put the desired values in the appropriate registers and then use **intdos( )** to call service function 0x2d to make the changes. The same registers are used in services 0x2c (get time) and 0x2d (set time). Function **set—time( )** shows how to call service 0x2d.

```
/* function to set current time; information is passed
   in four pieces : hours, minutes, seconds, hundredths of a second.
*/
int set_time ( int hours, int minutes, int seconds, int hundredths)
{
     /* Ask for DOS service 0x2d */
        inreg.h.ah = 0x2d;

        inreg.h.ch = hours;      /* send required values to service */
        inreg.h.cl = minutes;
        inreg.h.dh = seconds;
        inreg.h.dl = hundredths;

     /* Call DOS interrupt 0x21, the function dispatcher */
        intdos ( &inreg, &outreg);

        return ( !outreg.h.al);  /* BECOMES true is successful */
}


/* routine to let user exercise set_time () function. */
void test_set_time ()
{
        int     outcome, index, hour, min, sec, hundredth;
        char    info [ MAX_STR];

     /* get required information */
        printf ( "hour? ");
        gets ( info);
        hour = atoi ( info);
        printf ( "minute? ");
        gets ( info);
        min = atoi ( info);
        printf ( "second? ");
        gets ( info);
        sec = atoi ( info);
        printf ( "1/100's of a second? ");
        gets ( info);
        hundredth = atoi ( info);
        outcome = set_time ( hour, min, sec, hundredth);
        if ( outcome)
                printf ( "time set was successful\n");
        else
                printf ( "time set was UNsuccessful\n");
}
```

The hours and minutes are stored in the high and the low bytes of the CX register, respectively. The value of CH (**hours**) must be between 0 and 23, inclusive; the contents of the CL byte (**minutes**) must be between 0 and 59, inclusive. Similarly, the

seconds stored in DH must be between 0 and 59, inclusive, and the **hundredths** in DL must be between 0 and 99, inclusive.

As with service 0x2b, the AL byte of **outreg** contains 0 if the time was successfully changed and 0xff if the change was not made.

0x39, 0x3a, 0x3b: Manipulating Subdirectories

If you use directories and subdirectories in your work, you're probably familiar with some or all of the following DOS commands: **mkdir**, or **md**; **rmdir**, or **rd**; and **chdir**, or **cd**. These are commands for creating and deleting subdirectories and for moving from one subdirectory to another.

Service function 0x39 lets you create a directory. This service function works like the **mkdir** or **md** command. The **mk_dir( )** function in the following listing shows how to call this service function:

```
/* Program to test service for creating a directory. */

#include <stdio.h>
#include <dos.h>

#define TRUE     1
#define FALSE    0
#define MAX_STR  80

union REGS inreg, outreg;

int   mk_dir ( char *);
int   test_mk_dir ( void);

/* Create a directory having the specified name. */
int mk_dir ( char *name)
{
        inreg.h.ah = 0x39;        /* service request code */
     /* starting address of name string goes in DX register. */
        inreg.x.dx = (unsigned) &name [ 0];

        intdos ( &inreg, &outreg);  /* call function dispatcher */

        if ( outreg.x.cflag)   /* cflag is nonzero on error */
        {
                printf ( "Error. No subdirectory created. ");
                if ( outreg.x.ax == 3)   /* if error code == 3*/
                        printf ( "Path not found.\n");
                else                     /* other error code */
                        printf ("Not allowed or unable to create.\n");
                return ( FALSE);         /* report failure */
        }    /* end if directory creation error. */
        else /* if directory created */
                return ( TRUE);          /* report success */

}
```

```
int test_mk_dir ()
{
        char info [ MAX_STR];
        int  outcome;

        printf ( "Name of directory to create? ");
        gets ( info);
        outcome = mk_dir ( info);
        if ( outcome)
                printf ( "Directory created.\n");
        else
                printf ( "No directory created.\n");
        return ( outcome);
}

main ()
{
        int result;

        result = test_mk_dir ();
}
```

To use service function 0x39, you need to pass the address of the directory name—including any drive and path information—in **inreg.x.dx**. The contents at the specified memory location should be an ASCII string terminated by a null character (' \0 '). Such a string is often called an ASCIIZ string.

If the service function is unable to create a subdirectory under the specified name, the **outreg.x.cflag** member is set to a nonzero value, and a code for the reason for failure is specified in **outreg.x.ax**. The primary reasons for failure are that the pathname does not exist, there is already a subdirectory with the specified name and path, or there is no room to create a directory.

Service functions 0x3a and 0x3b take the same argument, the location of an ASCIIZ string containing the directory name. To delete the specified directory, call **intdos()** for service function 0x3a, as shown in function **rm_dir()** below. As with service function 0x39, the **outreg.x.cflag** member is nonzero if the call was unsuccessful. The service function will be unable to remove the subdirectory if the directory is not found, if it is the current directory, or if there are still files in the subdirectory.

To change to a new subdirectory, assign the location of the ASCIIZ string containing the subdirectory name to **inreg.x.dx**. Service 0x3b will make the specified directory the new current directory or will return an error value in **outreg.x.cflag** and an error code in **outreg.x.ax**. The only error code returned by this service function is 3, when the subdirectory is not found.

Functions **rm—dir( )** and **ch—dir( )** illustrate the use of service functions 0x3a and 0x3b, respectively.

```
/* Program to test services for removing a directory
   and switching directories.
*/

#include <stdio.h>
#include <dos.h>

#define TRUE      1
#define FALSE     0
#define MAX_STR   80

union REGS inreg, outreg;

int   ch_dir ( char *);
int   test_ch_dir ( void);
int   mk_dir ( char *);
int   test_mk_dir ( void);
int   rm_dir ( char *);
int   test_rm_dir ( void);


/* Create a directory having the specified name. */
int mk_dir ( char *name)
{
        inreg.h.ah = 0x39;        /* service request code */
    /* starting address of name string goes in DX register */
        inreg.x.dx = (unsigned) &name [ 0];

        intdos ( &inreg, &outreg); /* call function dispatcher */

        if ( outreg.x.cflag)    /* cflag is nonzero on error */
        {
                printf ( "Error. No subdirectory created. ");
                if ( outreg.x.ax == 3)    /* if error code == 3*/
                        printf ( "Path not found.\n");
                else                      /* other error code */
                        printf ("Not allowed or unable to create.\n");
                return ( FALSE);          /* report failure */
        }    /* end if directory creation error. */
        else /* if directory created */
                return ( TRUE);           /* report success */

}


int test_mk_dir ()
{
        char info [ MAX_STR];
        int  outcome;

        printf ( "directory name? ");
        gets ( info);
        outcome = mk_dir ( info);
        if ( outcome)
                printf ( "Directory created.\n");
        else
                printf ( "No directory created.\n");
        return ( outcome);
}
```

```c
/* Remove the specified directory */
int rm_dir ( char *name)
{
        inreg.h.ah = 0x3a;    /* service code to remove directory */
        inreg.x.dx = (unsigned) &name [ 0];

        intdos ( &inreg, &outreg);   /* call function dispatcher */

        if ( outreg.x.cflag)   /* cflag is nonzero on error */
        {
                printf ( "Error. Subdirectory not deleted. ");
                switch ( outreg.x.ax)   /* which error code? */
                {
                        case 3 :
                                printf ( "Path not found.\n");
                                break;
                        case 6 :
                                printf ( "Can't delete current ");
                                printf ( "directory.\n");
                                break;
                        default :
                                printf ( "Possibly not empty.\n");
                                break;
                }
                return ( FALSE);    /* report failure */
        }    /* end of error condition */
        else  /* if directory deleted */
                return ( TRUE);    /* report success */
}


int test_rm_dir ()
{
        char info [ MAX_STR];
        int  outcome;

        printf ( "Name of directory to remove? ");
        gets ( info);
        outcome = rm_dir ( info);
        if ( outcome)
                printf ( "Directory removed.\n");
        else
                printf ( "No directory deleted.\n");
        return ( outcome);
}


/* Change to the specified directory */
int ch_dir ( char *name)
{
        inreg.h.ah = 0x3b;    /* service code to change directories */
        inreg.x.dx = (unsigned) &name [ 0];

        intdos ( &inreg, &outreg);  /* call function dispatcher */

        if ( outreg.x.cflag)          /* cflag is nonzero on error */ .
        {
                printf ( "Error. No move made. ");
                if ( outreg.x.ax == 3)   /* if error code == 3 */
                        printf ( "Path not found.\n");
                else                     /* if other error code */
                        printf ( "Unable to move.\n");
                return ( FALSE);         /* report failure */
        }    /* end of error condition */
        else  /* if directory created */
                return ( TRUE);          /* report success */
}
```

```
int test_ch_dir ()
{
        char info [ MAX_STR];
        int   outcome;

        printf ( "Name of new directory? ");
        gets ( info);
        outcome = ch_dir ( info);
        if ( outcome)
                printf ( "Moved to new directory.\n");
        else
                printf ( "No move made.\n");
        return ( outcome);
}


main ()
{
        int result;

        result = test_ch_dir ();
        result = test_rm_dir ();
}
```

0x3c, 0x5b, 0x3d, 0x3e: Manipulating File Handles

DOS versions 2.0 and later give you access to files by means of integer values called *file handles*. There is a file handle associated with every open file, including five files that the system opens automatically: **stdin, stdout, sterr, stdaux,** and **stdprn.**

Thus, when a DOS service creates or opens a file, the function will return a file handle associated with that file. This handle serves as a "name" by which to refer to the file when using service functions. Although you can have up to 99 file handles, any single program can have only 20. Moreover, five of these file handles are used immediately to open the five default files.

DOS provides two service functions, 0x3c and 0x5b, for creating a new file. Service function 0x3c truncates an existing file to length 0; so the contents of any existing file are lost. On the other hand, if the file you want to create with 0x5b already exists, service 0x5b returns an error code about the existing file but does not destroy the file. Thus, service function 0x5b is the safer of the two ways to create a file, since it will prevent you from accidentally losing a file.

To call one of these service functions, put the function's code, 0x3c or 0x5b, in **inreg.h.ah,** put any special file attributes in **inreg.x.cx,** and put the starting location of the ASCIIZ string, containing the file name and path, into **inreg.x.dx**. By default, files opened with these service functions are read/write files. To specify this explicitly, put 0x0 in the CX register; to make the file read only, set this register to 0x1 before calling **intdos( )**; to make it a hidden file, put 0x2 in the CX register; finally, set this register to 0x4 if the file is to be a system file. These values actually correspond to turning individual bits on.

If successful, the service function returns the file handle in the AX register; if it's unsuccessful, the register contains one of the following error codes:

- 0x3, if the path was not found
- 0x4, if no handle was available—that is, if you already have the maximum allowable number of files open
- 0x5, if the service function was denied access to the file—for example, if an existing file with the same name was read only

An error code of 0x50 in the AX register indicates that the file could not be created because a file with the specified name already exists. This code is valid only for function 0x5b and *not* for 0x3c, since the latter service doesn't check. The **cflag** member is zero on return if the file was created and nonzero if there was an error. Both these service functions are illustrated in the next listing.

Service function 0x3d lets you open an existing file. In addition to the function's code in the AH byte, you can specify the file's attributes in the rightmost bits (0-2) of the AL byte. A value of 0x0 indicates read only, 0x1 indicates write permission, and 0x2 indicates read/write.

The starting location of the file's name should be stored in the DX register before you call **intdos( )**. When the file is opened, its pointer—which indicates where in the file the next action will take place—is set to the beginning of the file. Check one of the references mentioned earlier to see how to use DOS service 0x42 to move the file pointer—an action similar to that accomplished in Chapter 6 by using the **fseek( )** Run-Time library function.

Service function 0x3d returns information about the outcome of its efforts in the **cflag** member of the REGS **union** and in the AX register. If **outreg.x.cflag** is 0, the task was carried out successfully; the value of **outreg.x.ax** is the file handle. If the **cflag** member is nonzero, then **outreg.x.ax** contains one of the following error codes:

- 0x2, if the file could not be found
- 0x3, if the path could not be found
- 0x4, if the maximum allowable number of files are already open
- 0x5, if access was denied to the file for some reason
- 0xc, if the access code was invalid

Service function 0x3e lets you close the function specified with the file handle argument. The service function reads the handle of the file to be closed from the BX register. Outcome information is again returned in **outreg.x.cflag** and in **outreg.x.ax**. The only error code currently valid is 0xc, which indicates an invalid file handle.

The following listing lets you exercise functions for calling the service functions you've just seen:

```
/* Program to test services for creating, deleting,
   and opening files.
*/

#include <stdio.h>
#include <dos.h>

#define TRUE     1
#define FALSE    0
#define MAX_STR  80

union REGS inreg, outreg;
char  *null_str = "";

int   cl_file ( int);
int   test_cl_file ( void);
int   mk_file ( char *, int);
int   test_mk_file ( void);
int   op_file ( char *, int);
int   test_op_file ( void);
int   safe_mk_file ( char *, int);
int   test_safe_mk_file ( void);
```

```
main ()
{
        int result;

        /* result = test_mk_dir ();
        result = test_ch_dir (); */
        do
                result = test_safe_mk_file ();
        while ( result > 0);
        do
                result = test_cl_file ();
        while ( result > 0);
}


/* create a file and return file handle, if successful.
   WARNING: any existing file with the specified name will be
   overwritten. To avoid this, use safe_mk_file ();
*/
int mk_file ( char *name, int attrib)
{
        inreg.h.ah = 0x3c;      /* code for file creation service */
        inreg.x.cx = attrib;    /* file attribute -- e.g. read-only */

    /* starting location of file name, including path info */
        inreg.x.dx = (unsigned) &name [ 0];

        intdos ( &inreg, &outreg);   /* call function dispatcher */

        if ( outreg.x.cflag)  /* cflag is nonzero on error */
        {
                printf ( "Error code %d: \n", outreg.x.ax);
                if ( outreg.x.ax == 3)  /* if error code == 3 */
                        printf ( "path not found.\n");
                else if ( outreg.x.ax == 4)  /* error code == 4 */
                        printf ( "too many files open.\n");
                else            /* other error code */
                        printf ( "file is read-only.\n");
                return ( FALSE); /* report failure */
        }      /* end of error condition */
        else   /* if file was created */
                return ( outreg.x.ax);  /* return file handle  */
}


int test_mk_file ()
{
        char name [ MAX_STR], info [ MAX_STR];
        int  outcome = 0, attribute;

        printf ( "Name of file to create? ");
        gets ( name);
        if ( strcmp ( name, null_str) == 0)
                outcome = -1;

        if ( outcome >= 0)  /* if file name is not null string. */
        {
                /* 0 == read/write; 1 == read-only; 2 == hidden;
                   32 == archive;
                */
                printf ( "File attribute? (0, 1, 2, 4, 32)? ");
                gets ( info);
                attribute = atoi ( info);

                outcome = mk_file ( name, attribute);
```

```
                    if ( outcome)   /* if successful */
                            printf ( "File created, handle == %d.\n",
                                        outcome);
                    else
                            printf ( "No file created.\n");
            }  /* if file name was not empty */
            return ( outcome);
}


/* open an existing file and return file handle, if successful. */
int op_file ( char *name, int attrib)
{
        inreg.h.ah = 0x3d;     /* code for file opening service */
        inreg.x.cx = attrib;  /* file attribute -- e.g. read-only */

    /* starting location of file name, including path info */
        inreg.x.dx = (unsigned) &name [ 0];

        intdos ( &inreg, &outreg);  /* call function dispatcher */

        if ( outreg.x.cflag) /* cflag is nonzero on error */
        {
                printf ( "Error code %d: \n", outreg.x.ax);
                if ( outreg.x.ax == 3)  /* if error code == 3 */
                        printf ( "path not found.\n");
                else if ( outreg.x.ax == 4)  /* error code == 4 */
                        printf ( "too many files open.\n");
                else if ( outreg.x.ax == 5)
                        printf ( "file is read-only.\n");
                else
                        printf ( "File not found?\n");
                return ( FALSE);  /* report failure */
        }     /* end of error condition */
        else  /* if file was created */
                return ( outreg.x.ax);  /* return file handle  */
}


int test_op_file ()
{
        char name [ MAX_STR], info [ MAX_STR];
        int  outcome = 0, attribute;

        printf ( "Name of file to open? ");
        gets ( name);
        if ( strcmp ( name, null_str) == 0)
                outcome = -1;

        if ( outcome >= 0)  /* if file name is not null string. */
        {
            /* 0 == read/write; 1 == read-only; 2 == hidden;
               32 == archive;
            */
                printf ( "File attribute? (0, 1, 2, 4, 32)? ");
                gets ( info);
                attribute = atoi ( info);

                outcome = op_file ( name, attribute);

                if ( outcome)   /* if successful */
                        printf ( "File opened, handle == %d.\n",
                                    outcome);
                else
                        printf ( "No file opened.\n");
```

```
        }  /* if file name was not empty */
        return ( outcome);
}



/* close the file specified by the handle */
int cl_file ( int handle)
{
        inreg.h.ah = Ox3e;     /* code for file closing service */
        inreg.x.bx = handle;   /* file handle, to identify file */

        intdos ( &inreg, &outreg);

        if ( outreg.x.cflag)  /* cflag is nonzero on error */
        {
                printf ( "Error code %d: \n", outreg.x.ax);
                printf ( "Invalid handle or file not open.\n");
                return ( FALSE);    /* report failure */
        }    /* end error condition */
        else
                return ( TRUE);    /* report success */
}


int test_cl_file ()
{
        char info [ MAX_STR];
        int  outcome = 0, handle;

        printf ( "File handle? \n");
        gets ( info);
        handle = atoi ( info);

        if ( handle > 0)
                outcome = cl_file ( handle);

        if ( outcome)
                printf ( "File with handle == %d closed.\n",
                        handle);
        else
                printf ( "No file closed.\n");
        return ( outcome);
}



/* create a file and return file handle, if successful. */
int safe_mk_file ( char *name, int attrib)
{
        inreg.h.ah = Ox5b;     /* code for file creation service */
        inreg.x.cx = attrib;   /* file attribute -- e.g. read-only */

    /* starting location of file name, including path info */
        inreg.x.dx = (unsigned) &name [ 0];

        intdos ( &inreg, &outreg);  /* call function dispatcher */

        if ( outreg.x.cflag)  /* cflag is nonzero on error */
        {
                printf ( "Error code %d: \n", outreg.x.ax);
                if ( outreg.x.ax == 3)  /* if error code == 3 */
                        printf ( "path not found.\n");
                else if ( outreg.x.ax == 4)  /* error code == 4 */
```

```
                        printf ( "too many files open.\n");
                else if ( outreg.x.ax == 5) /* error code == 5 */
                        printf ( "no room to create file.\n");
                else if ( outreg.x.ax == 0x50) /* error code == 80 */
                        printf ( "file already exists.\n");
                else                           /* other error code */
                        printf ( "unknown error, no file created.\n");
                return ( FALSE);   /* report failure */
        }     /* end of error condition */
        else  /* if file was created */
                return ( outreg.x.ax);  /* return file handle  */
}


int test_safe_mk_file ()
{
        char name [ MAX_STR], info [ MAX_STR];
        int  outcome = 0, attribute;

        printf ( "Name of file to create? ");
        gets ( name);
        if ( strcmp ( name, null_str) == 0)
                outcome = -1;

        if ( outcome >= 0)  /* if file name is not null string. */
        {
                /* 0 == read/write; 1 == read-only; 2 == hidden;
                   32 == archive;
                */
                printf ( "File attribute? (0, 1, 2, 4, 32)? ");
                gets ( info);
                attribute = atoi ( info);

                outcome = safe_mk_file ( name, attribute);

                if ( outcome)   /* if successful */
                        printf ( "File created, handle == %d.\n",
                                        outcome);
                else
                        printf ( "No file created.\n");
        } /* if file name was not empty */
        return ( outcome);
}
```

0x3f, 0x40: Reading and Writing Files

You can read a specified number of bytes from a file by using service function 0x3f. This service assumes you've used a DOS service to open the file for reading. You need to provide the following information when calling **intdos( )** for this service:

- The handle of the file from which the service function should read

- The number of bytes to read

- The starting location of the variable to which the information read will be assigned

The last item will generally be a string. You should make sure you have sufficient storage available for the string to store the amount you expect to read.

When this service function is done, the AX register will contain either the number of bytes actually read or an error code, depending on the value of **cflag**. If there is no error (if **cflag** = 0), AX will contain a number between 0 and the number of bytes that should have been read.

If AX contains 0, you have reached the end of the file, and it's not possible to read anything more. If AX is nonzero but is less than the number that should have been read, only some of the material was read. Most likely this will happen near the end of the file, where you may finish with too few characters to fill the entire buffer you wanted to read.

Service function 0x40 lets you write to a file. You need to provide the following information: file handle (stored in **inreg.x.bx**), number of bytes to write to file (stored in **inreg.x.cx**), and starting location of bytes to write (in **inreg.x.dx**).

If successful, the service function returns the number of characters written or 0 in the AX register. The **outreg.x.cflag** member is 0 in this case. If the value of **outreg.x.ax** is 0 on return, the disk is full; if **outreg.x.ax** is less than the number of bytes you wanted to write, there may be an error.

If the service function was unable to write anything to the file, **outreg.x.cflag** is nonzero, and **outreg.x.ax** contains an error code. A value of 5 in the AX register indicates that the file is probably read only; a value of 6 indicates that the file handle is invalid or that the file is not open.

The following listing shows how to read from and write to a file. Notice that the file specification is by means of an **int** parameter, which indicates the handle associated with the file. This parameter format is different from the parameter passed when using C Run-Time functions, such as **fopen()**, **fclose()**, and **fprintf()**. These higher-level functions use a pointer to a file as their parameter. Although the two types of parameters provide access to similar kinds of information, pointers to file (FILE *) and file handles (**int**) are different.

```
/* Program to test services for reading and writing files. */

#include <stdio.h>
#include <dos.h>

#define TRUE      1
#define FALSE     0
#define MAX_STR   80
#define BUFF_SIZE 50

union REGS inreg, outreg;
char  *null_str = "";

int   cl_file ( int);
int   test_cl_file ( void);
int   mk_file ( char *, int);
int   test_mk_file ( void);
int   op_file ( char *, int);
int   test_op_file ( void);
int   safe_mk_file ( char *, int);
int   test_safe_mk_file ( void);
int   rd_file ( int, int, char *);
int   wr_file ( int, int, char *);


main ()
{
        int  r_handle, w_handle, r_result, w_result;
        char str [ MAX_STR];

        r_handle = test_op_file ();
        w_handle = test_mk_file ();
        if ( r_handle && w_handle)     /* if both files were opened */
        {
                do  /* work as long as source file not empty */
                {
                        r_result = rd_file (r_handle, BUFF_SIZE, str);
                        if ( r_result < 0)   /* if read error  */
                        {
                                printf ( "Error reading file.\n");
                                exit (1);
                        }
                        if ( r_result == 0) /* end of source file */
                                printf ( "End of file reached.\n");
                        /* if only a partial read */
                        else if ( r_result < BUFF_SIZE)
                                str [ r_result] = '\0';
                        else    /* if a full read */
                                str [ BUFF_SIZE] = '\0';
                        printf ( "%s\n", str);
                        /* Notice r_result is used for write length.
                        Otherwise, garbage characters get written.
                        */
                        if ( r_result > 0) /* if something read */
                                w_result = wr_file ( w_handle,
                                                r_result, str);
                }
                while ( r_result > 0);
                cl_file ( r_handle);
                cl_file ( w_handle);
        }
}
```

```
/* create a file and return file handle, if successful.
   WARNING: any existing file with the specified name will be
   overwritten. To avoid this, use safe_mk_file ();
*/
int mk_file ( char *name, int attrib)
{
        inreg.h.ah = 0x3c;      /* code for file creation service */
        inreg.x.cx = attrib;  /* file attribute -- e.g. read-only */

    /* starting location of file name, including path info */
        inreg.x.dx = (unsigned) &name [ 0];

        intdos ( &inreg, &outreg);  /* call function dispatcher */

        if ( outreg.x.cflag)  /* cflag is nonzero on error */
        {
                printf ( "Error code %d: \n", outreg.x.ax);
                if ( outreg.x.ax == 3)  /* if error code == 3 */
                        printf ( "path not found.\n");
                else if ( outreg.x.ax == 4)  /* error code == 4 */
                        printf ( "too many files open.\n");
                else        /* other error code */
                        printf ( "file is read-only.\n");
                return ( FALSE);  /* report failure */
        }   /* end of error condition */
        else  /* if file was created */
                return ( outreg.x.ax);  /* return file handle  */
}


int test_mk_file ()
{
        char name [ MAX_STR], info [ MAX_STR];
        int  outcome = 0, attribute;

        printf ( "Name of file to create? ");
        gets ( name);
        if ( strcmp ( name, null_str) == 0)
                outcome = -1;

        if ( outcome >= 0)  /* if file name is not null string. */
        {
            /* 0 == read/write; 1 == read-only; 2 == hidden;
               32 == archive;
            */
                printf ( "File attribute? (0, 1, 2, 4, 32)? ");
                gets ( info);
                attribute = atoi ( info);

                outcome = mk_file ( name, attribute);

                if ( outcome)   /* if successful */
                        printf ( "File created, handle == %d.\n",
                                  outcome);
                else
                        printf ( "No file created.\n");
        } /* if file name was not empty */
        return ( outcome);
}
```

```
/* open an existing file and return file handle, if successful. */
int op_file ( char *name, int attrib)
{
        inreg.h.ah = 0x3d;      /* code for file opening service */
        inreg.x.cx = attrib;   /* file attribute -- e.g. read-only */

    /* starting location of file name, including path info */
        inreg.x.dx = (unsigned) &name [ 0];

        intdos ( &inreg, &outreg);  /* call function dispatcher */

        if ( outreg.x.cflag)  /* cflag is nonzero on error */
        {
                printf ( "Error code %d: \n", outreg.x.ax);
                if ( outreg.x.ax == 3)  /* if error code == 3 */
                        printf ( "path not found.\n");
                else if ( outreg.x.ax == 4)  /* error code == 4 */
                        printf ( "too many files open.\n");
                else if ( outreg.x.ax == 5)
                        printf ( "file is read-only.\n");
                else
                        printf ( "File not found?\n");
                return ( FALSE);  /* report failure */
        }     /* end of error condition */
        else  /* if file was created */
                return ( outreg.x.ax);  /* return file handle */
}


int test_op_file ()
{
        char name [ MAX_STR], info [ MAX_STR];
        int  outcome = 0, attribute;

        printf ( "Name of file to open? ");
        gets ( name);
        if ( strcmp ( name, null_str) == 0)
                outcome = -1;

        if ( outcome >= 0)  /* if file name is not null string. */
        {
            /* 0 == read/write; 1 == read-only; 2 == hidden;
               32 == archive;
            */
                printf ( "File attribute? (0, 1, 2, 4, 32)? ");
                gets ( info);
                attribute = atoi ( info);

                outcome = op_file ( name, attribute);

                if ( outcome)   /* if successful */
                        printf ( "File opened, handle == %d.\n",
                                    outcome);
                else
                        printf ( "No file opened.\n");
        } /* if file name was not empty */
        return ( outcome);
}
```

```
/* close the file specified by the handle */
int cl_file ( int handle)
{
        inreg.h.ah = 0x3e;    /* code for file closing service */
        inreg.x.bx = handle;  /* file handle, to identify file */

        intdos ( &inreg, &outreg);

        if ( outreg.x.cflag) /* cflag is nonzero on error */
        {
                printf ( "Error code %d: \n", outreg.x.ax);
                printf ( "Invalid handle or file not open.\n");
                return ( FALSE);    /* report failure */
        }    /* end error condition */
        else
                return ( TRUE);     /* report success */
}


int test_cl_file ()
{
        char info [ MAX_STR];
        int  outcome = 0, handle;

        printf ( "File handle? \n");
        gets ( info);
        handle = atoi ( info);

        if ( handle > 0)
                outcome = cl_file ( handle);

        if ( outcome)
                printf ( "File with handle == %d closed.\n",
                        handle);
        else
                printf ( "No file closed.\n");
        return ( outcome);
}


/* create a file and return file handle, if successful. */
int safe_mk_file ( char *name, int attrib)
{
        inreg.h.ah = 0x5b;    /* code for file creation service */
        inreg.x.cx = attrib;  /* file attribute -- e.g. read-only */

    /* starting location of file name, including path info */
        inreg.x.dx = (unsigned) &name [ 0];

        intdos ( &inreg, &outreg);  /* call function dispatcher */

        if ( outreg.x.cflag) /* cflag is nonzero on error */
        {
                printf ( "Error code %d: \n", outreg.x.ax);
                if ( outreg.x.ax == 3)   /* if error code == 3 */
                        printf ( "path not found.\n");
                else if ( outreg.x.ax == 4)  /* error code == 4 */
                        printf ( "too many files open.\n");
                else if ( outreg.x.ax == 5) /* error code == 5 */
                        printf ( "no room to create file.\n");
                else if ( outreg.x.ax == 0x50) /* error code == 80 */
                        printf ( "file already exists.\n");
```

```
                else                            /* other error code */
                        printf ( "unknown error, no file created.\n");
                return ( FALSE);  /* report failure */
        }    /* end of error condition */
        else  /* if file was created */
                return ( outreg.x.ax);  /* return file handle  */
}


int test_safe_mk_file ()
{
        char name [ MAX_STR], info [ MAX_STR];
        int  outcome = 0, attribute;

        printf ( "Name of file to create? ");
        gets ( name);
        if ( strcmp ( name, null_str) == 0)
                outcome = -1;

        if ( outcome >= 0)  /* if file name is not null string. */
        {
            /* 0 == read/write; 1 == read-only; 2 == hidden;
               32 == archive;
            */
                printf ( "File attribute? (0, 1, 2, 4, 32)? ");
                gets ( info);
                attribute = atoi ( info);

                outcome = safe_mk_file ( name, attribute);

                if ( outcome)    /* if successful */
                        printf ( "File created, handle == %d.\n",
                                 outcome);
                else
                        printf ( "No file created.\n");
        } /* if file name was not empty */
        return ( outcome);
}



/* Write specified number of bytes to file */
int wr_file ( int handle, int size, char *message)
{
        inreg.h.ah = 0x40;
        inreg.x.bx = handle;
        inreg.x.cx = size;
        inreg.x.dx = (unsigned) &message [ 0];

        intdos ( &inreg, &outreg);

        if ( outreg.x.cflag)
        {
                printf ( "Error writing, code == %d\n",
                        outreg.x.ax);
                if ( outreg.x.ax == 5)
                        printf ( "file is read only?\n");
                else
                        printf ( "file not open?\n");
                return ( -1);
        }
        else    /* if no error */
        {
```

```
                if ( outreg.x.ax == 0)
                        printf ( "end of file reached.\n");
                else if ( outreg.x.ax < size)
                {
                        printf ( "Partial file write of %d chars.\n",
                                outreg.x.ax);
                }
        }
        return ( outreg.x.ax);
}


/* Read specified number of bytes from file */
int rd_file ( int handle, int size, char *message)
{
        inreg.h.ah = 0x3f;
        inreg.x.bx = handle;
        inreg.x.cx = size;              /* bytes to read */
        inreg.x.dx = (unsigned) &message [ 0];

        intdos ( &inreg, &outreg);

        if ( outreg.x.cflag)    /* cflag is nonzero on error */
        {
                printf ( "Error reading, code == %d\n",
                        outreg.x.ax);
                if ( outreg.x.ax == 5)
                        printf ( "file is read only?\n");
                else
                        printf ( "file not open?\n");
                return ( -1);
        }   /* end error condition */
        else    /* if no error */
        {
                if ( outreg.x.ax == 0)
                        printf ( "end of file reached.\n");
                else if ( outreg.x.ax < size)
                {
                        printf ( "Partial file read of %d chars.\n",
                                outreg.x.ax);
                }
        }
        return ( outreg.x.ax);
}
```

0x43: Reading and Setting
File Attributes

Service function 0x43 lets you determine whether a file is read
only, hidden, or otherwise. You can also use this service to set the
file's attribute to one of these values. Unlike the service functions
you've just seen, however, 0x43 does not use a file handle to identify the file; rather, it uses the file's name.

As always, **inreg.h.ah** will contain the function service code. If
you want to *get* the file's attribute, set **inreg.h.al** to 0x0; set it to
0x1 if you want to *change* the file's attribute. To change the attri-

bute, put the new attribute value in **inreg.x.cx**. A value of 0x0 indicates read only, 0x2 indicates a hidden file, 0x4 indicates a system file, and 0x20 indicates an archive file. To specify the file, pass the starting location of the file's name in **inreg.x.dx**.

The following listing shows an example using service function 0x43:

```c
/* Program illustrating use of DOS service for setting
    or reading file attributes.
*/

#include <stdio.h>
#include <string.h>
#include <dos.h>

#define MAX_STR  100

union REGS  inreg, outreg;

int attribute ( char *, int, int);

int attribute ( char *name, int action, int setting)
{
        inreg.h.ah = 0x43;      /* code for attribute service */
        inreg.h.al = action;    /* 0 == get; 1 == set */
        if ( action)            /* if set, specify new attributes(s) */
                inreg.x.cx = setting & 0xff;
        inreg.x.dx = (unsigned) &name [ 0]; /* address of file name */

        intdos ( &inreg, &outreg);   /* call function dispatcher */

        if ( outreg.x.cflag)         /* cflag is nonzero on error */
        {
                printf ( "Error code %d\n", outreg.x.ax);
                switch ( outreg.x.ax)
                {
                        case 0x1:
                                printf ( "invalid request.\n");
                                break;
                        case 0x2:
                                printf ( "file not found.\n");
                                break;
                        case 0x3:
                                printf ( "invalid path.\n");
                                break;
                        case 0x5:
                                printf ( "access denied.\n");
                                break;
                        default:
                                printf ( "unknown error code.\n");
                } /* switch on outreg.x.ax */
                return ( -outreg.x.ax);
        }    /* end error condition */
        else
        {
                if ( !action)   /* if just reading attributes */
                        return ( outreg.x.ax);
                else            /* if setting and no error */
                        return ( setting);
        } /* end if no error */
}
```

```
main()
{
        int result, action, setting = 0;
        char info [ MAX_STR], name [ MAX_STR];

        printf ( "file name? ");
        gets ( name);
        printf ( "Set or get? (g to get) ");
        gets ( info);
        if ( ( info [ 0] == 'g') || ( info [ 0] == 'G'))
                action = 0;
        else
        {
                action = 1;
                printf ( "Setting? (0, 1, 2, 4, 32, or sums) ");
                gets ( info);
                setting = atoi ( info);
        }

        result = attribute ( name, action, setting);
        printf ( "result == %d\n", result);
}
```

0x56: Renaming a File

Service function 0x56 lets you rename a file. In fact, you can actually move a file to a new subdirectory on the same disk during this renaming process.

To use this service function, you need to provide the starting addresses of the string containing the current file name (stored in **inreg.x.dx**) and of the string containing the new file name (stored in **inreg.x.di**) before calling **intdos( )**. DI is a register we haven't used yet. It is one of the two index registers, which are commonly used to store addresses. This register's name comes from *destination index*. Recall that the full-register version of the REGS **union** contains both **di** and **si** (the *source index* register) members.

There are some restrictions on the possible file names. First, you can't use wild-card characters in the name. Second, you can't use this service to transfer a file from one drive to another, although you can transfer the file to a different directory simply by including the necessary path information in the new name string. You should *not* rename or transfer special files, such as hidden files or subdirectories, and you should *never* use this service to rename open files.

The service sets **outreg.x.cflag** to a nonzero value if the call was unsuccessful. Again, the AX register contains the error code in this case: 0x2 if the specified file was not found, 0x3 if the path was not found, 0x5 if the function was denied access (for example, because a file with the new name already existed), or 0x11 if you tried to move the file to a different drive.

The following listing shows how to call this service function:

```c
/* Function for renaming a file */

#include <stdio.h>
#include <string.h>
#include <dos.h>

#define FALSE    0
#define TRUE     1
#define MAX_STR  100


union REGS inreg, outreg;
int ren_file ( char *, char *);


int ren_file ( char *old_name, char *new_name)
{
        inreg.h.ah = 0x56;   /* rename service code */
    /* store locations of old and new file names */
        inreg.x.dx = (unsigned) &old_name [ 0];
        inreg.x.di = (unsigned) &new_name [ 0];

        intdos ( &inreg, &outreg);   /* call function dispatcher */

        if ( outreg.x.cflag)  /* cflag is nonzero on error */
        {
                printf ( "Error code %d.\n", outreg.x.ax);
                switch ( outreg.x.ax)
                {
                        case 0x2:
                                printf ( "file not found.\n");
                                break;
                        case 0x3:
                                printf ( "path not found.\n");
                                break;
                        case 0x5:
                                printf ( "access denied.\n");
                                break;
                        case 0x11:
                                printf ( "invalid drive.\n");
                                break;
                        default:
                                printf ( "unknown error.\n");
                                break;
                }   /* end switch on outreg.x.ax */
                return ( FALSE);  /* report failure */
        }  /* end error condition */
        else
                return ( TRUE);   /* report success */
}


main ()
{
        char old [ MAX_STR], new [ MAX_STR];
        int  result;

        printf ( "Current file name? ");
```

```
gets ( old);
printf ( "New file name? ");
gets ( new);

result = ren_file ( old, new);

if ( result)
        printf ( "File name changed: %s --> %s\n",
                old, new);
else
        printf ( "Name not changed.\n");
}
```

INTERRUPTING WITHOUT
A DISPATCHER

The service functions we've looked at so far have all done their work in an orderly fashion, through the mediation of the DOS function dispatcher. In this section, we'll look at a few services you can use by interrupting the BIOS (Basic Input Output System) on your computer directly. To invoke these services, you need to use the **int86()** Run-Time library function.

Software interrupts through the function dispatcher are more likely to work the same way on different hardware than are service calls that interrupt the BIOS directly. Some of the services available through BIOS interrupts will work as stated only on machines that are completely compatible with the IBM PC, XT, and AT machines.

Caution: Be very careful when using BIOS interrupts. If you are changing something, make certain you are passing in exactly the values you want and that you are making the correct calls. You can overwrite essential portions of your disk if you are not careful.

int int86 (int nr—of—intrpt,
union REGS *inreg,
union REGS *outreg)

Run-Time library function **int86()** gives you direct access to software interrupts without going through the function dispatcher (interrupt 0x21), as **intdos()** and **bdos()** do. The **int86()** function takes three parameters: the interrupt's code number and two REGS union parameters, which are used to put the appropriate values in registers. Let's look at a few simple examples.

0x11, 0x12: Determining Equipment and Memory

BIOS interrupt 0x11 lets you determine the configuration of your machine. This interrupt has a very simple calling process: Just call **int86( )** with the appropriate parameters. You don't need to set any registers before calling the interrupt; thus, the following line will call BIOS interrupt 0x11:

```
int86 ( 0x11, &inreg, &outreg);
```

All equipment information is returned in **outreg.x.ax**. The individual bits of this register contain the following information about your configuration:

- Bit 0 (rightmost bit) is set to 1 if you have any disk drives connected to your computer; it's set to 0 otherwise.

- Bit 1 is set to 1 if your AT has an 80287 coprocessor. This bit is not used by non-ATs.

- Bits 2 and 3 specify the amount of memory on the system board in early IBM PCs. This information is not used by more recent machines.

- Bits 4 and 5 specify the video mode on your machine. Bit pattern 01 (0x1) indicates a color graphics adapter in 40-column text mode, bit pattern 10 (0x2) indicates a color graphics adapter in 80-column text mode, and bit pattern 11 (0x3) indicates a monochrome adapter in 80-column text mode. Bit pattern 00 is unused.

- Bits 6 and 7 specify the number of disk drives in your configuration. Bit patterns range from 00 for one drive up to 11 for four drives. If bit 0 is 0, indicating that you have no drives attached, then these two bits are ignored.

- Bit 8 specifies that a direct memory access chip is present on the PCjr. This bit is not used by other machines.

- Bits 9 through 11 specify the number of serial ports installed on your machine.

- Bit 12 is set to 1 if a game adapter is attached.

- Bit 13 is set to 1 on the PCjr if a serial printer is attached. This bit is not used by other machines.

- Bits 14 and 15 specify the number of printers installed on your machine.

BIOS interrupt 0x12 lets you determine the amount of RAM installed on your machine. As with interrupt 0x11, you don't need to set any values before calling this interrupt. Again, the results are returned in **outreg.x.ax**. The value of the AX register represents the amount of RAM, in 1K byte units. For example, a value of 384 indicates that your machine has 384K of memory.

The following listing shows the use of BIOS interrupts 0x11 and 0x12:

```
/* Program to illustrate use of interrupts to determine
   hardware configuration and available memory.
*/

#include <stdio.h>
#include <dos.h>

#define MAX_STR    80
#define FALSE       0
#define TRUE        1

union REGS inreg, outreg;
char *null_str = "";

main ()
{
        int86 ( 0x11, &inreg, &outreg);
        printf ( "AX register == %x\n", outreg.x.ax);
        int86 ( 0x12, &inreg, &outreg);
        printf ( "AX register == %d kbytes available\n", outreg.x.ax);
}
```

0x10: An Interrupt for Video Functions

BIOS interrupt 0x10 is particularly important because it gives you access to the video input and output. This interrupt actually provides access to over a dozen *function requests*, each of which lets you check or change some aspect of the video input or output.

For example, request 0xf lets you determine the current video mode, and request 0x0 lets you set the current video mode. Certain requests will work only with certain graphics adapters and monitors. You should read the documentation for your graphics board and your monitor before exploring this interrupt. In this section, you'll look at just a few of the available video functions. For examples using the video functions and for doing graphics, see a book such as Nelson Johnson's *Advanced Graphics in C* (Osborne/McGraw-Hill, 1987).

Function request 0xf under BIOS interrupt 0x10 lets you determine the current video mode. The following listing shows how to use this request. Before calling **int86( )**, you need to put the request code into the AH byte—that is, set **inreg.h.ah** to 0xf. The following statement shows how to call interrupt 0x10 for function request 0xf once you've put the appropriate value in **inreg.h.ah**:

```
int86 ( 0x10, &inreg, &outreg);
```

When done, the request returns its results in three bytes of **outreg**. The value of **outreg.h.ah** specifies the code for the current video display mode, and **outreg.h.al** specifies the number of characters per line in the current video mode; this will generally be 40 or 80. Finally, **outreg.h.bh** specifies the currently active video page. Depending on the mode, you may have one, four, or eight pages that can be displayed: In graphics mode, you have only one page (0); in 80-column text mode, you have four pages (0-3); and in 40-column text mode, you have eight pages (0-7).

The following list summarizes the possible video modes. Modes listed with column and row information are text modes; the others are graphics modes. Number of columns per line and number of lines per screen are indicated as an ordered pair. For example, (80, 25) indicates 80 columns per line, 25 lines per screen. Pixel count for graphics mode is shown as

```
<horizontal count> x <vertical count>
```

For example, 640 $\times$ 200 indicates 640 pixels per line and 200 pixels per column.

- 0x0: Medium-resolution text mode for color graphics adapter (CGA), running in monochrome mode (40, 25)
- 0x1: Medium-resolution text mode for CGA, using up to 16 colors (40, 25)
- 0x2: High-resolution text mode for CGA, running in monochrome mode (80, 25)
- 0x3: High-resolution text mode for CGA, using up to 16 colors (80, 25)
- 0x4: Medium-resolution graphics mode for CGA, using up to four colors (320 × 200)
- 0x5: Medium-resolution graphics mode for CGA, running in monochrome mode (320 × 200)
- 0x6: High-resolution graphics mode for CGA, running in monochrome mode (640 × 200)
- 0x7: High-resolution text mode for monochrome adapter (80, 25)
- 0x8: Low-resolution graphics mode for PCjr, using up to 16 colors (160 × 200)
- 0x9: Medium-resolution graphics mode for PCjr, using up to 16 colors (320 × 200)
- 0xa: High-resolution graphics mode for PCjr, using up to 4 colors (640 × 200)
- 0xb, 0xc: Unused
- 0xd: Medium-resolution graphics mode for enhanced graphics adapter (EGA), using up to 16 colors (320 × 200)
- 0xe: High-resolution graphics mode for EGA, using up to 16 colors (640 × 200)
- 0xf: Very-high-resolution graphics mode for EGA, using up to 16 colors (640 × 350)

Function request 0x0 lets you change the current video mode. You can put your machine into a different video mode provided your hardware can work in that mode. For example, to change from medium- to high-resolution graphics mode with an EGA, you would set **inreg.h.ah** to 0x0 to specify the appropriate function request. Then you would set **inreg.h.al** to 0xe for the desired video mode. After setting these two bytes, you would call **int86()** with 0x10 as the first argument.

This function request does not return any report on its success; therefore, it's a good idea also to call function request 0xf to verify that a change has actually been effected.

Function request 0x1 lets you change the shape of the cursor. The cursor is drawn with dots, just like any other character. With a color graphics adapter, characters are drawn using eight rows, numbered 0 (top row) through 7 (bottom row); with a monochrome adapter, 14 rows are used (0 through 13). The default cursor uses the bottom two lines—6 and 7 for a CGA, and 12 and 13 for a monochrome adapter.

The following function lets you redefine the cursor's shape and location. The first parameter specifies the top line to be turned on for the cursor. This value is put into **inreg.h.ch** before being passed to the function request. The second parameter specifies the bottom line and is stored in **inreg.h.cl**. All lines between these two are also turned on. For example, calling **set_cursor()** with arguments 0 and 4 would change the cursor so that the top five lines of the character would be turned on.

```
/* Program to illustrate how to change cursor size and location */

#include <stdio.h>
#include <string.h>
#include <dos.h>

#define MAX_STR     80
#define FALSE        0
#define TRUE         1
#define MONO_MAX    13
#define COLOR_MAX    7


union REGS inreg, outreg;
char  *null_str = "";

void new_cursor ( int, int, int);


void new_cursor ( int top, int bottom, int max_val)
{
        inreg.h.ah = 0x01;   /* request code */
    /* bring out of range values within bounds */
```

```
        if ( (top < 0) || ( top > max_val))
                top = 0;;
        inreg.h.ch = top;
/* bring out of range values within bounds */
        if ( (bottom < 0) || ( bottom > max_val))
                bottom = max_val;
        inreg.h.cl = bottom;

        int86 ( 0x10, &inreg, &outreg);   /* call video interrupt */
}


main ()
{
        int curr_mode, top, bottom;
        char info [ 80];

/* get coordinates for top and bottom of cursor */
        printf ( "Top row of cursor? ");
        gets ( info);
        top = atoi ( info);
        printf ( "Bottom row of cursor? ");
        gets ( info);
        bottom = atoi ( info);

        new_cursor ( top, bottom, MONO_MAX);
}
```

Function requests 0x2 and 0x3 let you set and read the cursor position, respectively. You can use request 0x2 to control where your programs write their output. To call this function request, you need to provide three values in addition to the request code.

You must specify the row to which you want to move the cursor. The top row of the screen is row 0 and the bottom row is, generally, 24. This value is put into **inreg.h.dh**. The column number is placed in **inreg.h.dl**. This will be a value between 0 and 79 or between 0 and 39, depending on the text mode. Column 0 is the leftmost column.

Finally, you need to specify the video-page number for which you are setting the cursor. This value will be stored in **inreg.h.bh**. The page number must be 0 in graphics mode. The following function shows how to move the cursor to an arbitrary location:

```
/* Program to illustrate use of function request
   to change cursor location
*/

#include <stdio.h>
#include <string.h>
#include <dos.h>
```

```
#define MAX_STR    80
#define FALSE      0
#define TRUE       1
#define MID_ROW    12      /* middle value in rows 0 -- 24 */
#define MID_COL    39      /* approximate middle in cols 0 -- 79 */


union REGS inreg, outreg;
char  *null_str = "";

void move_cursor ( int, int);
void test_move_cursor ( void);

/* move the cursor to the position specified,
   using BIOS interrupt 0x10 (video) for access to request.
*/
void move_cursor ( int row, int column)
{
        inreg.h.ah = 0x2;        /* function request code */
        inreg.h.dh = row;        /* new row position */
        inreg.h.dl = column;     /* new column position */
        inreg.h.bh = 0;          /* page 0 */

        int86 ( 0x10, &inreg, &outreg);  /* BIOS interrupt */
}


void test_move_cursor ()
{
        int   row = MID_ROW, col = MID_COL,
              index, rand_val, seed;
        char  info [ MAX_STR];

    /* Get seed for generating random walk */
        printf ( "seed? ");
        gets ( info);
        seed = atoi ( info);
        srand ( seed);

    /* write each character to screen, at random position */
        for ( index = 97; index <= 122; index++)
        {
                move_cursor ( row, col);
                printf ( "%c", index);

            /* decide whether to move up (odd #) or down */
                rand_val = rand ();
                if ( rand_val % 2)
                        row++;
                else
                        row--;
            /* decide whether to move left (odd #) or right */
                rand_val = rand ();
                if ( rand_val % 2)
                        col--;
                else
                        col++;
        }   /* for index == 'a' through 'z' */
}


main ()
{
        test_move_cursor ();
}
```

Function request 0x3 tells you not only where the cursor is but also its shape. After you specify the video page for which you want to know the cursor position, the function returns the column and the row for the current cursor position on that page. The function also returns the top and bottom rows of the cursor's shape.

To specify the video page, set **inreg.h.bh** to the desired page number. To determine the current row, check the value of **outreg.h.dh**. This will be a value between 0 and 24, as for request 0x2. The current column coordinate will be stored in **outreg.h.dl** after the call to **int86( )**. The top row of the cursor will be in **outreg.h.ch**, and the bottom row will be in **outreg.h.cl**.

Video pages are stored in the memory set aside for creating screen output. For example, the CGA allocates 16KB of memory for this purpose. The number of video pages available depends on the amount of memory required to display one screen in the current video mode. For example, in text mode, it takes two bytes for every character to be displayed on the screen—one byte for the character and one byte for its attributes (color, blinking, and so forth).

In medium-resolution text mode (40 columns by 25 rows), you need about 2KB (1000 characters * 2 bytes per character) to display one screen. This means you can have up to eight pages of information stored, ready to be displayed instantly. In 80 columns by 25 lines, you can have only four video pages, since each screen requires 4KB.

You can have information stored on each of the video pages and display them in whatever order you like, using request 0x5. This function request displays the video page you specify on the screen. To specify the page, put its value in **inreg.h.al** before calling **int86( )**. Naturally, you need to put 0x5, the request's code, into **inreg.h.ah**. The following function lets you set the currently active video page:

```
/* Function for setting the currently active video page.
   NOTE: Function assumes dos.h header file and external
         variables, inreg and outreg.
         Function passes row and column position on page selected,
         but does nothing with the information about
         cursor's shape that is also returned by request 0x05.
*/
```

```
void set_video_page ( int page, int *row, int *col)
{
        inreg.h.ah = 0x5;
        inreg.h.bh = page;

        int86 ( 0x10, &inreg, &outreg);

        *row = outreg.h.dh;
        *col = outreg.h.dl;
}
```

There are literally dozens of other DOS and BIOS services available, both directly and through the function dispatcher. This chapter is intended to give you an introduction to such services and to provide some examples on how to use them. You may want to explore other services on your own—but be *very* careful if you use services that will change something on your disk or even certain things in memory.

SUMMARY

In this chapter, you learned how to use three Run-Time library functions to generate interrupts for DOS or the BIOS. Through these interrupts you can request access to various DOS and BIOS services, such as input and output handling; file handling; checking time, date, and other system information; controlling the screen; and so forth.

The interrupts let you interact with the operating system and machine at very low levels, which can be a great help sometimes. This capability also makes it possible to cause damage if you're not careful.

The next chapter focuses on a very different topic: random numbers and how to generate them.

8

GENERATING RANDOM NUMBERS

In many situations, you may want a program to make an arbitrary selection from among several possibilities. For example, in Chapter 5, the sentence-generator program selected arbitrary subjects and predicates to build sentences. In Chapter 6, one encryption strategy involved making an arbitrary substitution for each character. This encryption method was contrasted with the offset strategy, in which the entire substitution pattern was determined by the selection of an offset.

In such cases, *arbitrary* does not mean the selection can be anything at all; rather, the term refers to the fact that you can't predict in advance what selection or substitution will be made. The decisions are never completely arbitrary: The sentence generator will never select q as a subject; the encryption strategy will never substitute γ for the letter a. The "arbitrary" selection is always made from among a predetermined set of possibilities.

Such arbitrary choices are often called *random selections*. In both of the examples mentioned, the basis for the selections was a number returned by the Run-Time library function **rand()**. This function returns an integer between 0 and 32,767, inclusive. A function such as **rand( )** is known informally as a *random number generator* but is, more precisely, a *pseudorandom* number generator. We'll look at what this means in the next section.

In this chapter, you'll find a discussion of randomness based on mathematical properties. You'll also learn why computers can generate only pseudorandom numbers. The chapter contains some algorithms for generating such numbers as well as some means of evaluating the randomness of the numbers generated with these algorithms. Random number generators will be very useful in chapters 9 and 10.

RANDOM NUMBERS

To begin our discussion of (pseudo)random numbers, let's use a simple program to generate some. The following program calls **rand( )** to generate 500 (MAX__RAND) integers between 0 and 32,767. The program writes the values returned, with PER__ LINE values on each line.

```
/* Program to generate 500 random integers */

#include <stdio.h>
#include <stdlib.h>

#define MAX_SIZE   500
#define PER_LINE   10

main ()
{
        int index;

        for ( index = 0; index < MAX_SIZE; index++)
        {
                printf ( "%7d", rand ());
                if ( ( index % PER_LINE) == 9)
                        printf ( "\n");
        }
}
```

This program produces and displays the following sequence of integers, 10 values per line:

41	18467	6334	26500	19169	15724	11478	29358	26962	24464
5705	28145	23281	16827	9961	491	2995	11942	4827	5436
32391	14604	3902	153	292	12382	17421	18716	19718	19895
5447	21726	14771	11538	1869	19912	25667	26299	17035	9894
28703	23811	31322	30333	17673	4664	15141	7711	28253	6868
25547	27644	32662	32757	20037	12859	8723	9741	27529	778
12316	3035	22190	1842	288	30106	9040	8942	19264	22648
27446	23805	15890	6729	24370	15350	15006	31101	24393	3548
19629	12623	24084	19954	18756	11840	4966	7376	13931	26308
16944	32439	24626	11323	5537	21538	16118	2082	22929	16541
4833	31115	4639	29658	22704	9930	13977	2306	31673	22386
5021	28745	26924	19072	6270	5829	26777	15573	5097	16512
23986	13290	9161	18636	22355	24767	23655	15574	4031	12052
27350	1150	16941	21724	13966	3430	31107	30191	18007	11337
15457	12287	27753	10383	14945	8909	32209	9758	24221	18588
6422	24946	27506	13030	16413	29168	900	32591	18762	1655
17410	6359	27624	20537	21548	6483	27595	4041	3602	24350
10291	30836	9374	11020	4596	24021	27348	23199	19668	24484
8281	4734	53	1999	26418	27938	6900	3788	18127	467
3728	14893	24648	22483	17807	2421	14310	6617	22813	9514
14309	7616	18935	17451	20600	5249	16519	31556	22798	30303
6224	11008	5844	32609	14989	32702	3195	20485	3093	14343
30523	1587	29314	9503	7448	25200	13458	6618	20580	19796
14798	15281	19589	20798	28009	27157	20472	23622	18538	12292
6038	24179	18190	29657	7958	6191	19815	22888	19156	11511
16202	2634	24272	20055	20328	22646	26362	4886	18875	28433
29869	20142	23844	1416	21881	31998	10322	18651	10021	5699
3557	28476	27892	24389	5075	10712	2600	2510	21003	26869
17861	14688	13401	9789	15255	16423	5002	10585	24182	10285
27088	31426	28617	23757	9832	30932	4169	2154	25721	17189
19976	31329	2368	28692	21425	10555	3434	16549	7441	9512
30145	18060	21718	3753	16139	12423	16279	25996	16687	12529
22549	17437	19866	12949	193	23195	3297	20416	28286	16105
24488	16282	12455	25734	18114	11701	31316	20671	5786	12263
4313	24355	31185	20053	912	10808	1832	20945	4313	27756
28321	19558	23646	27982	481	4144	23196	20222	7129	2161
5535	20450	11173	10466	12044	21659	26292	26439	17253	20024
26154	29510	4745	20649	13186	8313	4474	28022	2168	14018
18787	9905	17958	7391	10202	3625	26477	4414	9314	25824
29334	25874	24372	20159	11833	28070	7487	28297	7518	8177
17773	32270	1763	2668	17192	13985	3102	8480	29213	7627
4802	4099	30527	2625	1543	1924	11023	29972	13061	14181
31003	27432	17505	27593	22725	13031	8492	142	17222	31286
13064	7900	19187	8360	22413	30974	14270	29170	235	30833
19711	25760	18896	4667	7285	12550	140	13694	2695	21624
28019	2125	26576	21694	22658	26302	17371	22466	4678	22593
23851	25484	1018	28464	21119	23152	2800	18087	31060	1926
9010	4757	32170	20315	9576	30227	12043	22758	7164	5109
7882	17086	29565	3487	29577	14474	2625	25627	5629	31928
25423	28520	6902	14962	123	24596	3737	13261	10195	32525

These numbers don't seem to follow any immediately discernible pattern: Even and odd numbers occur with roughly equal frequency; no obvious repetitions of the same value or values occur; and no "local" patterns (series of consecutive numbers or series of numbers differing by 2, for example) seem to occur. At an intuitive level, these numbers will probably strike you as "arbitrary," or random.

Mathematically, a selection from a range of values is considered random if each possible value within that range has an equal chance of being selected on any given turn, or *trial*. This means you can't predict what the next number will be. A second requirement for a selection process to be considered random is that a number will have the same chance of being selected on *each* turn. This is known as an *independence requirement*.

One implication of this requirement is that any *pair* of numbers from the collection also has an equal chance of being selected, as does any sequence (or subsequence) of three, four, or more numbers. In fact, the same number is just as likely to be selected twice in succession as to be followed by a specific other number. (This is one place where intuitive conceptions of randomness may differ from the mathematical definition.)

For example, suppose the only possible values to choose from were 1, 2, and 3. The explicit requirement for a random selection says that any of these three values is equally likely to be selected on a turn. The independence requirement then says essentially that once a value has been selected, any of the three values is again equally likely to be selected as the next value. Thus, each of the following pairs of values is equally likely:

```
1-1     1-2     1-3     2-1     2-2     2-3     3-1     3-2     3-3
```

Similarly, each of the following triples is equally likely to occur:

```
1-1-1   1-1-2   1-1-3   1-2-1   1-2-2   1-2-3   1-3-1   1-3-2   1-3-3
2-1-1   2-1-2   2-1-3   2-2-1   2-2-2   2-2-3   2-3-1   2-3-2   2-3-3
3-1-1   3-1-2   3-1-3   3-2-1   3-2-2   3-2-3   3-3-1   3-3-2   3-3-3
```

Suppose you select three values, and each is a 1. Does this mean your selections were not random? Not necessarily. This triple does have a certain likelihood of occurring—in this case, 1 in 27. In fact, the triple 1-1-1 is just as likely as the triple 2-3-1, which may seem more random at an intuitive level but which also has a 1-in-27 chance of occurring. In fact, it is possible (but extremely unlikely) to get 1-1-1-1-1-1-1-1-1-1 as a sequence of random values. The likelihood of this happening "at random" is 1 in 59,049, but so is the likelihood of the seemingly more random 1-3-3-2-1-3-2-1-3-2.

The definition of a random sequence seems to differ from an intuitive conception of what constitutes an arbitrary collection of values. One difference is that our intuitive evaluation of randomness is based on the resulting values, whereas the definition implies that the randomness is based on the selection process rather than on the outcomes.

Another difference concerns the expectations for the next value after you've generated some values. For example, suppose you had already selected the following series of values: 1-2-3-1-2-3-1-2. The intuitive expectation is that, in a "nice" random sequence, the next value should be a value other than 3, since 3 is a predictable value. However, the definition says that 3 is just as likely to be the next value as either 1 or 2.

Evaluating a Selection Process for Randomness

Random sequences are important in many different contexts. For example, experimental research designs often require that some participants be assigned to one condition while others are assigned to different conditions. These assignments should be done "at random."

Historically, researchers have used both informal and formal methods to make such assignments. Among the most popular "random" selection methods are

- Flipping coins to assign participants to either of two conditions (heads get assigned to one condition, tails to another)
- Rolling a die or dice to assign participants to any of two or more different conditions
- Selecting objects (for example, numbered or colored balls) from an urn
- Using playing cards to "deal" participants to the appropriate conditions
- Using a table of random numbers

Such methods can be adequate for many purposes, depending on how they are carried through. For example, coin flipping or dice rolling may suffice if you have a "fair" coin or die and if you toss it well. A fair coin is one that is equally likely to come up heads or tails; a fair die is one that is equally likely to land with any of its six faces up. Biased coins and dice are generally weighted to increase the likelihood that certain sides will come up more often.

When you're flipping a coin, it's easy to get into a rhythm or pattern in which you throw the coin to roughly the same level each time. Such tosses can easily lead to biased sequences of heads and tails; thus, you can inadvertently favor one or the other side of the coin. To avoid this, you might throw the coin to different heights each time. Similarly, you can roll dice by letting them drop out of your hand onto the table or by shaking them vigorously in your cupped palms and then tossing them into the air, letting them fall onto the table. The latter method is more likely to ensure that the faces on the dice are mixed and shaken and is, therefore, likely to give you a more random selection of values.

Urn selection methods can be effective for generating random sequences, provided the urn is shaken vigorously after the selected ball is replaced and before another one is selected. Cards can also be useful for randomly assigning participants to conditions, provided the cards can be well shuffled between assignments. It is much more difficult to shuffle cards thoroughly than it is to mix objects in a container, however.

The use of random tables has become quite common, particularly since the RAND corporation published a table of one million random digits in the 1950s. Portions of this table are reproduced in many statistics books.

Using Computers to Generate Pseudorandom Numbers

Because randomness is defined in terms of probability—the probability of being selected—you can't tell in advance what the next number will be in a sequence of truly random numbers. The best you can do is state the *probability* that the next random number will be a particular value.

As you'll see, the algorithms used to generate numbers on a computer do enable you to predict the next number—provided you know the algorithm—because these algorithms generally use one number to generate the next one. This is why you'll generally see references to *pseudo*random numbers when discussing computer-generated sequences of values. Such algorithms are called *deterministic*, because each value in a sequence is determined by the first element and the algorithm. Although the algorithms you find in the next few pages all produce pseudorandom numbers, we'll use *random* and *pseudorandom* interchangeably, except when it would be confusing in the context in which the term is needed.

Deterministic algorithms are useful, even if they generate only pseudorandom numbers: The user rarely knows the algorithm underlying the sequence and therefore has no way of predicting subsequent values. It also turns out that pseudorandom numbers generated by a good algorithm have many of the properties considered desirable in random numbers.

ALGORITHMS FOR GENERATING PSEUDORANDOM NUMBERS

When you are generating values over a given range, you want each value to have an equal chance of being selected. This means each value should occur roughly an equal number of times, provided the total number of trials is several times larger than the total range of values. In such a case, you are generating a sequence of values having a *uniform distribution*. For example, suppose you generated a random sequence of values over the range 0 through 9. If you generated 10,000 such values, you would expect each of the ten digits to occur about 1000 times.

If you generated this sequence using a good algorithm, you could probably be reasonably confident that all possible combinations of digit pairs would also occur roughly an equal number of times; that is, you could expect each of the combinations between 0-0 and 9-9, inclusive, to occur about 100 times.

In this section, you'll look at some strategies for generating values that have such properties. All these algorithms are deterministic in that they use the current value to generate the next one. One consequence of generating a value from the preceding one is that as soon as a value is repeated, subsequent values will also be repetitions.

For example, suppose the starting value for a particular algorithm is 7. Suppose further that the algorithm produces 4 when 7 is the current value, 5 when 4 is the current value, 8 when 5 is the current value, and 7 when 8 is the current value. This algorithm would begin repeating from this last value on. Thus, the first 10 values produced with this algorithm would be

7   4   5   8   7   4   5   8   7   4

Each group of unique values is called a *cycle*, and the number of unique values is the cycle's *period length*. Thus, the preceding example has a cycle consisting of 7, 4, 5, and 8 and has a period length of 4.

Linear Congruential Algorithms

One of the most common strategies for generating sequences of pseudorandom values is the *linear congruential method*, developed by D.H. Lehmer around 1950. This method uses the following four integer parameters to generate a pseudorandom sequence:

- The starting (or current) value, X_0 (or X_n)
- The multiplier, a
- The increment, c
- The modulus, m

The properties and quality of a sequence are determined by the values of the parameters. Of the four parameters, the modulus must always be the largest. The modulus must always be greater than 0, whereas the other parameters must be greater than or equal to 0. These parameters are used in the following formula to produce pseudorandom sequences:

$$X_{n+1} = (aX_n + c) \% m$$

The % in the formula represents the *modulus operator*, as in C. Recall that this returns the remainder after dividing the left operand by the operand value following the modulus operator.

Caution: Be careful not to confuse the modulus parameter (m) and the modulus operator (%).

This formula will let you generate random values between 0 and $m - 1$, inclusive. For example, if m were 10, you could generate random values between 0 and 9, inclusive. There is no guarantee that you will generate all ten possible values, as you saw in an earlier example (7,4,5,8). Nor can you be sure that the formula will produce a particularly good set of pseudorandom values.

The largest number of unique values you can produce with a simple linear congruential algorithm is m, because the modulus operator will leave remainders only within this range. Thus, with a modulus of 10, you can produce a random sequence with a period length of up to 10 (0 through 9, inclusive). You can modify the algorithm to increase the period length beyond the range of possible values, as you will see later. However, most parameter values will produce cycles with shorter periods. For example, the preceding example (7-4-5-8, with period = 4) was generated using the following formula:

$$X_{n+1} = (3 * X_0 + 3) \% 10$$

Thus, both multiplier and increment were 3 and the modulus was 10. The starting value, 7, was given. Subsequent values were computed using the formula.

$$(3 * 7 + 3) \% 10 == (21 + 3) \% 10 == 24 \% 10 == 4$$

$$(3 * 4 + 3) \% 10 == (12 + 3) \% 10 == 15 \% 10 == 5$$

$$(3 * 5 + 3) \% 10 == (15 + 3) \% 10 == 18 \% 10 == 8$$

$$(3 * 8 + 3) \% 10 == (24 + 3) \% 10 == 27 \% 10 == 7$$

With this last value, repetition begins. As you'll notice, this set of parameter values does not make a very good generator, since the formula has such a short period.

A great deal of research has been done on determining values for the four parameters that will produce "good" random sequences—that is, sequences with long periods as well as other desirable properties we'll look at in a bit. One of the most comprehensive summaries of this research is the second volume of Donald Knuth's *The Art of Computer Programming*, 2d ed. (Reading, Mass.: Addison-Wesley Pub. Co., Inc., 1981).

Choice of Modulus

The modulus parameter determines the range of values and also the maximum possible period length for a linear congruential generator. You'll generally want m to be large. This is true even if you want pseudorandom values only within a small range.

For various reasons, values for m close to the largest signed **int** on your machine generally tend to produce good generators. In particular, if MAX_INT represents the largest signed **int** on your machine, modulus values of MAX_INT + 1 (which must be defined as a **long int**) or MAX_INT − 1, and possibly even MAX_INT, tend to be good ones.

Thus, on a PC, with a 16-bit word size, MAX_INT is generally 32,767. This means values of 32,766, 32,767, or 32,768L are good candidates. Notice that, of these three, only 32,768L will produce values in the range 0 through 32,767.

Another possibility for modulus is the largest prime number less than the MAX—INT value. For 32,767, this would be 32,749. Recall that a prime number is one that is divisible without remainder by only 1 and itself. For example, 2, 3, 5, 7, 13, and 29 are all primes, whereas 4, 8, 9, 21, and 111 are not.

In our programs, we'll use 32,768L as the modulus value. It turns out that using MAX—INT tends to produce values whose right-hand digits are sometimes less random than their left-hand digits. To use 32,768L as the modulus, you'll need to specify it as a **long int**; otherwise, the value would wrap around, and you would actually have −32,768. You should experiment with generators using other values for the modulus.

Choice of Multiplier and Increment

The multiplier and increment help determine the actual period length; therefore, a major criterion to use in selecting values for these parameters is that the values should provide the longest period possible.

If the modulus is a power of 2 (as is the case with 32,768), you can get the maximum period length if the multiplier and increment have the following properties:

- The increment is odd.
- The multiplier leaves a remainder of 1 when divided by 4, that is, *multiplier* % 4 == 1.

Thus, the following pairs would all be good values for multiplier and increment:

Multiplier	Increment
37	293
129	73
1201	1111

For the special case in which the increment equals 1 and the modulus is a power of 2, as above, select your multiplier according to the following criteria:

- The multiplier should have one digit less than the modulus.
- The multiplier should end in 21, and the digit to the left of the 21 should be even.

For example, 3621, 4821, 1421, and 9021 should all produce good generators.

Implementing a Generator

The following program implements a generator accoring to our discussion of linear congruential algorithms:

```
/* Program containing linear congruential random number generator */

#include <stdio.h>
#include <stdlib.h>
#include <string.h>

#define MODULUS     32768L
#define MAX_STR     80
#define MAX_RAND    5000
#define PER_LINE    10

int     even_count ( int []);
int     get_int ( char *);
int     linear ( int, int, int *);

int     curr_seed;
int     r_vals [ MAX_RAND];     /* contains random values generated */


main ()
{
        int     index, start, mult, incr;
        char    info [ MAX_STR];

        start = get_int ( "Starting seed? ");
        mult = get_int ( "Multiplier? ");
        incr = get_int ( "Increment? ");

        printf ( "Starting seed = %d\n\n", start);

        for ( index = 0; index < MAX_RAND; index++)
        {
                r_vals [ index] = linear ( mult, incr, &start);
            /* remove comments around following lines
                to see values generated.
            */
            /*
                printf ( "%7d", r_vals [ index]);
                if ( ( index % PER_LINE) == PER_LINE - 1)
                        printf ( "\n");
```

```
                */
        }
        printf ( "\n\n%d even values\n", even_count ( r_vals));
}

/* Prompt user for integer value, read and return the value */
int get_int ( char *message)
{
char info [ MAX_STR];

        printf ( "%s", message);
        gets ( info);
        return ( atoi ( info));
}

/* count the # of even values in the array */
int even_count ( int vals [])
{
        int count = 0, index;

        for ( index = 0; index < MAX_RAND; index++)
                if ( (vals [ index] % 2) == 0)
                        count++;
        return ( count);
}

/* generate a random integer, using linear congruential algorithm */
int linear ( int multiplier, int increment, int *seed)
{
        long int  temp;

        temp = ( (long) multiplier * *seed + increment) % MODULUS;
        *seed = (int) temp;
        return ( *seed);
}
```

get_int( )

This function prompts the user for a value, displaying the message passed as a parameter. The function reads the user's response as a string, converts it to an **int**, and returns this value.

even_count( )

This function simply counts the number of even values generated by the random number generator being used. You'll find that for the algorithms presented here, this value is always half the number of trials. It turns out that linear congruential generators alternate between even and odd returns, owing to mathematical properties of the parameters—basically because both multiplier and increment are odd.

linear( )

This function implements a linear congruential algorithm. If you want to generate usable numbers (as opposed to wanting simply to test some particular parameter values), follow the suggestions mentioned above for cases where the increment is 1 or for the more general case.

The program uses several values and data structures that are worth mentioning. First, note that MODULUS is defined as a **long**: 32,768 is too large to be represented as an **int**. The **r_vals[]** array holds the pseudorandom values generated with one of the algorithms.

Exploring the Generator's Period Length

Earlier, we claimed that certain parameter values would give you the maximum period length for a linear congruential generator. How can we test this claim? The simplest approach would be simply to create an array of **int**, with a cell for each possible value in the range. Unfortunately, this would require static data space larger than the 64K allowed by memory models available in QuickC.

The following listing provides a way of accomplishing this without exceeding the limits of available data space. (You could also accomplish it with Microsoft C 5.0 by using the huge memory model.) This method works, in its current form, only for simple linear congruential generators—where values are based on only one earlier value and where the modulus is 32,768L. Rather than having a cell for each possible value, the program uses half as many cells as would be required and makes each cell store information about two values.

The double duty is accomplished by changing the value in the cells by specific powers of 2 whenever an appropriate value is generated by the functions. Thus, an array of 16,384 cells is defined. The value of cell 0 will change if either a 0 or a 16,384 (subscript + SEMI_MOD) is generated. Cell 1 stores information about 1 and 16,385, and the pattern continues up to the cell with subscript 16,383, whose value changes when either a 16,383 or a 32,767 is generated. The latter is MAX—INT, the largest value possible with a modulus of 32,768L.

If a "lower" value (that is, one less than SEMI—MOD—for example, 358) is generated, the value of the appropriate cell (the one with subscript 358) changes by 1 (0x1). On the other hand, if the "higher" value corresponding to the cell is generated, the cell changes by 16 (0x10). Thus, the rightmost four bits of the cell's storage are changed when lower values are generated, and the next four bits are changed when higher values are generated. This makes it possible to keep tabs on both values in the same array cell.

For example, suppose you start with an array of SEMI—MOD elements—with each cell initialized to 0—and suppose your generator produces the following values:

```
1
16386
12133
16385
16385
12133
1
16386
12133
```

Cells 1, 2, and 12133 will be affected. These cells will have the following values after all nine values are generated:

```
[ 1]    : 34    /* 1 twice, 16,385 twice */
[ 2]    : 32    /* 16,386 twice */
  ...
[ 12133] : 3    /* 12,133 three times */
  ...
```

Cell 12133 shows what happens when the same low value occurs three times: The cell value becomes 3 (3 occurrences * 1 "point" per occurrence). Cell 2 shows the case when a high value occurs twice: The cell value becomes 32 (2 occurrences * 16 "points" per occurrence). Finally, cell 1 shows what happens when both the high and low values for the cell occur twice: 2 points for the low value plus 32 for the high value.

If a cell has a value greater than 1 but less than 16, you know that the low value for the cell was repeated. Similarly, if a cell has a value of at least 32, you know the high value was repeated.

By using only four bits to represent the frequency of occurrence, the program allows a maximum of 15 occurrences of a single value. After that, the four bits allotted for the occurrences overflow to the next set of bits. Since the purpose of the array is really to catch the first repetition—thereby letting you determine the period length—this restriction is not a problem.

If you needed to work with a case in which a value might occur more than 15 times, you would simply need to use an entire byte to store frequencies for the low and high values.

Like the previous program, the following one lets you specify a starting seed value, a multiplier, and an increment. Instead of calling the random generator functions directly, the program calls a testing routine. This **do—run( )** function generates a large number of values—larger than the modulus; so there must eventually be repetition. Each value is processed—the appropriate cell frequency is changed, and the function calls **test—cell( )** to check for repetition. If the function finds repetition, it informs the user.

```
/* Program to generate random integers, and to watch for
   repetitions.
*/

#include <stdio.h>
#include <stdlib.h>
#include <string.h>

#define MODULUS      32768L
#define SEMI_MOD     16384
#define MAX_STR      80
#define MAX_RAND     32769L
#define PER_LINE     10
#define LOW          0x1
#define HI           0x10
#define MASK_FOR_LO  0xf
#define MASK_FOR_HI  0xf0

int    even_count ( int []);
int    get_int ( char *);
int    linear ( int, int, int *);
void   test_cell ( int, long int);
void   do_run ( int, int, int);
void   wait ( void);
void   do_modulo ( int nr_read, int little_cycle, int big_cycle);

int    curr_seed;
int    all_vals [ SEMI_MOD];
```

```
main ()
{
        int    index, start, mult, incr;
        char   info [ MAX_STR];

        start = get_int ( "Starting seed? ");
        mult = get_int ( "Multiplier? ");
        incr = get_int ( "Increment? ");

        printf ( "Starting seed = %d\n\n", start);

        do_run ( start, mult, incr);
}


/* Prompt user for integer value, read and return the value */
int get_int ( char *message)
{
char info [ MAX_STR];

        printf ( "%s", message);
        gets ( info);
        return ( atoi ( info));
}


/* count the # of even values in the array */
int even_count ( int vals [])

{
        int count = 0, index;

        for ( index = 0; index < MAX_RAND; index++)
                if ( (vals [ index] % 2) == 0)
                        count++;
        return ( count);
}


/* generate a random integer, using linear congruential algorithm */
int linear ( int multiplier, int increment, int *seed)
{
        long int  temp;

        temp = ( (long) multiplier * *seed + increment) % MODULUS;
        *seed = (int) temp;
        return ( *seed);
}


/* generate a sequence of random values, using the parameters
   passed as arguments.
*/
void do_run ( int start, int  mult, int incr)
{
        int seed = start, result;
        long int index;

        for ( index = 0; index < MAX_RAND; index++)
        {
                result = linear ( mult, incr, &seed);
                do_modulo ( index, 10, 500);
                if ( result < SEMI_MOD)
                {
                        all_vals [ result] += LOW;
                        test_cell ( all_vals [ result], index);
```

```
                }
                else
                {
                        all_vals [ result - SEMI_MOD] += HI;
                        test_cell ( all_vals [ result - SEMI_MOD], index);
                }
        }
}


/* Test whether an array cell has a value that indicates whether
   a value has been repeated. If the value is in the rightmost 4 bits
   > 1, then a low end value has been repeated. If the value in bits
   4 through 7 > 16, then a high end value has been repeated.
*/
void test_cell ( int val, long int index)
{
        if ( ( val & MASK_FOR_LO) > LOW)
        {
                printf ( "Repetition on trial %ld: val == %d\n",
                        index, val);
                wait ();
        }
        if ( ( val & MASK_FOR_HI) > HI)
        {
                printf ( "Repetition on trial %ld: val == %d\n",
                        index, val);
                wait ();
        }
}


/* Wait for user to continue */
void wait ()
{
        char info [ MAX_STR];

        printf ( "Press <Return> to continue.");
        gets ( info);
}


/* Write symbols at specified intervals ---
   to let user know something is actually happening.
   PARAMETERS :
           int nr_read : value being checked for current count;
           int little_cycle : value to decide when to write INDICATOR.
           int big_cycle : value to determine when to do a line feed.
*/
void do_modulo ( int nr_read, int little_cycle, int big_cycle)
{
#define INDICATOR '.'

        if ( (nr_read % little_cycle) == little_cycle - 1)
                printf ( "%c", INDICATOR);
        if ( (nr_read % big_cycle) == big_cycle - 1)
                printf ( "      %6d\n", nr_read);
}
```

Try running this program with parameter values that conform to the guidelines listed earlier and also with values that vio-
late them. You'll find that the "good" values have periods whose

length is equal to the number of possible random values; other parameter values will almost certainly have shorter periods. You should also find that the starting seed value does not affect the period length; rather, it simply affects the actual sequence of values in the cycle.

do__run()

This function actually generates the values and records the **int** returned in the appropriate array cell. Notice how the cell values are changed: by adding HI to the cell frequency when a high value (> SEMI__MOD) is generated and LOW otherwise. Notice also that the array subscript must be adjusted so that the subscript is always within the valid range for the array. Effectively, this means restricting the subscript values to the lower half of the range of values.

test__cell()

This function tests whether the cell's high and low values have been repeated. The strategy is to mask off the irrelevant nibble (four bits) and then to test the value in the remaining bits. Thus, to check for repetition of a low value, the function masks all but the rightmost four bits (0xf); to check for repetition of a high value, the function masks all but the next four bits (0xf0).

do__modulo()

This is a convenience function that can help relieve anxiety while a program is running. Essentially, the function lets you know that something is actually happening so that you need not worry while the program does its time-consuming work.

The function writes a dot to the screen after a specified number of trials have been completed. After a larger number of trials have been completed, the program also writes a new-line character. To keep track of how many times something has been done, the function uses the value of some parameter that is presumably incremented every time the action of interest is performed.

QUADRATIC ALGORITHMS

Linear generators work with formulas of the following form:

$$(a * X + c) \text{ \% } m$$

A simple extension is to add a term involving the square of the previous random value. The following is the template for such a quadratic algorithm:

$$(d * X^2 + a * X + c) \text{ \% } m$$

If the modulus is a power of 2, then values that satisfy the following conditions provide a quadratic generator whose period length is the range of possible values:

- The greatest common divisor of the modulus (m) and the increment (c) must be 1. This means that c must be odd, since m is a power of 2.
- The *quadratic multiplier* (d) must be even, and the *linear multiplier* (a) must be odd.
- If d leaves a remainder of x when divided by 4, then ($a - 1$) must also leave a remainder of x when divided by 4.

For example, 194 leaves a remainder of 2 when divided by 4. If you select $a = 1771$, you will see that 1770 ($a - 1$) also leaves a remainder of 2 when divided by 4. Therefore, 1771 and 194 would serve as linear and quadratic multipliers, respectively. For the increment, you could select a number such as 32,749, the largest prime less than the modulus.

The following function implements a quadratic random number generator:

```
/* Function for generating random int using quadratic algorithm. */

/* Definition needed for function */
extern int curr_seed;
```

```
/* Random number generator using a quadratic algorithm of the form:
   (D * X^2 + A * X + C) % MODULUS
   Function assumes MODULUS has been defined, and that curr_seed has
   a value.
*/
int quadr ()
{
#define D       194L        /* quadratic multiplier */
#define A       1771L       /* additive multiplier */
#define C       32749L      /* increment */
        unsigned long int temp, rv;

        rv = curr_seed;
        temp = D * rv * rv + A * rv + C;
        curr_seed = (int) (temp % MODULUS);
        return (curr_seed);
}
```

quadr( )

This function generates a random value using a quadratic algorithm. The parameter values were chosen to satisfy the preceding criteria. The values for the parameters—quadratic and additive multipliers, increment, and modulus—are defined as manifest constants. You can, of course, change this, and you can define global variables that you can initialize or whose values you can let the user specify.

Try generating some random sequences using this algorithm. You'll see that this algorithm also produces even and odd values in alternation, like the linear congruential generator. This can lead to unexpected results, as you'll see in Chapter 9.

ADDITIVE ALGORITHMS

Another simple extension of the linear congruential method is using two earlier random values to generate another one. For example, all of the following would be additive generators of this type. The first version would use the two values generated just previously—X_n and X_{n-1}, respectively—to generate the new value, X_{n+1}. The third version uses the previous value and the value generated 16 steps earlier.

$$X_{n+1} = (X_n + X_{n-1}) \% m$$

$$X_{n+1} = (X_n + X_{n-15}) \% m$$

$$X_{n+1} = (X_n + X_{n-16}5) \% m$$

Such algorithms have period lengths up to m^2. It turns out to be a tricky matter to decide which earlier values to use, however. For example, in generators such as those in the list, the offset for the earlier of the two numbers should be at least 16. Thus, the first two generators would fail to meet some of the criteria for a good random number generator.

A variant of such an additive algorithm may prove to be one of the best random number generators. The algorithm was developed by G.J. Mitchell and D.P. Moore in the late 1950s. It has a period length on the order of $2^{55} - 1$ when the modulus is a power of 2 determined by the computer's word size.

The algorithm uses the following expression to generate a random number:

$$X_n = (X_{n-24} + X_{n-55}) \% m$$

That is, the algorithm uses the random values generated 24 and 55 steps earlier to compute the current random value. These offsets are "magic numbers," selected for theoretical reasons having to do with the bit patterns they generate. These 55 values are kept in an array that starts out with 55 arbitrary integers, at least one of which must be odd. As each new value is generated, it becomes the new 55th element in the array. Thus, the array is constantly being updated. Notice that the first random value actually generated by the algorithm is the 56th value, since the array presumably contains 55 random values generated by other means.

It turns out that you can implement this algorithm quite efficiently if you manipulate this array as if it were a circular queue. However, you can accomplish this very simply here without needing all the power of an actual queue structure.

The following listing shows how to implement this algorithm:

```
/* Function for generating random numbers using additive algorithm. */

/* Variable definitions required by function addit () */
int  two_four = 24, five_five = 55;
/* cell 0 is unused; cells 1 -- 55 contain 55 random values needed */
int  add_seed [ 56];


/* Random number generator using an additive algorithm.
   The function assumes a global array of 55 integers, add_seed [],
   has been generated, and is accessible.
   The function also assumes that two global integers,
           two_four and five_five
   are defined and have values.
*/
int addit ()
{
        unsigned long int temp;

        /* compute next value, using values generated 24 and 55
        trials ago.
        */
        temp = ( (long) add_seed [ five_five]
                    + add_seed [ two_four]) % MODULUS;
        /* assign the new value to the "oldest" cell,
        the one with subscript correspnding to five_five.
        */
        add_seed [ five_five] = ( int) temp;
        /* adjust the counters. */
        five_five--;
        if ( five_five == 0)
                five_five = 55;
        two_four--;
        if ( two_four == 0)
                two_four = 55;
        return ( (int) temp);
}
```

addit()

This function assumes you have generated an array containing 55 "random" values for use. You might use **rand()** or one of the other generators developed in this chapter to generate these values. The actual array, **add_seed[ ]**, is defined as having 56 elements. Cell 0 is unused. This definition just makes it easier to implement the algorithm.

The algorithm uses two counters, **two_four** and **five_five**, to store the subscripts for what will be the 24th and 55th earlier elements when generating a new random value. The array actually stores the elements in reverse order. Thus, the first "random" number is put into cell 55 and the second, in cell 54, because the "oldest" random value will be the first one that was generated. It will also be the one with the largest offset value when compared with the current value. By storing the numbers in reverse order, the subscript represents the desired offset value directly.

After a new value is generated, it is put into cell 55 of the array. The two counters are then decremented. The second value generated originally will now be the one that was generated 55 steps earlier (than the 57th value). After each value is generated, the cell with subscript **five_five** is assigned the new random value, and both counters are decremented by 1. When either counter reaches 0, that counter is reset to 55, as in a circular queue. Cell 0 is never read or changed.

Again, try generating some sequences using this algorithm. By all indications this is a very powerful algorithm. Unfortunately, there is not enough research available on the algorithm to make everyone feel comfortable about such an expectation.

OTHER APPROACHES

Another approach to generating random numbers within a given range is to generate values using a longer word size and then cut the result down to the appropriate size. Depending on how this is done and on the parameter values chosen, such generators can also be very powerful.

A properly designed algorithm of this sort provides at least two advantages. First, the period length will be longer than the range of possible values, since the modulus may be longer than the *maximum value* − 1. For example, if you used **long int** parameter values, or even **unsigned long int** values, you could have a much larger modulus than the one in our programs.

A second advantage concerns the randomness of individual digits in the values returned. For many generators, the low-order and high-order digits may not be equally random. Generally, it is the low-order digits—those farthest to the right—that are not as random as one might wish. One way of getting around this is to compute your large random value and then right-shift the value so as to move new bits into the portion of the value that will be returned as an **int**. For example, after computing a **long** value, such an algorithm might right-shift the value by 16 bits before returning the value cast as an **int**.

The Microsoft Run-Time library **rand( )** function uses such an approach. The **rand( )** function is a very good random number generator, with a suitably long period and with acceptable behavior. If you're interested and you have access to the Microsoft Run-Time library source code, you may want to look at the code for the **rand( )** function.

In the next section, you'll learn how to do some informal tests on your generators to see how well they do their job. The examples will use the linear congruential generator. Run the same tests with quadratic and additive generators as well as with the Run-Time library generator, **rand( )**. You should find the results interesting.

EVALUATING RANDOM NUMBER GENERATORS

In this section you will look at some techniques you can use to decide whether the values your generator is producing are reasonably random. The discussion and examples will use the **linear( )** function, rather than one of the other algorithms. This is by no means the best generator, but it is useful for illustrating certain properties (and shortcomings) of such generators.

You should explore the behavior of the other generators as we go along and compare their properties with those you find for the linear congruential generator. Using your results, you should pick the generator that seems most suitable for your purposes. In chapters 9 and 10, you'll make extensive use of random number generators. Later programs will call function **house—rand( )**. This function should contain the random number generator you want to use as you work through the programs and suggested projects.

In a later chapter we'll say more about the tests used to make such evaluations. You've already seen that the period length is important for a good pseudorandom number generator: The longer the period, the more different values the generator can produce before starting the next cycle. Another way of testing the quality of a random generator is by examining how uniform the distribution of values is. If you generate fewer values than the period length, then not all numbers will be represented. This makes it difficult to determine whether the generator might, for example, generate low numbers early in the sequence and higher numbers later.

You can get a rough idea of this by dividing your range of values into intervals and generating many values to get a good mix of numbers. For example, you can divide the range of possible values into groups of 100 (say, 0-99, 100-199, or 10,000-10,099). In this case, all but the last of your intervals would be the same size. The number of intervals needed depends on the range of values and the size of each interval.

For example, with a range of 32,768 (the value of MODULUS) and an interval size of 100 values, you need to have 328 intervals to span the range. Of these, 327 are the same size — 100 elements — and account for 32,700 of the possible values (0 through 32,699); the last interval has only 68 elements (32,700 through 32,767).

If you generated 5000 pseudorandom values, you should expect each of the intervals to have about 15 of their values (10 for the last interval) selected by a good generator. More precisely, the number of values you would expect from a given interval — assuming the generator was a good one — is given by the following formula:

$$\frac{(total\ nr\ values\ selected) * (nr\ values\ per\ interval)}{(range\ of\ values)}$$

This formula gives the *expected values* for the intervals. In this case, this amounts to 5000*100/32,768 (= 15.26) for all but the last interval and 5000*68/32,768 (= 10.38) for the last interval.

The following program includes a function to let you compute the actual frequencies for each interval. Try calling it several times using each of the generators you've developed—**linear( )**, **quadr( )**, and **addit( )**.

```c
/* Program to generate random integers, and
   compute frequencies with which values in different intervals
   occur.
*/

#include <stdio.h>
#include <stdlib.h>
#include <string.h>

#define MODULUS        32768L
#define MAX_STR        80
#define MAX_RAND       5000
#define PER_LINE       10

#define INTERV_SIZE    100
#define NR_INTERVALS   MODULUS / INTERV_SIZE + 1

int     even_count ( int []);
int     linear ( int, int, int *);
void    distribution ( int [], int [], long int, int, int);

int     curr_seed;
int     r_vals [ MAX_RAND];      /* contains random values generated */
int     group [ NR_INTERVALS];

main ()
{
        int     index, start, mult, incr;
        char    info [ MAX_STR];

        start = get_int ( "Starting seed? ");
        mult = get_int ( "Multiplier? ");
        incr = get_int ( "Increment? ");

        printf ( "Starting seed = %d\n\n", start);

        for ( index = 0; index < MAX_RAND; index++)
        {
                r_vals [ index] =  linear ( mult, incr, &start);
              /* remove comments around following lines
                 to see values generated.
              */
              /*
                printf ( "%7d", r_vals [ index]);
                if ( ( index % PER_LINE) == PER_LINE - 1)
                        printf ( "\n");
              */
        }
```

```
        printf ( "\n\n%d even values\n", even_count ( r_vals));

        distribution ( group, r_vals, MODULUS, INTERV_SIZE, MAX_RAND);
}


/* Prompt user for integer value, read and return the value */
int get_int ( char *message)
{
char info [ MAX_STR];

        printf ( "%s", message);
        gets ( info);
        return ( atoi ( info));
}



/* count the # of even values in the array */
int even_count ( int vals [])
{
        int count = 0, index;

        for ( index = 0; index < MAX_RAND; index++)
                if ( (vals [ index] % 2) == 0)
                        count++;
        return ( count);
}



/* generate a random integer, using linear congruential algorithm */
int linear ( int multiplier, int increment, int *seed)
{
        long int  temp;

        temp = ( (long) multiplier * *seed + increment) % MODULUS;
        *seed = (int) temp;
        return ( *seed);
}



/* Determine number of values from each interval that occur in the
   random sequence. Display the resulting frequencies.
*/
void distribution ( int group [], int raw [],
                    long int range, int size, int nr_trials)
{
        int nr_intervals, index, actual_size;

        nr_intervals = range / size + 1;

        for ( index = 0; index < nr_trials; index++)
                group [ raw [ index] / size]++;

        for ( index = 0; index < nr_intervals; index++)
        {
                printf ( "%7d", group [ index]);
                if ( ( index % PER_LINE)  == PER_LINE - 1)
                        printf ( "\n");
        }
}
```

distribution( )

This function analyzes pseudorandom values generated and stored in **r_vals[ ]**. For each value in **r_vals[ ]**, the function determines the interval in which the value belongs and increments the frequency count for that interval. Frequencies are stored in another array, **group[ ]**, which has a cell for each interval.

The function then displays the frequency in each cell of **group[ ]**. Try running the program with "good" sets of parameter values and also with "bad" sets. You'll find that, although there is considerable variation, the distribution of values generated by the good parameters is much better than that generated by the bad parameter values.

For example, for a multiplier of 4821 and an increment of 1, the program produced the following distribution of values. The intervals go in order across the line; thus, the first line contains the 10 intervals 0-99 through 900-999.

```
Starting seed = 12

2500 even values
    20      21      18      11      11       9      11      14      13      25
    18      15      15      20      18      14      13      11      14      19
    16      18      14      16      17      16      16      16      14      17
    13      18      15      11      13      16      20      13      10      26
    11      11      16      16      21      16      14      13      14      15
    17      13       9      19      17      17      16      17      13      17
    17      14      11      17      10      14      15      20      15      14
    14      20      15      16      12      21      14      17      16      18
    16      21      16      15      10      16      16      15      16      16
    14       9      17      14      15      15      18      14      15      20
    14      15      11      13      17      15      15      20      15      18
    22      21      14      17      13      17      18      21       9      16
    12      10      11      17      18      13      14      20      16      18
    14      15      22      13      16      17      17      17      13      17
     8      14      17      18      15      17      13      19      12      22
    15      11      12      11      21      21      23       9      11      18
    16      12      14      20      14      12      13       8      16      22
    10      17      14      15      15      13      20      14       8      20
    14      20      16      16      16       9      17      18      12      16
    17      15      20      15      19      15      18      16      13      12
    14      14      22      17      21      16      18      19      22      16
    22      21      18      16      10      16      14      18      10      17
    16       7      14      16      13      22      20      13      25      13
    18      10      14      12      10      14      10      13      18      15
    17      19      13      10      11      15      17      14      12      19
    12      18      18      19      23      15      13      11      11       8
    10      20      19      21      14      14      13      23      14      13
    17      12      13      12      23      14      13       9      13      13
    18      14      15      16      17      16      15      16      18      12
    14       9      12      14      10      11      16      13      17      13
    16      11      11      14      21      11      10      15      18      10
    17      14      13      14      17      18      18      13      15      14
    18      14      17      13      18      13       7       5
```

Most of the frequencies are within 30% or so of the expected values (between 11 and 19, roughly). There are only a few cells that are very far from the expected values—for example, the 26 in interval 3900-3999 and the 7 in 32,600-32,699.

Compare these numbers with the following distribution, which uses the same seed and increment but a multiplier of 56.

```
Starting seed = 12

0 even values
       0      0      0      0      0      0      1      0      0      0
       0      0      0      0      0      0      0      0      0      0
       0      0      0      0      0      0      0      0      0      0
       0      0      0      0      0      0      0      0      0      0
       0      0      0      0      0      0      0      0      0      1
       0      0      0      0      0      0      0      0      0      0
       0      0      0      0      0      0      0      0      0      0
       0      0      0      0      0      0      0      0      0      0
       0      0      0      0      0      0      0      0      0      0
       0      0      0      0      0      0      0      0      0      0
       0      0      0      0      0      0      0      0      0      0
       0      0      0      0      0      0      0      0      0      0
       0      0      0      0      1      0      0      0      0      0
       0      0      0      0      0      0      0      0      0      0
       0      0      0      0      0      0      0      0      0      0
       0      0      0      0      0      0      0      0      0      0
       0      0      0      0      0      0      0      0      0      0
    4996      0      0      0      0      0      0      0      0      0
       0      0      0      0      0      0      0      0      0      0
       0      0      0      0      0      0      0      0      0      0
       0      0      0      0      0      0      0      0      0      0
       0      0      0      0      0      0      0      0      0      0
       0      0      0      0      0      0      0      0      0      0
       0      0      0      0      0      0      0      0      0      0
       0      0      0      0      0      0      0      0      0      0
       0      0      0      0      0      0      0      0      0      0
       0      0      0      0      0      0      0      0      0      0
       0      0      0      1      0      0      0      0      0      0
       0      0      0      0      0      0      0      0
```

This generator starts out generating different values (indicated by the 1s in the listing), but quickly comes to a value (19,065) at which it gets stuck. Thereafter, the generator always produces the same number.

Other parameter values may also give you a nice distribution of values over the intervals but may have short period lengths. For example, with a multiplier of 63 and an increment of 3, you get a very even distribution for a starting seed of 12. However, the period length for these values is only 1024, as you can determine by using the parameter values with an earlier program. On the other hand, using a multiplier of 65 with an increment of 3 gives you a reasonably distributed set of values and a period whose length is the entire range. The quadratic and additive generators will give you even longer period lengths and will also give you good distributions, provided any required parameters are well chosen.

Remember, both distribution and period length are important when evaluating the adequacy of a random number generator. There are literally dozens of other aspects you can look at — distribution of individual digits, runs of consecutive ascending or descending values, and so forth. The second volume of Donald Knuth's *The Art of Computer Programming* discusses many such tests. We can't get into such tests here, although you'll learn more about random number generators in the next few chapters.

Chi-Square Tests for Evaluating Distributions

In the last section, you "evaluated" a random number generator by determining its period length and then "eyeballing" the distribution of the values over intervals. In this section, you'll look at a test that lets you get a more quantitative measure of confidence in the generator's adequacy — at least as far as distribution of values is concerned.

The chi-square (χ^2) test is used to assess the likelihood that a given distribution of values could arise at random. The test works with a value based on the deviation between the actual and expected values for each interval.

For reasons we can't go into here, the test uses the following formula, computed for each interval, as a measure of the deviation between actual and expected value:

$$\frac{(actual\ value - expected\ value)^2}{expected\ value}$$

The larger the discrepancy between actual and expected values, the larger this value will be and the less likely it will be that the distribution was generated at random.

The actual χ^2 statistic is computed by adding these values for all the intervals. Thus, the formula for the chi-square statistic is

$$\chi^2 = \sum_{i=1}^{nr\ intervals} \frac{(actual_i - expected_i)^2}{expected_i}$$

The index, i, specifies the interval.

The following function lets you compute a chi-square statistic for the values generated using your random number generators:

```
/* Function for computing a chi-square statistic, given
   an array of interval frequencies, the range of values,
   interval size, and number of trials.
*/
double chi_square ( int group [], long int range, int size, int trials)
{
        int     nr_intervals, index;
        double expected, deviation, last_size, sum = 0.0;

        nr_intervals = range / size + 1;
        expected = ( (double) trials * size) / range;

        for ( index = 0; index < nr_intervals - 1; index++)
        {
                deviation = group [ index] - expected;
                sum += deviation * deviation / expected;
        }

    /* for last, smaller, interval */
        last_size = range - (long) ( nr_intervals - 1) * size;
        expected = ( (double) trials * last_size) / range;
        deviation = group [ nr_intervals - 1] - expected;
        sum += deviation * deviation / expected;

        printf ( "\n\nchi-square for %d intervals == %.4lf\n",
                nr_intervals, sum);
        return ( sum);
}
```

chi_square()

This function computes the sum shown in the formula above. For each interval except the last, the expected value is the same, so this needs to be computed only once. Because the last interval will generally be smaller, its expected value must be computed separately. The function sums the deviation terms computed for each interval and returns the result as a **double**.

Notice the use of the **cast** operator to prevent intermediate **int** values from overflowing and becoming negative, thereby invalidating the computations.

For the generator shown earlier (seed = 12, multiplier = 4821, increment = 1), this function returns a value of 262.13. "Very interesting," you say, "but what does this number tell me?"

It turns out that this number can be compared against other, cutoff values to get a measure of the probability that the distribution you got was generated at random rather than through some bias or other systematic process. These cutoff values are based on theoretical distributions and are generally called *critical values.*

Let's begin with a concrete example, to help the discussion. For 328 intervals, as we have, the values shown in Table 8-1 are used as cutoffs. Notice that cutoff values vary with the probability.

Suppose your random generator produced a distribution with a χ^2 value of 299.31. According to the table, this value lies somewhere between the 0.10 and 0.25 probabilities. The fact that 299.31 is less than the 309.39 associated with a probability of 0.25 means, according to this table, that the probability of getting a value of 299.31 with a random distribution is less than approximately 0.25.

Table 8-1.   Cutoff Values for 328 Intervals

Probability	Cutoff
0.01	270.47
0.05	286.07
0.10	294.53
0.25	309.39
0.50	326.33
0.75	343.89
0.90	360.20
0.95	370.20
0.99	389.40

The table also tells you, indirectly, that the probability is about 0.90 that you'll get a value larger than 294.53: You'll get a value *smaller* than 294.53 about 10% of the time; so by implication, you'll get a value larger than this about 90% of the time—using a random distribution.

A probability between 0.10 and 0.25 is not bad. Of course, a probability will never let you be certain that the distribution was or was not generated by a random process. Rather, the probability associated with your χ^2 statistic can only increase or decrease your confidence in such an assertion.

The cutoff values depend on two factors: the probability level and the number of intervals. The latter factor is generally called the *degrees of freedom* for the computations. The value that is actually used for degrees of freedom when computing cutoff values is 1 less than the number of intervals. Thus,

$$(degrees\ of\ freedom) = (number\ of\ intervals) - 1$$

The following listing shows two functions you can use for computing critical values and probabilities against which you can check your χ^2 statistic. The **cutoffs( )** function generates the critical values for the probabilities in Table 8-1 and for the degrees of freedom corresponding to your intervals. The **show__probability( )** function displays information about the probability levels corresponding to the cutoff values between which your χ^2 value lies.

```
/* Definitions and functions for computing cutoff values
   for chi-square statistic, and for determining probability
   associated with observed chi-square value.
*/

#include <math.h>   /* needed for sqrt () function */

#define MAX_FACTOR     9

int    cutoffs ( double, int);
void   show_probability ( int);

int    r_vals [ MAX_RAND];     /* contains random values generated */
int    group [ NR_INTERVALS];

/* contains "magic numbers" for computing cutoff values for
   evaluating chi-square statistic.
   Magic numbers correspond to the following probabilities:
   .01, .05, .10, .25, .50, .75, .90, .95, .99
```

```
*/
double chi_factors [ MAX_FACTOR] =
                { -2.3253, -1.6449, -1.2816, -.6745,
                  0.0, .6745, 1.2816, 1.6449, 2.3253};


/* Compute the cutoff, or critical, value just less than
   you observed chi-quare statistic, given the observed
   chi-square value and the degrees of freedom.
*/
int cutoffs ( double chi_val, int df)
{
        double df_root, df_term, approx_term, cut_off = 0.0;
        int     index;

        df_root = sqrt ( 2 * df);
        printf ( "df_root == %.41f\n", df_root);

        for ( index = 0; ( index < MAX_FACTOR) &&
                         ( chi_val > cut_off); index++)
        {
                df_term = df + df_root * chi_factors [ index];
                approx_term = 2.0 / 3.0 *
                                ( chi_factors [ index] *
                                  chi_factors [ index] - 1);
                cut_off = df_term + approx_term;
                printf ("%d: term == %.41f; approx == %.41f; ",
                        index, df_term, approx_term);
                printf ( "df == %d; cut_off == %.41f\n",
                        df, cut_off);
        }
        printf ( "after loop, index == %d\n", index);
        if ( chi_val > cut_off)
                return ( index);
        else
                return ( index - 1);
}




/* Determine and display the probabilities that bound the chi-square
   statistic observed for a random distribution.
*/
void show_probability ( int level)
{
        double lower, upper;

        switch ( level)
        {
                case 0:
                        lower = .00;
                        upper = .01;
                        break;
                case 1:
                        lower = .01;
                        upper = .05;
                        break;
                case 2:
                        lower = .05;
                        upper = .10;
                        break;
                case 3:
                        lower = .10;
                        upper = .25;
                        break;
```

```
        case 4:
                lower = .25;
                upper = .50;
                break;
        case 5:
                lower = .50;
                upper = .75;
                break;
        case 6:
                lower = .75;
                upper = .90;
                break;
        case 7:
                lower = .90;
                upper = .95;
                break;
        case 8:
                lower = .95;
                upper = .99;
                break;
        case 9:
                lower = .99;
                upper = 1.00;
                break;
        default:
                lower = 0;
                upper = 0;
                break;
        }
        printf ( "Probability of value is between %.21f and %.21f\n",
        lower, upper);
}
```

cutoffs()

This function uses the following formula to compute approximate critical values for selected probabilities and for the appropriate number of degrees of freedom. In the formula, df represents the degrees of freedom, and x_p represents a "magic" number from the **chi_factors[ ]** array.

$$df + \sqrt{2df}\, x_p + \frac{2}{3}x_p{}^2 - \frac{2}{3}$$

The function computes an approximate cutoff for each of the probabilities in Table 8-1. The magic numbers correspond to the probabilities in the order in which they appear in the table. Thus, -2.3253 corresponds to a probability of 0.01, -1.2816 corresponds to a probability of 0.10, and so on through 2.3253, which corresponds to a probability of 0.99. The **cutoffs()** function returns an **int** representing the index of the smallest probability whose critical value is higher than your χ^2 value.

Table 8-2.   Selected Cutoff Values for χ^2 Statistic

Probabilities / $df \rightarrow$	5	10	15	20	25	30
0.01	.554	2.558	5.229	8.260	11.524	14.954
0.05	1.146	3.940	7.261	10.851	14.611	18.493
0.10	1.610	4.865	8.547	12.443	16.437	20.599
0.25	2.675	6.737	11.036	15.452	19.939	24.478
0.50	4.351	9.342	14.339	19.337	24.337	29.339
0.75	6.626	12.549	18.245	23.828	29.339	34.800
0.90	9.236	15.987	22.307	28.412	34.382	40.256
0.95	11.070	18.307	24.996	31.410	37.652	43.773
0.99	15.086	23.209	30.578	37.566	44.314	50.892

The **cutoffs()** function provides reasonable approximations to the cutoffs only if you have more than 30 intervals. If you have fewer intervals, use Table 8-2, which provides the cutoff values for selected degrees of freedom. Remember that the degrees of freedom value is one less than the number of intervals you have.

If you can't find the cutoff values you need, you'll need to consult a more extensive table of χ^2 critical values. You can find such tables in most statistics books. Be careful, however: Some tables give you the cutoffs for the probability that you'll get a value *larger* than the cutoff value by chance.

show—probability()

This function uses the **int** returned by **cutoffs()** to determine and display the probabilities bounding your χ^2 value. The 299.31 value used in an earlier example resulted from a run of the random number generator using 7171 as the seed, 65 as the multiplier, and 3 as the increment. If you use 111 as the seed, the resulting χ^2 value will be 280.88, which lies between the 0.01 and 0.05 probability levels.

Although a smaller chi-square value indicates a more even distribution, this second result may actually be *too* even; that is, it's possible to get distributions that are too well-behaved as well as those that are too unevenly distributed. Consider, for example, the sequence 0, 100, 200, ... 32700, 1, 101, ... In general, the most acceptable values for a good random number generator would be those that fall somewhere in the middle of the probability distribution: You don't want your generator to produce distributions that are always too "clean," nor do you want the distributions to be too uneven.

There's no hard and fast rule for deciding what values are acceptable. Ordinarily, when you're looking for parameters for a good generator, you should generate multiple sets of values and compute chi-square values and probabilities for all of them.

An acceptable and easy decision rule is provided by Knuth in the book mentioned earlier. He suggests generating at least three sets of random values with the same parameter values, using a different seed each time. If any of the three χ^2 values lies in the most extreme probabilities—that is, less than 0.01 or greater than 0.99—the generator should be rejected. Values lying within the next level of probabilities (between 0.01 and 0.05 or between 0.95 and 0.99) should be considered suspect. If at least two of your values are suspect, you should reject the generator.

Other authors may have different rules of thumb. For most ordinary purposes, generators that satisfy Knuth's criterion should be adequate. If your work requires a "better" random number generator, you'll need to investigate the issues more thoroughly.

OTHER RANDOM DISTRIBUTIONS

The discussion and algorithms in this chapter have concerned random number generators that produce uniformly distributed integer values. You may need other kinds of random values in certain circumstances.

Noninteger Random Values

If you were trying to build a simulation involving probabilities, you would need random values between 0.0 and 1.0, inclusive. In fact, the random number generators for some languages produce such random values rather than random integers.

You can produce such values by using your random number algorithm to generate random integers and then bringing these values into the desired range. Do this by dividing the integer by the largest random value possible—in our case, 32,767. The following function, **zero—one—rand()**, shows how to do this:

```
/* Function to return a pseudorandom value between 0.0 and 1.0. */

double zero_one_rand ()
{
#define  MAX_VAL  32767.0    /* NOTE: defined as floating point type */
        int  rand ();        /* returns a pseudorandom integer */
        int  rand_result;

        rand_result = rand (); /* get a pseudorandom integer */
        return ( rand_result / MAX_VAL);
}
```

zero—one—rand()

The currrent version of this function calls the Run-Time library function **rand()** for a random integer and then divides the value by MAX—VAL. You should substitute a call to one of your random number generators or develop a different version of this function, as you'll do later.

Notice that MAX—VAL is defined as a floating point value rather than an integer, because dividing one **int** by another yields another **int**; you would always get either a 0 or a 1, with a 1 only if **rand()** returned 32767.

Generating Nonuniform Distributions

Most random number generators produce uniformly distributed values—at least in principle. Sometimes, however, you may want to get a different distribution of values. For example, some situations call for a *normal distribution*, which has a familiar bell shape, as shown in Figure 8-1.

Other situations require still other distributions of values. For example, if you were doing a simulation of population growth, you might use an *exponential distribution*. To simulate a line in a

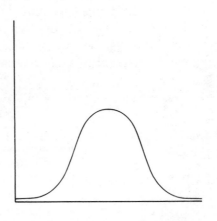

Figure 8-1.   A bell-shaped, or normal, distribution

bank, you might want to generate something called a *Poisson distribution.*

In the next chapter, you'll learn how to create simulations that may require such nonuniform distributions.

Combining Random Number Generators

Earlier, you saw a program in which you could specify which random number generator the program would use to generate an entire sample of values. You can also create a random sample by using different random generators on different turns.

These alternative generators can be different algorithms, or they can be the same algorithm using different parameter values. The simplest case selects between two different calls with equal probabilities. The following program illustrates this:

```
#include <stdio.h>
#include <stdlib.h>
#include <string.h>
#include <math.h>

#define MODULUS        32768L
#define SEMI_MOD       16384
#define MAX_STR        80
#define MAX_RAND       5000
#define PER_LINE       10

#define INTERV_SIZE    100
#define NR_INTERVALS   MODULUS / INTERV_SIZE + 1
#define MAX_FACTOR     9


double chi_square ( int [], long int, int, int);
int    cutoffs ( double, int);
int    even_count ( int []);
int    get_int ( char *);
void   get_params ( int *, int *);
int    linear ( int, int, int *);
void   distribution ( int [], int [], long int, int, int);
void   show_probability ( int);

int curr_seed;
int    r_vals [ MAX_RAND];      /* contains random values generated */
int    group [ NR_INTERVALS];

/* contains "magic numbers" for computing cutoff values for
   evaluating chi-square statistic.
   Magic numbers correspond to the following probabilities:
   .01, .05, .10, .25, .50, .75, .90, .95, .99
*/
double chi_factors [ MAX_FACTOR] =
                    { -2.3253, -1.6449, -1.2816, -.6745,
                      0.0, .6745, 1.2816, 1.6449, 2.3253};

int outcome;

main ()
{
        int    index, start, test_df;
        int    mult1, mult2, incr1, incr2;
        double result;
        char   info [ MAX_STR];

        start = get_int ( "Starting seed? ");
        get_params ( &mult1, &incr1);
        get_params ( &mult2, &incr2);

        printf ( "Starting seed = %d\n\n", start);

        srand (start);
        for ( index = 0; index < MAX_RAND; index++)
        {
                /* r_vals [ index] = rand(); */
                if ( (start = rand ()) >= SEMI_MOD)
                        r_vals [ index] = linear ( mult1,
                                                   incr1, &start);
                else
                        r_vals [ index] = linear ( mult2,
                                                   incr2, &start);
                printf ( "%7d", r_vals [ index]);
                if ( ( index % PER_LINE) == PER_LINE - 1)
                        printf ( "\n");
        }
```

```
        printf ( "\n\n%d even values\n", even_count ( r_vals));

        distribution ( group, r_vals, MODULUS, INTERV_SIZE, MAX_RAND);
        result = chi_square ( group, MODULUS, INTERV_SIZE, MAX_RAND);
        outcome = cutoffs ( result, NR_INTERVALS - 1);
        show_probability ( outcome);
}



/* Get multiplier and increment */
void get_params ( int *mult, int *incr)
{
        char info [ MAX_STR];

        printf ( "Multiplier? ");
        gets ( info);
        *mult = atoi ( info);

        printf ( "Increment? ");
        gets ( info);
        *incr = atoi ( info);
}


/* Prompt user for integer value, read and return the value */
int get_int ( char *message)
{
char info [ MAX_STR];

        printf ( "%s", message);
        gets ( info);
        return ( atoi ( info));
}


/* count the # of even values in the array */
int even_count ( int vals [])
{
        int count = 0, index;

        for ( index = 0; index < MAX_RAND; index++)
                if ( (vals [ index] % 2) == 0)
                        count++;
        return ( count);
}


/* generate a random integer, using linear congruential algorithm */
int linear ( int multiplier, int increment, int *seed)
{
        long int  temp;
        temp = ( (long) multiplier * *seed + increment) % MODULUS;
        *seed = (int) temp;
        return ( *seed);
}


/* Determine number of values from each interval that occur in the
   random sequence. Display the resulting frequencies.
*/
void distribution ( int group [], int raw [],
                    long int range, int size, int nr_trials)
{
        int nr_intervals, index, actual_size;

        nr_intervals = range / size + 1;
```

```
        for ( index = 0; index < nr_trials; index++)
                group [ raw [ index] / size]++;

        for ( index = 0; index < nr_intervals; index++)
        {
                printf ( "%7d", group [ index]);
                if ( ( index % PER_LINE)  == PER_LINE - 1)
                        printf ( "\n");
        }
}


/* Function for computing a chi-square statistic, given
   an array of interval frequencies, the range of values,
   interval size, and number of trials.
*/
double chi_square ( int group [], long int range, int size, int trials)
{
        int    nr_intervals, index;
        double expected, deviation, last_size, sum = 0.0;

        nr_intervals = range / size + 1;
        expected = ( (double) trials * size) / range;

        for ( index = 0; index < nr_intervals - 1; index++)
        {
                deviation = group [ index] - expected;
                sum += deviation * deviation / expected;
        }

    /* for last, smaller, interval */
        last_size = range - (long) ( nr_intervals - 1) * size;
        expected = ( (double) trials * last_size) / range;
        deviation = group [ nr_intervals - 1] - expected;
        sum += deviation * deviation / expected;

        printf ( "\n\nchi-square for %d intervals == %.4lf\n",
                 nr_intervals, sum);
        return ( sum);
}


/* Compute the cutoff, or critical, value just less than
   you observed chi-quare statistic, given the observed
   chi-square value and the degrees of freedom.
*/
 int cutoffs ( double chi_val, int df)
 {
        double df_root, df_term, approx_term, cut_off = 0.0;
        int    index;

        df_root = sqrt ( 2 * df);
        printf ( "df_root == %.4lf\n", df_root);

        for ( index = 0; ( index < MAX_FACTOR) &&
                          ( chi_val > cut_off); index++)
        {
                df_term = df + df_root * chi_factors [ index];
                approx_term = 2.0 / 3.0 *
                              ( chi_factors [ index] *
                                chi_factors [ index] - 1);
                cut_off = df_term + approx_term;
                printf ("%d: term == %.4lf; approx == %.4lf; ",
                        index, df_term, approx_term);
                printf ( "df == %d; cut_off == %.4lf\n",
                         df, cut_off);
```

```
        }
        printf ( "after loop, index == %d\n", index);
        if ( chi_val > cut_off)
                return ( index);
        else
                return ( index - 1);
}


/* Determine and display the probabilities that bound the chi-square
   statistic observed fora random distribution.
*/
void show_probability ( int level)
{
        double lower, upper;

        switch ( level)
        {
                case 0:
                        lower = .00;
                        upper = .01;
                        break;
                case 1:
                        lower = .01;
                        upper = .05;
                        break;
                case 2:
                        lower = .05;
                        upper = .10;
                        break;
                case 3:
                        lower = .10;
                        upper = .25;
                        break;
                case 4:
                        lower = .25;
                        upper = .50;
                        break;
                case 5:
                        lower = .50;
                        upper = .75;
                        break;
                case 6:
                        lower = .75;
                        upper = .90;
                        break;
                case 7:
                        lower = .90;
                        upper = .95;
                        break;
                case 8:
                        lower = .95;
                        upper = .99;
                        break;
                case 9:
                        lower = .99;
                        upper = 1.00;
                        break;
                default:
                        lower = 0;
                        upper = 0;
                        break;
        }
        printf ( "Probability of value is between %.2lf and %.2lf\n",
                lower, upper);
}
```

get_params()

This function is for convenience in reading and writing the **main()** function. The function gets multiplier and increment values for an arbitrary generator.

main()

The core of the **for** loop has been modified to select **linear()** with either of two sets of parameter values. To decide which parameter values to use, the program calls **rand()**. By actually returning the result from the call to **rand()** and using it as the next seed for **linear()**, the program avoids the cycle of even and odd numbers, since **rand()** does not alternate between even and odd values. You can also accomplish this by using the **addit()** function, but not the **quadr()** function, since that also alternates between odd and even. Try using **quadr()** to make the selection, and see what happens. Remember to generate values for the array **add_seed[ ]** before using **addit()**.

The test condition looks at the size of the value returned. You could just as easily check whether the value is even or odd. To select from more than two sets of parameter values, you may want to use **zero_one_rand()** to return a value. For example, you might select parameter set 1 if the resulting value is between 0.0 and 0.25, set 2 if the value is between 0.25 and 0.75, and set 3 if the value is greater than or equal to 0.75. Just remember to be careful about cutoff values. For example, in this case, you would take parameter set 1 if the value was less than 0.25 and parameter set 2 if the value was greater than *or equal to* 0.25 but less than 0.75.

Run several samples for the same parameters, and see how the chi-square values for the distributions look. You may want to try exploring the period length of such hybrid generators.

Think about how you might modify the linear congruential generator routines so that odd and even values would not necessarily alternate, while still using odd parameter values. You should also develop hybrid generators involving quadratic or additive generators.

EXAMPLE: A TRIVIA PROGRAM FOR TWO PLAYERS

In this section, you'll find a simple program that uses random number generators in various ways. The program "runs" a question-and-answer game in which two players compete with each other. The program reads questions selected at random from a question file. The player whose turn it is tries to answer the question first. The other player can also provide an answer. The player who provides the correct answer gets a point added to his or her score.

The program decides which player will get to answer the next question first. The decision is based on a random calculation weighted to take into account the scores of the two players. If both players have the same score, each player has an equal chance of getting the next turn. On the other hand, if player *1* has 60% of the points, then player *2* will have a 60% chance of getting the next turn.

The program uses random number generators to make decisions in several places: **pick—player( )**, **show—qn( )**, and **house—rand( )**. To start things off, you need to provide a seed and two sets of parameter values.

The program assumes all questions are stored in a file with the extension **.qn** and that the answers are stored in a file with the same name as the question file but with the extension **.ans**.

```
/* Program to ask questions selected at random, and to let two
   players compete against each other until one scores the required number
   of points.
*/

#include <stdio.h>
#include <string.h>
#include <stdlib.h>

#define MODULUS     32768L
#define MAX_STR     100
#define MAX_QNS     1000
#define MORE_CH     '/'        /* if question takes 2 or more lines */
#define QN_EXT      ".qn"      /* extension for question file */
#define ANS_EXT     ".ans"     /* extension for answer file */
#define PTS_TO_WIN  5          /* # correct answers needed to win */
#define MAX_PLAYER  2          /* # players allowed */
#define TRUE        1
#define FALSE       0
```

```
/* Function DECLARATIONS */

int     get_int ( char *);
void    get_params ( int *mult, int *incr);
int     house_rand ( void);
double  house_zero_one ( void);
int     linear ( int multiplier, int increment, int *seed);
int     pick_player ( int one, int two);
void    show_answer ( int depth);
int     show_qn ( int nr_qns);
void    triv_wait ( void);


FILE *qptr,    /* question file */
     *aptr;    /* answer file */

int        curr_seed;
int        mult1, mult2, incr1, incr2;    /* parameter sets */
int        pts [ MAX_PLAYER];             /* scores for players */
int        qn_asked [ MAX_QNS];           /* was qn [ index] asked? */
char       *null_str = "";

main ( int argc, char *argv [])
{
        char   info [ MAX_STR];
        int    index, nr_qns = 0,    /* # qns in file */
               depth,                /* question # */
               player,               /* player whose turn it is */
               pts_val = 1;          /* gain for each correct answer */

        if ( argc < 2)
        {
                printf ( "Usage: Trivia <qnfile>(no extension) \n");
                exit ( 1);
        }

    /* open files */
        strcpy ( info, argv[ 1]);
        strcat ( info, QN_EXT);
        qptr = fopen ( info, "r");
        strcpy ( info, argv[ 1]);
        strcat ( info, ANS_EXT);
        aptr = fopen ( info, "r");

    /* if files not both opened */
        if ( ( qptr == NULL) || ( aptr == NULL))
        {
                printf ( "File not found.\n");
                exit ( 1);
        }

    /* find out how many questions are in the file. */
        fgets ( info, MAX_STR, qptr);
        nr_qns = atoi ( info);

        curr_seed = get_int ( "Seed? ");

    /* get parameter sets from user */
        get_params ( &mult1, &incr1);
        get_params ( &mult2, &incr2);

        do   /* play until someone wins or questions are used up. */
        {
```

```
              /* pick player */
                  player = pick_player ( pts [ 0], pts [ 1]) - 1;
                  printf ( "Player %d:\n", player + 1);

                  depth = show_qn ( nr_qns);     /* show a question */
                  if ( depth == 0)               /* if no more qns */
                          break;
                  triv_wait ();                  /* let players answer */
                  show_answer ( depth);
                  printf ( "Outcome? (player #)");  /* who got ans? */
                  gets ( info);
                  player = atoi ( info);
              /* change score of player who got correct answer */
                  if ( player && ( player <= MAX_PLAYER))
                          pts [ player - 1] += pts_val;
              /* show scores */
                  for ( index = 0; index < MAX_PLAYER; index++)
                  {
                          printf ( "pts [ %d] == %d; ",
                          index + 1, pts [ index]);
                          if ( ( index % 2) == 1)
                                  printf ( "\n");
                  }
          }
          while ( ( pts [ 0] < PTS_TO_WIN) &&
                  ( pts [ 1] < PTS_TO_WIN) &&
                  ( depth != 0));

      /* show final scores */
          printf ( "\n\n\nFinal scores:\n\n");
          for ( index = 0; index < MAX_PLAYER; index++)
                  printf ( "Player %d: %3d pt.\n",
                          index + 1, pts [ index]);
          fclose ( qptr);
          fclose ( aptr);
}


/* Determine whose turn it will be;
   player with higher score has lower chance of being selected.
*/
int pick_player ( int one, int two)
{
          int     total;
          double  cutoff, result;

          total = one + two;
          if ( total == 0)
                  cutoff = 0.5;
          else
                  cutoff = ( double) two / total;

          result = house_zero_one();
      /* uncomment following statement to see
          selection process.
      */
      /*
          printf ( "Result == %.4lf; cutoff == %.4lf\n",
                  result, cutoff);
      */
          if ( result < cutoff)
                  return ( 1);
          else
                  return ( 2);
}
```

```
/* return a random integer between 0 and 32767 */
int house_rand ()
{
#define SEMI_MOD    (MODULUS % 2)

        if ( curr_seed >= SEMI_MOD)
                return ( linear ( mult1, incr1, &curr_seed));
        else
                return ( linear ( mult2, incr2, &curr_seed));
}


/* Function to return a pseudorandom value between 0.0 and 1.0. */
double house_zero_one ()
{
#define  MAX_VAL  32767.0        /* NOTE: defined as floating point type */
        int  rand_result;

        rand_result = house_rand ();  /* get a pseudorandom integer */
        return ( rand_result / MAX_VAL);
}


/* Select an unasked question number, and display the question. */
int show_qn ( int nr_qns)
{
        int  index, depth;
        char qn [ MAX_STR];
        static nr_asked = 0;
        rewind ( qptr);
    /* search for a qn number until
       an unasked question # is found, AND
       the question # is not 0, AND
       there are still questions to ask
    */
        do
                depth = house_rand () % ( nr_qns + 1);
        while ( ( (qn_asked [ depth]) || ( depth == 0)) &&
               ( nr_asked < nr_qns));

        if ( nr_qns == nr_asked)  /* if all qns have been asked */
        {
                printf ( "no more questions to ask.\n");
                return ( 0);
        }

    /* find the question */
        for ( index = 0; (index <= depth) && !feof ( qptr); index++)
        {
                fgets ( qn, MAX_STR, qptr);
            /* skip over continuation lines */
                while ( qn [ 0] == MORE_CH)
                        fgets ( qn, MAX_STR, qptr);
        }
        qn_asked [ depth] = TRUE;        /* mark qn as asked */
        printf ( "%s\n", qn);
        fgets ( qn, MAX_STR, qptr);      /* ask qn */
    /* display continuation lines of question */
        while ( !feof ( qptr) && ( qn [ 0] == MORE_CH))
        {
                printf ( "%s\n", qn);
                fgets ( qn, MAX_STR, qptr);
        }

        nr_asked++;              /* anbother question asked */
        return ( depth);
}
```

```
/* Show the answer for the question selected. */
void show_answer ( int depth)
{
        int    index;
        char   ans [ MAX_STR];

        rewind ( aptr);
        for ( index = 0; index < depth; index++)
                fgets ( ans, MAX_STR, aptr);
        printf ( "\n%s\n", ans);
}


/* Get values for multiplier and increment, to use for generator */
void get_params ( int *mult, int *incr)
{
        char info [ MAX_STR];

        printf ( "Multiplier? ");
        gets ( info);
        *mult = atoi ( info);
        printf ( "Increment? ");
        gets ( info);
        *incr = atoi ( info);
}



/* return a random integer, based on
   curr_seed, multiplier, and increment
*/
int linear ( int multiplier, int increment, int *seed)
{
        long int  temp;

        temp = (multiplier * *seed + increment) % MODULUS;
        *seed = (int) temp;
        return ( *seed);
}


/* Wait for user to press a key */
void  triv_wait ()
{
        char  info [ MAX_STR];

        printf ( "Press <Return> to see answer.");
        gets ( info);
}


/* Prompt user for integer value, read and return the value */
int get_int ( char *message)
{
        char info [ MAX_STR];

        printf ( "%s", message);
        gets ( info);
        return ( atoi ( info));
}
```

house_rand()

This function selects either of two parameter sets, using the value of **curr_seed** to make the decision. The **house_rand** function then calls **linear()** with the appropriate parameter set. You should substitute your random number generator for **linear()** or substitute your own function for **house_rand()**. If you keep the name **house_rand()**, the programs in the following chapters won't need to be changed.

The function needs five **extern int** values: **curr_seed, mult1, mult2, inc1**, and **inc2**.

house_zero_one()

This function returns a random **double** value between 0.0 and 1.0, inclusive. The function calls **house_rand()** instead of **rand()** for its random integer.

pick_player()

This function decides which of two players should get to answer first for the next question. In making its decision, the function uses each player's point value to weight the selection probabilities: Essentially, the player with fewer points is more likely to get the next turn.

show_qn()

This function selects a question number at random, reads this question from a file, and displays the question for the players. In generating its random question number, function **show_qn()** keeps generating values until it selects a question that has not already been asked.

Questions in the source file must be on separate lines. If a question extends over more than one line, the first character of the continuation line must be MORE_CH. This information enables **show_qn()** to skip over continuation lines without counting them and also to show the entire question if the current question takes more than one line.

The function skips over "question" 0 in the **.qn** file, since this line contains information about the number of questions in the entire file. The function returns the number of the question asked; if all questions have been asked, it returns 0.

show_answer()

This function reads the answer with the number corresponding to the question number from a file and displays the answer.

triv_wait()

This function is the same as the **wait()** function you've used in earlier chapters, except that **triv_wait()** displays a different prompt.

The following listing shows the contents of a question file. You can type in this file to see how the program works, or you can make up your own questions. Notice the use of the continuation character, '/', in several of the questions.

```
25
1. Who was president earlier, William Henry Harrison or Benjamin
/ Harrison?
2. Which has a longer life expectancy, an elephant or a human?
3. Which animal's milk has the highest fat content?
/ Cow, northern fur seal, goat.
4. What is the plural of nudibranch? (nudibranchs)
5. How many colors are there in the rainbow?
6. Which of the following authors was born most recently?
/ Dostoievsky, Dickens, Disraeli
7. Which is hotter, 21 degrees Centigrade or 72 degrees Fahrenheit?
8. How long is a furlong?
9. How many presidents had last names beginning with 'H'?
10. What is the second largest country in area?
11. What is the third largest country in area?
12. Who was older, Charlotte or Emily Bronte?
13. Within 10%, what is the total number of letters in the names of
/ all 50 states?
14. What is the tallest building in the United States?
15. In what country is the longest tunnel?
16. Which has a higher population density: Monaco or Vatican City?
17. Which air distance is longer: Boston -- San Francisco or
/ Boston -- Seattle?
18. Which has a greater land area: Iceland or Czechoslovakia?
19. Which of the following has the greatest atomic weight:
/ Iodine, Iron, Krypton?
```

20. Who discovered conditional reflexes by studying salivation in
/ dogs?
21. Who of the following was born in a different century
/ from the others?
/ Beethoven, Emerson, Henry David Thoreau, Bertrand Russell
22. How long does it take light from the sun to reach Jupiter:
/ 30 minutes, 45 minutes, 60 minutes
23. Which is heavier: 750 ounces or 20000 grams?
24. Which of the following letters begins the names of the most
/ state capitals? 'A', 'C', or 'J'
25. Name two birds whose names begin with 'e'

To give you an opportunity to try the questions even after you type them in, here are the contents of the answer file—but encrypted using the encryption program from Chapter 6 and an offset algorithm. For the answers where the length would give it away, only the first few characters are shown. For some answers, extra letters have been added to keep you from getting the correct answer just on the basis of the number of letters. All answers are encrypted using the same offset.

1. Pbeaxg
2. anf
3. lxt
4. ...tgval
5. lxoxgvhehkl
6. Whlm
7. Ytak
8. 220 rw
9. yboxwbw
10. Vtg
11. Vabgt
12. Vatke
13. yhnkangwkxwmpxeox
14. Lxtkl Mhpxk, Vab
15. Ctitgwhxl
16. Fhg
17. Uhlmhg -- Ltg
18. Vsx
19. Bh
20. Itoeho
21. Uxxm
22. 45 fbgnmxl
23. hs
24. 'V'
25. xtzex, xzkxm, xfn, xkgx

Suggestions and Extensions

The current version of the trivia program asks questions until one player reaches a predetermined number of points or until it runs out of questions. Each question is worth one point.

You can modify this program in several ways. For example, the game might continue for a predetermined number of questions or for a predetermined amount of time; the player with the most points at the end wins. Or questions might have a point value selected at random by the program or determined by the question's position in the file. You might also modify the program to enable more than two players to play; in this case, you'd need to modify the player-selection function.

Another version might give players money with which to bet on questions. Each player could then bet a given amount, based on current holdings, before seeing the question. In this version, both players may be able to offer their answers. If a player gives the correct answer, that player gets an amount of money equal to his or her bet; players who give incorrect answers lose the money they bet.

Yet another version might determine which player gets the next turn by how quickly the players "ring in." Each player might get a particular key to press. When the question is displayed, each player tries to be the first to press his or her key if he or she knows the answer. You might use DOS service 0xb to determine when a key has been pressed and DOS service 0x1 to see what it is. The key echoed will be that of the first player who responded; that player gets to answer the question first. You will need to get rid of any characters in the keyboard buffer prior to showing the next question; find out about DOS service 0xc for this.

To keep players from simply pressing their buttons whether or not they know the answer, you might want to have the program impose a time limit on a player's answer. To do this, you'll need to use the **get_time()** and **how_long()** functions or devise another way of reading the system time information at regular intervals.

Random Walk

In Chapter 7, you used **rand()** in conjunction with the ROM video function for placing the cursor and writing at random positions on the screen. That program was a simplified version of something called a *random walk*. In a random walk, a person begins at some starting position, selects one of the four directions at random, and takes a step in that direction. Random walks have all sorts of interesting mathematical properties that you might want to explore.

A simple random walk program might start the cursor at the center of the screen, move at random in one of the four directions, and check that position to see whether there is anything written at that position. You can use video function request 0x8 to do the last step.

Call **int86( )** with 0x10 (video function code) as its first argument. The **inreg.h.ah** member should contain the function request code (0x8); **inreg.h.bh** should contain the video page you want to read (this value will usually be 0). After the call to **int86( )**, **outreg.h.al** will contain the ASCII code for the character or 0 if there is no character at that position.

You might have your program write a letter or number based on the frequency with which a location has been visited. For example, if you were counting in hexadecimal, you could visit a spot 16 times before you would need to repeat a character. Thus, if your random walk took you to a particular cell that had already been visited 9 times (had the digit 9 written at that spot), your program would then write *a* to indicate that another visit had been made.

SUMMARY

In this chapter, you looked at pseudorandom number generators. You learned about some of the general algorithms for creating such generators and developed some functions to implement these algorithms and to generate collections of random values. The chapter also included some techniques and simple tests for evaluating the adequacy of a random number generator. You'll find more about such tests, and others, in Chapter 10.

Finally, the chapter included a simple, competitive question-and-answer program that used random number generators for various purposes.

The examples and discussion in the chapter have used the simplest and probably best-studied algorithm for generating random numbers, the linear congruential method. Generators based on this algorithm are by no means the best. You should explore the behavior of the simple quadratic algorithm discussed briefly as well as that of the additive algorithm. Both of these algorithms can give you better generators with very long periods—longer than the range.

The main random number generator developed by the end of the chapter, **house__rand( )**, is designed to make it easy for you to substitute your own random number generator. We'll continue to use the linear congruential generator in the next two chapters.

In Chapter 9, you'll learn how to use your random number generator to create samples of random values having specified properties.

9

SIMULATIONS

A *simulation* is a means of modeling certain aspects of a real-world process or phenomenon in a simpler context, such as a computer program. Simulations can enable you to study processes that are too inconvenient, too slow, too expensive, or too dangerous to study in the real world.

A SIMPLE SIMULATION AND SOME VARIANTS

In a simulation, you'll often repeat the process under investigation many times, with different values for the elements, and look at the "average" behavior over these repeated runs, or trials. For example, you can simulate coin tossing or dice rolling by generating random integers on a computer. The following program "flips a coin" as many times as you want, writing "H" or "t," depending on the outcome. The program uses function **coin_flip()** to "toss" the coin. To get information from the user, the program calls function **get_int()**, which you've seen in other programs.

```
/* Program to simulate coin tosses. */

#include <stdio.h>
#include <stdlib.h>
#include <string.h>
#include <math.h>

#define MAX_STR   100

#include "rand.c"            /* contains random number routines */


/* Function DECLARATIONS */
int coin_flip ( void);
int get_int ( char *message);

main ()
{
        int    index, start, nr_trials;
        int    head = 0, tail = 0;
        char   info [ MAX_STR];

        curr_seed = get_int ( "Starting seed? ");
        nr_trials = get_int ( "Toss coin how often? ");

        printf ( "Starting seed = %d\n\n", curr_seed);
        printf ( "Generating random values ... \n");

        for ( index = 0; index < nr_trials; index++)
        {
                start = coin_flip ();
                if ( start)
                {
                        head++;
                        printf ( "H");
                }
                else
                {
                        tail++;
                        printf  ("t");
                }
                /* */
                if ( ( index % 10) == 9)
                        printf ( " ");
                if ( ( index % 50) == 49)
                        printf ( "\n");
                /* */
        }
        printf ( "%3d heads; %3d tails\n", head, tail);
        printf ( "\n Done\n");
}
```

```
/* Return a "head" or "tail," depending on the random value
   generated. This function always assumes the probability
   of a head (hit) is 0.5.
*/
int coin_flip ()
{
        double hit = 0.5;     /* probability of a head */
        long   int cutoff;    /* int value corresponding to hit */
        int    result;

        cutoff = (long) floor ( MODULUS * hit);

        result = house_rand ();
        if ( result < cutoff)
                return ( 1);     /* return "head" */
        else
                return ( 0);     /* return "tail" */
}



/* Prompt user for a value, read and return an int */
int get_int ( char *message)
{
        char info [ MAX_STR];

        printf ( "%s\n", message);
        gets ( info);
        return ( atoi ( info));
}
```

coin—flip( )

Function **coin—flip( )** simulates a coin toss by generating a random integer. The function checks whether **result** is less than some value, **cutoff**. If so, the function reports that the coin came up heads; otherwise, the coin comes up tails. With a fair coin, heads and tails should come up about equally often. For this reason, **cutoff** divides the range of possible values in half.

'   Function **coin—flip( )** uses **house—rand( )**, the random number generator developed in the preceding chapter.

house—rand( )

This function generates pseudorandom integers between 0 and 32,767, inclusive. To do its work, the generator selects either of two parameter sets and then uses a linear congruential method to generate the value. This function is declared and defined in the file **rand.c**, along with the external variables the function uses.

You should substitute your own random number generator for this function, or at least for the call to **linear( )** currently used.

Why Simulations?

You can use simulations to support or refute hypotheses you already have, or you can use them to explore new aspects of a process. For example, you can count the number of heads in 500 tosses to help confirm (or contradict) the intuitive hypothesis that this side should come up about 250 times with a fair coin.

You can also explore the relationship between the number of heads and the number of tails with the same simulation. The following program also simulates a specified number of coin tosses. In addition, the program counts the number of heads and the number of tails. Finally, after each toss, the program checks whether there have been more heads or more tails tossed up to that point.

If more heads have been tossed, the counter **h—lead** is increased by one; if more tails have been tossed, the other counter, **t—lead**, is increased by one. After the tosses, you can check which side led more often and by how much. Before running the program or looking at the output below, formulate your own hypothesis. For discussion, assume 500 tosses.

The listing contains only the main program, since the **coin—flip( )** function is the same one used earlier. Other routines are now in the files **misc.c** and **rdist.c**.

```
/* Program to simulate coin tosses.
   Program keeps track of # heads and tails so far, and
     # of tosses during which each side had occurred more often.
*/

#include <stdio.h>
#include <stdlib.h>
#include <string.h>
#include <math.h>

#define MAX_STR    100
```

```
#include "rand.c"      /* contains random number generator */
#include "rdist.c"     /* contains coin_flip () */
#include "misc.c"      /* contains get_int () */

main ()
{
        int     index, start, nr_trials;
        int     head = 0, tail = 0, h_lead = 0, t_lead = 0;

        curr_seed = get_int ( "Starting seed? ");
        nr_trials = get_int ( "Toss coin how often? ");

        printf ( "Starting seed = %d\n\n", curr_seed);
        printf ( "Generating random values ... \n");

        head = 0;
        tail = 0;
        h_lead = 0;
        t_lead = 0;
        for ( index = 0; index < nr_trials; index++)
        {
                start = coin_flip ();
                if ( start)
                {
                        head++;
                        printf ( "H");
                }
                else
                {
                        tail++;
                        printf ("t");
                }
                if ( head > tail)
                        h_lead++;
                else if ( tail > head)
                        t_lead++;
                if ( ( index % 10) == 9)
                        printf ( " ");
                if ( ( index % 50) == 49)
                        printf ( "\n");
        }
        printf ( "%3d heads; %3d tails; ", head, tail);
        printf ( "H leads = %3d; T leads = %3d\n",
                h_lead, t_lead);
}
```

The following listing shows the output from this program:

```
Starting seed = 1951

Generating random values ...
tttHttHHtt HHtHHttHHH ttttHHHHHH HttttttHttt HtHttttttt
ttttttttHtH ttHttHHHHt tttHHtHHtH ttHHHtHHHt tHHttttHtt
HttHHtHtHH HHtHttHtHt ttttHHHHHH HHttttttttt tttHtHHttt
HHHHttttHH HttHtHHtHH tttHttttttH ttHHtHtttH tHHtttHHHH
tHtHHtHttt ttttttHtHt HtHtHHHHHH HtHttHtHtt ttHHHttHtH
HtHHHtHtt tHtttttHtt tttHttHttH HHHttttttHt HHtHtHHHHH
HHHHtHHttt HtttHHHHHt HttHtHtttH HHHttHtttH ttHHHtHHHt
HHHHHtHHHH HtHHHtHHHt ttHtHtHtHHH tHtHHHHHHH HHtHHtttHt
HHHHHtttHH tHttHHHHtt tHHttHHtHH ttHHHtHttH HttHHHttHt
HHtHtHHtHt ttttHtHHtH tHttttHttt HttHHHHtHtt tttHHHHttH
243 heads; 257 tails; H leads =   5; T leads = 492
```

The function generated almost equal numbers of heads and tails, as you would expect. Notice, however, that the value of the counter **t_lead** was larger on almost all the trials. Although the difference will generally be much smaller, it turns out that the two sides of the coin will rarely be in the lead roughly the same number of times in a sample. One or the other side will generally be in the lead more often — and by a wide margin.

This unexpected finding holds up even if you run dozens of coin-tossing samples. For example, the following program will generate 100 samples of 100 coin tosses. The program counts heads and tails and updates **h_lead** and **t_lead**.

After a sample has been generated, the program computes the proportion of times that the more frequent side occurred. For example, if the 100 tosses produced 57 tails, the proportion for the more frequent side would be 0.57; if the sample had 63 heads, the proportion would be 0.63.

The program also computes the proportion of trials on which the side with the higher **X_lead** value was ahead. Thus, if the variable **h_lead** were 57 and **t_lead** were 39, the lead proportion would be 0.59 (57 / (57 + 39)); if **t_lead** were 82 and **h_lead** were 10, the proportion would be 0.89 (82 / 92).

```
/* Program to generate multiple coin toss samples */

#include <stdio.h>
#include <stdlib.h>
#include <string.h>
#include <math.h>

#define MAX_ITER      1
#define MAX_STR       100
#define MAX_RAND      2000
#define MAX_INTERVAL  300

#include "rand.c"
#include "rdist.c"
#include "misc.c"

void    draw ( int vals [], int nr_interv);

double d_vals [ MAX_RAND];        /* for storing the proportion info */

main ()
{
        int     index, start, nr_trials, nr_iter;
        int     head = 0, tail = 0, h_lead = 0, t_lead = 0;
        int     iter;
        double ratio, lead_sum = 0.0, side_sum = 0.0;
```

```
    curr_seed = get_int ( "Starting seed? ");
    nr_trials = get_int ( "Sample size?" );
    nr_iter = get_int ( "Number of samples to generate? ");


    printf ( "Starting seed = %d\n\n", curr_seed);
    printf ( "Generating random values ... \n");
/* Generate nr_iter different samples */
    for ( iter = 0; iter < nr_iter; iter++)
    {
        /* reset counters for each sample */
        head = 0;
        tail = 0;
        h_lead = 0;
        t_lead = 0;
        /* Flip coin nr_trials times */
        for ( index = 0; index < nr_trials; index++)
        {
                start = coin_flip ();
                if ( start)
                {
                        head++;
                    /* printf ( "H"); */
                }
                else
                {
                        tail++;
                    /* printf  ("t"); */
                }
                if ( head > tail)
                        h_lead++;
                else if ( tail > head)
                        t_lead++;
                /*
                if ( ( index % 10) == 9)
                        printf ( " ");
                if ( ( index % 50) == 49)
                        printf ( "\n");
                */
        }

        /* Display information about sample */
        printf ( "%3d heads; %3d tails; ", head, tail);
        printf ( "H leads = %3d; T leads = %3d; ",
                h_lead, t_lead);
        if ( h_lead > t_lead)
                ratio = (double) h_lead / ( h_lead + t_lead);
        else
                ratio = (double) t_lead / ( h_lead + t_lead);
        d_vals [ iter] = ratio;
        lead_sum += ratio;
        side_sum += (head > tail) ?
                        ( (double) head / nr_trials) :
                        ( (double) tail / nr_trials);

        printf ( "ratio = %.4lf\n", ratio);
    }   /* for each sample */
    printf ( "\n Done\n");
    printf ( "side sum == %.4lf; mean side lead == %.4lf\n",
            side_sum, side_sum / nr_iter);
    printf ( "lead sum == %.4lf; mean lead == %.4lf\n",
            lead_sum, lead_sum / nr_iter);

}
```

The program contains calls to **printf( )** that are currently commented out. If you want to display the values for each of the samples, remove the comments from these statements.

When this program was run for 100 samples, each of size 100, the average proportion for the *more frequent* side was 0.54; the average proportion for the *lead* was 0.84! There were even times when one side came up more often than the other but the **X—lead** advantage was in favor of the less frequent side. For example, in one sample, heads came up 49 times to 51 tails, but **h—lead** was 83, to a 9 for **t—lead**. Similarly, the two sides each came up 50 times in one sample, but heads led on 91 trials, to only 3 for tails.

These results illustrate that your intuitive notions about how a process behaves can be surprised when you actually run a simulation of the process.

DISTRIBUTIONS FOR FAIR AND WEIGHTED COIN TOSSES

Suppose you had a coin. How would you know if the coin were unevenly weighted; that is, how could you tell whether the coin was more likely to land with one face up than with the other? One way is to toss the coin many times. You would end up with some proportion of heads. To decide whether this proportion was typical, you would have to go through more rounds of coin tossing.

Since this chapter is about simulation, another possible answer should occur to you right away: Run some simulations. In a simulation, you would generate multiple samples of coin tosses. For example, suppose your first sample produced 9 heads in 15 tosses. You might generate 50 or 100 more samples of this size, noting the proportion of heads each time.

You could draw the distribution of the frequencies with which each proportion of heads occurred in the 100 or so samples. Such a distribution is called a *sampling distribution*. Each point represents a sample.

The following program lets you generate coin-tossing samples. You can generate as many samples as you wish and draw the distribution of the frequency with which each number of heads occurs. Function **fancy_coin_flip()** from file **rdist.c** is also included here, since this routine must replace the **coin_flip()** function for simulations with hit rates other than 0.5.

```c
/* Program to simulate coin tosses with a possible "biased" coin. */

#include <stdio.h>
#include <stdlib.h>
#include <string.h>
#include <math.h>

#include "defs.h"
#include "rand.c"
#include "rdist.c"
#include "analysis.c"
#include "misc.c"

/* to store frequency with which head appears X times,
   where X goes from 0 through sample size.
*/
int     group [ MAX_INTERVAL];

main ()
{
        int     index, start, samples, size, nr_samples;
        int     head = 0, tail = 0;

        double hit_rate;

        curr_seed = get_int ( "Starting seed? ");
        hit_rate = get_dbl ( "Hit rate? ");
        size = get_int ( "Sample size? ");
        nr_samples = get_int ( "Number of samples? ");

        printf ( "Starting seed = %d\n\n", curr_seed);
        printf ( "Generating random values ... \n");

        for ( samples = 0; samples < nr_samples; samples++)
        {
                head = 0;
                tail = 0;
                for ( index = 0; index < size; index++)
                {
                        start = fancy_coin_flip ( hit_rate);
                        if ( start)
                                head++;
                        else
                                tail++;
                        /*
                        printf ( "%d", start);
                        if ( ( index % 10) == 9)
                                printf ( " ");
```

```
                if ( ( index % 50) == 49)
                        printf ( "\n");
                */
        }
        /* printf ( "%3d heads; %3d tails\n ",
                head, tail); */
        /* increment frequency with which head occurred
           head times.
        */
        group [ head]++;
    }
    printf ( "\n Done\n");
/* Display frequency breakdown */
    for ( index = 0; index < size; index++)
    {
        printf ( "%7d", group [ index]);
        if ( ( index % PER_LINE) == PER_LINE - 1)
            printf ( "\n");
    }
/* draw a graph of frequency breakdown.
   Graph contains relative frequency with which each
   possible number of heads occurred.
*/
    pct_draw ( group, size, nr_samples, 0);
}
```

fancy—coin—flip( )

This function tosses a coin, coming up heads with the probability specified in **hit—rate**. To compute its outcome, the function divides the range of possible random integers into two intervals. The relative size of the first interval corresponds to the value of **hit—rate**.

The programs throughout this and the next chapter rely heavily on several routines. These functions are in the include files listed at the beginning of the preceding program. A complete listing of these files is provided at the end of this chapter.

The following listing shows the output when this program was run with a starting **seed** of 229 and a **hit—rate** of 0.5, running 500 samples of 15 tosses each:

```
Starting seed? 229
Hit rate? .5
Sample size? 15
Number of samples? 500

Done
       0       0       4      10      24      35      66     110     116      69
      40      10      13       3       0
```

```
 0|
 1|
 2|*
 3|**
 4|****
 5|*******
 6|********** ****
 7|********** ********** **
 8|********** ********** ****
 9|********** ****
10|*******
11|**
12|***
13|*
14|
15|
```

The graph shows the proportion of times that each number of heads occurred in the 500 samples. Each asterisk represents 1% of the total occurrences. Thus, 12 heads occurred about 3% of the time; 7 and 8 each occurred roughly 22% of the time. The frequency with which each number of heads occurred reaches a peak at seven and eight and tapers off evenly and fairly quickly on either side.

You would expect the middle values, 7 and 8, to be the most common frequencies, since you expect heads to come up about 7.5 times in 15 tosses. The symmetry around the middle is also something you would expect from an evenly weighted coin.

This graph shows the distribution of the relative frequencies with which one of two possible outcomes occurred over many samples of a particular size. Such a distribution of frequencies when there are two possible outcomes is called a *binomial distribution*.

Run the program again, and this time ask it to generate a sampling distribution for a coin that is weighted so that heads comes up 60% of the time—that is, **hit_rate** is 0.60. The following listing shows the results for a **seed** of 731.

```
Starting seed? 731
Hit rate? .6
Sample size? 15
Number of samples? 500

Done
     0      0      0      4      5     12     26     50     97    121
    89     44     38     13      1
```

```
 0|
 1|
 2|
 3|*
 4|*
 5|***
 6|******
 7|*********
 8|********* *********
 9|********* ********* *****
10|********* ********
11|*********
12|********
13|***
14|*
15|
```

Notice that the peak of this distribution is shifted toward the high end, as you would expect if heads were more likely to occur. The binomial distributions for **hit_rate** = .5 and **hit_rate** = .6 could both handle a sample in which heads occurred nine times. How could you decide whether the coin is likely to be biased, based on your single sample? In the next chapter you'll look at some tests that will let you assign a numerical value to this likelihood.

Monte Carlo Methods

Let's look again at what's going on here. You draw random samples of a specific size; for each of these samples you determine the number of heads. After repeating this process many times, you'll have a collection of values, with each value representing the number of heads in a given random sample.

These values can be grouped so that you can determine the frequency and relative frequency with which each number of heads occurs. These frequencies can then be used to draw an approximation to a binomial distribution having a fixed probability of a head, or **hit**.

The process of generating multiple random samples to simulate the behavior of a phenomenon or problem is often known as *Monte Carlo simulation*. As you'll see, Monte Carlo simulation is a very flexible technique. You can use such random assignment methods to generate values fitting various distributions, as you'll be doing throughout this chapter and the next.

WAITING IN LINE

In the past, bank customers formed a separate line before each teller's window. Several years ago, most banks switched to a single line; the person at the front of the line waits for the next available teller. Feeding multiple tellers from a single line moves people through the bank more quickly.

To provide sample results to confirm or refute this claim, you need to simulate the processes of adding new people at the end of the line and of finishing with (that is, completing the transaction of) the person at the teller's window; in other words, you need to maintain a queue. New people are added to the queue at random intervals based on some decision rule; at the same time, the tellers finish with customers according to some decision rule. When done, the teller immediately gets the next person from the line, unless the line is empty.

You can formulate this problem as one for which a binomial distribution might apply if you think in terms of the number of people likely to be added to the line in a given amount of time. Although the content could be represented by a binomial distribution, the values involved make this distribution a bad choice.

If you break the situation down to small-enough time chunks, you end up with a very low hit rate for the binomial distribution. A hit here is a person added to the line. At the extremes of the distribution, the samplings can fluctuate drastically, which means computations can sometimes give misleading results.

It turns out that another distribution is well suited for this low-probability situation. The *Poisson distribution* provides information about the likelihood that a specified number of people will be added to the line in a given time interval.

The Poisson distribution represents integers corresponding to the number of people added during that interval. Thus, 0, 1, 2, . . . people will be added in a given interval, with each value occurring with a frequency proportional to the value's probability of occurrence, according to the distribution.

A Poisson distribution is defined in terms of μ, the average number of additions in a given unit of time. For example, suppose μ is 2.5 and the time interval is 5 minutes. A Poisson distribution would represent the number of people added to the line in 5-minute intervals over a large sample of such intervals.

It turns out to be surprisingly easy to generate a value for a Poisson distribution. For reasons we can't go into here, the following steps will provide a very good means of transforming a uniformly distributed random value between 0.0 and 1.0 into a value for the Poisson distribution:

1. Use the Run-Time library function **exp( )** to compute the value of $e - \mu$. Let's call this value the *target*.

2. Initialize a running product to 1.0.

3. Generate a random value between 0.0 and 1.0, and multiply the running product by this value. Increment a counter that keeps track of how many random values have been generated.

4. Compare the running product with the target. If the running product is less than or equal to the target, return (**count** −1); otherwise return to step 3.

The following function generates values for such a distribution:

```
/* Function to generate random values for a Poisson distribution */

/* Return a value based on a Poisson distribution,
   with a mean specified by the parameter. Algorithm computes

            -mean
          e

   then generates random values between 0.0 and 1.0,
   multiplying them until the product is less than e^(-mean).
   Result is # values generated, not including the value
   that ended the computation.
*/
int poisson ( double mean)
{
        double  val,        /* value of e^(-mean) */
                prod = 1.0;  /* running product */
        int     count = 0;   /* # of values generated */

        val = 1 / exp ( mean);

        do    /* multiply prod by random values */
        {
                count++;
                prod *= house_zero_one ();
        }
        while ( prod > val);    /* repeat until prod is smaller */
        return ( count - 1);
}
```

The following program lets you specify the average rate at which the line grows and the average rate at which it shrinks. Once these rates are specified, the program generates values for adding to the line and for removing from the line.

```c
/* Program to simulate a bank line growing and shrinking as people
   are added to the line, and as the teller finishes with customers.
*/

#include <stdio.h>
#include <stdlib.h>
#include <string.h>
#include <math.h>

#include "defs.h"
#include "rand.c"
#include "rdist.c"
#include "analysis.c"
#include "misc.c"

int     r_vals [ MAX_RAND];      /* contains random values generated */
double  d_vals [ MAX_RAND];
int     group [ MAX_INTERVAL];

main ()
{
        int     index, start;
        int     samples, size = 15, nr_samples = 500;
        int     line_lng = 0, max_lng = 0, remove;

        double poiss_add = 2.0, poiss_rem = 1.9;

        curr_seed = get_int ( "Starting seed? ");
        nr_samples = get_int ( "How many samples? ");
        poiss_add = get_dbl ( "Mean for addition to line? ");
        poiss_rem = get_dbl ( "Mean for removal from line? ");

        printf ( "Starting seed = %d\n\n", curr_seed);
        printf ( "Generating random values ... \n");

        for ( samples = 0; samples < nr_samples; samples++)
        {
            /* find out how many to add to line */
            start = poisson ( poiss_add);
            line_lng += start;
            group [ start]++;  /* count freq of start additions */

            /* find out how many to remove from line */
            remove =  poisson ( poiss_rem);
            if ( line_lng >= remove)
                    line_lng -= remove;
            else
                    line_lng = 0;
            if ( line_lng > max_lng)
                    max_lng = line_lng;
            r_vals [ line_lng]++;
        }
        printf ( "\n Done\n");
        for ( index = 0; index < size; index++)
        {
```

```
        printf ( "%7d", group [ index]);
        if ( ( index % PER_LINE) == PER_LINE - 1)
                printf ( "\n");
}
pct_draw ( group, size, nr_samples, 0);

printf ( "\n\nLine length == %d\n", line_lng);
for ( index = 0; index <= max_lng; index++)
{
        printf ( "%7d", r_vals [ index]);
        if ( ( index % PER_LINE) == PER_LINE - 1)
                printf ( "\n");
}
pct_draw ( r_vals, max_lng, samples, 0);
}
```

Values are generated by using the μ for the appropriate generator (add or remove) as the parameter to **poisson( )**. For each of the 500 trials, the program adds to the line with one value and removes from the line with one value. The **line—lng** variable holds information about the number of people currently waiting.

If the average rate at which people are added to the line is greater than the rate at which they are removed, the removal program is working inefficiently; the line will grow. On the other hand, if the mean rate of removal is higher than the rate at which people are added, there is hope that the line will sometimes get to 0 during the simulation.

Waiting Times for a Single Line Versus Separate Lines

Earlier you read that a single line with multiple tellers is, in general, more efficient than separate lines for separate tellers. In this section, you'll find a program that lets you test this assertion by enabling you to run Monte Carlo simulations for each situation and to compare the average line lengths.

The program currently assumes five tellers and five lines, or five tellers and one line. The tellers move an average of two or fewer people per unit interval. This means they tend to lose ground to the lines, which all add at 2.0 people per unit interval, on the average. Try changing some of these variables to see what happens to the line.

The major difference between the two versions is that the multiple lines alternate between adding and removing, once for each line-teller pair. In this situation, some tellers may be idle much of the time, while other tellers may be overworked, with long lines of waiting customers. In the single line, you need to add customers for each of the tellers as often as you remove them, adding the number of customers needed to keep all of the tellers busy for the designated period of time. Consequently, you'll rarely have a teller idle while other tellers have many customers to handle; rather, each teller always has access to customers.

The following program lets you run simulations of these two setups. The main difference between the versions is in the main program loop. For multiple lines, the loop repeats once for each line. Each time through the loop, the add-customers simulation is run, and then the remove-customers simulation is run. In the single-line case, the add loop is run once for each teller (that is, five times in its current form) and then the remove-customers simulation is run once for each teller.

```
/* Program to compare single and multiple lines when waiting for
   a teller in a bank.
*/

#include <stdio.h>
#include <stdlib.h>
#include <string.h>
#include <math.h>

#include "defs.h"
#include "rand.c"
#include "rdist.c"
#include "analysis.c"
#include "misc.c"

#define MAX_HELP     5

int    r_vals [ MAX_RAND];       /* contains random values generated */
double d_vals [ MAX_RAND];
int    group [ MAX_INTERVAL];
double help [ MAX_HELP] = { 1.8, 1.9, 2.0, 1.9, 1.8};
int    h_lng [ MAX_HELP];

main ()
{
        int    index, start, mult, incr, samples, size = 15,
        int    nr_samples = 200, line_lng = 0, max_lng = 0, remove;
        long int line_sum = 0;

        double poiss_add = 2.0, poiss_rem = 1.9;

        curr_seed = get_int ( "Starting seed? ");
        nr_samples = get_int ( "# of samples?") ;
```

```
poiss_rem = get_dbl ( "Mean # people removed?");
poiss_add = get_dbl ( "Mean # people added?");

printf ( "Starting seed = %d\n\n", curr_seed);
printf ( "Generating random values ... \n");

for ( samples = 0; samples < nr_samples; samples++)
{
        line_lng = 0;
        for ( index = 0; index < MAX_HELP; index++)
        {
                /* possibly add people to line */
                start = poisson ( poiss_add);
                h_lng [ index] += start;
                group [ start]++;
                line_lng += start;
        /* Currently set for multiple lines.
           For single lines, remove the pair of comments
           after the comment ending this warning.
        */
        }
        for ( index = 0; index < MAX_HELP; index++)
        {
                remove = poisson ( help [ index]);
                if ( h_lng [ index] >= remove)
                        h_lng [ index] -= remove;
                else
                        h_lng [ index] = 0;
                if ( line_lng >= remove)
                        line_lng -= remove;
                else
                        line_lng = 0;
        }

        r_vals [ line_lng]++;
        line_sum += line_lng;

        if ( line_lng > max_lng)
                max_lng = line_lng;
}

printf ( "\n Done\n");
for ( index = 0; index < size; index++)
{
        printf ( "%7d", group [ index]);
        if ( ( index % PER_LINE) == PER_LINE - 1)
                printf ( "\n");
}
pct_draw ( group, size, samples * MAX_HELP, 0);

printf ( "\n\nLine length == %d\n", line_lng);
printf ( "Mean line length == %.4lf\n",
        (double) line_sum / nr_samples);
for ( index = 0; index < max_lng; index++)
{
        printf ( "%7d", r_vals [ index]);
        if ( ( index % PER_LINE) == PER_LINE - 1)
                printf ( "\n");
}
pct_draw ( r_vals, max_lng, samples * MAX_HELP, 0);
}
```

The program works by calling **poisson( )** with the specified mean. This function returns an **int**, representing the number of people to be added to or removed from the line on the current turn.

This program was used to generate single- and multiple-line simulations for each of five different seeds. The program keeps track of the line length (number of customers waiting) after each trial and then computes the average line length at the end. In every case, the average line length was shorter for the single-line version than for multiple lines. Table 9-1 shows the results.

Suggestions and Projects

The simulations using the Poisson distribution provide information about the frequency with which different line lengths occur during the simulation and the frequency with which different numbers of people are added to the line in an interval. Modify the programs so they will also provide you with information about the length of the line after each interval. This enables you to see how the line grows and shrinks over time.

The programs given in the preceding pages are simple and inflexible. If you're running a simulation with a single line and a single teller and the line suddenly gets a lot of new customers, the teller may never catch up. Modify the program so that an addi-

Table 9-1.   Average Line Lengths for Bank Simulation

Seed	Multiple Lines	Single Line
27	3.23	2.12
424	3.18	2.02
815	3.02	1.96
1111	2.44	2.02
1951	2.73	2.16

tional teller will be put into service if the line becomes too long and will be dropped out of service once the line shortens again. Note that in this case, your add-customer simulation will run once for each teller, and the remove-customer simulation will also run once for each teller you have in service.

MAKING RULERS AND OTHER ACTIVITIES

Earlier, you took repeated samples of coin tosses and recorded the number of heads. The results of many samples were collected. These results approximated a binomial distribution. In the preceding section, you looked at some simulations based on the Poisson distribution.

In this section, you'll find some examples whose results approximate yet another distribution: the familiar bell-shaped distribution, known as the *normal*, or Gaussian, *distribution*. The latter name is in honor of Carl Friedrich Gauss, who discovered many of the distribution's properties.

Cutting Rulers

Suppose you are manufacturing one-foot rulers and that you are automating the process. One step in the process is slicing single pieces of wood from a longer piece of wood. For example, you might have a big piece of wood about 5.5 feet long. You could cut this piece into five smaller pieces, each just about the size of a ruler.

You might have a machine to cut these pieces. Suppose you have the machine calibrated to move 13 inches after cutting a piece. The machine's movement will have some error in it, so the machine will move sometimes less and sometimes more than 13 inches. For example, the machine may move 12.93 inches one time and 13.05 inches the next time.

In such a situation, the actual distances moved approximate a normal distribution: Distances slightly less or slightly more than 13 inches will be most probable, and distances much less or much more than 13 inches will be rare. The dropoff comes at a predictable distance from 13 inches and is of a predictable magnitude.

When discussing the distribution of values such as the distances moved, two summary numbers are important. The first one is the average distance moved. In this case, the average distance should be the calibrated value, 13 inches. To compute one form of the average, you add the distances moved on all the trials and divide by the total number of trials. This version of the average is known as the *mean*.

The other number provides a measure of how precisely or loosely the machine is calibrated. For example, a high-precision machine will tend to deviate less from the average distance than one with lots of play in its motion. Thus, this number will provide some idea of how spread out the observed distance values are likely to be: The more spread out, the less precise the calibration. One such measure of spread is known as the *standard deviation* for the distribution.

The following listing shows the distributions from two samples of movements by a ruler cutter. The first sample comes from a machine whose movement has a standard deviation of 0.1 inch; the second sample is from a machine with a standard deviation of 0.2 inch. Each distribution is based on 2000 trials, and each sample has a mean movement of about 13.0 inches.

```
Machine 1:
Starting seed = 815
Distribution mean = 13.0000; sd =  0.1000

Sample mean ==  13.001; SD ==    0.100
Interval size = 0.0700
Start = 12.3010; Finish = 13.7010; Range = 1.4000

     0      0      0      0      1      8     23    124    312    531
   523    317    126     27      7      1      0      0      0      0
     0

Sample mean is in interval 10
Range =    0.716; smallest =   12.643; largest =   13.359
```

```
 0|
 1|
 2|
 3|
 4|*
 5|*
 6|**
 7|*******
 8|********** ******
 9|********** ********** *******
10|********** ********** *******
11|********** ******
12|*******
13|**
14|*
15|*
16|
17|
18|
19|
20|
```

Machine 2:
Starting seed = 424
Distribution mean = 13.0000; sd = 0.2000

Sample mean == 13.001; SD ==   0.199
Interval size = 0.0700
Start = 12.3015; Finish = 13.7015; Range = 1.4000

```
         0        6        8       22       44       73      142      175      257      274
       264      262      185      123       91       37       22        8        6        1
         0
```

Sample mean is in interval 10

Range =   1.270; smallest = 12.396; largest = 13.667

```
 0|
 1|*
 2|*
 3|**
 4|***
 5|****
 6|********
 7|********
 8|********** ***
 9|********** ****
10|********** ****
11|********** ****
12|**********
13|*******
14|*****
15|**
16|**
17|*
18|*
19|*
20|
```

Notice that both distributions have the same general shape, but the distribution for the machine with a standard deviation of 0.2 inch is considerably more spread out than the distribution for the more precisely calibrated machine. The difference in spread indicates that you are more likely to get a 12.75-inch piece for a ruler with the more loosely calibrated machine than with the machine calibrated to a standard deviation of 0.1 inch. In the next chapter, you'll find some routines that will help you quantify such probabilities.

Generating Random Values with a Normal Distribution

Before you look at some more examples that use the normal distribution, you need to develop a function to generate random values having such a distribution. The following sequence of steps summarizes the *polar method*, a common technique for generating normally distributed random values. In fact, this method actually generates two independent random values. Both values are from normal distributions, which have a mean of 0.0 and a standard deviation of 1.0.

1. Generate two random values between 0.0 and 1.0, inclusive. These values come from a uniform distribution.

2. Multiply each value by 2 and subtract 1. Whereas the original values were from the interval 0.0 to 1.0, the transformed values will lie between -1.0 and 1.0. Let's call these transformed values V_1 and V_2, respectively.

3. Compute $V_1^2 + V_2^2$. Assign this value to an intermediate variable, **circ**.

4. If **circ** is greater than or equal to 1.0, repeat steps 1 through 3. Otherwise, proceed to step 5.

5. Compute the two random values, X_1 and X_2, using the following formulas:

$$X_1 = V_1 \sqrt{\frac{-2\ ln(\text{circ})}{\text{circ}}}, \quad X_2 = V_2 \sqrt{\frac{-2\ ln(\text{circ})}{\text{circ}}}$$

In the formulas ln represents the *natural logarithm*, or the logarithm to the base e ($e \approx 2.71828 \ldots$). To compute this value, use the Run-Time library function **log( )**.

Either of the values computed (X_1 or X_2) can serve as the random value you need. Although you are computing two different random values, this method is still faster and easier than other algorithms for generating normally distributed values.

The following function generates normally distributed values using the polar algorithm:

```
/* Return a value based on a normal distribution ---
   having a mean of 0.0 and a standard deviation of 1.0.
*/
double gauss_fn ()
{
        double  gs1, gs2,  /* two "seed" values between 0.0 and 1.0 */
                circ,      /* used in intermediate computation */
                rv1, rv2;  /* normally distributed random values */

        do
        {
                gs1 = house_zero_one ();
                gs1 = 2 * gs1 - 1.0;      /* ranges between -1 and 1 */
                gs2 = house_zero_one ();
                gs2 = 2 * gs2 - 1.0;      /* ranges between -1 and 1 */

                circ = gs1 * gs1 + gs2 * gs2;
        }
        while ( circ >= 1.0);

    /* compute two normally distributed random values */
        rv1 = gs1 * sqrt ( -2 * log ( circ) / circ);
        rv2 = gs2 * sqrt ( -2 * log ( circ) / circ);

        return ( rv1);    /* return one of the values */
}
```

gauss__fn( )

This function computes two random values from independent normal distributions, using the polar algorithm to generate the values. The function returns the first of the values computed.

This function will return a random value from a normal distribution with an average value of 0.0 and a standard deviation of 1.0. This version of the normal distribution is known as the *unit normal distribution*.

You can transform the random value returned into a random value from any other normal distribution with a different mean and standard deviation. The following transformation will accomplish this:

*new value = mean + standard deviation * old value*

Since μ is generally used to represent the mean, and σ is used to represent the standard deviation, you'll often see this formula as

$$X_{new} = \mu + \sigma * X_{old}$$

Thus, to get the distributions for the preceding machine examples, you would just need to multiply the random value by 0.1 or 0.2 (depending on the desired standard deviation) and add 13.0 (the mean for the new distribution) to the original value returned.

The following program was used to generate the two distributions shown earlier:

```
/* Program to generate random samples,
   based on a normal distribution.
*/

#include <stdio.h>
#include <stdlib.h>
#include <string.h>
#include <math.h>

#include "defs.h"
#include "rand.c"
#include "rdist.c"
```

```
#include "analysis.c"
#include "misc.c"

/* Function DECLARATIONS */
void   nrml_sample ( double d_vals [], int size,
                        double mean, double sd, double *sum);
double s_dev ( double vals [], double sum, int size);

double d_vals [ MAX_RAND], mean_vals [ MAX_RAND];
int    group [ MAX_INTERVAL];
double extremes [ 2];   /* extreme [ LOW] == low value;
                           extreme [ HIGH] == high value
                         */

main ()
{
        int     index, start, nr_trials;
        int     nr_intervals = 10;

        double sample_sum = 0.0;
        double mean, sd, obs_mean, obs_sd, difference;

        curr_seed = get_int ( "Starting seed? ");
        mean = get_dbl ( "Mean? ");
        sd = get_dbl ( "Standard deviation? ");
        nr_trials = get_int ( "# of trials? ");
        nr_intervals = get_int ( "Number of Intervals? ");
        difference = get_dbl ( "Amount of deviation to graph? ");

        printf ( "Starting seed = %d\n\n", curr_seed);
        printf ( "Distribution mean = %7.4lf; sd = %7.4lf\n\n",
                mean, sd);
        printf ( "Generating random values ... \n");

        nrml_sample ( d_vals, nr_trials, mean, sd, &sample_sum);
        obs_mean = sample_sum / nr_trials;
        obs_sd = s_dev ( d_vals, sample_sum, nr_trials);
        printf ( "\n\nSample mean == %7.3lf; SD == %7.3lf\n",
                obs_mean, obs_sd);

        dbl_dist ( group, d_vals, obs_mean - difference,
                        obs_mean + difference, nr_intervals, nr_trials);
        printf ( "\n\nSample mean is in interval %d\n",
                what_interval ( obs_mean, obs_mean - difference,
                                obs_mean + difference, nr_intervals));
        printf ("Range = %7.3lf; smallest = %7.3lf; largest = %7.3lf\n",
                extremes [ HIGH] - extremes [ LOW], extremes [ LOW],
                extremes [ HIGH]);

        pct_draw ( group, nr_intervals, nr_trials, 0);
}


/* generate a sample of random values from a normal distribution
   having the specified mean and standard deviation.
*/
void nrml_sample ( double smpl_vals [], int size,
                   double mean, double sd, double *sum)
{
        double temp_sum = 0.0, result;
        int    index;

    /* to keep track of lowest and highest values encountered. */
        extremes [ LOW] = 99999.99;
        extremes [ HIGH] = 0.0;
```

```
/* generate values, and store in the array */
   for ( index = 0; index < size; index++)
   {
           result = mean + gauss_fn () * sd;
           temp_sum += result;
           if ( result < extremes [ LOW])
                   extremes [ LOW] = result;
           if ( result > extremes [ HIGH])
                   extremes [ HIGH] = result;
           smpl_vals [ index] = result;
           /*
           printf ( "%12.3lf", smpl_vals [index]);
           if ( ( index % 5) == 4)
                   printf ( "\n");
           */
   }
   *sum = temp_sum;
}
```

Computing the Standard Deviation

The program computes both the standard deviation of the values and the mean. The standard deviation is essentially a measure of the average deviation of values around the mean. As with the chi-square test, the deviation is actually computed using the square of the difference. Thus, the deviation for the ith value is given by

$$(x_i - \overline{x})^2$$

where $\overline{x}$ is the average, or mean, for the sample. To find the average deviation, the deviations for individual values are first summed, using the following formula:

$$\sum_{i=1}^{sample\ size} (x_i - \overline{x})^2$$

This value is divided by a measure of the sample size. In the case of the standard deviation, this value is $(n - 1)$, where n is the sample size. Finally, to get rid of the square term, the formula involves taking the square root of the average deviation.

$$\sqrt{\sum_{i=1}^{sample\ size} \frac{(x_i - \bar{x})^2}{n - 1}}$$

The following function uses a formula that makes the computations easier but also makes it harder to see the derivation of the standard deviation. The function assumes you know the sum of the values in the array for which the standard deviation is to be computed.

```
/* Function to compute the standard deviation of an array of values,
   given the array, the sample size, and sum of values in the array.
*/

/* compute the standard deviation of the vals array,
   given the sample size and the sum of values.
*/
double s_dev ( double vals [], double sum, int size)
{
        double result, sum_sq = 0.0;
        int     index;

        for ( index = 0; index < size; index++)
                sum_sq += vals [ index] * vals [ index];
        result = (sum_sq - ( sum * sum / size)) / ( size - 1);
        return ( sqrt ( result));
}
```

Checking Production: Properties of the Normal Distribution

Suppose you have a factory that manufactures light bulbs. After years of making and testing them, you know the light bulbs will burn for an average of 50 hours, with a standard deviation of 5 hours. This lifetime information is likely to be normally distributed, with the given mean and standard deviation.

Suppose you picked a bulb at random, tested it, and found that it burned for only 40 hours. How likely is it that this bulb came from a batch with the average lifetime and standard deviation given above?

One way to answer such a question is to run a simulation: Pick repeated bulbs from a supply having the appropriate mean and standard deviation, and count the frequency with which a bulb with a lifetime of 40 or fewer hours is picked at random from such a distribution. The following program lets you run such a simulation:

```
/* Program to generate multiple samples of values drawn from a
   normal distribution, with specified mean and standard deviation.
*/

#include <stdio.h>
#include <stdlib.h>
#include <string.h>
#include <math.h>

#include "defs.h"
#include "rand.c"
#include "rdist.c"
#include "analysis.c"
#include "misc.c"

/* Function DECLARATIONS */
void    nrml_sample ( double d_vals [], int size,
                            double mean, double sd, double *sum);
double s_dev ( double vals [], double sum, int size);
int     what_interval ( double val, double start, double stop,
                            int interv);
double how_likely ( int group [], double val, double start,
                            double range, int intervals, int trials);


double d_vals [ MAX_RAND], mean_vals [ MAX_RAND];
int     group [ MAX_INTERVAL];
double extremes [ 2];   /* extreme [ LOW] == low value;
                            extreme [ HIGH] == high value
                    */

main ()
{
        int     index, start, nr_trials, nr_intervals;
        double sample_sum = 0.0;
        double ref_val, mean, sd, obs_mean, obs_sd, difference;

        curr_seed = get_int ( "Starting seed? ");
        mean = get_dbl ( "Mean? ");
        sd = get_dbl ( "Standard deviation? ");
        nr_trials = get_int ( "# of trials? ");

        nr_intervals = get_int ( "Number of Intervals? ");
        difference = get_dbl ( "Amount of deviation to graph? ");
        ref_val = get_dbl ( "Value under consideration? ");

        printf ( "Starting seed = %d\n\n", curr_seed);
        printf ( "Distribution mean = %7.4lf; sd = %7.4lf\n\n",
                mean, sd);
        printf ( "Generating random values ... \n");
```

```
        nrml_sample ( d_vals, nr_trials, mean, sd, &sample_sum);
        obs_mean = sample_sum / nr_trials;
        obs_sd = s_dev ( d_vals, sample_sum, nr_trials);
        printf ( "\n\nSample mean == %7.3lf; SD == %7.3lf\n",
                 obs_mean, obs_sd);

        dbl_dist ( group, d_vals, obs_mean - difference,
                     obs_mean + difference, nr_intervals, nr_trials);
        printf ( "\n\nSample mean is in interval %d\n",
                 what_interval ( obs_mean, obs_mean - difference,
                                 obs_mean + difference, nr_intervals));
        printf ("Range: %7.3lf; min val = %7.3lf; max val = %7.3lf\n",
                 extremes [ HIGH] - extremes [ LOW], extremes [ LOW],
                 extremes [ HIGH]);

        printf ( "Probability of %7.3lf or lower: %.4lf\n", ref_val,
                 how_likely (group, ref_val, obs_mean - difference,
                             2 * difference, nr_intervals, nr_trials));

        pct_draw ( group, nr_intervals, nr_trials, 0);
}


/* generate a sample of random values from a normal distribution
   having the specified mean and standard deviation.
*/
void nrml_sample ( double smpl_vals [], int size,
                   double mean, double sd, double *sum)
{
        double temp_sum = 0.0, result;
        int    index;

    /* to keep track of lowest and highest values encountered. */
        extremes [ LOW] = 99999.99;
        extremes [ HIGH] = 0.0;

    /* generate values, and store in the array */
        for ( index = 0; index < size; index++)
        {
                result = mean + gauss_fn () * sd;
                temp_sum += result;
                if ( result < extremes [ LOW])
                        extremes [ LOW] = result;
                if ( result > extremes [ HIGH])
                        extremes [ HIGH] = result;
                smpl_vals [ index] = result;
                /*
                printf ( "%12.3lf", smpl_vals [index]);
                if ( ( index % 5) == 4)
                        printf ( "\n");
                */
        }
        *sum = temp_sum;
}


/* compute the standard deviation of the vals array,
   given the sample size and the sum of values.
*/
double s_dev ( double vals [], double sum, int size)
{
        double result, sum_sq = 0.0;
        int    index;
```

```
for ( index = 0; index < size; index++)
        sum_sq += vals [ index] * vals [ index];
result = (sum_sq - ( sum * sum / size)) / ( size - 1);
return ( sqrt ( result));
}
```

If you run this program, you'll find that the simulations tend to return a value around 0.03. This is the probability that you would get a bulb with a lifetime no longer than 40 hours in a batch with an expected lifetime of 50 hours and a standard deviation of 5 hours. To compute the actual percentage for the distribution you generated, add the frequencies in each of the cells preceding and including the target value, and divide the sum by the total number of trials.

It turns out that the normal distribution has certain properties that make it possible to answer such questions by referring to a table of probabilities, instead of having to run such simulations each time you need an answer. These tables serve the same purpose as the simple table in Chapter 8, which listed the cutoff values for the chi-square statistic at different probability levels and for different numbers of intervals.

For a normal distribution, about 68% of the values lie within one standard deviation of the mean. Thus, if your bulbs actually did come from a normally distributed batch with a standard deviation of 5 hours, you would expect to find that just over two-thirds of the bulbs had lifetimes between 45 and 55 hours. Because the normal distribution is symmetric around its mean, about 34% of the bulbs would have lifetimes between 45 and 50 hours, and another 34% would have lifetimes between 50 and 55 hours.

Similarly, about 95% of the bulbs would lie within two standard deviations—in our case, between 40 and 60 hours. Thus, only 5% of the bulbs would last 40 or fewer hours or more than 60 hours. Since our original question concerned only short-lived bulbs, the theoretical answer to the original question would be that about 2.5% of the bulbs would last 40 hours or less—which is quite close to our results of about 3%. In the next chapter, you'll learn more about the probabilities associated with the normal and other distributions.

MAKING YOUR DATA GO FURTHER WITH JACKKNIFE AND BOOTSTRAP METHODS

Sometimes, you'll have the data from a sample but won't have access to the larger population of values from which that sample came. In most instances, you will simply assume you know something about the population from which the sample came—for example, that it is normally distributed or what the mean and standard deviation are. The quality of your conclusions and results will depend on how warranted these assumptions are.

There are alternatives to such an assumption-based approach. Two of these, the *jackknife* and the *bootstrap* methods, rely on computer-generated values based on the data from your original sample. The strategy behind both these methods is to generate more samples and then see where your original results fit within the distribution of the samples you generated. The methods differ in how many samples they generate and the starting pool from which sample values are selected.

The Jackknife

Suppose you have the following set of lifetimes for a sample of 25 light bulbs. You would like to know whether you can be confident that this sample is representative of your usual batch of bulbs or whether it's more likely that the results in your sample are just a fluke.

```
46.051    64.472    48.364    56.422    45.183
59.261    52.051    44.763    46.113    54.275
52.113    52.791    46.294    53.975    50.071
56.316    54.995    51.896    42.382    44.130
52.829    50.771    52.889    54.631    44.641
```

```
Sample mean == 51.107; SD == 5.331
```

The jackknife technique generates additional samples from your original sample. More specifically, if you have 25 bulbs in your sample, the jackknife generates 25 additional samples, each containing 24 bulbs. A different one of the 25 bulbs is omitted when creating each jackknife sample.

The observed mean from your original sample is compared to the distribution of means from the additional samples. If your original mean was a representative one, you would expect the jackknife means to have a fairly small range of variability, and you would expect your original mean to lie somewhere near the middle in the distribution of jackknife means.

The following listing shows the results of using the jackknife method with the sample data:

```
Generating random values ...
        46.051      64.472      48.364      56.422      45.183
        59.261      52.051      44.763      46.113      54.275
        52.113      52.791      46.294      53.975      50.071
        56.316      54.995      51.896      42.382      44.130
        52.829      50.771      52.889      54.631      44.641
Sample mean ==  51.107; SD ==    5.331
Generating Jackknife values ...
        51.318      50.550      51.221      50.886      51.354
        50.767      51.068      51.372      51.315      50.975
        51.065      51.037      51.308      50.988      51.150
        50.890      50.945      51.074      51.471      51.398
        51.035      51.121      51.033      50.960      51.377

Interval size = 0.1000
Start = 50.1072; Finish = 52.1072; Range = 2.0000

        0       0       0       0       1       0       1       2       4       6
        2       1       7       1       0       0       0       0       0       0
        0
LOW ==  50.550; HIGH ==  51.471; actual ==   51.107
Sample mean is in interval 10
Range =   0.920; smallest =   50.550; largest =   51.471

   0|
   1|
   2|
   3|
   4|****
   5|
   6|****
   7|********
   8|********* ******
   9|********* ********* ****
  10|********
  11|****
  12|********* ********* ********
  13|****
  14|
  15|
  16|
  17|
  18|
  19|
  20|
```

Notice that most of the observed jackknife means are very close to the originally observed mean; so it is likely that your sample is a representative one rather than one containing many extreme values.

The following program was used to generate the original sample and the jackknife information based on that sample. The sample was generated with a starting seed of 1111 from a normal distribution with mean of 50.0 and standard deviation of 5.0. The graphing used 20 intervals.

```
/* Program to generate samples and jackknife samples. */

#include <stdio.h>
#include <stdlib.h>
#include <string.h>
#include <math.h>

#include "defs.h"
#include "rand.c"
#include "rdist.c"
#include "analysis.c"
#include "chisq.c"
#include "misc.c"

#define MAX_SAMP_SIZE   200

/* Function DECLARATIONS */
void    jackknife ( double vals [], double means [],
                    int size, double sum);
void    nrml_sample ( double d_vals [], int size,
                    double mean, double sd, double *sum);
double s_dev ( double vals [], double sum, int size);


double d_vals [ MAX_RAND], mean_vals [ MAX_RAND];
double sample_vals [ MAX_SAMP_SIZE];
int    group [ MAX_INTERVAL];
double extremes [ 2];    /* extreme [ LOW] == low value;
                           extreme [ HIGH] == high value
                    */

main ()
{
        int    index, samples, smpl_size = 25, nr_intervals = 10;;
        double sample_sum = 0.0;
        double difference, mean, sd, obs_mean, obs_sd;

        curr_seed = get_int ( "Starting seed? ");
        mean = get_dbl ( "Mean? ");
        sd = get_dbl ( "Standard deviation? ");
        smpl_size = get_int ( "Sample size? ");

        nr_intervals = get_int ( "Number of Intervals? ");
        difference = get_dbl ( "Deviation from mean to graph?" );
        printf ( "Starting seed = %d\n\n", curr_seed);
        printf ( "Distribution mean = %7.4lf; sd = %7.4lf\n\n",
                mean, sd);
        printf ( "Generating random values ... \n");
```

```
        nrml_sample ( d_vals, smpl_size, mean, sd, &sample_sum);
                obs_mean = sample_sum / smpl_size;
        obs_sd = s_dev ( d_vals, sample_sum, smpl_size);
        printf ( "\n\nSample mean == %7.3lf; SD == %7.3lf\n",
                obs_mean, obs_sd);
        jackknife ( d_vals, mean_vals, smpl_size, sample_sum);

        dbl_dist ( group, mean_vals, obs_mean - difference,
                    obs_mean + difference, nr_intervals, smpl_size);
        printf ( "\nInterval range: %7.3lf to %7.3lf\n",
                extremes [ LOW], extremes [ HIGH]);
        printf ( "\n\nSample mean is in interval %d\n",
                what_interval ( obs_mean, obs_mean - difference,
                            obs_mean + difference, nr_intervals));
        printf ( "Actual Range = %7.3lf; smallest = %7.3lf; ",
                extremes [ HIGH] - extremes [ LOW], extremes [ LOW]);
        printf ( "largest = %7.3lf\n", extremes [ HIGH]);

        pct_draw ( group, nr_intervals, smpl_size, 0);
}


/* generate jackknife samples, given array of original values,
    sample size, and some of original values.
*/
void jackknife ( double vals [], double means [],
                int size, double sum)
{
        int     index;

        extremes [ LOW] = 99999.99;
        extremes [ HIGH] = 0.0;
        printf ( "\nGenerating Jackknife values ...\n");
        for ( index = 0; index < size; index++)
        {
                means [ index] = ( sum - vals [ index]) /
                            ( size - 1);
                if ( means [ index] < extremes [ LOW])
                    extremes [ LOW] = means [ index];
                if ( means [ index] > extremes [ HIGH])
                    extremes [ HIGH] = means [ index];
                /**/
                printf ( "%12.3lf", means [index]);
                if ( ( index % 5) == 4)
                    printf ( "\n");
                /**/
        }
}


/* generate a sample of random values from a normal distribution
    having the specified mean and standard deviation.
*/
void nrml_sample ( double smpl_vals [], int size,
                double mean, double sd, double *sum)
{
        double temp_sum = 0.0, result;
        int    index;

    /* to keep track of lowest and highest values encountered. */
        extremes [ LOW] = 99999.99;
        extremes [ HIGH] = 0.0;

    /* generate values, and store in the array */
        for ( index = 0; index < size; index++)
        {
```

```
          result = mean + gauss_fn () * sd;
          temp_sum += result;
          if ( result < extremes [ LOW])
                  extremes [ LOW] = result;
          if ( result > extremes [ HIGH])
                  extremes [ HIGH] = result;
          smpl_vals [ index] = result;
          /*
          printf ( "%12.3lf", smpl_vals [index]);
          if ( ( index % 5) == 4)
                  printf ( "\n");
          */
     }
     *sum = temp_sum;
}


/* compute the standard deviation of the vals array,
   given the sample size and the sum of values.
*/
double s_dev ( double vals [], double sum, int size)
{
     double result, sum_sq = 0.0;
     int    index;

     for ( index = 0; index < size; index++)
             sum_sq += vals [ index] * vals [ index];
     result = (sum_sq - ( sum * sum / size)) / ( size - 1);
     return ( sqrt ( result));
}
```

nrml—sample()

This function generates a random sample of the specified size. The values are generated according to a normal distribution, with specified **mean** and **sd**. The function also returns the **sum** of all the values generated. This value, when divided by the sample size, gives the average of the values actually generated.

jackknife()

This function generates jackknife samples based on the original array of values. The function computes the mean of each sample and stores this mean in the appropriate cell of **means[]**. The parameter **sum** is the sum of all the values generated in the original sample.

To compute the mean of a jackknife sample, the function simply subtracts the value being omitted from **sum** and computes the mean of the remaining values.

The jackknife is a quick-and-dirty means of gauging the confidence you can have in your data. The method is easy to compute and provides a convenient way to check on your data. Because it is based on a limited number of samples, however, the jackknife can sometimes give the wrong impression about your information.

The Bootstrap

The bootstrap method is quite new. It was invented in 1977 by Bradley Efron and arose largely because of the availability of computers for doing fast computations. The bootstrap is similar to the jackknife in that it uses your existing sample to get more information about your data. The bootstrap is somewhat more powerful, partly because it works much more to get additional samples.

The basic strategy behind the bootstrap can be summarized in the following four steps, with steps two and three being the heart of the bootstrap:

1. Generate your original sample.
2. Duplicate your original sample many times—ideally, thousands or even millions of times—and mix the resulting "combined sample" well.
3. From this generated population, take multiple random samples of the same size as your original sample.
4. Plot the results of the sampling.

Essentially, you are sampling repeatedly from the sample data. Instead of physically copying the sample over and over, you can associate each element in the original sample with an interval or a value and then generate random numbers to decide which element is selected.

For example, a quick method—adequate for our purposes— would be to divide up the interval between 0.0 and 1.0 into as many intervals as there are values in the original sample. Each of these intervals would then correspond to one element in the original sample. The bootstrap samples would be created by generating random values between 0.0 and 1.0 and determining the interval within which this value falls. The sample value corresponding to that index is assigned as the value in the bootstrap sample.

Thus, if you have your original samples in the array **d—vals[]**, you will assign values from this array to the array in which the bootstrap sample is being stored. If the random value falls in interval 12, then **d—vals[11]** is assigned to the next available cell in the bootstrap sample array.

For each of these bootstrap samples, you need to compute a mean (and, perhaps, a standard deviation). The variability of these means will provide information about how representative your sample is.

The following program lets you compute and display the results of a bootstrap process applied to the same sample we used earlier to illustrate the jackknife. The program generates 200 bootstrap samples, each consisting of 25 bulbs.

```
Program to generate sample and bootstrap samples. */

#include <stdio.h>
#include <stdlib.h>
#include <string.h>
#include <math.h>

#include "defs.h"
#include "rand.c"
#include "rdist.c"
#include "analysis.c"
#include "chisq.c"
#include "misc.c"

#define MAX_NR_SAMPLES   500

/* Function DECLARATIONS */
void    bootstrap ( double vals [], double smp_vals [],
                        int size, int nr_samples);
void    nrml_sample ( double d_vals [], int size,
                        double mean, double sd, double *sum);
double s_dev ( double vals [], double sum, int size);

double d_vals [ MAX_RAND];
double sample_vals [ MAX_NR_SAMPLES];
int     group [ MAX_INTERVAL];
double extremes [ 2];   /* extreme [ LOW] == low value;
                            extreme [ HIGH] == high value
                    */
```

```
main ()
{
        int     index, samples, nr_samples = 25, smpl_size = 25;
        int     nr_intervals = 10;
        double  sample_sum = 0.0;
        double  difference, mean, sd, obs_mean, obs_sd;

        curr_seed = get_int ( "Starting seed? ");
        mean = get_dbl ( "Mean? ");
        sd = get_dbl ( "Standard deviation? ");
        smpl_size = get_int ( "Sample size? ");
        nr_samples = get_int ( "Generate how many samples? ");
        if ( nr_samples > MAX_NR_SAMPLES)
        {
                printf ( "Maximum is %d samples.\n", MAX_NR_SAMPLES);
                nr_samples = MAX_NR_SAMPLES;
        }

        nr_intervals = get_int ( "Number of Intervals? ");
        difference = get_dbl ( "Deviation from mean to graph?" );
        printf ( "Starting seed = %d\n\n", curr_seed);
        printf ( "Distribution mean = %7.4lf; sd = %7.4lf\n\n",
                mean, sd);
        printf ( "Generating random values ... \n");

        nrml_sample ( d_vals, smpl_size, mean, sd, &sample_sum);
                obs_mean = sample_sum / smpl_size;
        obs_sd = s_dev ( d_vals, sample_sum, smpl_size);
        printf ( "\n\nSample mean == %7.3lf; SD == %7.3lf\n",
                obs_mean, obs_sd);
        dbl_dist ( group, d_vals, obs_mean - difference,
                obs_mean + difference, nr_intervals, smpl_size);
        bootstrap ( d_vals, sample_vals, smpl_size, nr_samples);

        for ( index = 0; index < MAX_INTERVAL; index++)
                group [ index] = 0;
        dbl_dist ( group, sample_vals, obs_mean - difference,
                obs_mean + difference, nr_intervals, nr_samples);
        printf ( "\nInterval range: %7.3lf to %7.3lf\n",
                extremes [ LOW], extremes [ LOW]);
        printf ( "\n\nSAMPLE mean is in interval %d\n",
                what_interval ( obs_mean, obs_mean - difference,
                        obs_mean + difference, nr_intervals));
        printf ( "Actual Range = %7.3lf; smallest = %7.3lf; ",
                extremes [ HIGH] - extremes [ LOW], extremes [ LOW]);
        printf ( "largest = %7.3lf\n", extremes [ HIGH]);

        pct_draw ( group, nr_intervals, nr_samples, 0);
}


/* generate a sample of random values from a normal distribution
   having the specified mean and standard deviation.
*/
void nrml_sample ( double smpl_vals [], int size,
                   double mean, double sd, double *sum)
{
        double temp_sum = 0.0, result;
        int    index;

    /* to keep track of lowest and highest values encountered. */
        extremes [ LOW] = 99999.99;
        extremes [ HIGH] = 0.0;
```

```
/* generate values, and store in the array */
   for ( index = 0; index < size; index++)
   {
           result = mean + gauss_fn () * sd;
           temp_sum += result;
           if ( result < extremes [ LOW])
                   extremes [ LOW] = result;
           if ( result > extremes [ HIGH])
                   extremes [ HIGH] = result;
           smpl_vals [ index] = result;
           /* */
           printf ( "%12.3lf", smpl_vals [index]);
           if ( ( index % 5) == 4)
                   printf ( "\n");
           /* */
   }
   *sum = temp_sum;
}


/* compute the standard deviation of the vals array,
   given the sample size and the sum of values.
*/
double s_dev ( double vals [], double sum, int size)
{
       double result, sum_sq = 0.0;
       int    index;

       for ( index = 0; index < size; index++)
               sum_sq += vals [ index] * vals [ index];
       result = (sum_sq - ( sum * sum / size)) / ( size - 1);
       return ( sqrt ( result));
}


/* Generate bootstrap samples, given array containing original sample,
sample size, and number of samples to generate.
Return means of bootstrap samples in smp_vals array.
*/
void bootstrap ( double vals [], double smp_vals [],
                 int size, int nr_samples)
{
       double width, value, sum = 0.0;
       int    index, sample, level;

    /* used in computing which value from original sample to use */
       width = 1.0 / size;

       printf ( "\nInterval Width == %.4lf\n", width);
       printf ("Generating bootstrap samples (means) ...\n");

       extremes [ LOW] = 99999.99;
       extremes [ HIGH] = 0.0;

       for ( sample = 0; sample < nr_samples; sample++)
       {
               sum = 0.0;
               for ( index = 0; index < size; index++)
               {
                       value = house_zero_one ();
                       level = floor ( value / width);
                       sum += vals [ level];
```

```
        }
        smp_vals [ sample] = sum / size;
        if ( smp_vals [ sample] < extremes [ LOW])
                extremes [ LOW] = smp_vals [ sample];
        if ( smp_vals [ sample] > extremes [ HIGH])
                extremes [ HIGH] = smp_vals [ sample];
        /**/
        printf ( "%12.3lf", smp_vals [sample]);
        if ( ( sample % 5) == 4)
                printf ( "\n");
        /**/
    }
}
```

The following listing shows part of the output from such a bootstrap process:

```
Distribution mean = 50.0000; sd =  5.0000

Generating random values ...
        46.051       64.472       48.364       56.422       45.183
        59.261       52.051       44.763       46.113       54.275
        52.113       52.791       46.294       53.975       50.071
        56.316       54.995       51.896       42.382       44.130
        52.829       50.771       52.889       54.631       44.641

Sample mean ==  51.107; SD ==    5.331

Interval Width == 0.0400
Generating bootstrap samples ... (means)
        49.606       48.883       50.245       50.152       50.605
        50.860       52.459       52.817       50.612       50.606
        50.875       51.765       50.981       51.967       52.339
        51.207       51.161       52.401       50.221       51.048
        52.166       50.517       51.212       50.125       51.293
        51.222       50.043       51.864       50.982       52.862
        52.161       52.523       49.157       50.622       49.946
        51.091       51.959       50.901       51.069       51.356
        50.675       50.113       51.139       50.340       52.251
        50.494       49.940       50.247       53.843       52.489
        50.277       52.263       52.655       50.861       51.981
        49.735       50.753       49.794       50.991       50.184
        52.961       50.306       52.614       52.355       50.456
        49.635       50.880       51.794       50.488       50.764
        50.808       50.722       49.554       51.905       51.227
        51.709       51.959       51.610       49.821       52.339
        50.563       51.880       50.941       50.460       52.611
        51.976       50.678       50.651       52.695       49.426
        49.336       50.706       51.620       49.779       52.364
        51.563       52.076       53.633       51.682       48.995
        50.097       51.315       49.940       52.330       51.735
        52.808       52.045       51.200       51.935       52.208
        51.512       49.082       51.776       50.029       50.649
        51.044       51.174       49.754       52.270       51.051
        50.147       49.456       51.148       50.128       50.540
        51.506       52.258       51.414       50.020       50.123
        49.629       49.692       52.258       50.002       52.776
        50.125       50.651       49.425       50.493       50.864
```

```
49.878    52.382    52.685    51.501    51.188
49.216    49.525    50.397    51.993    50.595
50.329    51.511    49.751    48.865    51.041
49.358    49.930    51.397    50.871    51.488
49.787    52.735    50.877    52.120    52.795
51.117    50.812    51.761    51.985    51.545
50.541    52.232    51.193    50.772    51.446
52.226    50.360    49.343    52.522    50.636
50.962    49.783    51.162    47.250    51.643
50.267    51.908    51.181    51.627    51.963
50.827    51.277    52.197    50.756    51.462
50.689    49.091    51.914    51.553    50.885
```

Interval size = 0.4000
Start = 47.1072; Finish = 55.1072; Range = 8.0000

```
     1      0      0      0      5      8     15     23     26     28
    25     19     25     16      7      0      2      0      0      0
     0
```
Interval range: 47.250 to 53.843

SAMPLE mean is in interval 10
Actual Range =   6.593; smallest = 47.250; largest = 53.843

```
 0|*
 1|
 2|
 3|
 4|***
 5|****
 6|********
 7|********** **
 8|********** ***
 9|********** *****
10|********** ***
11|**********
12|********** ***
13|********
14|****
15|
16|*
17|
18|
19|
20|
```

The distribution of the bootstrap means is not necessarily a normal, bell-shaped curve. One real advantage of the bootstrap method is that it can provide empirical information, even if the data have an odd distribution. With such distributions, you can still get some assessment of your sample by checking the middle of the distribution.

Recall that in the normal distribution, over two-thirds of the values lie within one standard deviation to either side of the mean, and about 95% lie within two standard deviations. Even though the distributions generated from the bootstrap samples may not be symmetrical, you can still find the 68% of the values lying closest to the center of the distribution. This means that if you generate random samples, the resulting mean will lie within the range determined from the distribution just under 70% of the time.

Thus, if your original sample mean falls within this range, you can be reasonably confident that the data are representative. On the other hand, if your sample mean falls near the extremes in the bootstrap distribution, you may want to be wary of your data.

Both the bootstrap and the jackknife can be used to study values other than the mean. For example, the following version of the bootstrap function computes bootstrap samples of the standard deviation rather than the mean. The main program has also been changed to compute a standard deviation for the original sample.

```
/* Program to compute bootstrap samples for standard deviation. */

#include <stdio.h>
#include <stdlib.h>
#include <string.h>
#include <math.h>

#include "defs.h"
#include "rand.c"
#include "rdist.c"
#include "analysis.c"
#include "chisq.c"
#include "misc.c"

#define MAX_NR_SAMPLES    500

/* Function DECLARATIONS */
void    bootstrap_sd ( double vals [], double smp_vals [],
                              int size, int nr_samples);
void    nrml_sample ( double d_vals [], int size,
                          double mean, double sd, double *sum);
double  s_dev ( double vals [], double sum, int size);

double  d_vals [ MAX_RAND];
double  sample_vals [ MAX_NR_SAMPLES];
int     group [ MAX_INTERVAL];
double  extremes [ 2];   /* extreme [ LOW] == low value;
                            extreme [ HIGH] == high value
                    */

main ()
{
        int     index, samples, nr_samples = 25, smpl_size = 25;
        int     nr_intervals = 10;
        double  sample_sum = 0.0;
        double  difference, mean, sd, obs_mean, obs_sd;
        char    info [ MAX_STR];

        curr_seed = get_int ( "Starting seed? ");
        mean = get_dbl ( "Mean? ");
        sd = get_dbl ( "Standard deviation? ");
```

```
        smpl_size = get_int ( "Sample size? ");
        nr_samples = get_int ( "Generate how many samples? ");
        if ( nr_samples > MAX_NR_SAMPLES)
        {
                printf ( "Maximum is %d samples.\n", MAX_NR_SAMPLES);
                nr_samples = MAX_NR_SAMPLES;
        }

        nr_intervals = get_int ( "Number of Intervals? ");
        difference = get_dbl ( "Deviation from mean to graph?" );
        printf ( "Starting seed = %d\n\n", curr_seed);
        printf ( "Distribution mean = %7.4lf; sd = %7.4lf\n\n",
                mean, sd);
        printf ( "Generating random values ... \n");

        nrml_sample ( d_vals, smpl_size, mean, sd, &sample_sum);
                obs_mean = sample_sum / smpl_size;
        obs_sd = s_dev ( d_vals, sample_sum, smpl_size);
        printf ( "\n\nSample mean == %7.3lf; SD == %7.3lf\n",
                obs_mean, obs_sd);
        dbl_dist ( group, d_vals, obs_mean - difference,
                obs_mean + difference, nr_intervals, smpl_size);
        bootstrap_sd ( d_vals, sample_vals, smpl_size, nr_samples);

        for ( index = 0; index < MAX_INTERVAL; index++)
                group [ index] = 0;
        dbl_dist ( group, sample_vals, obs_sd - 2.0,
                obs_sd + 2.0, nr_intervals, 200);

        printf ( "\nInterval range: %7.3lf to %7.3lf\n",
                extremes [ LOW], extremes [ HIGH]);
        printf ( "\n\nSample sd is in interval %d\n",
                what_interval ( obs_sd, obs_sd - 2.0,
                                obs_sd + 2.0, nr_intervals));
        printf ( "Actual Range = %7.3lf; smallest = %7.3lf; ",
                extremes [ HIGH] - extremes [ LOW], extremes [ LOW]);
        printf ( "largest = %7.3lf\n", extremes [ HIGH]);

        pct_draw ( group, nr_intervals, nr_samples, 0);
}


/* generate a sample of random values from a normal distribution
   having the specified mean and standard deviation.
*/
void nrml_sample ( double smpl_vals [], int size,
                   double mean, double sd, double *sum)
{
        double temp_sum = 0.0, result;
        int    index;

    /* to keep track of lowest and highest values encountered. */
        extremes [ LOW] = 99999.99;
        extremes [ HIGH] = 0.0;

    /* generate values, and store in the array */
        for ( index = 0; index < size; index++)
        {
                result = mean + gauss_fn () * sd;
                temp_sum += result;
                if ( result < extremes [ LOW])
                        extremes [ LOW] = result;
                if ( result > extremes [ HIGH])
                        extremes [ HIGH] = result;
                smpl_vals [ index] = result;
```

```
                        /*
                        printf ( "%12.3lf", smpl_vals [index]);
                        if ( ( index % 5) == 4)
                                printf ( "\n");
                        */
                }
                *sum = temp_sum;
        }


/* compute the standard deviation of the vals array,
   given the sample size and the sum of values.
*/
double s_dev ( double vals [], double sum, int size)
{
        double result, sum_sq = 0.0;
        int    index;

        for ( index = 0; index < size; index++)
                sum_sq += vals [ index] * vals [ index];
        result = (sum_sq - ( sum * sum / size)) / ( size - 1);
        return ( sqrt ( result));
}


/* Generate bootstrap samples, given array containing original sample,
sample size, and number of samples to generate.
Return standard deviations of bootstrap samples in smp_vals array.
*/
void bootstrap_sd ( double vals [], double smp_vals [],
                    int size, int nr_samples)
{
        double width, value, sum = 0.0, sum_sq = 0.0;
        int    index, sample, level;

        width = 1.0 / size;
        printf ( "\nInterval Width == %.4lf\n", width);
        printf ("Generating bootstrap samples (sd) ...\n");

        extremes [ LOW] = 99999.99;
        extremes [ HIGH] = 0.0;

        for ( sample = 0; sample < nr_samples; sample++)
        {
                sum = 0.0;
                sum_sq = 0.0;
                for ( index = 0; index < size; index++)
                {
                        value = house_zero_one ();
                        level = floor ( value / width);
                        sum += vals [ level];
                        sum_sq += vals [ level] * vals [ level];
                }
                value = ( sum_sq - sum * sum / ( size)) / ( size - 1);
                smp_vals [ sample] = sqrt ( value);
                if ( smp_vals [ sample] < extremes [ LOW])
                        extremes [ LOW] = smp_vals [ sample];
                if ( smp_vals [ sample] > extremes [ HIGH])
                        extremes [ HIGH] = smp_vals [ sample];
                /**/
                printf ( "%12.3lf", smp_vals [sample]);
                if ( ( sample % 5) == 4)
                        printf ( "\n");
                /**/
        }
}
```

We've only touched on some of the most general issues and simplest situations related to the jackknife and bootstrap methods. Both of these methods have extensions and variations. If you're interested in finding out more about such methods, you might start with an article by Persi Diaconis and Bradley Efron, "Computer-Intensive Methods in Statistics" (*Scientific American*, May 1983).

CAUTIONS WHEN GENERATING SIMULATION DATA

You may sometimes want to generate random numbers only within a small range of possible values. For example, if you wanted to simulate the role of a die, you would want to divide your random values into six groups.

The following listing shows two ways you can do this. The first way is to use the modulus operator (%). Find the remainder when you divide the random integer by 6. Since this will be a value between 0 and 5, you'll need to add 1 to every result to bring it within the desired 1-6 range.

This method is very quick, and it's adequate for most purposes. The drawback is that the rightmost digit is sometimes not so random as other parts of the number. Thus, there is a danger of biasing the results toward certain values. You can run a simulation to see whether your generator is biased in this way. Generate samples of random values, and plot their distributions. If the values 1 through 6 appear roughly an equal number of times in a high majority of your samples, your generator is probably adequate for explorations of the sort you're doing here.

A second danger, discussed later in this chapter, associated with this method can show up when you try to combine two random values generated in this way.

The second method for simulating the roll of a die divides the range of possible values into six intervals. This strategy works with random values between 0.0 and 1.0. The first sixth of this range is associated with a roll of 1, the next sixth with 2, and so forth. Both methods are shown in the following program:

```
/* Program to roll a die, using 2 different methods. */

#include <stdio.h>
#include <stdlib.h>
#include <string.h>
#include <math.h>

#include "defs.h"
#include "rand.c"
#include "rdist.c"
#include "analysis.c"
#include "chisq.c"
#include "misc.c"

#define MAX_SAMP_SIZE    500
#define DIE_FACES          6
#define NR_DICE            1

/* Function DECLARATIONS */
void   nrml_sample ( double d_vals [], int size,
                        double mean, double sd, double *sum);
double s_dev_int ( int vals [], double sum, int size);

int    r_vals [ MAX_RAND];       /* contains random values generated */
double d_vals [ MAX_RAND], mean_vals [ MAX_RAND];
double sample_vals [ MAX_SAMP_SIZE];
int    group [ MAX_INTERVAL];
double extremes [ 2];   /* extreme [ LOW] == low value;
                           extreme [ HIGH] == high value
                         */


main ()
{
        int    index, samples, nr_trials = 1200, smpl_size = 25;
        int    level, nr_intervals = 10;
        double result, sample_sum = 0.0;
        double width, mean, sd, obs_mean, obs_sd, low_val, hi_val;

        curr_seed = get_int ( "Starting seed? ");
        nr_trials = get_int ( "Number of Rolls? ");

        printf ( "Starting seed = %d\n\n", curr_seed);
        printf ( "Generating random values ... \n");

        /* METHOD 1 --- modulus operator */
        for ( index = 0; index < nr_trials; index++)
        {
                r_vals [ index] = (house_rand ( ) % 6) + 1;
                sample_sum += r_vals [ index];
        }

        obs_mean = sample_sum / nr_trials;
        obs_sd = s_dev_int ( r_vals, sample_sum, nr_trials);
        printf ( "\n\nSample mean value == %7.3lf; SD == %7.3lf\n",
                obs_mean, obs_sd);

        distribution ( group, r_vals, (long) (NR_DICE * DIE_FACES),
                        1, nr_trials);
        pct_draw ( group, NR_DICE * DIE_FACES, nr_trials, 0);

        for ( index = 0; index < MAX_INTERVAL; index++)
                group [ index] = 0;

        for ( index = 0; index < MAX_RAND; index++)
                r_vals [ index] = 0;
```

```
                /* METHOD 2 --- intervals between 0.0 and 1.0 */
                sample_sum = 0.0;
                width = 1.0 / 6;
                for ( index = 0; index < nr_trials; index++)
                {
                        result = house_zero_one ( );
                        level = floor ( result / width) + 1;
                        r_vals [ index] = level;
                        sample_sum += level;
                }

                obs_mean = sample_sum / nr_trials;
                obs_sd = s_dev_int ( r_vals, sample_sum, nr_trials);
                printf ( "\n\nSample mean == %7.3lf; SD == %7.3lf\n",
                        obs_mean, obs_sd);

                distribution ( group, r_vals, (long) (NR_DICE * DIE_FACES),
                            1, nr_trials);
                pct_draw ( group, NR_DICE * DIE_FACES, nr_trials, 0);
        }


/* generate a sample of random values from a normal distribution
   having the specified mean and standard deviation.
*/
void nrml_sample ( double smpl_vals [], int size,
                   double mean, double sd, double *sum)
{
        double temp_sum = 0.0, result;
        int     index;

        /* to keep track of lowest and highest values encountered. */
        extremes [ LOW] = 99999.99;
        extremes [ HIGH]  = 0.0;

        /* generate values, and store in the array */
        for ( index = 0; index < size; index++)
        {
                result = mean + gauss_fn () * sd;
                temp_sum += result;
                if ( result < extremes [ LOW])
                        extremes [ LOW] = result;
                if ( result > extremes [ HIGH])
                        extremes [ HIGH] = result;
                smpl_vals [ index] = result;
                /*
                printf ( "%12.3lf", smpl_vals [index]);
                if ( ( index % 5) == 4)
                        printf ( "\n");
                */
        }
        *sum = temp_sum;
}


/* compute the standard deviation of an array of integers,
   given the sample size and the sum of values.
*/
double s_dev_int ( int vals [], double sum, int size)
{
        double result, sum_sq = 0.0;
        int     index;

        for ( index = 0; index < size; index++)
                sum_sq += vals [ index] * vals [ index];
        result = (sum_sq - ( sum * sum / size)) / ( size - 1);
        return ( sqrt ( result));
}
```

The following listing shows the results from two samples of 1200 rolls. Notice that both strategies seem to generate a reasonably uniform distribution.

```
Starting seed = 7171

Sample mean value ==   3.532; SD ==    1.693
        0     188    200     204     201     208     199

  0|
  1|********** ******
  2|********** *******
  3|********** *******
  4|********** *******
  5|********** ********
  6|********** *******


Sample mean ==     3.470; SD ==    1.717
        0     208    201     203     195     193     200

  0|
  1|********** ********
  2|********** *******
  3|********** *******
  4|********** *******
  5|********** *******
  6|********** *******
```

Rolling Two Dice

Suppose you wanted to simulate rolling two dice. This simulation will have possible outcomes ranging from 2 through 12. A first guess might be to generate random values between 0 and 10 and then add 2. With this approach, all eleven possible values would come up equally often.

This is not the case when you roll real dice, however. Although each value between 1 and 6 is equally likely when you are rolling a single die, some values are more likely than others when you roll two dice, since there may be several ways of getting the same total on the two dice. For example, you have only one way to get a 2: Roll a 1 on each die. But there are three ways of rolling a 4: 1 and 3, 3 and 1, and 2 and 2. Table 9-2 shows the possible values and how to get them.

Table 9-2. Value When Rolling Two Dice

Value	How to Get It
2	1—1
3	1—2, 2—1
4	1—3, 3—1, 2—2
5	1—4, 4—1, 2—3, 3—2
6	1—5, 5—1, 2—4, 4—2, 3—3
7	1—6, 6—1, 2—5, 5—2, 3—4, 4—3
8	2—6, 6—2, 3—5, 5—3, 4—4
9	3—6, 6—3, 4—5, 5—4
10	4—6, 6—4, 5—5
11	5—6, 6—5
12	6—6

Thus, to simulate rolling two dice, you need some way of generating values so that the relative frequencies above are found in the samples generated. One possibility is to roll each die individually and then add their values. This amounts to generating two independent random values between 1 and 6 and adding the results.

The following program shows how to do this; it generates a 1200 roll sample:

```
/* Program to roll two dice, using two different methods. */

#include <stdio.h>
#include <stdlib.h>
#include <string.h>
#include <math.h>

#include "defs.h"
#include "rand.c"
#include "rdist.c"
#include "analysis.c"
#include "chisq.c"
#include "misc.c"

#define MAX_SAMP_SIZE    500
#define DIE_FACES          6
#define NR_DICE            2
```

```
/* Function DECLARATIONS */
void    nrml_sample ( double d_vals [], int size,
                        double mean, double sd, double *sum);
double s_dev_int ( int vals [], double sum, int size);

int     r_vals [ MAX_RAND];      /* contains random values generated */
double d_vals [ MAX_RAND], mean_vals [ MAX_RAND];
double sample_vals [ MAX_SAMP_SIZE];
int     group [ MAX_INTERVAL];
double extremes [ 2];   /* extreme [ LOW] == low value;
                            extreme [ HIGH] == high value
                        */


main ()
{
        int     index, samples, nr_trials = 1200, smpl_size = 25;
        int     level, nr_intervals = 10;
        double result, sample_sum = 0.0;
        double width, mean, sd, obs_mean, obs_sd, low_val, hi_val;

        curr_seed = get_int ( "Starting seed? ");
        nr_trials = get_int ( "Number of Rolls? ");

        printf ( "Starting seed = %d\n\n", curr_seed);
        printf ( "Generating random values ... \n");

        /* METHOD 1 --- modulus operator */
        for ( index = 0; index < nr_trials; index++)
        {
                /* roll first die */
                r_vals [ index] = (house_rand ( ) % 6) + 1;
                /* roll second die */
                r_vals [ index] += (house_rand ( ) % 6) + 1;
                sample_sum += r_vals [ index];
        }

    /* Alternative for method 1:
       generate a second die roll separately
    */

    /*
        for ( index = 0; index < nr_trials; index++)
        {
                r_vals [ index] += (house_rand ( ) % 6) + 1;
                sample_sum += r_vals [ index];
        }
    */

        obs_mean = sample_sum / nr_trials;
        obs_sd = s_dev_int ( r_vals, sample_sum, nr_trials);
        printf ( "\n\nSample mean value == %7.3lf; SD == %7.3lf\n",
                obs_mean, obs_sd);

        distribution ( group, r_vals, (long) (NR_DICE * DIE_FACES),
                        1, nr_trials);
        pct_draw ( group, NR_DICE * DIE_FACES, nr_trials, 0);

        for ( index = 0; index < MAX_INTERVAL; index++)
                group [ index] = 0;

        for ( index = 0; index < MAX_RAND; index++)
                r_vals [ index] = 0;
```

```
        sample_sum = 0.0;
        width = 1.0 / 6;
/* METHOD 2  --- interval between 0.0 and 1.0 */
        for ( index = 0; index < nr_trials; index++)
        {
                result = house_zero_one ( );
                level = floor ( result / width) + 1;
                r_vals [ index] = level;
                sample_sum += level;
        }

/* generate rolls for second die */
        for ( index = 0; index < nr_trials; index++)
        {
                result = house_zero_one ( );
                level = floor ( result / width) + 1;
                r_vals [ index] += level;
                sample_sum += level;
        }

        obs_mean = sample_sum / nr_trials;
        obs_sd = s_dev_int ( r_vals, sample_sum, nr_trials);
        printf ( "\n\nSample mean value == %7.3lf; SD == %7.3lf\n",
                obs_mean, obs_sd);

        distribution ( group, r_vals, (long) (NR_DICE * DIE_FACES),
                1, nr_trials);
        pct_draw ( group, NR_DICE * DIE_FACES, nr_trials, 0);
}


/* generate a sample of random values from a normal distribution
   having the specified mean and standard deviation.
*/
void nrml_sample ( double smpl_vals [], int size,
                double mean, double sd, double *sum)
{
        double temp_sum = 0.0, result;
        int    index;
    /* to keep track of lowest and highest values encountered. */
        extremes [ LOW] = 99999.99;
        extremes [ HIGH] = 0.0;

    /* generate values, and store in the array */
        for ( index = 0; index < size; index++)
        {
                result = mean + gauss_fn () * sd;
                temp_sum += result;
                if ( result < extremes [ LOW])
                        extremes [ LOW] = result;
                if ( result > extremes [ HIGH])
                        extremes [ HIGH] = result;
                smpl_vals [ index] = result;
                /*
                printf ( "%12.3lf", smpl_vals [index]);
                if ( ( index % 5) == 4)
                        printf ( "\n");
                */
        }
        *sum = temp_sum;
}


/* compute the standard deviation of an array of integers,
   given the sample size and the sum of values.
```

```
*/
double s_dev_int ( int vals [], double sum, int size)
{
        double result, sum_sq = 0.0;
        int     index;

        for ( index = 0; index < size; index++)
                sum_sq += vals [ index] * vals [ index];
        result = (sum_sq - ( sum * sum / size)) / ( size - 1);
        return ( sqrt ( result));
}
```

Both methods for generating a die roll seemed to produce uniformly distributed values in an earlier listing; the methods perform quite differently when you try to add two values. When using the modulus operator, successive values can become coupled with each other because of the properties of the linear congruential algorithm when certain parameters are odd. In this case, the generator will produce all odd sums. Thus, only values of 3, 5, 7, 9, and 11 are found, as you can see in the following results from this program:

```
Starting seed = 931

Sample mean value ==    7.005; SD ==    2.416
        0        0      0      135      0      308      0      336      0      261
        0      160      0

   0|
   1|
   2|
   3|********** **
   4|
   5|********** ********** ******
   6|
   7|********** ********** ********
   8|
   9|********** ********** **
  10|
  11|********** ****
  12|


Sample mean value ==    6.994; SD ==    2.406
        0        0     34       71     92      132    173      191    177      133
      101       66     30

   0|
   1|
   2|***
   3|******
   4|********
   5|********** *
   6|********** *****
   7|********** ******
   8|********** *****
   9|********** **
  10|*********
  11|******
  12|***
```

For most purposes, such behavior will not become a problem. Thus, using the simple linear congruential algorithm in function **house_rand()** has caused no trouble until this case.

Before applying a generator to a new situation, it's always a good idea to run some simulations first. Try the generator in the new situation, and look at the resulting means, spread, and distribution. If anything seems odd, you may need to use a different generator.

Tasks and Suggestions

In this chapter, you've looked at some examples involving different distributions: binomial, Poisson, and normal. In the process, you've had an opportunity to explore some properties of these distributions. Build some simulations involving other distributions, such as the exponential distribution, which is useful for modeling such phenomena as radioactive decay and bacterial growth.

Function **exp_fn()** will generate random values from a version of the exponential distribution. This function is included in the file **rdist.c**, whose listing is included in the next section.

Pick a problem or event of interest to you, and develop a simulation of it.

MISCELLANEOUS ROUTINES

Several routines are used extensively by programs in this and the next chapter. To keep the listings in this chapter more readable, these routines were "hidden" in header files. In this section, you'll find the contents of these files.

Notice that some functions are included here that were also included in some of the programs. If you want to compile these programs with the header files, you'll need to make sure you have only one version of the function in your code.

defs.h

This header file contains the manifest constants and some macros used throughout the program.

```
/* Contents of File Defs.H.
   Contains manifest constants and macros used by programs.
*/

#include <stdio.h>
#include <stdlib.h>
#include <string.h>
#include <math.h>
#include <ctype.h>


#define MAX_STR         80
#define MAX_RAND        2000
#define PER_LINE        10      /* # of integers to write per line */
#define LOW             0
#define HIGH            1

#define INTERV_SIZE     100
#define MAX_INTERVAL    300
#define NR_INTERVALS    MODULUS / INTERV_SIZE + 1
#define ABS_VAL(x)      ((x) >= 0) ? (x) : ( 0 - (x))
```

rand.c

This file contains the main random number generators, **house_rand( )** and **house_zero_one( )**. These routines are called by the functions that generate data from various distributions.

```
/* Contents of File Rand.C
   Contains random number generators .
*/

#define MODULUS         32768L

/* Function DECLARATIONS */
int     house_rand ( void);
double  house_zero_one ( void);
int     linear ( int, int, int *);

/* External variables used by random number generators */
int     curr_seed = 27;
int     mult1 = 65, mult2 = 3621,
        incr1 = 3, incr2 = 1;


/* generate a pseudorandom integer between 0 and 32,767.
   Depending on the previous value returned, the
   function uses either of two parameter sets to generate the
   next value.
```

```
        The function uses the external variables, multX, incrX,
        and curr_seed.
*/
int house_rand ()
{
#define SEMI_MOD    (MODULUS % 2)    /* split range in half */
        long int temp;

        if ( curr_seed >= SEMI_MOD)
                temp = ((long) mult1 * curr_seed + incr1) % MODULUS;
        else
                temp = ((long) mult2 * curr_seed + incr2) % MODULUS;
        curr_seed = (int) temp;
        return ( curr_seed);
}



/* Function to return a pseudorandom value between 0.0 and 1.0.
   Note format of function heading:
   <type specifier> <function name> ()
*/
double house_zero_one ()
{
#define  MAX_VAL 32767.0    /* NOTE: defined as floating point type */
        int  rand_result;

        rand_result = house_rand ();   /* get a pseudorandom integer */
        return ( rand_result / MAX_VAL);
}


/* Linear congruential algorithm for generating random integer */
int linear ( int multiplier, int increment, int *seed)
{
        long int  temp;
        temp = ((long) multiplier * *seed + increment) % MODULUS;
        *seed = (int) temp;
        return ( *seed);
}
```

rdist.c

This file contains the functions for generating random values
from specific distributions, such as the binomial (**coin_flip( )** and
fancy_coin_flip( )), the Poisson (**poisson( )**), and the normal
(**gauss_fn( )**). There is also a function (**exp_fn( )**) for generating
values from an exponential distribution.

```
/* Contents of file Rdist.C.
   Functions for generating random values from
   various distributions.
   File assumes Rand.C has been read in first.

   coin_flip (), fancy_coin_flip () assume MODULUS is defined.
*/
```

```
/* Function DECLARATIONS */
int    coin_flip ( void);
double exp_fn ( void);
int    fancy_coin_flip ( double hit);
double gauss_fn ( void);
int    poisson ( double mean);



/* generates value from exponential distribution with mean == 1;
   to generate exponential distributions with another mean,
   multiply resulting value by the desired mean ---
   either here or after returning the "unit" exponential value.
*/
double exp_fn ()
{
        double  temp;

        do   /* to avoid log of 0, which is undefined */
                temp = house_zero_one ();
        while ( temp <= 0.0);
        temp = -log ( temp);
        return ( temp);
}



/* Return a value based on a normal distribution ---
   having a mean of 0.0 and a standard deviation of 1.0.
*/
double gauss_fn ()
{
        double  gs1, gs2,  /* two "seed" values between 0.0 and 1.0 */
                circ,      /* used in intermediate computation */
                rv1, rv2;  /* normally distributed random values */

        do
        {
                gs1 = house_zero_one ();
                gs1 = 2 * gs1 - 1.0;      /* ranges between -1 and 1 */
                gs2 = house_zero_one ();
                gs2 = 2 * gs2 - 1.0;      /* ranges between -1 and 1 */

                circ = gs1 * gs1 + gs2 * gs2;
        }
        while ( circ >= 1.0);

        /* compute two normally distributed random values */
        rv1 = gs1 * sqrt ( -2 * log ( circ) / circ);
        rv2 = gs2 * sqrt ( -2 * log ( circ) / circ);
        /* printf ( "rv1 == %.4lf; rv2 = %.4lf\n", rv1, rv2); */

        return ( rv1);    /* return one of the values */
}



/* Return a "head" or "tail," depending on the random value
   generated. This function always assumes the probability
   of a head (hit) is 0.5.
*/
int coin_flip ()
{
```

```
        double hit = 0.5;      /* probability of a head */
        long    int cutoff;    /* int value corresponding to hit */
        int     result;

        cutoff = (long) floor ( MODULUS * hit);

        result = house_rand ();
        if ( result < cutoff)
                return ( 1);      /* return "head" */
        else
                return ( 0);      /* return "tail" */
}


/* Return a "head" or "tail," depending on the random value
   generated.
   This function always returns head with a probability
   specified by the hit parameter.
*/
int fancy_coin_flip ( double hit)
{
        long    int cutoff;   /* int corresponding to hit */
        int     result;

        cutoff = (long) floor ( MODULUS * hit);

        result = house_rand ();    /* get a random integer */
        if ( result < cutoff)
                return ( 1);       /* return "head" */
        else
                return ( 0);       /* return "tail" */
}


/* Return a value based on a Poisson distribution,
   with a mean specified by the parameter. Algorithm computes

                -mean
           e

   then generates random values between 0.0 and 1.0,
   multiplying them until the product is less than e^(-mean).
   Result is # values generated, not including the value
   that ended the computation.
*/
int poisson ( double mean)
{
        double val,          /* value of e^(-mean) */
               prod = 1.0;   /* running product */
        int    count = 0;    /* # of values generated */

        val = 1 / exp ( mean);

        do    /* multiply prod by random values */
        {
                count++;
                prod *= house_zero_one ();
        }
        while ( prod > val);      /* repeat until prod is smaller */
        return ( count - 1);
}
```

analysis.h

This file contains several functions that are useful for looking at various aspects of the data. The two most commonly used functions are **dbl—dist()** and **pct—draw()**.

Function **dbl—dist()** breaks the range of values into intervals and counts the number of values that fall into each of these intervals. Function **pct—draw()** plots the relative proportion in each of the intervals built with **dbl—dist()**.

Function **how—likely()** lets you determine how likely you are to get a value as small as or smaller than **ref—val**. The function simply counts the number of values that meet this criterion and determines what proportion of the values this number represents.

```
/* Contents of file Analysis.C
Routines for grouping and analyzing data.
*/

/* Function DECLARATIONS */
void    dbl_dist ( int [], double [], double, double, int, int);
void    distribution ( int [], int [], long int, int, int);
int     even_count ( int [], int);
double  how_likely ( int group [], double val, double start,
                     double range, int intervals, int trials);
void    pct_draw ( int vals [], int nr_interv, int nr_samples,
                   int offset);
int     what_interval ( double val, double start, double stop,
                        int interv);


/* count the number of even values in the specified array */
int even_count ( int vals [], int size)
{
        int count = 0, index;

        for ( index = 0; index < size; index++)
                if ( (vals [ index] % 2) == 0)
                        count++;
        return ( count);
}


/* compute frequencies with which values in each interval occur
   --- works with array of int.
*/
void distribution ( int group [], int raw [],
                    long int range, int size, int nr_trials)
{
        int nr_intervals, index, actual_size;

        nr_intervals = range / size + 1;
```

```
        for ( index = 0; index < nr_trials; index++)
                group [ raw [ index] / size]++;

        for ( index = 0; index < nr_intervals; index++)
        {
                printf ( "%7d", group [ index]);
                if ( ( index % PER_LINE)  == PER_LINE - 1)
                        printf ( "\n");
        }
}


/* compute frequencies with which values in each interval occur
   --- works with array of double.
*/
void dbl_dist ( int group [], double raw [],
                double start, double stop, int nr_interv, int nr_trials)
{
        int     index, count;
        double  size, curr, range;

        range = ABS_VAL ( stop - start);
        size = range / nr_interv;
        printf ( "\nInterval size = %.4lf\n", size);
        printf ( "Start = %.4lf; Finish = %.4lf; Range = %.4lf\n\n",
                start, stop, range);

        /* group values into appropriate intervals */
        for ( index = 0; index < nr_trials; index++)
        {
                if (( raw [ index] < start) || ( raw [ index] > stop))
                {
                        count = 0;
                        printf ( "index == %d; value == %.4lf\n",
                                index, raw[ index]);
                }
                else
                        count = floor ( (raw [ index] - start) / range
                                        * nr_interv);
                if ( count >= nr_interv)
                        count = nr_interv;
                group [ count]++;
        }

        /* display frequencies for values */
        for ( index = 0; index <= nr_interv; index++)
        {
                printf ( "%7d", group [ index]);
                if ( ( index % PER_LINE)  == PER_LINE - 1)
                        printf ( "\n");
        }
}


/* determine how likely a value less than or equal to val is,
   by counting the proportion of such values in the sample.
*/
double how_likely ( int group [], double val, double start, double range,
                    int intervals, int trials)
{
        int index, subscript, freq_sum = 0;

        subscript = floor ( val - start) / range * intervals + 1;
```

```
        if ( subscript < 0)
                subscript = 0;
        for ( index = 0; index < subscript; index++)
                freq_sum += group [ index];
        return ( (double) freq_sum / trials);
}


/* determine the interval in which a particular value falls */
int what_interval ( double val, double start, double stop,
                    int interv)
{
        int     level;
        double range;

        range = ABS_VAL ( stop - start);
        if ( val < start)
                level = 0;
        else
                level = floor ( (val - start) / range * interv);
        if ( level >= interv)
                level = interv;
        return ( level);
}



/* Graph the contents of the vals array, grouping
   contents into nr_interv cells.
   Actually graphed: the relative proportion of time
   values in the cell occurred --- that is,
   # in cell / nr_samples.
   The offset is intended for case such as dice rolls,
   where 1 -- 6 would be better subscripts than 0 -- 5.
*/
void pct_draw ( int vals [], int nr_interv, int nr_samples,
                int offset)
{
#define MAX_DOTS     60   /* maximum # dots on a graph line */
        int     dots, index, count;
        double ratio;

        printf ( "\n\n");
        /* write information for each interval */
        for ( index = 0; index <= nr_interv; index++)
        {
                printf ( "%3d|", index + offset);
                ratio = (double) vals [ index] / nr_samples;
                /* 1 dot per 1% or fraction thereof */
                dots = ceil ( ratio * 100);
                /* truncate if too many dots. */
                if ( dots > MAX_DOTS)
                        dots = MAX_DOTS;
                for ( count = 0; count < dots; count++)
                {
                        printf ( "*");
                        /* leave space after every 10 dots */
                        if ( ( count % 10) == 9)
                                printf ( " ");
                }
                if ( count == MAX_DOTS)  /* if more to write */
                        printf ( "...");
                printf ( "\n");
        }   /* end for each interval */
}
```

chisq.c

This file contains the functions (from Chapter 8) for computing chi-square values, critical values, and probability information.

```
/* Contents of file Chisq.C
   Routines for computing chi-square values for uniformly
   distributed data, and for displaying the appropriate probabilities.
*/


#define MAX_FACTOR   9    /* # of magic values needed for chi-square */

/* Function DECLARATIONS */
double chi_square ( int [], long int, int, int);
int    cutoffs ( double, int);
double dbl_chi_square ( int group [], double range, double size,
                        int trials);
void   show_probability ( int);


/* contains "magic numbers" for computing cutoff values for
   evaluating chi-square statistic.
   Magic numbers correspond to the following probabilities:
   .01, .05, .10, .25, .50, .75, .90, .95, .99
*/
double chi_factors [ MAX_FACTOR] =
                  { -2.3253, -1.6449, -1.2816, -.6745,
                    0.0, .6745, 1.2816, 1.6449, 2.3253};


/* compute a chi-square statistic to evaluate the uniformness of
   of a sample of random values. Assumes all values are integers.
*/
double chi_square (int group [], long int range, int size, int trials)
{
        int    nr_intervals, index;
        double expected, deviation, last_size, sum = 0.0;

        nr_intervals = range / size + 1;
        expected = ( (double) trials * size) / range;

        for ( index = 0; index < nr_intervals - 1; index++)
        {
                deviation = group [ index] - expected;
                sum += deviation * deviation / expected;
        }

    /* for last, smaller, interval, expected value is smaller */
        last_size = range - (long) ( nr_intervals - 1) * size;
        expected = ( (double) trials * last_size) / range;
        deviation = group [ nr_intervals - 1] - expected;
        sum += deviation * deviation / expected;

        printf ( "\n\nchi-square for %d intervals == %.4lf\n",
                nr_intervals, sum);
        return ( sum);
}
```

```c
/* compute a chi-square statistic to evaluate the uniformness
   of a sample of random values. Assumes raw values are double.
*/
double dbl_chi_square ( int group [], double range,
                        double size, int trials)
{
        int     nr_intervals, index;
        double expected, deviation, last_size, sum = 0.0;

        nr_intervals = floor ( range / size);
        expected = ( (double) trials * size) / range;
        printf ( "intervals == %d; expected == %.4lf\n",
                 nr_intervals, expected);

        for ( index = 0; index < nr_intervals; index++)
        {
                deviation = group [ index] - expected;
                sum += deviation * deviation / expected;
        }

        /* for last, smaller, interval */
        last_size = range - ( nr_intervals - 1) * size;
        expected = ( (double) trials * last_size) / range;
        deviation = group [ nr_intervals - 1] - expected;
        sum += deviation * deviation / expected;

        printf ( "\n\nchi-square for %d intervals == %.4lf\n",
                 nr_intervals, sum);
        return ( sum);
}


/* Compute critical, or cutoff, chi-square values, given
   degrees of freedom information
*/
int cutoffs ( double chi_val, int df)
{
        double df_root, df_term, approx_term, cut_off = 0.0;
        int     index;

        df_root = sqrt ( 2 * df);
        printf ( "df_root == %.4lf\n", df_root);

        for ( index = 0; ( index < MAX_FACTOR) &&
                          ( chi_val > cut_off); index++)
        {
                df_term = df + df_root * chi_factors [ index];
                approx_term = 2.0 / 3.0 *
                              ( chi_factors [ index] *
                                chi_factors [ index] - 1);
                cut_off = df_term + approx_term;
                printf ("%d: term == %.4lf; approx == %.4lf; ",
                        index, df_term, approx_term);
                printf ( "df == %d; cut_off == %.4lf\n",
                         df, cut_off);
        }
        printf ( "after loop, index == %d\n", index);
        if ( chi_val > cut_off)
                return ( index);
        else
                return ( index - 1);
}
```

```
/* compute the probability of getting a chi-square value
   between the critical values specified by the parameter.
*/
void show_probability ( int level)
{
        double lower, upper;

        switch ( level)
        {
                case 0:
                        lower = .00;
                        upper = .01;
                        break;
                case 1:
                        lower = .01;
                        upper = .05;
                        break;
                case 2:
                        lower = .05;
                        upper = .10;
                        break;
                case 3:
                        lower = .10;
                        upper = .25;
                        break;
                case 4:
                        lower = .25;
                        upper = .50;
                        break;
                case 5:
                        lower = .50;
                        upper = .75;
                        break;
                case 6:
                        lower = .75;
                        upper = .90;
                        break;
                case 7:
                        lower = .90;
                        upper = .95;
                        break;
                case 8:
                        lower = .95;
                        upper = .99;
                        break;
                case 9:
                        lower = .99;
                        upper = 1.00;
                        break;
                default:
                        lower = 0;
                        upper = 0;
                        break;
        }
        printf ( "Probability of value is between %.2lf and %.2lf\n",
                lower, upper);
}
```

misc.c

This file contains various functions for getting information from
the user.

```
/* Contents of file Misc.C
   Miscellaneous functions
*/

/* Function DECLARATIONS */
void   do_modulo ( int nr_read, int little_cycle, int big_cycle);
double get_dbl ( char *);
int    get_int ( char *);
void   get_params ( int *mult, int *incr);


/* Get multiplier and increment from user. */
void get_params ( int *mult, int *incr)
{
        char info [ MAX_STR];

        printf ( "Multiplier? ");
        gets ( info);
        *mult = atoi ( info);

        printf ( "Increment? ");
        gets ( info);
        *incr = atoi ( info);
}


/* Prompt user for a value, read and return a double */
double get_dbl ( char *message)
{
        char info [ MAX_STR];

        printf ( "%s\n", message);
        gets ( info);
        return ( atof ( info));
}


/* Prompt user for a value, read and return an int */
int get_int ( char *message)
{
        char info [ MAX_STR];

        printf ( "%s\n", message);
        gets ( info);
        return ( atoi ( info));
}


/* Write symbols at specified intervals ---
   to let user know something is actually happening.
   PARAMETERS :
           int nr_read : value being checked for current count;
           int little_cycle : value used to decide when to write INDICATOR.
           int big_cycle : value used to determine when to do a line feed.
*/
void do_modulo ( int nr_read, int little_cycle, int big_cycle)
{
#define INDICATOR '.'

        if ( (nr_read % little_cycle) == little_cycle - 1)
                printf ( "%c", INDICATOR);
        if ( (nr_read % big_cycle) == big_cycle - 1)
                printf ( "     %6d\n", nr_read);
}
```

SUMMARY

In this chapter, you learned how to simulate some simple processes by generating random data having specific values for certain properties (mean, standard deviation, and so forth) and coming from particular distributions (normal and Poisson). In the next chapter, you'll learn about some statistical tools you can use to help evaluate your simulations.

10

DATA ANALYSIS AND STATISTICS

Like it or not, you are surrounded by statistics. There are financial statistics, sports statistics, vital statistics, and so forth. In this chapter, you'll learn about a few of the concepts and tools used to create and analyze statistics. Although you'll learn about only a small number of topics, there are enough functions developed to provide you with a simple but handy collection of data-analysis tools.

Statistical methods and tools are used to describe and summarize information and to guide decision-making and inference processes. Various methods are also used to find mathematical models that fit a collection of values. In Chapter 9, you used the mean and the standard deviation to provide summary information about a sample of data. In Chapter 8, you used critical values for a chi-square statistic to decide how probable it was that your collection of values came from a random number generator that selected uniformly distributed values.

In this chapter, you'll learn more about descriptive statistics, and you'll learn about inferential statistics. You'll also learn how to use chi-square statistics to test how well your data fit nonuniform distributions, such as the normal or binomial.

DESCRIPTIVE STATISTICS

The mean and standard deviation, which you saw in Chapter 9, are two values that can be used to tell you something about a collection of data. The mean gives you a sort of "typical," or "average," value. The standard deviation gives you an idea of how spread out the values in your data collection are. Both of these values are *descriptive statistics*, since they serve to characterize or summarize a larger collection of values.

Mean and Standard Deviation

The following functions let you compute the mean and the standard deviation of an array of values. The standard deviation function here differs from the one in the last chapter in that the version here needs to know only the array and its size. In function **s—dev()**, you also had to pass the sum of the values to the function.

```
/* Compute and return the mean of an array of double */
double comp_mean ( double vals [], int size)
{
        double sum = 0.0;
        int    index;

        for ( index = 0; index < size; index++)
                sum += vals [ index];

        return ( sum / size);
}


/* compute the standard deviation of an array of double */
double s_dev ( double  vals [], int size)
{
        double result, sum = 0.0, sum_sq = 0.0;
        int    index;

        for ( index = 0; index < size; index++)
        {
```

```
            sum += vals [ index];
            sum_sq += vals [ index] * vals [ index];
    }

    result = (sum_sq - ( sum * sum / size)) / ( size - 1);
    return ( sqrt ( result));
}
```

comp—mean( )

This function computes and returns the mean of an array of values, given the array and the number of values in the array. To compute the mean of a set of values, add all the values, and then divide by the total number of values.

The mean is a measure of *central tendency*. In computing the mean, you take the magnitude of each value in the distribution into account. The amount of influence a value has in determining the mean depends on the value's magnitude; thus, very large and very small values can have more effect on the mean than do intermediate values, which are nearer the center of the distribution. If each value in your distribution were weighted by an amount proportional to the value's magnitude and the values were "hung" on the distribution, the mean would be the balance point for the distribution. The sum of the magnitudes greater than the mean is exactly equal to the sum of the magnitudes less than the mean. In this sense, the mean is a central, or typical, value.

s—dev( )

This function computes and returns the standard deviation of an array of values, given the array and the number of values in the array.

The standard deviation is a measure of *spread,* or *dispersion;* it provides an index of the amount by which values in the distribution differ from the mean. Recall that for the standard deviation, each value's deviation from the mean is given by a squared term:

$$(x_i - \bar{x})^2$$

One reason for this is that the sum of straight deviations,

$$\sum_{i=1}^{nr\ values} (x_i - \overline{x})$$

would always equal 0 — by definition of *mean* as the balance point of the distribution.

One consequence of squaring the deviations is that you'll need to take the square root of the sum of the squared deviations to bring the value back to the same size level as the original data. This square root is computed in function **s_dev( )**.

For some statistical work, it actually turns out to be useful to keep the squared values. In that case, the computations are the same as for the standard deviation, except that no square root is computed at the end. This measure of spread, called the *variance*, is simply the square of the standard deviation. Modify function **s_dev( )** to create a **variance( )** function.

The Median as an Alternative to the Mean

Ordinarily, when people talk about "average" values, they are thinking of the mean. There are times, however, when the mean does not really provide a representative value. This is because the mean is sensitive to, and influenced by, the magnitude of each value in the sample. As a consequence, very large values can have undue influence in determining the value of the mean.

For example, consider the mean of the following values:

```
12235.50
17500.00
22890.45
25455.00
33981.75
35000.00
43125.00
44100.00
45500.00
5239890.00
```

This example illustrates the sensitivity of the mean to extreme values. The mean of these values is 551,967.77, which is clearly not a typical or representative value for this data set. A more likely value is one in the middle of these ranked values — a value around 34,000 or 35,000. Such a "middle" value is known as the *median*. More specifically, the median is the value in an ordered collection that has an equal number of values smaller and larger than it in the array.

The median is also a measure of central tendency. Whereas the mean is the value around which the sum of all the magnitudes is balanced, the median is the ranked value that has as many values above it as below it.

To compute the median, you need to sort your values. You'll need to pick one of the sorting routines from Chapter 4 to perform this task before computing the median. Once the values are sorted, determine the median as follows:

- If there are an odd number of values, the median is the middle value. For example, if there are seven values, the median is the fourth value.

- If there are an even number of values, use the mean of the two middle values as the median. For example, in a ten element data set, the median would be a value between the fifth and sixth values. If these values were 55 and 65, the median would be 60, which is the mean of 55 and 65.

The median uses rank order to determine the middle value. Because it uses rank positions rather than actual values, the median is not sensitive to extreme values.

The following functions sort an array of **double** values and find the median value for the array. We'll use a Shell sort function like the one in Chapter 4, but the function here will sort arrays of **double**. Function **median( )** automatically distinguishes between the even and odd cases.

```
/* Sort an array of double, using Shell sort algorithm */
void  shell_sort ( double vals [], int size)
{
        int    low, hi, gap = 1;
        double temp;
```

```
      /* generate gap sizes */
      do
              gap = 3 * gap + 1;
      while ( gap < size);
      gap /= 3;    /* to avoid using gaps that are too big */
      gap /= 3;    /* to avoid using gaps that are too big */

   /* for decreasing gap sizes do the following loop */
      for ( ; gap >= 1; gap /= 3)
      {
              printf ( "gap == %d\n", gap);
              for ( hi = gap; hi < size; hi++)
              {
                      /* value currently being moved */
                      temp = vals [ hi];
                      /* compare from previous cell downward */
                      low = hi - gap;
                      /* while still cells to compare,
                         and while new value still goes lower
                      */
                      while ( (low >= 0) && ( temp < vals [ low]))
                      {
                              /* move the earlier cells upward */
                              vals [ low + gap] = vals [ low];
                              /* move to next lower cells */
                              low -= gap;
                      }    /* while still not ready to insert */
                      /* store current value */
                      vals [ low + gap] = temp;
              }    /* for hi < size */
      }    /* for gap >= 1 */
}


/* compute the median of an array of double */
double median ( double vals [], int size)
{
      double low, hi;

      if ( size % 2)  /* if an odd number */
              return ( vals [ size / 2]);
      else
      {
              hi = vals [ size / 2];
              low = vals [ size / 2 - 1];
              return ( (low + hi) / 2);
      }
}
```

shell_sort( )

This function sorts the values in an array of **double**, given the
array and the number of values to sort. This function is very similar to the Shell sort function developed in Chapter 4 to sort an
array of integers.

median( )

This function returns the median of the sample values, that is, the value closest to the middle rank. If there are an odd number of values, the median is the value of the middle cell. If there are an even number of values, the median is the mean of the two cells closest to the middle of the distribution.

Percentile Ranges as Alternatives to the Standard Deviation

As you saw, the median is an alternative measure of central tendency, based on rankings of the values; 50% of the values are below the median, and 50% are above it. Because of this position, the median is said to be at the 50th *percentile*. A percentile is a division of the range of values corresponding to 1% of the sample.

You can get a rough idea of the amount of dispersion in your values by looking at the values associated with other percentiles. For example, the value at the 25th percentile is the one that is preceded by one-fourth of the values; the value at the 75th percentile is the one *followed* by one-fourth of the values. If 25% of the values are below the 25th percentile and 25% of the values are above the 75th percentile, 50% of the values will be in the range between these two values.

The difference, or range of values, between the values corresponding to the 75th and 25th percentiles is known as the *interquartile range*, since it represents the range of values between the upper and lower quartiles. You can, of course, compute other ranges. For example, the range from the 33rd through 67th percentiles gives you the middle third of the values. In a unit normal distribution (one with a mean of 0.0 and a standard deviation of 1.0), the range of values between the 16th and 84th percentiles gives you the proportion of values (0.68) within one standard deviation to either side of the mean; thus, 68% of the values in a normal distribution lie within one standard deviation to either side of the mean.

The following functions let you compute the value closest to a specified percentile and the difference between two specified percentiles. The functions assume the values in the array have already been sorted.

```
/* Compute range of values lying between percentiles specified
   by l_val and h_val
*/
double range  ( double vals [], double l_val, double h_val, int size)
{
        double l_bound, h_bound;

        l_bound = pct2val ( vals, l_val, size);
        h_bound = pct2val ( vals, h_val, size);
        return ( h_bound - l_bound);
}


/* compute the value corresponding to the specified percentile */
double  pct2val ( double vals [], double pct, int size)
{
        int     index;
        double val, temp;

    /* The commented statement is a quick and dirty way of
       computing the value, which will always be in a cell.
    */
    /* index = ceil ( pct * size) - 1; */
        if ( pct <= 0.0)
                return ( vals [ 0]);
        if ( pct >= 1.0)
                return ( vals [ size - 1]);

        val = pct * ( size + 1);
        printf ( "val == %7.3lf\n", val);
        index = floor ( val);
        if ( ( val - index) <= CUTOFF)
                return ( vals [ index - 1]);
        index = ceil ( val);
        if ( ( index - val) <= CUTOFF)
                return ( vals [ index - 1]);
         temp = ( index - val) * vals [ index - 2] +
                ( val - index + 1) * vals [ index - 1];
        return ( temp);
}
```

pct2val()

This function returns the value closest to the specified percentage. In its current form, the function will use a weighted mean based on the values in adjacent cells to compute the value corresponding to the specified percentile.

A simpler version of the function always returns a value from the cell closest to but below the specified percentile. The first line in the function, currently commented out, shows how to compute the subscript for this value. To use this simpler version, remove the comments from the first line of the function, comment out the remaining statements in the function, and add instructions to return the appropriate cell value.

range( )

This function computes the range of values between the specified starting and ending percentiles.

Exploratory Data Analysis with Percentiles

In a very innovative book, *Exploratory Data Analysis* (Reading, Mass.: Addison-Wesley, 1977), John Tukey describes how to use certain key percentiles to help characterize the distribution of a sample of values and provides some rules of thumb for identifying extremely deviant values.

Tukey points out that the median splits a sample of values in half. The 25th and 75th percentiles, which Tukey calls *hinges*, split each of those halves in half. The hinge points are determined by ranks, not values.

To characterize a distribution of sample values, you could use 5 values, which make up a *5-number summary*. These would be values corresponding to the lowest and highest ranks (the extreme values), to the median (middle value), and to the hinges (quartile values). The difference between a hinge value and the extreme below or above it gives you some idea of how spread out the rare values are; for example, if there is little difference between the lowest value and the hinge corresponding to the 25th percentile, then your values are more likely to be tightly grouped.

If the differences between the left hinge (25th percentile) and the lowest value is about the same as the difference between the highest value and the right hinge, your distribution is more likely to be symmetric. This would be strongly supported if the median of all the values were close to the mean of the hinges.

For example, suppose you have the following data values. The five values of interest are marked *e*, for extreme, *h* for hinge, and *m* for median.

```
1  2  3  4  5  6  7  8  9  10  11  12  13  14  15  16  149
e        h        m            h                 e
```

The middle portion of the distribution appears to be symmetric: The median, 9, equals the average of the two hinge values, (5 + 13) / 2. The lower and upper quartiles are not symmetric, however, since the difference between the highest value and the right hinge (136) is much larger than the difference at the other end (4).

The following function returns a 5-number summary for your sample. The function returns the values in an array of **double** to keep the five values together.

```
/* Return the five values used in a 5-number summary:
   smallest value, left hinge, median, right hinge, largest value.
*/
void summary5 ( double vals [], double five_pt [], int size)
{
        five_pt [ 0] = vals [ 0];
        five_pt [ 1] = pct2val ( vals, .25, size);
        five_pt [ 2] = median ( vals, size);
        five_pt [ 3] = pct2val ( vals, .75, size);
        five_pt [ 4] = vals [ size - 1];
}
```

summary5( )

This function computes the values that make up the 5-number summary for the specified array. Note that the function returns these values in an array.

The function calls **pct2val( )** to compute the values. Because the current version of **pct2val( )** weights the values, the two hinge values will actually differ from the values computed by hand. The simpler version, which always returns a cell value, will give the same hinge values as the hand analysis did. The symmetry of the distribution within the hinges is not affected by the formula used; thus, the median will still be the mean of the two hinge values for this sample.

To identify values that are "far out"—that is, so different from other values as to be suspect—you can use the values in the 5-number summary. To compute a boundary beyond which values will be considered suspect, Tukey defines a unit of distance that is 1.5 times the difference between the values of the right and left hinges. He calls this unit a *step*.

To identify suspect values, or *outliers*, as they are commonly known, find the values that are two steps beyond the left and right hinges; that is, find a low-end value that differs from the left hinge by 2 * *step*, and find a high-end value that differs from the right hinge by more than two steps. Any values more extreme than these two boundaries can be considered outliers.

For example, the values above have a step size of 12 (1.5 * 8). The lower boundary would be 24 points less than the left hinge, giving the boundary a value of −19; the right boundary would be at 13 + 24, or 37. Thus, the largest value in the array, 149, would be considered suspect.

The following function identifies suspect values in a given array and displays those values, along with information about step size and boundary values. The function also returns the number of outliers found in the array.

```
/* identify suspect values --- those more than 2 steps beyond a hinge.
   Function displays each suspect value, counts the number of suspect
   values and returns this number. Function also passes the smallest
   (*lower) and the largest (*upper) non-suspect values back.
*/
int suspect ( double vals [], int size, double *lower, double *upper)
{
        double lval, hval, step, lbound, hbound;
        int    count = 0, index;

        lval = pct2val ( vals, .25, size);
        hval = pct2val ( vals, .75, size);
        step = 1.5 * ( hval - lval);
        lbound = lval - 2 * step;
        hbound = hval + 2 * step;
        printf ( "\n\nlow hinge = %7.3lf; high hinge = %7.3lf\n",
                 lval, hval);
        printf ( "step = %7.3lf; low = %7.3lf; high = %7.3lf\n",
                 step, lbound, hbound);
```

```
for ( index = 0; ( index < size) &&
                 ( vals [ index] < lbound); index++)
{
        count++;
        printf ( "%d: %7.3lf\n", index, vals [ index]);
}
*lower = vals [ index];
for ( index = size - 1; ( index >= 0) &&
                 ( vals [ index] > hbound); index--)
{
        count++;
        printf ( "%d: %7.3lf\n", index, vals [ index]);
}
*upper = vals [ index];
return ( count);
}
```

suspect( )

This function identifies outliers and displays them. The function also counts the number of suspect values found. Finally, the function passes the two most extreme nonsuspect values back through ***lower** and ***upper**. These values are, respectively, the smallest and the largest nonsuspect values.

Note that outliers must be *very* different in order to be identified as such. In a normal distribution, you would expect to find values so extreme fewer than five times in ten million values. Tukey's rule of thumb for identifying suspect values is quite conservative.

What to Do with Suspect Data

If your sample includes suspect values, you need to decide how to deal with them. Leaving the values untouched makes it likely that conclusions you draw will be incorrect, because very extreme values may have too much weight in the values computed. If you discard the values, you run the risk of throwing out an actual data point.

One way of dealing with suspect data points is to keep them but bring their values more into line. *Winsorization* is a technique in which the values of suspect data points are replaced by the value of the most extreme point that is not suspect; for example, the 149 in the sample we used earlier would be changed to 16.

The following function lets you Winsorize the extreme values in your data array. The function assumes your array is already sorted and requires you to pass the boundary values in as parameters.

```
/* Winsorize extreme values in a sorted array, by replacing
   outliers with the most extreme non-suspect values.
*/
int winsor ( double vals [], int size, double lower, double upper)
{
        int index, count = 0;

    /* Winsorize low values */
        for ( index = 0; ( index < size) &&
                            ( vals [ index] < lower); index++)
        {
                printf ( "%d: %7.31f --> %7.31f\n",
                        index, vals [ index], lower);
                vals [ index] = lower;
                count++;
        }

    /* Winsorize high values */
        for ( index = size - 1; ( index >= 0) &&
                                ( vals [ index] > upper); index--)
        {
                printf ( "%d: %7.31f --> %7.31f\n",
                        index, vals [ index], upper);
                vals [ index] = upper;
                count++;
        }
        return ( count);
}
```

winsor( )

This function Winsorizes the extreme values in the specified array. The function is passed the array, the number of values in the array, and the two most extreme nonsuspect values. These nonsuspect values will be substituted during the Winsorization process—**lower** for the extreme values on the left, and **upper** for the suspect values on the right of the distribution.

Exercising the Descriptive Statistics Functions

The following program lets you exercise the functions for computing and displaying descriptive statistics for your data. The program lets you generate samples of up to 1000 values from a normal distribution. You can specify the mean and the standard deviation. Once you've generated the values, you can compute the mean and the standard deviation, sort the values, display them, and so forth. The program uses the **show—menu( )** function, which you've seen in other exerciser programs, to display the possible options.

```
/* Program to exercise descriptive statistics functions */

#include <stdio.h>
#include <stdlib.h>
#include <string.h>
#include <math.h>

#include "defs.h"
#include "rand.c"
#include "rdist.c"
#include "analysis.c"
#include "misc.c"
#include "mnu.c"

#define MAX_SAMP_SIZE   500
#define DIE_FACES       6
#define NR_DICE         1
#define MAX_PRINT       100
#define FALSE           0
#define TRUE            0
#define CUTOFF          .25
#define NR_MENU         11

/* Function DECLARATIONS */
void    draw_vals ( int vals [], double start, double stop,
                    int nr_interv, int nr_samples);
void    binom_sample ( double smpl_vals [], int size,
                       double hits, double *sum);
double comp_mean ( double vals [], int size);
void    disp_vals ( double vals [], int size, int first, int last);
int     get_data ( double vals []);
double median ( double vals [], int size);
void    nrml_sample ( double d_vals [], int size,
                      double mean, double sd, double *sum);
double pct2val ( double vals [], double pct, int size);
void    poiss_sample ( int smpl_vals [], int size,
                       double mean, double *sum);
double range ( double vals [], double l_val, double h_val, int size);
double s_dev ( double vals [], int size);
void    shell_sort ( double vals [], int size);
void    summary5 ( double vals [], double five_pt [], int size);
```

```
int     suspect ( double vals [], int size,
                      double *lower, double *upper);
void    wait ( void);
int     winsor ( double vals [], int size, double lower, double upper);


/* menu for the selections possible with this program */
char *menu [ MAX_MENU] = { "0) Quit",
                            "1) Generate Sample", "2) Sort Values",
                            "3) Central Tendency", "4) Spread",
                            "5) Percentiles", "6) Explore Data",
                            "7) Winsorize", "8) Display Values",
                            "9) Graph Data", "10) Enter Data"};
double d_vals [ MAX_RAND];       /* contains random values generated */
int     group [ MAX_INTERVAL];
int     sorted = FALSE;
double five_pts [ 5];    /* extreme, hinge, median, hinge, extreme */
double extremes [ 2];    /* extreme [ LOW] == low value;
                            extreme [ HIGH] == high value
                         */
char   *null_str = "";


main ()
{
        int     index, nr_trials = 1200;
        int     start = -1, finish = -1, nr_intervals = 10;
        int     selection;

        double sample_sum = 0.0;
        double test_pct, spread;  /* deviation when distributing */
        double mean = 0.0, sd = 1.0;
        double obs_mean, obs_sd, obs_med;
        double smpl_mean, smpl_sd, pop_mean, pop_sd;
        double smpl2_mean, smpl2_sd;
        double lower, upper; /* smallest & largest non-suspect vals */
        char   info [ MAX_STR];

        curr_seed = get_int ( "Starting seed? ");
        nr_trials = get_int ( "Number of Trials? ");
        nr_intervals = get_int ( "Number of Intervals? ");

        srand ( curr_seed);
        for ( index = 0; index < 56; index++)
                add_seed [ index] = rand ();

        /* repeat this loop until user wants to quit */
        do
        {
                show_menu ( menu, NR_MENU);
                gets ( info);
                selection = atoi ( info);

                /* switch on user's menu selection */
                switch ( selection)
                {
                        default:
                                break;
                        case 0:
                                break;
                        case 1:              /* generate sample */
                                printf ( "Generating values ...\n");
                                nrml_sample ( d_vals, nr_trials,
                                                mean, sd, &sample_sum);
                                break;
```

```
case 2:             /* sort values */
        printf ( "Start shell_sort ()...\n");
        shell_sort ( d_vals, nr_trials);
        sorted = TRUE;
        printf ( "End shell_sort ()...\n");
        break;
case 3:             /* central tendency */
        obs_mean = comp_mean ( d_vals,
                               nr_trials);
        printf ( "\n\nmean == %7.3lf\n",
               obs_mean);
        obs_med = median ( d_vals, nr_trials);
        printf ("Median = %7.3lf\n", obs_med);
        break;
case 4:          /* spread */
        obs_sd = s_dev ( d_vals, nr_trials);
        printf ( "\n\nSD == %7.3lf\n",
                obs_sd);
        break;
case 5:             /* percentiles */
        printf ("Interqtile range = %7.3lf\n",
               range ( d_vals, .25, .75,
                       nr_trials));
        do
        {
                test_pct = get_dbl("Pctile?");
                printf ( "Pctile == %7.3lf\n",
                        pct2val (d_vals,
                                 test_pct,
                                 nr_trials));
        }
        while ( test_pct > 0.0);
        break;
case 6:             /* explore */
        printf ( "%d suspect values\n",
                suspect ( d_vals, nr_trials,
                          &lower, &upper));
        summary5 ( d_vals, five_pts,
                 nr_trials);
        for ( index = 0; index < 5; index++)
                printf ( "   %d: %7.3lf",
                        index,
                        five_pts [ index]);
        printf ( "\n");
        break;
case 7:             /* Winsorize */
        winsor ( d_vals, nr_trials,
               lower, upper);
        break;
case 8:             /* display */
        start = get_int ( "First value?");
        finish = get_int ( "Last value?");
        disp_vals ( d_vals, nr_trials,
                  start, finish);
        break;
case 9:             /* graph */
        for ( index = 0; index < MAX_INTERVAL;
            index++)
                group [ index] = 0;
        spread = get_dbl (
                "Deviation to graph?");
        dbl_dist ( group, d_vals,
                 obs_mean - spread,
                 obs_mean + spread,
                 nr_intervals,
                 nr_trials);
```

```
                            draw_vals ( group,
                                        obs_mean - spread,
                                        obs_mean + spread,
                                        nr_intervals,
                                        nr_trials);
                            break;
                    case 10:          /* Enter values */
                            nr_trials = get_data ( d_vals);
                            break;
                }
                wait ();
        }
        while ( selection != 0);
}



/* generate a sample of random values from a normal distribution
   having the specified mean and standard deviation.
*/
void nrml_sample ( double smpl_vals [], int size,
                   double mean, double sd, double *sum)
{
        double temp_sum = 0.0, result;
        int    index;

    /* too keep track of lowest and highest values encountered. */
        extremes [ LOW] = 99999.99;
        extremes [ HIGH] = 0.0;

        /* generate values, and store in the array */
        for ( index = 0; index < size; index++)
        {
                result = mean + gauss_fn () * sd;
                temp_sum += result;
                if ( result < extremes [ LOW])
                        extremes [ LOW] = result;
                if ( result > extremes [ HIGH])
                        extremes [ HIGH] = result;
                smpl_vals [ index] = result;
                /*
                printf ( "%12.3lf", smpl_vals [index]);
                if ( ( index % 5) == 4)
                        printf ( "\n");
                */
        }
        *sum = temp_sum;
}



/* generate a sample of random values from a binomial distribution
   having the specified hit rate.
*/
void binom_sample ( double smpl_vals [], int size,
                    double hits, double *sum)
{
        double temp_sum = 0.0, result;
        int    index;

    /* too keep track of lowest and highest values encountered. */
        extremes [ LOW] = 99999.99;
        extremes [ HIGH] = 0.0;

        /* generate values, and store in the array */
        for ( index = 0; index < size; index++)
        {
```

```
                    result = fancy_coin_flip ( hits);;
                    temp_sum += result;
                    if ( result < extremes [ LOW])
                            extremes [ LOW] = result;
                    if ( result > extremes [ HIGH])
                            extremes [ HIGH] = result;
                    smpl_vals [ index] = result;
                    /*
                    printf ( "%12.3lf", smpl_vals [index]);
                    if ( ( index % 5) == 4)
                            printf ( "\n");
                    */
            }
            *sum = temp_sum;
    }



/* generate a sample of random values from a Poisson distribution
   having the specified mean.
*/
void poiss_sample ( int smpl_vals [], int size,
                    double mean, double *sum)
{
        double temp_sum = 0.0;
        int     result;
        int     index;

    /* too keep track of lowest and highest values encountered. */
        extremes [ LOW] = 99999.99;
        extremes [ HIGH]  = 0.0;

        /* generate values, and store in the array */
        for ( index = 0; index < size; index++)
        {
                result = poisson ( mean);
                temp_sum += result;
                if ( result < extremes [ LOW])
                        extremes [ LOW] = result;
                if ( result > extremes [ HIGH])
                        extremes [ HIGH] = result;
                smpl_vals [ index] = result;
                /*
                printf ( "%12.3lf", smpl_vals [index]);
                if ( ( index % 5) == 4)
                        printf ( "\n");
                */
        }
        *sum = temp_sum;
}



/* compute the standard deviation of an array of double */
double s_dev ( double  vals [], int size)
{
        double result, sum = 0.0, sum_sq = 0.0;
        int    index;

        for ( index = 0; index < size; index++)
        {
                sum += vals [ index];
                sum_sq += vals [ index] * vals [ index];
        }
```

```
        result = (sum_sq - ( sum * sum / size)) / ( size - 1);
        return ( sqrt ( result));
}



/* shell sort function */
void  shell_sort ( double vals [], int size)
{
        int    low, hi, gap = 1;
        double temp;

    /* generate gap sizes */
        do
                gap = 3 * gap + 1;
        while ( gap < size);
        gap /= 3;    /* to avoid using gaps that are too big */
        gap /= 3;    /* to avoid using gaps that are too big */

    /* for decreasing gap sizes do the following loop */
        for ( ; gap >= 1; gap /= 3)
        {
                printf ( "gap == %d\n", gap);
                for ( hi = gap; hi < size; hi++)
                {
                    /* value currently being moved */
                    temp = vals [ hi];
                    /* compare from previous cell downward */
                    low = hi - gap;
                    /* while still cells to compare,
                    and while new value still goes lower
                    */
                    while ( (low >= 0) && ( temp < vals [ low]))
                    {
                        /* move the earlier cells upward */
                          vals [ low + gap] = vals [ low];
                        /* move to next lower cells */
                          low -= gap;
                    }    /* while still not ready to insert */
                    /* store current value */
                    vals [ low + gap] = temp;
                }    /* for hi < size */
        }    /* for gap >= 1 */
}



/* return the median of an array of values */
double median ( double vals [], int size)
{
        double low, hi;

        if ( size % 2)  /* if an odd number */
                return ( vals [ size / 2]);
        else
        {
                hi = vals [ size / 2];
                low = vals [ size / 2 - 1];
                return ( (low + hi) / 2);
        }
}
```

```
/* compute the mean of an array of values */
double comp_mean ( double vals [], int size)

{
        double sum = 0.0;
        int    index;

        for ( index = 0; index < size; index++)
                sum += vals [ index];

        return ( sum / size);
}


/* compute the range between two xpecified percentiles. */
double range  ( double vals [], double l_val, double h_val, int size)
{
        double l_bound, h_bound;


        l_bound = pct2val ( vals, l_val, size);
        h_bound = pct2val ( vals, h_val, size);
        return ( h_bound - l_bound);
}


/* compute the value corresponding to the specified percentile. */
double  pct2val ( double vals [], double pct, int size)
{
        int    index;
        double val, temp;

        /* index = ceil ( pct * size) - 1; */
        if ( pct <= 0.0)
                return ( vals [ 0]);
        if ( pct >= 1.0)
                return ( vals [ size - 1]);

        val = pct * ( size + 1);
        printf ( "val == %7.3lf\n", val);
        index = floor ( val);
        if ( ( val - index) <= CUTOFF)
                return ( vals [ index - 1]);
        index = ceil ( val);
        if ( ( index - val) <= CUTOFF)
                return ( vals [ index - 1]);
         temp = ( index - val) * vals [ index - 2] +
                ( val - index + 1) * vals [ index - 1];
        return ( temp);
}


/* Return the five values used in a 5-number summary:
   smallest value, left hinge, median, right hinge, largest value.
*/
void summary5 ( double vals [], double five_pt [], int size)
{
        five_pt [ 0] = vals [ 0];
        five_pt [ 1] = pct2val ( vals, .25, size);
        five_pt [ 2] = median ( vals, size);
        five_pt [ 3] = pct2val ( vals, .75, size);
        five_pt [ 4] = vals [ size - 1];
}
```

```
/* identify suspect values --- those more than 2 steps beyond a hinge.
   Function displays each suspect value, counts the number of suspect
   values and returns this number. Function also passes the smallest
   (*lower) and the largest (*upper) non-suspect values back.
*/
int suspect ( double vals [], int size, double *lower, double *upper)
{
        double lval, hval, step, lbound, hbound;
        int    count = 0, index;

        lval = pct2val ( vals, .25, size);
        hval = pct2val ( vals, .75, size);
        step = 1.5 * ( hval - lval);
        lbound = lval - 2 * step;
        hbound = hval + 2 * step;
        printf ( "\n\nlow hinge = %7.3lf; high hinge = %7.3lf\n",
                 lval, hval);
        printf ( "step = %7.3lf; low = %7.3lf; high = %7.3lf\n",
                 step, lbound, hbound);

        for ( index = 0; ( index < size) &&
                         ( vals [ index] < lbound); index++)
        {
                count++;
                printf ( "%d: %7.3lf\n", index, vals [ index]);
        }
        *lower = vals [ index];

        for ( index = size - 1; ( index >= 0) &&
                         ( vals [ index] > hbound); index--)
        {
                count++;
                printf ( "%d: %7.3lf\n", index, vals [ index]);
        }
        *upper = vals [ index];
        return ( count);
}


/* Winsorize extreme values in a sorted array, by replacing
   outliers with the most extreme non-suspect values.
*/
int winsor ( double vals [], int size, double lower, double upper)
{
        int index, count = 0;

    /* Winsorize low values */
        for ( index = 0; ( index < size) &&
                         ( vals [ index] < lower); index++)
        {
                printf ( "%d: %7.3lf --> %7.3lf\n",
                         index, vals [ index], lower);
                vals [ index] = lower;
                count++;
        }

    /* Winsorize high values */
        for ( index = size - 1; ( index >= 0) &&
                             ( vals [ index] > upper); index--)
        {
                printf ( "%d: %7.3lf --> %7.3lf\n",
                         index, vals [ index], upper);
```

```
                        vals [ index] = upper;
                        count++;
                }
                return ( count);
        }


/* display elements from vals array.
   Elements are specified by first and last.
   first and last are specified as ordinal units, rather than as
   array subscripts. E.g., to specify that the second through 10th
   cells should be written, use 2 for first.
   Special values:
   first == 0: display from start of array;
   last == 0; display to end of array.
   first < 0: value of first specifies an offset from value of last.
   last < 0: value of last specifies an offset from value of first.
   First and last cannot both be negative.
   E.g., set first = -10, last = 0 to display last 10 values in array.
*/
void disp_vals ( double vals [], int size, int first, int last)
{
        int offset1 = FALSE, offset2 = FALSE;
        int index, count = 0;  /* count used for formatting output */

        if ( first > 0)
                first--;
        if ( ( last == 0) || ( last > size))
                last = size;

        if ( ( first < 0) && ( last < 0))
        {
                first = 0;
                last = 0;
        }
        else
        {
                if ( first < 0)
                {
                        first = last + first;
                        if ( first < 0)
                                first = 0;
                }
                else if ( last < 0)
                {
                        last = last + first;
                        if ( last < 0)
                                last = size;
                }
        }

        printf ( "Printing elements %d through %d\n",
                first, last);
        for ( index = first; index < last; count++, index++)
        {
                printf ( "%7.3lf", vals [ index]);
                if ( ( count % 5) == 4)
                        printf ( "\n");
                if ( ( count % 50) == 49)
                        wait ();
        }
        printf ( "\n");
}
```

```
/* wait for user to press return */
void wait ()
{
        char info [ MAX_STR];

        printf ( "<Return> to continue");
        gets ( info);
}



/* Graph the contents of the vals array, grouping
   contents into nr_interv cells.
   Actually graphed: the relative proportion of time
   values in the cell occurred --- that is,
   # in cell / nr_samples.
*/
void draw_vals ( int vals [], double start, double stop,
                 int nr_interv, int nr_samples)
{
#define MAX_DOT    52   /* maximum # dots on a graph line */
        int    dots, index, count;
        double ratio, size, label, lower = start, upper;

        size = (ABS_VAL ( stop - start)) / nr_interv;
        printf ( "\nInterval size for graphing == %7.3lf\n",
                 size);
        printf ( "\n\n");
        /* write information for each interval */
        for ( index = 0; index <= nr_interv; index++)
        {
                upper = lower + size;
                label = ( lower + upper) / 2;
                printf ( "%7.3lf|", label);
                lower = upper;
                ratio = (double) vals [ index] / nr_samples;
                /* 1 dot per 1% or fraction thereof */
                dots = ceil ( ratio * 100);
                /* truncate if too many dots. */
                if ( dots > MAX_DOT)
                        dots = MAX_DOT;
                for ( count = 0; count < dots; count++)
                {
                        printf ( "*");
                        /* leave space after every 10 dots */
                        if ( ( count % 10) == 9)
                                printf ( " ");
                }
                if ( count == MAX_DOT)  /* if more to write */
                        printf ( "...");
                printf ( "\n");
        }    /* end for each interval */
}


/* get values for an array from user */
int get_data ( double vals [])
{
        int    index = 0;
        char   info [ MAX_STR];
        printf ( "? ");
        gets ( info);
```

```
        while ( strcmp ( info, null_str))
        {
                vals [ index++] = atof ( info);
                printf  ( "? ");
                gets ( info);
        }
        return ( index);
}
```

nrml—sample( )

This function generates a random sample of the specified size. The sample is generated from a normal distribution having the specified mean and standard deviation.

get—data( )

This function lets you enter your own data for analysis. This will be very useful in the second part of the chapter, when we talk about statistical tests you can run on sample data. The function puts values into the **vals[ ]** array, just as **nrml—sample( )** does.

disp—vals( )

This function displays values from the specified array. You can specify the first and last elements to be displayed. For example, to specify that you want to see the first 10 elements of the array, call the function with 0 or 1 for the third argument, **first**, and 10 for the fourth argument, **last**.

A value of 0 means to display either from the start of the array (if **first** = 0) or to the end of the array (if **last** = 0). Element numbers are in ordinal terms. Thus, to start displaying with the third element in the array, call the function with 3 as the value for **first**. The function will translate this value to a subscript. Thus, calling **disp—vals( )** with 3 and 15 for the third and fourth arguments, respectively, means to display the 3rd through the 15th elements; elements with subscripts 2 through 14 will be displayed.

You can specify an offset from the start or the end of the array by passing a negative value for **first** or **last**. For example, using −20 and 0 for the third and fourth arguments would specify that the function was to display the last 20 values in the array: The 0 sets **last** to the end of the array, and the minus sign indicates that **first** is to get a value 20 less than the value of **last**.

Once all this adjustment and checking is done, the function simply displays the values in cells **first** -1 through **last** -1.

draw—vals( )

This function graphs the relative frequencies with which values in different intervals occur. The function assumes you have grouped your sample values into intervals, using the **dbl—dist( )** function from Chapter 9.

The function uses the midpoint of the interval as the value on the left. Each (*) represents 1% of the relative frequency or fraction thereof.

Tasks and Suggestions

The functions available for exploring and summarizing data include a routine for determining the value associated with a particular percentile. Write a function **val2pct( )** that returns the percentile associated with a particular value. In designing this function, think of how to find the element in the array. Remember that the array must be sorted if this request is to be meaningful. You might try adapting the binary search function from Chapter 4 to work with **double** values.

Generating Distributions

Compare the properties and the values of a sample distribution generated and analyzed by you with the properties of a theoretical normal distribution. Try this with several random number generators. Generate a very large (say, 5000-element) sample of random values from a normal distribution with a mean of 0.0 and a standard deviation of 1.0, and group these values into small intervals (such as 0.1).

In this unit normal distribution, the value of an element can be interpreted as the number of standard deviations that element is from the mean; thus, large values correspond to greater distances from the mean and should occur less frequently.

Compare your empirically generated distribution with a theoretical distribution, which you can find in a table in most statistics books. Compare values such as the mean, the median, the standard deviation, and the interquartile range. For example, the interquartile range in the theoretical normal distribution is about 1.34, since the 25th and 75th percentiles correspond to values of about -0.67 and 0.67, respectively. See how this value compares with your observed interquartile range.

You learned earlier that about 68% of the values in a normal distribution lie within one standard deviation to either side of the mean—between the values of -1.0 and 1.0 in a normal distribution with mean of 0.0 and standard deviation of 1.0. To determine what percentage of the values in your distribution lie between these two values, subtract the percentage that lies below -1.0 from the percentage that lies below 1.0.

Modifying draw—vals( )

The **draw—vals( )** function does an adequate job of presenting your results graphically. However, the function's vertical graph display makes it somewhat difficult to read at times. Write a graphing function that will display the results horizontally. Think about how you'll know where to start graphing and how you'll represent the interval values.

A More Flexible Winsorization Function

The current version of **winsor( )** assumes that the values in the array have already been sorted. Write a version that will use an unordered array and the 5-number summary information to determine the cutoff points for outliers. The Winsorization process would work the same way as in the current **winsor( )** function—with the exception that each cell of the array would be checked and would be Winsorized, if necessary.

Describing Relationships
Between Two Variables

So far, all of our examples have involved one variable at a time, such as light bulb lifetime. Sometimes, however, you may want to know whether high values on one variable also mean high values on a second variable.

If two variables tend to vary together, they are said to be *correlated*. For example, scores on math and verbal aptitude tests tend to be correlated because people who do well on one type of test also tend to do well on the other. The relationship is not perfect, however, since there are people who are very good in one area but not the other. Thus, there is a correlation between performances on math and verbal tests, but only on the average.

As another example, suppose you wanted to know whether there is a relationship between the size of a body of water and its deepest point—that is, do large bodies of water tend to be deeper than smaller bodies of water? Let's look at some data regarding this question.

The following listing contains approximate areas and maximum depths of the 15 largest oceans and seas:

```
Body of water    Area (sq mi)    Max. depth
Pacific Ocean    64,000,000      37,800
Atlantic Ocean   31,800,000      30,250
Indian Ocean     25,300,000      24,500
Arctic Ocean      5,500,000      18,500
Mediterranean     1,150,000      15,200
Caribbean         1,050,000      22,800
South China Sea     900,000      16,500
Bering Sea          890,000      15,700
Gulf of Mexico      615,000      12,400
Okhotsk Sea         614,000      12,000
East China Sea      482,000       9,100
Hudson Bay          476,000         600
Japan Sea           389,000      12,300
Andaman Sea         308,000      12,400
North Sea           222,000       2,200
```

Looking at this list, you can see a fairly strong trend: Larger bodies of water tend to be deeper. There are a few exceptions, such as Hudson Bay, which seems too shallow for its size, and the Andaman Sea, which seems too deep. By and large, however, the relationship between area and maximum depth seems to be quite strong. You'll see how to quantify this apparent relationship after looking at another example.

Let's see whether a similar relationship between area and maximum depth holds for lakes. The following listing provides the data:

```
Lake              Area (sq mi)    Max. depth
Caspian Sea       152,300         3100
Lake Superior     31,800          1330
Lake Victoria     26,800          270
Lake Aral         25,600          225
Lake Huron        23,000          750
Lake Michigan     22,400          925
Lake Tanganyika   12,700          4700
Lake Baikal       12,200          5700
Great Bear Lake   12,000          270
Lake Nyasa        11,600          2300
Great Slave Lake  11,200          2000
Lake Chad         9,950           25
Lake Erie         9,930           210
Lake Winnipeg     9,100           200
Lake Ontario      7,500           780
```

Glancing over this set of values, it is much harder to discern a relationship. Several very large lakes are shallow (for example, Lake Victoria and Lake Aral), and some smaller lakes are very deep (for example, Lake Baikal). On the whole, the relationship between area and maximum depth seems to hold for oceans and seas, but not for lakes. Let's develop a measure for testing these two informal conclusions.

The *correlation coefficient* (r) provides an index of the degree to which the values of two variables are correlated in a linear fashion; that is, it provides a measure of the extent to which extreme scores in one sample tend to be associated with extreme scores in another set of values. When two variables tend to be associated in this way, they are said to have a high *covariation*.

Recall that the standard deviation (or variance) of a value from its mean is computed by squaring the difference between the value and its mean. The covariation of two values from different data sets is computed by finding the difference between each value and the mean for its sample and multiplying the two differences. Thus, the covariation between the first terms in the lakes data is given by the following:

$$(152,300 - 25,205.33) * (3100 - 1519)$$

After computing the covariation for all the data pairs in the sample, you would divide by the number of data pairs to get the average covariation.

Essentially, the correlation coefficient provides a measure of the degree to which two sets of data covary. In particular, the correlation coefficient is based on the covariation of the two variables, standardized by dividing the covariation by a value based on the variances for the individual samples. The following formula is generally used to compute the correlation coefficient between two data sets, x and y, where each value in x has a corresponding value in y. Using the formula is computationally more efficient than computing the difference between each value and its mean.

$$r = \frac{N * \sum_1^N x_i * y_i - \sum_1^N x_i * \sum_1^N y_i}{\sqrt{(N * \sum_1^N x_i^2 - (\sum_1^N x_i)^2) * (N * \sum_1^N y_i^2 - (\sum_1^N y_i)^2)}}$$

In the formula, N is the size of each sample, that is, the number of value pairs used in the computation. The x_i and the y_i represent the ith score in the first and the second data set, respectively.

Because of the standardization, the correlation coefficient is always between -1.0 and 1.0. Values near the extremes represent high correlations; values near 0.0 represent low or nonexistent correlations. A correlation coefficient near -1.0 indicates a strong *inverse* relationship; that is, large values on one variable tend to be associated with small values in the other variable.

The following program lets you enter data and then compute the correlation coefficient:

```
/* Program to compute correlation coefficient */

#include <stdio.h>
#include <stdlib.h>
#include <string.h>
#include <math.h>

#define MAX_STR      100
#define MAX_VALS     50
```

```
int       get_data ( double vals []);
double    sum_vals ( double vals [], int nr_vals);
double    var_term ( double vals [], int nr_vals);
double    correl ( double vals1 [], double vals2 [], int size);
double    cov ( double vals1 [], double vals2 [], int nr_vals);


char      *null_str = "";
double    d_vals [ MAX_VALS];
double    c_vals [ MAX_VALS];


main ()
{
        int     n1, n2;
        double  coeff;

        printf ( "Enter values for group 1.\n");
        n1 = get_data ( c_vals);

        printf ( "Enter values for group 2.\n");
        n2 = get_data ( d_vals);

        if ( n1 = n2)
                coeff = correl ( c_vals, d_vals, n1);
        else
                printf ( "Arrays must be the same size.\n");
}


/* compute the sum of an array of values */
double sum_vals ( double vals [], int nr_vals)
{
        int     index;
        double temp = 0.0;

        for ( index = 0; index < nr_vals; index++)
                temp += vals [ index];

        return ( temp);
}


/* get values for an array from user */
int get_data ( double vals [])
{
        int    index = 0;
        char   info [ MAX_STR];

        printf  ( "? ");
        gets ( info);
```

```
        while ( strcmp ( info, null_str))
        {
                vals [ index++] = atof ( info);
                printf  ( "? ");
                gets ( info);
        }
        return ( index);
}


/* compute the variance term used when computing correlation
   coefficient.
   NOTE: This value is the sum of all the squared deviation terms,
         NOT the average covariance.
*/
double var_term ( double vals [], int nr_vals)
{
        double temp = 0.0;
        int     index;

        for ( index = 0; index < nr_vals; index++)
                temp += vals [ index] * vals [ index];

        return ( temp);
}


/* Compute the covariance term used when computing correlation
   coefficient.
   NOTE: This value is the sum of all the covariance terms, NOT
         the average covariance.
*/
double cov ( double vals1 [],  double vals2 [], int nr_vals)
{
        double temp = 0.0;
        int     index;

        for ( index = 0; index < nr_vals; index++)
                temp += vals1 [ index] * vals2 [ index];

        return ( temp);
}


/* compute the correlation coefficient between two sets of values */
double correl ( double vals1 [], double vals2 [], int nr_vals)
{
        double   sum1, sum2, co_vari, var1, var2;
        double   coeff, numer, denom;
```

```
sum1 = sum_vals ( c_vals, nr_vals);
sum2 = sum_vals ( d_vals, nr_vals);

co_vari = cov ( c_vals, d_vals, nr_vals);
co_vari *= nr_vals;

numer = co_vari - ( sum1 * sum2);

var1 = var_term ( vals1, nr_vals) * nr_vals;
var2 = var_term ( vals2, nr_vals) * nr_vals;

denom = ( var1 - sum1 * sum1) * ( var2 - sum2 * sum2);
denom = sqrt ( denom);

coeff = numer / denom;
printf ( "r == %7.3lf\n", coeff);
return ( coeff);
}
```

correl( )

This function returns a correlation coefficient, given two arrays containing the first and second data sets and information about the number of data pairs.

With this function, you can test whether your guesses regarding relationships in the data for oceans and seas were correct. If you compute the correlation coefficients, you should find that the correlation between area and maximum depth for oceans and seas is about 0.825, which is quite close to 1.0. The correlation between the same variables for lakes is only 0.207— close enough to 0.0 to suggest that there is no relationship between area and maximum depth of lakes.

The correlation coefficient assumes that the relationship between the two variables is linear; so it is possible to actually try to predict the value of one variable once you know the other. In a later section, you'll learn about a technique for doing this.

You may want to add the functions for computing a correlation coefficient to the exerciser program. If you do this, keep in mind that the paired values used when computing the correlation coefficient cannot simply be arbitrary pairs. In particular, do *not* sort your arrays before computing a correlation coefficient. Generally, the values will represent two different pieces of information about the same body of water, person, or whatever else you are examining. If you sorted the arrays for lakes, the values for any one body of water would no longer correspond, and there would be no way for the **correl( )** function to know which values to pair up.

It's important to keep in mind that the correlation coefficient tells you only whether there is a relationship between two variables; it tells you nothing about the nature of this relationship. In particular, it does not tell you whether the value of one variable causes the other variable to have a particular value. For example, just because the areas and the maximum depths of oceans and seas are correlated does not allow you to claim that a large area "causes" a deep body of water, or vice versa. Don't be tempted to draw such causal conclusions.

USING STATISTICS TO MAKE DECISIONS

The discussion and the functions so far have concerned the use of statistics — the mean, the standard deviation, and the median — to summarize or characterize a collection of information. Statistics are also used to draw inferences about these values and to provide measures indicating the confidence with which we can draw various conclusions.

In this section, you'll find routines for doing *inferential statistics*. You'll run tests on your sample values to determine whether certain conclusions are warranted or how likely it is that the values you obtained came from a distribution with certain properties. In such cases, you'll be drawing inferences, based on your sample information, about the larger population of values from which the sample was drawn.

Some terminology will be useful here: A *sample* is a collection of data values obtained or generated by some means; a *population* is the larger collection of values from which a sample is taken. In some cases, a population may consist of a finite number of values, such as every person on Earth or all the stars in the Milky Way galaxy. In other cases, a population will be a theoretical distribution, such as a normal distribution with a particular mean and standard deviation or a Poisson distribution with a particular mean.

The task of inferential statistics is to enable you to make inferences about populations based on the samples you draw from them. For example, a public opinion poll, such as the Gallup poll, collects data from a sample representative of the population of registered voters. Using the sample results, you can try to infer the likely voting patterns of the larger population from which the sample was drawn.

A second task of inferential statistics is to draw conclusions about samples based on the populations from which the samples have supposedly been derived. For example, you would use inferential statistics to estimate the probability that the sample of coin tosses in which you got 650 heads and 350 tails actually used a fair coin, that is, one whose tosses came from a binomial distribution with a hit rate of 0.5.

Values such as the mean, the standard deviation, and the median are known as *statistics* when they are based on data from a sample; they are known as *parameters* when they refer to population characteristics.

Let's return to the light bulb manufacturing plant from Chapter 9. Suppose the plant produces bulbs with an average lifetime of 50.0 hours and a standard deviation of 10.0 hours. Years of experience have convinced you that bulb lifetime is normally distributed with the stated mean and standard deviation.

Now, suppose you've developed a new manufacturing technique that is expected to increase the lifetime of a light bulb. You manufacture a batch of such bulbs and select a sample of 100 bulbs. Suppose the mean lifetime ($\bar{x}$) of the bulbs is actually 52.5, and the sample standard deviation (s) is 11.5.

You might ask how likely you are to get the statistics you computed for your sample bulbs if there were really no difference between the batch manufactured with your new process and the batches made with the traditional process. This amounts to asking how likely it is that you would generate a random sample as deviant as the one observed if you were selecting at random from the usual bulb batches.

It turns out that the probability of this happening by chance is less than 0.01; that is, there is less than one chance in 100 that you would select such a sample at random from the normal distribution under consideration. Thus, you would probably conclude that there was something different about the batch from which your sample was taken.

The z Test: A Simple Example of Hypothesis Testing

When you try to answer questions about possible differences between your sample and a population, you need to formulate your questions precisely so that you will know what values you need to test. In inferential statistics, your "question" generally takes the form of two competing hypotheses.

The first hypothesis generally states that your sample values are not unusual in any way. This is known as the *null hypothesis*, and is generally denoted by H_0. For the bulb example, the null hypothesis says essentially that there's nothing special about your new bulbs.

The alternative hypothesis generally states that your sample values are different from the usual batches. Thus, the alternative hypothesis for the example might say that the batch from which your sample was selected has a longer lifetime than the usual bulbs.

Let's see how to use inferential statistics to select between these two competing hypotheses. In Chapter 9, you saw that one way to evaluate the likelihood of something was to simulate the situation by generating lots of random samples having the desired characteristics and then see how many of the outcomes had the properties whose likelihood you were testing.

In this case, that would mean generating lots of 100-element samples of bulbs from the usual batches. You could then graph the distribution of the means obtained in these simulations. Such a distribution of summary statistics from many samples is called a sampling distribution. It consists of summary statistics (in this case, means), rather than raw scores.

By seeing where in the distribution your observed mean is found, you could estimate the probability of getting such a result by chance. Earlier, you saw that a value from a unit normal distribution could be interpreted as indicating the number of standard deviations the value was removed from the mean; thus, a value of 1.5 was 1.5 standard deviations above the mean.

You can always "standardize" a score from any normal distribution by using the following formula to convert a value from an arbitrary normal distribution to a score from the unit, or standard, normal distribution having $\mu = 0.0$ and $\sigma = 1.0$:

$$standardized\ value = \frac{(score - \mu)}{\sigma}$$

μ is the mean of the distribution from which the sample was drawn, and σ is the standard deviation for this population.

Such standardized scores for a normal distribution are generally known as *normal deviates*, or *z scores;* you'll often see a *z* used to represent such a value. This formula transforms the value to one from a normal distribution with mean of 0.0 and standard deviation of 1.0. If you work out the algebra, you'll see that the preceding formula is just the inverse of the one used to generate a normal value with a particular mean and standard deviation in **gauss_fn( )**. The formula in that function is

$$new\ value = \mu + (standardized\ value) * \sigma$$

In the bulb problem, the conversion formula would have the following form:

$$standardized\ value = \frac{(52.5 - 50)}{\sigma}$$

Although you know the standard deviation for the distribution of bulb lifetimes (10.0), you don't know the standard deviation for the *sampling* distribution of sample means. (Although we won't go into detail here, it turns out that there is a formula for this standard deviation.) For a case such as our problem—large sample (over 30), known population parameters—the standard deviation for the sampling distribution is given by

$$\frac{\sigma}{\sqrt{N}}$$

where σ is the standard deviation for the distribution of bulb lifetimes and N is the sample size. Thus, in our case, the standard deviation for the sampling distribution is 1.0. Compare this with the standard deviation you get if you run a few hundred samples of size 100, graphing the resulting sampling distribution.

After carrying out the computations, you'll find that the standardized value for the bulb experiment is

$$\frac{(52.5 - 50.0)}{1.0} = \frac{2.5}{1.0} = 2.5$$

The result, 2.5, can be interpreted as the number of standard deviations the value is from the mean.

Table 10-1 provides a list of the probabilities associated with a range of *z values*, which represent the number of standard deviations a value is from the mean. For example, $z = -2.5$ means the value is 2.5 standard deviations *below* the mean. The probability represents the proportion of values in a normal distribution with a smaller or equal z score. For more extensive information, check a statistics book with a table of z values. This table will tell you the probability of getting a value as large as that or larger by chance.

For the example, you'll find that the probability is actually about 0.006 of getting a z score of 2.50 or greater. Because the probability of getting such a value from a usual bulb population is

Table 10-1.   Probabilities for Selected z Values

z	Probability
-3.0	.001
-2.5	.006
-2.0	.023
-1.75	.040
-1.5	.067
-1.25	.106
-1.0	.159
$-.75$	.227
$-.5$	.308
$-.25$	.401
0.0	.500
$.25$	.599
$.5$	.692
$.75$	.773
1.0	.841
1.25	.894
1.5	.933
1.75	.960
2.0	.977
2.5	.994
3.0	.999

so small, it seems reasonable to reject the null hypothesis that the sample actually came from the usual population. The cutoff probability for rejecting the null hypothesis is not fixed. One common cutoff probability is 0.05; that is, if the probability of getting such a value is less than 0.05—less than one chance in 20—then you reject H_0.

Congratulations! You've just run your first inferential statistical test in this chapter. This test is generally known as a z *test*. The conditions under which a z test is appropriate include the following:

- You want to compare a sample mean against a population mean.

- You know the population mean and standard deviation.

- You can assume the population has a normal distribution.

If these conditions are met, you can compute a *z* score using the standardization formula along with the formula for the standard deviation of a sampling distribution:

$$z\ score = \frac{(\bar{x} - \mu)}{\sigma/\sqrt{N}}$$

The following function, **z—score( )**, computes and returns a *z* score, given the sample mean, the population mean, and the population standard deviation.

```
/* Function to compute a z-score, or normal deviate */
double z_score ( double smpl_mean, double pop_mean,
                 double pop_sd, int size)
{
        double temp;

        temp = (smpl_mean - pop_mean) / pop_sd * sqrt ( size);
        return ( temp);
}
```

Comparing Two Samples with Each Other

Sometimes you may have two *samples* that you want to compare with each other, rather than with a population. In such cases, you will essentially be asking how likely it is that both the samples were drawn from the same population.

For example, suppose you have a new strain of tomato that you think will produce more abundantly than another strain. To test this, you might select several fields at random, planting the new strain of tomato in some rows and the tomato strain usually planted in other rows. It's important that field-selection and row-assignment decisions be made at random—to avoid bias due to differences in soil quality, climate, and so forth. The new strain will be the experimental tomatoes, and the rows planted with this strain will be the experimental rows. The other, usual strain will be the control strain, and it will be planted in the control rows.

To test your expectation, you need to formulate your hypotheses, collect your data, compute the appropriate statistics, evaluate the results, and formulate your conclusions. The null hypothesis will essentially state that there is no reason to conclude that the tomato strains are different; that is, H_0 assumes both strains of tomato come from the same population. The alternate hypothesis would state that, based on the yields of the two strains you're comparing, you can conclude that the experimental strain most likely is a different tomato than the control strain and that the experimental strain will produce a greater yield than the control strain. Both hypotheses would concern the mean yield of the strains.

The test used to evaluate the competing hypotheses when comparing two samples is called a *t test*. There are actually several versions of the t test, each intended for somewhat different situations. The distributions for evaluating the results from *t* tests were first published by William S. Gosset in 1908. Gosset was a chemist and, later, brewmaster for the Guinness Brewing Company. Because of company restrictions, he was not allowed to publish the results under his own name; he published them under the name "Student." The distribution is often known as *Student's t distribution*.

The *t* test assumes that your values are independent of each other and that the values come from a random sample. You should also have grounds for assuming that your data come from a population that is normally distributed.

As with the *z* test, the strategy for the *t* test will be to compute a difference between means and standardize it on the basis of some measure of spread. In this case, the difference is between the means for the two samples. The measure of spread is more complex and is based on the variances of the two samples.

Suppose you had 60 experimental rows and 40 control rows, with the following statistics:

Experimental rows: $\bar{x} = 58.6$ pounds per row; $s = 8.2$ pounds

Control rows: $\bar{x} = 53.4$ pounds per row; $s = 10.9$ pounds

The following formula allows you to compute a t score for this problem:

$$ t = \frac{(\overline{x}_1 - \overline{x}_2)}{\sqrt{\frac{s_1^2}{n_1} + \frac{s_2^2}{n_2}}} $$

In the formula, $\overline{x}_1$ and $\overline{x}_2$ are the means of the experimental and control samples, respectively. Similarly, s_1^2 and s_1^2 are the variances for these two samples. (Recall that the variance is simply the square of the standard deviation.)

To determine whether you have grounds for rejecting the null hypothesis, you need to check the probability of getting, simply by chance, a t score as extreme as the one you got. In the example, the t score is 2.57.

The actual cutoff values for the t distribution depend essentially on the size of the smaller sample. This parameter is again called the degrees of freedom. As with the chi-square test in Chapter 8, the critical t values will differ for the same probability, depending on the degrees of freedom. The degrees of freedom for this test would be one less than the smaller sample size—that is, 39.

For reasons we won't go into here, the regular z score for a normal distribution provides a good estimate of the critical t values when you have more than 30 degrees of freedom. Thus, you can simply find the probability corresponding to a z score of 2.57 in a table of normal deviates, such as Table 10-2, for a small number of z scores. The resulting probability turns out to be about 0.005; that is, there are about 5 chances in 1000 that you would get a mean so much larger than the control sample mean just by chance if the samples came from the same population. Again, this result is unlikely enough so that you can reject the null hypothesis.

For samples smaller than about 30, you'll need to look up the critical t value in Table 10-2 or in a more extensive table in a statistics book. To use Table 10-2:

1. Find the highest number of degrees of freedom less than or equal to your degrees of freedom.

2. Find the largest *t* value less than or equal to your *t* value.

3. The probability associated with this critical *t* represents the probability of getting a *t* value greater than or equal to your *t* value.

The following function computes and returns a *t* value, given the sample statistics you pass in:

```
/* Function to compute a t-score */
double t_score ( double mean1, double mean2,
                 double sd1, double sd2, int size1, int size2)
{
        double temp, numer, denom;

        numer = mean1 - mean2;
        denom = sqrt ( sd1 * sd1 / size1 + sd2 * sd2 / size2);
        temp = numer / denom;
        return ( temp);
}
```

Table 10-2.   Selected Critical Values for *t* Statistic

df	Probabilities			
	.01	.025	.05	.1
5	3.36	2.57	2.02	1.48
10	2.76	2.23	1.81	1.37
15	2.60	2.13	1.75	1.34
20	2.53	2.09	1.72	1.32
25	2.48	2.06	1.71	1.32
30	2.46	2.04	1.70	1.31

Tossing Coins Revisited: Testing Proportions

The z and t tests are for comparing the means of two samples or of a sample and a population. There are also tests for comparing proportions.

In Chapter 9, you ran some simulations to determine the probability of getting some small number of heads with a balanced coin. By generating lots of samples of the desired size and counting the number of heads in each sample, you were able to generate a binomial distribution of relative frequencies with which a particular number of heads occurred.

There are tests to help you decide how likely the observed number of hits is in a task with two possible outcomes, hit or miss. Such tests generally rely on a table whose values depend on the probability of a hit, the sample size, and the number of hits you want to test.

However, if your samples are larger than 100, you can actually use formulas that will give you a z score. For example, to test whether a sample of 200 coin tosses was made with a fair coin— that is, proportion of hits (heads) = proportion of misses (tails) = 0.5—compute a z score by starting with the following formula and taking the square root of the resulting z^2 value. The $|hits - misses|$ indicates the absolute value of that difference.

$$z^2 = \frac{(|hits - misses| - 1)^2}{tosses}$$

The basic strategy is to get a standardized measure of the difference between hits and misses. The larger this difference, the greater the proportion of one or the other side.

For example, to decide between the null hypothesis that the coin is unbiased and the alternative hypothesis that it is biased,

generate a sample of coin tosses, count the number of heads and
tails, and compute a z score using the following function:

```
/* Function to compute a z-score as approximation to binomial value.
   This version assumes p (hit) = 0.5; > 100 trials.
*/
double z_binom ( int hits, int trials)
{
        double temp;
        int    misses;

        misses = trials - hits;
        temp = ((double) (ABS_VAL ( hits - misses)) - 1);
        printf ("top temp = %7.3lf\n", temp);
        temp = temp * temp / trials;
        return ( sqrt ( temp));
}
```

Once you've computed a z score, you can look up this value in your
table to determine how likely your result was.

For smaller samples, or for samples where you're testing
whether the proportion of hits will be something other than 0.5,
you need to modify the preceding formula somewhat. This modified formula will work with samples of 10 or more, provided that
the expected numbers of both hits and misses are at least 5.

The cases that are likely to run afoul of this requirement are
small samples and large proportions. For example, if you have a
sample of size 10 and you think the population hit rate is 0.6, you
won't have large-enough expected values in both cells (6 in one
cell, but only 4 in the other). Similarly, even if you have a sample
of size 200, you may run into problems trying to test whether your
sample comes from a population with a hit rate of 0.98, since you
would expect only 4 misses in such a sample.

To compute a z score, you need information about the expected
values for hits and misses. We'll use e_h and e_m to refer to these two
expected values, respectively, and use the information in the
formula:

$$z^2 = \frac{tosses * (|hits - e_h| - .5)^2}{e_h * e_m}$$

The following function accomplishes this modified computation.
The function will compute the expected values for you.

```
/* Function to compute a z-score as approximation to binomial value.
   This version assumes each expected value >= 5.
*/
double z_binom2 ( int hits, int trials, double p_hit)
{
        double temp, e_hit, e_miss, numer, denom;

        e_hit = trials * p_hit;
        e_miss = trials - e_hit;
        printf ( "ehit = %7.3lf; emiss = %7.3lf\n", e_hit, e_miss);
        denom = e_hit * e_miss;
        temp = ((ABS_VAL ( hits - e_hit)) - .5);
        printf ("top temp = %7.3lf\n", temp);
        temp = trials * temp * temp;
        return ( sqrt ( temp / denom));
}
```

There are numerous other tests for this and similar types of problems involving means or proportions and even measures of spread. An excellent book that includes many statistical tests and very clear guidelines on when and how to use them is Richard Darlington's *Radicals and Squares* (Ithaca, N.Y.: Logan Hill Press, 1975).

USING STATISTICS TO FIT MODELS TO DATA

Suppose you have the following set of math and verbal aptitude test scores for a sample of students:

Student	Math	Verbal
1	765	720
2	695	733
3	680	625
4	660	580
5	650	660
6	625	735
7	615	650
8	600	570
9	580	610
10	550	550
11	535	585
12	535	600
13	520	500
14	480	460
15	460	580

The correlation between the two values is 0.754 for this sample. This indicates that there is, on the whole, a linear relationship between these two variables. The correlation coefficient does not tell you very much about the details of that relationship, however.

There is a technique that you can use to find out more about the nature of the relationship indicated by the correlation. This technique, called *linear regression*, lets you compute the two coefficients you need to define a line that relates one variable, *y*, to another variable, *x*. Recall from algebra that the formula for a line is

$$y = a + bx$$

where *a* is the value of *y* when *x* = 0. The coefficient *a* is generally known as the *intercept*. The *b* in the formula determines how "steep" the line is—that is, how large the change in *y* will be for a one-unit change in *x*. This coefficient is called the *slope* of the line.

Such lines are graphed on the two-dimensional coordinate system that you learned about in algebra. Notice in Figure 10-1 that the *y* value is represented on the vertical axis and the *x* value is on the horizontal axis. Positive values are at the top and to the right for *y* and *x*, respectively.

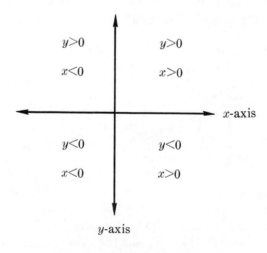

Figure 10-1.   A two-dimensional coordinate system

For example, if $y = 3 + x$, the intercept is 3 and the slope is 1 (which is implicit when there is no coefficient for x in such a formula). This means that increasing x by 1 would increase y by 1. Had the slope been 2—that is, had the formula been $y = 3 + 2*x$—each unit change in x would change y by 2.

When the slope is positive, the line goes up and to the right. This means large values of x are associated with large values of y. If the slope is negative, the line goes *down* and to the right. This means that large values of x are associated with *small* values of y.

Linear regression will provide a formula for such a line relating the two variables. Keep in mind that, since the relationship is not perfect in most cases, any formula you derive will provide only an estimate. For example, if you use x to refer to math scores, then the formula would let you predict a person's verbal score (y) given that person's math score. There will generally be some difference between the predicted value and the actual score; this difference, or deviation, is essentially error for your data.

There are several criteria you can use to select the "best" estimate, that is, the estimate that produces the smallest errors. A common criterion is one that minimizes the *square* of the deviations between predicted and actual values. Not surprisingly, this is known as the *least squares criterion*.

The slope coefficient is based on both the covariation between x and y and the variance of the x values. More specifically, to compute the slope, compute the covariance using a formula such as the following, and then compute the variance for x:

$$covariance_{xy} = \frac{\sum_{i=1}^{N} x_i * y_i}{N} - mean_x * mean_y$$

For reasons we won't go into here, you need to divide by n, rather than by $n - 1$, when computing the variance for x. To compute this value if you've already computed the standard deviation using the $n - 1$ divisor, just multiply the standard deviation by the term $(n - 1) / n$.

Once you have both the covariance and the variance, divide the former by the latter. This gives you the slope of the regression line for your sample data.

$$slope_{xy} = \frac{covariance_{xy}}{variance_x}$$

The intercept for the regression line is given by

$$intercept_{xy} = mean_y - slope * mean_x$$

The following function computes the coefficients for a regression line, given two arrays containing the values and the number of pairs of values:

```
/* Compute regression line slope and intercept. */
void regress ( double vals1 [], double vals2 [], int size,
               double *intercept, double *slope)
{
        double covar, var1, sum = 0.0, mean1, mean2;
        int    index;

    /* compute means */
        for ( index = 0; index < size; index++)
                sum += vals1 [ index];
        mean1 = sum / size;
        printf ( "mean1 = %7.3lf\n", mean1);

        sum = 0.0;
        for ( index = 0; index < size; index++)
                sum += vals2 [ index];
        mean2 = sum / size;
        printf ( "mean2 = %7.3lf\n", mean2);

    /* compute covariance */
        covar = cov ( vals1, vals2, size);
        printf ( "raw covariance = %7.3lf\n", covar);
        covar /= size;
        covar -= mean1 * mean2;

    /* compute variance */
        var1 = var_term ( vals1, size);
        printf ( "raw variance = %7.3lf\n", var1);
        var1 /= size;
        var1 -= mean1 * mean1;
        printf ("covar = %7.3lf; var_x = %7.3lf\n",
                covar, var1);

        *slope = covar / var1;
        printf ( "slope = %7.3lf\n", *slope);

        *intercept =  mean2 - *slope * mean1;
        printf ( "intercept = %7.3lf\n", *intercept);
}
```

regress( )

This function computes the intercept and the slope for a regression line that summarizes the relationship between two variables. The values for the variables are passed in two arrays. The function also needs to know the number of values in each array.

After doing its work, **regress( )** passes the intercept and the slope back in the fourth and fifth arguments, respectively.

If you call **regress( )** with the test values from earlier in this chapter, you get an intercept of 187.363 and a slope of 0.709 for the regression line. You can then use this formula to predict the verbal score of a person if you know the person's math score. To do this, use the formula

$$\hat{y}_i = intercept + slope * x_i$$

The predicted value, $\hat{y}_i$, is your best guess, given the formula you created based on the original sample data.

The following function returns the predicted y value, given an intercept, a slope, and an x value:

```
/* predict a new y-value based on the x-value and
   the coefficients for the regression equation.
*/
double predict ( double intercept, double slope, double val)
{
        return ( intercept + slope * val);
}
```

Suppose you had a person whose math score was 655. What would be the predicted verbal score for this person? If you use **predict( )**, the function returns 651.76 as the predicted verbal score.

We've just looked at a few simple examples involving linear regression. If you need to compute regression equations for an actual application or client, you'll need more than the routines developed in this section. To find out more about the conditions and restrictions for using the technique, to get more information related to the regression line (such as a measure of prediction error), and for extensions to the linear regression model you used here, check a statistics book.

EVALUATING SAMPLE DISTRIBUTIONS

In the nineteenth century, Gregor Mendel, an Austrian monk, grew some peas to study the distribution of characteristics in the peas over several generations. In his work, Mendel crossed seeds from peas having particular characteristics to observe the frequency with which these characteristics would show up in successive generations. Such crosses are known as hybrids.

For example, Mendel crossed plants having green seeds with those having yellow seeds. The first generation all had yellow seeds. In the second generation, however, one-fourth of the plants had green seeds. Similarly, plants with round seeds were crossed with those that had wrinkled seeds. The first hybrid generation all had round seeds, but in the next generation, one-fourth of the plants had wrinkled seeds.

Mendel then crossed plants with round, yellow seeds and plants with wrinkled, green seeds. The first-hybrid-generation plants all had round, yellow seeds. In the second generation, Mendel got the following distribution of 556 plants:

315 plants with round, yellow seeds

101 plants with wrinkled, yellow seeds

108 plants with round, green seeds

32 plants with wrinkled, green seeds

For reasons we won't go into here, Mendel expected a distribution ratio of 9:3:3:1 for the four categories of plants; that is, he expected 9 plants with round, yellow seeds to every 3 plants with wrinkled, yellow seeds, and so forth.

How well did Mendel's data fit his expected distribution? In Chapter 8, you computed a chi-square statistic to determine whether the random values you had generated fit a uniform distribution well enough for you to be confident that the values were generated at random from such a distribution.

That test was actually a special case of a chi-square *goodness of fit test.* You can compute a chi-square value for any distribution of values, provided you have a means of specifying the expected values or the expected proportion of values in each cell.

For example, to test Mendel's data using a chi-square value, you need to specify expected values for four cells. The first cell should contain 56.25% of the scores (9 / (9+3+3+1)), the second and third cells should each contain 18.75% of the scores, and the fourth cell should have 6.25% of the scores.

Thus, Mendel's four groups should have the following expected frequencies in the four cells:

556 (total plants) * 0.5625 = 312.75 plants

556 (total plants) * 0.1875 = 104.25 plants

556 (total plants) * 0.1875 = 104.25 plants

556 (total plants) * 0.0625 = 34.75 plants

The chi-square value for Mendel's results is 0.470, computed using the formula shown in Chapter 8:

$$\frac{(315 - 312.75)^2}{312.75} + \frac{(101 - 104.25)^2}{104.25} + \frac{(108 - 104.25)^2}{104.25} + \frac{(32 - 34.75)^2}{34.75} = 0.470$$

There are only three degrees of freedom for this value, since there are only four cells. The probability of getting a chi-square of this size by chance from a distribution having the specified expected frequencies is between 0.05 and 0.10. As shown earlier, extreme probabilities are suspicious. If you get a chi-square larger than the critical value for a 0.95-or-so probability, your results are too different from the expected distribution to allow you to conclude that the data came from such a distribution. If the value is *smaller* than the cutoff value for a probability of 0.05, then you should also be suspicious, because the data may be too good.

Since the observed chi-square value lies between these extremes, there is moderate support for Mendel's expectation that the data came from a 9:3:3:1 distribution.

Actually, in computing a chi-square value, looking up a probability, and deciding what conclusion to draw, you tested a hypothesis, just as you did earlier when doing z and t tests. The null hypothesis was that the data came from the specified distribution; the alternative hypothesis said that the data were more likely to be from a different distribution. In this case, you should reject the alternative hypothesis if your observed probability lay between 0.05 and 0.95. If you want to be more stringent in accepting that the data fit a distribution, you might move the cutoff probabilities inward—to 0.10 and 0.90, for example.

You can compute a chi-square statistic for any sample of values, provided you can specify intervals and expected values for those intervals. Sometimes, these expected values can be computed; at other times, you simply need to specify them cell by cell. For the modified chi-square test to be developed here, we'll assume the required expected-value information is available in a file.

The following function reads values from a file into an array. The values should represent the expected proportion of values for the interval having the same index as the cell. For example, you would have put the values 0.5625, 0.1875, 0.1875, and 0.0625 into a file for Mendel's data. These values would be used to help compute the expected frequencies.

```
/* read values from specified file, convert to double, and
   store in specified array.
*/
int f_get_data ( char *name, double vals [])
{
        int    count = 0;
        char   info [ MAX_STR];
        FILE   *fp;

        fp = fopen ( name, "r");
        if ( fp != NULL)
        {
                while ( !feof ( fp))
                {
                        fgets ( info, MAX_STR, fp);
                        if ( !feof ( fp))
                                vals [ count++] = atof ( info);
                }
        }
        fclose ( fp);
        return ( count);
}
```

f—get—data( )

This function reads values from a file into an array of **double**. You must provide the name of the file—which must not be open—and the name of the array into which the function is to write the values. The function will open the file, read the values, and store them in the array. The function returns the number of values read as an **int**.

Once you have an array of frequencies and an array of expected proportions, you can compute a chi-square statistic using the following function:

```
/* compute a chi-square value to estimate the goodness of fit
   between the observed grouping values and the expected groupings
   based on a theoretical distribution.
*/
double good_fit ( int group [], double wts [],
                  int size, int trials)
{
        int     index;
        double expected, deviation, last_size, sum = 0.0;

        for ( index = 0; index < size; index++)
        {
                expected = trials * wts [ index];
                printf ( "%d: expected = %7.4lf\n", index, expected);
                deviation = group [ index] - expected;
                sum += deviation * deviation / expected;
                /* printf ( "%d: dev == %.4lf; sum == %.4lf\n",
                        index, deviation, sum); */
        }

        /* for last, smaller, interval */
        /*
        last_size = range - ( nr_intervals - 1) * size;
        expected = ( (double) trials * last_size) / range;
        deviation = group [ nr_intervals - 1] - expected;
        sum += deviation * deviation / expected;
        */

        printf ( "\n\nchi-square for %d intervals == %7.4lf\n",
                size, sum);
        return ( sum);
}
```

good—fit( )

This function computes a chi-square value for a goodness of fit test. The function has four parameters: array of frequencies, array of expected proportions for each interval, total number of values and number of intervals. The function returns the computed chi-square as a **double**.

Once you have the chi-square for your goodness of fit test, you can use the **cutoffs( )** and **show‾probability( )** routines from Chapter 8 to tell you more.

Tasks and Suggestions

Develop functions for displaying a graph of data pairs, such as those used to compute correlation coefficients. On the horizontal axis you might put the x value, with the y value on the vertical axis. One way of making this more manageable is to standardize all values so that each value is expressed as a value between 0.0 and 1.0. These endpoints would be defined by the maximum and minimum values for the sample on that variable.

SUMMARY

In this chapter, you learned about some common statistical methods for describing and analyzing data. These included techniques for computing measures of central tendency and spread, routines for running various statistical tests, and functions for describing the relationship between two variables, based on sample values for the variables.

This chapter used functions and concepts developed in chapters 8 and 9. Together, the three chapters provide a handy collection of routines for simulating phenomena and then analyzing the results of those simulations. However, this collection is very simple and quite minimal; there is much more that could be said about the topics in each of these chapters. If you plan to do serious work in this area, you will need to consult other sources and develop additional routines.

11

GRAPHS

If you fly, you've probably seen the map in the magazine on board, showing all the cities between which the airline flies. Such a picture can be viewed as a *graph*, and an example is shown in Figure 11-1.

The graph consists of cities (dots) and routes (edges). Cities between which the airline flies have routes connecting them. Not all cities are on the routes flown by the airline; so some dots have no edges coming off them. Some cities are connected, but not by nonstop flights; for example, you might have to fly from Boston to Chicago and then on to Minneapolis, rather than being able to fly directly from Boston to Minneapolis. On the other hand, all routes go somewhere; thus, all edges connect two dots.

This type of map simply shows whether or not there is a route between two cities. You might also see a similar map for people enrolled in a frequent flyer program, as in Figure 11-2. This map shows the mileage between cities served by the airline.

There can be a large number of cities on such a map. For large airlines with lots of routes, the map will be filled with many connections between cities. Small airlines, with just a few flight routes, will have relatively few connections on the map. The graph of flights for such an airline will look quite sparse compared to the flights for a large airline.

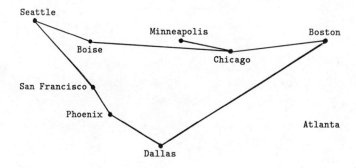

Figure 11-1.   A simple airline route collection summarized as a graph

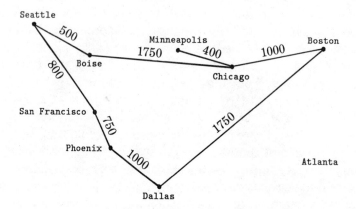

Figure 11-2.   A simple airline distance collection as a weighted graph

SOME GRAPHIC TERMS

A graph is nothing more than a collection of dots and edges that connect pairs of dots. The dots are known as *nodes*, or *vertices*, and the edges are known as *arcs*.

With such a simple definition for a graph, it shouldn't be surprising that you can come up with lots of variants on the basic idea of dots and edges. For example, a graph that not only shows air routes but also the mileage between cities on the route is a *weighted graph*, since the edges are marked, or "weighted," by the distance between the cities. On the other hand, a map that just shows whether there is a flight between two cities is an *unweighted graph*, since each edge has the same "weight."

In maps of airline routes, you generally take it for granted that you can fly in either direction; that is, you assume that the existence of a route between A and B means you can fly from A to B as well as from B to A. There are situations where this might not be the case, however. For example, consider a graph of the delivery routes for a West Coast strawberry farm. The farm may deliver strawberries to major cities in the Midwest and in the East; it is unlikely, however, that strawberries would be shipped *to* the West. In a graph of strawberry delivery routes, direction matters.

A graph in which you can assume that a connection (edge) means you can move in either direction (such as a graph of airline routes) is an *undirected graph*. A graph in which you need to specify the direction of a connection is a *directed graph*, or digraph.

There are lots of ways in which two nodes in a graph can be connected to each other. If there is a single edge between them, the nodes are *adjacent* to each other. Thus, all nonstop flights are between adjacent cities. When two nodes are adjacent, the edge connecting them is said to be *incident* to each of the nodes.

Two nodes might also be connected by a sequence of edges, with each edge connecting two intermediate nodes. When this is the case, there is a *path* of a particular length connecting the nodes. The path's length is the number of edges you need to follow to get from the starting node to the target. For example, Boston and Minneapolis are connected, but only via Chicago; because it would take two flights to get from Boston to Minneapolis, the two cities have path of length 2 between them. Cities connected by nonstop routes have paths of length 1.

It's a good idea to get in the habit of thinking of nodes in terms of being adjacent or having a path between them, rather than in terms of being connected. The term *connected* has a special meaning in relation to graphs: A graph is connected if there is a path between every pair of nodes in a graph—that is, if you can always "get there from here," no matter where in your graph "here" and "there" are. For example, each of the graphs in Figures 11-3*a* and 11-3*b* is connected; the graph in Figure 11-3*c* is not, because there is no path between the nodes on the left and those on the right. Similarly, Figure 11-3*d* is not connected, because node C is not adjacent to any other node.

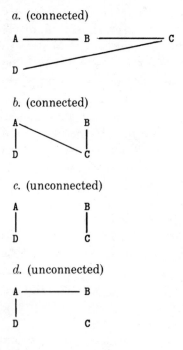

a. (connected)

b. (connected)

c. (unconnected)

d. (unconnected)

Figure 11-3.   Examples of connected and unconnected graphs

If every node in your graph is *adjacent* to every other node, then the graph is *complete*, as in Figure 11-4. In a complete graph of airline routes, you would have a nonstop route between any two cities on the map.

Sometimes you can find a route that starts in one city, continues through several others, and returns to the starting city by a different route. For example, you might go from Boston to Chicago to Boise to Seattle to San Francisco to Phoenix to Dallas to Boston. This is essentially a (restricted) path from a city to itself. Such a path is known as a *cycle*. In a cycle, you cannot repeat any flight between two intermediate cities, regardless of direction. This restriction is what makes a cycle's path a true "round" trip, as opposed to a trip that merely returns by flying back through some of the same cities in the other direction.

Not all graphs have cycles in them. If a graph has no cycles, the graph is said to be *acyclic*. You've already seen some examples of acyclic graphs: linked lists and trees. These structures are simply collections of nodes connected by pointers (edges)—that is, they are graphs. You can also create a cyclic list structure. A *circular list* is one in which the last element in the list points to the first element.

In a graph, you might have many or few edges relative to the number of vertices. In particular, you can have anywhere from zero edges through a number of edges based on the number of nodes: $(1 / 2) N * (N - 1)$, where N is the number of nodes. For example, in a graph with two nodes (A, B), you can have at most one edge (AB); in a graph with three nodes (A, B, C) you can have at most three edges (AB, AC, BC), and so forth. A complete graph has the maximum number of edges. A *sparse* graph has relatively few edges, and a *dense* graph has almost all of its possible edges.

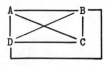

Figure 11-4.   A complete graph

REPRESENTING GRAPHS

There are two very common ways to represent graphs in programs: as a two-dimensional array (matrix) and as a collection of linked lists. In an *adjacency matrix*, the nodes define both the rows and the columns. A cell has a nonzero value if the nodes identified by the row and column subscripts are adjacent. In an *adjacency list*, on the other hand, you keep a separate linked list for each node in the graph. The list consists of all the nodes that are adjacent to the node whose list it is.

The most appropriate data structure for a particular graph depends on several things. If the graph is sparse, then lists will take up less space than a matrix, since a matrix will always require N^2 cells (where N is the number of nodes). On the other hand, for a dense graph, the random access features of an array can become an advantage.

What you intend to do with the graph also has consequences for the most appropriate representation. If you will need to check whether arbitrary nodes are adjacent, an array is much faster than other structures, since in an array you need to check just the cell relating to the nodes in question. If you will want to determine all the nodes adjacent to a particular node, the list structure is the most efficient, since the answer is simply the linked list representing the node under consideration.

Basic Graph Functions

Let's develop some general-purpose functions for reading and displaying information about graphs. To start, let's see what capabilities will be needed.

You'll need to be able to initialize a graph structure. For example, you may want to start out with all nodes isolated from each other, that is, with no edges. You'll then build the graph by getting information about edges and updating the graph structure. Thus, you'll need a routine for getting edge information and incorporating this into the graph. The other function required in a minimal set is the ability to display the contents of a graph—at least those nodes that are connected.

In the next sections, you'll develop these routines. To provide more flexibility, and to illustrate the parallels and differences, you'll develop some of the routines for both an adjacency matrix and an adjacency list representation of a graph.

Data Structures for Graphs: Array Representation

In this chapter, assume that (1) all nodes are represented by single-character names, and (2) only alphabetic characters will be used for names. For now, you'll use only uppercase characters to represent nodes. Later, you'll see how to extend the number of possible nodes and how to get around the naming restriction.

The following listing shows the data structures for represent-ing a graph of up to 26 nodes:

```
/* Data structure for adjacency matrix representation of graph.
   Main structure is 2-dimensional array of int.
   Subscripts 1 -- 26, 1 -- 26 each represent a possible node
   name (alphabetic character).
*/
typedef int  GRAPH_T [ MAX_NODES] [ MAX_NODES];

GRAPH_T  gr;      /* external variable for representing a graph. */
```

The basic structure for the adjacency matrix representation of a graph is a two-dimensional array of **int**. Subscripts 1 through 26 correspond to A through Z, respectively; subscript 0 is unused in this version. Each row of the matrix represents the adjacency information for a particular node. If a cell in the row has a non-zero value, the "row node" is adjacent to the node corresponding to the column with the nonzero value.

For example, Figure 11-5 shows a graph and its representa-tion in an adjacency matrix.

You'll develop some graph-handling routines in two versions— for adjacency matrix and adjacency list representations. To sim-plify this, **typedef** renames the data structure being used. In this way, routines will work with variables of type GRAPH—T,

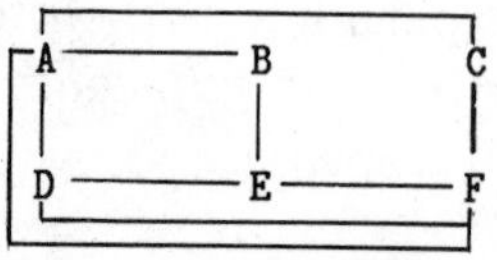

```
  ┌A───────B        C
  │        │        │
  D────────E───────F
  └─────────────────┘
```

Adjacency matrix

Node	A	B	C	D	E	F
A	0	1	1	1	0	1
B	1	0	0	0	1	0
C	1	0	0	0	0	1
D	1	0	0	0	1	1
E	0	1	0	1	0	1
F	1	0	1	1	1	0

Figure 11-5.   Graph and adjacency matrix representation

regardless of whether this is a synonym for an array or for a collection of linked lists.

The following program contains routines for initializing, reading, and displaying a graph, represented as an adjacency matrix. To make it easier to get an overview, definitions and general utility functions are in separate files. The contents of these files will be shown after we discuss the program.

The graph input routine, **f_get_graph( )**, reads edge information from a file and adds the edge to the adjacency matrix by changing the contents of the appropriate cells to nonzero values.

The information should consist of starting node and ending node written together, with no intervening spaces. For example, AB and QT are valid edges, but A B and !T are not: The first invalid edge has a space between the node names; the second has an invalid node name (!). Each edge entry should be on a separate line in the file.

Thus, if **f_get_graph()** reads AD from the file, the routine would add this edge by changing the contents of cell [1][4] in the adjacency matrix to a nonzero value (in this case, 1). Because the function implicitly assumes an undirected, unweighted graph, it would also change cell [4][1] to the same value.

The output routine simply displays the subscripts and the value of each cell that has a nonzero value.

```c
/* Program for building and displaying a graph, using
   adjacency matrix representation.
*/

#include "gdefs.h"
#include "gmisc.c"

/* Data structure for adjacency matrix representation of graph.
   Main structure is 2-dimensional array of int.
   Subscripts 1 -- 26, 1 -- 26 each represent a possible node
   name (alphabetic character).
*/
typedef int  GRAPH_T [ MAX_NODES][ MAX_NODES];

GRAPH_T  gr;      /* external variable for representing a graph. */

/* initialize each cell in an adjacency matrix to 0 */
void init_graph ( GRAPH_T gr, int size)
{
        int outer, inner;

        for ( outer = 0; outer < size; outer++)
                for ( inner = 0; inner < size; inner++)
                        gr [ outer] [ inner] = 0;
}


/* read graph information from specified file, and
   store in specified array for a graph.
   A file entry will have a form such as the following:
   AB
   CE
   which mean that nodes A and B are adjacent, as are nodes C and E.
   Function returns the number of edges entered.
*/
int f_get_graph ( char *name, GRAPH_T gr, int size)
{
        int    count = 0,           /* # edges read */
               dim1, dim2;          /* subscripts for endpoints */
        char   info [ MAX_STR];
        FILE   *fp;

        /* Open file if possible. */
        fp = fopen ( name, "r");
        if ( fp != NULL)
        {
```

```
                    while ( !feof ( fp))
                    {
                            fgets ( info, MAX_STR, fp);
                            if ( !feof ( fp))
                            {
                                    dim1 = ch_index ( info [ 0]);
                                    dim2 = ch_index ( info [ 1]);
                                    /* if both subscripts are valid */
                                    if ( dim1 && dim2)
                                    {
                                            gr [ dim1] [ dim2] = TRUE;
                                            gr [ dim2] [ dim1] = TRUE;
                                    }
                            }   /* end if !feof () */
                            count++;
                    }   /* end while not end of file. */
                    fclose ( fp);
            }
            return ( count);
    }


/* display the graph, by listing each pair of connected nodes
   and the weight between them.
*/
void show_edges ( GRAPH_T gr, int size)
{
        int outer, inner, count = 0;

        for ( outer = 0; outer < size; outer++)
                for ( inner = 0; inner < size; inner++)
                {
                        /* if the nodes are adjacent, display edge */
                        if ( gr [ outer][ inner])
                        {
                                printf ( "%c%c: %5d   ",
                                        index_ch ( outer),
                                        index_ch ( inner),
                                        gr [ outer][ inner]);
                                if ( ( count % 5) == 4)
                                        printf ( "\n");
                                if ( ( count % 50) == 49)
                                        wait ();
                                count++;
                        }
                }
}


main ()
{
        char  info [ MAX_STR];
        int   nr_edges;

        printf ( "File name? ");
        gets ( info);
        /* initialize graph array */
        init_graph ( gr, MAX_NODES);
        /* read graph info and build adjacency matrix */
        nr_edges = f_get_graph ( info, gr, MAX_NODES);
        /* display graph */
        show_edges ( gr, MAX_NODES);
}
```

init—graph()

This function initializes each element of the graph to 0. Notice that the first parameter is a GRAPH—T, which in this representation is a two-dimensional array of **int**. The second parameter is simply the size of the array that should be initialized. If your graph uses fewer than 26 nodes, you can save time by passing a value of **size** that is smaller than MAX—NODES.

f—get—graph()

This function is similar to the **f—get—data()** function in Chapter 10. The function opens the file specified by the first parameter and reads values from the file into the graph represented by the second parameter. The function returns the number of edges added.

Note how the function does its work: It assumes the nodes to which the edge is incident will be specified in the first and second characters of the string read. If both of these are valid alphabetic characters, the function makes the appropriate changes in **gr**. Because **f—get—graph()** assumes an undirected graph, two cells are updated for every edge read.

show—edges()

This function displays all the adjacent nodes, five to a line. For each pair of adjacent nodes, the function displays the nodes and the value associated with the edge. In an unweighted graph, this weight will always be 1.

When processing this program file, the compiler reads the contents of two other files, **gdefs.h** and **gmisc.c**. The first of these contains the usual manifest constant definitions, which are shown in the following listing:

```
/* include instructions and manifest constants for graph programs */

#include <stdio.h>
#include <stdlib.h>
#include <string.h>
#include <math.h>
#include <ctype.h>

#define MAX_STR      80
#define MAX_NODES    27      /* current version allows 26 nodes */
#define TRUE          1
#define FALSE         0
```

The program also uses some general utility functions that are defined in file **gmisc.c**. These functions are independent of a particular graph representation. As such, the functions are appropriate for use with functions for an adjacency matrix as well as for an adjacency list representation. The contents of **gmisc.c** are shown in the following listing. Function **wait( )** should already be familiar to you from earlier programs.

```
/* Miscellaneous functions, useful for both list and matrix
   graph representations.
*/

/* Function DECLARATIONS */
int     ch_index ( int ch);
int     index_ch ( int ch);
void    wait ( void);


/* wait for user to press a key */
void wait ()
{
        char info [ MAX_STR];

        printf ( "Press <Return> to continue.");
        gets ( info);
}


/* return the subscript corresponding to a particular character */
int ch_index ( int ch)
{
        if ( isalpha ( ch))
                return ( tolower ( ch) - 'a' + 1);
        else
                return ( 0);
}


/* return the character corresponding to a particular subscript */
int index_ch ( int ch)
{
        return ( toupper ( ch + 'a' - 1));
}
```

ch—index

Essentially, this function is used to determine a subscript for the array cell corresponding to the node name encountered. The function returns an **int** corresponding to the ordinal position, in the alphabet, of the alphabetic character passed as an argument. For example, for *M*, the function returns 13; for *T*, 20; and so forth. If the character is not an alphabetic character, the function returns 0; for this reason, the cell of the adjacency matrix with subscript 0 is not used.

index—ch( )

This function is the inverse of **ch—index( )**. The **index—ch( )** function returns the character corresponding to a specified subscript in an array. This is useful when writing the name of a node, as in **show—edges( )**.

The following listing shows a sample file of the sort that **f—get—graph( )** expects to read. Notice that each pair of adjacent nodes is on a separate line. The listing contains the information for an unweighted graph; each edge is assumed to have a weight of 1.

```
AB
AC
CD
CE
BC
BF
EF
HI
HJ
IJ
JK
```

To read information about weighted or directed graphs, you need to make a few simple changes in **f—get—graph( )**. The following listing contains the functions needed to build weighted undirected graphs, unweighted digraphs, and weighted digraphs.

To handle weighted graphs, as in **f—get—wgraph( )**, you need to include the weight information on the same line as the adjacent nodes and then call **atoi( )** to convert the weight into a number. This number becomes the cell entry—instead of 1—for the edge connecting the nodes.

To handle digraphs, you need to remove the statements that mark the edge from the second node to the first. For example, to indicate that nodes A and C are adjacent, **f—get—graph( )** first makes cell [1][3] (corresponding to A,C) nonzero and then makes cell [3][1] nonzero. For a directed graph, this second cell would be changed only if there were an explicit edge going from C to A in your file. Functions **f—get—dgraph( )** and **f—get wdgraph( )** are the corresponding functions for building directed graphs.

```
/* Functions for reading information about
    undirected, weighted graphs
    directed, unweighted graphs
    directed, weighted graphs
    Functions use adjacency matrix representation for graphs.
*/

/* Function DECLARATIONS */
int f_get_dgraph ( char *name, GRAPH_T gr, int size);
int f_get_wdgraph ( char *name, GRAPH_T gr, int size);
int f_get_wgraph ( char *name, GRAPH_T gr, int size);

/* read graph information from specified file, and
    store in specified array for an undirected, weighted graph.
    A file entry will have a form such as the following:
    AB  84
    CE  12
    which mean that nodes A and B are adjacent and have weight 84,
    nodes C and E are adjacent with weight 12.
    Function returns the number of edges entered.
*/
int f_get_wgraph ( char *name, GRAPH_T gr, int size)
{
        int    count = 0, dim1, dim2, wt;
        char   info [ MAX_STR],
               *temp; /* used to point to weight string *
        FILE   *fp;

        fp = fopen ( name, "r");
        if ( fp != NULL)
        {
                while ( !feof ( fp))
                {
                        fgets ( info, MAX_STR, fp);
                        if ( !feof ( fp))
                        {
                                dim1 = ch_index ( info [ 0]);
                                dim2 = ch_index ( info [ 1]);
                            /* remainder of line has weight info */
                                temp = &info [ 2];

                                wt = atoi ( temp); /* build weight */
                                /* if both subscripts are valid,
                                mark both cells.
                                */
                                if ( dim1 && dim2)
                                {
                                        gr [ dim1] [ dim2] = wt;
                                        gr [ dim2] [ dim1] = wt;
                                }
                        }
                        count++;
                }
                fclose ( fp);
```

```
        }
        return ( count);

}


/* read graph information from specified file, and
   store in specified array for a directed, unweighted graph.
   A file entry will have a form such as the following:
   AB
   CE
   which mean that node A is adjacent to node B, and
   node C is adjacent to node E.
   Function returns the number of edges entered.
*/
int f_get_dgraph ( char *name, GRAPH_T gr, int size)
{
        int    count = 0, dim1, dim2, wt;
        char   info [ MAX_STR];
        FILE *fp;

        fp = fopen ( name, "r");
        if ( fp != NULL)
        {
                while ( !feof ( fp))
                {
                        fgets ( info, MAX_STR, fp);
                        if ( !feof ( fp))
                        {
                                dim1 = ch_index ( info [ 0]);
                                dim2 = ch_index ( info [ 1]);
                                if ( dim1 && dim2)
                                        gr [ dim1] [ dim2] = TRUE;
                        }
                        count++;
                }
                fclose ( fp);
        }
        return ( count);
}


/* read graph information from specified file, and
   store in specified array for a directed, weighted graph.
   A file entry will have a form such as the following:
   AB  84
   CE  12
   which mean that nodes A and B are adjacent and have weight 84,
   nodes C and E are adjacent with weight 12.
   Function returns the number of edges entered.
*/
int f_get_wdgraph ( char *name, GRAPH_T gr, int size)
{
        int    count = 0, dim1, dim2, wt;
        char   info [ MAX_STR], *temp;
        FILE *fp;

        fp = fopen ( name, "r");
        if ( fp != NULL)
        {
                while ( !feof ( fp))
                {
```

```
                    fgets ( info, MAX_STR, fp);
                    if ( !feof ( fp))
                    {
                            dim1 = ch_index ( info [ 0]);
                            dim2 = ch_index ( info [ 1]);
                            temp = &info [ 2];
                            wt = atoi ( temp);
                            if ( dim1 && dim2)
                                    gr [ dim1] [ dim2] = wt;
                    }
                    count++;
            }
            fclose ( fp);
        }
        return ( count);
}
```

f—get—dgraph()

Like function **f—get—graph()**, this function assigns a default weight of TRUE to each edge. Unlike **f—get—graph()**, this function marks only the cell with subscripts in the order specified in the file. Thus, if AB were found in the file, only **gr** [A][B] would be updated; for an *undirected* graph, **gr** [B][A] would also be updated.

f—get—wgraph() and f—get—wdgraph()

These functions work just like functions **f—get—graph()** and **f—get—dgraph()**, respectively, with respect to identifying nodes. Instead of assigning weights of 1 to any edges, these functions first try to build a weight from the information found in the rest of the line on which each node is specified in the file. The weight built using the **atoi()** Run-Time library function is assigned to the appropriate cell or cells.

Once the graph has been built, most of the other routines will simply do their work by checking each cell for adjacency. Based on the value, these functions will do what they need to; consequently, the functions will work for weighted and unweighted graphs and for directed and undirected graphs.

Data Structures for Graphs: List Representation

Before looking at graph traversal functions, let's look at another way of representing graphs. In the previous section, you used N^2 cells of an array to represent the adjacency information of a graph with up to N nodes. In this section, you'll find how to represent graph connections as a collection of linked lists, which provides an alternative representation for a graph.

An *adjacency list* consists of several linked lists—one for each node. Each list consists of the nodes adjacent to one of the nodes. For example, Figure 11-6 shows a graph and its representation in an adjacency list.

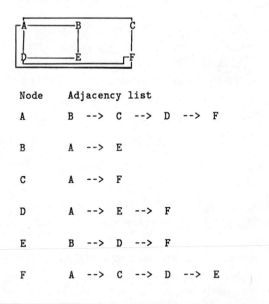

Node	Adjacency list
A	B --> C --> D --> F
B	A --> E
C	A --> F
D	A --> E --> F
E	B --> D --> F
F	A --> C --> D --> E

Figure 11-6.   Graph and adjacency list representation

These lists are generally represented in an array. Each array cell contains a pointer to a linked list node. Thus, each array cell is actually the root of a linked list.

The following listing contains the declaration for a GRAPH—T using linked lists instead of a matrix. The main data structure is a variant on the **lnode** you've used in programs involving linked lists.

You'll have a linked list for each node. The roots for these lists are gathered together in an array.

```
/* Data structure for representing graphs using adjacency list.
   Main component is an lnode;
   Each node in the graph has its own linked list, and
   the array contains pointers to each of these lists.
*/
typedef struct lnode *GRAPH_T [ MAX_NODES];

GRAPH_T  gr;    /* external variable to represent a graph. */
```

In this application, the **lnode** template has been modified to hold information about the node name and the weight (0 or 1 for unweighted graphs, 0 or a nonzero value for weighted graphs) as well as a pointer to the next **lnode**. The following listing shows the template for such an **lnode**:

```
/* Node for a linked list for graphs.
   Three members: node name, data, and a pointer to another lnode.
*/
struct lnode {
        int   name;
        int   data;
        int   done;
        struct  lnode *next;      /* pointer to another lnode */
};
```

The following program contains the functions for initializing and building a graph using adjacency lists. Notice that the program uses the utilities in file **gmisc.c**. The program also needs the list-handling functions included in file **glist.c** and shown in the listing after the program.

```
#include "gdefs.h"
#include "gmisc.c"
#include "glist.c"
#include "gstack.c"
#include "gql.c"

/* Data structure for representing graphs using adjacency list.
   Main component is an lnode;
   Each node in the graph has its own linked list, and
   the array contains pointers to each of these lists.
*/
typedef struct lnode *GRAPH_T [ MAX_NODES];


GRAPH_T  gr;      /* external variable to represent graph. */
int      visited [ MAX_NODES];
int      when_visited, nr_visits;


/* initialize graph structure, by setting each linked list to NULL */
void init_graph ( GRAPH_T grl, int size)
{
        int index;

        for ( index = 0; index < size; index++)
                grl [ index] = NULL;
}


/* add a node to the appropriate linked list ---
   to indicate adjacency and also weight of edge between the
   starting and ending node.
*/
struct lnode *process_node ( struct lnode *root, int ch, int val)
{
        struct lnode *temp;

        /* get storage for an lnode */
        temp = get_node ( temp);
        /* put information into lnode */
        temp -> name = ch;
        temp -> data = val;
        /* attach new node to list */
        root = middle_of_list ( temp, root);
        return ( root);
}


/* read graph information from specified file, and
   store in specified array for a graph.
   A file entry will have a form such as the following:
   AB
   CE
   which mean that nodes A and B are adjacent, as are nodes C and E.
   Function returns the number of edges entered.
*/
int f_get_graph ( char *name, GRAPH_T gr, int size)
```

```
{
        int    count = 0, dim1, dim2;
        struct lnode *temp;
        char  info [ MAX_STR];
        FILE  *fp;

        fp = fopen ( name, "r");
        if ( fp != NULL)
        {
                while ( !feof ( fp))
                {
                        fgets ( info, MAX_STR, fp);
                        if ( !feof ( fp))
                        {
                                dim1 = ch_index ( info [ 0]);
                                dim2 = ch_index ( info [ 1]);
                                if ( dim1 && dim2)
                                {
                                        /* add node to appropriate
                                        list.
                                        */
                                        gr [ dim1] = process_node (
                                                        gr [ dim1],
                                                        info [ 1],
                                                        TRUE);
                                        /* add node to appropriate
                                        list --- in other direction.
                                        */
                                        gr [ dim2] = process_node (
                                                        gr [ dim2],
                                                        info [ 0],
                                                        TRUE);
                                } /* end if both subscripts valid */
                        }   /* end if !feof () */
                        count++;
                } /* end while still something to read */
                fclose ( fp);
        }
        return ( count);
}


/* display edges of the graph. */
void show_edges ( GRAPH_T gr, int size)
{
        int index, count = 0;

        for ( index = 0; index < size; index++)
                show_list ( gr [ index], index_ch ( index), &count);
        printf ( "\n");
}


main ()
{
        char  info [ MAX_STR];
        int   nr_edges;

        printf ( "File name? ");
```

```
      gets ( info);
      /* initialize graph */
      init_graph ( gr, MAX_NODES);
      /* get graph from file, and build adjacency list */
      nr_edges = f_get_graph ( info, gr, MAX_NODES);
      /* display graph */
      show_edges ( gr, MAX_NODES);
}
```

init—graph( )

This function initializes the adjacency list by setting each cell in the array of pointers to NULL. This effectively starts the graph as a collection of isolated nodes, none of which is connected to the other.

f—get—graph( )

This function reads the adjacency information from a file and adds each edge to the adjacency list. Because the function assumes an undirected, unweighted graph, each edge is added to two adjacency lists. To add a node to the appropriate list, the function calls **process—node( )**.

process—node( )

This function actually allocates storage for an **lnode**, assigns the appropriate values to the node, and adds the node to the appropriate list.

disp—graph( )

This function displays the adjacent nodes as well as the weighting associated with each edge. In the current program, these weights would all be 1, since function **f—get—graph( )** does not read in any weightings.

The following listing contains the list-handling functions for adjacency lists. The functions have been modified somewhat from the versions in earlier chapters to work with the customized **lnode** template.

```
/* Contents of Glist.C
   Functions for handling linked lists for graphs
*/

#include <malloc.h>

/* Node for a linked list for graphs.
   Three members: node name, data, and a pointer to another lnode.
*/
struct lnode {
        int   name;
        int   data;
        int   done;
        struct  lnode *next;      /* pointer to another lnode */
};

/* **********
   linked list function DECLARATIONS
********** */
struct lnode *back_of_list ( struct lnode *, struct lnode *);
struct lnode *del_val_node ( struct lnode *base, struct lnode *prev,
                             int val);
int          find_val_node ( struct lnode *, int);
struct lnode *front_of_list ( struct lnode *, struct lnode *);
struct lnode *get_node ( struct lnode *);
struct lnode *middle_of_list ( struct lnode *, struct lnode *);
void         show_list ( struct lnode *, int, int *);


/* **********
   linked list function DEFINITIONS
********** */

/* allocate space for and initialize a structure;
   return pointer to it
*/
struct lnode *get_node ( struct lnode *item)
{
        void *malloc ( size_t);

        /* allocate enough space to store an lnode */
        item = (struct lnode *) malloc ( sizeof ( struct lnode));

        /* if allocated, initialize the structure */
        if (item != NULL)
        {
                item->next = NULL;
                item -> name = ' ';
                item->data = 0;
                item -> done = 0;
        }
        else
                printf ( "Nothing allocated\n");
        return ( item);              /* return the pointer */
}



/* add the structure pointed at by new to front of the list pointed
   at by list.
```

```
*/
struct lnode * front_of_list ( struct lnode *new, struct lnode *list)
{
        new->next = list;
        list = new;
        return (list);
}


/* add lnode to which new points to end of list
   to which list points.
*/
struct lnode *back_of_list ( struct lnode *new, struct lnode *list)
{
        if ( list == NULL)
        {
                list = new;
                return ( list);
        }
        else
        {
                /* return results of most recent search. */
                list->next = back_of_list ( new, list->next);
                return ( list);
        }
}


/* add lnode to list at position corresponding to data member's
   relative position
*/
struct lnode *middle_of_list ( struct lnode *new, struct lnode *list)
{

        if ( list == NULL)
        {
                list = new;
                return ( list);
        }
        else if ( list->data > new->data)
        {
                new->next = list;
                list = new;
                return ( list);
        }
        else
        {
                /* return results of most recent search. */
                list->next = middle_of_list ( new, list->next);
                return ( list);
        }
}



/* display contents of the list */
void show_list ( struct lnode *list, int ch, int *count)
{
        if ( list != NULL)
        {
                printf ( "%c%c: %5d   ", ch,
                        list -> name, list->data);
```

```
                        if ( ( *count % 5) == 4)
                                printf ( "\n");
                        if ( ( *count % 50) == 49)
                                wait ();
                        (*count)++;
                        if ( list->next != NULL)
                                show_list ( list->next, ch, count);
                }
        }


/* Find the node with the value specified in val from the list.
   Identical to show_val_node () except that this function
   produces no output to the screen.
*/
int find_val_node ( struct lnode *base, int val)
{
#define INF   32767

        struct lnode *curr;

        curr = base;   /* make curr point to first element of list */

    /* find the node whose data member has the specified value */
        for ( ; ( curr != NULL) &&
                ( curr -> name != val); )
                curr = curr -> next;

    /* if the value was not found in the list */
        if ( curr == NULL)
                return ( INF);
        else
                return ( curr -> data);
}


/* Delete the node with the value specified in val from the list,
   and return a pointer to root of the revised list.
*/
struct lnode *del_val_node ( struct lnode *base, struct lnode *prev,
                             int val)   /* val is node name */
{
        struct lnode *curr;
        int     index = 1;

        curr = base;   /* make curr point to first element of list */
        prev = NULL;   /* first element has no predecessor */

    /* if there is nothing to delete */
        if ( base == NULL)
        {
                printf ( "ERROR : Empty list; no node deleted.\n");
                return ( base);
        }

    /* if the first node matches the value to be deleted. */
        if ( base -> name == val)
        {
                base = base -> next;
                return ( base);
        }
```

```
/* find the node whose data member has the specified value */
   for ( ; ( curr != NULL) &&
           ( curr -> name != val); )
   {
           prev = curr;
           curr = curr -> next;
   }

/* if the value was not found in the list */
   if ( curr == NULL)
   {
           printf ( "Value not found; nothing deleted.\n");
           return ( base);
   }

   if ( curr != NULL) /* if there is a current element, delete it */
   {
           curr = curr -> next;
           prev -> next = curr;
   }

   return ( base);
}
```

front_of_list( ), back_of_list( ), and middle_of_list

These functions are used to add a new node at the appropriate spot in a linked list. The adjacency lists are built using function **middle_of_list( )**, since this is easiest when searching weighted graphs for paths.

find_val_node( )

This function returns the weight associated with the specified node in a particular adjacency list.

del_val_node( )

This function deletes the **lnode** having a specified value and returns a pointer to the modified list.

Finally, here are the functions for building weighted and directed graphs for adjacency list representations:

```
/* Functions for reading information about
    undirected, weighted graphs
    directed, unweighted graphs
    directed, weighted graphs
    Functions use adjacency matrix representation for graphs.
*/
```

```
/* Function DECLARATIONS */
int f_get_dgraph ( char *name, GRAPH_T gr, int size);
int f_get_dwgraph ( char *name, GRAPH_T gr, int size);
int f_get_wgraph ( char *name, GRAPH_T gr, int size);


/* read graph information from specified file, and
   store in specified array for a directed, weighted graph.
   A file entry will have a form such as the following:
   AB  84
   CE  12
   which mean that nodes A and B are adjacent and have weight 84,
   nodes C and E are adjacent with weight 12.
   Function returns the number of edges entered.
*/
int f_get_wgraph ( char *name, GRAPH_T gr, int size)
{
        int    count = 0, dim1, dim2, wt;
        char   info [ MAX_STR], *temp;
        FILE   *fp;

        fp = fopen ( name, "r");
        if ( fp != NULL)
        {
                while ( !feof ( fp))
                {
                        fgets ( info, MAX_STR, fp);
                        if ( !feof ( fp))
                        {
                                dim1 = ch_index ( info [ 0]);
                                dim2 = ch_index ( info [ 1]);
                                if ( dim1 && dim2)
                                {
                                        temp = &info [ 2];
                                        wt = atoi ( temp);
                                        /* add node to appropriate
                                        list.
                                        */
                                        gr [ dim1] = process_node (
                                                        gr [ dim1],
                                                        info [ 1],
                                                        wt);
                                        /* add node to appropriate
                                        list --- in other direction.
                                        */
                                        gr [ dim2] = process_node (
                                                        gr [ dim2],
                                                        info [ 0],
                                                        wt);

                                } /* end if both subscripts valid */
                        }   /* end if !feof () */
                        count++;
                } /* end while still something to read */
                fclose ( fp);
        }
        return ( count);
}
```

```
/* read graph information from specified file, and
    store in specified array for a directed, weighted graph.
    A file entry will have a form such as the following:
    AB  84
    CE  12
    which mean that nodes A and B are adjacent and have weight 84,
    nodes C and E are adjacent with weight 12.
    Function returns the number of edges entered.
*/
int f_get_wdgraph ( char *name, GRAPH_T gr, int size)
{
        int    count = 0, dim1, dim2, wt;
        char   info [ MAX_STR], *temp;
        FILE   *fp;

        fp = fopen ( name, "r");
        if ( fp != NULL)
        {
                while ( !feof ( fp))
                {
                        fgets ( info, MAX_STR, fp);
                        if ( !feof ( fp))
                        {
                                dim1 = ch_index ( info [ 0]);
                                dim2 = ch_index ( info [ 1]);
                                if ( dim1 && dim2)
                                {
                                        temp = &info [ 2];
                                        wt = atoi ( temp);
                                        gr [ dim1] = process_node (
                                                gr [ dim1],
                                                info [ 1],
                                                wt);
                                }
                        }
                        count++;
                }
        }
        fclose ( fp);
        return ( count);
}


/* read graph information from specified file, and
    store in specified array for a directed, unweighted graph.
    A file entry will have a form such as the following:
    AB
    CE
    which mean that node A is adjacent to node B, and
    node C is adjacent to node E.
    Function returns the number of edges entered.

*/
int f_get_dgraph ( char *name, GRAPH_T gr, int size)
{
        int    count = 0, dim1, dim2;
        char   info [ MAX_STR];
        FILE   *fp;
```

```
fp = fopen ( name, "r");
if ( fp != NULL)
{
        while ( !feof ( fp))
        {
                fgets ( info, MAX_STR, fp);
                if ( !feof ( fp))
                {
                        dim1 = ch_index ( info [ 0]);
                        dim2 = ch_index ( info [ 1]);
                        if ( dim1 && dim2)
                        {
                                gr [ dim1] = process_node (
                                        gr [ dim1],
                                        info [ 1],
                                        TRUE);
                        }
                }
                count++;
        }
}
fclose ( fp);
return ( count);
}
```

f—get—wgraph( ) and f—get—wdgraph( )

The weights on a graph often represent distances, as in our original examples, or prices, such as air fares. In such cases, a common task is to find the shortest or cheapest route between two points.

The solution to such a task involves traversing the graph, or at least a portion of it. For a weighted traversal, the solution will involve moving down the edge with the smallest weight. To make this the "natural" method, the graph-building functions build the lists in order of increasing weight.

TRAVERSING GRAPHS

Earlier, you saw that trees are just graphs. In the chapter on trees, you developed functions to traverse the tree, using either a depth-first or a breadth-first strategy.

Such traversal functions are also important for graphs. For example, you can use a traversal to determine whether a graph is connected. You can also use a specialized version of a traversal function to determine whether there is a path between two nodes.

Depth-First Traversal

Recall that for trees, a breadth-first traversal keeps following the node on one branch (left or right) of the tree until the search reaches a leaf. The algorithm then backtracks to the parent of that node, searches to the bottom of the other branch, and writes the local root value. The order of the latter two steps depends on whether the traversal is postfix or infix.

The recursion makes sure you don't write the same node twice. Essentially, the sequence of recursive calls provides a stack that keeps the traversal process in the correct sequence. This works because a tree is an acyclic graph; you would never visit the same node twice. With graphs, however, you need to keep track of where you've been. Function **depth( )** keeps track of visits by marking the appropriate cell in the **visited[]** array when a node is visited in the traversal.

Beyond this, **depth( )** visits nodes in an order determined by the list of nodes adjacent to the starting node for the traversal. For example, suppose you had the graph and the adjacency list from Figure 11-6. An annotated list is shown in Figure 11-7. The new figure includes a number for each **lnode**, corresponding to the position in which the node would be visited when the traversal function is at the adjacent node heading the list. For example, in the list representing node D, node E would be visited second, as indicated by the 2; this "version" of the E node can be called "D2" in the adjacency list for D.

These numbers would be the order *if* the traversal algorithm didn't get sidetracked. However, the digressions are exactly what characterize a depth-first, as opposed to a breadth-first, search. The actual order in which nodes would be visited also is shown in Figure 11-7. Nodes in square brackets *should* be—but are not—visited at that point because they have already been visited. Nodes in parentheses represent the actual names. For example, B1 is the first adjacent node in the list for B. This turns out to be node A, as indicated by B1(A). Thus, in a depth-first search, the nodes would be visited in the order shown in Figure 11-7.

The following functions let you do a depth-first traversal of a graph, writing the name of the node and when it was visited.

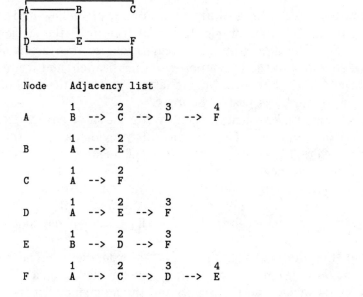

```
Node      Adjacency list

          1           2           3           4
A         B  -->  C  -->  D  -->  F

          1           2
B         A  -->  E

          1           2
C         A  -->  F

          1           2           3
D         A  -->  E  -->  F

          1           2           3
E         B  -->  D  -->  F

          1           2           3           4
F         A  -->  C  -->  D  -->  E


Depth-first traversal sequence. (X) indicates actual node name;
[ ] indicates node would be next in visit sequence,
but has already been visited.

A
A1(B)
[B1(A)]
B2(E)
[E1(B)]
E2(D)
[D1(A)]
[D2(E)]
D3(F)
[F1(A)]
F2(C)
```

Figure 11-7.   Graph, adjacency list, and sequence of node visits for
depth-first traversal

Function **prepare_for_visit()** initializes the **visited[ ]** array.
Any node names that do not occur in the graph are marked as
visited; so the traversal function does not need to worry about
them and does not try to write them.

```
/* Functions for doing a depth-first search of a graph */

/* depth-first traversal of a graph:
   gr is the array of adjacency lists;
   which is the starting node.
*/
void depth ( GRAPH_T gr, int which)
{
        struct lnode *temp;
        int          new_cand;

        /* mark each node with info about when in sequence
        the node was visited.
        */
        visited [ which] = ++when_visited;
        printf ( "%c (%3d) ", index_ch ( which), when_visited);
        if ( ( when_visited % 5) == 4)
                printf ( "\n");
        /* get first node adjacent to specified node */
        temp = gr [ which];
    /* find next node in the list that has not yet been visited */
        while ( temp != NULL)
        {
                new_cand = ch_index ( temp -> name);
                /* if new node hasn't been visited, visit it. */
                if ( !visited [ new_cand])
                        depth ( gr, new_cand);
                temp = temp -> next;
        } /* while not at end of adjacency list for starting list */
}


/* set any unused nodes to 1 in visits [], so these nodes
   will not be written out by depth first function.
   Function returns the number of nodes used.
*/
int prepare_for_visit ( GRAPH_T gr, int visits [], int size)
{
        int index, count = 0;

        for ( index = 1; index < size; index++)
        {
                if ( gr [ index] == NULL)
                        visits [ index] = 1;
                else
                        count++;
        }
        return ( count);
}
```

If your graph is not connected, **depth( )** will not traverse the entire graph; rather, the function will visit only the nodes in a connected component. To make sure all such connected groups of nodes are visited, you can call **depth( )** inside a loop that makes sure the function at least tries to traverse every node. The following loop would enable you to write out the entire graph, even if the graph were not connected:

```
/* Loop to enable depth-first traversal to visit every
   node in the graph, in each connected cluster of nodes.
*/

for ( index = 1; index < MAX_NODES; index++)
{
        /* if the node hasn't been visited yet,
        start the traversal with the node.
        */
        if ( !visited [ index])
        {
                printf ( "\n");
                nr_visits++;
                depth ( gr, index);
        }
}
```

If the graph is connected, then the first call will visit each node. The **if** clause executes only once in that case. This can help you determine whether the graph is connected: Count the number of times **depth( )** is called inside the loop—that is, nonrecursively; this number will tell you the number of connected clusters in the entire graph.

To determine whether there is a path between two nodes, you can modify the depth-first search to check whether the target node has been reached. This function will merely find you *a* path, not necessarily the shortest one. You can write an **is—path( )** function by literally modifying **depth( )**. However, to make it easier to record the nodes on the path found—and to see other ways of manipulating graphs—let's use the following iterative function for finding a path between two nodes:

```
/* Function to determine whether a path exists between two nodes. */

/* return TRUE if there is a path from start to finish in graph.
   Function keeps the path in a stack.
   As a dead-end is reached, the node is popped from the stack
   and the new top node is explored.
   Nodes are marked as they are visited.
   When the target node is found, the stack will contain the path.
   If the stack is empty, no path was found.
*/
int is_path ( GRAPH_T gr, int start, int finish, int size)
{
        struct stack   ps;  /* path stack, to hold viable nodes */
        struct lnode   *temp;
        int            new_cand,   /* index for node being explored */
                       done = FALSE;
        int            solved = FALSE;  /* path search is over */
        int            hold, index, visited [ MAX_NODES];

        /* initialize visited array: not node visited at start. */
        for ( index = 0; index < MAX_NODES; index++)
                visited [ index] = FALSE;

        init_stack ( &ps);
        new_cand = ch_index ( start);
        /* put starting node on stack. */
        hold = push_stack ( gr [ new_cand], start, &ps);
        ps.names [ ps.top - 1] = start;
        visited [ new_cand] = TRUE;

    /* process the list until list is finished or path is found */
        while ( !stack_is_empty ( &ps) && !solved)
        {
                /* find out what node to explore next */
                new_cand = ps.names [ ps.top - 1];
                new_cand = ch_index ( new_cand);
                /* find adjacency list for the node */
                temp = gr [ new_cand];
                done = FALSE;
                /* while no unexplored node is found in list,
                search for one.
                */
                while ( !done)
                {
                        if ( temp == NULL)
                                done = TRUE;
                        else if ( !visited [ ch_index ( temp -> name)])
                                done = TRUE;
                        else
                                temp = temp -> next;
                }

                /* if all the adjacent nodes have been visited,
                pop the next node from stack, to explore its nodes.
                */
                if ( temp == NULL)
                        temp = pop_stack ( &ps, &hold);
```

```
                              /* else add the unvisited node to stack */
                              else
                              {
                                      new_cand = ch_index ( temp -> name);
                                      hold = push_stack ( gr [ new_cand],
                                                             index_ch ( new_cand),
                                                             &ps);
                                      visited [ new_cand] = TRUE;
                              }

                              /* check whether new node is the target node */
                              new_cand = ps.names [ ps.top - 1];
                              /* if node is target, a path has been found. */
                              if ( new_cand == finish)
                                      solved = TRUE;
                              else
                                      new_cand = ch_index ( new_cand);
                      }
                      disp_stack ( &ps);     /* show the path */
                      if ( stack_is_empty ( &ps))
                              return ( FALSE);      /* no path found */
                      else
                              return ( TRUE);
}
```

This function uses a stack to keep track of the nodes already visited. The stack also provides the means of backtracking if the function notices that a particular path has reached a dead end. The function knows this is the case if the current node has no more adjacent nodes to explore but is still not the current node.

The function stops when the target node is found or when there are no more nodes to explore. If there is a path between the two specified nodes, the stack contains the nodes on this path. To show the path, the function displays the stack.

The stack handling is done using a data structure and functions similar to those in Chapter 1. The declarations and functions are assumed to be in the file **gstack.c** and are shown in the following listing. Notice that the **stack** structure has two arrays in this version—one for pointers and one for names.

```
/* File Gstack.C
   Macros and functions for manipulating stacks for graph-handling
   routines.
*/

#define STACK_EMPTY(A)    (!((A)->top))              /* is stack empty? */
#define STACK_FULL(A)     ((A)->top == MAX_VALS)     /* is stack full? */
#define STACK_SIZE(A)     ((A)->top)       /* # elements in stack */
#define MAX_VALS          100
```

```
struct stack {
    /* vals is a MAX_VALS element array of *lnode */
        struct lnode *vals [ MAX_VALS];
    /* vals is a MAX_VALS element array of node names */
        int        names [ MAX_VALS];
        int  top;   /* indicates the next stack cell to be filled */
};


/* **************
    stack function DECLARATIONS
************** */
void        disp_stack ( struct stack *);
void        init_stack ( struct stack *);
struct lnode *pop_stack ( struct stack *, int *);
int         push_stack ( struct lnode *, int, struct stack *);
int         stack_is_empty ( struct stack *);
int         stack_is_full ( struct stack *);


/* **************
    stack function DEFINITIONS
************** */

/* Initialize each cell in the stack to NULL_STR;
   set top of stack (next element to add) to 0.
*/
void init_stack ( struct stack *stack_ptr)
{
        int  index;

        for ( index = 0; index < MAX_VALS; index++)
        {
                stack_ptr -> vals [ index] = NULL;
                stack_ptr -> names [ index] = ';
        }
        stack_ptr -> top = 0;
}


/* Test whether stack_ptr is empty.
   If the_stack.top == 0, then stack is empty,
   so negating value returns the correct answer.
*/
int stack_is_empty ( struct stack *stack_ptr)
{
        return ( !(stack_ptr -> top));  /* if zero, return true */
}


/* Test whether stack_ptr is full.
   If stack_ptr -> top == MAX_VALS, then stack is full.
*/
int stack_is_full ( struct stack *stack_ptr)
{
        /* if equal, return true */
        return ( stack_ptr -> top == MAX_VALS);
}


/* Add an element to a stack, first checking whether stack is full.
   If the stack is full, the function does nothing.
```

```
*/
int push_stack ( struct lnode *gnode, int name,
                 struct stack *stack_ptr)
{
    /* if stack is not full, add the element,
       AND increment the top of stack marker.
    */
        if ( !STACK_FULL ( stack_ptr))
        {
                stack_ptr -> vals [ (stack_ptr -> top)] = gnode;
                stack_ptr -> names [ (stack_ptr -> top)++] = name;
                return ( TRUE);
        }
    /* if stack is full, indicate that push was unsuccessful */
        else
                return ( FALSE);
}



/* Remove an element from a stack, if possible;
   return the element to the calling function;
   adjust the top of the stack to reflect the pop.
*/
struct lnode *pop_stack ( struct stack *stack_ptr, int *nm)
{
        if ( !STACK_EMPTY ( stack_ptr))
        {
                *nm = stack_ptr -> names [ stack_ptr -> top - 1];
                return ( stack_ptr -> vals [ --stack_ptr -> top]);
        }
        else
                return ( 0);
}


/* Display the contents of the stack. */
void disp_stack ( struct stack *st)
{
        int index;

        for ( index = st -> top - 1; index >= 0; index--)
                printf ( "stack.top == %d : name == %c\n",
                        index, st -> names [ index]);
}
```

Breadth-First Traversal

A depth-first traversal starting at node A visits the first node
adjacent to A (say, B), then the first node adjacent to B (say, C),
then the first node adjacent to C (say, D), and so forth. When the
algorithm reaches the deepest point of such a path, it backtracks
one level and repeats the process with the next node adjacent to
the one at this level.

A breadth-first traversal, on the other hand, first visits all the nodes (say, B, C, and D) adjacent to the starting node (say, A). The algorithm then visits all nodes adjacent to B (say, E and F), then all nodes adjacent to C, and so on. After D has been visited, nodes E and F are visited, since these are the first nodes on the next level below B, C, and D.

In Chapter 3, you kept track of the nodes and the sequence in which they should be visited by using a queued list. The same strategy will work here: Before actually "visiting" a node, put all its adjacent nodes in the queue; nodes will be visited in the order in which they are added to the queue. The following function implements a breadth-first graph traversal:

```
/* Perform a breadth-first traversal of the specified graph.
   Function assumes an adjacency list representation.
   Function uses a queued list of pointers to lnode to keep track
   of what node to explore at each turn.
   As a new node is visited, all unvisited nodes adjacent
   to it are added to the queue.
*/
void breadth ( GRAPH_T gr, int which)
{
        /* qlnodes are the basic elements in the queued list. */
        struct qlnode *ps = NULL, *temp;
        struct lnode  *ltemp;
        int    new_cand, index, start, finish, hold;

        when_visited = 0;
        /* index of node to explore */
        new_cand = ch_index ( which);
        /* mark node as visited */
        visited [ new_cand] = TRUE;
        /* get storage for a qlnode to add to queued list. */
        temp = get_qnode ( temp);
        temp -> tn = gr [ new_cand];
        temp -> name = which;
        /* add qlnode to queued list */
        ps = back_of_qlist ( temp, ps);
        /* while there are still nodes in queued list to process. */
        while ( ps != NULL)
        {
                /* process the front node */
                start = ps -> name;
                printf ( "%d (%d) ", start, ++when_visited);
                if ( ( when_visited % 5) == 0)
                        printf ( "\n");

                /* save information about the node just processed */
                ltemp = ps -> tn;
                /* remove node from queued list when processed. */
                ps = deq ( ps);
                /* add nodes adjacent to the one just processed
                to queued list.
```

```
                        */
                        while ( ltemp != NULL)
                        {
                                new_cand = ch_index ( ltemp -> name);
                                /* if unvisited, add node to queued list */
                                if ( !visited [ new_cand])
                                {
                                        visited [ new_cand] = TRUE;
                                        temp = get_qnode ( temp);
                                        temp -> tn = gr [ new_cand];
                                        temp -> name = index_ch ( new_cand);
                                        ps = back_of_qlist ( temp, ps);
                                }
                                ltemp = ltemp -> next;
                        }
                }
        }
```

The data structure and functions to support this function are assumed to be in the file **gql.c** and are shown in the following listing:

```
/* File Gql.C
   Functions to create a simple queue using linked lists
*/

#include <malloc.h>

/* Node for a queued list, for use with graph-handling functions.
   Three members: tn, an int, and a pointer to another node like this one.
*/
struct qlnode {
        struct  lnode   *tn;        /* pointer to a node in a list */
        int             name;
        struct  qlnode *next;       /* pointer to another qlnode */
};


/* ***********
   linked list function DECLARATIONS
*********** */
struct qlnode *back_of_qlist ( struct qlnode *, struct qlnode *);
struct qlnode *deq ( struct qlnode *);
struct qlnode *front_of_qlist (struct qlnode *, struct qlnode *);
struct qlnode *get_qnode ( struct qlnode *);


/* ***********
   linked list function DEFINITIONS
*********** */

/* Allocate space for and initialize a queued list structure;
   return pointer to the structure.
*/
struct qlnode *get_qnode ( struct qlnode *item)
{
        void *malloc ( size_t);
```

```
        /* allocate enough space to store a qlnode */
        item = (struct qlnode *) malloc ( sizeof ( struct qlnode));

        /* if allocated, initialize the structure */
        if (item != NULL)
        {
                item->next = NULL;
                item->tn = NULL;
                item->name = ';
        }
        else
                printf ( "Nothing allocated\n");
        return ( item);              /* return the pointer */
}


/* Add new queued list node to the front of an existing list. */
struct qlnode *front_of_qlist ( struct qlnode *new,
                                struct qlnode *list)
{
        new->next = list;
        list = new;
        return (list);
}


/* Add new queued list node to the back of an existing list. */
struct qlnode *back_of_qlist (struct qlnode *new, struct qlnode *list)
{
        if ( list == NULL)
        {
                list = new;
                return ( list);
        }
        else
        {
                /* return results of most recent search. */
                list->next = back_of_qlist ( new, list->next);
                return ( list);
        }
}


/* remove front element from queued list */
struct qlnode *deq ( struct qlnode *front)
{
        if ( front != NULL)
                front = front -> next;
        return ( front);
}
```

You can also modify this function to determine whether there
is a path between two nodes. As for depth-first searches, the
major modification is to make the function check whether the
current node is the target.

```
/* Return TRUE if there is a path between the specified nodes.
   Function uses an adjacency list representation, and
   uses a breadth-first traversal.
*/
int bfs_path ( GRAPH_T gr, int start, int finish)
{
        /* used for queued list */
        struct qlnode *ps = NULL, *temp;
        struct lnode  *ltemp;
        int    new_cand, curr_node, hold, solved = FALSE;

        when_visited = 0;
        /* get first node */
        new_cand = ch_index ( start);
        visited [ new_cand] = TRUE;
        temp = get_qnode ( temp);
        temp -> tn = gr [ new_cand];
        temp -> name = start;
        /* add starting node to queued list */
        ps = back_of_qlist ( temp, ps);
        /* while there are nodes in the queued list, process */
        while ( (ps != NULL) && !solved)
        {
                /* process node at front of list */
                curr_node = ps -> name;
                printf ( "%d (%d)  ", curr_node, ++when_visited);
                /* if the node is the target, you're done */
                if ( curr_node == finish)
                {
                        printf ("%c == %c\n", curr_node, finish);
                        solved = TRUE;
                        continue;
                }
                if ( ( when_visited % 5) == 0)
                        printf ( "\n");

                ltemp = ps -> tn;
                /* remove front node */
                ps = deq ( ps);
                /* add any unvisited nodes adjacent to node just
                processed to queued list.
                */
                while ( ltemp != NULL)
                {
                        new_cand = ch_index ( ltemp -> name);
                        if ( !visited [ new_cand])
                        {
                                visited [ new_cand] = TRUE;
                                temp = get_qnode ( temp);
                                temp -> tn = gr [ new_cand];
                                temp -> name = index_ch ( new_cand);
                                ps = back_of_qlist ( temp, ps);
                        }
                        ltemp = ltemp -> next;
                }
        }

        if ( solved)
                return ( TRUE);
        else
                return ( FALSE);
}
```

FINDING SHORTEST PATHS

Both depth-first and breadth-first search strategies can find you a path between any two nodes, if a path exists. However, neither strategy will necessarily provide the shortest path, that is, the path having the fewest edges (in an unweighted graph) or the lowest total weight (in a weighted graph).

An algorithm by Edsger Dijkstra finds the shortest path in a directed weighted graph. Interestingly, Dijkstra's algorithm finds the shortest paths between the starting node and all other nodes connected to the starting node—at no extra cost. Because the algorithm goes through all the nodes in the outer loop and then all the nodes in the inner loop, the algorithm runs in n^2 time; thus, doubling the size of the graph would increase the running time by a factor of four.

Dijkstra's algorithm passes through portions of the graph repeatedly. At each turn, a node is added to the collection of shortest paths. On the first turn, the closest adjacent node (the one with the smallest weight) is added to the shortest paths; on the second turn, the smallest of the remaining paths is added; and so forth.

After a node is added to the shortest path collection, the distances to the remaining nodes are updated. For example, suppose you have the graph in Figure 11-8, for which you would like to find the shortest paths from A.

To begin with, initialize the weights between A and every other node. If a node is not adjacent to A, set the weight of the edge to some very large number—larger than any weight that actually occurs in the graph.

The first node added after the starting node will be B, since the weight for the edge AB (10) is the smallest one. Distances to the other nodes are adjusted after this addition. For example, the distance AC (50) can be reduced to 40 (AB + BC, or 10 + 30), since the two-step path, in this case, is shorter than the direct one. Similarly, the weight for AF can be reduced from "infinity" to 60, since there is a two-step path from A to F—through B, which is already in the shortest-path list.

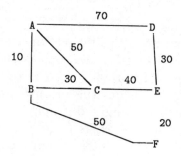

Figure 11-8. A weighted graph

The next node selected will be C, since the weight of the edge AC (50) is the smallest of the remaining edges incident to A. The weight for AD remains unchanged, since the direct distance, AD, is only 70, whereas AC + CE + ED would be 120. Thus, while the shortest route from A to D is the direct route, a roundabout route (through B) is the shortest route from A to C.

F will be selected next, since the 60 weight is less than the 70 for D or the "infinity" for E. Adding F changes none of the values. D is selected next, and it retains its direct value of 70. The node E is added, with a total minimum weight of 80 (AB + BC + CE, or 10 + 30 + 40).

When the algorithm is finished, you have the following weights: AB 10; AC 40; AD 70; AE 100; AF 60. The following listing implements Dijkstra's algorithm for an adjacency list representation:

```
/* Function to find shortest paths between starting node and all
   other nodes.
*/
void dijkstra ( GRAPH_T gr, int start)
{
#define INF    32767   /* distance between unconnected nodes */
```

```c
/* path is used for building shortest path */
struct lnode *path = NULL, *ptemp;
/* wtlist used to keep track of what node to add next */
struct lnode *wtlist = NULL, *wtemp, *wt2, *prev;
int         wts [ MAX_NODES],  /* weights for each node */
            index, new_cand, cand;
int         newest, count, nr_written = 0;;
long int    q1, q2;  /* used to compute minimum distances */

/* initialize weights array to maximum distance */
for ( index = 0; index < MAX_NODES; index++)
        wts [ index] = INF;

/* get index of starting vertex */
new_cand = ch_index ( start);

/* change weights for nodes adjacent to start */
for ( ptemp = gr [ new_cand]; ptemp != NULL;
      ptemp = ptemp -> next)
{
        cand = ch_index ( ptemp -> name);
        wts [ cand] = ptemp -> data;
}

/* put weights in ordered list */
for ( index = 1; index < MAX_NODES; index++)
{
        if ( index != new_cand)
        {
                wtemp = get_node ( wtemp);
                wtemp -> data = wts [ index];
                wtemp -> name = index_ch ( index);
                wtlist = middle_of_list ( wtemp, wtlist);
        }
}

for ( wtemp = wtlist; wtemp != NULL; wtemp = wtemp -> next)
{
        /* add closest node to front of path list */
        ptemp = get_node ( ptemp);
        ptemp -> name = wtemp -> name;
        printf ( "Adding %c\n", ptemp -> name);
        ptemp -> data = wtemp -> data;
        path = front_of_list ( ptemp, path);

        for ( wt2 = wtemp; wt2 != NULL; wt2 = wt2 -> next)
        {
                cand = ch_index ( wt2 -> name);
                newest = ch_index ( path -> name);
                q2 = find_val_node ( gr [ newest],
                                        wt2 -> name);
                q1 = wts [ newest] + q2;
                if ( q1 < wts [ cand])
                        wts [ cand] = (int) q1;
                if ( wts [ cand] < wt2 -> next -> data)
                {
```

```
                                        printf ( "wts [%c] < %c: ",
                                                index_ch ( cand),
                                                wt2->next->name);
                                        printf ("%d < %d: ",
                                                wts [ cand], wt2->next->data);
                                        wtemp = del_val_node (
                                                wtemp, prev,
                                                index_ch ( cand));
                                        prev = get_node ( prev);
                                        prev -> data = wts [ cand];
                                        prev -> name = index_ch ( cand);
                                        wtemp = middle_of_list ( prev, wtemp);
                        }
                }
        }

        /* Display the distances from start to each other vertex */
        printf ( "\n");
        /* Version commented out displays in alphabetical order */
        /*
        for ( index = 1; index < MAX_NODES; index++)
        {
                if ( wts [ index] != INF)
                {
                        printf ( "%c%c: %3d    ", start,
                                index_ch ( index), wts [ index]);
                        nr_written++;
                        if ( ( nr_written % 5) == 4)
                                printf ( "\n");
                }
        }
        */
        /* show nodes in order of appearance on list. */
        show_list ( path, 'A', &nr_written);
}
```

dijkstra( )

This function computes the shortest distance from a specified starting node to all other nodes connected to the starting node. To do its work, the function keeps an array and two lists. The array is used to store the weights between the starting node and each other node in the graph. One list keeps the nodes still to be processed, ordered so that the smallest remaining node will be selected next. The other list is the list containing the currently shortest path.

The function builds the ordered list of unprocessed nodes by reading the weight information from the array into the list. The outer **for** loop (involving **wtemp**) goes through this ordered list, adding the first node to the path each time through the loop and then advancing to the next node. The inner loop adjusts the distances to the remaining nodes according to the relative sizes of the nonstop distances from the starting node and the distance from the newest shortest path.

The function checks whether a newly computed distance is smaller than the one that currently heads the ordered list of nodes to be selected next. If so, the function moves the newly adjusted node to the front of the list—after removing the node from its original position in the list.

By setting the "distance" between two nonadjacent nodes to a very large number, you make every node adjacent to (has a non-zero edge with) every other node. When **show—list( )** displays the path generated by **dijkstra( )**, you'll find that every node is in the adjacency list.

USING MORE NODES

So far, you've limited graphs to 26 nodes by insisting that each node name be a single alphabetic character and by treating uppercase and lowercase characters as equivalent.

To double the number of nodes you can use in your graphs, you need only treat node names as case sensitive. Thus, a node named 'a' would be different from one named 'A'. (This will also increase the running time of an n^2 algorithm, such as Dijkstra's, by a factor of four.)

The only two functions affected by such a change would be **ch—index( )** and **index—ch( )**. The following listing shows the revised versions of these functions for handling the expanded set of node names. The functions assume that names 'A' through 'Z' are represented by subscripts 1 through 26 in any array and nodes 'a' through 'z' are represented by subscripts 27 through 52.

```
/* return the subscript corresponding to a particular character */
int ch_index ( int ch)
{
    /* uppercase characters have subscripts 1 -- 26 */
        if ( isupper ( ch))
                return ( ch - 'A' + 1);
    /* lowercase characters have subscripts 27 -- 52,
        or 70 less than the ASCII code for the character.
    */
        else if ( islower ( ch))
                return ( ch - 70);
        else
                return ( 0);
}


/* return the character corresponding to a particular subscript */
int index_ch ( int ch)
{
    /* if the index is for an uppercase character ( 1 -- 26) */
        if ( ch <= ( MAX_NODES / 2))
                return ( ch + 'A' - 1);
        else
                return ( ch + 70);
}
```

Notice that the offset used to process the lowercase characters is a specific numerical value (70) rather than the ASCII code for a specific character. This is because the first lowercase character name will have subscript 27, which is exactly 70 less than the ASCII code for *a* (97).

You can build graphs with even more nodes by "naming" your nodes using index numbers. For example, if you were willing to "name" your nodes '1' through '100', you could do this by making **index—ch()** and **ch—index()** functions that return the value passed in, if it's between 1 and 100, or return 0. You would need to change display functions and statements, since you could not just use printable characters to represent these names.

EXAMPLE: SOLVING MAZES

A graph is an abstract concept. You can use it to represent lots of different situations. Earlier, graphs were used to show air routes between cities.

Think of a node as a decision point from which you can take any of several different steps (follow any incident edges). Seeing it this way, you can use a graph to represent choice points and dead ends in a maze. Once you've represented the maze as a graph, you can "solve" the maze by finding a path from the starting point to the target point.

For example, Figure 11-9 shows a maze based on the maze at Hampton Court Palace in England, along with a list of adjacent nodes in the graph of the maze. Next to the maze is a graph that represents the maze. This is done by marking all dead ends in the

Graph for maze
AB
AC
CD
CE
DE
EF
EG
GH
GI
HI
IJ
JK
JL

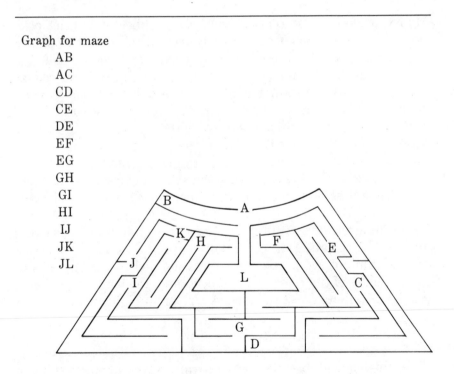

Figure 11-9.   Maze from Hampton Court Palace, and graph representation

maze, such as B. All points in the maze where you could choose from two or more moves in addition to returning to the preceding node are also labeled.

To determine whether there is a path from A to L, you can use function **is_path( )**. If you put weights on the edges—to indicate distance, for example—you can use **dijkstra( )** to find the shortest path or paths.

EXAMPLE: USING GRAPHS
TO REPRESENT PUZZLES

Many puzzles can be represented by a number of distinct positions, or states. If you use nodes to represent these states, you can let node adjacency represent a valid move between two states.

For example, the following puzzle, which goes back at least as far as the eighth century, can be solved using graphs. A man needs to get a wolf, a goat, and a cabbage across a river. His rowboat can carry only himself and either the wolf, the goat, or the cabbage. The man can't leave the wolf and the goat alone together because the wolf will eat the goat. Similarly, he can't leave the goat with the cabbage because the goat will eat the cabbage. How does he manage to get everything across the river?

This puzzle is one of a class known as "river-crossing" problems. These are favorite problems for research in problem solving and also for certain Artificial Intelligence programs. To solve this puzzle, think of the problem states as defined by the contents of the two sides of the river and the location of the boat. Three items can be distributed on two sides of a river in eight ways:

wgc/-, wg/c, wc/g, gc/w, w/gc, g/wc, c/wg, -/wgc

Since the boat can be on either side, this makes 16 possible states in all. However, only some of these states are "legal," meaning that both the goat and the cabbage will survive. To solve the puzzle, you need to get from the starting state (wgc/-, with the boat on the occupied side) to the target state (-/wgc, with the boat on the occupied side).

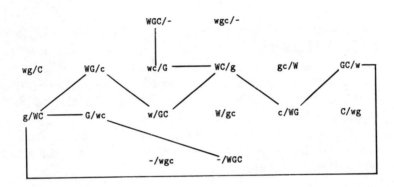

Figure 11-10. Graph representation of river-crossing problem

States that are adjacent represent valid moves, that is, moves that do not result in either cabbage or goat being eaten. To be valid, a move must also be physically possible. For example, you can't "magically" get the cabbage from one side of the river to the other without moving the boat at least once.

Figure 11-10 shows the graph for this puzzle. Letters for the side on which the boat is located are capitalized. For example, WC/g means the wolf and cabbage are on the same side of the river as the boat, and the goat is on the other side.

To solve this problem, read the appropriate edges into the graph program, and then use **is—path( )** to find the solution.

TASKS AND SUGGESTIONS

Graph theory is a branch of mathematics that abounds with theorems and algorithms. Many of these are accessible even to someone with minimal formal training in mathematics. Learn about some of these algorithms and try to implement them.

The Traveling Salesman Problem

A *Hamiltonian circuit* is a cycle in a graph that visits every node exactly once. If the edges have weights on them, you can search for a Hamiltonian circuit in the graph to solve what is known as the *traveling salesman problem.* The problem is as follows: A traveling salesman must visit all the cities on his route, and he would like to do it in the shortest distance possible.

An algorithm for finding *a* solution to this problem (but not necessarily the best one) finds a Hamiltonian circuit in the graph. The algorithm is as follows:

1. Select a starting node.
2. Add this node to the list representing the path.
3. Set the total weight for the trip to 0.
4. Mark the node most recently added to the path as "visited."
5. Choose the unmarked node closest to the most recently added node.
6. Add the weight between these two nodes to the total weight.
7. Add this closest node to the path. While there are unvisited nodes, repeat steps 4 through 7.
8. Add the weight between the starting node and the last node added to the path to the total weight.
9. Add the starting node to the path to complete the cycle.

Implement this algorithm.

Naming Nodes

Currently, the only valid names for nodes are single characters. You can get around this restriction by keeping an array of strings wherein each element is a string associated with a particular node. Your functions and programs would still use single-character names, but each would be associated with a longer name stored in the array. Implement such an array.

Adjacency Matrix Routines

Earlier, you saw a representation of graphs as an adjacency matrix. Only the functions for building a graph from information in a file and for displaying the edges in a graph were developed for this data structure. Implement the traversal functions, **depth()** and **breadth()**, as well as **is_path()** and **dijkstra()** for adjacency matrix representations.

SUMMARY

In this chapter, you learned about graphs and were introduced to two ways of representing graphs. The chapter also contained routines for searching graphs and for finding the shortest paths between two nodes on the graph.

You now have enough tools—data structures and functions— to build very powerful programs. What you do with these tools is up to your imagination, and your energy. Happy programming.

A

A QUICK C REVIEW

C is a very versatile programming language. It has often been called a *middle-level language* because it offers you the powerful control constructs and data structures of high-level languages (such as Pascal or Modula-2) but also gives you the access to individual bits provided by low-level languages (such as assembly language). Because of such multilevel features, C is an ideal language for writing systems programs (which must take advantage of hardware and operating system features) as well as for performing general programming tasks. Table A-1 lists some high-level and low-level features of C.

C is a very small language, having a vocabulary of only about 30 reserved words, or *keywords*. However, C has an exceptionally large and varied collection of operators. In fact, C has more operators than keywords! C supports numerous data types, including both simple (for example, integer) and aggregate (for example, array) data types. Finally, C provides a pointer type that you can use in very flexible ways. You can even do arithmetic on pointer values. These features—a small vocabulary, a rich collection of operators, a broad range of data types, and powerful pointers—make C such a versatile language.

Table A-1. Language Properties

High-level Languages	C		Low-level Languages
Structured	yes	yes	Fast
Easy to use	yes	yes	Compact
Safeguards	yes/no	yes	(Can be) efficient
Complex Data Structures	yes	yes	Address and bit manipulation

Table A-2 contains C's keywords. The words in parentheses have been added in the new proposed ANSI standard. Some older compilers also include the following reserved words: **asm, entry,** and **fortran.**

The following sections provide a very brief summary of the major features and components of C's syntax and rules. The discussion can only serve to refresh what you already know about C; you will not have much luck learning C from this summary, since the subtleties of C's syntax and data structures would require more detailed presentation.

Table A-2. C Keywords

auto	double	int	struct
break	else	long	switch
case	enum	register	typedef
char	extern	return	union
(const)	float	short	unsigned
continue	for	(signed)	void
default	goto	sizeof	(volatile)
do	if	static	while

PROGRAM STRUCTURE

C programs consist of functions (similar to subroutines in other programming languages); functions consist of statements. Statements serve to define or express something or to carry out some action. The following program illustrates these program components. The listing contains two functions (**main( )** and **message( )**), and three statements (one in **main( )** and two in **message( )**).

```
/* Sample C program to illustrate three components of a program:
   program; functions; statements.
*/

message ()    /* a simple function; writes two words on screen. */
{
        printf ( "hello,");
        printf ( " world");
}

main()  /* the main program */
{
        message ();   /* call function message */
}
```

Statements

Statements are the main components of functions; they are essentially instructions to do certain things or to define something. C allows *simple* and *compound statements*. Statements can be used in various contexts (for example, if-then tests, loops), and can serve many purposes, such as assigning a value, returning from a function, or continuing a loop.

The following are all simple statements in C:

```
printf ( "this is a simple statement in C\n");

curr_int = 23;

return ( 8.5);

continue;
```

In C, each simple statement must end with a semicolon.

You can "collect your thoughts" by grouping several statements together and treating them as a single, extended statement. Such a statement is known as a compound statement. A compound statement consists of zero or more statements (simple or compound) bounded by left and right curly braces ({ and }).

The following listing contains two compound statements:

```
{
        printf ( "This is not");
        printf ( " a simple statement,\n");
        printf ( "since it consists of several simple statements");
        printf ( " followed by a right brace.\n");
        printf ( "The entire collection of statements makes up a");
        printf ( " compound statement.\n");
}
{
        ;
}
```

Identifiers and Naming Rules

The naming rules for C variables and functions are similar to the rules in other languages. An identifier, or name, consists of some combination of valid characters. The only real trick is remembering what characters are valid and when each is valid. Valid characters for C identifiers are:

- the letters A through Z and a through z (letters)
- the underscore character, __ (underscore)
- the characters 0 through 9 (digits)

Identifiers *must* start with a letter or an underscore. A digit is not allowed as the first character of an identifier, and spaces are not allowed at all in C identifiers.

In C, the case of the characters in a name *does* matter. Thus, **hello**, **HELLO**, and **Hello** are all different names.

You may not use reserved words as identifiers.

Variable Definitions

In order to associate a name, or identifier, with a particular memory location, and to use this location in a program, you need to *define* the variable. To define a variable, you need to specify a type and a name for the variable. When you do this, a particular data type is associated with the name, and storage is allocated for the variable to hold values of the specified type.

The following line shows how to define two integer variables, **i1** and **i2**.

```
int i1, i2;
```

FUNCTION DEFINITIONS AND PROTOTYPES

Functions are collections of statements that are used together to accomplish some task. Think of functions as specialists that you call when the need arises.

Function Definitions

A *function definition* serves to specify the details of the function for the compiler. There are two major components to a function definition: the *function declarator* and the *function body*.

The top line of a function is called the function declarator, or *function heading*. Essentially, a function declarator contains a type name that indicates the type of information the function is returning to the calling routine, an identifier (the function name, such as **main** or **message**), and a set of parentheses that may contain additional information; the material in the parentheses is the formal parameter list.

There is no semicolon at the end of the function declarator. The absence of a semicolon tells the compiler that you are defining the function, rather than simply declaring it so that another function will know what type of value the original routine is returning.

The second component is the function body—the actual instructions the function will carry out. The function body is essentially a compound statement (hence the curly braces at top and bottom).

If a function does not return any values, the return type is **void**. If no return type is specified, the compiler assumes the function returns an integer.

If you need to provide information for the function to use when doing its work, you can pass this information to function parameters. A *parameter* is essentially a slot through which you can pass information of a particular type to a function.

In the function heading, you declare any *formal parameters* for the function. The formal parameters represent the slots through which information will be passed to the function. When you call the function elsewhere and actually pass specific values into these slots, you are passing the *actual parameters*, or *arguments*, to the function. Thus, formal parameters refer to the slots in the function definition, and actual parameters refer to values passed during a function call.

When using what is known as the prototype form of a function definition—the form specified by the Proposed ANSI Standard C—you need to provide both a type identifier and a name for each parameter. This information is provided between the parentheses in the function declarator.

The following illustration shows the heading for a function that returns no value but that takes two integer parameters:

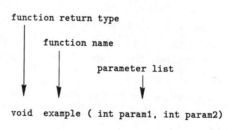

```
function return type
        |
        |     function name
        |          |
        |          |       parameter list
        |          |           |
        |          |           |
        v          v           v
void  example ( int param1, int param2)
```

An older, nonprototype syntax puts only the parameter names in parentheses and includes definitions for these parameters on a separate line, before the function body.

Unless you specify pointer variables as parameters, all parameter information in C is passed by value, which means you are passing a copy rather than an actual variable that could be changed.

Function Prototypes

The concept of a function prototype was introduced into C in the Proposed ANSI Standard C. The intent was to make it possible for the compiler to do the kind of type checking common in other high-level languages, such as Pascal.

To accomplish this, the compiler must see either a function definition or a function declaration in prototype form before it sees a call to the function. Such a prototype can occur as a declaration inside the body of another function, along with the variables definitions for the function, or it can appear outside of any function.

The function protoype is similar to the function heading line in a function definition, but with two important differences. First, the function prototype must end with a semicolon. Second, in the prototype, you need to list only the types for the parameter within the parentheses; you may, but need not, include names for the parameters. The following listing shows the function declaration that corresponds to the heading in the previous listing:

```
void  example ( int, int);
```

C'S SIMPLE DATA TYPES

C provides the simple data types shown in Table A-3.

The following program shows how to define and use such variables:

```
/* Sample program to illustrate properties of simple data types
   and certain syntactic rules and conventions for using these types.
*/

main ()
{
        char c1, c2, c3;     /* define three variables of type char */
        int i1, i2, i3;      /* ...                       type int */
        float f1, f2;        /* ...                       type float */
        double d1, d2;       /* ...                       type double */

    /* assignment statements involving chars; note different uses. */
        c1 = 'a';       /* assign character constant 'a' to c1 */
        c2 = 97;        /* substitute 353 (255 + 98); what happens? */
        c3 = c1 + 3;    /* what types are in "addition" expression? */

    /* display the information; note differences between the lines */
        printf ( "char as char: c1 = %c; c2 = %c; c3 = %c\n",
                c1, c2, c3);
        printf ( "char as int : c1 = %d; c2 = %d; c3 = %d\n\n",
                c1, c2, c3);

    /* assignments for ints; note types in third assignment */
        i1 = 23;
        i2 = i1 + 3;
        i3 = i2 + c1;   /* note types being added. */

    /* write the int values */
        printf ( "ints: i1 = %d; i2 = %d; i3 = %d\n\n",
                i1, i2, i3);

    /* assignment statements for floats. */
        f1 = 23.000000000000001;
        f2 = f1 + 3.00000000000000; /* see result of this addition. */

    /* write float results; note use of formatting */
        printf ( "float : f1 = %f; f2 = %40.37f\n\n", f1, f2);

    /* assignment statements for doubles. */
        d1 = 23.00000000000001;
        d2 = d1 + 3.00000000000000; /* see result of this addition. */

    /* write double results; compare output with that for float. */
        printf ( "double: d1 = %lf; d2 = %40.37lf\n", d1, d2);

    /* write double results AS INTS; compare output with above. */
        printf ( "\nThe following is INVALID OUTPUT.\n");
        printf ( "double as int: d1 = %d; d2 = %40d\n", d1, d2);
}
```

A **char** is an 8-bit value that is generally used to represent an alphanumeric character, special symbol, or simple control sequence. The **char** variables are processed internally as integers. A **signed char** is used to represent values between -128 and 127; an **unsigned char** lets you represent values between 0 and 255. The default representation for **char** is generally the signed version.

Table A-3.   Summary of Simple Data Types

Type	Range of Values in QuickC
char	−128 .. 127
signed char	−128 .. 127
unsigned char	0 .. 255
int	−32768 .. 32767
signed int	−32768 .. 32767
unsigned int	0 .. 65535
short	−32768 .. 32767
long	−2147483648 .. 2147483647
float	−3.4e+48 .. 3.4e+48
double	−1.7e+308 .. 1.7e+308

The **int** type is used to represent whole numbers over a range determined by the amount of storage allocated for a variable of this type. As you can determine from the table, QuickC allocates 2 bytes for such variables. As with the **char** type, you can specify whether the leftmost bit should be used in computing the magnitude of a positive value (**unsigned**) or for indicating that a value is negative (**signed**). As with **char**, the signed version of the integer type is the default.

You can also define whole-number variables over a broader range, by using the **long** type. QuickC allocates 4 bytes for such a variable. There is also a **short** type, which explicitly specifies that only 2 bytes are to be allocated for a variable of the specified type. In both cases, the type is implicitly assumed to be an integer.

Variables of type **float** and **double** are used to represent real numbers—that is, numbers that may have a fractional part. QuickC allocates 4 bytes for a variable of type **float** and 8 bytes for a variable of type **double**. Thus, a **double** is essentially a long **float**.

The **char** type and the various forms and versions of the **int** type are known collectively as *integral data types*. The types **float** and **double** are known as *floating-point types*.

When working with integral types, you must be careful to avoid overflow, which occurs when you perform operations that result in a value larger than the maximum value you can represent in the type. For example, $16,384 + 16,384 = -32,768$, because the binary representation of the actual sum (1000 0000 0000 0000) is interpreted as a negative number by default.

Internally, all floating-point computations are carried out with **double** values. You will probably find **double** values easier to work with than **float** variables in your programs.

In C, variables in expressions with multiple types undergo something called *type promotion*. What this means is that, *for the purposes of evaluating the expression*, variables of a "lower" type are "promoted" to—that is, treated as—variables of the highest type appearing in the expression. In general, integral types are lower than floating-point types; more specifically, a **char** type is lower than an **int**, an **int** is lower than a **float**, and a **float** is lower than a **double**.

In the case of an expression such as 35 / 7.0, the 35 would be "promoted" to a **float**; that is, it would be treated as 35.0. On the other hand, 35 / 7 involves only integers; since both variables are at the same level, there is no need to do any type promotion. The rules for type promotion (or coercion, as it is sometimes called) are as follows:

- All **char** and **short** variables are *automatically* promoted to **int**.

- All **unsigned char** and **unsigned short** variables are automatically promoted to **unsigned int**.

- After any of the above conversions have been made, additional promotions are made, as needed, up the following hierarchy (from lowest to highest): **int** to **unsigned** to **long** to **float** to **double**.

C'S AGGREGATE DATA TYPES

Aggregate variables are made up of multiple components—which may all be of the same type or of different types. C has three aggregate types: arrays, structures, and unions.

Arrays

In C, an *array* is an aggregate variable consisting of a collection of elements, each of the same type. The array identifier is the name given to the entire collection; an individual element is identified in terms of its location in the array. Location of an individual element is specified by a subscript associated with the element.

For example, to store daily temperature readings for a one-month period, you could define an array as follows:

```
double daily_temp [ 31];
```

This definition creates an array variable named **daily—temp**. The type specifier indicates that the variable contains information of type **double**. The square brackets ([]) with number following the identifier indicate that the variable is an *array* of **double** values containing 31 elements.

To define an array containing variables of a particular type, you need to specify the type (as in other variable definitions), give the array a name, and indicate the array's size within square brackets. The brackets indicate that the variable is an array.

When the variable **daily—temp** is defined, the compiler allocates enough contiguous storage for 31 variables of type **double**. The first array element has the lowest address in the array, and represents the address of the entire array variable.

To access a particular element in the array, specify the array name followed by square brackets containing the subscript corresponding to the element's position in the array. In C, all arrays start with the subscript 0; thus, the subscript values in the array **daily—temp[ ]** range from 0 to 30, *not* from 1 to 31.

You can also define multidimensional arrays. For example, a two-dimensional array is essentially an array each of whose elements is itself an array. To specify such an array, you need to provide two sets of dimensions within square brackets, as in the following listing, which defines a two-element array, each of whose elements is a three-element array:

```
double two_by_three [ 2][ 3];
```

You can also access individual cells in such a matrix by specifying the two subscripts associated with the cell. For example, **two_by_three[0][1]** refers to the middle element (1) of the first row (0) of the matrix.

Structures

A *structure* is an aggregate variable that consists of several *components*, or *members*. Members can be of different types. For example, to keep track of the average temperature and wind speed on a given day, you might want to use a structure with two members, **temp** and **wind**, to record the information. The following listing shows how to specify a template for such a structure:

```
struct weather {
        double temp;
        double wind;
}
```

This declaration merely creates a structure description, or template, based on the members specified. The declaration does *not* allocate any storage for such a structure. The declaration begins with the keyword **struct**, which specifies that what follows is a structure; **weather** is the *tag*, or *tag name*, of the structure being created.

The material between the paired left and right curly braces represents the structure's members. Each of these members is declared as if it were a variable of the specified type; thus, **temp** and **wind** are both specified as being of type **double**. The right brace ends the structure template, and each semicolon ends a declaration statement.

Then, to define a variable of type **weather**, you could write something like the following:

```
struct weather {
        double temp;
        double wind;
}
```

```
main ()
{
        struct weather  today;

        /* main function body here */
}
```

This listing describes a global structure named **weather**. A local variable (named **today**) of that type is defined in **main()**. The definition contains the keyword, **struct**; the tag name associated with the structure, **weather**; and an identifier for the variable itself, **today**.

Once you've allocated space for a structure, by defining a variable of the appropriate type, you can use the *structure member*, or *dot*, *operator* (.) to access individual members of the structure. This operator takes two operands. The left operand is the name of a variable of the structure's type, and the right operand is a member within that structure. The result of applying the operator is the specified structure element itself or its value, depending on the context.

The following listing shows how to use the dot operator:

```
struct weather {
        double temp;
        double wind;
}
main ()
{
        struct weather  today;
        today.temp = 84.5;   /* access temp member to assign a value */
        today.wind = 20.5;
        printf ( "Temp == %.21f; wind == %.21f\n",
                today.temp, today.wind);
}
```

The member list for a structure is essentially a variable declaration list. You simply specify the type and an identifier for each member of the structure. Members can be of any type, but a structure can't be a member of itself. You can, however, have a pointer to the structure as a member.

Unions

Unions are aggregate types that have members, like structures. Unlike structures, however, unions may hold, *at different* times, different types of information; that is, the same variable may be used to store different members at different times. For example, the **union** variable **value**, declared in the following listing, may contain an **int** at some times, a **double** at other times, and a complex number on other occasions. At any one time, however, only one of these types is stored there.

```
struct complex {
        double re, im;
}

union value {
        int     int_val;
        double dbl_val;
        struct complex com_val;
}
```

This data structure can store the value for *either* an **int**, *or* a **double**, *or* a **struct complex** variable at any one time. The union does *not* have three members, each of which can be present at the same time; rather, the union has a certain amount of space allocated, which can contain information that may be interpreted *in any of three ways*, depending on context.

POINTERS

A *pointer* is a variable type whose value is an address. The address will be that of another variable of a particular type. For example, a properly initialized pointer to **int** (denoted by *int) contains the address of an integer variable.

Pointers are distinguished by the type of variable to which they point. Thus, a pointer to **double**, or *double, contains an address that will be interpreted as the starting address of an 8-byte variable; a pointer to **int**, or *int, on the other hand, will contain the starting address of a 2-byte variable.

There is a close relationship between pointers and C's address operator (&). The address operator takes one operand, a variable, and returns the memory location associated with that variable. Thus, the value returned after applying the address operator is the type of value you would store in a pointer. For example, suppose you have the following definitions:

```
double target, *dbl_ptr;
```

To make **dbl—ptr** reference **target**, you need to assign the address of **target** to **dbl—ptr**. To do this, use the address operator, as follows:

```
dbl_ptr = &target;
```

Dereferencing Pointers

To make use of the memory location pointed to, or referenced by, a pointer variable, you need to be able to specify the target variable. C's *indirection operator* (*) enables you to do this. The indirection operator takes a pointer variable as its operand and returns the value stored at the location referenced by the pointer. You can also use the indirection operator on the left-hand side of an assignment statement to change the value of the variable referenced by the pointer. The following listing shows an example:

```
main ()
{
        double target, *dbl_ptr;

        target = 5.0;
        dbl_ptr = &target;    /* make dbl_ptr point to target */

    /* Use indirection operator to return the value stored in
       target, the variable referenced by dbl_ptr.
       Both values will be 5.00.
    */
        printf ( "target == %.2lf; *dbl_ptr == %.2lf\n",
                target, *dbl_ptr);

    /* Assign the value 12.5 to the variable referenced by dbl_ptr */
        *dbl_ptr = 12.5;
```

```
    /* Since *dbl_ptr is just another name for target,
       both values will be 12.50.
    */
       printf ( "target == %.2lf; *dbl_ptr == %.2lf\n",
                target, *dbl_ptr);
}
```

The indirection operator "dereferences" the pointer variable: Whereas the pointer variable contains an address, the indirection operator returns the value stored at that address.

Pointer Arithmetic

The type of a pointer's target variable determines the size of an *address unit* for the pointer. For example, an address unit for a ***double** is 8 bytes, because C allocates 8 bytes of storage for a **double**. Address units are used when doing pointer arithmetic. For example, if you had a ***double** variable with value 4000—that is, with memory location 4000 as the pointer's contents—then adding one address unit to the contents of this pointer would change the contents to 4008 (4000 + 8 bytes). The following listing shows the statements that carry out the necessary pointer arithmetic:

```
double    *dbl_ptr;  /* define a pointer to double */
double    dbl_val;   /* define a variable of type double */
...
dbl_ptr = &dbl_val;    /* store address of dbl_val in dbl_ptr */
dbl_ptr = dbl_ptr + 1; /* add 1 address unit to contents of dbl_ptr */

/* contents of dbl_ptr will now be
   &dbl_val + 8
*/
```

Note that adding address units to pointer values looks the same as adding to an integer variable. The only way the compiler knows how to interpret the addition operator is by checking whether the variables involved are pointers or integral variables. When doing pointer arithmetic, the compiler will make sure it's working with pointer variables; it's your responsibility to make sure the location computed with the pointer arithmetic contains the appropriate type of value.

Using Pointers to Pass by Reference in Function Calls

Ordinarily, parameters for functions are passed by value; that is, a copy of the value stored in the argument is actually passed to the function. This means the original variable cannot be changed in the function.

To change a variable within a function, you need to declare a pointer to a variable of the appropriate type as one of the function's parameters, and you then need to call the function with the address of the variable you want to change as an argument. This is known as *passing by reference*, since you are passing information about the actual variable, rather than just the value stored there. The following listing shows an example of this by defining and calling a function to swap the contents of two **double** values:

```c
/* Program to swap two values.
   Program shows use of pointers to pass parameters by reference.
*/

/* Function to actually swap two values. Uses pointer parameters. */
void swap_dbl ( double *first, double *second)
{
        double temp;       /* to store one of the values during swap */

        temp = *first;       /* store *first in safe place */
        *first = *second;    /* move *second */
        *second = temp;      /* restore first to new location */
}


main ()
{
        double d1 = 12.3, d2 = 39.5;
        void    swap_dbl ( double *, double *);

        printf ( "d1 = %lf; d2 = %lf\n\n", d1, d2);
        swap_dbl ( &d1, &d2); /* notice use of address operators. */
        printf ( "d1 = %lf; d2 = %lf\n", d1, d2);
}
```

C'S OPERATORS

C provides more than 40 operators for use with its data types. Table A-4 summarizes these operators, in order of precedence from highest (top) to lowest (bottom). Operators at the same level have the same precedence.

Table A-4.   Precedence Hierarchy for C Operators

Operator	Comments
() [ ] –>	Function and access operators
! ~ & * (cast) + – sizeof() ++ ––	Unary operators
* / %	Arithmetic (multiplication)
+ –	Arithmetic (addition)
<< >>	Shift operators
< <= > >=	Relational operators
== !=	Equality operators
&	Bitwise AND
^	Bitwise XOR
|	Bitwise OR
&&	Logical multiplication
||	Logical addition
?:	Conditional operator
= += –= *= /= %= &= ^= |= <<= >>=	Assignment operator
,	Comma operator

Function Call Operator (())

This operator takes a function name and an argument list and indicates a call to the function specified. The following examples all use the function call operator:

```
printf ( "hello\n");      /* call function printf, 1 argument */
my_val = sqrt ( 35.0);    /* call function sqrt, 1 argument */
scanf ( "%d", &my_int);   /* call function scanf, 2 arguments */
result = rand ();         /* call function rand, 0 arguments */
```

Array Subscript Operator ([])

This operator lets you access a specific cell in an array. When used in a variable definition, the operator also serves to indicate that the variable is an array containing elements of the specified type, rather than a simple variable. The following listing displays the value of the first cell in the array **int—array[]**:

```
printf ( "%d\n", int_array [ 0]);
```

Structure Member Operators (. and —>)

These operators let you access specific members of a structure variable. The dot operator (.) lets you access a member of a structure that you specify directly. The *arrow operator* (—>) lets you access a member of a structure by specifying a pointer to the structure. The following listing shows how to use each of these operators:

```
struct weather {
        double temp, wind;
};

main ()
{
        struct weather today;    /* define variable of type weather */
        struct weather *we_ptr; /* define a pointer to a structure */

        we_ptr = &today;       /* make we_ptr point to today */

     /* use . to access temp member of today */
        today.temp = 85.7;

     /* use -> to access wind member of *we_ptr (same as today) */
        we_ptr -> wind = 12.9;
}
```

Unary Operators

The following operators all take a single operand. Whereas operators with equal precedence are generally evaluated from left to right, unary operators—all of which have the same precedence—are evaluated from right to left. For example, the following listing shows a statement involving indirection and increment operators:

```
#include <stdio.h>

main()
{
        int val1 = 50, val2 = 100;
        int *ptr = &val2;

        printf ( "&val1 = %u; &val2 = %u; ptr = %u; +++ptr = %u\n",
                &val1, &val2, ptr, +++ptr);
}
```

The last value displayed is 101, rather than the address of **val1**. The indirection operator is applied first to get at **val2**, and then the increment operator is applied to the variable returned by the indirection operator, changing the value of **val2** by 1.

Address (&) and Indirection (*) Operators

These two operators are inverses of each other. The address operator returns the location of its variable operand; the indirection operator returns the variable stored at the address operand (the contents of a pointer).

Increment (++) and Decrement (−−) Operators

These operators change the value of the variable operand by adding (increment) or subtracting (decrement) 1 from the current value. These operators can be used in prefix or postfix form.

When the operator precedes its operand (prefix form), the variable's value is changed, and the *new* value is used in whatever expression the operator and operand are encountered. When the operator follows its operand (postfix form), the *current* value of the variable is used in the expression, and *then* the value is changed. The following program illustrates the difference between prefix and postfix forms of the increment operator:

```
/* Program to illustrate use of increment operator, and
   to show different effects of prefix and postfix forms of operator.
*/

main ()
{
        int result, test = 0;

        /* PREFIX increment: increment then use */
        if ( ( result = ++test) == 1)
                printf ( "result == %d\n", result);
        /* else do nothing */
        printf ( "after ++test, value of test == %d\n", test);

        test = 0;               /* reinitialize test to 0 */

        /* POSTFIX increment: use then increment */
        if ( ( result = test++) == 1)
                printf ( "result == %d\n", result);
        else            /* if test is still zero at assignment time */
                printf ( "nothing to do, so test must still == 0\n");
        printf ( "after test++, value of test == %d\n", test);

}
```

This program produces the following output:

```
result == 1
after ++test, value of test == 1
nothing to do, so test must still == 0
after test++, value of test == 1
```

sizeof Operator

The **sizeof** operator takes a variable of a specific type (for example, **my_int** or **my_array**) or a type specifier (for example, **int**, **double**, **int [50]**) as its operand and returns the number of bytes needed to store a variable of the specified type. The following listing uses the operator to determine the storage allocated to simple types:

```
/* Program to show the amount of storage allocated for each of C's
   simple types.
   NOTE : sizeof() is an operator that returns an integer
          indicating the number of bytes of storage allocated to
          for the base type of the variable passed as an argument.
*/
main ()
{
        printf ( "TYPE      SIZE (in Bytes)\n\n");
        printf ( "char     %d bytes\n", sizeof ( char));
        printf ( "short    %d bytes\n", sizeof ( short));
        printf ( "int      %d bytes\n", sizeof ( int));
        printf ( "unsigned %d bytes\n", sizeof ( unsigned));
        printf ( "signed   %d bytes\n", sizeof ( signed));
        printf ( "long     %d bytes\n", sizeof ( long));
        printf ( "float    %d bytes\n", sizeof ( float));
        printf ( "double   %d bytes\n", sizeof ( double));
}
```

Cast Operator ((type))

This operator lets you temporarily convert the value of a variable to a specified type before using the value. For example,

```
(int) my_dbl
```

converts the value of **my_dbl** to an integer value before using it.

Arithmetic (−), Logical (!), and Bitwise (~) Negation Operators

These operators transform the values of their operands.

The *arithmetic negation,* or *minus, operator* (−) changes a positive value to a negative one, and vice versa. For example, −(325) yields −325; −(−325) yields 325.

The *logical negation operator* (!) changes TRUE (nonzero) values to FALSE (zero), and vice versa. For example, !(7) yields 0, and !(0) yields a nonzero value (generally, 1).

The *bitwise negation operator* (~) changes individual bits of its variable operand. Bit values of 1 are changed to 0, and values of 0 are changed to 1. For example ~1111000011110000 would yield 0000111100001111.

Arithmetic Operators

The arithmetic operators in C are the operators you know and love from elementary school. The operators are split over two levels of precedence, corresponding to a level for *multiplicative operators* and one for *additive operators.*

Multiplicative Operators (*, /, and %)

The *multiplication operator* (*) returns the product of its left and right operands; for example, 5 * 4 yields 20.

The *division operator* (/) returns a quotient with decimal part if your division involves floating-point types. For example, 34 / 4.0 yields 8.5, since 4.0 is a floating-point value. If your division involves only integral values, the operator returns the quotient from the division, but without a fractional part. For example, 34 / 4 yields 8 in this case, since the remainder from the division (2) is discarded. The compiler will determine which version of the division operator should be used.

The *modulus operator* (%) works *only* with integral types. This operator returns *only* the remainder when one integral value is divided by another. For example, 34 % 4 yields 2, the remainder from an integer division, after discarding the quotient.

Additive Operators (+ and −)

These are the familiar addition and subtraction operators. If used with floating-point values, the operators return a floating-point value; if used with integral values, the operators return an integral value. For example, 8.0 − 3 yields 5.0, whereas 8 − 3 yields 5.

Shift Operators

The *left* and *right shift* operators modify variables at the level of individual bits. Each operator takes two operands: a variable or value and the number of bits to shift. The left and right shift operators have equal precedence.

Left Shift Operator (<<)

This operator shifts bits leftward, filling the vacated positions on the right with zeros. Bits at the left end of the value are simply discarded during the shifting process. For example, 1110001110001111 << 4 yields 0011100011110000.

Right Shift Operator (>>)

This operator shifts bits rightward, discarding bits at the right end of the value during the shifting process. C compilers differ with respect to how the vacated positions on the left are filled in.

Some compilers use a *logical shift* to fill in the bits on the left. In a logical shift, these positions are always filled with zeros. With an *arithmetic shift*, on the other hand, the positions on the left are filled in with the value of the sign bit when the shifting process begins; positions on the left are filled with 1s when right-shifting a negative number and with 0s when shifting a positive number. To ensure that a logical shift is used, cast the value to be shifted to an **unsigned** before shifting.

Relational and Equality Operators

These operators return a nonzero value (TRUE) if the specified relation holds between the left and the right operands and a zero value (FALSE) otherwise.

Relational Operators (<, <=, >, and >=)

These operators are used to compare two numerical values with respect to magnitude. You should *not* use these operators to compare two string values.

Equality Operators (== and !=)

These operators are used to determine whether two numerical values are equal (==) or unequal (!=) in magnitude. Because the equality operator (==) and the simple assignment operator (=) are quite similar, be very careful when you want to use ==. Make certain you do not accidentally use the assignment operator.

Bitwise Operators

The following operators work by applying an operation to corresponding bits in the left and right operands. The operators return a new bit pattern that is the result of these bitwise operations. Each of the bitwise operators has a different precedence level.

The bitwise operators have lower precedence than most common operators. This means you should use parentheses around bitwise operations in expressions involving operators with higher precedence, especially relational or equality operators.

Bitwise And Operator (&)

This operator "multiplies" corresponding bits. This multiplication produces a 1 only if both bits are 1. The multiplication produces a 0 otherwise. For example, 1111000011110000 & 0000111111110000 yields 0000000011110000, because only the group of 1s on the right is found in each of the operands.

Bitwise Exclusive Or Operator (^)

This operator examines corresponding bits from each operand and returns a 1 if *exactly* one of the operands has a 1 at that bit. The operator returns a 0 if both bits are 0 or both bits are 1. For example, 1111000011110000 ^ 0000111111110000 yields 1111111100000000, because the two operands have different values at corresponding bits for the eight bits on the left and the same values for the eight bits on the right.

Bitwise Or Operator (|)

This operator "adds" corresponding bits. This addition produces a 0 only if both bits are 0. The operator produces a 1 otherwise. There are no carries. For example, 1111000011110000 | 0000111111110000 yields 1111111111110000, because one or the other operand has 1s in all positions except the rightmost four bits.

Logical and Conditional Operators

The logical operators return values representing TRUE or FALSE, depending on the results of applying the operator to the two operands. The conditional operator returns one of two values, depending on whether the specified condition is TRUE or FALSE.

Logical And Operator (&&)

This operator returns a nonzero value (TRUE) if *both* the left and the right operands are TRUE. For example, (7) && (0) yields FALSE, since the right operand is zero.

Logical Or Operator (||)

This operator returns a nonzero value (TRUE) if *either* the left or the right operand is true *or* if *both* are TRUE. For example, (7) || (0) yields TRUE, since the left operand is nonzero.

Conditional Operator (?:)

This operator takes three operands: a condition and two alternatives. The operator tests the condition. If TRUE, the operator returns the alternative to the left of the :; if FALSE, the operator returns the alternative to the right of the :. For example,

```
z = (x < 0) ? -x : x;
```

assigns −**x** to **z** if **x** is negative and assigns **x** to **z** otherwise.

Assignment Operators

C provides a *simple assignment operator* and several *compound assignment operators* that make it very easy to carry out certain common types of assignments more efficiently.

Simple Assignment Operator (=)

This operator needs a variable with a known memory location as its left operand. The operator assigns the value of the right operand to the memory location associated with the left operand.

This operator is very similar to the equality operator (==), so be careful not to confuse the two.

Compound Assignment Operators (+=, −=, *=, /=, %=, &=, ^=, |=, <<=, and >>)

These operators change the left operand by an amount determined by the right operand and the operator involved. Each compound assignment operator consists of a simple assignment operator (=) preceded by another operator; this other operator determines the change in the left operand.

For example, if an integer variable, **val**, has a value of 7, then **val** += 5 assigns 12 (7 + 5) as the new value to **val**. Thus, **val** += 5 is equivalent to **val** = **val** + 5. Similarly, if **val** == 7, then **val** %= 3 assigns 1 as the new value of **val**, since 7 % 3 yields 1 — because the expression involving the compound assignment operator is equivalent to **val** = **val** % 3.

Comma Operator

In certain situations, such as a loop, you may need to change several variables each time through the loop. These changes are often simple assignments, increments, or decrements. The *comma operator* (,) lets you accomplish this in a concise way. The following listing illustrates the use of the comma operator in a loop:

```
/* Program to count up from 1 to 20,
   and down from 20 to 1 at the same time.
   Program illustrates use of the comma operator.
*/

main ()
{
        int up, down;

        for ( up = 1, down = 20; (up <= 20) && ( down >= 1);
              up++, down--)
                printf ( "up %5d; down %5d\n", up, down);
}
```

CONTROL CONSTRUCTS

C includes the same kinds of control constructs as other high-level languages: conditional constructs for selecting among possible conditions and actions, and constructs for looping. C's selection constructs include the **if-else** and **switch** statements; looping constructs include the **while**, **do-while**, and **for** statements.

if-else

The **if** construct is used for making decisions within your programs. There are two major components to an **if** construct: a condition and an action. There may also be a third component: an alternative action. The condition is an expression that the system evaluates. If the result is a nonzero value (that is, TRUE, in C), then C carries out the action specified in the next statement. The action may be simple or may consist of several actions (compound statement). If the condition evaluates to 0 (that is, FALSE), then the program does nothing at that point, or it carries out an alternative action you may have specified.

If you specify such alternative actions, the **if** construct will also include an **else** component. The **else** part is not necessary, however.

The following listing computes the absolute value of a number and shows how to use the **if-else** construct:

```
/* Program to compute the absolute value of an integer entered.
   Program illustrates use of if construct.
*/

main ()
{
        int  val_read, result;

    /* get value */
        printf ( "Please enter an integer: ");
        scanf ( "%d", &val_read);

    /* compute absolute value */
        if ( val_read >= 0)
                result = val_read;
        else                    /* if val_read is negative */
        {
                printf ( "Changing sign\n");
                result = -val_read;
        }

        printf ( "result = %d\n", result);        /* display result */
}
```

The program illustrates the syntax for a simple **if-else** statement. The construct begins with the keyword, **if**, followed by the condition to be tested. This condition, which represents the test for the **if** clause, must be in parentheses. The expression in the test must evaluate to an integer value: zero if the condition is FALSE and a nonzero value if the condition is TRUE.

If the condition is TRUE (in this case, if the value stored in **val_read** is greater than or equal to zero), then C carries out the next statement. In the listing, this is a simple statement. If the condition is FALSE (that is, if **val_read** is negative), the **else** portion of the control construct is carried out. In this case, the program does two things: It prints a message that the sign is being changed, and it assigns −**val_read** to **result**. To make sure that both of these actions are carried out, the two actions are in a compound statement, which the system processes as a single statement.

The following example illustrates a somewhat different, but commonly used, form of the **if-else** construct:

```
/* Program to determine whether an integer entered is
   positive, negative, or zero.
   Program illustrates else--if construct.
*/

main ()
{
        int  val_read;

        printf ( "Please enter an integer: ");
        scanf ( "%d", &val_read);

        if ( !val_read)                     /* if val_read == 0 */
                printf ( "Number == zero\n");
        else if ( val_read < 0)
        {
                printf ( "Not zero ...\n");
                printf ( "Negative\n");
        }
        else                            /* if val_read is positive */
        {
                printf ( "Not zero ...\n");
                printf ( "Positive\n");
        }
}
```

The program uses a common logical construction: *if* A then Z *else if* B then Y *else if* C then X. In this construction, the conditions are tested in order, from top to bottom. As soon as the system finds one that is true, the actions associated with that condition are carried out, and the rest of the clauses are bypassed. The program then exits the **if-else** construct.

The switch Statement

The **switch** statement is a useful selection construct when you want to test whether any of several constant values is found. For example, suppose you want to read a character and determine whether it is a digit or whitespace. The following listing shows how to use the **switch** construct to make such a decision and to act accordingly:

```
/* Program to illustrate use of switch construct to determine whether
   a character is a digit, whitespace, or neither.
*/

main ()
{
        char char_read;

        printf ( "Please enter a character: ");
        scanf ( "%c", &char_read);

        switch ( char_read)
        {
                case '0':
                case '1':
                case '2':
                case '3':
                case '4':
                case '5':
                case '6':
                case '7':
                case '8':
                case '9':
                        printf ( "Digit\n");
                        break; /* force exit from switch */
                case ' ':
                case '\t':
                case '\n':
                        printf ( "Whitespace\n");
                        break; /* force exit from switch */
                default :      /* if neither digit nor whitespace */
                        printf ( "Neither\n");
                        break; /* force exit from switch */
        }
        printf ( "Done\n");
}
```

The **switch** construct begins with the keyword, **switch**, followed by an expression in parentheses. This expression must evaluate to an integer in most implementations. QuickC and Microsoft C 5.0 allow the expression to evaluate to any integral type. The main body of the **switch** construct is contained in a compound statement, which consists of two types of components: labels (for example, **case '0':**), which are used to make decisions, and statements (for example, **printf ("Whitespace \n");**).

Each label represents a possible value for the expression at the top of the **switch** statement. Most labels begin with the keyword, **case**, followed by a value and a colon. In the preceding listing, the values are characters (which are treated as integers internally). Notice that each value must get its own label—you can't have a label such as **case '0', '1', '2':**, for example. No two labels can represent the same value—you can't have **case '0':** in two different places in the **switch**.

The **default** keyword represents the case in which none of the other labels applied. In our example, this label captures any characters that are neither digits nor whitespace. You need not include a **default** label in your **switch** statement; if you do, you can have *at most* one such label.

When the program encounters a **switch** construct, it evaluates the expression and searches through the labels in sequence until it finds the case that corresponds to the current value of the expression. If there are no matches, the program uses the **default** label, if it's present.

The program starts executing from the first statement it finds after the matching label; for example, for an input of '\t' (a tab key), the preceding program would start executing at the statement **printf ("Whitespace \n")**. The program continues processing until it encounters a **break** statement or until it reaches the end of the **switch** construct.

The **break** command causes the program to exit from the **switch** construct immediately. Thus, after printing 'Whitespace,' the program exits from the **switch** and continues executing from the instruction right after the end of the **switch** body. Thus, in our case, the program displays **Done** after exiting from the **switch**.

If there were no **break** after the call to **printf( )**, the program would keep executing any statements it encountered until it encountered a **break** elsewhere or until the end of the **switch** construct. For example, if you removed the first break (after the instruction to write "Digit") and then entered '8' when running the program, the program would produce the following output:

```
Digit
Whitespace
Done
```

Ifthe program finds no **case** label that matches the current value of the expression at the top of the **switch** construct, it starts executing from the statement immediately after the **default** label. If it finds no match and there is no **default** label, the program simply "drops through" the **switch** construct, doing nothing.

The while Loop

The main type of loop in C is the **while** loop, which comes in two different forms and in a more compact variant, called the **for** loop. The following listing illustrates a **while** loop:

```
/* Program to compute and display cubes and sums of cubes
    of first 10 integers.
    Program illustrates use of while loop.
*/

#define CUBE(x)   ((x) * (x) * (x))

main ()
{
        int i1, running_sum = 0;

        i1 = 1;
        while ( i1 <= 10)
        {
                running_sum += CUBE ( i1);
                printf ( "%2d: CUBE == %4d; running_sum == %4d\n",
                        i1, CUBE ( i1), running_sum);
                ++i1;
        }
}
```

This program prints the cubes and the sum of the cubes for the first ten integers. The first statement in **main( )** initializes the "counter," or looping, variable, **i1**, to 1. The value of this counter variable is incremented by 1 each time through the loop (**++i1**), and the loop continues while **i1** is less than or equal to 10.

In the case of a **while** loop, the test to determine whether the following statement should be executed is called the *continuation condition*. The loop repeats while the continuation condition remains TRUE. The expression representing the continuation condition must be in parentheses.

The actions associated with the **while** loop are those in the (simple or compound) statement immediately following the continuation condition. The program carries out each of the actions in the body of the loop; then it goes back to the top of the loop and checks the continuation condition. If this condition is still TRUE, the program carries out the actions in the loop once again.

The increment statement, **++i1**, is a very common way of modifying the counter variable in a loop, since most loops simply change the counter by 1 each time through. This statement is crucial to the loop: Without it, the value of the counter variable would never change, and the loop would never end, since the continuation condition would always be TRUE (1 is always less than or equal to 10).

There are four main components to the **while** loop. The following illustration identifies them:

```
i1 = 1;                            ◄——————— /* Initialization */
while ( i1 <= 10)                  ◄——————— /* Continuation condition */
{                                  ◄——————— /* Loop body */
        running_sum += CUBE ( i1);
        printf ( "%2d: CUBE == %4d; running_sum == %4d\n",
                 i1, CUBE ( i1), running_sum);
        ++i1;                      ◄——————— /* Change in looping variable */
}
```

"Initialization" refers to the looping variable. It is generally a good idea to initialize the control variable just before starting the loop, to make sure you know exactly what value the loop starts with. The "continuation condition" is the test that will determine how long the loop continues. The *loop body* contains the actions to be done when executing the loop. These actions are the main purpose of the loop; the other components are really administrative, to make sure the loop executes the proper number of times and with the correct values. Finally, the "change in the looping variable" is designed to ensure that you get closer to making the continuation condition FALSE each time you go through the loop.

In the illustration, the looping variable was changed at the bottom of the main loop body. You can change it anywhere in the body; be aware, however, that changing it in different places may affect what happens in the loop.

The preceding illustration represents the "vanilla flavored" form of the **while** loop. Sometimes, in actual practice, one or more of these components might be missing or might be present only in an implicit form, as in the following example:

```
/* Program to read characters until a blank is entered.
   Program uses while loop with implicit looping variable.
*/

main ()
{
        int ch;

        while ( (ch = getche()) != ' ')
                printf ( "%c", ch);
}
```

The **while** loop in this program has no initialization for the looping variable (**ch**, in this case). The looping variable is changed, but not necessarily in a manner that will eventually make the continuation condition false. Essentially, this program relies on the user eventually getting tired and ending the input.

The do-while Loop

The **while** loop tests the continuation condition at the top of the loop. If the condition is FALSE from the start, the loop does not execute at all; thus, a **while** loop executes zero or more times. Sometimes, your programs need to have an action carried out *at least* once. For example, suppose you wanted to get a value between 1 and 10 from the user. The following program would accomplish this:

```
/* Program to prompt user until value between 1 and 10 is entered */

main ()
{
        double val;

        do
        {
                printf ( "Please enter a number between 1 and 10 ");
                scanf ( "%lf", &val);
                if ( (val < 1) || ( val > 10))
                        printf ( "Number must be between 1 and 10\n");
        }
        while ( ( val < 1) || ( val > 10));
        printf ( "You entered %lf\n", val);
}
```

The loop in this program will always execute at least once, since the program will not know what the continuation condition is until it reaches the **while** statement at the end of the loop body. If the continuation condition still holds—that is, if the value that has been read is *outside* the desired range—the program goes back to the top of the **do-while** loop and tries again.

The syntax for the **while** portion of the **do-while** loop is the same as for the regular **while** loop: the keyword **while** followed by a continuation condition in parentheses. However, this **while** statement is at the *end* of the **do-while** loop, whereas it is at the *start* of the regular **while** loop.

The for Loop

C provides a very convenient form of the loop construct: the **for** loop. Recall that three of the components of a **while** loop are the initialization of the looping variable, the continuation condition, and the changing of the looping variable's value. The **for** loop lets you gather all three of these components in one place—at the top of the loop. The **for** loop makes it possible to write the code in a very compact but very readable manner, as shown in the following example. The **for** loop is, in fact, equivalent to a **while** loop.

```
/* Program to count from 1 to 20.
   Program illustrates for loop syntax and use.
*/

main ()
{
#define TOP_VAL  20      /* highest value in count */

      int index;

    /* start at 1;
       continue while still below maximum value;
       increment index each time through loop
    */
      for ( index = 1; index <= TOP_VAL; index++)
            printf ( "%d\n", index);
}
```

In a **for** loop, the parentheses following the keyword, **for**, usually contain three expressions, separated by semicolons. In our example, the first expression, **index** = 1, initializes the looping variable. The second expression, **index** <= TOP__VAL, represents the continuation condition. Finally, the third expression, **index++**, uses the increment operator to change the looping variable each time through the loop. The semicolon after each expression is necessary.

The **for** loop in the preceding listing is equivalent to the following **while** loop:

```
index = 1;
while ( index <= TOP_VAL)
{
        printf ( "%d\n", index);
        index++;
}
```

In a sense, the **for** loop simply takes these three elements of a loop from the specific places where they would ordinarily be found and groups them at the top of the loop. When the program encounters a **for** loop, it takes the following actions:

1. It evaluates the first expression once and makes any initializations. The first expression is not used again in the loop.

2. It evaluates the continuation condition (second expression). If the expression is FALSE, the loop terminates, and no further action is taken in the loop body or in the expressions. If the continuation condition is TRUE, the program executes the loop body.

3. After the loop body has executed, the program processes the third expression. This will generally change the looping variable.

4. The program goes back to the top of the **for** loop and repeats the cycle beginning with step 2 (testing the continuation condition).

break and continue

Sometimes you need to be able to get out of a loop quickly, before the current iteration of the loop has been completed. The **break** statement terminates the innermost loop or **switch** in which the statement is found; at that point, program control transfers to the next statement in the immediately surrounding block. The **break** statement can be used only inside a loop or in a **switch** construct.

The **continue** statement is similar to **break** in that both allow exits from a loop. The two types of statements differ, however, in what happens after the exit: The **continue** statement exits to the top of the loop in which the statement was found, thus preparing the program to start the next iteration of the loop. The **continue** statement does not apply to **switch** statements.

Remember: The **break** statement exits from the innermost loop or **switch** in which the statement is found. The **continue** statement exits from the innermost loop (but *not* **switch**) in which the statement is found. The **continue** statement transfers control to the top of the loop in which the statement was found. The **break** statement transfers control to the next statement in the immediately surrounding block.

SUMMARY

The overview of C in this appendix has covered only the most important concepts and constructs. The intent was mainly to refresh your memory about information you haven't used in a long time, not to provide you with new information. You'll need to consult other resources, such as the *Language Reference* that comes with your QuickC or C 5.0 compiler, for more extensive treatment of C's syntax.

B

BUILDING LIBRARIES IN QuickC

One of C's most important features is the ease with which it allows you to build and use *function libraries*, precompiled collections of functions that you can use in your programs. The advantage of using such libraries, as opposed to having the source code for the library functions in your program, is in the time saved because the compiler doesn't have to compile the functions every time you make changes to your program.

QuickC is particularly flexible in the way it lets you work with libraries. You can build two types of libraries in QuickC. The first type, *Quick libraries*, are built for use when you want to run your program *inside* the QuickC environment, as opposed to building an executable version of your program. That is, Quick libraries are used when you want to compile your program to memory while inside QuickC, and then run the program. Quick libraries have the extension **.qlb**. You don't need to use a Quick library if you plan to compile the function to executable code each time — that is, if you're going to create an **.exe** file whenever you compile. Quick libraries can only be used with QuickC.

The second type of library is a *stand-alone library,* which contains precompiled functions that can be linked into your program when you're building an executable version. Such libraries generally have the extension **.lib**. Stand-alone libraries have the same format as the libraries included with QuickC or Microsoft C 5.0.

In this appendix, you'll learn how to build both types of libraries. You'll build a Quick library containing Run-Time library functions that are used in our example programs, but that are not built into QuickC. Chapter 6 of the *QuickC Programmer's Guide* contains a table of the functions built into QuickC. As you'll notice, several of the functions we've used—including **rand( )**, **pow( )**, and **ecvt( )**—are not built into QuickC. In the next section, you'll see how to build a Quick library file, **qcstuff.qlb**, that contains these functions. You must build the **qcstuff.qlb** library yourself; it is not part of QuickC. Quick libraries work only with QuickC.

You'll also learn how to build a stand-alone library, and how to link this library into your programs. We'll only be looking at a small number of the possibilities here; read the discussion in your *QuickC Programmer's Guide* for more details.

BUILDING QUICK LIBRARIES

We'll look at the steps involved in building a Quick library by developing one that includes the functions used in the example programs for this book.

To create a Quick library for a program or programs, you need to do three things:

1. Create a source file that includes calls to the functions you want to include in the Quick library.

2. Compile and link this source file to create a compiled version of the file with the extension **.qlb**.

3. Load the Quick library when you want to run your program within QuickC.

Creating the Source File

The source file you create just needs a **main( )** function that contains calls to each of the functions you want. The following listing represents the source file used to build a file, **qcstuff.qlb**, usable for compiling the programs in earlier chapters within the QuickC environment.

```
/* Source file containing calls to the commonly used functions
   that are not predefined in QuickC.
   File is eventually compiled and linked to create qcstuff.qlb.
*/

#include <math.h>
#include <stdio.h>

main ()
{
        char    ch, *str;
        double  dbl1, dbl2;
        int     i1, i2, i3;
        FILE    *fp;
        fpos_t  *pos;

        rand();
        srand();
        fgetchar();
        fputchar( ch);
        _ftol();
        pow ( dbl1, dbl2);
        sqrt ( dbl1);
        perror ( str);
        ecvt ( dbl1, i1, &i2, &i3);
}
```

As you can see, the format for this file is simple. The entire "program" consists of calls to the desired functions. The program does nothing with the results of these function calls.

The basic strategy is to get QuickC to link the desired functions into a file that really does nothing with them. The resulting object file is then transformed into a **.qlb** file having the format required for QuickC to be able to use these functions when you compile and run your program within QuickC.

Compiling and Linking
to a .qlb File

Once you've created your source file, you need to create a Quick library from it. The following line contains a batch file you can use to build the file **qcstuff.qlb**:

```
qcl /AM \qc\lib\quicklib %1.c /Fe%1.qlb /link /Q
```

Let's look at the elements in this rather long command line. The first "word" on the line, **qcl**, lets you compile and link files outside of the QuickC environment. The **qcl** program, which is included with QuickC, compiles and (if you wish) links the specified files without bringing you into the QuickC window environment.

The /AM specifies that a medium memory model is to be used. This memory model is necessary for a Quick library. Compiler and linker options are case-sensitive in QuickC and in Microsoft C 5.0, partly because of the large number of options available.

Remember: Quick libraries *must* use a medium memory model.

The purpose of **\qc \inc \quicklib** is to tell the **qcl** program where the **quicklib.obj** file is to be found. The **quicklib.obj** file is needed for building Quick libraries. If you set up your QuickC files using the default directories, you only need to specify **quicklib** here—that is, you don't need to specify an entire path.

The next word (**%1.c**) specifies the file to be compiled. The **%1** is a placeholder in this batch file, just as it would be in a **printf()** string argument. When you call this batch file, you need to specify **qcstuff** as a command line argument. You could just as well write **qcstuff** instead of **%1** in this file, thereby making the batch file capable of building just the one Quick library, **qcstuff.qlb**. The **.c** extension is necessary when specifying a file name here.

The **/Fe%1.qlb** specifies that the "run" file is to have the same name as your source file (the name substituted for **%1**), and the extension **.qlb**. Ordinarily, when you compile a file to become a stand-alone program, the resulting file will have the extension

.exe, since this is the extension DOS expects. However, in this case, you don't want DOS to deal with the file; you want QuickC to run it. QuickC expects the **.qlb** extension.

The **/link** command invokes the linker, and the **/Q** option tells it to create a Quick library out of the compiled file. This Quick library file will have the format appropriate for use by QuickC.

You can accomplish the same thing with a two-step process. The following listing shows the two command lines needed:

```
qcl /c /AM qcstuff.c
link \qc\lib\quicklib.obj + qcstuff.obj, qcstuf.qlb, , /Q;
```

The first line invokes the **qcl** program as in the earlier example. The **/c** option specifies that you just want to compile, not to link. The **/AM** option again specifies the medium memory model, and the **qcstuff.c** tells **qcl** what file you want to compile.

The second command line invokes the linker. The lengthy expression **\qc \libquicklib.obj + qcstuff.obj** tells the linker what compiled files to link together. Such files will generally have the extension **.obj**, but they may also be stand-alone libraries — that is, **.lib** files.

The **qcstuff.qlb** argument specifies the "run" file you want the linker to create, just as in the one-line version. Notice that linker parameters, or fields, are separated by commas. This tells the linker where one type of information, or set of parameters (object files, for example), stops and the next type (run files, for example) starts.

Two commas with nothing between them indicate that the linker can use its default values for that field. In this case, the space between **qcstuff.qlb,** and the next comma indicates that the linker can use its default names for a file known as the *map* file, which the linker can create. (Such a file contains information about where in the module the segments of a program are to be found. For most purposes, you won't need this file.) By default, in this case, the linker would write this information to **qcstuff.map**.

You could also specify additional libraries for the linker to search for routines needed in other modules. In our case, there were no other libraries that needed to be searched. Ordinarily, the linker would prompt for additional libraries if none were specified. The semicolon suppresses this prompt.

Finally, the /Q option tells the linker to create a Quick library. Linker options can be included just about anywhere on the command line.

The commands in the previous listing produce three files in addition to the **qcstuff.c** file that started it all: **qcstuff.obj** (created by the compiler), **qcstuff.map**, and **qcstuff.qlb** (created by the linker). The following pair of command lines would have accomplished the same thing, except that no **.map** file would be built:

```
qcl /c /AM qcstuff.c
link /Q \qc\lib\quicklib.obj + qcstuff.obj, qcstuf.qlb;
```

Notice that the /Q option has been moved to an earlier part of the line. This makes no difference, but the semicolon immediately after the name of the run file is important. This tells the linker not to worry about the remaining two fields: map file and additional libraries. The result is that no **.map** file is created and the linker doesn't ask about whether to search additional library files.

Loading the Quick Library

Once you've created your Quick library, you're ready to use it in any programs that rely on more than the functions built into QuickC. To start QuickC with your Quick library loaded, use the /l option, followed by the name of the Quick library file, as in the following command line. This line will let you compile the file **srcfile** to memory, once you're in QuickC, even though this program uses more than the built-in QuickC functions.

```
qc /lqcstuff srcfile
```

BUILDING STAND-ALONE LIBRARIES

You can use the Microsoft Library Manager, **lib**, to build stand-alone libraries. Such libraries consist of compiled routines that can be added to any program you're building and can be used in the program. Once they are in compiled form, the compiler need not process these routines each time you compile a program that uses them.

For example, the following listing collects generally applicable functions, most of which we've already defined in this book. We'll build a library containing these functions; you can link this library when you build programs that use them.

```
/* File containing commonly used functions.
   File is used to illustrate how to build a stand-alone library.
*/

#include <stdio.h>
#include <dos.h>

#define NULL_CHAR    '\0'
#define FALSE        0
#define TRUE         1
#define TOLERANCE    1e-12
#define INVALID_VAL  -99999.999


/* double get_time ()
   Returns the number of seconds elapsed on system clock since midnight.
   NOTE : Assumes <dos.h> (Microsoft) or equivalent.
   USAGE : time_elapsed = get_time ();
*/
double get_time ()
{
        double hrs, mins, secs, hundredths;
        union  REGS inregs, outregs;

        /* Request DOS service 0x2c */
        inregs.h.ah = 0x2c;

        /* call interrupt 0x21 with DOS service request # 0x2c */
        intdos ( &inregs, &outregs);

        hrs = (double) outregs.h.ch;        /* hrs elapsed returned in CH */
        mins = (double) outregs.h.cl;       /* mins elapsed returned in CL */
        secs = (double) outregs.h.dh;       /* secs elapsed returned in DH */
        hundredths = (double) outregs.h.dl; /* 1/100's secs returned in DL */
```

```
        /* Total elapsed time (in seconds) =
            3600 (secs / hr)  * hrs +
            60 ( secs / min) * mins +
            1 ( secs / sec) * secs +
            .01 ( secs per 1/100th sec) * hundredths.
        */
        return ( hrs * 3600.0 + mins * 60.0 + secs + hundredths / 100.0);
}


/* double how_long ( double start, double finish)
    Returns the time elapsed between finish and start.
    Routine compensates for tasks that started before and finished
    after midnight.
    USAGE :  time_required = how_long ( start, finish);
*/
double how_long ( double start, double finish)

{
#define FULL_DAY 86400.0  /* seconds in a 24 hr day */

        /* start == first elapsed time measurement;
            finish == second elapsed time measurement.
            If start > finish then the time must have passed midnight
            between start and finish of process.
            In that case, a formula adjustment is necessary.
        */
        if ( start > finish)
                return ( FULL_DAY - start + finish);
        else
                return ( finish - start);
}


/* void make_str_lower ( char *str)
    Convert a string to lowercase characters
    USAGE :  make_str_lower ( my_str);
*/
void make_str_lower ( char *str)
{
        int index;

        for ( index = 0; str [ index] != NULL_CHAR; index++)
                str [ index] = tolower ( str [ index]);
}


/* void make_str_upper ( char *str)
    Convert a string to uppercase characters
    USAGE :  make_str_upper ( my_str);
*/
void make_str_upper ( char *str)
{
        int index;

        for ( index = 0; str [ index] != NULL_CHAR; index++)
                str [ index] = toupper ( str [ index]);
}


/* int non_zero ( double val)
    Return true if val differs from zero by more than a predefined amount.
    USAGE : test_result = non_zero ( val_to_test);
*/
int non_zero ( double val)
{
```

```
        if ( (( val - 0.0) > TOLERANCE) || ((val - 0.0) < -TOLERANCE))
                return ( TRUE);
        else
                return ( FALSE);
}


/* double safe_division ( double numer, double denom)
   Divide num by denom, checking for division by zero before doing so.
   Return quotient or a default value ( INVALID_VAL) on division by zero.
   USAGE : quotient = safe_division ( num, den);
*/
double safe_division ( double numer, double denom)
{
        int non_zero ( double);

        if ( non_zero ( denom))
                return ( numer / denom);
        else
                return ( INVALID_VAL);
}


/* void swap_dbl ( double *first, double *second)
   Exchange the values stored in *first and *second.
   USAGE : swap_dbl ( first, second);
*/
void swap_dbl ( double *first, double *second)
{
        double temp;       /* to store one of the values during swap */

        temp = *first;
        *first = *second;
        *second = temp;
}


/* void swap_int ( int *first, int *second)
   Exchange the values stored in *first and *second.
   USAGE : swap_int ( first, second);
*/
void swap_int ( int *first, int *second)
{
        int temp;       /* to store one of the values during swap */

        temp = *first;
        *first = *second;
        *second = temp;
}


/* double zero_one_rand ()
   Returns a pseudorandom value between  0 and 1, inclusive.
   USAGE : pseudo = zero_one_rand ();
*/
double zero_one_rand ()
{
#define  MAX_VAL  32767.0        /* NOTE: defined as floating point type */
        int  rand ( void);       /* returns a pseudorandom integer */
        int  rand_result;

        rand_result = rand ();   /* get a pseudorandom integer */
        return ( rand_result / MAX_VAL);
}
```

To build a stand-alone library, you need to do two things:

1. Compile the source file(s) to an **.obj** file.
2. Build a **.lib** library file from this object file, using the library manager program, **lib**.

A batch file containing the following two command lines will let you build a stand-alone library file from a source file. In the discussion, assume the file containing the preceding listings is named **utils.c**.

```
qcl /c %1.c
lib %1.lib +%1.obj;
```

The first line invokes the **qcl** program to compile the source file specified in the command line argument when starting the batch file. In our case, this argument would be **utils**, without an extension (since the extension is added in the batch file). You would include this argument on your command line when you invoked the batch file.

The output from the first line would be a file named **utils.obj**. The second line in the batch file builds the stand-alone library. The first field specifies the name of a library file to be modified. If no file with this name exists, the library manager will create a new one, which is what we want in this case. The second field specifies that the library manager should add (+) the contents of the object file specified (in this case, **utils**) to the **.lib** file. The semicolon again indicates that the program should not look for additional fields or options. (See Chapter 10 of the *QuickC Programmer's Guide* for details on these additional fields.) The outcome from executing this command line is that a file named **utils.lib** is created.

Using a Stand-alone Library

Once the **utils.lib** file has been created, you can link it into any programs you want to build that use functions in this library. For example, suppose you had the following program, which uses several of the functions in **utils.lib:**

```
/* Program to generate pseudorandom values betwen 0 and 1, and
   to keep track of the current maximum ratio between successive values.
   Program also illustrates use of stand-alone library files.
*/

#include <stdio.h>
#define MAX_TRIALS 20
main ()
{
        double first, second, ratio, max_ratio = 0.0;
        double start, finish;
        double zero_one_rand ( void), get_time ( void);
        double how_long ( double, double);
        double safe_division ( double, double);
        int    index;

        start = get_time ();
        first = zero_one_rand ();
        for ( index = 1; index <= MAX_TRIALS; index++)
        {
                second = zero_one_rand ();
                ratio = safe_division ( first, second);
                printf ( "%10.4lf\n", ratio);
                if ( ratio > max_ratio)
                {
                        printf ( "old max == %10.4lf;  new max == %10.4lf\n",
                                max_ratio, ratio);
                        max_ratio = ratio;
                }
                ratio = safe_division ( second, first);
                printf ( "%10.4lf\n", ratio);
                if ( ratio > max_ratio)
                {
                        printf ( "old max == %10.4lf;  new max == %10.4lf\n",
                                max_ratio, ratio);
                        max_ratio = ratio;
                }
                first = second;
        }
        finish = get_time ();
        printf ( "%10.2lf seconds\n", how_long ( start, finish));
}
```

The following command line would let you compile this program, which we'll call **ratios.c**, linking in the **utils.lib** library while creating the executable file.

```
qcl ratios.c /Feratios1.exe·/link utils.lib;
```

This line says to compile the file **ratios.c**, ultimately writing the executable file, **ratios.exe**. The linking instructions specify that the library file, **utils.lib**, is to be searched for any functions not found in the **ratios.obj** file or in the standard libraries.

The resulting **ratios.exe** file behaves just as if the program had been built out of a large source file containing the functions included in both **ratios.c** and in **utils.c**, or out of two source files compiled separately or compiled together by including an instruction to read the contents of **utils.c** while compiling **ratios.c**. The difference is in the compilation time required. In this case, compiling just **ratios.c**, then linking in **utils.lib**, is almost 20% faster than working with the source files alone.

You can explore additional options and ways of using the linker on your own. One thing to notice is that we didn't include the **/AM** option. By default, QuickC compiles with a small memory model. The resulting files are different than they would be if they had been compiled with a medium memory model. When you link in libraries, make sure the libraries and the source files are compiled under the same memory models.

SUMMARY

In this appendix, we've looked at two ways to use precompiled files to make program development quicker and more convenient. Quick libraries let you compile and run your programs within QuickC, which has the advantages of speed and ease of modification. This means you can create, compile, and revise without ever leaving QuickC—one of the nicest features of the software.

Once you've got the program working the way you want it to, you can compile it to an executable file. During this process you'll often want to save time by linking in precompiled libraries that have been tested, and can now be used in any of your programs. This approach makes the compilation process faster, and also gives you flexibility for building modular programs. By collecting related functions in libraries and then linking these libraries into the programs you're building, you can make your programs smaller (since only the libraries for needed functions will be linked in) and also make your programming tools more widely usable.

C

QuickC COMMAND SUMMARY

This appendix summarizes the commands and options available in QuickC. In the commands, special notation is used in a few places.

The vertical bar, |, means "or," so that 0 | 1 means "0 or 1," as in the command to set warning levels for **qcl.exe**, for which any of the following would be valid:

```
qcl first /W0

qcl first /W1

qcl first /W2

qcl first /W3
```

Material between curly braces, {}, is optional, as in the command to add watch variables. This material may be repeated more than once. Both of the following would be valid watch variable selections:

```
val
val; even
```

Angle brackets, < and >, around material mean that you are to provide information of the sort specified between these brackets. Do not include the brackets in your text. For example, the first of the following calls to QuickC is valid, but the second call is not valid:

```
/* the following call is valid */
qc /lqcstuff

/* the following call is NOT valid */
qc /l<qcstuff>
```

COMMANDS FOR
CALLING QuickC

Start the QuickC program   qc

You can use the following commands as command-line arguments when you invoke QuickC—that is, when you use the **qc** command.

Start QuickC in black-and-white mode   /b

```
qc /b
```

Start QuickC when using a color   /g
graphics adapter

```
qc /g
```

Use as many screen lines as possible,   /h
given the display adapter being used

```
qc /h
```

Load a Quick library for use when   /l<*library name*>
compiling to memory

`qc /lqcstuff`

Start QuickC with a source file as the   <*file name*>
working file

`qc first`

USEFUL COMMANDS IN THE QuickC ENVIRONMENT

The following predefined keys are very convenient, especially in dire situations. The on-line help feature provides a brief listing of the QuickC commands. The exit command can get you out of many tough situations.

On-line help   F1

  On-line help about a C keyword or
  Run-Time library function (assumes
  cursor is on keyword or function
  name)   SHIFT-F1

Exit from QuickC   ALT-F-X

EDITING COMMANDS

The following commands are available while editing a file. Many of these commands accomplish the same thing as QuickC menu options, eliminating the need to call up a menu.

Movement Commands

Move up one line	UP ARROW or CTRL-E
Move down one line	DOWN ARROW or CTRL-X
Move right one character	RIGHT ARROW or CTRL-D
Move left one character	LEFT ARROW or CTRL-S
Move right one word	CTRL-RIGHT ARROW or CTRL-F
Move left one word	CTRL-LEFT ARROW or CTRL-A
Move to top of screen	CTRL-Q-E
Move to bottom of screen	CTRL-Q-X
Move to beginning of line	HOME or CTRL-Q-S
Move to end of line	END or CTRL-Q-D
Move to beginning of file	CTRL-HOME or CTRL-Q-R
Move to end of file	CTRL-END or CTRL-Q-C

Move to next error	SHIFT-F3
Move to previous error	SHIFT-F4
Scroll up one line	CTRL-W
Scroll down one line	CTRL-Z
Scroll up one screen, or window	PGUP
	or
	CTRL-R
Scroll down one screen, or window	PGDN
	or
	CTRL-C
Scroll left one window	CTRL-PGUP
Scroll right one window	CTRL-PGDN
Find text to be specified	CTRL-Q-F
Find next occurrence of text just found	F3
Find selected text	CTRL-\
Find and change text to be specified	CTRL-Q-A

The following command is available after CTRL-Q-A has been specified:

Switch to **Change To** text box	ALT-T

Selection Commands

Select preceding character	SHIFT-LEFT ARROW
Select current character	SHIFT-RIGHT ARROW
Select preceding "word"	SHIFT-CTRL-LEFT ARROW
Select current "word"	SHIFT-CTRL-RIGHT ARROW
Select preceding line	SHIFT-UP ARROW
Select current line	SHIFT-DOWN ARROW
Select to beginning of file	SHIFT-CTRL-PGUP
Select to end of file	SHIFT-CTRL-PGDN

Insertion Commands

Insert text from Clipboard	SHIFT-INS
Insert line below current line	CTRL-B
Insert line above current line	CTRL-N
Insert line deleted using CTRL-Y	SHIFT-INS
Insert tab at current cursor position	TAB
	or
	CTRL-I
Copy selected text to Clipboard	CTRL-INS

Deletion Commands

Delete character at current cursor position	DEL
	or
	CTRL-G
Delete preceding character	BACKSPACE
	or
	CTRL-H
Delete to end of current word	CTRL-T
Delete current line	CTRL-Y
Delete to end of current line	CTRL-Q-Y
Delete selected text without saving in Clipboard	DEL
Delete selected text, saving in Clipboard	SHIFT-DEL
Delete control character	CTRL-P *<character>*

Miscellaneous Commands

Toggle between overtype and insert modes	INS
	or
	CTRL-V
Mark section of text	CTRL-K 0 | 1 | 2 | 3
Jump to marked section of text	CTRL-Q 0 | 1 | 2 | 3
Find matching left brace	CTRL-{

Find matching left bracket	CTRL-[
Find matching left angle bracket	CTRL-<
Find matching left parenthesis	CTRL-(
Find matching right brace	CTRL-}
Find matching right bracket	CTRL-]
Find matching right angle bracket	CTRL->
Find matching right parenthesis	CTRL-)
Move to next tabstop	TAB
Move to previous tabstop	SHIFT-TAB

MENU COMMANDS

This section summarizes the commands and options available through QuickC menus. These commands are grouped by menu.

Files Menu (ALT-F)

The File menu serves to create, open, and save files of various sorts. It also includes some miscellaneous options for getting access to DOS and printing a file.

File Manipulation Commands

Create new file	ALT-F-N
Open existing file	ALT-F-O
Open file edited before current file	F2
	or
	ALT-F-F
Merge specified file into work file at current cursor location	ALT-F-M
Save current file	ALT-F-S
Save current file under a new name, leaving original file intact	ALT-F-A

Program List Commands

The following commands let you create, modify, and delete program list files, which contain the names of all the source files that make up a large program.

Create a program list for current file	ALT-F-L
Edit program list for current file	ALT-F-E

The following options and commands are available when either of the preceding options has been set. That is, the following assume either ALT-F-L or ALT-F-E.

File name for program list (.**mak**) file	*<file name>*

Once QuickC has created or opened the specified program list file, the following commands can be used:

File name to be added to program list	*<file name>*
Add file name to list, if not present, or remove name from list, if present	RETURN
Select Add/Remove option, if not currently selected	ALT-A
Clear program list	ALT-C
Save program list	ALT-S
Clear, or delete, program list for current file	ALT-F-C

Miscellaneous File Commands

Print current file	ALT-F-P
Suspend QuickC, exit temporarily to DOS shell	ALT-F-D

Edit Menu (ALT-E)

This menu makes it possible to modify the contents of the working file and possibly of other files as well. By default, your actions will affect your work file.

Clear, or delete, text from file; do not copy to Clipboard	DEL or ALT-E-E
Cut, or delete, text from file; copy text to Clipboard	SHIFTDEL or ALT-E-T
Copy text to Clipboard; do not delete from file	CTRL-INS or ALT-E-C
Paste text from Clipboard to Target (requires text in Clipboard)	SHIFT-INS or ALT-E-P
Make working file read only	ALT-E-R
Undo last action on current line	ALT-BACKSPACE or ALT-E-U

View Menu (ALT-V)

This menu lets you see various files associated with your current program file. It also lets you change the way Quick C appears on your screen.

View a program source file (that is, a file on the program list)	ALT-V-S
View an include file for the current program	ALT-V-I
View display format options	ALT-V-O
View output screen	F4 or ALT-V-T
Open/close Error window	ALT-V-E

Search Menu (ALT-S)

This menu lets you find and modify specified text, find the definition of a function in the source file, and so on.

Find specified text	ALT-S-F
Find and change specified text	ALT-S-C

The following all work with the preceding options. Each of the following options toggles:

Require self-standing word	ALT-W
Require uppercase or lowercase matching	ALT-M
Regular Expression	ALT-R

The following commands assume the ALT-S-C option has been specified:

Switch to **Change To** text box	ALT-T
Change all occurrences of specified text, without verifying	ALT-C
Set default action to skip current occurrence of text	S
Set default action to change current occurrence of text	C

The following special characters are allowed in regular expressions, and assume that ALT-R has been specified:

Match any single character appearing in specified position	. (dot)
Match one or more occurrences of the character preceding *	*<character>**
Treat the next character literally	\
Match if specified phrase appears at *end* of line	*<text>*$
Match if specified phrase appears at *beginning* of line	^*<text>*
Match occurrence of any one of the characters between the brackets	[*<text>*]

The following are special characters that can be used within the square brackets:

To search for any ASCII values between those of the starting and ending characters, use '-'	[<*char*>-<*char*>]
To match any characters *except* those listed between the brackets, use '^' in regular expressions	[^<*text*>]
Repeat search for last text found	F3
	or
	ALT-S-R
Find marked, or selected, text	CTRL-\
	or
	ALT-S-S
Find function definition	ALT-S-U
Find next error	SHIFT-F3
	or
	ALT-S-N
Find previous error	SHIFT-F4
	or
	ALT-S-P

Run Menu (ALT-R)

This menu lets you compile and run your program, or continue running your program if it has been stopped for some reason.

Start compilation and execution	SHIFT-F5
	or
	ALT-R-S
Continue interrupted program execution	F5
	or
	ALT-R-N

Restart interrupted program execution at next statement	ALT-R-R
Set compile-time options	ALT-R-C

Compile-time options include the following. All these options assume ALT-R-C has been selected.

Warning Levels (0 through 3)	UP ARROW or DOWN ARROW

The following five commands toggle:

Compile for subsequent debugging	D
Compile with pointer checks	P
Compile with stack checks	S
Allow Microsoft language extensions	L
Optimize for speed	Z

The following four options for specifying output from compilation process are mutually exclusive:

Compile to object file	O
Compile to memory	M
Compile to executable file	X
Syntax check only	Y

In the Compiler option dialog box, the following additional commands are allowed:

Search in additional paths for include	I or ALT-I
Specify definitions for current compilation	D or ALT-D

In the Compiler option dialog box, the following commands, in addition to Cancel, are valid:

Build program	B
	or
	RETURN
Compile file	C
Rebuild all	R
Set run-time options	ALT-R-O

The following options all assume ALT-R-O has been selected:

Specify information to be passed to program on command line for use in programs just being compiled in memory	*<command line information>*
Specify memory to allocate for global and static program data (*near data*)	ALT-N
Specify amount of memory to allocate for local variables (stack)	ALT-S

Debug Menu (ALT-D)

This menu lets you set up your program to watch changes in the variables of interest to you, and to step through the program to watch these values change.

The following options both toggle:

Turn program tracing on/off	ALT-D-T
Turn screen swapping on/off	ALT-D-S

The following options all assume the program has been compiled with the Debug compiler option turned on:

Add one or more watch variables   ALT-D-A

The following assumes ALT-D-A has been selected:

Specify the watch variable(s) to be
added   <*name*>{;<*name*>;}

You can also specify the output format for the watch variables, using the following specifiers. These specifiers are included after the watch variable name, and are separated by a comma from this name.

Signed decimal integer	d
	or
	i
Unsigned decimal integer	u
Unsigned octal integer	o
Hexadecimal integer	x
Real number in floating point format	f
Real number in scientific notation format	e
Real number in either floating point or scientific notation format, whichever is more compact	g
Single character	c
String (characters up to first null character)	s
Delete the last watch variable set	SHIFT-F2
	or
	ALT-D-E
Clear all watch variables currently set	ALT-D-L
Toggle breakpoint on/off	F9
	or
	ALT-D-B
Clear all breakpoints currently set	ALT-D-C

The following keyboard commands will let you step through the program in the debugger:

Execute the next program statement, tracing execution through the function	F8
Execute the next program statement, tracing execution around the function	F10
Execute the program until it reaches the current cursor position	F7
Execute program to next breakpoint	F5
Display the current output screen	F4

COMPILING AND LINKING OUTSIDE OF QuickC

The following commands and options can be used with the **qcl.exe** program. Defaults are in parentheses. Case is important for many of these options.

Get help about **qcl** commands	/help
Set warning level (/W1)	/W0 | 1 | 2 | 3
Compile only to object file; no linking (off)	/c
Debug mode (off)	/Zq *and* Zi *and* Zd
Pointer checks on (off)	/Zr
Stack checks off (on)	/Gs
Syntax check only (off)	/Zs
Language extensions off (on)	/Za
Optimize for speed/time (off)	/Ot
Optimize loops (off)	/Ol
Optimize for everything (off)	/Ox
Specify directories to search for include files	/I<*path name*>

Do not search usual places for include files (off)	/X
Specify definitions of current program/run (none)	/D<*definitions*>
Set stack size (0x400)	/F<*hexadecimal value*>
Specify name of executable file to be created (same name as main source file, **.exe** extension)	/Fe<*file name*>
Specify name of map file to be created (none)	/Fm<*file name*>
Specify name of object file to be created (same name as main source file, **.obj** extension)	/Fo<*file name*>
Specify language underlying function-calling and naming conventions used by program (for mixed-language programming)	/Gc fortran | pascal | cdecl

Memory Models

The following commands let you specify the memory models and library files to use:

Use small memory model—one 64KBdata segment, one 64KB code segment (default for **qcl**)	/AS
Use medium memory model—one 64KB data segment, multiple 64KB code segments (default for **qc**)	/AM
Use compact memory model—multiple 64KB data segments, one 64KB code segment	/AC
Use large memory model—multiple 64KB data segments, multiple 64KB code segments	/AL

Specify size threshold for including data structure in a new data segment	/Gt{<*number*>}
Emulate 8087 or 80287 for floating point math (default)	/FPi
Generate code for an 8087 or 80287 for floating point math	/FPi87
Use instruction set for 8086 (default)	/G0
Use instruction set for 80286	/G2
Pack structure members	/Zp
Do not use the default library or libraries	/Zl

Controlling the Preprocessor

The following commands let you use the preprocessor and also save files after the preprocessor has finished with them.

Preserve comments in source files (observe case of command)	/C
Write preprocessed output to a disk file	/P
Write preprocessed output to **stdout**	/E
Write preprocessed output to disk file *and* **stdout**	/EP
Undefine the specified predefined name	/U <*name*>
Undefine all predefined names	/u

CONTROLLING THE LINKER

The following commands are available when linking files to build a program or library. Note that linker options are not case-sensitive. For the following commands, you don't necessarily have to write out the entire command. The capitalized characters are necessary; the lowercase characters can be omitted when referring to the option.

Get help about linker options	/HElp
Pause for disk swap before writing .exe file	/PAUse
Display information during linking	/Information
Don't prompt if linker can't find a file	/Batch
Do not search in default libraries	/NODefaultlibrary-search
Create a map file	/Map
Include line numbers in output file	/LInenumbers
Prepare executable file for use with Codeview	/COdeview
Do not ignore case	/NOIgnorecase
Create a Quick library	/Quicklib
Make executable file as small and accessible as possible	/Exepack
Optimize use of far calls to functions	/Farcalltranslation
Do not optimize use of far calls to functions	/NOFarcall-translation
Pack contiguous program segments	/PACkcode
Do not pack contiguous program segments	/NOPackcode
Order program segments using Micro soft high-level language defaults	/DOsseg

The following linker options let you control various values relating to the program being compiled.

Maximum number of program segments (default == 128)	/SEgments: $<number>$
Maximum amount of space needed by program in memory	/CParmaxalloc: $<number>$
Maximum stack size (in bytes)	/STack:$<number>$

TRADEMARKS

IBM®	International Business Machines Corporation
Microsoft®	Microsoft Corporation
MS-DOS®	Microsoft Corporation
PCjr™	International Business Machines Corporation
QuickC™	Microsoft Corporation
UNIX®	AT&T
XENIX®	Microsoft Corporation

INDEX

699

Microsoft. QuickBASIC 4.0. Instant programming means instant results!

Microsoft QuickBASIC 4.0 gives you the remarkable ability to run, edit and debug, then continue to run your program without a time-consuming compile step!

The new instant environment gives you everything you need for quick and efficient program development. Edit your program and see

your mistakes right away with automatic syntax checking; debug using breakpoints, watchpoints, and watch expressions; and write multiple-module programs easily with the built-in code outliner. All without having to leave the instant environment.

Microsoft QuickBASIC 4.0 is a revolution in BASIC programming! Come in and see why.

For the name of your nearest Microsoft dealer, call (800) 541-1261, Dept. D69.

Advanced C, Second Edition
by Herbert Schildt

Experienced C programmers can become professional C programmers with Schildt's nuts-and-bolts guide to advanced programming techniques. Now thoroughly revised, *Advanced C, Second Edition* covers the new ANSI standard in addition to the Kernighan and Ritchie C used in the first edition. All the example code conforms to the ANSI standard. You'll find information you need on sorting and searching; queues, stacks, linked lists, and binary trees; dynamic allocation, interfacing to assembly language routines and the operating system; expression parsing; and more. When you finish reading *Advanced C*, you'll be ready for the slick programming tricks found in Schildt's twelfth book for Osborne, C: Power User's Guide.

$21.95 p
0-07-881348-4, 353 pp., 7³/₈ x 9¹/₄

Artificial Intelligence Using C
by Herb Schildt

With Herb Schildt's newest book, you can add a powerful dimension to your C programs—artificial intelligence. Schildt, a programming expert and author of seven Osborne books, shows C programmers how to use AI techniques that have traditionally been implemented with Prolog and LISP. You'll utilize AI for vision, pattern recognition, robotics, machine learning, logic, problem solving, and natural language processing, Each chapter develops practical examples that can be used in the construction of artificial intelligence applications. If you are building expert systems in C, this book contains a complete expert system that can easily be adapted to your needs. Schildt provides valuable insights that allow even greater command of the systems you create.

$21.95 p
0-07-881255-0, 432 pp., 7³/₈ x 9¹/₄

C: Power User's Guide
by Herbert Schildt

Make your C programs sizzle! All the bells, whistles, and slick tricks used to get professional results in commercial software are unveiled to serious programmers in *C: Power User's Guide*. In his eleventh book for Osborne/McGraw-Hill, Schildt shows you how to build a Borland type interface, develop a core for a database, create memory resident programs, and more. Schildt combines theory, background, and code in an even mix as he excites experienced C programmers with new features and approaches. Learn master techniques for handling menus, windows, graphics, and video game programming. If hashing is what you're after, it's here too, along with techniques for using the serial port and sorting disk files. OS/2™ level programming with specific OS/2 functions is also covered. Before you send your programs out to market, consult Schildt for the final touches that set professional software apart from the rest.

$22.95 p
0-07-881307-7, 384 pp., 7³/₈ x 9¹/₄

Advanced Graphics in C: Programming and Techniques
by Nelson Johnson

Add graphics to your C programs and you'll add significant capabilities to your software. With *Advanced Graphics in C* you'll be able to write graphics programs for the IBM® EGA (Enhanced Graphics Adapter), the de facto standard for high-quality graphics programming on the IBM PC. *Advanced Graphics in C* features a special, complete graphics program called GRAPHIQ, that provides a whole toolkit of all the routines you'll need for graphics operations, and even gives you code for a rotatable and scalable character set. Johnson shows you how to use GRAPHIQ to implement or adapt graphics in your C programs. GRAPHIQ is full of tools not available elsewhere. *Advanced Graphics in C* also offers an entire stroke/front character set; code for the AT&T Image Capture Board; and information on serial and parallel interfacing to mice, light pens, and digitizers.

$22.95 p
0-07-881257-7, 670 pp., 7³/₈ x 9¹/₄

C: The Complete Reference
by Herbert Schildt

For all C programmers, here's an encyclopedia of C terms, functions, codes, and applications. Arranged for quick fact-finding, *C: The Complete Reference* includes sections covering C basics, C library functions by category, various algorithms and C applications, and the C programming environment. You'll also find coverage of C++, C's newest direction, as well as full information on the UNIX® C de facto standard and the new proposed ANSI standard. Includes money-saving coupons for C products.

$27.95 p
0-07-881313-1, 740 pp., 7³/₈ x 9¹/₄
$24.95 p
0-07-881263-1, 740 pp., 7³/₈ x 9¹/₄

C: The Pocket Reference
by Herbert Schildt

Speed up your C programming with *C: The Pocket Reference*, written by master programmer Schildt, the author of twelve Osborne/McGraw-Hill books. This quick reference is packed with vital C commands, functions, and libraries. Arranged alphabetically for easy use.

$5.95 p
0-07-881321-2, 120 pp., 4¹/₄ x 7

Using Turbo C®
by Herbert Schildt

Here's the official book on Borland's tremendous new C compiler. *Using Turbo C®* is for all C programmers, from beginners to seasoned pros. Master programmer Herb Schildt devotes the first part of the book to helping you get started in Turbo C. If you've been programming in Turbo Pascal® or another language, this orientation will lead you right into Turbo C fundamentals. Schildt's emphasis on good programming structure will start you out designing programs for greater efficiency. With these basics, you'll move on to more advanced concepts such as pointers and dynamic allocation, compiler directives, unions, bitfields, and enumerations, and you'll learn about Turbo C graphics. When you've finished *Using Turbo C®*, you'll be writing full-fledged programs that get professional results.

$19.95 p
0-07-881279-8, 350 pp., 7³/₈ x 9¹/₄
The Borland-Osborne/McGraw-Hill Programming Series

Advanced Turbo C®
by Herbert Schildt

Ready for power programming with Turbo C®? You'll find the expertise you need in *Advanced Turbo C®*, the Borland/Osborne book with the inside edge. In this instruction guide and lasting reference, Herb Schildt, the author of five acclaimed books on C, takes you the final step of the way to Turbo C mastery. Each stand-alone chapter presents a complete discussion of a Turbo C programming topic so you can pinpoint the information you need immediately. *Advanced Turbo C®* thoroughly covers sorting and searching; stacks, queues, linked lists, and binary trees; operating system interfacing; statistics; encryption and compressed data formats; random numbers and simulations; and expression parsers. In addition, you'll learn about converting Turbo Pascal® to Turbo C and using Turbo C graphics. *Advanced Turbo C®* shows you how to put the amazing compilation speed of Turbo C into action on your programs.

$22.95 p
0-07-881280-1, 325 pp., 7³/₈ x 9¹/₄
The Borland-Osborne/McGraw-Hill Programming Series

Turbo C®: The Complete Reference
by Herbert Schildt

Herb Schildt's *C: The Complete Reference* which has topped best-seller charts across the country, is now followed by a special edition for Borland's highly acclaimed Turbo C® compiler. In *Turbo C®: The Complete Reference*, programmers at every level of Turbo C expertise will find all commands, functions, codes, and applications listed and described. *Turbo C®: The Complete Reference* also includes coverage of Borland's new Turbo C version 1.5, including the graphics functions and the Turbo C Librarian. Schildt describes the elements in the Turbo C language and environment, considers algorithms and applications, and discusses software development in Turbo C. An informative appendix points out the differences between Turbo C and Kernigan and Richie's C compiler. Add another bonus — money-saving coupons for popular Turbo C add-on products from Borland.

$27.95 p, Hardcover Edition
0-07-881373-5, 850 pp., 7³/₈ x 9¹/₄
$24.95 p, Paperback Edition
0-07-881346-8, 850 pp., 7³/₈ x 9¹/₄
The Borland-Osborne/McGraw-Hill Programming Series

Using Turbo BASIC®

by Frederick E. Mosher and David I. Schneider

Using Turbo BASIC® is your authoritative guide to Borland's incredible new compiler that offers faster compilation speeds than any other product on the market. *Using Turbo BASIC®* is packed with information for everyone from novices to seasoned programmers. Authors Mosher and Schneider, two accomplished programmers, introduce you to the Turbo BASIC® operating environment on the IBM® PC and PC-compatibles, and discuss the interactive editor and the BASIC language itself. You'll learn about recursion, math functions, graphics and sound functions, and conversions from IBM BASICA to Turbo BASIC.

$19.95 p
0-07-881282-8, 350 pp., 7⅜ x 9¼
The Borland-Osborne/McGraw-Hill Programming Series

Advanced Turbo Prolog™ Version 1.1

by Herbert Schildt

Herb Schildt now applies his expertise to Borland's remarkable Turbo Prolog™ language development system, specifically designed for fifth-generation language programming and the creation of artificial intelligence on your IBM® PC. *Advanced Turbo Prolog™* has been extensively revised to include Turbo Prolog version 1.1. The new Turbo Prolog Toolbox™, which offers more than 80 tools and 8,000 lines of source code, is also described in detail. Schildt focuses on helping you progress from intermediate to advanced techniques by considering typical AI problems and their solutions. Numerous sample programs and graphics are used throughout the text to sharpen your skills and enhance your understanding of the central issues involved in AI. Expert systems, problem solving, natural language processing, vision and pattern recognition, robotics, and logic are some of the applications that Schildt explains as he leads you to Turbo Prolog mastery.

$21.95 p
0-07-881285-2, 350 pp., 7⅜ x 9¼
The Borland-Osborne/McGraw-Hill Programming Series

Using Turbo Pascal® Version 4

by Steve Wood

Using Turbo Pascal®, the book that gives you a head start with Borland's internationally acclaimed compiler, now appears in a special edition that covers the new Turbo Pascal® version 4. This version offers significantly faster compilation speed, separate compilation of units, project management facilities, and the Borland Graphics Interface. Author Steve Wood provides programming examples that run under MS-DOS®, as well as information on memory-resident applications, in-line codes, interrupts, and DOS functions. If you're already programming in Pascal or any other high-level language, you'll be able to write programs that are more efficient than ever. *Using Turbo Pascal®, Version 4* discusses program design and Pascal's syntax requirements, and thoroughly explores Turbo Pascal's features. Wood also develops useful applications and gives you an overview of some of the advanced utilities and features available with Turbo Pascal version 4. *Using Turbo Pascal®, Version 4* helps you develop the skills to become a productive programmer—and when you're ready for more, you're ready for *Advanced Turbo Pascal® Version 4*.

$19.95 p
0-07-881356-5, 500 pp., 7⅜ x 9¼
The Borland-Osborne/McGraw-Hill Programming Series

Advanced Turbo Pascal® Version 4

by Herbert Schildt

This separate edition of *Advanced Turbo Pascal®* is devoted exclusively to Borland's newly released version 4 which features faster compilation speed. Schildt provides many programming tips to take you on your way to high performance programming with Turbo Pascal. You'll refine your skills with techniques for sorting and searching; stacks, queues, linked lists, and binary trees; dynamic allocation; expression parsing; simulation; interfacing to assembly language routines; and efficiency, porting, and debugging. *Advanced Turbo Pascal Version 4* also covers the Turbo Pascal Database Toolbox®, which speeds up database searching and sorting, and the Turbo Pascal Graphix Toolbox®, which lets you easily create high-resolution graphics. This is the best single resource for serious Turbo Pascal 4 programmers.

$21.95 p
0-07-881355-7, 625 pp., 7⅜ x 9¼
The Borland-Osborne/McGraw-Hill Programming Series

The manuscript for this book was prepared and submitted to Osborne/McGraw-Hill in electronic form. The acquisitions editor for this project was Jeffrey Pepper, the technical reviewer was Nelson Johnson, and the project editor was Fran Haselsteiner.

Text design uses Century Expanded for both text body and for display.

Cover art by Bay Graphics Design Associates. Color separation by Colour Image. Cover supplier, Phoenix Color Corp. Book printed and bound by R.R. Donnelley & Sons Company, Crawfordsville, Indiana.